W9-AHV-207

Multiple Paths to Literacy

Assessment and Differentiated Instruction for Diverse Learners, K–12

JOAN P. GIPE

Professor Emeritus, University of New Orleans
Lecturer Emeritus, California State University, Sacramento
Faculty, EdD Program in Teacher Leadership, Walden University

PEARSON

Boston   New York   San Francisco
Mexico City   Montreal   Toronto   London   Madrid   Munich   Paris
Hong Kong   Singapore   Tokyo   Cape Town   Sydney

In memory of Tillie, who sent me a new helper, Cocoa.
Cocoa knows how to make me take breaks!

As always, thanks to Charlie, my technology guru.

Continued thanks to Mom and Dad for their constant love,
support, and frequent Webcam visits.

A special thanks to Matt, whose early artistic talent,
as seen on page iii and the back cover of this edition,
supports the theories that provide the basis for this text.

Lastly, to my sister, Judy, who somehow
manages to live her life without S. J.

Executive Editor: *Aurora Martínez Ramos*
Editorial Assistant: *Jacqueline Gillen*
Executive Marketing Manager: *Krista Clark*
Production Editor: *Janet Domingo*
Editorial Production Service: *Nesbitt Graphics, Inc.*
Composition Buyer: *Linda Cox*
Manufacturing Buyer: *Megan Cochran*
Electronic Composition: *Nesbitt Graphics, Inc.*
Interior Design: *Nesbitt Graphics, Inc.*
Photo Researcher: *Annie Pickert*
Cover Administrator: *Linda Knowles*
Illustration on page iii and back cover: *James Matthew Gipe*

For related titles and support materials, visit our online catalog at www.pearsonhighered.com.

Between the time website information is gathered and then published, it is not unusual for some sites to have closed. Also, the transcription of URLs can result in typographical errors. The publisher would appreciate notificaton where these errors occur so that they may be corrected in subsequent editions.

Library of Congress Cataloging-in-Publication data was unavailable at press time.
ISBN-10: 0-132-08089-3
ISBN-13: 978-0-132-08089-7

Printed in the United States of America

Photo Credits: pp. 3, 265, 307, Anne Vega/Merrill Education; pp. 17, 95, 109, 163, 193, Scott Cunningham/Merrill Education; p. 47, Lindfors Photography; p. 69, Corbis RF; p. 145, IndexOpen; p. 233, Anthony Magnacca/Merrill Education; p. 329, Bob Daemmrich Photography; p. 355, Frank Siteman

10 9 8 7 6 5 4 3 2 1   HAM   13 12 11 10 09

www.pearsonhighered.com

ISBN-10:   0-132-08089-3
ISBN-13: 978-0-132-08089-7

About Matt

Matt was about five years old when he drew this picture. Matt is a fun-loving, charismatic, and bright young man who is now studying to become an architect. But Matt's early experience with school was all too typical for students who struggle with literacy tasks. While Matt demonstrated talents for drawing, athletics, math, and making friends, he had difficulty with phonics even though he had no difficulty with phonemic awareness tasks. But rather than celebrate his strengths, Matt and his parents were made to feel less than successful because of his difficulty with reading. I only recall one teacher who paired Matt with another boy who could easily write while Matt would provide the drawings to accompany their stories.

Matt clearly demonstrates that there are many ways to be intelligent, and each individual has his or her own unique blend of intelligences. Traditionally, schools have rewarded those with a linguistic intelligence, and have not seriously considered how to tap the other intelligences to help students learn the content of the curriculum. It is time for educators to celebrate the diversity that learners bring to the classroom, rather than look for ways to categorize or label students who need to develop their linguistic intelligence. The intent of this text is to help teachers learn more about their students' abilities through assessment and to then plan the differentiated instruction that accomplishes multiple paths to literacy.

Contents

Preface

Once again I begin this preface by saying that throughout this text I hope to demonstrate the profound respect I have for teachers as knowledgeable, thinking professionals. There remains a specific need for such a statement when the federal government and state legislatures continue to mandate curriculum, resulting in decisions that expect teachers to serve mainly as technicians of a particular program rather than be recognized as valued and trusted professional educators allowed to make instructional decisions that benefit individual students. Teaching is very hard work. It requires a view of oneself as a lifelong learner. Our best teachers also view themselves as researchers, constantly questioning their methods and trying new ideas that might help them meet the needs of all the students entrusted to them.

Just as classroom teachers are continually developing as professionals, so am I, as the author of this text. Between editions I regularly read professional literature, attend conferences, work with students who struggle with literacy, and discuss ideas with colleagues for the express purpose of identifying the methods and theories related to literacy assessment and instruction that represent the best of what is known in the field of literacy education. Therefore, as I have done for prior editions, I offer information based on the most current research in the field and the best thinking of literacy experts representative of a variety of viewpoints to present a comprehensive look at what we educators can do to help all learners, of all ages, achieve literacy. A continuing goal is also to provide teacher education students, classroom teachers, literacy coaches, and reading teachers with a guide and a resource for meeting the needs of their diverse learners, including English learners and students with special needs found in most classrooms throughout the United States. The use of quality multicultural literature as a means to help learners broaden their understanding of their own and others' cultures remains a recommendation of this edition, and one that is practical in educating for a democratic society.

This edition continues to strongly support a view of literacy development that includes multiple forms of literacy. From text-based forms to technology-related literacy to visual literacy and the performing arts, incorporating a variety of forms is essential to meeting the needs of learners in today's world. The conceptual framework that best illuminates this view is Howard Gardner's (1983, 1999) multiple intelligences (MI) theory, which provides the foundation for the instructional recommendations made in this edition. MI theory also supports differentiated instruction, and this text describes analytic teaching as essential to achieving effective differentiation. Additionally, this edition makes explicit what has been an underlying premise in earlier editions; that is, an emphasis on educating students in ways that make literacy education equally available for all students. Such a focus is certainly consistent with the concept of differentiated instruction and multiple intelligences theory.

A conscious effort has been made to present techniques appropriate to, or easily modified for, any grade level from primary through secondary school. Students can experience difficulty at any point in their literacy development. Difficulty might be first noticed when students are asked to read expository text that requires strategic reading behaviors different from reading narrative text. Difficulties also occur with expository writing, or academic writing. This book recognizes that competence in reading and writing is critical to entry into the world of knowledge and societal power. In fact, my hope is for all students to acquire the skills, knowledge, and dispositions needed to respond to their public responsibilities as citizens. I also hope to help teachers empower all students to enjoy the confidence that good readers and writers share, identify and solve problems of social injustice, and act as wise consumers and decision-makers in our technologically advancing society. This I see as the main task of literacy instruction.

What Is New in This Edition?

This edition provides teachers with an analytic approach and techniques for (a) recognizing learners' literacy strengths and needs, (b) identifying learners' special needs, and (c) planning and differentiating instruction that takes into account the special talents and multiple intelligences of their students. The following list describes the focus of this new edition.

- While earlier editions recognized that students learn differently and the importance of valuing this uniqueness, the connections among multiple intelligences, differentiated instruction, and democratic values have not been crystal clear. In this edition, the reader is exposed to **explicit and specific ways to incorporate democratic ways of teaching within the context of literacy instruction.**

- **Clarifications of the connections between analytic teaching and differentiated instruction are provided.** The analytic process is vital for teachers who wish to differentiate instruction. Technology integration is also an important element in differentiating instruction to make literacy education inclusive for all students.

- **A new chapter on early literacy, chapter 7,** has been added to correspond with components of literacy as delineated by No Child Left Behind (NCLB) and the National Reading Panel Report. While earlier editions did address emergent and early literacy, this edition presents expanded material on emergent literacy in a prominent place as a separate chapter.

- **Updated coverage of comprehension topics** is presented for both upper and lower grades, to include reading comprehension and the Internet. There remains a separate chapter on meaning vocabulary, followed by chapters on foundations of comprehension, strategic reading for both narrative and expository material, and study skills and test-taking strategies. This results in essentially five chapters that deal specifically with comprehension—the heart of reading.

- **More integration of technology** occurs throughout the text with updated websites, annotated and located at the end of each chapter. New to this edition is access to **MyEducationLab**, a course-specific website that offers readers opportunities to view video footage of authentic classrooms as well as simulations, artifacts and case studies, activities, and discussion questions. Connections to MyEducationLab multimedia assets occur in each chapter and link to the concepts discussed in the text, demonstrating lessons and employing similar teaching and learning strategies presented in the text.

- **Integration of the visual and communicative arts** is accomplished throughout most chapters to better enable readers to know when and how such integration might occur.

- Updates were made throughout the text for content and references. **Updates to the Appendix put the focus on forms of assessment.**

How Is This Edition Organized?

For teachers to effectively build cooperative learning communities and provide opportunities for critical thinking and problem solving, important goals in a democratic society, they first need to know their students' learning profiles. The bulk of this text explains how to profile students, identify their individual needs, and address those needs. The organization of this text supports those teaching goals.

The text is divided into two major sections: Part I, "Foundations," and Part II "The Major Domains." Part I presents the fundamental dimensions of literacy, literacy as a linguistic intelligence, the concept of civic literacy, prevalent views about literacy instruction, and the goals of effective literacy programs; describes analytic teaching and the analytic process and its relationship to differentiated instruction; summarizes perspectives on linguistic diversity as related to literacy instruction; discusses factors that influence literacy learning, such as physical, psychological, and environmental correlates; and describes ways to assess and evaluate literacy performance. Part II provides specific information on instructional techniques and integrating multiliteracies through visual and communicative arts for each of the major literacy domains. The literacy domains addressed are early literacy; oral and written language, including spelling and academic writing; word recognition; meaning vocabulary; reading comprehension; strategic reading for narrative text; strategic reading for expository text; and study skills, including test-taking strategies. The extensive coverage of research-based instructional techniques for all literacy domains and applicable to all grade levels is a particular strength of this text.

The chapters in Part I are best studied in the order presented, whereas the chapters in Part II are independent of one another and can be studied in any order. The text organization corresponds especially well to a course organization that includes action research, a field experience, or a practicum or clinic experience. Although the basis of the text is well supported by research and theory, the overall flavor of the text remains applied and practical.

Special Features

Certain format features aid learning from the text. Each chapter begins with a list of learning objectives and important vocabulary words. The terms listed as important vocabulary for each chapter are boldfaced within the text for quick location. There is also a glossary that provides definitions for these boldfaced terms. These features aid the reader in preparing to read each chapter and in studying the material, and they aid the instructor in anticipating topics that may need additional explanation or hands-on experience. Within each chapter are margin notes that refer the reader to specific examples of classroom instruction, student artifacts, and other valuable resources located on the MyEducationLab website accessible to adoptees at **www.myeducationlab.com**. Within each domain chapter, margin notes also make explicit connections between teaching activities or strategies and the multiple intelligences. In addition, within each domain chapter there are Spotlight on English Learners and Arts Connection features that highlight particularly effective strategies for English learners and activities for addressing multiliteracies by integrating the visual and communicative arts.

The Assessment Resources provides a compendium of assessment tools for both teachers and students. These tools include materials for assessing instructional environments, determining students' areas of literacy strength and instructional need, examining readers' attitudes toward reading and self-concept, determining spelling development, analyzing writing samples, communicating student progress to parents, self-assessment for phonics terminology, and many more. A glossary and index are provided for quick reference.

Supplements for Instructors and Students

The following supplements comprise an outstanding array of resources that facilitate learning about reading assessment and differentiated instruction. For more information, ask your local Allyn & Bacon Merrill Education representative or contact the Allyn & Bacon Merrill Faculty Field Support Department at 1-800-526-0485. For technology support, please contact technical support directly at 1-800-677-6337 or http://247.pearsoned.com. Many of the supplements can be downloaded from the Instructor Resource Center at www.pearsonhighered.com/irc.

Help your students get better grades and become better teachers.

Instructor's Manual, Resource Masters, and Test Bank. For each chapter, the instructor's manual features a summary of important concepts and terms with their definitions, in-class activities, field-based activities, journal questions. The summary gives an overview of what is discussed in each text chapter. The important terms highlight the major concepts of each chapter. The in-class activities provide ideas for experiences that can be accomplished within the university setting to enhance understanding of the concepts presented in the text. The field-based activities help build portfolio materials. The journal questions help students engage personally with the concepts. The manual also provides resource pages that can be used either as handouts or transparency masters. The test bank provides multiple-choice questions for each chapter. (Available for download from the Instructor Resource Center at http://www.pearsonhighered.com/irc.)

PowerPoint™ Presentation. Ideal for lecture presentations or student handouts, the PowerPoint™ Presentation created for this text highlights key concepts and major topics for each chapter and provides dozens of ready-to-use graphic and text images. (Available for download from the Instructor Resource Center at http://www.pearsonhighered.com/irc.)

MyEducationLab (myeducationlab.com) is a research-based learning tool that brings teaching to life. Through authentic in-class video footage, interactive simulations, rich case studies, examples of authentic teacher and student work, and more, MyEducationLab prepares you for your teaching career by showing what quality instruction looks like.

MyEducationLab is easy to use! In the textbook, look for the MyEducationLab logo in the margins and follow the simple link instructions to access the multimedia "Activities and Application" and "Building Teaching Skills and Dispositions" assignments in MyEducationLab that correspond with the chapter content. "Activities and Application" exercises offer opportunities to understand content more completely and to practice applying content. "Building Teaching Skills and Dispositions" assignments help students practice and strengthen skills that are essential to quality teaching through analyzing and responding to instructional encounters and artifacts.

MyEducationLab includes:

Video: The authentic classroom videos in MyEducationLab show how real teachers handle actual classroom situations.

Case Studies: A diverse set of robust cases illustrates the realities of teaching and offers valuable perspectives on common issues and challenges in education.

Simulations: Created by the IRIS Center at Vanderbilt University, these interactive simulations give you hands-on practice at adapting instruction for a full spectrum of learners.

Student & Teacher Artifacts: Authentic preK-12 student and teacher classroom artifacts are tied to course topics and offer you practice in working with the actual types of materials you will encounter daily as teachers.

Lesson & Portfolio Builders: With this effective and easy-to-use tool, you can create, update, and share standards-based lesson plans and portfolios.

Acknowledgments

Thanks to colleagues and students across the country, and to the staff at Allyn & Bacon, this text is now in its seventh edition. Suggestions for improving the instructional strategies offered and the explicit text connections to differentiated instruction come from a variety of valuable sources. First, the feedback from my own students and from other instructors and students who used the previous editions provided the impetus for the changes in this edition. I sincerely thank all who offered suggestions for this new edition. Second, I extend a special thank you to reviewers Diane Bottomley, Ball State University; John Barnitz, University of New Orleans; James C. Dillon, Southern University; Leslie Ann Prosak-Beres, Xavier University, Cincinnati. Your thorough and thoughtful reviews and comments were invaluable in the development of this new edition. Special thanks to Janet C. Richards for her contributions from chapter 14 of the sixth edition that now appear in each of the thirteen Arts Connection features. Special thanks also to Linda Bishop, Executive Editor, for her careful listening and her wonderful suggestions for ways to accomplish the many ideas we wanted to include in this edition. I hope all of you find the result even more appealing and helpful than the previous editions.

Joan P. Gipe

About the Author

Joan P. Gipe is Research Professor Emeritus from the University of New Orleans and Lecturer Emeritus from California State University, Sacramento. She is currently engaged in online teaching and mentoring for Walden University's EdD Program in Teacher Leadership. After graduating from the University of Kentucky with a BA and MA in education, and Purdue University with a PhD emphasizing reading education, Joan spent many years working with learners of all ages: in Kentucky as a reading specialist, in Indiana as a fifth-grade teacher, and in several university contexts as faculty, supervisor of student teachers, department chairperson, coordinator for teaching enhancement, university/school liaison for professional development schools, coordinator of field-based teacher education cohorts, and now mentor for numerous doctoral students engaged in research toward the EdD in Teacher Leadership. Many publications, including this text, share with the professional community what was learned during this career. Joan now resides in the charming town of Healdsburg, California, nestled in the heart of Sonoma County's Wine Country. She savors life there with her husband, and her four-legged companion, Cocoa, a Field Spaniel, who appears in the accompanying photograph that earned an Honorable Mention in Sonoma County's Best in Show.

Joan may be contacted at PO Box 1553, Healdsburg, CA 95448. E-mail joan.gipe@waldenu.edu.

CHAPTER 1

Fundamental Aspects of Literacy Learning

OBJECTIVES

After you have read this chapter, you should be able to:
1. Identify dimensions of literacy.
2. Discuss how the various dimensions of literacy interact.
3. Explain the importance of literacy teachers educating for a democratic society.
4. Describe several characteristics of your own philosophy about literacy learning.
5. Describe the two major goals of an effective literacy program.

VOCABULARY ALERT

For this list, and all the others that accompany each chapter, you might find the following steps helpful. First, review the entire list. If you see words that are mostly new, you know you will need to spend more time with the chapter. If you find the list contains many familiar concepts, you will need to spend less time. Know that your instructor has access to a quiz on these terms to correspond to each chapter. You might wish to request to take these quizzes before or after you study each chapter as a way to gauge your understanding of these important chapter concepts. Also be aware that these terms can be found in the glossary of this text, as well as defined within the context of the chapter where the word appears in boldface type.

academic literacy	graphophonic cue system	proficient reader
aesthetic reading	holistic view	recreational literacy
aliterates	interactive view	schematic cue system
best practices	language	semantic cue system
civic literacy	language comprehension	semantics
comprehensive view	language cue systems	skills-based view
early reader	language production	syntactic cue system
efferent literacy	morphology	syntax
emergent literacy	multiple intelligences	viewing
emergent reader	phonology	visual language
fluent reader	pragmatic cue system	visually representing

As teachers, we are concerned with creating class-rooms that are places of learning for *all* our students. Such classrooms, and the schools that house them, are responsive to issues of social justice and democratic values (Dewey, 1916). By explicitly educating for dem-ocratic life, we will empower our nations' youth to par-ticipate "in community life and take actions that balance the rights of individuals with the collective needs of society" (Robelen, 1998, p. 1). Teachers charged with literacy instruction are in a unique posi-tion to have a significant impact on students' develop-ment as literate and wise citizens (Mantle-Bromley & Foster, 2005). Certain skills, knowledge, and disposi-tions are needed for participation in a democratic soci-ety. Most of these capabilities come under the heading of critical thinking and inquiry skills, but others reflect a disposition that strives for the common good or the high moral ground. A few of the most important skills and dispositions related directly to literacy instruction are:

- Knowing how to ask questions, what to ask, and when to ask.
- Being able to consider multiple points of view on an issue or situation.
- Being capable of evaluating information, arguments, or data for accuracy and legitimacy.
- Having broad and deep multicultural understandings.
- Knowing how to read the implied message.
- Being able to communicate clearly both in speaking and in writing.

In addition, teachers recognize that students of all ages sometimes need alternative and supplementary instruction to support their literacy development. Such assistance is one of the most important tasks facing classroom teachers at all levels. Providing this assistance is challenging because paths to literacy development are as unique and distinct as our stu-dents. Hands-on activities, computer technology, music, art, drama, group work, and self-evaluation, as well as creative writing and reading material of one's choice, can each allow pupils to cultivate their linguistic intelligence even when their strengths may lie elsewhere (Gardner, 1983, 1999).

DIMENSIONS OF LITERACY

The development of literacy is complex and multidimensional; it involves reading, writ-ing, speaking, listening, viewing, visually representing, and thinking. It is much more than being able to decode print. How the various dimensions work together is not clear, but the dimensions that usually interact during literacy learning have been identified.

Literacy Is a Language Process

The sophisticated system through which meaning is expressed is **language**. The symbol systems of a language can be oral, written, or visual. Language enables individuals to communicate—to give and receive information, thoughts, and ideas. Communication does not exist in a vacuum. A message has both a sender and a receiver. The sender, who has specific intentions, produces a message that is reconstructed by the receiver, such as sharing a personal experience, asking a question, or complaining. The sender can also use language to persuade, inspire, comfort, or encourage others.

Sending a message is called **language production**, which can be oral, written, or visual; receiving or decoding the message is **language comprehension**. Speaking, therefore, is the production of oral language; listening is the comprehension of oral language. Similarly, writing and reading are the production and comprehension, respectively, of written language. As young children learn to read and write, they are already giving and receiving information by speaking and listening. A strong oral language base facilitates reading and writing development. Likewise, **visually representing** and **viewing** are the production and comprehension of visual language. For instance, producing a chart or a drawing can visually represent the learner's comprehension of text, while understanding the symbols found in visual media is viewing. Young children who have experience responding to picture books also have a background of producing and comprehending **visual language** (meaning in images) that can be further developed through instruction (Piro, 2002). Reading, writing, speaking, listening, viewing, and visually representing comprise the language arts and are mutually supportive, so they must be seen as interrelated and developing concurrently. As just discussed, reading, listening, and viewing share common receptive and constructive processes; and writing, speaking, and visually representing share common expressive processes.

Components important to the development of oral and written language are phonology, syntax, morphology, and semantics. Briefly, **phonology** refers to the system of speech sounds; **syntax** to word order and the way words are combined into phrases and sentences; **morphology** to the internal structure of words and meaningful word parts (prefixes, suffixes, word endings and inflections, compound words); and **semantics** to word meanings or to understanding the concepts represented by the language.

A firm language base, resulting from many hours spent experiencing oral, written, and visual language through activities such as telling stories or sharing books, is crucial to literacy growth. The language heard by participating in these activities becomes source material for written expression. Fortunately, all students bring to school a wealth of language and cultural experiences from which teachers can build literacy. The work of Kenneth Goodman (1968, 1973, 1994, 1996) is especially relevant because it helps us understand **language cue systems**. Goodman's work in analyzing students' oral reading behaviors and demonstrating how readers use specific language cues to recognize words and predict meaning in the reading process provides us with tremendous insight into what readers do when they read. He terms these language cues the *graphophonic, syntactic,* and *semantic cue systems.* As users of language, students bring to the reading task expectations about language that are basic to their ability to make sense of printed text. For example, assume a student encounters the unknown word *sidewalk* in the sentence "The dog ran down the _____." The reader may rely on one or all of the following: (a) the **syntactic cue system**, which indicates the part of speech for the unknown word, in this case a noun; (b) the **semantic cue system**, which indicates the possible words that would make sense (for example, street, alley, path, stairs, hill, sidewalk) in the context of the sentence; and (c) the **graphophonic cue system**, which provides sound and symbol clues, in this case an initial sound of *s,* a final sound of *k,* and a possible long *i* because of the vowel–consonant–silent *e* pattern.

Additionally, language is only really meaningful "when functioning in some environment" (Halliday, 1978, p. 28). Therefore, language users also develop a **pragmatic cue system**—rules related to the use of language in social or cultural contexts. For example, consider the sentence "This is cool," which can be interpreted several ways depending on the context of the situation. Consider the two different meanings of the sentence if it were spoken by a person tasting some coffee that has just been served or by two teenagers enjoying a rock concert. Similarly, one might say in an informal conversational setting, "Nice to meet ya"; in a more formal context, such as an academic gathering, this statement might become, "It is a pleasure to meet you."

The **schematic cue system** is viewed by some as separate from the semantic system and is defined as information from an individual's prior knowledge or personal associations with both the content and the structure of the text. For example, reading about a familiar topic or within a familiar format (for example, narratives) allows readers to use their schematic cue system (see the next section). Because language is so critical as an underlying process for success in literacy, students who are linguistically diverse require special attention. This topic is discussed in more depth in Chapter 3.

Literacy Is a Cognitive Process

Cognition refers to the nature of knowing, or the ways of organizing and understanding our experiences. The system of cognitive structures that represents knowledge about events, objects, and relationships in the world is called a *schema* (pl. *schemata*). The formation of concepts is basic to cognition. The more experience learners have with their environment, and the richer that environment, the more concepts they develop. A limited conceptual development affects literacy growth. For instance, even if a reader correctly pronounces the words in a written text, understanding is hindered unless those words represent familiar concepts. Active involvement with their world provides students with the necessary background for concept development and, ultimately, for literacy development. Schema theory and cognitive development are crucial to reading comprehension and are discussed in more detail in Chapter 11.

Literacy Is a Psychological or Affective Process

The student's self-concept, attitudes in general, attitudes toward reading and writing, interests, and motivation to read and write affect literacy development. Each of these factors is closely related to the student's experiential background in home, school, and community and the feelings associated with those experiences, which can have long-term impacts. For example, many adults who dislike reading point to some traumatic reading event as the cause (such as round robin reading or reading aloud without previous practice before their peers).

Psychological factors are crucial to literacy development. Students must have the desire to learn or improve an area of literacy; unless they experience success, they tend to avoid the literacy situation. This is only human nature; all of us avoid the things we do poorly or that we associate with negative feelings. On the other hand, success will encourage risk taking—an important step for learners who struggle.

Developing a positive self-concept and attitude is often the most important part of a student's literacy program. This dimension of literacy is discussed in more detail in Chapters 4 and 6.

Literacy Is a Social/Cultural Process

Learners are influenced by their social culture. For example, the various forms of oral literacy that connect generations of families, such as stories told around the dining table during holidays, provide a basis for using literacy as a tool in learning how to relate to others. Even past social experiences can influence present reading. An adult reader fondly recalls being read to by a parent at bedtime and now carries on that literacy tradition with his or her own child. In addition, the meaning that readers bring to text reflects the knowledge, attitudes, concerns, and social issues of their particular communities or cultures at a particular point in time. This explains how books read several years ago might now be reread with completely different understandings or appreciations.

Language and culture also play a critical role in building social capital (Delgado-Gaitan, 2002). *Social capital* refers to the connections within and between social networks that allow one to achieve success in the workings of a community or in society. For example, preserving traditional ethnic values while becoming bilingual enables immigrants to both integrate socially and maintain solidarity and often leads to academic success (Putnam, 2000). Civic literacy is another aspect of literacy as a social process and is the foundation by which a democratic society functions. **Civic literacy** is the knowledge of how to actively participate and initiate change in one's community and in the whole of society.

Probably the most common application of literacy as a social and cultural process occurs through discussion, or dialogue, as it relates to comprehension and learning from text through reading, speaking, and listening. Sharing what has been read obviously requires a social interaction with at least one other person. There is increasing evidence that, as students participate in small-group discussions such as literature circles, book clubs, or reader response groups, they acquire a deeper understanding of the text, increase higher-level thinking and problem-solving ability, and improve communication skills (Almasi, 1996; McMahon & Raphael, 1997; Morrow & Smith, 1990; Palincsar, 1987; Villaume & Hopkins, 1995). Communication skills are an important foundation for civic literacy, as they will enable the discussion, agenda setting, debating, and coalition building necessary for democratic participation in a multicultural society.

On the other hand, in multicultural classrooms where the conventions for conversation might vary among cultures, misunderstanding can easily occur. Children come to school knowing the rules for communicating used in their home culture. For example, a shoulder shrug that means "I don't know" to the child can be misinterpreted by the teacher as "I don't care." Therefore, it is incumbent on the teacher to become familiar with the cultural values and traditions represented by the students in the classroom.

Literacy Is a Physiological Process

Anticipating a literacy act activates certain language and cognitive processes (nonvisual information). Depending on the specific literacy act, certain physical processes are also activated. For the reading act, the brain must receive printed stimuli (visual information) that normally enter through a visual process. If the reader is blind, the stimuli may enter through a tactile process, as in using Braille, or through auditory means, as in listening to a taped reading. Under normal circumstances the reader must be able to focus on the printed stimuli, move the eyes from left to right, make return sweeps, discriminate likenesses and differences, and distinguish figure–ground relationships. In addition to visual acuity, physiological factors include good health, auditory acuity, and neurological functioning. Physiological (including neurological), psychological, and environmental factors are discussed further in Chapter 4.

Literacy Is an Emerging Process

Emergent literacy is a term describing the transformation that occurs when young children, having been exposed to printed material, actively construct for themselves how oral, written, and visual languages work. Viewed from the child's perspective, early literacy learning (the topic of Chapter 7) is as much a social activity as it is a cognitive one. Researchers such as Teale and Sulzby (1989), who have observed children in their homes and communities, provide the basis for the following insights:

1. Literacy begins at birth as children encounter print in their environment (for example, alphabet books, being read to, labels, signs, logos, computer screens). Experimentation with writing begins as scribbles.

2. Children view literacy as a functional activity. Their experiences show literacy events as ways to get things done (such as reading a recipe to bake cookies, writing a grocery list, paying bills online, viewing a city map to find a particular street).

3. Aspects of literacy development occur simultaneously in young children and in relationship to oral language development. As reading or viewing experiences influence oral language, writing and drawing (visually representing) experiences influence reading, and developing reading ability influences writing. Thus each of these areas provides support for the development of the others.

4. Children learn through active involvement, constructing for themselves an understanding of written language. Through a process of trial and error, of forming and testing hypotheses about the symbols used in written language and the sounds used in oral language, children learn how written language works. Their emerging knowledge is revealed by their attempts at spelling.

These insights have implications for the early literacy learning environment and strongly imply a need to connect reading and writing instruction more closely than has been traditionally done. These important components of effective literacy instruction are discussed in Chapters 7 and 8.

Emergent literacy also supports the view that literacy develops continuously over time when children are helped to explore and interact with written language (Brassell, 2004). Children develop from what many refer to as **emergent readers**, or readers who engage in pretend reading and who are just beginning to understand the nature and meaning of print; to **early readers**, who are learning strategies for word recognition and comprehension; to **proficient readers**, who demonstrate skills, strategies, and reading achievement appropriate to their age and grade level; and finally to **fluent readers** who read comfortably with both accuracy and comprehension at levels beyond normal expectations. To further specify, emergent readers are beginning to understand letter–sound relationships for consonants and the use of context clues as an aid to word identification. Early readers understand letter–sound relationships including the vowels, recognize common rimes (for example, *-an, -ake*), are able to segment multisyllabic words, and use context clues. Proficient readers understand structural clues in words, such as prefixes and suffixes along with Greek and Latin roots, and can combine the use of context to determine both pronunciation and meaning of words.

Literacy Represents the Linguistic Intelligence

In 1983 Howard Gardner published *Frames of Mind*, proposing a theory of **multiple intelligences**, or an expanded framework for thinking about intelligence. In *Intelligence Reframed: Multiple Intelligences for the 21st Century* (1999), Gardner refined and expanded this theory of multiple intelligences (MI theory) and clarified implications for its use. He defines an intelligence as "a biopsychological potential to process information that can be activated in a cultural setting to solve problems or create products that are of value in a culture" (pp. 33–34). In other words, these potentials are essentially neural in nature, and every member of the species has them. These intelligences are, however, realized only as a consequence of experiential, cultural, and motivational factors. A person is, therefore, not "smart" or "stupid" across the board. Depending on the values of a person's culture, opportunities, and personal decisions by the individual, his or her family and teachers, and others, these biopsychological potentials will or will not be activated. For example, the ability to use language and explore mathematical concepts is especially valued in our society, whereas spatial intelligence is valued in Eskimo cultures "because noticing subtle differences in snow and ice surfaces is critical to survival" (Cecil & Lauritzen, 1994, p. 5).

Gardner proposes eight intelligences, leaving open the possibility of others; for example, he is exploring the parameters of a ninth intelligence, one with the core ability of pondering "ultimate" issues that he refers to as an "existential intelligence" (Gardner, 1999). To determine the intelligences, Gardner established eight criteria for judging whether a "candidate" could be considered a separate intelligence. He believed the establishment of these criteria[1] to be one of the enduring contributions of multiple intelligences theory. Briefly, the eight current intelligences are described as follows:

1. *Linguistic:* language competence, using words effectively, orally or in writing
2. *Musical:* competence in perceiving, discriminating, transforming, and expressing musical forms and having a strong sensitivity to rhythm, melody, and tone
3. *Logical-mathematical:* competence in using numbers, inductive and deductive reasoning, and abstract patterns
4. *Spatial:* three-dimensional thinking and ability to form mental images and perceive the visual world accurately
5. *Bodily-kinesthetic:* competence in using one's whole body in skilled ways for expressive or for goal-directed purposes
6. *Interpersonal:* social understanding of other people's moods, intentions, motivations, and feelings

---

[1]Gardner's eight criteria for considering an intelligence:
1. The potential of isolation by brain damage
2. An evolutionary history and evolutionary plausibility
3. An identifiable core operation or set of operations
4. Susceptibility to encoding in a symbol system
5. A distinct developmental history, along with a definable set of expert "end-state" performances
6. The existence of idiot savants, prodigies, and other exceptional people
7. Support from experimental psychological tasks
8. Support from psychometric findings

7. *Intrapersonal:* self-understanding and awareness of one's own strengths and limitations and the capacity for self-discipline

8. *Naturalist:* competence in the recognition and classification of the many species of flora and fauna in the environment

MI theory is especially relevant to anyone who recognizes that learners are unique and can benefit from a variety of pathways to literacy. MI theory also provides teachers a way of revaluing learners and a way for learners to revalue themselves. Too often our perception of students who sometimes struggle with literacy tasks is to view these students as slow, as individuals with problems, or even as lazy. However, all learners are unique individuals, each with his or her own natural strengths and preferences for learning. By looking for the diverse ways in which learners demonstrate what they know and how they think best, educators will begin to appreciate each learner's individual learning profile.

MI theory encourages us to perceive the best in learners and to appreciate that there are several ways to reach a common goal. As Gardner (1999) stated, "a commitment to some common knowledge does not mean that everyone must study these things in the same way and be assessed in the same way" (p. 152).

The focus of this text is literacy development. We can also think of literacy development as cultivating linguistic intelligence:

> Linguistic intelligence is activated when people encounter the sounds of language or when they wish to communicate something verbally to others. However, linguistic intelligence is not dedicated only to sound. It can be mobilized as well by visual information, when an individual decodes written text; and in deaf individuals, linguistic intelligence is mobilized by signs (including syntactically arranged sets of signs) that are seen or felt. (Gardner, 1999, pp. 94–95)

Reading, as a discipline or domain in and of itself, can be realized through the use of several intelligences. By recognizing which intelligences represent strengths in our students, especially those students experiencing difficulty with linguistic tasks, we can then capitalize on their demonstrated intelligences to enhance the underdeveloped linguistic intelligence. Integrating linguistic activities with those that represent a student's demonstrated intelligences does this. In other words, for students with an underdeveloped linguistic intelligence, we must provide more experiences with books, stories, and print, not fewer (Allington, 1994). But these experiences can be embedded within the context of a student's intelligences profile. For example, the student who demonstrates a propensity toward the logical-mathematical intelligence could be asked to write triangle poems.[2] The student with a strong interpersonal intelligence could be group leader for a literature circle discussion (Campbell, Campbell, & Dickinson, 1999).

Several checklists are available for observing multiple intelligences (see Appendix P and the Web links for Multiple Intelligences at the end of this chapter). However, it is *not* appropriate to use these observation checklists to label a learner according to particular intelligences—recall that humans possess all of the intelligences but may not have had the opportunity to develop each one. It is also *not* appropriate to distort the multiple intelligences by simplifying them. For example, having students stand up and move around or do stretching exercises may be helpful to get blood to flow to the brain, but it does not enhance or use the bodily-kinesthetic intelligence. Likewise, having a student sing a list to remember it is only a mnemonic device and does not enhance or use musical

Go to MyEducationLab and select the topic *Formal Assessments*. Then, go to the Activities and Applications section, and watch the video entitled "Multiple Intelligences in the Classroom" to observe two teachers collaborating on how they will incorporate the multiple intelligences of their students into their instruction. Next respond to the accompanying questions.

---

[2]Triangle poems consist of three lines. Each line represents one side of the triangle, and each line leads into the next. Thus, there is no predetermined starting or ending point. Any line can be the first or last.

Arts Connection _____

Acknowledging an expanded perspective of literacy and recognizing the power and benefits of a strong, integrated language arts curriculum for all students, the *Standards for the Arts* (National Standards for Arts Education, 1994), adopted by 47 states (Anonymous, 1997), and the *Standards for the English Language Arts* (International Reading Association/National Council for the Teachers of English Language Arts, 1996) reflect the transformation and extension of the term *literacy* beyond reading and writing. Listings of communicative standards in these two documents that particularly apply to literacy and arts linkages include the following:

1. Making connections between the visual arts, music, dance, and other disciplines
2. Comparing and incorporating art forms by analyzing methods of presentation and audience response for theater and dramatic media (such as films, television, and electronic media) and other art forms
3. Listening to, analyzing, and describing music
4. Developing a wide range of strategies for comprehending, interpreting, and evaluating texts

The Arts Connection boxes that appear throughout this text are offered to broaden your awareness and stimulate your thinking about the possibilities of literacy and arts connections as you work with students.

intelligence. MI theory may help us most by reminding us of these three key principles: "we are not all the same; we do not all have the same kinds of minds . . . ; and education works most effectively if these differences are taken into account rather than denied or ignored" (Gardner, 1999, p. 91).

PREVALENT VIEWS ABOUT LITERACY INSTRUCTION

Knowledge about the ways in which humans learn, along with increasing knowledge about the emergence and development of literacy, will influence one's beliefs about literacy instruction. For example, proponents of a **holistic view** of literacy growth (also referred to as "top-down") claim that students should be exposed to a form of literacy instruction more like the process of learning to talk, in which experimentation and approximation are accepted and encouraged. Learning activities are based on students' interests and needs and are placed in meaningful contexts. Students are encouraged to integrate new information with what they have already learned. Fragmenting and fractionalizing areas of literacy learning are avoided, so not only are reading, writing, listening, speaking, viewing, and visually representing integrated *within* language arts instruction, they are often integrated *across* the curriculum. In other words, learning is not subdivided into artificial subject area time periods but is often organized around themes. Such classrooms generally encourage students to take an active part in their own learning with much cooperation and collaboration among students and teachers. Evaluation focuses on what learners *can* do, not on what they cannot do.

Proponents of a **skills-based view** of literacy growth (also referred to as "bottom-up") focus on the products of reading and writing. They believe there are important subskills related to reading and writing that students must learn before becoming adept in the area of literacy (for example, recognizing long and short vowel sounds, stating main ideas, drawing conclusions, comparing and contrasting, identifying pronouns, writing adverbial clauses, using guide words). They emphasize that learning the code for written language is a key subskill in learning to read. Teaching subskills and then assessing student mastery of subskills are common activities found in such programs as well as a set of basal reading materials. Advocates of a skills-oriented reading program believe that a carefully controlled reading program, in which behaviors are examined one by one, will lead more students to maturity in reading and that, without specific and direct subskills instruction, many students may not become proficient readers.

Many educators find something of value in both these views and talk about balance in reading instruction. But *balanced reading* instruction is not just a blending of different views. Routman (2000), who prefers the term **comprehensive view**, talks about the teacher providing "the balance of skills, strategies, materials, and social and emotional support [learners] need" (p. 15). Blair-Larsen and Williams (1999) define a balanced approach as "a decision-making approach through which a teacher makes thoughtful decisions each day about the best way to help each child become a better reader and writer" (p. 13). This particular definition is consistent with an **interactive view**, which says that "reading is a cognitive process, meaning results from the interaction between reader and text, [and] processing proceeds from whole to part and part to whole. . . . [As a result,] different emphases in instruction are appropriate at different times" (Lipson & Wixson, 1991, p. 12). Cantrell's (1998/1999) research further indicated that skills instruction provided within meaningful contexts according to students' needs is most effective in primary classrooms.

Jill Fitzgerald (1999) views balanced reading not as an approach but rather as a philosophical perspective based on a set of beliefs about the kind of knowledge, who has the knowledge, and how the knowledge can be learned:

> Local knowledge about reading is important, such as being able to read words at sight, knowing how to use various strategies to figure out unknown words, and knowing word meanings. Global knowledge about reading is important, such as understanding, interpreting, and responding to reading. Love of reading is important. There are equally effective multiple knowledge sources, including the teacher, parents, and other children. There are equally important multiple ways of learning through which children can attain the varied sorts of knowledge about reading. . . . As a result, a teacher who holds a balanced philosophical view of the reading process values multiple ways of learning and arranges her or his reading program to incorporate diverse instructional techniques and settings. (p. 103)

Each of these viewpoints has merit. There is no one best way to develop literacy. But for teachers to be able to meet the literacy learning needs of all students, we must continuously seek greater knowledge about literacy development. Fortunately, the research on literacy development has provided a strong knowledge base for the improvement of literacy instruction (see Braunger and Lewis, 2006). Recent insights from this research are readily shared in the form of scholarly works, conference presentations, and reports available online. This knowledge base has led to the use of the term **best practices** in literacy instruction. Gambrell and Mazzoni (1999, p. 14) compiled a list of 10 research-based practices that are descriptive of the methods and techniques discussed throughout this text:

1. Teach reading for authentic meaning-making literacy experiences: for pleasure, to be informed, and to perform a task.
2. Use high-quality literature.
3. Integrate a comprehensive word study–phonics program into reading/writing instruction.
4. Use multiple texts that link and expand concepts.
5. Balance teacher- and student-led discussions.
6. Build a whole class community that emphasizes important concepts and builds background knowledge.
7. Work with students in small groups while other students read and write about what they have read.

8. Give students plenty of time to read in class.

9. Give students direct instruction in decoding and comprehension strategies that promote independent reading. Balance direct instruction, guided instruction, and independent learning.

10. Use a variety of assessment techniques to inform instruction.

We also need to regularly reexamine our personal beliefs and knowledge about literacy instruction. Spiegel (1999) poses several questions that teachers should ask themselves: "Do I have a comprehensive view of literacy?"; "Do I have a clear understanding of a broad range of options for promoting literacy development?"; and "Can I match children with strategies?" (pp. 20–21). One of my goals for this text is to help you better match learners with strategies. I attempt to do this by providing a wide variety of strategy options and by associating a strategy with specific intelligences when that strategy functions beyond the linguistic intelligence (noted by the Multiple Intelligences margin notes), as well as how the arts might be integrated within literacy instruction (noted in Arts Connections boxes). Through continued professional reading and teaching experience, belief systems and knowledge about learning change; as belief systems change and knowledge increases, instruction will change accordingly. These changes are never easy, and they take time. Routman (1991, p. 27) shared the stages of her own change process:

1. I can't do this. It's too hard, and I don't know enough.

2. Maybe if I find out about it, it's possible.

3. I'll do exactly what the experts say.

4. I'll adapt the experts' work to my own contexts.

5. I trust myself as an observer-teacher-learner-evaluator.

A teacher's philosophy or theoretical orientation about literacy instruction can make a significant difference in the approach (basal, intensive phonics, language experience, literature-based), materials (basal readers, skill sheets, workbooks, children's literature), and techniques or methods (directed reading-thinking activity, cloze procedure, book sharings, creative bookmaking, literature circles, reading response logs) chosen to help students read (Richards, 1985; Squires & Bliss, 2004). Teachers who believe that literacy learning basically involves a sequential set of subskills will undoubtedly stress those subskills in their instruction. Those who believe that literacy is primarily about processing language will approach literacy instruction quite differently. Even authors of literacy instructional materials reflect their own beliefs, and perhaps those of the marketplace, in the materials they produce. Thus a teacher's beliefs, approach, and techniques may not always be in harmony with the materials available in the classroom, although knowledgeable teachers with firm beliefs can easily manipulate most materials in ways consistent with their beliefs. As Gambrell and Mazzoni (1999) stated, "Teachers are ultimately the instructional designers who develop practice in relevant, meaningful ways for their particular community of learners" (p. 13).

I encourage you to examine the professional literature and formulate your own beliefs about literacy instruction so that you can better evaluate suggestions in this and other texts, in materials such as basal reader manuals, and in federal regulations and legislative mandates. Your beliefs will help you make decisions about what to teach and how best to teach it. Don't be afraid to change your beliefs or your instructional practices as you read more and gain experience working with students. Practice informs theory, and a continuous cycle of interaction between practice and theory begins. Every teaching experience helps us construct knowledge about teaching and learning.

TWO MAJOR GOALS OF AN EFFECTIVE LITERACY PROGRAM

When planning a literacy program, a teacher is responsible for addressing long-term goals for student literacy achievement. These goals generally fall into two categories:

1. Academic or instructional literacy
2. Recreational or independent literacy

Academic Literacy

Academic literacy, or instructional literacy, deals primarily with learning from textbooks and other forms of scholarly or informational oral, written, or visual language. Rosenblatt (1991, as cited in Harris & Hodges, 1995) referred to this type of literacy as **efferent**, meaning "the attention is focused on abstracting out, analyzing, and structuring what is to be retained after the reading, as, e.g., information, logical argument, or instructions for action" (p. 69).

Effective literacy instructional programs usually have well-specified goals. Some teacher objectives for academic reading include (a) increasing proficiency in strategies for comprehending what one reads; (b) expanding sight vocabulary and improving ability to decode words; and (c) instructing to locate and organize information and to understand the special and technical vocabularies of the various content subjects. These teacher objectives are based on curriculum content standards. The International Reading Association (IRA) and the National Council of Teachers of English (NCTE), two major organizations devoted to furthering understanding of literacy development, together developed Standards for the English Language Arts (International Reading Association & National Council of Teachers of English, 1996). These standards only provide guidance toward developing curriculum and instruction and are not prescriptions for particular approaches.

Most states or school districts also publish content standards for language arts, as well as other content areas. These content standards further specify and define goals for what students should know and be able to do as a result of being educated in their particular schools. However, as with the IRA/NCTE standards, the means teachers choose to achieve these goals will reflect their individual philosophies about literacy instruction, and the way teachers combine theory and practice will determine the effectiveness of the literacy program. The teacher is the key to the success of any instructional program.

Recreational Literacy

Recreational literacy, or independent literacy, deals primarily with affective dimensions: fostering positive interests, attitudes, and habits concerning the areas of the language arts—reading, writing, speaking, listening, viewing, and visually representing. If teachers and others fail to encourage the desire for literate behavior in children and young adults, specifically reading, many students will become **aliterates**: people who can read but choose not to. Too often the learning environment works against instilling a love of reading or, at the very least, an appreciation for its value in a democratic society. Building positive attitudes toward reading and writing (recreational literacy) and developing the skills necessary for obtaining information (academic literacy) are both critical for developing an informed citizenry.

To access the content standards for any state, go to MyEducationLab and select the Lesson Plan Builder link within the Resources section. Once in the Lesson Plan Builder, go to Lesson Planner and click Begin. Visit the Academic Standards section and click on Close and then the Browse Standards tab. You will then see a map of the United States that allows you to click on a state in order to choose the content standard(s) your lesson addresses.

Learners who engage in recreational reading are also engaging in *aesthetic reading* (Rosenblatt, 1978). This type of reading focuses attention on the emotional and psychological dimension of literacy. According to Rosenblatt (1978, as cited in Harris & Hodges, 1995), **aesthetic reading** is "what is being lived through, the idea and feelings being evoked during the [literacy] transaction" (p. 5).

As Goodman and Marek (1996) stated:

> Schools have already produced too many people who can read but do not choose to do so. . . . Teachers must patiently help . . . students to find reading materials that give them personal satisfaction and pleasure. They must help them realize that reading is something they can do when traveling, when waiting, when there is some time available for a quiet, personal activity, or when there is nothing interesting on television or nobody to talk to. Students must reach the point where they choose to read when there is nobody to make them do it before educators can really claim success. (p. 20)

Some example teacher objectives for recreational reading include (a) providing students with the opportunity to practice reading in a relaxed atmosphere, (b) sharing good literature with students, and (c) making provisions for students to share books with one another. To achieve these objectives, teachers will want to provide their students with quality children's literature that includes a variety of ethnic groups (including African, Asian-Pacific, Latin, Mexican, and Native American). "Multicultural affirmations are especially important for students from divergent cultures" (Hoover & Fabian, 2000, p. 475). Students achieve better when given materials and themes relevant to their cultures (Freire, 1992). For teachers working in today's increasingly diverse classrooms, providing and sharing children's literature that reflects their students' own cultures is imperative for effective communication (Diller, 1999). Au (1993) summarized the benefits of using multiethnic literature:

- Students of diverse backgrounds feel pride in their own identity and heritage.
- Both mainstream students and students of diverse backgrounds learn about diversity and the complexity of American society.
- All students gain more complete and balanced views of the historical forces that shaped American society.
- All students can explore issues of social justice. (p. 178)

The two goals of an effective literacy program should be maintained and balanced at least throughout the elementary school years, although emphasis may change according to the literacy needs of the students. Both goals are equally important for students' literacy growth at all levels of education.

The remainder of this text focuses on helping teachers expand their repertoire of methods, materials, and techniques for supporting students as literacy learners and as active, effective citizens living in a democracy; analyzing their specific strengths, intelligences, and needs; and providing appropriate instruction. A process to help teachers plan literacy instruction that meets their students' needs is addressed in a discussion of the analytic process, analytic teaching, and the analytic teacher (Chapter 2). Chapter topics range from gathering and interpreting relevant information and differentiating instruction (Chapters 2 through 6) to the implementation of effective instructional techniques for the major domains of literacy learning (Chapters 7 through 14). Many useful assessment and instructional procedures for early literacy development, integrating reading and writing, word recognition, meaning vocabulary, comprehension, strategic reading, and study skills are provided. Ideas and examples for how literacy instructional strategies, multiple intelligences, and the arts can be interwoven are integrated throughout the domain chapters, along with references to instructional video clips, useful articles, and student artifacts available through Allyn and Bacon's MyEducationLab website.

Summary

To provide effective literacy instruction for the wide range of abilities and talents found in today's diverse classrooms, teachers must be able to recognize in their students' behaviors signs of how best to assist and support their learning efforts. This chapter reviews the dimensions of literacy and discusses the importance of teachers developing a personal philosophy about literacy instruction. Two major goals of an effective literacy instructional program are identified. Teachers can achieve these goals in a variety of ways, depending on their individual beliefs about literacy.

Recommended Websites

The Theory of Multiple Intelligences
www.edwebproject.org/edref.mi.intro.html and
http://surfaquarium.com/MI/inventory.htm
These sites provide good introductory information on the multiple intelligences as well as a self-assessment survey.

Reading Online: An Electronic Journal
www.readingonline.org
Hundreds of articles on all aspects of literacy. This website will prove useful throughout the entire text.

Effective Teachers of Literacy: Knowledge, Beliefs, and Practices
www.acs.ucalgary.ca/~iejll/volume3/wray.html
This article reports the results of research into the characteristics of teachers who effectively teach literacy to elementary school students (from the March 22, [Volume 3] 1999 issue of *International Electronic Journal for Leadership in Learning*).

The IRA/NCTE Standards, National, and Statewide Standards
www.ncte.org/about/over/standards, www.literacy.uconn.edu/litstan.htm, and www.education-world.comm/standards/
These sites provide listings of the literacy standards with access to other subject area standards.

Reference to IRA's Standards for Reading Professionals (2003)
www.reading.org/resources/issues/reports/professional_standards.html
IRA's new standards for reading professionals.

Multicultural Children's Literature, Carol Hurst's Children's Literature Site, and Latino Children's Literature
www.multiculturalchildrenslit.com, www.carolhurst.com/, and clnet.sscnet.ucla.edu/Latino_Bibliography.html
These sites contain a wealth of information about children's literature and ways to use the recommended books in the classroom.

Read across America
www.nea.org/readacross
To encourage recreational reading, participate in this annual event for promoting literacy development. Several valuable book lists are also provided, as well as other ideas for making reading fun.

Learning to Read: Resources
www.toread.com
Check out this website for information on nearly every aspect of literacy discussed throughout this text. This site also explains why DIBELS is *not* discussed in this text.

MyEducationLab is a research-based learning tool that brings teaching to life. Go to the Gipe 7th Edition MyEducationLab for Reading Assessment site at www.myeducationlab.com to:

- Engage in multimedia exercises to help you build a deeper and more applied understanding of chapter content.
- Use extensive resources including videos from real classrooms, Praxis and licensure preparation, a lesson plan builder, and materials to help you in your teaching career.

CHAPTER 2

The Analytic Process
Preparation for Differentiating Instruction

OBJECTIVES

After you have read this chapter, you should be able to:

1. Define, describe, and justify the analytic process, and then contrast it with assumptive teaching.
2. Describe analytic teaching and its relationship to differentiated instruction.
3. Explain the importance of ongoing teacher observation as a function of the analytic teacher.
4. Compare and contrast the teaching models of nondirective and direct instruction.
5. Differentiate teacher objectives and correlated student learning objectives.
6. Discuss the difference between didactic and discovery teaching.
7. Contrast problem-solving questions and facilitating questions.

VOCABULARY ALERT

action research
analytic process
analytic teaching
assumptive teaching
deductive teaching
diagnosis
didactic teaching
differentiated instruction
direct instruction
discovery teaching

EL
entry point
evaluation activity
facilitating questions
guided practice
independent practice
inductive teaching
learning profile
learning style
nondirective teaching

paradigm
problem-solving questions
readiness
reflective thinking
structured practice
teachable units
teaching hypothesis
tiered activities
transactive
transfer of training

Today's teachers are under enormous pressure to ensure that their students achieve high academic standards whether or not these students are native speakers of English or have other special needs. Federal mandates, such as the No Child Left Behind (NCLB) Act of 2001, and individual state standards combine to place a heavy layer of accountability on teachers, especially in areas of literacy and mathematics.

While our understanding of literacy development recognizes the importance of the learner, the text, and the context of the literacy task, the current emphasis on testing is resulting in less attention to learners' specific needs. But educators realize there is no social justice in denying the uniqueness of learners. If all students are to truly achieve, their unique needs must be addressed within a learning environment that actually engages them in meaningful activities and at their multiple levels of ability. Rather than rely on test instruments, even nonstandardized ones such as informal reading inventories, teachers should initially gain insights into students' literacy abilities by observing their individual competence in areas such as oral reading, story retellings, written summaries, answers to key questions, and background knowledge. Thus, teachers must become not only more analytical and better observers of their students but also more knowledgeable about literacy learning and various methods for literacy instruction. To meet these demands, classroom teachers in any curricular area can use the **analytic process**, defined here as a systematic way to help teachers observe and assess aspects of literacy learning in their students, identify areas of strength and need for individual students, and provide instruction for specific literacy domains.

JUSTIFICATION FOR THE ANALYTIC PROCESS

Problems Associated with Assumptive Teaching

Sometimes teachers make inappropriate assumptions about the literacy status of their pupils. Herber (1970) called the resulting instruction **assumptive teaching**. Although teachers make many unfortunate specific assumptions, most fall into two general categories.

First, teachers often assume their pupils need to learn something when, in fact, they already have learned it. When this assumption is made, those pupils are in a minimal-growth instructional setting. The teacher may spend a great deal of time and energy teaching something that is already known to those students. This leads to student boredom, inattentiveness, and disruptive behavior. Second, teachers may assume their pupils have learned something when, in fact, they have not. If this occurs regularly, learning deficits will accrue and students will slip into a no-growth instructional setting. Teaching a lesson well does not guarantee that pupils learn; student learning must be confirmed. Figure 2.1 lists common assumptions that teachers should try to avoid.

Figure 2.1	Common Assumptions Classroom Teachers Should Avoid

1. Assuming that a child has attained readiness for a particular learning
2. Assuming that a report card grade reflects a child's instructional level
3. Assuming that a report card grade from one teacher means the same as that from another teacher
4. Assuming that all teachers develop independent reading habits in all pupils in the primary grades
5. Assuming that all teachers use instructional material diversified in difficulty and content in each grade
6. Assuming that readers having difficulty are able to use material on a frustration level of difficulty
7. Assuming that group instruction is the best method to meet the literacy needs of all pupils
8. Assuming that a basal reader series constitutes an entire literacy program
9. Assuming that children can learn a new skill without direct instruction
10. Assuming that children who read well will read widely
11. Assuming that teacher–pupil relationships are unimportant to growth in literacy
12. Assuming that mastery of reading skills and mastery of reading are identical
13. Assuming that instruction for "different" children is identical to instruction for "normal" children
14. Assuming that all children have the same capacity for learning
15. Assuming that reading deficiencies are nonexistent when the class average on standardized reading tests reaches or exceeds the norm
16. Assuming that the child's reading/writing abilities remained unchanged over school breaks
17. Assuming that individual difficulties in word analysis in the intermediate grades will correct themselves
18. Assuming that all materials are adequate and appropriate as instructional materials
19. Assuming that teachers make only fortunate assumptions

Adapted from Delwyn G. Schubert and Theodore L. Torgerson, *Improving the Reading Program,* 5th ed. Copyright © 1981 by William C. Brown. Used with permission.

Assuming too much about students can lead to a mismatch between the learner and the instructional program. For example, if a sixth-grade teacher gives everyone in the class a sixth-grade text at the beginning of the school year, the teacher has assumed that all the students are reading at the level of the text and will profit from instruction at this level. This is a dangerous assumption to make. Teachers must verify that each student in the class can respond appropriately to assigned reading materials.

Similarly, faulty assumptions about individual students can lead to inappropriate teaching. Consider the following example: A fifth-grade teacher accurately determines each student's *instructional reading level* (grade level of material that is challenging but not frustrating for the student to read successfully with normal classroom instruction). Two boys are reading at third-grade level, according to test results. The teacher gives both of them appropriate reading materials, assuming that instruction can proceed in a manner similar to that of a typical basal reading program, in this case, guided reading followed by reviewing the stories and workbook exercises at the third-grade level. This teacher has done well in finding each boy's proper instructional reading level but has failed to pursue the *reasons* why each boy is unsuccessful with age-appropriate material. One boy may be reading at third-grade level because he is having difficulty with word meanings and comprehension, while the other boy may be having difficulty recognizing the printed form of the words. Each needs supplementary instruction designed for his particular reading needs. After learners are given appropriate-level materials, deeper

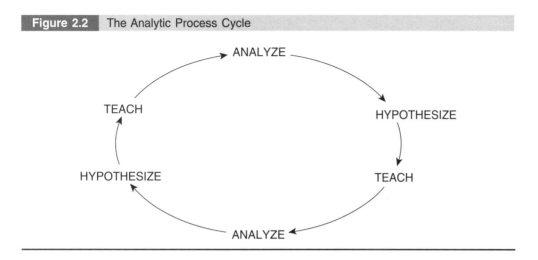

Figure 2.2   The Analytic Process Cycle

analyses of strengths and weaknesses within that level are essential to avoid inappropriate teaching assumptions.

Assumptions have features similar to hypotheses. Both terms connote a hunch or a notion about something. They differ in that the word *assumption* implies that the hunch is accepted or taken for granted, whereas the word *hypothesis* always implies tentativeness and the need for verification, after which acceptance or rejection occurs.

The Analytic Process Paradigm

A loose and unstructured literacy instructional program, based on unverified assumptions, often perpetuates literacy problems in the classroom. Employing the analytic process alleviates many of the unfortunate results of faulty teacher assumptions. The reason is that the analytic process follows a **paradigm**, or pattern. The teacher (a) analyzes literacy behaviors, (b) forms teaching hypotheses, (c) teaches, and (d) reexamines literacy behaviors. This paradigm can be expanded to allow for necessary specificity in terms of individual strengths and difficulties and also to allow for *teacher* self-assessment. The process is simple in that it parallels a natural instructional progression. As you will see later in this chapter, however, this process can become quite intricate when put to use, and it requires a knowledgeable teacher—one who knows what to look for and how to interpret behaviors observed. Figure 2.2 presents a graphic representation of the analytic process cycle.

ANALYTIC TEACHING: TEACHING FOR DEMOCRACY AND SOCIAL JUSTICE

Analytic teaching supports all literacy learners by recognizing their unique strengths, interests, and competencies and meeting their specific instructional needs. Analytic teaching is rooted in assessment (not necessarily testing) and offers ways of observing and determining students' literacy development that respect students as naturally creative persons who possess a broad range of human aptitudes and who learn in different ways. Irrespective of one's beliefs about literacy instruction, analytic teaching begins with a teacher's firm convictions that:

1. All students can learn and have the capabilities to become successful readers and writers.

2. Diversity has value within the classroom community because it prepares students to function in a society where people must work and learn together across culture, ethnicity, language ability, and gender.

3. All students deserve opportunities to develop their unique competencies and strengths.

4. Students who are afforded varied ways of interrelating new information and concepts with previously acquired background knowledge, or schemata, will have greater opportunities to reach their fullest potential.

Analytic teaching consists of activities that foster student–teacher communication, student choice, student discovery, student self-expression, and student engagement. Analytic teaching is democratic teaching; it encourages students to construct meaning from their interactions with print, set goals for achievement, acquire new literacy concepts, enhance their problem-solving abilities using their preferred combinations of aptitudes or intelligences (for example, through linguistic, musical, spatial, or bodily-kinesthetic activities), and assume some responsibility for evaluating their own achievements and instructional needs.

Analytic teaching is also highly consistent with a focus on differentiated instruction. **Differentiated instruction** is designed to engage students through their different learning modalities and interests by using varied rates of instruction and/or varied degrees of complexity (Tomlinson, 1999). Principles similar to those that guide analytic teaching also guide differentiated instruction:

1. The teacher focuses on the essential concepts, principles, and skills of a subject area.

2. The teacher attends to student differences.

3. Assessment and instruction are inseparable.

4. The teacher modifies content, process, products, and the learning environment.

5. All students participate in respectful work.

6. The teacher and students collaborate in learning.

7. The teacher balances group and individual norms.

8. The teacher and students work together flexibly.

The analytic process is the first step toward differentiating instruction because it will reveal the readiness or skill levels, the interests, and the learning styles and/or multiple intelligences of the students. This information is critical for the teacher who wishes to differentiate, or "personalize," instruction (Tomlinson, 1999).

The Analytic Teacher

Analytic teachers are committed to teaching for democracy; that is, they work hard to ensure that they and their students work together as a community of learners, sharing their individual talents and special ways of solving problems. They help students think critically, question, consider a variety of perspectives, and gain multicultural understandings. Analytic teachers are good listeners; they listen to their students' ideas and encourage them to share opinions. They often use whole-class meetings in which students and teacher face one another in a seated circle to foster group communication and facilitate student–teacher communication (Glasser, 1969, 1975).

Analytic teachers are also reflective practitioners. It is well documented that **reflective thinking** (questioning and trying to solve educational problems in a thoughtful and deliberate manner) helps teachers make quality decisions about students and their instruction. For example, analytic teachers determine what their students already know about reading and writing, and they figure out what concepts and cognitive tasks are causing confusion for students.

Another aspect of being a reflective practitioner is constant examination of one's own teaching and learning. For example, effective analytic teachers need to know how to tap resources in all the multiple intelligences to meet the needs of all their students. Therefore, analytic teachers examine their own profile of multiple intelligences so they can develop those that are underdeveloped and thus expand their teaching repertoires. A teacher with a strong interpersonal intelligence might readily use cooperative learning strategies; likewise, a teacher having an underdeveloped spatial intelligence might avoid using visuals or graphic materials. Although we cannot be masterful in all the intelligences, awareness of our own profiles will encourage us to ask for the help of colleagues, students, or parents in certain areas, or to know when to incorporate available technology (such as music CDs, videotapes, or calculators).

Analytic teachers are most concerned with teaching all their students effectively— not with covering a specified amount of reading material or teaching a predetermined number of writing lessons. Thus, analytic teachers are decision makers—teachers who adapt programs to their students' needs. They engage in **action research**, or systematic inquiry into their teaching practices to gather information about how their methods affect student learning (Mills, 2003). Analytic teachers constantly observe their students to determine how their students learn best, to recognize what their students are ready to learn next, and to watch for the emergence of reading and writing patterns and achievements. Teacher observation is never wasted time. Observation also helps the teacher assemble instructional materials. In fact, materials for literacy instruction (basal readers, developmentally appropriate literature, content-area texts, pictures, art and creative bookmaking supplies, and magazines) are more wisely assembled *after* students' literacy instructional strengths, needs, and interests are determined (see Chapter 6 for more on observation).

Because analytic teachers are effective observers of students and reflective practitioners, they feel confident in their abilities to formulate literacy instructional plans and long-range goals for individuals and groups of students. Professional decisions are made before, during, and after instruction. See Figure 2.3 for the kinds of questions teachers ask themselves in order to make professional decisions.

Analytic teachers often work collegially to enhance their teaching skills. Through capacity-building activities such as peer coaching and lesson study, analytic teachers grow professionally. These collegial activities help teachers increase not only their subject matter knowledge and their knowledge of instruction, but also their ability to observe students—an ability crucial to analytic teaching.

The Analytic Process and Multiple Intelligences Theory

Even though enhancing literacy ability is the focus of this text, it is important to observe during the analytic process that students can, and likely do, excel in other areas. While some learners may demonstrate an overall underdeveloped linguistic intelligence, they may demonstrate strength in at least one aspect of linguistic intelligence and likely in at least one of the other intelligences (see Appendix N). For example, a student who has difficulty reading a story may be able to *tell* a wonderful story (both are linguistic acts) and is also observed to be very popular with classmates (interpersonal). This information

| Figure 2.3 | Questions for Professional Decision Making |

A teacher might ask the following questions during the course of one school day while reflecting on various students:

1. Is this student reading as well as he can? If not, why? What reading or writing instructional technique might help? Will an individual conference help? Will peer tutoring help? What are this student's unique talents and aptitudes? How can I build on this student's personal interests and particular talents and strengths to enhance his reading and writing abilities?
2. Should this student remain in the reading group that is exploring poetry? If so, what additional instructional techniques may enable her to grasp the ideas and concepts represented (for example, artwork, writing, peer discussions, dramatization, composing a melody, researching the lives of some poets)?
3. What quality literature selections could I use to introduce our unit on immigration?
4. How can I plan literacy activities that will stimulate my passive learners?
5. What are effective literacy activities for English language learners that will encourage their use of oral language?
6. What lesson modifications can I make to help my students with special needs?
7. How can I motivate my students to become avid, wide readers and/or enthusiastic writers?
8. How can I structure the classroom environment to provide a blend of learning experiences that promote all students' growth in reading and writing?

will assist the analytic teacher in instructional planning. MI theory would describe this approach to planning as using the concept of the **entry point**, or finding ways to engage learners and at the same time place them centrally within the desired literacy task. See Table 2.1 for a description of Gardner's seven entry points and an example literacy activity for each (Gardner, 1999). Any of the intelligences can serve as entry points to another intelligence. Each person possesses all intelligences, but they function in ways unique to each person depending on his or her biology, personal life history, and cultural background. Thus, the analytic process helps teachers focus on appreciating and welcoming diversity within the classroom and ultimately helps students revalue themselves as learners. Information gained from the analytic process with respect to forming an intelligences profile is crucial for teachers wanting to differentiate instruction because the intelligences profile is directly related to a student's learning profile. In Sonia Nieto's words, "Learning begins when students begin to see themselves as competent, capable and worthy of learning" (1999, p. 123).

The following example suggests how one student who demonstrates spatial, bodily-kinesthetic, and intrapersonal intelligences can be helped to develop his linguistic intelligence (IRI/Skylight Publishing, 1995):

Trevor [12 years old] is a seventh grader who is just as proud of his collection of doodles and pictures as he is of his good grades [in math]. Many of his drawings are done during school in classes that are lecture-based or "just plain boring," as Trevor puts it. Others are a result of long hours of detailed work on sketches and designs. While his classmates make simple book covers, Trevor creates covers with intricate and complex geometrical designs or cartoon characters.

Trevor is drawn to classrooms that are picture rich. Slides, mobiles, photos, overhead transparencies, and other visuals that reinforce the lesson make all the difference in his motivation and understanding. He is easily frustrated by an overdose of words, whether he's reading, writing, or listening to them. His frustration about long writing assignments quickly changes to excitement, however, when he is encouraged to include visuals. . . . Trevor's

Table 2.1	Gardner's Seven Entry Points	
Entry Point	**Description**	**Example Literacy Activities**
Narrational (can align with linguistic, spatial, and interpersonal intelligences)	For students who enjoy learning through stories, in either linguistic or film form	"Tell the story of what you saw (or heard)." "Work with a partner to create a story for the pictures you drew."
Quantitative/Numerical (closely aligns with logical mathematical intelligence)	For students motivated by numbers and their patterns and operations	Creation of triangle poems or some of the "formula" poems (e.g., haiku)
Logical (closely aligns with logical-mathematical intelligence)	For deductive thinkers	Syllogisms (e.g., teacher covers the *th* in the word *that* and points to the *at,* and says, "If this word is /at/, and if this word starts like the *t-h* in /the/, then the word is /th/ + /at/, or /that/.")
Foundational/Existential (can align with intrapersonal intelligence and the "potential" ninth intelligence, existential)	For learners attracted to the "larger" questions	"Why is reading important?" "How can it affect your life?" "How does reading make you feel?"
Aesthetic (aligns with spatial, musical, and naturalist intelligences)	For learners drawn to works of art or features in nature that represent symmetry, balance, and harmony	"Describe the shapes of the letters/words. How are they alike/different?" "Choose some music that could accompany this story."
Hands-on (aligns with bodily-kinesthetic intelligence)	For students who learn when active and fully engaged	Manipulating letter cubes to form words: "How many words can you make out of the word *student*?" "Design a dance that shows the meaning of the word *swarm.*"
Social (aligns with interpersonal intelligence)	For learners who function best in a group setting	Participating in literature circle discussions with a variety of job roles over time

teacher can identify Trevor's reports without his name because they always have one picture on the front, one on the back, and several throughout.

Trevor spends most of his free time putting together and painting models. . . . He loves math class this year because, as he says, the teacher "keeps us really busy when we learn. We move around to different centers and use manipulatives."

Trevor is definitely not a social butterfly. . . . He has a small group of close friends and is happy to spend time alone. His mental and physical well-being are very important to him, as is his academic achievement. (pp. 45–46)

Arts Connection

Artistic engagements provide opportunities for students with special literacy learning requirements to use their distinctive multiple intelligences (Gardner, 1983, 1999). Students who are encouraged to augment the literacies of reading and writing with their MI strengths (for example, spatial, musical, bodily-kinesthetic) can more easily solve problems creatively, explore their reasoning, and extend and express their points of view. Gardner further maintains that authentic constructions of knowledge occur only when a learner can transform ideas, information, and skills from one domain to another (such as the transformation of oral or written language to the languages of music, dance, or the visual arts). Such a view is an important rationale for weaving the arts with literacy instruction. For example, the idea for a scripted and rehearsed puppet show emerged from reading the book *Saint George and the Dragon* (Hodges, 1990). A fifth-grade teacher and his students constructed the puppet stage from a large discarded board they found behind a local grocery store. After covering the board with dark green paper and sketching a castle scene on the paper with chalk and tempera paint, the teacher drilled holes at various places in the board so that students could simultaneously use the top of the board and the drilled holes to enable their sock puppet characters to interact. The dragon puppet was especially striking. It was created from a bright electric-green-and-black striped sock. Black buttons formed the dragon's eyes and a red triangular piece of felt served as the dragon's glistening tongue. Because the students became so fascinated with dragons, the teacher extended the story reading and drama production into a three-week unit of instruction about dragons. The students used the Internet to obtain photographs and facts about Komodo dragons. They visited the library to get *National Geographic* photos and maps about Komodo dragons and wrote in their dialogue journals from the points of view of dragons, dragon slayers, people chased by dragons, and fantasy dragon families.

These representative behaviors reveal Trevor's strengths and propensities for learning as well as showing his linguistic intelligence as an area in need of further cultivation. To develop his linguistic intelligence, Trevor's teacher provides opportunities that allow Trevor to use his strong intelligences when engaged in tasks involving his underdeveloped linguistic intelligence. For example, when asked to read a book, Trevor is encouraged to draw a picture that shows how the book made him feel or what it meant to him. This instructional technique, appropriately implemented with seventh graders, is called *sketch-to-stretch* (Whitin, 1996). Sketch-to-stretch readily combines two of Trevor's strong intelligences—spatial and intrapersonal—to nurture the linguistic task of reading a book. By applying the principles of differentiated instruction, analytic teachers provide opportunities for students to use their particular combinations of intelligences to support and enhance literacy efforts and development.

It should be noted that MI theory is not the same concept as **learning style**. Proponents of learning styles suggest that the learner approaches different contents (such as language, numbers, music) in the same way (for example, global, analytical, impulsive, reflective). MI theory supports the possibility that a learner may have more than one learning style. For example, a learner might respond reflectively in the music realm but analytically while working a jigsaw puzzle (spatial realm). With such complexity, it is not possible for teachers to completely individualize their teaching to match each of their students' learning styles, nor is it necessarily appropriate. However, it is possible for teachers to expand their instructional methods to provide a variety of activities within their literacy curriculum that link learning to as many intelligences and learning styles as possible. Armstrong (2000, p. 41) provides characteristics of instructional strategies that link MI theory with learning information:

- Listen to it, talk, read, or write about it (linguistic).
- Draw, sketch, color, or visualize it (spatial).
- Dance it, act it out, build a model of it, or find some other hands-on activity related to it (bodily-kinesthetic).

- Create a song or chant about it, find music that illustrates it, or put on back-ground music while learning it (musical).
- Relate it to a personal feeling or inner experience, reflect on it (intrapersonal).
- Conceptualize it, quantify it, or think critically about it (logical-mathematical).
- Teach it, work on it with another person or group of people (interpersonal).
- Connect it to living things and natural phenomena (naturalist).

ANALYZING COMPONENTS OF LITERACY LEARNING TO ASSIST DIFFERENTIATED INSTRUCTION

Literacy learning is recognized as a process that is complex, dynamic, and **transactive** (learners actively construct meaning as they interact with print); representing its components in isolation and in static form is actually a distortion of the process itself. Some distortion is acceptable, however, if it helps teachers attain the level of specificity needed for direct and/or differentiated instruction. Additionally, teachers must examine the kinds of materials students read and the nature of the methods, materials, and tasks they use in the classroom, as well as the social and cultural environment of the classroom (see Appendix A for an instructional environment self-assessment survey). Such analysis can lead to changes in a teacher's methods, materials, tasks, and approach.

Levels of Analysis and Correlative Diagnostic Questions

Following observation of literacy behaviors, three levels of analysis help answer the question, "What strategies and lessons should I plan to help my students?" Each level has a correlative diagnostic question, and some questions have important related subquestions. A summary of the levels of analysis and correlative diagnostic questions can be seen in Figure 2.4. These questions and levels of analysis can also be used as a record-keeping tool or diagnostic tool for monitoring student progress (Appendix B). Because literacy learning is complex, teachers should always approach analysis of literacy behaviors with the knowledge that the resulting hypotheses may be imprecise or only partially correct. During the teaching phase, hypotheses and instructional practices can be verified, modified, and further adapted to the needs of the students. This again points out the integrated nature of instruction and assessment.

Level 1: Determining Lack of Success in Literacy. At the initial level of analysis, only one diagnostic question needs to be answered:

- Is the learner experiencing a lack of success in literacy?[1]

A teacher may find the answer to this question in several ways. To see how well the learner can read, the teacher listens to the student read. Informal reading inventories and use of running records are common means of assessing reading behaviors (see Chapter 6). As part of compiling a learning profile for each student, teachers are strongly advised to assess (collect information about) their students' literacy abilities using the trade books, textbooks, basal readers, and skill development books available in the classroom.

---

[1]Note that for this question, as with all the diagnostic questions that follow, a follow-up question needs to be asked: "Under what conditions or in what situations?"

Figure 2.4   Summary of Levels of Analysis and Correlative Diagnostic Questions

Level 1: Determining Lack of Success in Literacy
- Is the learner experiencing a lack of success in literacy?

Under what conditions or in what situations?

(*Note:* This question should be asked after *every* diagnostic question that follows.)

Level 2: Determining the Domain(s) in Which Difficulty Occurs
- Does the learner demonstrate underdeveloped oral or written language ability?
- Does the learner have difficulty with word recognition?
- Does the learner have difficulty with comprehension of narrative text?
- Does the learner have difficulty with strategic reading of expository text or with study skills?

Level 3: Determining the Area(s) within the Domain(s)
Oral and Written Language Ability
- Does the learner demonstrate underdeveloped oral (i.e., speaking or listening) and written language ability, to include spelling?

Word Recognition
- Does the learner have a limited sight vocabulary and a word recognition strategy?
- Does the learner have difficulty in the area of word analysis (i.e., visual analysis and decoding)?
- Can the learner reassemble (or blend) word parts that have been visually or auditorily analyzed?
- Does the learner have knowledge of word morphology (structural analysis)?
- Does the learner have difficulty using context clues?
- Can the learner use a dictionary to assist word recognition?

Reading Comprehension and Strategic Reading for Narrative Text
- Does the learner have a limited meaning vocabulary?
- Does the learner have difficulty with thinking or problem-solving skills associated with comprehension of narrative text, such as identifying story features, predicting events, or evaluating a character's actions?
- Does the learner have difficulty recognizing his or her own inability to understand what was read?
- Does this apparent comprehension problem result from difficulty with word recognition?
- Does the learner's apparent comprehension problem result from difficulty in strategic reading for expository text or study skills?

Strategic Reading for Expository Text and Study Skills
- Does the learner have difficulty with content-specific vocabulary?
- Does the learner have difficulty with content-specific skills, such as reading visual displays, formulas, or other unique symbols?
- Does the learner have difficulty recognizing whether the text is meaningful to him or her?
- Does the learner have difficulty locating information?
- Does the learner have difficulty organizing information?

Physical, Psychological, and Environmental Factors
- Does this learner demonstrate the influence of a physical factor?
- Does this learner demonstrate the influence of a psychological factor?
- Does this learner demonstrate the influence of an environmental factor?
- Has this learner had opportunities for reading and writing related to his or her needs and interests?

Figure 2.4 *continued*

- Does the learner have a negative attitude toward reading/writing?
- Does the learner lack interest in reading/writing?
- If someone asked this learner, "What is reading?" or "What is writing?" would the response be one that would please me?
- Is my curriculum so skills oriented that this learner never has the opportunity to read or write for his or her own purposes?
- Have I examined my own beliefs and attitudes about the way this learner might need to learn?
- Have I explored alternative instructional approaches that might benefit this learner?

Another indication of literacy ability may be the student's scores on a standardized achievement test, usually readily available in the student's cumulative folder. But be careful not to let one test score identify a student's level of success. Achievement tests probably do a good job of identifying good readers, so by comparison teachers can identify students who are less successful in reading. On the other hand, be careful not to assume that students who score high have the reading abilities necessary for any reading tasks not represented on the test (Farr & Carey, 1986).

The teacher may notice a discrepancy between a student's reading scores on an achievement test and mathematics achievement test scores. Reading difficulties *may* be indicated if the mathematics scores are higher. Achievement test scores alone may also suggest further analysis if, for example, the scores on the vocabulary and comprehension subtests vary significantly.

A teacher might also look for patterns in a student's achievement records. One pattern could reveal a student whose test results indicate that from the beginning of literacy instruction, the student failed to achieve as rapidly as average intellectual ability would warrant (that is, one year's growth for each year in school). Such a pattern might indicate the influence of a physical, psychological, or environmental factor (see Chapter 4). Aspects of emergent or early literacy might also be examined (see Chapter 7).

Another pattern might indicate the student had a successful beginning, but progress gradually slowed. This second pattern may not be recognized until a student has already experienced difficulty. Teachers must be alert to the proportionate gains that a student makes through the years, as in the following example: Six-year-old Jody makes good progress through first grade, and her end-of-the-year test shows an average level of achievement. By the end of second grade, Jody's achievement is slightly below average. At that point Jody's teacher might feel concern about her progress or decide that her score merely reflects the imprecise nature of tests. When the third-grade test reveals that Jody is further below average, however, this teacher should recognize the pattern and decide that Jody needs assistance.

A third pattern could indicate the student had a successful beginning, but progress suddenly dropped. Good progress followed by a sudden drop may have a number of causes: an omission of instruction; an emotional factor interfering with the student's learning rate, such as a recent divorce or a death in the family; or something as simple as the student not feeling well on the day of the test. In any case, the teacher should continue with the analytic process to pinpoint possible learning gaps.

Level 2: Determining the Domain(s) in Which Difficulty Occurs. Once teachers have identified students displaying difficulty in their literacy development, they must begin to determine where the difficulty lies. Literacy development can be characterized by the following four major domains: *oral and written language ability, word recognition, comprehension and strategic reading for narrative text*, and *strategic reading for expository text and study skills* (this last domain is often referred to as "reading to learn," or content-area reading). Four primary diagnostic questions to be answered are:

1. Does the learner demonstrate underdeveloped oral and/or written language ability?
2. Does the learner have difficulty with word recognition?
3. Does the learner have difficulty with comprehension of narrative text?
4. Does the learner have difficulty with strategic reading of expository text or with study skills?

When the answer to a question in Level 2 is no, analysis in that domain ends. When the answer to a question is yes, that domain is analyzed further to define the difficulty more precisely. If the answer to all the questions in Level 2 is no, the teacher must consider other factors and may require the help of a specialist to meet the student's needs. If the answer to several of the questions is yes, the teacher should consider whether difficulty in one domain is influencing another and, if so, provide instruction in the dominant domain. Physical, psychological, or environmental factors may also be involved (see Chapter 4).

Level 3: Determining the Area(s) within the Domain(s). Experts disagree about dividing the domains into smaller segments. Some label the segments differently, and others resist the separation process even for the purpose of analysis. Thus, neither empirical data nor the consensus of experts directly supports the manner in which the domains will be segmented here for analytical purposes.

Nevertheless, the domains are divided into smaller parts for communication and instructional purposes. From a practical point of view, you should be aware that these areas are discussed at length in the literature, that the category labels can be found in many texts on literacy instruction, and that these smaller **teachable units** are acknowledged and used in many literacy instructional systems today. Even for those with a holistic philosophy, the search for answers to why a student experiences lack of success with literacy tasks must include consideration of these areas so that appropriate instructional opportunities can be provided.

Oral and written language ability. This component of literacy development lies at its core and is of concern when a student performs very poorly on assessment instruments or when a beginning reader has trouble with simple reading tasks. It is a major focus for students who are English learners, or **ELs** (learners whose first language is not English). A correlative diagnostic question to be asked when a student performs so poorly is:

- Does the learner demonstrate underdeveloped oral (that is, speaking and/or listening, or phonemic awareness) and/or written language ability, to include spelling?

Teachers at all levels should ask themselves whether their students have the oral and written language competencies needed for a particular reading or writing task, whether students are native speakers of English or nonnative speakers of English reading in their native language or reading English. As the concept of emergent literacy implies, oral and written language competence develops only in a learning environment that provides students with frequent opportunities to use language and to hear or see language being used in meaningful, communicative contexts. Teachers of English learners (ELs) (also referred to as English language learners—ELLs or limited

English proficient—LEP) are especially interested in providing appropriate language environments (see Chapter 3).

Word recognition. If a student has difficulty with word recognition, more specific information must be sought by asking the following diagnostic questions:

- Does the learner have a limited sight vocabulary?
- Does the learner lack a word recognition strategy?
- Does the learner have difficulty in the area of word analysis (that is, visual analysis and decoding, or phonics)?
- Can the learner reassemble (or blend) word parts that have been visually or auditorily analyzed?
- Does the learner have knowledge of word morphology (structural analysis)?
- Can the learner use context clues to assist word recognition?
- Is the learner able to use a dictionary to assist word recognition?

Answers to these questions tell the teacher where to begin an instructional focus or the content that needs to be differentiated for particular students. Chapter 9 details these areas of word recognition and provides suggestions for assessment and instruction. The important point to remember here is that any area(s) associated with word recognition can be out of balance for a particular student. When the imbalance becomes too great, some learners demonstrate word recognition difficulties so severe that they cannot reach the heart of reading—comprehension.

Reading comprehension and strategic reading for narrative text. Much has been learned about reading comprehension in recent years, and it is clear that comprehension is deeply intertwined with memory, thinking, and language. When a student demonstrates poor comprehension, carefully consider these diagnostic questions:

- Does the learner have a limited meaning vocabulary?
- Does the learner have difficulty with thinking or problem-solving skills associated with comprehension of narrative text, such as identifying story features, predicting events, or evaluating a character's actions?
- Does the learner have difficulty recognizing his or her own inability to understand what was read?

Answers to these questions help the teacher determine a starting point for differentiating the content of instruction and choosing appropriate instructional strategies.

Some students, especially in the early elementary grades, appear to have trouble with comprehension when the difficulty actually lies in the domain of word recognition. Therefore, when students of any age are experiencing difficulty typically associated with primary-grade students, teachers should ask:

- Does this apparent comprehension problem result from difficulty with word recognition?

Similarly, especially in the upper grades, an apparent comprehension problem may in reality reflect difficulty with strategic reading of expository text and/or study skills. If the student is experiencing difficulty with content-area material, this question is suggested:

- Does the learner's apparent comprehension problem result from difficulty in strategic reading for expository text and/or study skills?

This question and the preceding one probably should be considered transitional questions. They demonstrate how reading comprehension overlaps the other domains discussed. Chapters 10, 11, and 12 provide suggestions for assessment and instruction in the domain of reading comprehension and strategic reading for narrative text.

Strategic reading for expository text and study skills. When students have problems in the domain of strategic reading for expository text and study skills, ask these questions:

- Does the learner have difficulty with content-specific vocabulary?
- Does the learner have difficulty with content-specific skills, such as reading visual displays, formulas, or other unique symbols?
- Does the learner have difficulty recognizing whether the text is meaningful to her or him?
- Does the learner have difficulty locating information?
- Does the learner have difficulty organizing information?

The answers to these questions help the teacher decide what instructional content is needed and choose appropriate instructional strategies. Chapters 10, 13, and 14 provide suggestions for assessment and instruction in the domain of strategic reading for expository text and study skills.

Additional factors. Almost any physical, psychological, or environmental influence may impede literacy development. For example, an inadequate background of experience or one divergent from the majority of students in the class can seriously affect comprehension, attitude toward reading, and perhaps the acquisition of word recognition strategies. These influences that exist outside the literacy domains (see Chapter 4) must be considered independent entities that may adversely affect *any* area of the school curriculum, not just literacy. These outside influences warrant considerable study and are more appropriately pursued in advanced and specialized coursework typically found at the graduate level.

Correlative diagnostic questions associated with physical, psychological, or environmental factors include:

- Does this learner demonstrate the influence of a physical factor?
- Does this learner demonstrate the influence of a psychological factor?
- Does this learner demonstrate the influence of an environmental factor?
- Has this learner had opportunities for reading and writing related to her or his needs and interests? (In other words, is the learner possibly a "victim" of the curriculum or of poor instruction?)

Poor attitudes toward and disinterest in reading and writing hinder literacy achievement. Teachers must ask questions about their students' attitudes and interests, their own teaching practices, and the curriculum itself, regardless of the literacy domain being addressed:

- Does the learner have a negative attitude toward reading/writing?
- Does the learner lack interest in reading/writing?
- If someone asked my students, "What is reading?" or "What is writing?" would they respond in a way that pleases me?

- Is my curriculum so skills oriented that students never have the opportunity to read or write for their own purposes? (See Appendix A for an instructional environment survey.)
- Have I examined my own beliefs and attitudes about the way this learner might need to learn?
- Have I explored alternative instructional approaches that might benefit this learner?

The answers to the correlative diagnostic questions for these additional factors are typically obtained through observation, surveys, interviews, and reflection.

BASIC STEPS IN THE ANALYTIC PROCESS

This section provides information on the basic steps involved in the analytic process. Use these steps to answer the questions posed for any of the domains, areas, or specific tasks mentioned earlier. The paradigm for the analytic process (refer back to Figure 2.2) will now be expanded.

Analysis of Literacy Behaviors

Step 1: Gathering Information. Many sources of information about students are available to teachers: the learner, cumulative records (containing relevant medical information, test scores, grades), discussion with others who have observed the student in the classroom (such as a previous teacher) and outside the classroom (such as parents), work samples (daily oral and written work, dated material such as that found in working portfolios), and additional assessment measures (results of informal reading inventories, interest and attitude surveys, teacher-made and classroom-based measures). Assembling all available information possible about students to better understand their strengths and needs is called *assessment*. This information can be compiled into a learning profile for each student and is valuable when planning differentiated instruction. This first step involves teacher action; the following steps represent the teacher's thought processes.

Step 2: Evaluating the Information. In Step 2, teachers judge the quality of the information gathered. They try to establish students' instructional reading levels, find a pattern or set of behaviors indicative of students' strengths and needs, and identify possible areas for development or assistance. If only such information as standardized test scores is available, teachers must verify these scores through other means. Most often teachers use classroom-based measures. Chapters 5 and 6 discuss specific assessment tools, and later chapters provide additional suggestions for classroom-based assessment of particular areas (see also the many appendixes to this text).

Steps 1 and 2 together are roughly equivalent to **diagnosis**, or identification of literacy difficulties from behaviors. The outcome can range from a global diagnosis, as determined by the first and second levels of analysis, to identification of specific areas of difficulty represented by the third level. The specific areas identified must then be translated into teacher objectives and, ultimately, an instructional plan.

Generation of Possible Teaching Hypotheses

Step 1: Determining Alternatives. Once teachers have identified what assistance students need, they next consider how best to provide that assistance. Numerous instructional procedures are available, and many of these will be detailed in the following chapters. For now, simply consider a **teaching hypothesis** to be a tentative instructional focus based on students' identified educational needs.

Step 2: Selecting a Tentative Hypothesis. The teacher evaluates the alternatives generated in Step 1 and decides how to differentiate an instructional plan to best meet the needs of the students. This decision may be influenced by information regarding students' interests, learning styles, self-concepts, or other strong intelligences. The teacher then develops or selects learning activities and the teaching phase begins.

Teaching

Although differentiated literacy instruction may be designed for individuals' needs, it is usually carried out in groups. By providing group instruction to students with similar needs, classroom teachers are implementing effective classroom management. Additionally, there are many alternative models of teaching, all with specific purposes and the power to help students learn (Joyce, Weil, & Calhoun, 2000). Different purposes or outcomes require different teaching models, so it is important for teachers to develop and use a large repertoire of teaching models. "When teachers are able to use different pedagogical approaches, they can reach more students in more effective ways" (Gardner, 1999, p. 168). Two quite different models are presented here—the nondirective teaching model and the direct instruction model. These examples represent ends of a continuum from student centered (nondirective) to teacher centered (direct). At times, teachers need to use both of these models as well as others in between to reach all learners.

Nondirective Teaching. The **nondirective teaching** model is an ideal choice when the instructional purpose is to help students set personal educational goals. "The nondirective teaching model focuses on facilitating learning. . . . [Nondirective teaching occurs when] the environment is organized to help students attain greater personal integration, effectiveness, and realistic self-appraisal . . . the teacher's goal is to help them understand their own needs and values so that they can effectively direct their own educational decisions" (Joyce et al., 2000, p. 288). This is accomplished primarily through a nondirective interview, basically a conversation in which the teacher mirrors students' thoughts and feelings. By using reflective comments, the teacher raises the students' consciousness of their own perceptions and feelings, thus helping them clarify their ideas. The nondirective interview has five phases.

Phase 1: Defining the helping situation. The teacher encourages free expression of feelings. Students who have not been successful in literacy learning are likely to have some feelings about their struggles. For example, a student who is having difficulty with writing may feel tense or defensive when asked to write. The teacher's first step is to help the learner release those feelings so that other, more positive aspects of his or her writing can be explored. The teacher might say, "When I'm asked to write a report for the school principal I have a hard time getting started—that makes me feel nervous and panicky. How do you feel when I ask you to write?"

Phase 2: Exploring the problem. Students are encouraged to define the problem while the teacher accepts and clarifies feelings. Once the problem area has been defined (for example, writing), the teacher encourages the student to express both positive and negative feelings and to explore the problem. Some teacher questions or responses might include the following:

- "You say you hate writing because it's too hard. Can you say more about that?"
- "Kind of like it doesn't matter what you do, it always turns out the same."
- "I see."
- "Perhaps you feel you won't succeed."
- "You are saying to me that the problem is . . ."

Phase 3: Insight. Students discuss problems, and the teacher supports the students. As students discuss their problems and become aware of the reason(s) for their feelings or behaviors, they can begin to see possible solutions more clearly. These new insights help the students set goals. Questions that might be asked at this step include:

- "What is difficult for you as a writer (reader)?"
- "What is easy for you as a writer (reader)?"
- "What do good writers (readers) do?"
- "What are your goals as a writer (reader)?"

Phase 4: Planning and decision making. Students plan initial decisions, and the teacher helps to clarify possible decisions. This is a difficult step for most teachers, who can readily provide suggestions. It is more important for the student to initiate a plan. Helpful comments might include the following:

- "You would do this because . . ."
- "It sounds as if your reasons for that are . . ."
- "What do you think of that?"
- "How might that idea help?"

Phase 5: Integration. In this final phase, students begin to take positive actions. These actions initially may be intermittent and/or unfocused, but eventually they begin to focus on a single area, giving students the direction they need. Thus, students gain further insight and can develop more positive actions. The teacher is supportive and can provide approval statements if genuine progress has been made. Approval statements should be used sparingly, though, to avoid returning to the expectation that the teacher knows best and makes the decisions. Some helpful comments are:

- "That's a very interesting comment and may be worth considering again."
- "I think we are really making progress together."

Because the nondirective teaching model is student centered, it is less activity oriented and more a set of principles for interacting with students in response to a situation. Teacher questions and responses are aimed at initiating and maintaining conversation to help students clarify their own thinking. Some additional examples:

- "How do you feel when that happens?"
- "Maybe you feel you will be wrong."
- "It sounds to me as though your reasons for your actions today are (restate student's reasons)."
- "The last idea you had was really strong. Could you explain it some more to me?"

Go to MyEducationLab and select the topic *Direct and Indirect Instruction.* Then, go to the Activities and Applications section, watch the video entitled "The Indirect Instruction Model," and notice how the teacher engages the students in the lesson to make this a more student-centered lesson. Next respond to the accompanying questions.

One possible outcome of nondirective teaching is that students will begin to feel more in control of their own learning.

Direct Instruction. Direct instruction refers to a model of teaching that is highly structured and teacher initiated. This model can be particularly effective, for example, in helping learners who have difficulty understanding how to read more strategically; the teacher begins the lesson by providing "mental modeling" to share the reasoning processes involved in expert reading (Herrmann, 1988). Direct instruction is necessary in any literacy program. Such lessons are not always completed in one class session. More often, strategies will be learned and practiced over a series of days.

Step 1: Orientation or overview. Students are informed of the purpose of the lesson and the teacher's expectations. The learning task is clarified and student accountability established.

Step 2: Direct instruction/modeling. The direct instruction model requires that the teacher be *actively* involved in the lesson by first explaining and then modeling or demonstrating the new skill or strategy. Once the particular strategy to be modeled has been identified, the teacher must plan how to introduce the lesson, what to say while modeling, and how to best show the reasoning process. Usually, a *thinking out loud* technique is used to reveal the actual reasoning process followed by the teacher while engaged in using the skill or strategy. For example, if the strategy is making predictions, the teacher may read a story to the class. After reading the title, the teacher stops, thinks out loud what the story might be about, *and states why*. The teacher proceeds to read the story, stopping and thinking out loud at points that provide information confirming or rejecting earlier predictions and always stating why the prediction was confirmed or not and how the text is helping to change the teacher's predictions. Usually the teacher checks for understanding (CFU) at this point to be sure the students understand what they will be expected to do before they apply the new skill or strategy during practice opportunities.

Step 3: Structured practice. Once the teacher has modeled a strategy, the students must be given the opportunity for **structured practice**—to practice what has been demonstrated with the teacher still directly involved. In this way the teacher begins to determine the accuracy of the teaching hypothesis as well as the effectiveness of the lesson. The teacher is checking to see how accurately students have interpreted the modeling, another instance of checking for understanding. Depending on students' responses, additional modeling may be needed. Often the whiteboard, chart paper, or an overhead projector is used during structured practice so students can see the applications while having access to the teacher's explanations. Routman (2000) refers to this step as *shared demonstration*. The teacher works interactively with the students to ensure that they understand the task.

Step 4: Guided practice. **Guided practice** allows students to apply the new information on their own or in small groups while the teacher is still available. In this phase, the teacher monitors students and provides corrective feedback when necessary. Differentiated activities occur at this step because students do not all need to be working with the same materials, in the same way, but only with the same concept, strategy, or skill. Thus, both content and process can be differentiated according to students' learning profiles.

Step 5: Independent practice. **Independent practice** provides an opportunity for students to apply what they have learned without the teacher's help. This kind of practice is often done as homework. It gives further information on the accuracy of the hypothesis and the effectiveness of the lesson. If students seem unable or unwilling to participate in independent practice, there are several possible reasons: The initial hypothesis about their needs may be inaccurate, the lesson procedures may need to be revised, or students may not have developed the ability to work independently. In any case, providing independent practice gives the teacher additional information.

Step 6: Evaluation activity. The **evaluation activity** is a way of directly judging the effectiveness of the lesson(s) and the accuracy of the hypothesis. These activities are usually teacher made and relate directly to the kinds of tasks demonstrated in the modeling and practice. If the teaching hypothesis was appropriate and learning occurred, opportunities for further practice or enrichment can be provided; if the hypothesis was not appropriate, alternative hypotheses should be considered and new lessons planned. Students may be given choices in how to demonstrate their new knowledge. In this way, the products of learning can be differentiated.

Reexamination of Literacy Behaviors

Step 1: Gathering Information. This second examination of literacy behaviors differs in several ways from the first. The first time that the teacher gathers information about a student, it is essentially new information. The second examination of behaviors, however, follows an instructional sequence of events, making the analysis much more dependent on the teacher's insights and observations. This analysis overlaps considerably with the preceding teaching stage: as the teacher teaches, information is gathered. In this sense, the teaching act itself is assessment.

Step 2: Evaluating the Information. Evaluation is based on feedback provided by the instructional sequence. Using this feedback, the teacher must decide whether the lesson was effective and whether the teaching hypothesis was appropriate.

Step 3: Generating Possible Teaching Hypotheses. New hypotheses are needed if the lesson is effective and the desired behaviors are learned. New hypotheses are also needed if the original one was inappropriate because the teacher will proceed to a new lesson. In both instances, this step depends on the teacher's perceptions of the lesson and the results of the evaluation activity.

Step 4: Selecting a Teaching Hypothesis. Based on *all* the available information, a new hypothesis is selected and a lesson planned. This takes the teacher back into the teaching phase and the whole cycle begins again (refer again to Figure 2.2).

FROM TEACHING HYPOTHESES TO LESSON PLANS

Once a teaching hypothesis has been selected, the teacher designs a corresponding lesson plan or set of lesson plans. The lesson plan(s) depicts the manner in which the desired literacy behavior is to be achieved. Good lesson planning addresses three important elements: (a) specific learner objectives, (b) learning activities and materials designed to help the learners achieve the objectives, and (c) assessment activities designed to evaluate whether the pupils have achieved these objectives. In addition, lesson procedures, materials, and activities reflective of teaching for democracy would encourage student

Go to MyEducationLab and first select the topic *Direct and Indirect Instruction.* Go to the Activities and Applications section, watch the video entitled "The Direct Instruction Model," and respond to the accompanying questions. Then select the topic *Word Recognition.* Go to the Activities and Applications section, watch the video entitled "Reading—Direct Instruction," and respond to the accompanying questions. These teacher-directed lessons at two diverse grade levels should seem very familiar as most of us have experienced direct instruction more than any other teaching model.

Go to MyEducationLab and first select the topic *Differentiating Instruction*. Go to the Activities and Applications section, watch the video entitled "Enhancing Learning through Technology," and respond to the accompanying questions. Then select the topic *Informal Assessments*. Go to the Activities and Applications section, watch the video entitled "Cooperative Learning," and respond to the accompanying questions. Observe how "Enhancing Learning through Technology" represents differentiated instruction for teaching about bar graphs, using tiered activities to meet students' needs, whereas in "Cooperative Learning" all the students are doing the same thing when working on the balance beam activity—they are merely doing the same activity in small groups.

voice and responsibility. Language arts teachers are familiar with interactive read alouds, cooperative groups, self-assessment using rubrics, and student choice of reading material (for example, uninterrupted sustained silent reading). Attention to questioning skills, critical and evaluative thinking skills, and considering multiple perspectives is needed to develop literate, thoughtful, and compassionate citizens.

Teachers should try to also provide diversity in learning activities to achieve the lesson objectives, to differentiate instruction, and to address a variety of intelligences. For example, many instructional formats are available for teaching initial consonant blends: children's literature (linguistic intelligence), puzzles and other visual presentations (spatial), oral problem-solving riddles (logical-mathematical), manipulatives or sandpaper tracings (bodily-kinesthetic), songs that teach (musical), and learning games (interpersonal). A teacher trying to achieve differentiated instruction can design or adapt a lesson by using **tiered activities** (Tomlinson, 1999), which provide the same essential skills or concepts but in ways that address learners' different strengths and needs. Thus, tiered activities are a way of differentiating instruction by differentiating the process learners use to achieve a common lesson objective.

The MyEducationLab video clip "Enhancing Learning through Technology" shows a classroom of students all working toward the same objective of extending and applying their knowledge of bar graphs (content), but through the use of learning centers that reflect tiered activities (the process is differentiated). Notice how the three learning center technology activities vary to accommodate a range of skill levels. Students were matched to a version of the activity based on their learning profiles. Compare this lesson example to the balance beam activity in the MyEducationLab video clip "Cooperative Learning" in which all students are working on the same activity even though they are in small groups. The students in the balance beam video clip are all working on the same task to achieve the same objective. While they may be working collaboratively and thus addressing the interpersonal intelligence, working in collaborative groups does not imply differentiated instruction. Flexible grouping can be one of the characteristics of differentiated instruction, but the instruction itself must vary in content, process, or product according to students' readiness, interests, or learning profiles to be truly differentiated. It is not reasonable to expect that every lesson provide differentiated instruction, but there are points within a unit or topic of study where differentiated instruction can be accomplished. The effective teacher takes advantage of these opportunities and uses a variety of instructional techniques whenever possible, employing different materials and procedures until learners experience successful evaluations. The domain chapters provide a wide array of instructional techniques for teaching literacy skills.

Distinguishing Teacher Objectives and Correlated Student Learning Objectives

Teachers, especially beginning teachers, are often understandably confused about lesson objectives because they tend to think about objectives from the teacher's point of view and which content standard or curriculum unit is being addressed rather than from the student learning point of view. To avoid this confusion, teachers can state objectives from both perspectives. When writing *teacher* objectives you can begin with the words "To teach . . ." and specify the content standard you want to address or that the student needs to learn. So teacher objectives reflect the curriculum standards. The correlated *student learning* objective, which helps the teacher and student focus on student behavior, should be stated in terms of indicators of student performance. Such objectives clarify what is expected of the students and lend themselves to evaluation of the lesson's effectiveness. For an example of a lesson in using context clues, the *teacher* objective might be:

> To teach use of context clues to aid in figuring out words unknown in print.

The correlated *student learning* objective might be:

> At the end of this lesson, students will be given a portion of their group-developed language experience story having five sentences, each containing a blank for a word omitted, followed by three word choices. The students will be able to underline words in the sentences that help in choosing the one word that correctly completes each sentence. Each student should be able to complete 80 percent, or four of the five sentences, accurately.

Writing Student Learning Objectives

Student learning objectives should include three components: (a) the condition, (b) the observable behavior, and (c) the criterion. The *condition* refers to the setting or context in which the behavior will occur. Following are examples:

> Using a 250-word section from a social studies text . . .
> Given a 10-item worksheet on sequence of events . . .
> Given a 100-word paragraph . . .
> Using a list of the 12 vocabulary words . . .
> During a silent reading of Taro Yashima's book *Umbrella* . . .

The *observable behavior* refers to the behavior that the teacher expects the student to demonstrate. For best results, use verbs that express observable, or overt, behaviors. Although several types of observable, or overt, behaviors can be prescribed, they fall into two general categories, motoric and verbal. *Avoid* verbs that require unobservable, or covert, mental activity because the activity cannot be verified easily. Examples of motoric, verbal, and covert verbs are:

Motoric: point, circle, mark, write, underline, draw
Verbal: say, read orally, tell, retell, paraphrase
Covert: know, learn, remember, decide, participate, listen

Figure 2.5 provides additional observable verbs that are useful for writing student learning objectives.

The primary strength of overt verbal behaviors is their ready accessibility to the teacher in a discussion-recitation setting. Answering the teacher's questions and reading

Figure 2.5	Useful Verbs for Writing Student Learning Objectives

Suggest	Discuss critically	Justify
Describe	Select	Report
Synthesize	Analyze	Operationalize
Explain	Identify	Differentiate
Obtain	Define	Evaluate
Implement	Listen	Match
Classify	Give examples	Compare
Construct	Contrast	State
Recognize	Predict	Integrate
List	Solve	Recall
Label	Apply	Measure

orally are common verbal literacy behaviors. Probably the greatest weakness of overt verbal behaviors is that they do not lend themselves to easy record keeping, particularly in a group or informal setting. Recording overt oral behaviors accurately requires that the teacher work with students individually. This may mean working directly with the student or listening to a taped reading by the student.

Motoric behaviors, especially marking or writing by students, have the advantage of being relatively permanent and readily scored. Motoric behaviors also can be recorded for more than one student at a time. Record keeping can be less time consuming than recording and scoring oral reading behaviors for each student, although interpreting students' written products, to include products such as a PowerPoint presentation, does require time and thought.

Learners who have not had many opportunities to write may find writing words and sentences difficult. Those who experience reading difficulties often write and spell at a lower developmental level than that of their reading level. This is all the more reason for these learners to be given opportunities to write, although the quantity of writing and spelling required for completing an activity might be limited initially until confidence and/or skill increases. Sometimes a drawing with captions can provide evidence of learning. Multiple-choice questions that require marking and questions requiring short written answers are suggested, particularly if a written model is available for copying. If a daily writing journal is employed for instructional practice, students' writing abilities will likely improve more rapidly. (More information about the reading/writing connection can be found in Chapter 8.)

The *criterion* element of a student learning objective serves as the basis for deciding whether the lesson helped learners reach a higher performance level than earlier behaviors indicated. The criterion itself is a matter of subjective judgment, and the teacher needs to take into account the fact that certain strategies are learned over a period of time. For example, when a new strategy is first introduced the criterion level, or expected level of performance, may be low, but as students gain practice, this level is raised. For instance, the teacher and Bill agree that Bill needs to self-correct his miscues more often. If currently he never self-corrects, the initial criterion may call for Bill to self-correct "at least once." Later, after he becomes aware of the nature of his miscues (see discussions of Retrospective Miscue Analysis in Chapters 6 and 9), this criterion may be raised to "most miscues will be self-corrected." Examples of criteria are:

- With seven out of ten correct
- With 85 percent accuracy
- At least five times

Here are two examples of complete student learning objectives:

Condition:	Following the shared reading of *Bringing the Rain to Kapiti Plain* and a minilesson on long *a* spelling patterns,
Behavior:	each student will locate and make a list of words from the story that have a long *a* sound
Criterion:	with both of the two long *a* patterns in the story represented (*ai, aCE*).
Condition:	Given a 200-word paragraph from his language experience story,
Behavior:	Hue will read out loud and show evidence of self-monitoring by verbally correcting
Criterion:	at least half his miscues.

The value of student learning objectives is not in their precise writing. These objectives cannot be written at all unless the teacher has thought about students' needs and how to help individual students. These objectives provide direction for the teacher as well as documentation for later reflection. Following a lesson, the teacher should review the student learning objective and ask questions such as, "Was this goal achieved? Why or why not? Is it still an important goal? Did I learn anything new about my students from this lesson? Should the goal be changed?"

Learning Activities

Many parts of a lesson, such as changing learning activities, reviewing the lesson, and preparing for independent practice activities, are procedural. These important steps are related to classroom management but are only peripheral to the teaching function, which is the focus here. The heart of every lesson resides in the planned learning activities. Teachers' roles change rather dramatically from analyzing literacy behaviors and forming teaching hypotheses to instructing. Teachers also use assessment procedures during their lessons. Wise teachers constantly evaluate whether students are grasping the various points of the lesson. Teachers who "reflect-in-action" can modify lessons while they are ongoing (Schön, 1987). When planning the learning activities for a lesson, teachers should focus on the following: the needs of the students, the type of teaching techniques, and the questions that will best guide learning.

Planning the Learning Activities

The Needs of the Learners. Lesson planning must always be responsive to the needs of the learners. Differentiated instruction represents an approach clearly responsive to three learner characteristics in particular: readiness, interest, and learning profile. **Readiness** refers to a student's level of preparedness for learning a certain skill or concept. As discussed earlier in this chapter, much assumptive teaching can occur if students' readiness levels are not taken into account. If a learning task is provided that is too easy, little learning will occur. Likewise, if a task is well beyond the student's readiness level, frustration rather than learning will occur. So it is important to know which students are ready to learn what new information or skill. This information can come only from some form of assessment. The interest a learner has for a particular topic can serve as a strong motivator for learning. By linking content to students' interests, teachers bring the content to life for the students. Providing some choice in reading material is an obvious way to connect student interest with source material for teaching a literacy skill. **Learning profile** refers to the combination of factors such as gender, culture, developed multiple intelligences, and learning style that affect the way a student learns best. Providing for several ways of learning will help each student learn more efficiently and effectively. The teacher who is responsive to the needs of his or her learners will adapt the three curricular elements of *content* (what is to be learned), *process* (how learning will happen, or activities), and *product* (evidence of student learning) so all students might be successful learners.

Two Types of Teaching Techniques. In addition to teaching approaches, such as differentiated instruction, teachers have options or alternative techniques for presenting new concepts. For contrast, two are mentioned here: didactic (deductive) and discovery (inductive) teaching techniques. In **didactic teaching**, also called **deductive teaching**, new information is given to pupils in a direct fashion. An example is "giving" a student a new word and telling him to learn it:

Teacher: Jimmy, the word is *tray, tray*. Now you say it.

The lesson may continue with the presentation of more new words and appropriate practice activities. This technique is direct and efficient and often works well for specific purposes. It is limited, however, in that it provides little opportunity for students to be actively involved or to learn to generalize the specific word recognition process to other unknown words (**transfer of training**). To be sure, some learners can make their own generalizations and transfer these learnings to other tasks. Typically, however, students who struggle academically have trouble transferring what they have learned from one task to another. The discovery approach to teaching may better help these students learn the process (for example, analyzing the word) as well as the product (the word itself, in this case).

In **discovery teaching**, also called **inductive teaching**, learners are encouraged to seek generalizations for themselves. The teacher's function is to observe how students carry out this process and to provide reinforcement and additional clues to aid learning as needed. Providing clues helps prevent undue frustration if pupils have trouble making the "discovery." The teacher also helps students learn how to discover knowledge, that is, the transfer process itself. The word *tray* can be used again as an example:

> *Teacher:* Jimmy, you have told me this word in your story is a new word (teacher points to the word *tray* in the sentence, *The cookie tray fell down*). How can you figure it out?
>
> *Jimmy:* (No response)
>
> *Teacher:* Look at the rest of the words in the sentence. Do they help you?
>
> *Jimmy:* (No response)
>
> *Teacher:* Do you see anything or any part of this word you might already know?
>
> *Jimmy:* It starts the same as *train*.
>
> *Teacher:* Good! Anything else?
>
> *Jimmy:* No.
>
> *Teacher:* How about the ending?
>
> *Jimmy:* Well, it ends like *say* and *may*.
>
> *Teacher:* Yes, go on.
>
> *Jimmy:* Tr-tr-tr-ay-tray. I think it's *tray*.
>
> *Teacher:* Very good, Jimmy. Now let's check it out in the sentence to see if it makes sense.
>
> *Jimmy:* The cookie *tray* fell down. Yes, that makes sense. The new word is *tray*.
>
> *Teacher:* That's great, Jimmy. You are becoming a good word detective. Let's make a card for your word bank . . . great! Now, on the back of the card I want you to write a new sentence using the word *tray* (or the teacher can write a dictated sentence). Then you can practice this word later so you can read it quickly. If you have trouble remembering this word, turn your card over and read your sentence for help. You might also want to add this word to your personal dictionary with a picture and your new sentence.

Notice how much more teacher time and effort are involved when the discovery approach is used. But notice also that the teacher is getting the pupil actively involved in developing a strategy for analyzing unknown words. The minimal clues given to the learner and the use of ample praise for risk taking help reduce negative feelings of failure and frustration. While these examples included a single student, the techniques described can also be used just as well with small groups of students.

Questions to Guide Learning. The third important consideration when planning a lesson is anticipating questions that may help the students during the lesson. The teacher cannot always plan the exact questions but should be prepared to use certain types of questions during the lesson. Two types are discussed in this section, and the use of teachers' questions is addressed frequently throughout the remainder of this text.

The use of **problem-solving questions** moves a student from thinking, "I don't know the answer" to a more dynamic frame of mind equivalent to, "How can I try to solve this problem?" An example of this type of question taken from the previous dialogue is:

"How can you figure out the word, Jimmy?"

Often a question of this type signals subtly to the pupil that the teacher accepts lack of knowledge—that it is OK if a person does not know the word or answer. The student can then focus on the problem without feeling a sense of embarrassment or failure if a guess is wrong. The teacher thereby increases the probability that active student participation will occur without the learner feeling threatened.

Frequently pupils are unable to solve a problem on their own. A second type of question, called a **facilitating question**, encourages continued thinking. The purpose of facilitating questions is to make discovery easier for the learner. Examples are paraphrased from the previous dialogue:

"Do the rest of the words in the sentence help you?"
"Do you see any part of this word you might know?"

Some facilitating questions encourage pupils to focus on a point they may have overlooked:

"How about the ending of the word?"

Other facilitating questions present clues in the form of questions:

"Do you think the new word ends like these that you already know?" (The teacher writes or says appropriate examples.)

Facilitating questions demonstrate the teacher's efforts to guide students to discovery through active participation. In the example, the teacher wants Jimmy to learn the word *tray*, but all that effort to teach one word is hardly justifiable. The underlying purpose of inductive (or discovery) teaching is to help students learn part of the *process* involved in figuring out new words. The teacher and students focus on the step-by-step process (a strategy) of analyzing a particular word so the steps in the thought processes can be learned and the general thinking strategy practiced with the aid of the teacher. Such practice will eventually transfer to other unknown words students encounter when the teacher is not present.

One purpose of problem-solving and facilitating questions is to help pupils actively seek answers to the immediate question. Far more important, however, is their role in helping students develop independent-thinking strategies that can be applied to many other situations.

Assessment and Evaluation during the Lesson. This section has briefly illustrated the teaching task and discussed significant parts of lesson planning. One important issue remains. During the lesson, while the teacher is teaching, the opportunity for direct assessment of student learning is always present. The most expeditious way to assess directly is to ask questions during the course of the lesson that elicit oral responses about each point being taught. Asking for examples or illustrations also provides assessment information. After reviewing content recently taught, open the lesson with general questions that start with, "Who remembers . . . ?" or "Can someone tell us . . . ?" If the students are having trouble, the teacher can give clues or hints, which often can be stated as facilitating or focusing questions.

One good teaching procedure is to provide a brief, structured practice session on the topic, but with new examples for students to solve. Students who struggle often learn content more quickly if they can practice with the teacher and classmates. Misperceptions and incorrect learnings can be corrected immediately. A written work sheet or chalkboard or transparency practice on the topic provides a common focus for the group and helps prepare them for any evaluation activity that may follow.

Once teachers become familiar with their students, they can use practice sessions as a guide to the students' readiness to take a quiz or to participate in some other evaluation activity. If the students do poorly during practice, defer the evaluation activity and give further instruction or a second practice period. Figure 2.6 provides guidelines and a template for developing a lesson plan. When planning lessons, teachers are also expected to address the particular content standards identified by their state's Department of Education. For more help understanding how to do this, complete the simulation activity "Content Standards" in MyEducationLab about connecting a standards-based curriculum to instructional planning.

Go to MyEducationLab and select the topic *Government Regulations*. Then, go to the Activities and Applications section, and complete the simulation entitled "Content Standards" to learn how to prepare standards-based lessons. Next respond to the accompanying questions.

Summary

This chapter defines and explains the analytic process and analytic teaching. The analytic process is contrasted with assumptive teaching, and a justification for the process is presented. The analytic process provides information teachers need to differentiate instruction.

A large portion of this chapter discusses the analysis of literacy domains to gather information needed to plan for differentiated literacy instruction. Three levels of analysis are described, and correlative diagnostic questions are provided for the major domains of oral and written language ability, word recognition, comprehension and strategic reading for narrative text, strategic reading for expository text and study skills, and additional components such as linguistic diversity and outside influences. Analysis ultimately leads to instruction. For example, analysis revealing a need in the use of context clues leads to an instructional plan to teach students how to use word-order clues.

Another major section of this chapter deals with moving from the formation of teaching hypotheses to the preparation of lessons. Suggestions for differentiated instruction are provided. Examples of teacher objectives and student learning objectives are discussed. Two teaching models, nondirective and direct instruction, are explained. Examples for deductive and inductive teaching procedures are provided. Problem-solving and facilitating questions, designed to promote active learner involvement and transfer of thought processes, are explained. Several video clips are referenced that correspond to chapter content. Finally, a lesson planning template is presented that provides guidelines for planning standards-based instruction.

Figure 2.6   Guidelines and Template for Lesson Planning

Follow these steps when beginning a new lesson plan. Begin by identifying which content standards and benchmarks you will be addressing. Then, consider what behaviors students will need to demonstrate in order to indicate they have met the content standard or benchmarks. Next, think about your students and what learning activities will help them achieve the indicator behaviors. Also identify a variety of assessments that will provide different ways students can show they have met the learning objective. Prepare criteria (e.g., scoring rubrics) you will use to evaluate your students' work.

> 1. Teacher Objective.
> Which *standard(s) (benchmark)* am I addressing?

> 2. Student Learning Objective.
> What *behaviors* will students need to be able to demonstrate that will indicate they have met the standard?

> 3. Learning Activities.
> What *learning activities* will accommodate the readiness levels of my students for meeting this standard? Which students have special needs that also must be accommodated? Which lesson components would best be introduced to the whole class? Which components would best be differentiated (i.e., based on readiness, interest, or learning profile)?

> 4. Assessment.
> What are some *assessment options* for this lesson? Consider students' particular intelligence strengths. For example, might some students be more successful with drawing or diagramming rather than being given a writing task?

> 5. Evaluation.
> What *criteria* will be used to evaluate students' work? Might a scoring rubric be the best tool, or a rating scale (see Chapter 6)?

Recommended Websites

A Teacher's Guide to the NCLB Act
   www.ed.gov/teachers/nclbguide/index2.html
A user-friendly guide to NCLB is provided in the "Teacher's Toolbox."

Fry's Readability Graph
   http://school.discoveryeducation.com/schrockguide/fry/fry.html
Directions for using and a large printable version of the Fry Graphs are available at this site to determine the suitability levels of materials. Links to other readability formulas are also found at this site.

Article by Carol Tomlinson on Standards-Based Teaching and Differentiated Instruction
   www.ascd.org/ed_topics/el200009_tomlinson.html
This is a helpful article for understanding the basis for differentiating instruction.

Article by Tracey Hall on Differentiated Instruction
   www.cast.org/publications/ncac/ncac_diffinstruc.html
A good application section on differentiated instruction as well as an extensive reference list and links for learning more about differentiated instruction can be found at this link.

Differentiated Instruction
   www.frsd.k12.nj.us/rfmslibrarylab/di/differentiated_instruction.htm
A hot list of websites that includes learning styles, multiple intelligences, lesson plans, and online tutorials.

Analytic Teaching: A Journal
   www.viterbo.edu/analytic
This URL provides access to the journal called Analytic Teaching.

Teaching Models
   www.funderstanding.com/thematic_instruction.cfm
Helpful links to thematic instruction, whole-brain teaching, mastery learning, cooperative learning, service learning, and many other teaching models can be found at this site.

Learning Styles
   www.geocities.com/educationplace/ls.html
This is a resource for information on learning styles.

Learning Styles Self-Test
   www.crc4mse.org/ILS/Index.html
Determine your own learning style by taking this self-test.

Lesson Study
   http://www.lessonresearch.net/AERAfinal.pdf
This paper reports results of a lesson study project in which teachers reflect on their lessons in order to improve instruction.

For resources related to *Effective Lesson Planning* for literacy teaching, visit the following sites:

   http://readwritethink.org
Sponsored by IRA and NCTE, this site provides access to high quality practices and resources in reading and language arts.

   www.thinkfinity.org
Sponsored by the Verizon Foundation, this site serves as a browser and links to many sources of lesson plans including those found in readwritethink.org.

   www.linkslearning.org
To view the ReadingLINKS video lessons on this site, you must use Internet Explorer. This site provides 18 multimedia literacy lessons, from preschool level through secondary, for all major literacy domains.

   www.sdcoe.k12.ca.us/resources/welcome.asp
This site provides links to K–12 educational resources.

   http://school.discoveryeducation.com/schrockguide
An extensive website for curriculum ideas, resources, and teaching ideas can be found here.

   www.pacificnet.net/~mandel
The *Teachers Helping Teachers* site provides access to lesson plans, teaching tips for new teachers, a forum, and new ideas in teaching methodologies.

   www.middleweb.com
Here is a place for middle-grade teachers to explore ideas for supporting middle grade students.

   www.fi.edu/fellows/fellow8/dec98/main.html
Created by a Title 1 teacher in Tennessee, this site provides a sample literature unit, *Treasures at Sea: Exploring the Ocean through Literature,* and is a useful site for ideas related to differentiating instruction.

   www2.scholastic.com
Printable lesson plans and classroom activities are provided at this site.

   http://scholastic.com/MagicSchoolBus/index.htm
The Magic School Bus site includes many science-related online field trips for children, as well as a resource area for teachers.

   www.teacherease.com
This site provides, for the first three teachers in a school to ask, a free online gradebook service that parents can also have access to.

MyEducationLab is a research-based learning tool that brings teaching to life. Go to the Gipe 7th Edition MyEducationLab for Reading Assessment site at www.myeducationlab.com to:

- Engage in multimedia exercises to help you build a deeper and more applied understanding of chapter content.
- Use extensive resources including videos from real classrooms, Praxis and licensure preparation, a lesson plan builder, and materials to help you in your teaching career.

CHAPTER 3

Linguistic Perspectives on Literacy Instruction for English Language Learners

John G. Barnitz
University of New Orleans

OBJECTIVES

After you have read this chapter, you should be able to:

1. Explain the relationship between communicative competence and literacy development.
2. Describe some of the basic characteristics of linguistic competence and sociolinguistic competence.
3. Summarize aspects of second language acquisition.
4. Describe how language characteristics vary across cultural groups.
5. Explain implications of linguistic diversity for assessing students' language and literacy abilities.
6. Explain basic principles for facilitating children's acquisition of standard English.
7. Appreciate and respect the language and culture of all learners and explore the many professional resources for future teaching of linguistically and culturally diverse learners who speak various vernacular dialects or other native languages.

VOCABULARY ALERT

African American vernacular English (AAVE)

Basic Interpersonal Communicative Skills (BICS)

Cognitive Academic Language Proficiency (CALP)

communicative competence

comprehensible input

dialects

dialogue (interactive) journals

discourse

ebonics

ELD (English language development)

EL (English learner)

ELL (English language learner)

ESL (English as a second language)

experience-text relationship method

language experience approach

language functions

lexicon

linguistic competence

morphemes

narrative ability

oral interaction

orthography

phonemes

pragmatics

psycholinguistic processing

regional dialects

SDAIE (specially designed academic instruction in English)

social dialects

sociolinguistic competence

standard dialects

style shifting

vernacular dialects

As teachers in the twenty-first century, we need to acquire as much professional knowledge as possible about diverse languages, dialects, cultures, and ways to address the language needs of students to facilitate literacy acquisition in our increasingly multicultural classrooms. **English language learners (ELLs),** whose native tongues are either vernacular dialects of English or another language altogether, often struggle in a new language or with standard English dialect. This chapter introduces some foundational concepts of language diversity that will help us to become successful literacy teachers in diverse instructional settings.

Before proceeding, explore your own personal awareness of linguistic diversity. Activate your own schemata about the many people from various cultures and languages in your life from childhood to the present. My own experiences in urban, suburban, and rural contexts have shaped my respect for diversity, such as experiences with extended family, schooling and teaching, folk dancing, and riding city buses, to name a few (Barnitz, 1997). In various social contexts, I can recall hearing diverse languages and dialects, for example:

- shopping at a suburban drugstore and hearing customers speak Spanish, Arabic, and various dialects of English
- attending church services that involved three languages for the culturally diverse congregation
- evacuating from Hurricane Katrina and experiencing the many dialects and languages spoken along the way as well as those of various relief and recovery workers who are rebuilding New Orleans
- watching baseball and basketball games on television and sitting in the bleachers of neighborhood playgrounds around the metropolitan area and listening to the spectators and players
- watching and listening to the Summer Olympics televised from Beijing and listening to many varieties of English spoken around the world
- viewing inspirational movies about teachers in urban and rural schools with variations in classroom discourse and speech features

Standing in line at gas stations, banks, and grocery stores is no longer boring when my ears are tuned in to the diverse pronunciations, sentence structures, and vocabulary of others in line. So take a few moments now to reflect on your exposure to linguistic similarities and differences. I am sure you will agree that linguistic diversity is all around us and certainly in our schools. Diversity in communication is natural.

This chapter first provides foundational information in three major areas: communicative competence, language variations and vernacular differences, and second

For more informa-
tion on diver-
sity, go to
MyEducationLab
and first select the
topic *Intervention
Programs*. Go to the
Activities and
Applications section,
complete the simula-
tion entitled
"Teachers at the
Loom," and respond
to the accompanying
questions. Then se-
lect the topic *English
Language Learners*.
Go to the Activities
and Applications
section, complete
the simulation enti-
tled "Teaching and
Learning in New
Mexico," and re-
spond to the accom-
panying questions.
Focus on the
Cultural and
Linguistic Diversity
and Learning sec-
tions (pages 3 and 4)
located under the
Perspectives and
Resources button.
You will be asked to
revisit the "Teaching
and Learning in New
Mexico" simulation
in Chapter 4 for the
portions related to
other aspects of di-
versity beyond cul-
tural and linguistic.

language acquisition. Next, you will gain knowledge of general principles for literacy instruction and assessment with linguistic diversity awareness in mind. The chapter concludes with information about developmental stages of English language acquisition that
may help you recognize the language proficiency level of English language learners and
corresponding instructional practices. Equipped with this knowledge base, you will be
able to choose wisely from among the many instructional strategies discussed in Chapters
7 through 14, and thus plan appropriate learning opportunities for maximum student participation and achievement among your English language learners.

COMMUNICATIVE COMPETENCE

Communicative competence is the knowledge and use of language for oral and written interaction or, more specifically, the internalized knowledge of the phonological
and syntactic structures of language (**linguistic competence**) and the ability to use
language in various social situations, or **sociolinguistic competence**. According to
Shuy (1981), the term *linguistic competence* generally refers to the mastery of the formal system of language (that is, sounds, sentences, vocabulary), whereas sociolinguistic
competence is the use of language "to get things done," which includes language functions (purposes for language) but also includes the social strategic use of language to
accomplish communicative goals. Sociolinguistic competence emphasizes how language is used for various functional purposes in various social situations (**pragmatics**).
Speakers of all languages and dialects have common communicative competence abilities as they use the various language arts (speaking, listening, writing, reading, visually representing, and viewing), although naturally variation exists across the many
languages and dialects of the world.

Regardless of dialect or language backgrounds, learners first develop their abilities
in speaking and listening and extend that ability to writing and reading. In addition,
learners develop communicative competence through the visual arts by viewing and visually representing. All the communicative/language arts involve **psycholinguistic processing**, or composing and comprehending the meaning of oral and written language by
using the various thinking processes (memory, knowledge, language, perception, and the
like). Communicative competence is the ability to compose meaning through talking,
writing, and visually representing and to comprehend meaning by listening, reading, and
viewing—all for functional purposes in social contexts.

Sociolinguistic competence includes, among other processes, social interaction abilities, language functions, narrative abilities, and *style shifting* (the ability to adapt a
language style to a social context) (Shuy, 1981). Consider the example of a social conversation (oral interaction). **Oral interaction** includes conversational abilities, switching topics, taking turns, and strategies for politeness and tact, as well as basic pragmatic abilities
such as knowing what and what not to say (or write). Such abilities transfer to reading and writing because literacy is also a sociocultural discourse process (Au, 2006;
Bloome, 1991; Gee, 2007). These competencies help us infer, for example, the social
motives of a speaker, writer, or visual representer, and better comprehend the oral interactions of characters in a story. Moreover, in the twenty-first century, the newer literacies,
such as digital and electronic communications, are manifested in the social practices of today's learners, no matter how diverse all of us are (see Coiro, et al., 2007; Gee, 2008;
Mahiri, 2004).

The functional use of language is basic to language production and comprehension
and usually precedes the perfection of formal structures. Language exists because it is

useful, and children learn language as they perceive the need. Children from various linguistic backgrounds use a variety of functions crucial to the effective use of language. For instance, in their **dialogue journals** (written conversations between child and teacher) students demonstrate a wide range of **language functions**: reporting opinions and personal and general facts, responding to questions, predicting future events, complaining, giving directives, apologizing, thanking, evaluating, offering, promising, and asking various kinds of questions (Shuy, 1988; Staton et al., 1988).

English language learners use language functionally. For example, a group of native Zulu speakers (ages 12 through 16) learning English used the language functions of teaching, inquiring, joking, informing, scolding, offering, seeking clarification, apologizing, explaining, expressing opinions, conversing, thanking, comforting, and reflecting in their dialogue journals (Lindfors, 1989).

The functional use of language to fluently express and sequence ideas, called **narrative ability**, is also central to literacy development in that the writer/speaker/visual representer must use language to facilitate a certain response in the reader/listener. Conversely, an effective reader/listener is aware of what the author is trying to do with language. Many ethnically diverse learners demonstrate strength in composing oral stories, telling lengthy jokes, and describing events such as traffic accidents. If students have an intuitive awareness of how narrative **discourse** (any oral or written communication longer than a single sentence) is ordered in text, they can make meaningful predictions in the reading comprehension process. Students may demonstrate strong narrative abilities (an aspect of linguistic intelligence) regardless of the language or dialect spoken.

Style shifting is another important language skill that refers to the ability of speakers and writers to adapt their language styles to various social contexts (depending on the different settings, participants, and topics). As such, style shifting is certainly a core operation of linguistic intelligence and can also be considered a facet of interpersonal intelligence (Gardner, 1999). Just as we vary our dress depending on the social situation (formal, semi-formal, casual), so do we shift our language styles. Language variety is a necessary part of language competence. The more variety in our language "wardrobe," the better we can interact in diverse social contexts. We need to express ourselves formally in formal situations (job interviews, professional presentations) and also informally in casual situations (visiting with a friend in a coffee shop or sitting in the bleachers at a basketball game). Code switching is a natural part of learning standard English literacy (see Wheeler & Swords, 2006).

Functional use of language is crucial to school success (Piper, 2003; Shafer, Staab, & Smith, 1983), while social use of language is critical for language and literacy acquisition. Social interaction is especially critical for diverse learners (Au, 2006; Bloome, 1991; Cary, 2007; Enright & McCloskey, 1988; Gee, 2008; Mahiri, 2004; Tharp & Gallimore, 1988). Thus, first and second language literacy development involves a complex interaction of social, cognitive, and linguistic processes (August & Shanahan, 2008; Bernhardt, 1991; Carrell, Devine, & Eskey, 1988; Ferdman, Weber, & Ramirez, 1994; Kamil et al., 2000; Koda & Zehler, 2007).

While the overall sociolinguistic, pragmatic, functional aspects of communication within and across any language are the most critical to learning, we must acknowledge the roles of the various linguistic structures. Linguistic competence related to oral and written language communication certainly involves: the *phonological system*, which includes the individual speech sounds (**phonemes**) and sound processes of a language (see also Chapter 9); the *morphological system*, which includes the meaningful word structures (**morphemes**) (see also Chapter 10); the *syntactic system*, which consists of the structures and processes of sentence formation; and the **lexicon**, or a language's systematic set of vocabulary and word meanings (also a part of the *semantic system*).

SOME LINGUISTIC VARIATIONS

Variations across Languages

Linguistic diversity includes variations across languages and variations within a language. A wide range of language varieties is spoken in today's classrooms. Nonnative speakers of English are found throughout the United States and the world, and these learners of **English as a second language (ESL)**, more recently called **English language learners (ELLs)** or **English learners (ELs)**, will need additional assistance from their teachers in learning to read. Many English learners will already have some literacy abilities in their first language (L1) and perhaps also in English (L2). Their native linguistic abilities transfer to English, although the extent of the transfer may depend on the specific languages and writing systems involved (Cowan & Sarmad, 1976; Koda & Zehler, 2007).

English learners often use the rules from their native language schema when reading or writing English as a second language. Many so-called errors are the result of the influence of the native language rather than linguistic or cognitive deficits (Flores, 1984). For example, a native Spanish speaker who writes, "We bought the book in the library" is likely influenced by the Spanish word for bookstore, which is *libreria*. Therefore, it is important for teachers to learn about similarities and contrasts between English and the languages spoken by their students. Although languages are too complex to be thoroughly discussed here, some phonological, syntactic, and lexical differences between English and Spanish and between English and Vietnamese are presented here in some detail.

Phonological Differences. Phonological contrasts should be considered when teaching phoneme–grapheme correspondences for learning to read and spell words. Not all languages have the same set of phonemes, and their relationship with the writing system can also vary. Because the phoneme systems vary, certain pairs of English words that normally are pronounced differently are pronounced or heard as homonyms by the native speaker. For example, the word pair *tin/thin* would sound the same to Spanish speakers since they do not have the /th/ sound in their language (note that when the sound for a written symbol, or phoneme, is referenced it is written inside backward slash marks). Geissal and Knafle (1977) explained that linguistically diverse learners use their native phonological systems when processing English and may not hear some of the English sounds or contrasts. This could result in what would seem to be a mispronunciation error by someone not knowledgeable about the particular language diversity. These pronunciations are certainly not the result of a language or speech disorder.

The following consonant contrasts are often not made by native Spanish speakers learning English because these contrasts are not made in Spanish (Troike, 1972, p. 312):

Sound	*Examples (pronunciation/target word)*
ch/sh	chair/share, watch/wash
s/z	sip/zip, racer/razor
m/mp	lam/lamp, ram/ramp
n/ng	sin/sing
n/nk	sin/sink
b/v	bat/vat, rabble/ravel
t/th	tin/thin
s/th	sin/thin
d/th	den/then, ladder/lather

Spanish, unlike English, has only five vowel phonemes. Thus Spanish speakers do not hear or pronounce contrasts such as the following:

bait/bet/bat
cut/cot
cheap/chip
pool/pull
coat/caught

Additionally, there are no Spanish words that begin with *s-* blends; there is no letter *k* or letter *w* (only in words of foreign origin); and the pronunciation of the soft *g*, or /j/, is often pronounced /h/ as *hiraffe* for *giraffe* or *huvenile* for *juvenile*. The only silent letter in Spanish is *h*. Any of these differences influence pronunciation or spelling of English. (See Freeman & Freeman, 2006, for more information.)

Here are some more phonological examples, this time from Vietnamese (Grognet et al., 1976). Vietnamese speakers learning English do not contrast such pairs of English words as the following:

Sound	*Examples*
z/s	flees/fleece, dyes/dice
ch/sh	much/mush
f/p	laugh/lap
p/b	pin/bin
k/g	back/bag
th/t	ether/eater
th/d	lather/latter/ladder
i/e	pit/Pete
e/a	bet/bat

Nonnative speakers of English (and dialect speakers) do not initially hear or pronounce contrasts not made in the native language. Vietnamese phonology does not allow certain consonant clusters at the ends of words; therefore, in pronouncing English words they may split consonant blends with vowels (for example, *stop* becomes *suhtop*) or they may delete consonants at the ends of words (and so *cold* becomes *col'*; *called* becomes *call)*. Thus, their auditory discrimination and oral reading may be influenced by the phonological organization of their native language. However, this is natural and not a sign of linguistic deficiency or disability (Flores, Cousin, & Diaz, 1998; Goodman & Buck, 1973/1997). In teaching the reading and writing of words, these pairs of words can be treated like any other set of homonyms; that is, teach them in meaningful contexts first. More contextual support reduces potential linguistic interference from phonological diversity. Therefore, meaning-based, holistic techniques supported by social discourse are especially important to successful literacy instruction of linguistically diverse learners (see Au, 2006; Barnitz, 1985; Carrell et al., 1988; Enright & McCloskey, 1988; Freeman & Freeman, 2006; Opitz, 1998; Peregoy & Boyle, 2004; Rigg & Allen, 1989; Spangenberg-Urbschat & Pritchard, 1994; Watts-Taffe & Truscott, 2000).

Syntactic Differences. Just as phonological systems of native languages influence performance in English, so do the syntactic systems. Davis (1972) presented, among other syntactic features, the following sentence structures likely produced by Spanish speakers learning English (also included in a teachers' guide by the New York City Board of Education, *Teaching English to Puerto Rican Pupils in Grades 1 and 2* [1956, 1963] (as cited by Davis, 1972, pp. 131–132):

Sentence Structure	*Examples*
Deletion of subject pronouns and articles	Is green. Is my sister.
Negative morpheme before verb	Jose not (no) is here.
Adjectives after nouns	The dress green. The dresses greens.
Deletion of /s/ inflections	He go to church. The pencil are here.
Present instead of progressive	He clean now.
Preposition contrasts	In the counter. In First St.
Have for *be*	She have nine years.

Similarly, teachers of Vietnamese learners need to be aware of syntactic differences (Grognet et al., 1976). The Vietnamese language does not use suffixes to convey meaning. Meaning is conveyed in other ways, as seen in sentences that translate into English as follows:

> I need book.
> I need one piece book.
> I need three piece book.
> I need few piece book.

Plurality is marked by separate words rather than suffixes. Similarly, tense is marked by separate words that are equivalent to the underlined words in the following sentences:

> I <u>often</u> drink tea.
> I <u>intend</u> to drink tea.
> I <u>past tense</u> drink tea.
> I <u>about to</u> drink tea.

Because Vietnamese does not use suffixes, its native speakers often omit or ignore them when speaking, writing, and reading English. Greene (1981) referred to this as the "morpheme conceptualization barrier" but found that Vietnamese speakers who also were competent in French, a language with suffixes, tended to recognize and produce English suffixes in their writing and reading. Instructional practices such as sentence expansion, choral reading, the language experience approach, creative writing, and the careful selection of children's literature can help students become sensitive to new syntactic structures being learned in English (these instructional strategies, as well as many others, are discussed in more detail in later chapters).

To more fully understand how important it is to show respect for a student's language and culture, go to MyEducationLab and select the topic *Spelling*. Then, go to the Activities and Applications section, and watch the video entitled "Teacher Rigidity" for one parent's perspective on this issue. Next respond to the accompanying questions.

Lexical Differences. Vocabulary varies across languages. For example, the Spanish *penitencia, realizar, libreria,* and *chanza* are not equivalent to the English *penitentiary, realize, library,* and *chance,* but rather *penance, accomplish an ambition, bookstore,* and *joke* (Thonis, 1976). French speakers learning English need to learn the meaningful contrasts between the English words *cut* and *carve,* for example, because French has only one word for both concepts, *couper.* For teaching vocabulary to all learners, recommended strategies include semantic mapping and semantic feature analysis (see Chapter 10). Teachers also might wish to learn and use at least 10 practical words from the native language of their English learners. For teachers who have four different nonnative languages represented in their classrooms, this would mean a minimum of 40 words should be learned. Such a gesture from the teacher will motivate English learners and show respect and appreciation for their native languages.

Likewise, idioms and various other figures of speech are also potentially problematic for learners not familiar with the metaphorical use of phrases such as *kick the bucket, factor into the equation,* and *the bottom line.* Because vocabulary and metaphorical language are closely related to meaning, there may be influences on reading comprehension unless learners understand how to use context and/or acquire the nonliteral meanings.

Variations within a Language

Dialects are variations of a language found among speakers of particular regions, social classes, or cultural groups. Variations identifiable to speakers in a particular geographical area are called **regional dialects**; variations identifiable to particular speakers in particular social classes or cultural groups are called **social dialects**.

Dialects normally vary in terms of phonological, grammatical, lexical, and functional dimensions. Phonologically, you can easily identify the many variations in pronunciations of words; for example, how do you, your classmates, or family and friends say, *"How now brown cow"*? *"Boil the oysters in oil"*? *"Park the car by the river"*? *"Will merry Mary find someone to marry"*? *"Give them these, not those"*? Many pronunciations exist within a language, and learners bring these various pronunciations to both reading and spelling words. Grammatically, can you identify people with variations in sentence structures? For example, have you heard someone say, *"Did you bring the camera with"*? *"Did daddy go a-huntin"*? *"My mama, she be tall"*? Similarly, do you know people from various regions, cultures, social classes, or age groups whose vocabulary varies? Do you or they say *soft drink, cold drink, soda,* or *pop? Bag* or *sack? Neutral ground* or *median strip? Hoagie, submarine,* or *po' boy? Bad, good,* or *cool?* And what about situational, functional differences in conversations, such as getting straight to the point or talking around a point? Discuss with your classmates or colleagues how dialects and discourse customs vary within our families, communities, and schools.

Dialects often identify us, sometimes unjustly, as educated or less educated, or as prestigious or of lower status, depending on the social values and norms about language in a community. The language varieties spoken and preferred by the dominant members of a society for conducting formal affairs are called **standard dialects** (Wolfram, 1991), while the varieties more likely used in informal settings and also pervasive among groups of lower social status are called **vernacular dialects**. It is important to note that vernacular dialects and the many variations among social situations are systematic, rule-governed, sophisticated sociolinguistic systems (see Adger, Wolfram, & Christian, 2007; Labov, 1975; Meier, 2008; and Rickford & Rickford, 2000).

Examples of Vernacular Dialects. African American vernacular English (AAVE) is a variety of English spoken in African American communities. AAVE consists of a range of speech from standard English (the language of wider communication) to the vernacular speech found in the community. As is true for any ethnic variety of English, AAVE (also referred to as "**ebonics**") is rule governed, containing a systematic set of phonological, syntactic, semantic, and discourse characteristics (Adger et al., 2007; Baugh, 1983, 1999; Labov, 1975; McWhorter, 2000; Meier, 2008; Rickford, 1999; Rickford & Rickford, 2000; Smitherman, 1985; Smitherman & Villenueva, 2003).

In addition, the rich lexical and discourse styles in the African American community make AAVE a fully developed communicative system that is beneficial to literacy development in standard English. The "ebonics" controversy of the 1990s and the earlier court case decided in Ann Arbor, Michigan, that legitimized AAVE (Wardhaugh, 2002) have led to our understanding of the advantages of acquiring standard English, but with respect

Table 3.1	Selected Phonological and Syntactic Features of a Vernacular Dialect
Phonological Patterns of AAVE	**Examples**
Consonant cluster simplification	des (desk)
Deletion of /l/	hep (help)
voiced *th*	den (then)
voiceless *th*	tin (thin)
vowel neutralization before nasal consonants	pin (pen)
Morphological and Syntactic Patterns of AAVE	**Examples**
Deletion of plural	ten cent (cents)
Deletion of third-person singular	The girl walk fast. (walks)
Deletion of past tense	The man call yesterday. (called)
Existential *it (there)*	It was two cars in the garage. (There were)
Invariant *be*	He be hollin' at us. (He hollers)
Deletion of *be*	My momma name Annie. (name is)

for the legitimacy of native vernacular varieties, which function like any language or dialect. African American varieties of English (like other ethnic varieties, such as rural Appalachian English) are considered fully developed linguistic systems capable of supporting the development of literacy. Table 3.1 includes just a few of many systematic characteristics found in vernacular English–speaking populations (see Adger et al., 2007 for a useful collection of vernacular dialect features).

Other Linguistic Variations

Other ways that languages vary include orthographic diversity and discourse diversity. **Orthography** refers to the writing system of a language. Some writing systems, like Chinese, have symbols that represent whole word meanings. Most writing systems have symbols that represent levels of the stream of speech; for example, *syllabaries* have symbols representing syllables, as in Japanese and Cherokee. The most common writing systems have symbols representing phonemes—for example, various alphabets. These alphabetic writing systems operate based on the spelling system that conveys the particular grapheme–phoneme representations in the language. Most languages of the world have alphabets of various kinds (for example, Greek, Arabic, Russian), but most alphabetic languages use the Roman alphabet, based on Latin, which spread through imperial conquests and missionary evangelization across many languages of the world. English, a Germanic language, has acquired the Roman writing system, which does not appear on the surface as "regular" as would be found in the Romance languages.

Also, the directionality of print varies across languages; for example, Arabic, Farsi, and Hebrew speakers read from right to left. Thus, nonnative speakers of English have to grapple with the unique alphabet connections to English. Although first- and second-language learners can readily acquire phonemic awareness, the connections to the writing system are more difficult and performance can vary. See Venezky (1999) and Wilde

(1997) for discussions of the writing system of English. See Coulmas (1989) for discussions of writing system characteristics of languages around the world. See Trabasso and colleagues (2005) for research on phonological and orthographic aspects of spelling and decoding; and Koda and Zehler (2007) for discussion of writing system characteristics related to learning to read a second language.

Oral and written discourse diversity also can influence learners acquiring literacy (see review by Barnitz, 1986, 1994, 1998). Research by Au (2006) has documented the role of culturally unique discourse strategies of conarration of responses to texts in reading lessons for Hawaiian minority children. Heath (1983) documented the unique "ways with words" of three communities in the Piedmont Carolinas impacting children's literacy if teachers are aware or unaware of the diversity. Discourse variations can be allowed in classrooms that involve children in talking naturally as a strategy for developing literacy (Au, 2006). In the same way, oral and written culture-specific variations in textual organization (Conner, 1996; Kaplan, 1966) can influence the comprehension and composing of texts by learners from various cultures (see Barnitz, 1986; Barnitz in Opitz, 1998).

Taken as a whole, language in any of its variations certainly is a rich foundation for literacy development. Linguistically informed teachers know how to minimize the potential negative effects of language differences on the reading, writing, speaking, and visual communication performance of their students. A brief overview of second language acquisition and some guiding principles for literacy development for language-diverse learners comprise the rest of this chapter.

ASPECTS OF SECOND-LANGUAGE ACQUISITION

The professional knowledge base for literacy instruction includes an understanding of language acquisition of native and nonnative language in addition to the structures of language (see Garcia, 2003; Piper, 2006; Wong Fillmore & Snow, 2000). A short summary of some general themes related to language acquisition follows.

In brief, language acquisition has been viewed from several different perspectives. Earlier views of language acquisition were based on behaviorism (see Skinner, 1957). According to behaviorism, acquisition is considered to be a habit formation process in which learners acquire language structures through imitation (stimulus-response mechanisms). This perspective underlies many repetitive, skill-drill approaches to language instruction, such as the audiolingual approach in which learners practice through drilling various structural patterns of oral language. Alternative perspectives on language acquisition emphasize the psycholinguistic creativity of learners. Chomsky (1972) and others argued that language is acquired through discovery and making hypotheses about how a language works by employing a "language acquisition device" innate to all human beings. Ensuing instructional approaches to language and literacy, such as the language experience approach, are based on the individual language competence and performance of the learners. Another third perspective on language acquisition emphasizes the sociocultural and sociolinguistic nature of human communication (see Vygotsky, 1962, and Tharp & Gallimore, 1988). From this perspective, learners acquire language through social interaction by using language in situated contexts to accomplish functions. Instruction based on this perspective would involve learners in using oral and written language in a variety of authentic communicative situations. In essence, language acquisition is a creative, developmental psycholinguistic process in which learners use language in social interactions to carry out various functional intentions. The functional use of language drives the creative acquisition of sociolinguistic and linguistic competence.

Figure 3.1	Ensuring Comprehensible Input

1. Use visuals.
2. Use gestures and body language (see Asher [1982] for information on Total Physical Response, or TPR).
3. Speak slowly and enunciate.
4. Use longer, natural pauses at phrase and sentence boundaries.
5. Use natural redundancy in speaking by providing more than one explanation of an idea; repeat and review often.
6. Use shorter sentences.
7. Use simpler syntax.
8. Use fewer pronouns.
9. Exaggerate intonation at appropriate times.
10. Stress high-frequency vocabulary.
11. Use fewer idioms and slang and avoid culturally bound clichés and metaphors.
12. Clarify meaning through context, definition, or paraphrasing.
13. Maintain a low anxiety level.
14. Stress participatory learning.
15. Be enthusiastic and use a warm tone of voice.

Communicative abilities in oral and written language are central to any language arts program for both native and nonnative English speakers. Enright and McCloskey's (1988) approach to second-language instruction involves at least four kinds of discourse in a classroom community: share discourse, fun discourse, fact discourse, and thought (critical thinking) discourse. Cummins (1994) argued that second-language learners need to acquire not only conversational abilities called **Basic Interpersonal Communicative Skills (BICS)** in the target language (L2) but also academic language competencies in both oral and written language, called **Cognitive Academic Language Proficiencies (CALPs)**, for learning cognitively demanding and undemanding content in various degrees of supportive contexts.

Within a social context, when language is used naturally and when the input is comprehensible, second-language and literacy acquisition is enhanced (Krashen, 2003). Krashen claims that the amount of **comprehensible input** (exposure to the L2 "that the learner can and is motivated to make sense of" [Cummins, 1994, p. 45]) is a critical factor in second-language acquisition (see Figure 3.1 for ways to achieve comprehensible input). Yet, to reach grade-level norms, the acquisition of many linguistic competencies in a second language often requires a minimum of two years for conversational abilities and five to seven years for academic language proficiency (Collier, 1987, 1989; Cummins, 1994). Also, Gee (2008) advanced our understanding that literacy for second-language learners involves situated action and various kinds of social discourse and genres. In recent years, dual language instruction and two-way immersion programs are advocated for language instruction of Language Learners. See Freeman and Freeman (2006); Freeman, Freeman, and Mercuri (2006); and Howard, Christian, and Genesee (2004) for more information on these programs.

SOME DIVERSITY-RELATED PRINCIPLES FOR LITERACY INSTRUCTION

All learners develop a certain degree of communicative competence in their native language or dialect; much of language development and ability is universal or common across all languages. For example, much of what we know about native English speakers learning to read in English also applies to English learners learning to read in their native language (L1) as well as in English (L2). Yet differences do exist and need to be considered by teachers. These differences can exist between the learner's language and the text, between the learner's language and that of the teacher, between the text and the teacher, and between the learner and other learners in a multicultural classroom community. The challenge is to minimize the impact of these differences in guiding learners in their development of literacy (the topic of the last section in this chapter).

Respect Differences in Languages and Dialects as Natural. Learners have communicative competence in their native dialects and languages on which to build English literacy. This implies that children can develop literacy if allowed to use their native dialect or language as they make the transition to reading and writing standard English. Respecting linguistic diversity allows learners to take risks to communicate in the various language arts modes. In our profession, we have come to appreciate linguistic diversity as difference rather than as deficit because negative attitudes toward language and cultural differences interfere with the success of learners acquiring literacy in standard English and their native language or dialect (Flores et al., 1998; Goodman & Buck, 1973/1997). We can minimize any potential negative effects of differences if we have the appropriate theoretical and practical professional knowledge and attitudes. Linguistic diversity is one of the professional knowledge bases for teaching culturally diverse learners.

Use Methods That Bridge Cultural Background Knowledge and Whatever Texts Are Being Read. Such methods allow learners to use the total language system, while it is still developing, in the literacy process. Holistic strategies such as the language experience approach (LEA) (see Spotlight on English Learners in Chapter 8) and the experience-text-relationship method (ETR) (see Spotlight on English Learners in Chapter 11) allow learners to make connections between their language and culture and that of the texts they are reading and writing. The **language experience approach** allows developing readers and writers to connect their oral language with the written language. The texts produced in language experience lessons become good "drafts" for further development of linguistic skills and processes (see Rigg, 1989). The **experience-text-relationship method** and related reading process approaches allow learners to use their authentic discourse and cultural background knowledge in constructing meanings for the texts they are reading (Au, 2006). English language learners have better opportunities to acquire competence in oral and written English when "comprehensible input" (Krashen, 2003) is provided for students in natural language lessons. Teachers can make input comprehensible if they base lessons on students' prior knowledge and use language that is predictable. Furthermore, adapting book club discussions and other classroom community discourse practices can assist language learners' comprehension and use of language by providing the support of classmates (Brock & Raphael, 2005).

Integrate Instruction on Language Structures and Skills within the Composing and Comprehending Process. Although process strategies are critical for successful development of language and literacy, English learners will also need direct instruction on specific aspects of the language system such as grammar structures, spelling patterns, meaning vocabulary, and discourse patterns. Teachers may use semantic maps or clusters to teach the relevant cultural background knowledge and vocabulary related to a story being read (see Chapter 10), or they may choose various *graphic organizers* or text pattern diagrams to represent the organizational pattern of a text, especially for learners who organize textual meaning differently (see Chapters 11 and 12). Teachers have available a variety of authentic approaches to teaching grammar structures (see Chapter 8), especially for learners who come from language backgrounds where the grammar structures are ordered differently (see Barnitz, 1998; Dean, 2008; Weaver, 1998; and Wheeler and Swords, 2006, for current practices in teaching grammar related to oral and written communication). Or, through systematic phonics instruction in comprehensive reading programs, teachers can provide direct instruction on the orthographic patterns, especially if the reader comes from a language that does not use an alphabetic writing system or uses one different from English (see Chapters 8 and 9). Many strategies that are successful with native speakers can also be adapted to nonnative speakers of English when combined with holistic strategies (Barnitz, 1985).

Use Authentic Materials from the Learner's Community. Literacy materials are all around us and readily available. Such materials include restaurant menus from ethnic restaurants, church bulletins printed in more than one language, directions for assembling a toy or installing camera batteries, and brochures from community businesses written in several languages. Meaningful materials from the community that are used in the classroom support literacy development. These authentic materials can be connected with role-playing strategies for developing communicative competence related to direct use in the community (for example, learning to order from a menu; also see Chapters 13 and 14). Moreover, authentic materials representing various cultural groups can be used for developing cross-cultural awareness, which builds classroom community and helps students develop respect for one another's languages and cultures.

Access Learners' Out-of-School Interests in the Community as Relevant to Literacy and Language Development. Learners are actively engaged in a variety of activities in their culturally diverse communities. Heath (1993) documented the rich communicative competence of urban youth in the situated contexts of drama clubs. Mahiri (1998, 2004) documented sophisticated ways in which urban youth use language in a basketball program sponsored by a recreation department. Barnitz (2003, 2004) documents his own linguistic awareness and literacy practices related to baseball experiences in alleys, parks, and playgrounds in an urban community. A growing body of research on popular culture in the lives of youth is yielding a professional understanding of natural connections to language and literacy acquisition (Alvermann, Moon, & Hagood, 1999; Krashen, 2004). Moreover, community resources such as zoos, museums, and sports arenas are rich contexts for acquiring language and literacy. Learners from diverse backgrounds can become literate when actively engaged in social, meaningfully enriching activities. Moreover, in times of personal and community crises, such as what many experienced after Hurricane Katrina, various aspects of literacy and language become critical for survival and recovery (see Barnitz, 2006; Bedford and Kieff, in press). Experiences outside of school are rich contexts for literacy and language performance (Gee, 2008; Mahiri, 2004).

Design Literature-Based Instruction for Developing Language Competence. Using literature as well as musical lyrics can provide the needed variety of language structures and functions to support English language acquisition. Exposure and interaction with literature and lyrics facilitates the acquisition of systems of language, multicultural understanding, and various cognitive and social processes. Literature in its different genres as well as literature with art illustrations and audio-recorded counterparts provides necessary "scaffolding" for children acquiring the language. Teachers can also have learners read familiar stories (such as "Cinderella") that may be represented in different ways and in various languages and cultures (see Chapter 12 for examples of ways to compare and contrast versions of familiar stories). For a review of the many benefits of literature-based instruction, see Barnitz, Gipe, and Richards (1999), Morrow and Gambrell (2000), and Morrow and Temlock-Fields (2004).

Use Technological and Other Communicative Arts to Facilitate Oral and Written Language Acquisition. Speaker and Barnitz (1999) presented a vision for a hypothetical culturally diverse classroom in the twenty-first century. Technology provides the multi-mediated support for language and literacy to be acquired, embedded within a classroom community that is communicatively interactive. Technological processes associated with various mediated language experiences are universal across languages. Native and non-native speakers of English can view and visually represent ideas in various electronic and linguistic forms to communicate. The more learners use whatever communicative systems are available to them, the better the chance that their general communicative abilities will develop. By incorporating the arts into language/literacy instruction, we especially help nonnative speakers of English acquire abilities of constructing meaning. Photography, dance, music, painting, and drama can allow communicative expressions to occur, which are foundationally related to oral and written language development. Wholesome musical lyrics from audio recordings can support literacy, especially for learners whose learning preferences are attuned to musical ways of representing meaning. Likewise, professionally published or teacher-made audio recordings of literature and content material can also support comprehension and language skills acquisition. Many of the visual and musical arts provide contextual support for oral and written language to develop, in addition to providing an avenue for students whose strong intelligences are bodily-kinesthetic, spatial, or musical in particular (Gardner, 1999). Both the performing and the technological arts are invaluable avenues to facilitating the language and literacy abilities of culturally diverse learners (see Coiro et al., 2007; Flood, Heath, & Lapp, 2007).

Facilitate Authentic, Functional Communication. Using language for various purposes or functions is what drives the language acquisition process (Halliday, 1978). Thus, writing and reading texts related to real purposes, aimed at real audiences, provides natural motivation for literacy. Dialogue journals, mentioned earlier, are one means of incorporating language functions. Whether in print or electronic formats (e-journals, e-mail), dialogue journals can encourage the development of functional discourse in which the English-speaking adult serves as a model for using the structures and functions of English in the natural writing/reading process. It is through natural, functional discourse that learners of any language or dialect acquire literacy. (See Piper, 2006; Shafer et al., 1983; and Staton et al., 1988 for discussions of function-based instruction.)

Base Literacy Assessment on Authentic Language and Literacy Tasks and Events. Through authentic tasks, students use the entire language system to express themselves in real literacy events (Garcia & Pearson, 1991). Potentially negative influences of dialect or language diversity are diminished when there is rich situational and textual context. Whatever a student's dialect, functional language use in narrating or retelling a story can be demonstrated. The following is a retelling[1] of the story *Jumanji* (Van Allsburg, 1981) by a sixth-grade African American female student. (Some of the dialect is represented by the spelling, but the focus here should be on the fluent cohesiveness of the narrative summary.)

> This story is about Judy an(d) Peter. Dey (their) mother an(d) father went to a reception; dey left the(m) home by theyself (theirselves). Judy an(d) Peter say it got a little boring; so, so, dey went outside across the street an(d) dey foun(d) a game. Judys, Judy say, "No, let's wait, let's rea(d) de instruction(s)." Judy read the instructions. Den they start(ed) playin the game. Lots of

---

[1]Retelling recorded by a former undergraduate student, Kelly Strahan, in an urban school as part of her teacher education program. See also Barnitz, Gipe, and Richards (1999).

Arts Connection _____

The arts clearly empower students who come from diverse ethnic and linguistic backgrounds. Students can use the arts along with their varied cultural experiences, values, identities, beliefs, and languages to convey their thinking. Blending literacy events with artistic pursuits also creates possibilities for students from nonmainstream backgrounds, nonstandard English–speaking families, or English learners to increase their oral and written language by constructing, extending, and sharing meaning from the texts they read and to generate new and novel texts. Most important, the arts provide cultural opportunities that are not related to social class, academic ranking, or standard English proficiency. In addition, the use of visuals or realia is recommended when working with English learners especially. Book-specific visuals that accompany the stories students read or hear pique students' interest in literature and enhance their imagination. In addition, visuals help students remember how the story elements of characters, settings, problems, and solutions relate to one another. Equally important, attractive visuals that represent various facets of stories provide opportunities for students to experience a language-based activity (reading) through a different system (the visual arts).[2] For example, when one teacher read the story *Goldilocks and the Three Bears* (a Brothers Grimm fairy tale retold by Brett, 1987) to her first-grade students, she assembled small, medium, and large-sized bowls, spoons, chairs, and toy beds. As she read the story, her students took turns manipulating the visuals when the bowls, spoons, chairs, and beds were mentioned in the story. At the end of the fairy tale, the students used the visuals to offer an informal drama improvisation for other students and teachers in the school. These types of activities allow teachers to observe and document students' ongoing abilities to retell, recreate, and extend a story. Teachers can also record children's developing abilities to understand story characters' thinking, goals, and actions.

thangs (things) happen(ed) to a game. Den, Peter roll(ed) de dice; den he stopped on a lion; his siste(r) said, "Peter, look behind you!" On top of the piano, they had a big lion lickin his lips. Den it was Judy turn. Den somethin' happen(ed) to her. An den other thangs. . . . Judy and dem, um, when Judy and dem finish(ed) the game, they brought it back across the street. Dey (their) fathe(r) and mothe(r) came home; dey were (a)sleep. Judy shoved at Peter to wake him up an den, his mo(ther), they started to finish the puzzles. Then this lady came an say, "My two son(s) don't, dey don't read the instructions," and den the, um the two boys went outside; dey went across the street an dey found a puzzle an brought it back.

This short retelling illustrates the student's ability to compose a narrative with an overall gist of the story. At first glance, a teacher might misjudge this student's language abilities by focusing only on the surface dialect features. (See Irwin and Mitchell, 1983, and Morrow, 1988, for ways of assessing retellings; also refer to Appendix I and Figure 12.1 in this text.)

Practice Ongoing, Continuous, and Varied Literacy Assessment. Multiple methods of assessment, discussed throughout this text, are needed to understand the full linguistic abilities and multiple literacies of children. But a teacher must also have a solid understanding of the linguistic requirements of literacy tasks. If the intended assessment task contains unfamiliar vocabulary or syntax, the purpose of the assessment is lost. Assessment must help to identify the learner's "zone of proximal development" (Vygotsky, 1978) in a given skill area; monitor progress toward achieving English language development, literacy, or academic content standards; include direct and indirect measures (see Chapters 5 and 6); and provide evidence that demonstrates students' abilities. Be sure to consider the strengths and weaknesses of the assessment approaches, especially if there is an overemphasis on particular skills. (See for example, Goodman, 2006, regarding the Dynamic Indicators of Basic Early Literacy Skills [DIBELS] assessment tools.)

_____

[2]The world is full of semiotic systems. Human beings give and get meaning through socially and culturally agreed upon semiotic systems. A traffic light is a semiotic system. Other semiotic systems include oral language, technology, print media, and the visual and communicative arts.

In Interpreting Assessment Data, Be Sensitive to Cultural and Linguistic Variation.
Hall and Freedle (1975) reviewed research demonstrating that students' performance on tests is better if the vocabulary matches their cultural backgrounds. In Louisiana, for example, the word *parish* is equivalent in meaning to the word *county* used in other parts of the country; the words *carnival, throw,* and *krewe* have particular meanings associated with Mardi Gras; and children play *cabbage ball* instead of 16-inch *softball.* If these items appeared on a standardized vocabulary test, non-Louisianians would probably be at a cultural disadvantage.

In a similar way, various cultural experiences affect the comprehension of prose. In a study by Reynolds and colleagues (1981), urban African American students comprehended a passage describing an event in a school cafeteria (involving the discourse style of playing the dozens) differently than agrarian European American students. Andersson and Gipe (1983) found that the cultural schemata the children possessed influenced the creative process required for inferential comprehension by New Orleans–area Catholic school children and New York Greek Orthodox children. Put simply, cultural background knowledge influences the comprehension and recall of information in text (see Au, 1993, 2006; Barnitz, 1986; Steffensen, 1987).

Another example of language and cultural influences with respect to assessment can be found in auditory discrimination tests (Geissal & Knafle, 1977). Linguistically diverse students may not hear contrasts between word pairs such as *thin/tin, sherry/cherry, cot/caught, oil/Earl,* and *Mary/merry/marry* because the linguistic rules and patterns of their dialects or native languages do not permit such contrasts. Teachers must know about features of linguistic diversity to attribute an "error" to the appropriate cause, that is, an auditory problem versus a dialect variation. In fluent reading, these dialect homonym pairs can be interpreted by context just like other homonym pairs, such as *knight/night.* Dialect differences are not a liability in literacy performance (Goodman & Buck, 1973/1997).

EFFECTIVE INSTRUCTIONAL PRACTICES FOR ENGLISH LEARNERS

The challenge for teachers of linguistically diverse learners is how to serve these students' needs as well as the needs of native English speakers and also to teach the grade level or content area curriculum. In reality, the diversity-related principles previously discussed, if followed, will result in meeting the needs of *all* learners. Even so, some instructional practices are distinctive—effective for native English speakers, but especially effective for English learners. In addition, teachers will want to choose instructional practices that are an appropriate fit for the developmental stage of the English learner.

A Developmental Stage Approach for English Language Acquisition

For instruction to be effective for English learners, it first needs to address their proficiency level in English. Krashen and Terrell (1983) introduced the concept of stages of proficiency in second-language acquisition. Referred to as the Natural Approach, the stages they described are: preproduction (the "silent period"), early production, speech emergence, intermediate fluency, early advanced fluency, and advanced fluency. These proficiency levels have since evolved into the five stages described in Figure 3.2. For growth to occur, instruction must be targeted to the learner's level of proficiency with

Figure 3.2   Developmental Stages of English Language Development

Stage	Characteristics	Instructional Strategies
1 Beginning (preproduction and early production)	• Becomes familiar with English sounds, rhythm, and patterns • Shows some comprehension of the gist of the language • Relies on picture clues for understanding during shared readings • Responds with one-word answers and by pointing, gesturing, nodding, drawing	• Use visuals, props, and real objects • Active listening • Use language through songs, chants, and simple poems • Cooperative learning groups • Shared readings with visual support (felt board, puppets) • Use physical movement in language activities (i.e., Total Physical Response [Asher, 1982]) • Use art, music, dance, and pantomime to represent meaning • Use the language experience approach for literacy
2 Early intermediate (speech emergence)	• Confidence increases; speaks with less hesitation • Listens with greater understanding • Identifies people, places, objects • Uses routine expressions • Can repeat and recite memorable language	• Provide opportunities for oral language • Use yes/no and either/or questions • Ask problem-solving questions (who, what, when, where, why) • Label pictures and objects • Use shared reading with a variety of text genres • Introduce dialogue journals coupled with face-to-face interaction
3 Intermediate (intermediate fluency)	• Produces grammatically accurate phrases/ sentences • Experiments with new vocabulary in spoken English • Participates in discussions of academic content • Responds to literature by explaining, describing, comparing, retelling • Engages in independent reading	• Oral presentations for an audience (author's chair, readers' theater, content area projects) • Ask open-ended questions • Use guided reading, such as a directed reading-thinking activity • Present a variety of resource materials (textbooks, trade books, newspapers, dictionaries, etc.)

continued

Figure 3.2 *continued*

Stage	Characteristics	Instructional Strategies
	• Writes for a variety of purposes	• Conduct conferences with students to discuss reading/writing progress • SDAIE techniques, such as visuals and graphic organizers to make content information more accessible
4 Early advanced (early advanced fluency)	• Produces connected discourse • Uses more extensive vocabulary • Uses language to persuade and evaluate • Understands both narrative and expository material with greater depth • Engages in research projects	• Facilitate group discussions • Use literature circles (book clubs) • Introduce use of reference material for research • Request creative oral and written narratives • Use writer's workshop to publish student-authored newsletters, bulletins, stories, poems, reports • Provide opportunities for performance-based assessment through art, music, dance, drama
5 Advanced (advanced fluency)	• Understands idiomatic expressions • Includes more creative and analytical writing using standard forms • Language comparable to native English speakers of the same age	• Integrated thematic units for content area subjects • Real-world literacy experiences to include classroom newsletters, pen pals, letters to the editor, creative writing contests, and so on

Information source: Tinajero, J. V., & Schifini, A. (1997). *INTO English!* Carmel, CA: Hampton-Brown Books.

many opportunities for the student to practice at that proficiency level but with scaffolded instruction also provided at the next level of proficiency. For example, students who are proficient at Level 3 can speak in complete English sentences. If the teacher is addressing the literacy standard of comparing two characters in a story, these students could be given sentence frames to complete at a Level 3 complexity ("Charlotte is _____. Wilbur is _____. They are both _____.") followed by Level 4 complexity to spur growth ("Charlotte and Wilbur are similar because they both _____, but different because she _____ and he _____.").

Achieving full proficiency in English, however, includes more than conversational fluency. It also means knowing English well enough to be fully competitive in academic uses of English with their age-equivalent English-speaking peers (Echevarria, Vogt, & Short, 2003;

Figure 3.3	Comparison of ELD and SDAIE Elements for Content Area Lesson Based on the Use of a Text Photograph

English Language Development	SDAIE (Social Studies/Science)
How do we reverse the order of words in a sentence to create a **question**? (Practice writing questions about the picture.)	What are these people doing? Why are they doing it? Where are they? (geography)
Describe what you see in the picture. (Practice using descriptive language.)	Who is working together? Are they part of a team? Are they working at a job?
Attempt to write an **explanation** of what you see. (Expository writing based on making inferences/arguments.)	Why are the plants yellow in the foreground and green on the mountains beyond? What kind of biome is this? What kind of forest?
Compare and contrast this photo to something that goes on in the United States.	Do you think this photo was taken in a developing country? Why?

Vocabulary is essential to both ELD and SDAIE. For this example, vocabulary might include common words like *forest*, *dry*, *rice*, *mountains* and more specific social studies or science words and phrases like *agriculture, bamboo forest, hill tribes, Southeast Asia, subtropical*. What students see in the pictures that correspond to this lesson will be based on what they already know. This may help or confuse their understanding, depending on their actual experiences. More important, however, is the notion that English learners can communicate what they know in school only *if they know the academic language*. Being able to ask questions, describe, write explanations, as well as understand concepts in a larger structural context (e.g., "It is subtropical" vs. "It feels hot") leads to school success. Knowledge without academic language skills often results in failure ("ELD/SDAIE worksheet," 2003).

Hakuta & Cancino, 2001). For example, in California teachers are expected to provide both appropriate **English language development (ELD)** instruction and academic content area instruction, often referred to as **SDAIE (specially designed academic instruction in English)** and influenced by the work of Cummins (1981, 1994) and Krashen (2003). The focus of ELD is on language teaching using English methods that correspond with lower levels of language proficiency. The emphasis is on listening, speaking, and early literacy learning, usually organized around themes. The focus of SDAIE is on teaching content with modifications such as use of visuals and graphic organizers. This instruction corresponds to at least the intermediate level of language proficiency, which emphasizes conceptual understanding. Refer to Figure 3.3 for a sample contrast between ELD and SDAIE within the context of a content area lesson.

Additional Considerations when Planning Instruction for English Learners

Overall, there are relatively few distinct components for teachers working with English learners toward academic achievement. Gersten (1996) identifies four instructional practices effective for English learners:

1. Rather than assign long lists of new vocabulary words, select only two or three evocative or critical words and provide rich instruction for them.

2. Explicitly teach comprehension strategies accompanied by frequent use of scaffolds (for example, praise a partially correct answer and then provide further explanation).

3. Point out parallels between the native language and English to facilitate the transfer of knowledge from the L1 to English.

4. Encourage English learners to talk about and write about their lives.

Anderson and Roit (1996, pp. 297–299) identify six abilities that teachers should foster in English learners to promote both oral language and reading comprehension:

1. English language flexibility (for example, encourage alternate phrasings; see Chapter 8)

2. Use of cohesion devices (for example, expand vocabulary instruction to include words such as *about, but, although, for, any, several;* see Chapter 10)

3. Consideration of the larger context (such as focus on the overall meaning; see Chapter 11)

4. Determination of important and unimportant text segments (for example, distinguish main ideas from details; see Chapters 13 and 14)

5. Elaboration of responses (for example, expand on short answers; see Chapter 8)

6. Engagement in natural conversations (participate in literature circle discussions in either the L1 or the L2; see Chapter 12)

Saunders and colleagues (1998) summarize guidelines for instruction focused on the academic achievement of English learners that include:

- Building and using vocabulary as a curricular anchor
- Using visuals and/or realia to reinforce concepts and vocabulary
- Implementing cooperative learning and peer tutoring strategies
- Using native language (L1) strategically
- Modulating cognitive and language demands (pp. 99–132)

English learners face a challenging task. They must learn both the language (phonology, syntax, vocabulary, forms, and cultural contexts) and the academic content, all the while learning alongside native English speakers. Thus, it is imperative for their teachers to address both language and content needs when planning instruction. Appendix C provides a self-assessment questionnaire for teachers of English learners that highlights important considerations for instructional planning. To demonstrate that these considerations are not burdensome additions to a lesson, refer once again to Figure 3.3, which shows the natural integration between the language aspects of a lesson and the content aspects of a lesson with English learners in mind. Attention to both these aspects could only enhance instruction for *all* students, not just English learners.

Summary

This chapter provided an overview of the linguistically related professional knowledge used in teaching diverse language learners to read and write standard English. To facilitate the necessary acquisition of standard English literacy, respecting the native

For some example lessons, go to MyEducationLab and first select the topic *English Language Learners*. Go to the Activities and Applications section, watch the video entitled "Teaching Diverse Learners," and respond to the accompanying questions. Then select the topic *English Language Learners*. Go to the Activities and Applications section, watch the video entitled "Think-Pair-Share," and respond to the accompanying questions. Then select the topic *English Language Learners*. Go to the Activities and Applications section, watch the video entitled "Peer Scaffolding," and respond to the accompanying questions. Look for examples of the practices and guidelines suggested by Gersten (1996), Anderson and Roit (1996, pp. 297–299), and Saunders and colleagues (1998). A wide variety of grade levels are represented in these videos so you can see how strategies are used in grades K–12.

languages and dialects of students is a necessary first step. Incorporating literacy strategies that allow diverse learners to connect to the full range of the communicative arts is especially critical to supporting their development of communicative competencies and learning to read and write. This chapter contains information teachers need for a solid understanding of the communicative nature of language and the arts and the value of continually growing in their understanding of the languages and dialects found among the children they teach. Finally, principles and guidelines for instructional practices that consider students' unique cultures and languages were presented. All of this knowledge contributes to classroom decisions that benefit all children in developing language and literacy.

Recommended Websites

For a variety of resources, consult the websites of the Center for Applied Linguistics (www.cal.org), National Council of Teachers of English (www.ncte.org), International Reading Association (www.reading.org), Teachers of English to Speakers of Other Languages (www.tesol.org), and the National Association for Bilingual Education (www.nabe.org).

Language Variations
www.mla.org/resources/map_main
Be sure to examine the MLA Language Map to see the extent of language variation in the United States.

Multicultural Children's Literature
www.multiculturalchildrenslit.com and http://icdlbooks.org
Books with appeal to African American, Chinese American, Japanese American, Jewish American, Korean American, Latino/Hispanic American, Native American, and others can be found at these sites.

Responding to the Demographic Challenge: An Internet Classroom for Teachers of Language-Minority Students
www.readingonline.org/electronic/elec_index.asp?HREF=/electronic/mora/index.html
An article by Dr. Jill Kerper Mora guides you through this elaborate website.

The ESL Standards for Pre-K–12 Students
www.tesol.org/s_tesol/seccss.asp?CID=95&DID=1565
The TESOL organization provides the entire text of the standards related to teaching English learners.

The SIOP Model
www.cal.org/siop
Information on the SIOP Model, a research-based approach to sheltered instruction, can be found on this site.

Integrated Thematic Planning: Lesson Planning for ELD Instruction
http://coe.sdsu.edu/people/jmora/Pages/4X4Guidelines.htm
This site presents a structure of the Four by Four Unit specifically for Sheltered English (ELD/SDAIE) that is helpful in modifying lessons for English learners.

Differentiating Instruction for Limited English Proficient Students
www.betac.org/pdf/spring_summer_04.pdf
This site provides examples of good differentiated instruction strategies for English learners.

Dave's ESL Café
www.eslcafe.com
An extensive collection of ESL information and links from Dave Sperling can be found here.

ESOL Online
www.tki.org.nz/r/esol/esolonline/index_e.php
This New Zealand–based site has ESOL teaching resources, professional readings, and classroom projects for students.

SOLOM
http://coe.sdsu.edu/people/jmora/Pages/solom914.htm and www.cal.org/twi/EvalToolkit/appendix/solom.pdf
These sites provide background information on the SOLOM as well as on scoring breakdowns, some interpretation of scores with directions, and the SOLOM matrix.

MyEducationLab is a research-based learning tool that brings teaching to life. Go to Gipe 7th Edition MyEducationLab for Reading Assessment site at www.myeducationlab.com to:

- Engage in multimedia exercises to help you build a deeper and more applied understanding of chapter content.
- Use extensive resources including videos from real classrooms, Praxis and licensure preparation, a lesson plan builder, and materials to help you in your teaching career.

CHAPTER 4

Physical, Psychological, and Environmental Factors Affecting Literacy Development

OBJECTIVES

After you have read this chapter, you should be able to:

1. Identify characteristics of the three factors that affect literacy development.
2. Explain the teacher's role with regard to each of the three factors: physical, psychological, and environmental.
3. Recognize symptoms of poor general health or possible visual, auditory, or neurological problems.
4. Prepare objective anecdotal records.
5. Suggest ways to establish a classroom environment that might help students who struggle with literacy learning or who have been "labeled" to revalue themselves as learners.

VOCABULARY ALERT

ADD/ADHD
affect
anecdotal records
assistive technology
  devices
at risk
attributional retraining
auditory acuity
auditory blending

auditory discrimination
auditory memory
auditory perception
bibliotherapy
brain-based learning
cognition
dyslexia
emotional maltreatment
learning disability

physical abuse
physical neglect
resiliency
sexual abuse
stuttering
visual acuity
visually impaired
visual perception

F or many years educators and others have been concerned because too many students fail to learn to read, or read and write so ineffectively that eventually the struggle leads to avoidance of literacy activities altogether. All teachers will find such students in their classrooms and should be prepared to help them as much as they can. When a student manifests symptoms such as poor health, hunger, homelessness, an inability to perceive objects or sounds, emotional outbursts, lack of motivation, or processing problems, plus many others, the chances for academic success are lessened. A student can be considered **at risk** if there are two or more physical, psychological, or environmental symptoms present. Unfortunately, only one aspect of the environmental factor, inappropriate teaching, can be directly controlled and substantially changed by educators.

Factors associated with potentially negative impacts on literacy development are discussed within this chapter in one of three basic categories: *physical* (including neurophysical or neurological), *psychological*, and *environmental* (which includes instructional factors). Teachers, by the very nature of their role and their training, should be held responsible for instructional factors associated with poor literacy achievement and for identifying the possible presence of other factors that might impede literacy development. The improvement of literacy instruction through better-informed teachers is a major goal of this text. This chapter can alert teachers to the wide range of learning needs that exist in classrooms today and help them to match learning needs to the instructional strategies presented throughout this text.

PHYSICAL FACTORS

General Health. Learning to read and write is a demanding task for many students. A student must be alert, attentive, and capable of working for a sustained period of time. Any physical condition that lowers stamina or impairs vitality can have a deleterious effect on learning. Serious illnesses and prolonged absences from school obviously may result in learning gaps. Many conscientious parents and teachers work hard to alleviate such problems; home instruction is also provided by many school systems for students who are bedridden or otherwise incapacitated for an extended time. Today's technology also offers great assistance in such situations.

More subtle forms of illness and physical problems sometimes elude parents and teachers. Chronic low-grade infections, glandular disturbances, allergies, and persistent minor illnesses such as mild respiratory problems can induce a general malaise and lower the vitality level. Insufficient sleep may inhibit learning, and malnutrition may lower ability to attend and learn.

Go to MyEducationLab and first select the topic *Instructional Decision Making*. Go to the Activities and Applications section, and complete the simulation entitled "What Do You See?" to learn more about your own perceptions about people with disabilities. Respond to the accompanying questions. Then select the topic *English Language Learners*. Go to the Activities and Applications section, and complete the simulation entitled "Teaching and Learning in New Mexico" to learn more about diversity beyond linguistic diversity. Respond to the accompanying questions.

Teachers, of course, are not physicians and cannot appropriately assume medical responsibilities. Yet they do function as substitute parents while school is in session and must be sensitive to the general well-being of each student in their class. When teachers are concerned about possible health problems, they should seek help from the school nurse and principal. Communication with the parents should be initiated according to local school policies.

Occasionally teachers encounter parents who resist counseling efforts regarding their child's health. Little can be done to help the student directly when this happens. If the problem is serious enough, however, legal procedures can be instigated. Usually other community agencies, such as the child welfare department, become involved in these cases.

When students are not in good health, teachers must try to accommodate their problems as much as possible. Let these students rest, put their heads on their desks, go to the nurse's office, or whatever seems reasonable for the particular problem.

Visual Acuity. Visual acuity is keenness of vision. Acuity problems are usually physiologically based and can be corrected by ophthalmologists or optometrists. The role of the classroom teacher is to identify students with visual acuity problems that may have gone unnoticed by parents or other teachers.

Although some students learn to read in spite of visual problems, the emphasis here is not so much on the relationship to difficulties in the literacy domains as it is on comfort and efficiency. When students can deal comfortably with print at a normal distance (about 14 to 18 inches), the chances are good that they will be able to attend to a task as long as is necessary. Discomforts such as headaches or burning or watery eyes diminish their chances considerably. Learners who see relatively clearly work more efficiently for longer periods of time without having to direct undue energy to accommodate visual deficiencies.

Assessment Techniques. Some school systems hire reading (or other) specialists who are trained to help identify students with vision problems. Even with special training, however, these people are not vision specialists, and their work should be considered as screening only. Instruments typically used for screening purposes are the *Keystone School Vision Screening Test* (Keystone View) and the *Master Ortho-Rater Visual Efficiency Test* (Bausch and Lomb). Other devices often used to screen vision are the *Rader Visual Acuity Screening Chart* (Modern Education Corporation), the *Snellen Chart*, and the *Spache Binocular Reading Test* (Keystone View).

Probably the most important assessment function for classroom teachers is to observe the behavior of their students. The Optometric Extension Program Foundation has compiled an excellent checklist to help teachers make reliable observations of visual behavior that could interfere with academic progress (Appendix D). If several of these behaviors are observed, especially within a single category, the teacher should refer the student to an appropriate vision specialist, whether inside or outside the school setting.

Teachers' Responsibilities. The classroom teacher does not initiate correction of visual acuity problems, which are often resolved through proper prescription of glasses. If the vision specialist believes a problem can be corrected through visual therapy, such activities typically are conducted by the parents under a doctor's supervision or by special teachers working with the student on a one-to-one basis outside the regular classroom.

Classroom teachers should ensure the best possible conditions to accommodate the needs of students with mild vision problems. Nearsighted students (those with *myopia*) should be able to see the chalkboard or screens used for projected visuals better when they are seated closer to what they need to see. Prescription lenses will reduce this problem, as well as farsightedness (*hyperopia*) and astigmatism. Ample light is necessary. Remind students occasionally to rest their eyes after lengthy reading assignments or computer usage. Emphasize ease of reading rather than speed.

Students who have been classified as **visually impaired** function quite well in a regular classroom. Sight-saving books printed in large type (12 to 24 point) can be requested for their use. In addition, methods using tactile discrimination and word tracing are useful.

Visual Perception. Visual perception skills include visual discrimination of form, visual closure, constancy, and visual memory. A student may have normal visual acuity skills but underdeveloped visual perception skills.

Visual discrimination of form, commonly called simply *visual discrimination*, requires recognizing similarities and differences among letters and words in print. For example, the student must be able to distinguish between *H* and *K* or *c*, *e*, and *o*.

Visual closure is the ability to identify or complete, from an incomplete presentation, an object, picture, letter, or word. The student must identify the whole even though the whole is not provided. For example, the student must be able to recognize that a face

 needs another feature or a comb has teeth missing, or that

f_ _tb_ ll represents the word *football*.

Constancy is a factor when a figure, letter, or word remains the same regardless of a change in shape, orientation, size, or color. This concept is critical for reading because many types of print fonts are used and students must not be confused by slight changes—for example, *a* and a. Also, many letters that are the same in shape are different letters because of their orientation, or placement—for example, *b* and *d*, *p* and *q*, or *n*, *u*, and *c*. In the world of objects, orientation doesn't matter—a chair is a chair no matter which way you turn it. However, when dealing with letters and words, orientation can make a difference.

Visual memory is the ability to remember the sequence of letters in words. This ability is most obviously reflected in spelling; however, it is also important in reading when words are encountered having the same or many similar letters but a different sequence. For example, a student lacking in visual memory may have difficulty distinguishing between *ate*, *eat*, and *tea*. Many mature readers have to tax their visual memory skills encountering *through*, *though*, and *thorough*.

Assessment Techniques. Several standardized instruments assess visual discrimination, visual closure, constancy, and visual memory skills. The following are examples:

- *Gates-MacGinitie Reading Tests—Level Pre-Reading (PR),* Riverside
- *Metropolitan Readiness Tests,* Harcourt Brace Educational Measurement
- *Murphy-Durrell Reading Readiness Analysis,* Harcourt Brace Educational Measurement

If teachers know the characteristics of the various visual perception skills, they can develop classroom activities to assess these visual abilities; for example, work sheets that request students to identify the "same letter or word" (o | c o c e; cake | coke cake coke) or the "letter or word that is different" (b b o b; bed bad bed bed).

Go to MyEducationLab and first select the topic *Special Needs*. Then go to the Activities and Applications section, and complete the simulation entitled "A Clear View" to learn more about how to accommodate the special needs of students with serious visual impairments, including blindness. Respond to the accompanying questions.

Visual closure tasks at an early stage usually involve picture or shape completion tasks. In one example, the student is asked to complete the second drawing so it looks like the first.

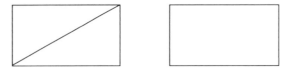

Constancy is often assessed as a specially designed visual discrimination task. Again, finding what is "alike" or "different" is the direction—for example, d | b b b d or p | p q p.

Visual memory is more difficult to assess. Initially, the teacher may use a modification of the party game in which several objects are presented on a tray for viewing, then covered, and participants are asked to write down as many as they can remember. For classroom use, you can show three or four objects. Then cover them, remove one, show the remaining objects, and ask the student what was removed. Letters and words can be assessed in a similar fashion. Show a word or letter for about two seconds. Then ask the student to locate the word or letter from a list of words or letters. Consistently poor performance on spelling tests or in written work beyond third or fourth grade may also indicate a need for visual memory practice.

Teachers' Responsibilities. Many practice activities for helping students develop visual perception skills are readily available in classroom reading materials and activity books. Some of the more representative exercises are provided here:

1. Have the student mark the letter that is like the one at the beginning of the row:

   B | E B D

2. Direct the student to identify "what's missing?" in a picture.

3. Direct the student to mark the letter or letter group that looks like the first item in each row:

   ap | pa la ap

   bl | lb bl bi

4. Show the student a series of letters, remove the series, and have the student write from memory what was seen. Reshow the series if necessary until the student succeeds.

Auditory Acuity. Auditory acuity is keenness of hearing. Students obviously need to hear adequately in school. Students with high-tone hearing deficits have more difficulties learning to read (specifically, *phonics*, or symbol–sound relationships) than those with low-tone deficits. The consonants that give distinction and meaning to speech in our language are relatively high-pitched (especially *s*, *l*, and *t*), whereas vowel sounds are lower in pitch. Most teachers of young children are female, and their voices are higher-pitched than those of males. Thus, it is understandable that high-tone deficits might be more critical than low-tone deficits when teaching sound–symbol relationships. Much early reading work involves oral-aural participation. Successful performance with phonics activities requires good auditory acuity.

Hearing loss is a medical matter best handled by a hearing specialist or otologist. The teacher can help, however, by identifying students suspected of having hearing deficits.

Assessment Techniques. Screening for auditory acuity with an audiometer is a reliable procedure. However, teachers must be specially trained in the use of this sensitive instrument, and even then results should be considered tentative. Students who do not pass the audio-metric screening should be referred to a hearing specialist in the school or to other appropriate personnel for professional diagnosis.

Classroom teachers must be sensitive to and observant of behaviors or physical symptoms that suggest hearing loss. The list of common symptoms found in Appendix E will help the teacher identify students who should be seen by the school nurse, speech and hearing specialist, or reading specialist. A decision can then be made whether to suggest medical assistance.

Fortunately, many school systems have speech and hearing specialists. The specialist usually screens young children entering school, so many potential problems are identified early.

Sometimes teachers can jump to the conclusion that there is a hearing deficit when a student shows particular physical symptoms. Some symptoms may be only temporary because of congestion from colds or an ear infection. The wise teacher observes behavior over a period of time, perhaps three to four weeks, to see whether the behaviors or symptoms persist. If they do, consider a referral.

Teachers can structure activities to help determine hearing loss. Some examples follow:

- *Simon Says*. The teacher plays Simon Says with small groups, telling the students to face away and follow the directions. If a student consistently has trouble keeping up with classmates, the teacher may suspect a hearing deficit.

- *Low-voice or whisper test*. The teacher stands about 20 feet away from the student, first on one side, then the other, and asks the student to repeat the words the teacher says in a normal, clear voice. A student who cannot do this task at 15 or fewer feet may have a hearing deficit. A variation of this procedure is to talk softly (or whisper) while standing just behind a student. If there is no response to words spoken at the same volume heard by other students, the student may have a hearing deficit.

- *Watch tick test*. The teacher holds a stopwatch or loudly ticking wristwatch about 12 inches from the student's ear, gradually extending the distance to about 48 inches. Students with normal hearing should hear the ticks 40 to 48 inches from the ear (Kennedy, 1977). If the distance is less than 40 inches, the student may have a deficit, and the teacher should consider referral.

Results of these assessment procedures vary depending on factors such as noise level of the environment, differences in teachers' voices, and loudness of watches. A good way to judge the adequacy of these procedures is to test several students and notice those who differ significantly from the overall group. If a student's responses consistently deviate from the peer group, consider requesting more reliable and sophisticated assessment procedures performed by the appropriate specialist.

Teachers' Responsibilities. Corrective work for students with auditory acuity impairments, particularly those who are deaf or hard of hearing, is an intricate task that requires specially prepared teachers. Facilities for these learners are usually provided in special schools or special education classes. A well-equipped school might have **assistive technology devices** (electronic devices designed or modified to improve the functional capabilities of persons with severe communication disorders or other disabilities) that can be helpful as well. However, most students with mild hearing impairments or with deficits corrected by prosthetic devices (such as hearing aids) function quite well in the regular classroom with only minor accommodations. Special provisions, such as seating the student close to where the teacher and others are talking, should be considered. It is also helpful for the speaker to face these students directly

Go to MyEducationLab, select the topic *Special Needs*, and go to the Activities and Applications section. Watch the video "SmartBoards for Students with Hearing Impairments" to learn more about one such device. Also view the video "Lily" to see how the TouchTalker device is used, and view the video "Using Technology for Special Needs" to see the use of an adaptive keyboard for a computer. Respond to the accompanying questions.

so they will have the advantage of watching lips closely if needed. Clear enunciation is essential.

Students who have hearing impairments may have difficulty when oral discussion and recitation are in progress. Listening to others read may be difficult, too. Teachers should stress silent reading and a visual approach to word analysis for these students. Phonics may be difficult or, for some, impossible to learn. Emphasis during instruction in word recognition (see Chapter 8) should be placed on the uses of visual and structural analysis techniques and context clues.

Auditory Perception. As with visual perception, a number of skills are included in the area of **auditory perception**, defined as the ability to discriminate, remember, and blend sounds. **Auditory discrimination** is the ability to distinguish sounds, **auditory memory** is the ability to remember a sequence of sounds, and **auditory blending** refers to the blending of phonemes to form a word.

Assessment Techniques. When their auditory discrimination skills are being assessed, students should face away from the teacher to eliminate the possibility of lip reading. Some common procedures follow:

1. Pronounce word pairs (for example, *big/pig, pat/pot, some/come, rug/run*). Direct the student to answer "same" if the two words sound the same, or "not the same" or "different" if the two words sound different in any way. Give several examples for practice and enough word pairs to assess all positions reliably (beginning, middle, end); probably about 10 pairs are adequate for each position.

2. The same concept can be modified for use with a group of students. Give each student a sheet of paper listing the item number followed by the words *same* and *not the same*, or *yes* and *no* (Figure 4.1). Again, the teacher stands behind the group and pronounces word pairs. Students circle "yes" or "same" if the two words sound the same and "no," "not the same," or "different" if they sound different.

The assessment of auditory memory evaluates a student's ability to follow oral directions and remember information presented orally in class. Generally, assessment requires

Figure 4.1 Sample Items for Protocol Sheet Used in Assessing Auditory Discrimination

1. yes   no

2. yes   no

                        or

3. same   not the same

                        or

4. same   different

                and so on

students to recall and reproduce a series of unrelated words. For example, the teacher may say, "Listen to these words and be ready to repeat them in the same order: *cow . . . tie . . . bed*. Now you say them." With young children, several practice items are needed. The number of words can be increased if three appear to be too easy.

Assessment of auditory blending requires that the learner articulate the sounds of a word together in order, as in spoken language. Blending is a relatively difficult skill and should not be expected from children younger than age 4. Initial consonant sounds are easier to blend than are final consonants, and continuant phonemes (/*m*/, /*s*/, /*sh*/) are easier to blend than noncontinuant-stop phonemes (/*p*/, /*b*/, /*t*/). Auditory blending assessments should consist of about 30 words. The first 10 should require the learner to blend two phonemes to pronounce a word (/*i*/-/*n*/ = in; /*i*/-/*s*/ = is; /*u*/-/*p*/ = up); the next 10 should require blending three or four phonemes segmented into two parts to pronounce a word (/*m*/-/*an*/ = man; /*n*/-/*et*/ = net; /*st*/-/*ep*/ = step); the last 10 should require blending three or four phonemes segmented into three or four parts to pronounce a word (/*m*/-/*a*/-/*p*/ = map; /*th*/-/*a*/-/*t*/ = that; /*c*/-/*l*/-/*o*/-/*ck*/ = clock; /*s*/-/*t*/-/*ar*/ = star; /*b*/-/*oo*/-/*k*/ = book). This task takes 5 to 10 minutes to administer, and kindergarten children typically achieve an average score of 20 out of 30 correct.

Teachers' Responsibilities. To develop auditory discrimination skill, begin with practice in listening for known sounds within known words. This not only provides success for the student but also a better idea of the nature of the task. The teacher must understand that "poor auditory discrimination is often accompanied by inaccurate or indistinct speech. The child who pronounces *with* as *wiv* is not likely to notice any difference between final *v* and *th* in words. It is hard for many children to discriminate among short vowel sounds because those sounds do not differ greatly" (Harris & Sipay, 1990, pp. 456–457). Therefore, in such cases the teacher must decide whether instruction in auditory discrimination would be time well spent, or whether visual learning should be emphasized until articulation has improved.

Useful activities for auditory discrimination development follow. The first three activities are particularly representative of those currently used in classroom settings that emphasize phonics instruction:

1. Students are asked to locate or mark pictures that begin or end with a particular sound.

2. Students are asked to listen to pairs of words and determine whether they begin or end with the same sound.

3. Pictures are provided, with a choice of two letters for each picture. Students are to choose the letter that represents the beginning or ending sound of the picture.

4. Using a familiar story or nursery rhyme, the teacher selects words to be changed to new words by altering one or two sounds. The teacher then reads the story slowly while the students listen for words that sound wrong. Students must identify the incorrect word and state what the word should sound like. The teacher then continues reading. For example,

   Jack and *Phil* went up the *wall*
   To fetch a *pile* of water.
   Jack *tall* down and *bright* his crown
   And Jill came *mumbling* after.

Auditory memory exercises are designed to develop the ability to attend to, recognize, and recall sequences of numbers, letters, and words. The following are representative activities:

1. Give students a series of numbers to dial on a telephone or type on a computer keyboard.

2. Require students to repeat clapping patterns (for example, clap/clap-clap/clap).

3. Require students to decide whether two sound patterns are alike. Claps, taps, or toy flutes can be used (for example, -/-/-; -/-/—). ·

4. Pronounce two words for the students, then repeat one of them. Have students note whether the repeated word was the first or second word of the pair.

5. Have students repeat a series of three to seven unrelated words in sequence, from memory.

A few auditory blending activities are presented here for explanatory purposes. Auditory blending is also discussed in Chapter 9:

1. Have students join beginning consonant sounds to ending phonograms (such as /b/ -ake, /k/ -ake, /f/ -ake, /l/ -ake, /m/ -ake).

2. Combine visuals with the preceding auditory task. While pronouncing /k/ -ake, show the word card for *cake* and continue by covering the initial consonant with the various other consonants, for example, *make.*

3. Provide riddles, such as, "I'm thinking of a word that starts like *man*, /m/, and ends like *lake*, /-ake/. What is the word?"

Neurological Factors. Neurological (also called neurophysical) factors refer to conditions that result in learning problems due to differences in the structure and functioning of the brain. Neurological factors affect approximately 15 percent of the U.S. population, resulting in 2.4 million school children having a learning disability. Of these, 80 to 85 percent experience difficulty in language and reading (International Dyslexia Association, 2000). Unfortunately, the incidence of neurological disorders is on the rise. For example, nearly six out of every 1,000 children now have autism spectrum disorders, and about two out of every 1,000 children have cerebral palsy (Hirtz, 2007).

Considerable confusion exists about students who have learning problems due to neurological involvement. A host of terms refer to these children: "learning disabled," "dyslexic," exhibiting "undifferentiated attention deficit disorder, or ADD," and "attention deficit hyperactivity disorder, or ADHD." Until recently, distinctions between these labels were not readily made. But these are very different conditions, each with its own set of characteristics. If descriptive criteria are unknown, labels of this nature can be counterproductive because they focus on deficits to the exclusion of competencies.

In general, a student with a **learning disability (LD)** demonstrates a severe discrepancy between achievement and intellectual ability in one or more academic areas (oral expression, written expression, listening comprehension, basic reading skill, reading comprehension, mathematics computation, mathematics reasoning). However, this discrepancy is not the result of visual, hearing, or motor handicaps; mental retardation; emotional disturbance; or environmental, cultural, or economic disadvantage (Mercer, 1997).

The International Dyslexia Association defines **dyslexia** as [a specific learning disability that is neurological in origin. It is characterized by difficulties with accurate and/or fluent word recognition and by poor spelling and decoding abilities. These difficulties typically result from a deficit in the phonological component of language that is often unexpected in relation to other cognitive abilities and the provision of effective classroom instruction. Secondary consequences may include problems in reading comprehension and reduced reading experience that can impede the growth of vocabulary and background knowledge.] (International Dyslexia Association, 2008, p. 1)

In other words, dyslexia does not result from a lack of motivation, sensory impairment, or lack of instructional or environmental opportunities. Those with dyslexia are bright people who happen to have a lifelong neurological disorder, but a disorder they can cope with if timely and appropriate interventions are provided. Teachers must be able to recognize the symptoms of those instances of dyslexia, the neurological deficit most often associated with reading difficulty, as distinct from symptoms of attention deficit disorders and other learning disabilities. But teachers also must recognize the specific talents of these children, and they are substantial. MI theory provides a framework for viewing any learning disability as just one part of a student's intelligences profile. For example, people with dyslexia often excel in areas that require visual, spatial, and motor integration. Thus, they are likely to reveal well-developed spatial, bodily-kinesthetic, and/or musical intelligences (Gardner, 1999).

Not all people with dyslexia demonstrate the same symptoms. Some have great difficulty using word analysis skills to read words not already committed to memory. They have trouble breaking spoken words into their component parts to assist their spelling and have particular difficulty with consonant clusters. Others read more slowly because they have difficulty blending component parts into words while reading. In oral reading, they often pronounce letter sounds in the wrong order and produce the wrong sound for given letters. Most will likely show a discrepancy between listening comprehension and reading comprehension. Individuals with dyslexia, being bright, have learned to use their language strengths (vocabulary, general knowledge, interpretive ability) to compensate for other weaknesses.

Many signs indicate dyslexia, but few dyslexics show all of these signs. In addition, the signs and symptoms of dyslexia may also be present among the student's relatives.

The more common signs and symptoms of dyslexia are:

- Reads slowly and painfully
- Shows wide disparity between listening comprehension and reading comprehension of some text
- Experiences decoding errors, especially with the sound order of letters, for example, *left–felt*; rhymes; or sequence of syllables, such as *soiled–solid*
- Has trouble with spelling
- May have difficulty with handwriting
- Exhibits difficulty recalling known words
- Has difficulty expressing thoughts with written language
- May experience difficulty with math computations because numbers are often reversed, as in 12–21; or with sequencing of steps or directionality
- Decodes real words better than nonsense words
- Substitutes one small sight word for another: *a, I, he, the, there, was*
- May have confusion about right- or left-handedness
- Has difficulty interpreting language that is heard

Attention Deficit Disorder (ADD) and Attention Deficit Hyperactivity Disorder (ADHD) on the other hand, involve an overall inability to attend during complex tasks that require a high degree of self-monitoring. The characteristics of ADD are as follows: can persist when task is interesting, chronic inattention when task is uninteresting, class clown, impulsive or erratic behavior, failure to start work, sloppy work, ignores rules, seeks attention, noisy, and disruptive. ADHD has the added characteristic of hyperactivity.

Arts Connection _____

The visual and communicative arts allow students to convey meaning without oral or written language. Therefore, visual arts activities are ideal for students who struggle with reading, writing, and speaking. They offer opportunities for students to think in pictures and see ideas. Further, the visual arts provide all sorts of options for personal expression because they can be combined with other forms of the language arts, such as reading, creative writing, and drama.

Music also provides opportunities for students who experience difficulty with language arts tasks to think and learn through another language that is repetitive, melodious, and emotional. Teachers can infuse music into every teaching session by bringing tapes and CDs of classical music into the classroom. Played as soft background music, the sonatas, etudes, concertos, and symphonies add peacefulness, unity, and creativity to our workplaces. Students and teachers also learn to appreciate a broad spectrum of classical music. Likewise, teachers who are reluctant to sing aloud in front of an audience can use taped instrumental or vocal music selections to set the mood for students' storytelling or to provide background music as students personally respond to literature read or heard. Famous pop vocalists, such as Little Richard and Ella Fitzgerald, offer "movement-oriented song collections on tape and CD for children" (Cornett, 1999, p. 389). In addition, many fine CDs combine music with dancing, such as the Hokey Pokey (Knapp & Knapp, 1976) and the Twist. Teachers and students also can use rhythm instruments to provide atmosphere and sound effects as students create or recreate stories (e.g., finger cymbals, tambourines, bells, sticks, small drums, and xylophones). Song lyrics can be made available so students can read along as they sing.

It is appropriate to mention children who stutter in this section on neurological factors. Although **stuttering** itself is termed a speech disorder, research shows that neurological components are probably involved. Also, stuttering has recently been recognized as a learning disability (National Stuttering Association, 2000). Stuttering affects about 1 percent of adults and 4 percent of children, generally starts between ages 2 and 5, and is five times more likely to affect boys than girls. The degree of stuttering can vary widely, and its cause is unknown. Nor is it known why people who stutter often do not stutter when they sing, whisper, or speak in chorus, or when they do not hear their own voice. Although stuttering does *not* reflect any diminished mental capability, it can limit a student's ability to participate in "speaking" assignments (such as readers' theater) or oral reading situations. These expectations would be very intimidating for students who stutter and could indirectly affect their literacy development by associating oral reading activities with negative feelings (feelings of anxiety, frustration, teasing by classmates). Teachers' responsibilities are to maintain a relaxed pace and moderate rate of speech and expect all classmates to do the same; model good listening behaviors; and provide opportunities for choral reading or singing with others.

Personal issues can accompany any of these learning disabilities. Understandably, students with a learning disability might exhibit a poor self-image. They sometimes have difficulty picking up on social signals from other children. They fear failure and new situations. Their feelings about themselves swing back and forth between positive and negative. Sometimes they have trouble finding the right words and remembering sequences of events. Feelings of frustration and anger are common. A caring teacher will watch for these signs and provide the necessary support.

Assessment Techniques. Accurately assessing neurological involvement is difficult even for medical and psychological specialists. Therefore, teachers must be extremely cautious and conservative regarding assessment. A teacher's best assessment technique is observation with the use of anecdotal records (see the next section and also Chapter 6). When neurological involvement is suspected, a teacher who can provide documentation in the form of dated records will greatly assist those specially trained to evaluate the presence of these conditions.

Teachers' Responsibilities. Teachers should follow established channels provided by the school system. The school principal will be able to advise the teacher on how to proceed. In addition to documenting the possible symptoms of dyslexia, ADD, and other learning disabilities, teachers might also consider those students who demonstrate such behavioral symptoms as poor balance or awkwardness, delayed speech, extreme distractibility, wide mood swings, and disorganization in time and space (Harris & Sipay, 1990) for referral to the school's reading specialist or school psychologist and the school principal. Together these professionals decide whether to recommend to parents that their child see a family physician or a pediatric neurologist for further evaluation.

Meanwhile, a teacher can help students use their strengths and pursue alternate routes to achieve academic success. As Armstrong (2000) stated, "By constructing a perspective of special-needs students as whole individuals, MI theory provides a context for envisioning positive channels through which students can learn to deal with their disabilities. . . . It's interesting to note that Braille, for example, has been used successfully with students identified as severe dyslexics who possessed special strengths in tactile sensitivity" (p. 105). Similarly, Schirduan and Case (2000) report on an elementary school curriculum that uses strategies consistent with MI theory as improving the self-concept of students with ADHD.

Relatively new findings from the area of brain research are also having an impact on teaching students with a variety of disabilities. Jensen (2008) and others have attempted to relate the results of this research to teaching and learning. However, many well-intentioned educators have gone beyond the research in their use of aromatherapy (for calming) and peppermint candy (for invigorating), for example. The emerging theory resulting from brain research is referred to as **brain-based learning**, or translating the findings from brain research into designing instructional environments intended to make the brain more receptive to learning. For example, brain research suggests that cooperative learning strategies represent brain-compatible learning because of the growing body of knowledge that says interpersonal intelligence is important to brain development (Lackney, 2004). Applications of brain-based learning need to be tested, similar to the testing of MI theory.

As part of the movement to inclusive classrooms, teachers will encounter students in their classrooms who are physically challenged. In addition to assistive devices, such as adaptations to computer keyboards or lapboards for students needing wheelchairs, there are ways to adapt instructional material that will benefit learners with disabilities. Depending on the specific disability, consider the following adaptations:

- Shorten assignments and tasks (for example, do the first four problems, read the first three pages, then listen to the tape of the rest of the story, choose one question to answer).

- Use larger font sizes in printed materials (enlarged materials can be easier to read and less intimidating for students).

- Place prompts on materials (for example, place a star on the starting point, use arrows to indicate direction, or use a green highlighter indicating to keep going).

- Add color to focus student attention (for example, highlight in yellow the part of an assignment to be done, put key vocabulary in color).

- Simplify the nature of a required response (for example, substitute pictures for words, change fill-in or multiple choice to true/false, provide only two choices rather than four for multiple choice, provide word boxes for cloze activities).

- Use pictures and graphics (such as graphic organizers help students organize information and remember more).

- Mask part of the page/work sheet/paper (for example, fold paper in half to reveal only part of the page, cut pages apart, use a "work window" in which only a small portion of the page can be seen; that is, cut a rectangle in a blank piece of paper to cover all but the sentence or word of interest).

- Use the same material over again but for a different purpose (for example, for a story read, now go back and find all the words that begin with a consonant blend, have four syllables, contain a suffix).

It is important to remember that students with physical challenges, to include neurological, are quite capable of performing well intellectually. They could experience frequent absences or fatigue associated with their particular impairment, and learning problems could begin in this way. However, students with a cognitive learning disability such as ADHD or a physical impairment such as cerebral palsy can benefit from these adaptations to instructional material. The instructional suggestions made in Chapter 3 for English learners could also be helpful.

PSYCHOLOGICAL FACTORS

Psychological factors refer to processes of the mind or psyche. Two psychological areas of concern to teachers are **cognition**, roughly the equivalent of thinking, and **affect**, which refers to feelings and attitudes. Cognition can be broadly conceptualized as reflecting a person's general ability to think, to act purposefully, and to solve problems. Recall from Chapter 1 that literacy is a cognitive process. The specific aspects of conceptual development, schema theory, and comprehension are discussed more fully in Chapters 11 through 13.

Literacy instruction is primarily concerned with students' thinking, but to be truly effective it must also be concerned with feelings. What people think and what they feel often are not the same, although the two processes are frequently so interrelated that it is difficult to separate them. How people perceive themselves and the world around them is a gauge of their emotional and social adjustment. People who do not feel good about themselves often have problems resolving inner conflicts and relating effectively with others in their environment. This generalization holds true for students who struggle in the area of literacy development.

Studies of the incidence of emotional maladjustment among effective and ineffective readers in general show no clear differences, although they suggest that serious reading problems are likely to be accompanied by adjustment problems. It would be very dangerous to conclude, however, that emotional instability causes problems in literacy. A more appropriate conclusion is that adjustment problems result from stress associated with difficulty learning. Behavior problems may also interact with other outside influences to make literacy learning even more difficult for learners who struggle. In fact, brain research does confirm that emotions are strongly linked to learning. Emotions trigger the release of chemicals into the endocrine system, which has the effect of intensifying the learner's conscious experience of a situation. Thus, decreasing anxiety or other stressors through cooperation, a risk-free learning environment, and a motivating classroom climate will increase positive emotions, in turn ensuring learning (Lackney, 2004).

Whether psychological adjustment problems are a cause or a result of difficulties in literacy learning is not clear, but the presence of these factors can be safely assumed to inhibit progress in literacy development. Quite often, students who improve in one of the literacy domains also improve in terms of self-concept. Thus, the classroom teacher should make every effort to help students feel good about themselves and feel successful, especially if they have difficulty with academic subjects because of a weakness in reading or writing.

Teachers' Responsibilities. Responsible classroom teachers are concerned with the well-being of their students, including their social and emotional well-being. Occasionally teachers observe students who seem to exhibit unusually severe maladjustment in these areas. Teachers may have an advantage over parents in identifying contributing social and emotional factors because they are not as close emotionally to the students and also because they can compare one student's behavior with that of many others. After teachers have taught for a few years, they have a fairly good idea of what constitutes bizarre or aberrant behavior. Although teachers should not dabble in amateur psychology, they should note unusual behaviors in students, particularly when those behaviors are frequent and persistent.

When teachers become aware of possible maladjustment, they should reflect on precisely what the student is doing to cause concern. Appendix F provides a checklist of some of the symptoms associated with psychosocial problems.

Many other behaviors are also possible symptoms. A checklist helps teachers organize their thoughts and prepare a case for referral to the school psychologist, guidance counselor, or school social worker. In many school systems these specialists have a heavy workload, and the waiting period after referral can be many months. A well-prepared and documented referral by a thoughtful teacher may expedite response.

Carefully prepared **anecdotal records**, a set of brief, highly objective written notes (see also Chapter 6), are a teacher's best tool in presenting a case for referral. Behaviors should be described objectively rather than presented as tentative conclusions. Valuable information is lost when conclusions are the only thing noted. The objective details will be helpful in revealing patterns of behavior when anecdotal records are reviewed over time. Consider the following examples:

Date	Conclusions	vs.	Objective Description
11/18	Jennifer had a temper tantrum.		Today, when Jennifer discovered she did not have her paper posted on the "my best effort" bulletin board, she ran up to the board, ripped off several papers belonging to classmates, then began to cry.
11/20	Jennifer fought with Susan in the cafeteria line.		Susan accidentally pushed Jennifer while they were in the cafeteria line. Jennifer then began to hit and kick Susan. Her facial expression frightened both Susan and me.
12/5	Jennifer refused to participate in the reading group and at other times today.		Jennifer was unusually quiet today. When I asked her comprehension questions, she dropped her head and eyes. I let someone else answer. Later when I tried to reengage her in the group activity, she still would not respond. I tried several other times to communicate with her today and had no luck. She did not talk with me all day.

The incomplete-sentence technique is often used to gain insights into the student's feelings about reading and self in general. Typically, a student will be asked to complete 20 to 50 sentence starters either orally or in writing. Some examples follow:

My reading group _____.
The teacher thinks I _____.
My books _____.

Information from such an instrument should be considered tentative and must be verified because students often respond as they think the teacher wants them to. This is a limitation of any self-reporting technique. A frequently used incomplete sentence test that was developed by Boning and Boning (1957) can be found in Appendix G.

Most school systems today have special classes for students displaying social or emotional maladjustment. Some students with relatively mild adjustment problems function quite well in the regular classroom. But sometimes these students do not learn well, and their response to failure and frustration from not learning academic subjects interacts with their already negative self-concept, leading to further maladjustment. This can create a negative spiral that worsens with time.

Failure can also have a devastating effect on well-adjusted people. Johnston and Winograd (1985) suggested that many of the problems exhibited by learners having difficulty are related to their passive involvement in literacy tasks. Therefore, the teacher can make a positive impact by providing a program that ensures active participation, strategy instruction, and **attributional retraining** (teaching pupils to accept responsibility for their successes and failures and to understand that effort and persistence may help to overcome failure) (Borkowski, Wehing, & Turner, 1986). Following are suggestions for helping students who display evidence of lowered self-esteem, whether from lack of accomplishment in literacy or for other reasons. They can also be appropriately used with most students:

1. *Create a facilitative learning environment.* Make special efforts to establish a warm, trusting working relationship with students and to listen carefully. Often students feel the need to discuss what is bothering them with a trusted adult, but teachers may be so preoccupied that they fail to hear the clues given. Dialogue journals can provide students and teachers a vehicle for "talking" to each other (Staton, 1988). Learners often need reassurance and specific suggestions, particularly regarding their troubles, whether they are academic or not. The teacher must establish a free and open atmosphere but at the same time set certain limits and maintain those limits, being pleasant but firm when necessary. The purpose of establishing rapport is to create an environment in which a learner's self-confidence and self-esteem are nurtured.

2. *Create opportunities for success.* The axiom "Nothing succeeds like success" is particularly appropriate for students who struggle with learning. Teachers help structure success experiences by ensuring that students work at a difficulty level that is easy enough for them. Find something they can read easily, even if it is their own name. Increasing the difficulty level if the literacy task is too easy is healthier than decreasing it after failure.

More difficult tasks can be spaced among easier ones. Students often can work with new and difficult tasks for only a few minutes before becoming too frustrated to continue. Interspersing success experiences among such tasks helps to relieve undue pressure and stress.

Older students often respond negatively to "baby stuff." Avoid this problem by using materials that appear more mature than they really are, such as high interest–low vocabulary books and stories without pictures of younger children. Some excellent picture books are available that lend themselves to sophisticated uses that will appeal to older students' sensibilities (see Benedict & Carlisle, 1992; Cassady, 1998; Danielson, 1992; Hadaway & Mundy, 1999; Miller, 1998; Neal & Moore, 1991/1992; Polette, 1989; Tiedt, 2000). Cross-age tutoring programs can also be effective in helping older students gain much needed practice with easier materials (Juel, 1991; Labbo & Teale, 1990; Morrice & Simmons, 1991).

A process called **bibliotherapy** can provide opportunities for distressed students to identify with a character or situation in a book and experience a catharsis or perhaps gain insight into their own problems (Dreyer, 1987). Bibliotherapy can help a student

Go to MyEducationLab and select the topic *Intervention Programs*. Then, go to the Activities and Applications section, and watch the video entitled "Extra Tutoring" to observe a middle school cross-age tutoring program. Next respond to the accompanying questions.

come to grips with personal problems and realize that reading can be a useful activity for personal growth (D'Alessandro, 1990). For example, *Golden Daffodils* (Gould, 1982) is a book about Janis, a fifth-grade student who has cerebral palsy, being mainstreamed into a regular classroom. Students with and without physical handicaps can better understand themselves and others when reading about the obstacles Janis must overcome. Other examples include *My Name is Brain/Brian* (Betancourt, 1993), a story about a sixth-grade boy diagnosed with dyslexia; *The Curious Incident of the Dog in the Night* (Haddon, 2004), a story about autism that explores an autistic boy's reactions to emotional losses; *Double Dutch* (Draper, 2002), a story about dyslexia and the fear of fitting in; and *Adam Zigzag* (Barrie, 1994), a novel about a teenage boy with dyslexia. (See Fouse and Morrison, 1997, for books to use with students diagnosed with ADD.)

A variation on bibliotherapy can be accomplished through a readers' theater format. *Readers' theater* is the oral presentation of a script. The script can be created from prose or poetry and presented by as few as two people. A portion of a script relevant to an emotional issue faced by many students, divorce, can be seen in Figure 4.2. This script would call for 10 participants and could be a lead-in for further discussion of this topic. (Other uses of readers' theater are discussed in Chapter 9 and in the Arts Connection feature in this chapter.)

3. *Develop authentic literacy tasks that reflect the popular culture.* Students who struggle, especially those in upper grades, often reject literacy tasks that lack purpose and interest (Pitcher et al., 2007). When only textbooks or whole-class activities are used, the teacher misses opportunities to engage in authentic literacy tasks. Today's concept of literacy goes beyond "text" to include not only print material such as newspapers and graphic novels but also media text and electronic messaging as well as nonprint media such as television shows, films, and songs. Developing literacy tasks that use these "new literacies" will increase student engagement in literacy (Phelps, 2006). In addition, "When we connect literacy to popular culture, our students can understand difficult content in new ways, as well as learn to question the media they are presented with on a daily basis" (Norton-Meier, 2005, p. 608). Fukunaga (2006) stated, "we may be able to find students' potential literacy skills and their multiple identities by paying attention to their activities with popular culture texts and the Internet." (p. 219).

Instant messaging, one example of an authentic literacy task used by today's students, can serve to motivate learners "to engage in decoding, encoding, interpretation, and

---

Figure 4.2   Readers' Theater Script Based on *Dinosaurs' Divorce*

This readers' theater script is a portion of a full script based on *Dinosaurs' Divorce: A Guide for Changing Families* (1986) by Laurene Krasny Brown and Marc Brown, originally published by Atlantic Monthly Press.

Narrator 1:	When your parents divorce, it's natural to feel
Dinosaur 1:	sad
Dinosaur 2:	angry
Dinosaur 3:	afraid
Dinosaur 4:	confused
Dinosaur 5:	ashamed
Dinosaur 6:	guilty
Dinosaur 7:	relieved
Dinosaur 8:	worried about who will take care of you.
Narrator 2:	The bad feelings won't last forever, and there is plenty you can do to help yourself feel better.
Narrator 1:	It helps to talk about these feelings and to let them show.

analysis, among other literacy processes" (Lewis & Fabos, 2005, p. 473). Lewis and Fabos (2005) found students used font color, font size, and icons to communicate sarcasm and visually represent emotional content. Word choice also received high levels of thoughtfulness during instant messaging. Students demonstrated themselves to be strategic language users to communicate their intended messages. Instructional strategies like dialogue journals and reading response logs can be easily adapted for use with instant messaging.

Song lyrics can also be quite useful for literacy lessons. Once carefully screened, using song lyrics of the performers students enjoy can help students connect their own experiences with the lesson objective. For example, instead of teaching about poetry techniques in the usual ways, the lyrics of some of their favorite songs and raps could be used to demonstrate the various poetry techniques (Weinstein, 2007). To illustrate, hyperbole, meaning a great exaggeration, can be demonstrated by well-chosen song lyrics (e.g., from *Where Is the Love?* sung by the Black Eyed Peas: "I feel the weight of the world on my shoulder."). Song lyrics could also be used to develop vocabulary (to explore synonyms, descriptive words, polysemantic words) and critical analysis skills (by uncovering intended meanings or political meanings).

4. *Provide ample reward and reinforcement.* Because many students who struggle have less than adequate confidence in their ability to engage in literacy tasks, they often need more encouragement than other students. Praise students when they succeed or when they attempt a task that is difficult and threatening. Social reinforcement can be given verbally ("very good," "nice try") or nonverbally (a reassuring smile, a pat on the back).

A more structured approach, using behavior modification techniques adapted to individual needs, often helps students having more serious problems. Extrinsic reinforcers applied by the teacher should in time be integrated into the learner's own personality structure. When this occurs and the student personally feels the reward of accomplishment, the reinforcement becomes the intrinsic satisfaction gained from doing the activity. One consideration teachers often overlook is that some students need considerable practice before they can attain a sense of satisfaction. Sometimes teachers try to push too fast for growth, changing learning tasks before the learner reaches the satisfaction of mastery.

5. *Encourage student participation.* Generally speaking, students who are involved in analyzing, planning, and evaluating their own literacy growth are those who profit most from instruction. Teachers should support students in understanding what they need to learn to develop their literacy skills. With the teacher's help, many students can verify, even if intuitively, the reality of their identified learning gaps. They can also demonstrate to the teacher their ability to be successful at certain tasks that an original analysis may have suggested were too difficult. Timely, meaningful interaction between pupil and teacher leads to efficient and enjoyable learning.

When students recognize their need and realize their desire to know a variety of literacy strategies, their goals become much clearer and attainment of those goals is consequently facilitated. Students like to keep track of their progress in attaining goals, and teachers should encourage them to make progress charts or other records of their growth. These charts and graphs become concrete evidence of success that helps the learner maintain goal-directed behaviors. They also become an important evaluation tool for both student and teacher. Maintaining a portfolio is a natural way for students to keep track of their own progress and development over time (Clemmons et al., 1993; DeFina, 1992; Glazer & Brown, 1993; Johnson & Rose, 1997; Sunstein & Lovell, 2000; Tierney, Carter, & Desai, 1991). For best results, at least four one-to-one teacher–student conferences are required each semester, with student self-analysis occurring more frequently (Farr, 1992). (See Chapters 6 and 8 for more on portfolios.)

Go to MyEducationLab and select the topic *Special Needs*. Then, go to the Activities and Applications section, and watch the video entitled "Reading and Writing" to see how praise and social reinforcement are used with one autistic student. Next respond to the accompanying questions.

ENVIRONMENTAL FACTORS

Much of what occurs in the environment or surrounding world directly and indirectly influences the people who live in that environment. Environmental factors that have a strong negative influence on school achievement and literacy progress include debilitating poverty, unfortunate conditions within the home, schools that are physically inadequate for or unresponsive to students' instructional needs, and societal ills. These environmental factors put students at risk and make them academically vulnerable.

Poverty. In recent years considerable evidence has demonstrated that economic differences have a strong relationship with school achievement. Low income and poverty have a positive correlation with low achievement (Dyer, 1968; Puma et al., 1997). Schools in economically distressed areas such as ghettos, barrios, urban housing developments, and certain rural areas generally do not offer the same benefits to students as the more affluent systems characteristic of suburban school districts. Poor students from minority groups, in particular, have been denied the benefits of a good education (Kozol, 1991), which has led to a "pedagogy of poverty" (Haberman, 1991) rather than a humanizing pedagogy with a commitment to social justice.

Students from impoverished circumstances, some perhaps homeless, come to school with experiences and backgrounds that vary considerably from those of their upper- and middle-class peers (Payne, 1998). Thus, the content of the school's literacy program may be inappropriate for these students. Although academically vulnerable due to their economic circumstances, these students are capable learners. They need enhanced and enriching conceptual, experiential, and language opportunities in school to ensure their literacy development. These students must also be made to see themselves as competent readers and writers, and they will do so as teachers help them accomplish literacy tasks. But first, they need teachers who believe in them. Educators need to acknowledge that their own particular values, beliefs, or attitudes undergird the pedagogy and curriculum provided their students. Teachers who seek to implement a framework of education for social justice will not approach children of poverty with preconceived notions about their needs. Nieto (1999) says it well:

> Many students are subjected to stale teaching and irrelevant curricula, but it is especially children of color, [and] those who live in poverty, speak a native language other than English, or attend poorly financed schools who are affected disproportionately and negatively by pedagogy and curriculum. This is true for several reasons. First, frequently these students are tracked into low-level ability groups . . . and very often they are thought by their teacher to need "basic skills" before moving on to more interesting knowledge and creative tasks. Second, teachers in poorly funded schools tend to be the least experienced and therefore they usually have scant knowledge of alternative pedagogical strategies or current curriculum thinking. . . . Finally, in the case of students with limited English proficiency, the singular focus on their learning English results in overshadowing all other considerations of curriculum and pedagogy. (p. 78)

Negative Home Environment. Unfortunate home environments are found in every social, cultural, and economic group. When a home is unstable and the family setting does not nurture feelings of security, learning problems may arise. Factors frequently mentioned are broken homes, family conflicts, sibling rivalry, and quarreling, overprotective, dominating, neglectful, or abusive parents. No one can deny that these factors have negative effects on a child. However, many children exposed to these conditions successfully learn to read. Hence the response to problems at home is a highly individual, idiosyncratic matter. The more resilient the child, the more likely the child will succeed. **Resiliency** is defined as the "capacity to spring back, rebound, successfully adapt in the face of adversity, and develop social competence despite exposure to severe stress" (R. Bowman, personal communication, January 23, 1999). (For more information, see the section on resiliency later in this chapter.)

Negative School Environment. Schools and instructional programs must also share the blame for failures in literacy development. Too often the common response to poor literacy achievement is to increase the amount of testing, demand national standards, or mandate a particular curriculum (Alexander, 1993; Farr, 1992; Frazee, 1993; Newmann & Wehlage, 1993). Such responses have led to mixed results, sometimes benefiting and sometimes hindering student learning.

Poor teaching is frequently cited as a reason for students not learning to read well (Shannon, 1989). Among the many complaints, the more common include: using unsuitable teaching methods; using overly difficult reading materials; using dull or otherwise inappropriate reading methods and materials; overemphasizing skills in isolation, especially phonics; giving too much or too little emphasis to reading skills; and teaching reading without integrating it into other curricular areas (see Shannon, 1990, for a historical treatment of the philosophies and practices of alternative literacy programs). The sooner educators and other school personnel recognize that there is no one way, no best method, no "magic bullet," and no "quick fix" for teaching reading, and that teaching approaches should accommodate students' different ways of knowing, the sooner all learners will make progress in literacy development (Allington & Walmsley, 1995; Nieto, 1999). Each learner is unique; even learners within the same cultural group are unique. Every learner comes to us knowing something, and it is our responsibility to find out what each learner knows and build on that knowledge.

Administrators and teachers working collaboratively can best facilitate improved instruction. Administrators can work to alleviate certain rigid school policies that lead to imbalanced curricula and other inappropriate outcomes. Examples of such policies are (a) requiring teachers to emphasize reading subskills to the detriment of reading as a transactive process; (b) overemphasizing the affective domain to the detriment of cognitive learnings; (c) requiring teachers to instruct students in a specific sequence at a specific time, to the detriment of students needing supplementary or corrective instruction; and (d) requiring students to attain a specified level of achievement before they are promoted, to the detriment of students who are doing their best and achieving, but below some arbitrary level. Teachers become frustrated and their efforts are hindered by such unfortunate administrative policies. On the other hand, teachers must work to remain as informed as possible about their students' needs and current pedagogical knowledge. They must also be willing to learn *with* their students to impress on students that teaching is more about learning than it is about "knowing everything." And finally, teachers must have the courage to be advocates for their students, which will sometimes mean "teaching against the grain" (Cochran-Smith, 1991).

Societal Ills. It is a major challenge of schools today to educate students who are at risk for their personal safety and survival. For instance, gangs can present a real threat to personal safety and survival and have infiltrated growing numbers of communities across the United States, from large cities to small and from the suburbs to rural areas. Teachers must be alert to all aspects of child maltreatment. Areas of child abuse and neglect include **sexual abuse** (sexual exploitation, molestation, child prostitution), **physical abuse** (nonaccidental injury to a child resulting in bruises, burns, broken bones, and/or internal injuries), **emotional maltreatment** (constant belittling, verbal abuse, inappropriate parenting, and neglect), and **physical neglect** (abandonment or inadequate provision of food, clothing, shelter, medical care, and supervision). Child abuse is far too common for teachers not to be knowledgeable about its physical and behavioral indicators (see Table 4.1). Teachers have the best opportunity to identify these students and, having done so, are

Go to MyEducationLab and first select the topic *Differentiating Instruction*. Go to the Activities and Applications section, and watch the video entitled "Teaching to Diverse Learning Styles" to learn more about the use of Guided Reading, scaffolds, role playing, addressing multiple intelligences, and including art and drama for effective literacy instruction. Respond to the accompanying questions. Then select the topic *Special Needs*. Go to the Activities and Applications section, and watch the video entitled "Accommodations for Heather" to learn more about addressing the needs of a student with learning disabilities in the classroom. Respond to the accompanying questions. If you want to learn more about accommodations and the inclusive classroom, select the topic *Overview of Reading Assessment*. Go to the Activities and Applications section, complete the simulation entitled "Accessing the General Education Curriculum," and respond to the accompanying questions.

Table 4.1	Signs and Symptoms of Child Abuse and Neglect		
Type	Physical Indicators	Behavioral Indicators	
Neglect (includes physical, educational, and emotional)	• Clothes are dirty, ill fitting, ragged, or not suitable for weather • Unwashed appearance • Offensive body odor • Consistent hunger • Consistent lack of supervision • Untreated rashes, colds, fevers, and other medical needs • Chronically tired • Delayed physical development (to include speech disorders) • Severe allergies, asthma	• Difficulty relating to people • Frequent absences or tardiness • Asks for, or steals, food • Goes through trash looking for food • Eats too fast • Eats more than fair share when food is available to a group • Sleeps in class	• Reports being home alone often • Disruptive behavior or withdrawal • Clinginess, neediness
Physical abuse	• Visible marks, such as cuts, bruises, welts, bite or hand marks • Well-defined burns (like cigarette burns) or bald spots • Unexplained fractures	• Reluctance to go home • Balks at physical contact • Extreme behaviors—either withdrawal or aggression • Runs away often	• Moves as if uncomfortable • Wears clothing inappropriate to weather, perhaps to cover marks • Self-destructive
Sexual abuse	• Discomfort in the genital area • Discomfort sitting or walking • Bruises or bleeding in genital area • Frequent urinary or yeast infections • Torn, stained, or bloody underwear	• Inappropriate interest in knowledge of sexual acts • Seductive behavior • Excessive aggression • Fear of a specific person or family member	• Noticeable change in weight • Sudden school difficulties • Chronic depression • Reluctance (or refusal) to undress in front of others • Attempts at suicide

continued

Table 4.1 *continued*

Type	Physical Indicators	Behavioral Indicators	
Sexual abuse *continued*	• Venereal disease	• Lack of confidence and poor self-esteem • Unusual concern for siblings • Pornography found on child's computer • Much online time at night • Child uses someone else's online account	• Lack of emotional control • Child receives phone calls (or gifts, mail, packages) from unknown persons • Quickly turns off computer monitor when someone approaches
Emotional abuse	• Outwardly hostile • Anger issues • Flashbacks and nightmares • Personality disorders • Speech disorders • Substance abuse • Ulcers • Delayed physical development	• Neurotic behaviors (rocking, sucking) • Self-destructive • Antisocial • Developmentally delayed • Delinquent behavior • Behavioral extremes (apathy, aggression)	• Difficulty with relationships • Anxiety • Depression

A single occurrence of any one of these indicators does not mean a child is being neglected or abused, but a number of physical indicators and a pattern of behaviors may indicate the need for further investigation or reporting.

required by law to report such cases. But a teacher's help does not stop there. All the suggestions made earlier with regard to emotional and social adjustment apply here as well.

Crack and cocaine have also had a serious impact on today's classrooms, but not in the way one might expect. Waller (1992, 1993) and DeSylvia and Klug (1992) estimate that between 400,000 to 700,000 children are born annually to mothers in all socioeconomic and cultural groups who used crack or cocaine during pregnancy. Although these children are at risk for physical, cognitive, and emotional difficulties most likely due to their environments, rigorous research efforts fail to link cocaine use and negative neonatal outcomes (Beattie, 2005). Chasnoff (1991) found that some children prenatally exposed to crack or cocaine exhibit no overt effects and goes on to state that these children are "more like drug-free children than they are different" (Chasnoff, 1992, p. 2). Barone's (1995, 1996) work also offers a more positive prognosis. She challenges us to reexamine our assumptions about children who were prenatally exposed to crack or cocaine as difficult to teach, hyperactive, late developers of language, and even violent. She has found that these children, like other children, respond to a supportive environment. Barone (1995) claimed that the only instructional recommendation that can be made for teachers is to provide these children the best instruction recommended for all children. Classrooms like those seen in Project DAISY (Developing Appropriate Intervention Strategies for the Young Child), which specifically targeted children between 3 and 5 years who had been prenatally exposed to drugs, support holistic, active learning; process-oriented, literature-based reading and writing; students' decision making; higher-level thinking document; and the success of these approaches with all children (pp. 52–53).

Resiliency. In spite of all the challenges that negative environmental factors present, the resilient child manages to survive and do well. The resilient child has the ability to bounce back. Goal-oriented, the resilient child believes that his or her efforts will lead to positive results. Resilient children can think critically and consider alternative solutions to both cognitive and social dilemmas, reflect on and learn from experiences, and are motivated to achieve. It is easy to see that resiliency has a direct relationship to student learning.

But resiliency is a learned capacity. Four key systems in a child's environment can present either risk factors or protective factors in the development of resiliency: family, peers, school, and community. The more risk factors present in these four key systems, the greater chance the child will engage in risky behaviors; whereas the more protective factors present in these four key systems, the greater chance the child will develop resiliency. Examples of risk factors grouped according to the four key systems are (a) unclear expectations for behavior; lack of monitoring; tobacco, drug, and alcohol abuse; low expectations for children's success (family); (b) antisocial behavior; rebelliousness; use of tobacco, alcohol, and other drugs (peers); (c) ill-defined or unenforced school policies, lack of student involvement, academic failure, identifying students as "high risk" (school); and (d) economic deprivation, community disorganization, lack of employment opportunities, tobacco and drugs readily available, and norms favorable to abuse (community). Examples of protective factors are (a) close bonding with the child, values and encourages education, clear expectations, nurturing and protective, shares family responsibilities (family); (b) respects authority, involved in drug-free activities (peers); (c) nurturing caretakers, encourages goal setting, high expectations, active student involvement, involves parents, fosters cooperative learning (school); and, (d) access to resources such as child care and job training, supportive networks, opportunities for youth in community service (community). Research by the Search Institute (1997) found that having at least one caring adult in a young person's life led to resiliency. They identified 40 assets, or protective factors, that lead to resiliency. The more protective factors possessed, the greater the chance for healthy, caring, responsible, resilient youth. They also found that even if a child possessed only just over half (or 21) of the 40 assets, he or she would be likely to succeed in school. Likewise, those with very few assets (0 to 10) had less than a C average.

Teachers' Responsibilities. It is very difficult to designate a specific environmental factor as the *cause* of a student's difficulties in literacy learning. Rather, this factor should be considered as a possible contributor to literacy difficulties. Teachers are not sociologists or social workers, and few have been trained in techniques that pinpoint contributing factors. The role of the teacher is one of identifying *possible* contributing factors and referring the student to appropriate specialists or agencies according to school policies. School districts often have social workers, counselors, and nurses to help teachers in the decision-making process.

Many schools have special programs for students who live in poverty, such as government-subsidized breakfast and lunch programs. Many communities today have mental health clinics that deal with family adjustment problems on a sliding fee basis.

Community welfare agencies often have child welfare departments concerned with children caught in untenable living conditions, including homelessness or abusive situations. Thus, a major responsibility of teachers is to be knowledgeable regarding community services available to the students they teach and to their families.

To assist any possible future referral, anecdotal records should be kept that document teacher observations with a high level of objectivity. This means the teacher must be careful to describe behaviors or indicators rather than simply assign labels, such as "This child's father is abusive." Remember not to overlook the privacy rights of students and their families. *Anecdotal records must never read like gossip.*

Teachers also must examine their own attitudes and beliefs about their students. I agree with Sonia Nieto (1999) when she says,

> Teaching and learning are primarily about relationships. . . . Consequently, teachers' beliefs and values, how these are communicated to students through teaching practices and behaviors, and their impact on the lives of students—these are the factors that make teaching so consequential in the lives of many people. . . . If we understand teaching as consisting primarily of social relationships and as a political commitment rather than a technical activity, then it is unquestionable that what educators need to pay most attention to are their own growth and transformation and the lives, realities, and dreams of their students. (pp. 130–131)

In addition, it is teachers' responsibility to make every effort to involve each student's parents in their child's literacy development. The very best advice to give parents is to read aloud with their child and to talk about the books their child is reading. Parental involvement is critical to student achievement. Parents and teachers who work together can make an outstanding positive contribution to a student's educational experiences. But sometimes parents need guidance and support to become effectively involved in their child's literacy development. Progress reports (see Appendix H) are one way to inform parents of what their child is experiencing in the classroom. Morningstar (1999) suggested the use of home response journals as a way for parents and teachers to communicate about a child's home and school language/literacy experiences. Other ways to keep parents informed include personal letters, especially positive notes about their child; classroom newspapers or newsletters; and invitations to visit the classroom at their convenience (Thomas, Fazio, & Stiefelmeyer, 1999a, 1999b). It is equally important to be prepared for parents' questions (see Figure 4.3). When meeting with parents for a conference, teachers should:

Go to MyEducationLab and select the topic *Involving Parents.* Then, go to the Activities and Applications section, and watch the video entitled "Beyond Instruction" to observe a parent-teacher conference. Use the five items listed here and in Figure 4.3 to critique this conference. Think about what this teacher could have done differently. Next respond to the accompanying questions.

1. Talk specifically about the child and use specific examples. They should especially mention the child's strengths.
2. Mention things that the child is enthusiastic about.
3. Ask parents for information about their child's interests and achievements at home.
4. Offer possible solutions to any problems. Engage their cooperation in joint efforts to help the child.
5. Discuss your criteria for grades (for example, what does the grade B mean in your class?) and state what you think is important about the report card or the student's progress report.

The most important thing is to keep the lines of communication open. Positive communication encourages further involvement between teacher and parents, removes barriers, and provides the school with greater parental support (Batey, 1996; Rasinski, 1995).

Instructional factors should be within the control of school personnel, specifically the classroom teacher and the principal. School-based personnel should assume responsibility for providing instruction that promotes rather than inhibits literacy learning. To maximize

Figure 4.3   Questions Parents Ask/Questions Teachers Consider when Preparing a Response

Parent Questions	Teacher Questions
Is my child doing as well as he should in school?	• Have I looked at this student's cumulative records? • What are the grade-appropriate standards? • Are there anecdotal records of this student's progress?
What group(s) is my child in and why?	• Can I clearly explain the grouping system I use? • How can I help this parent understand that all students are expected to meet the same content standards? • Is this student working at a developmentally appropriate level? • Does this student have special needs?
What kind of books is my child using?	• Do I readily know the textbook names and reading levels of this student? • Does this student use supplemental books? Why? • Do I have my students keep a record of books read?
May I see some of my child's work?	• Have I asked students to update their portfolios regularly, and have I looked at them recently? • How am I going to respond to the student's work that is less than satisfactory? • Do I have a system in place for periodically sending home students' work and monitoring whether a parent actually sees it?
Does my child get along well with the other children?	• Do I keep anecdotal records on problems that arise between students? • Do I give suggestions to students and parents about how behavior can be improved?
Have you noticed any special interests, aptitudes, or abilities?	• Do I encourage my students to do extra projects and exploration in their areas of expertise, and do I maintain records of what their interests are? • Do I provide opportunities for the students that will further develop their talents, and have I determined their multiple intelligences profiles?
Does my child obey you?	• Do I have an effective classroom management system in place that provides periodic feedback to parents? • Do I keep anecdotal records of specific incidents as documentation?
How can I help at home?	• Have I provided specific examples to parents on how to assist their child? • Have I provided materials to parents to assist them in helping their child?
What is my child's national standing?	• Do I provide parents with a complete copy of their child's standardized test scores? • Can I clearly explain test results to parents?

Figure 4.3   *continued*

Parent Questions	Teacher Questions
Does my child get to class and school on time?	• Are my attendance records up-to-date?
Is it all right to call you at home?	• Do I have a procedure informing parents of how and when to contact me?
Is it OK if I drop in anytime to see about my child?	• Do I have guidelines established concerning parental visits? Have I provided parents with this information? • Are guidelines established for the way parents should conduct themselves during a classroom visit?

instruction in the classroom, teachers must first consider their students—their needs and interests, how they learn best, and how they might learn the joy of a literate life. These considerations are of major concern throughout the instructional chapters that follow.

Summary

The intent of Chapter 4 is to help make teachers aware of the variety of factors that affect literacy development. Many of the factors mentioned, such as overall health, cognition, and emotional maladjustment, affect learning in general. Other factors, including visual and auditory acuity and perception, are more directly related to literacy learning.

In many cases the teacher can only refer students with such issues to other resources. Physicians, including neurologists and psychologists, may be needed if one of the outside influences is severe. In some cases, teachers can give specific help—for example, with visual perception skills or auditory comprehension. In all cases, teachers should be understanding and caring and attempt to make the educational environment comfortable and risk free for learners experiencing difficulty.

Recommended Websites

Educator's Quick Reference for Classroom Vision Problems
  www.oep.org/EducatorsHome.asp
Selected references and pamphlets for the most current information are placed here for teacher use.

The Blind Readers' Page
  blindreaders.info/index.html
This site is a guide to sources of information in alternative formats (Braille, recorded cassettes, large print, e-texts, web audio) accessible by people with print disabilities, to include those with dyslexia. There are extensive links, all evaluated, annotated, and organized by subject.

LD Online Home Page
  www.ldonline.org/
This respected website provides the latest research and teaching strategies related to students with LD and ADHD.

Learning Disabilities Association of America
  www.ldanatl.org
This site is designed to help people with learning disabilities, as well as their parents and teachers.

One A.D.D. Place
  www.oneaddplace.com/
A virtual neighborhood consolidating information and resources related to ADD, ADHD, and learning disabilities can be found here in one place.

Autism Society of America
  www.autism-society.org/
This site is a source of autism information.

Asperger Syndrome
www.asperger.org
Links to autism, Asperger syndrome, and related pervasive developmental disorders can be found at this site.

Stuttering Foundation of America
www.stuttersfa.org
This site provides information on stuttering as it relates to special education laws.

National Stuttering Association
www.nsastutter.org/
Information on stuttering as a communication disorder with suggestions for educators, parents, and students is provided here.

Asthma and Allergy Foundation of America
www.aafa.org/
This site has information and statistics on asthma and allergies, including food allergies.

Brain Connection: The Brain and Learning
www.brainconnection.com
This is a site devoted to applying brain science to teaching and learning.

International Dyslexia Association (formerly the Orton Dyslexia Society)
www.interdys.org
Dedicated to the study and treatment of dyslexia, this organization's website provides access to many resources related to this learning disability.

Hoagie's Gifted Education Page
www.hoagiesgifted.org
This site is designed for gifted students, parents, and teachers.

National Clearinghouse on Child Abuse and Neglect
www.childwelfare.gov/can/
Locate recent statistics, and other resources, regarding child abuse at this site.

School–Home Links: A Compact for Reading
www.ed.gov/pubs/CompactforReading/index.html
Read about ways to improve family involvement in education. This site provides hundreds of K–3 printable activities to send home with children.

Misunderstood Minds
www.pbs.org
Type in Misunderstood Minds in the Search box for companion websites to this outstanding PBS special on learning differences and disabilities.

National Down Syndrome Society
www.ndss.org
This website is the most comprehensive source on Down syndrome.

New Horizons for Learning
www.newhorizons.org/
Visit the Special Needs section for a database of inclusion teaching and learning resources and strategies.

American Sign Language Browser
http://commtechlab.msu.edu/sites/aslweb/index.htm
Learn American Sign Language to communicate with students who are deaf or who have hearing impairments.

Assistive Technology and Literacy Instruction
http://tiger.towson.edu/users/mmille30/assistive.htm
This site describes assistive technology and how/why such devices are useful in school.

National Assistive Technology Research Institute
http://natri.uky.edu/
This website is designed to support teachers, families, and administrators in planning and implementing assistive technology services.

Positive Behavioral Interventions & Supports
www.pbis.org
This site provides video clips of schoolwide behavior interventions and capacity-building information.

MyEducationLab is a research-based learning tool that brings teaching to life. Go to the Gipe 7th Edition MyEducationLab for Reading Assessment site at www.myeducationlab.com to:

- Engage in multimedia exercises to help you build a deeper and more applied understanding of chapter content.
- Use extensive resources including videos from real classrooms, Praxis and licensure preparation, a lesson plan builder, and materials to help you in your teaching career.

Formal Literacy Assessment

Indirect Measures

OBJECTIVES

After you have read this chapter, you should be able to:

1. Define and describe briefly the following measurement terms: *validity, reliability,* and *standard error of measurement.*
2. Interpret these scores: grade equivalent, percentile, NCE, and stanine.
3. Decide the value of a particular test score for instructional decision making.
4. Explain purposes of testing relevant to literacy instruction.
5. Describe the differences between norm-referenced and criterion-referenced tests.

VOCABULARY ALERT

assessment	high-stakes testing	reliability
at-level testing	indirect assessment	standard deviation
construct validity	mastery tests	standard error of
content validity	normal curve equivalent	measurement
correlation coefficients	(NCE) scores	standard scores
criterion-referenced tests	norm-referenced tests	standardized tests
direct assessment	norms	stanine scores
evaluation	out-of-level testing	validity
formal tests	percentile scores	
grade-equivalent scores	performance assessment	

This is not an easy period for administrators, teachers, and all those struggling to help learners achieve academically in today's culture of testing. Testing is about evaluation, while assessment is about gathering information. Often the terms are used as if they were synonymous. While educational assessment includes testing, it means more than test results. In its current stage of development, educational assessment is generally of two very different types: large-scale achievement testing (such as the *California Achievement Tests*, or CAT6) and **performance assessment** (students read, write, and solve problems in genuine ways such as taking and supporting a point of view on a specific issue). However, large-scale testing remains in the forefront due in large part to the NCLB Act and state legislatures' mandates of specific methods of instruction.

Peter Johnston (1992) cautions us to consider the language we use when we talk about assessment. As he points out,

> We refer to our own observations as "subjective," "informal," and "anecdotal," whereas we refer to tests as "objective" and "formal." Our own language devalues the close knowledge we have and values distance. It would be more helpful if we referred to our own assessments as "direct documentation" and test-based assessments as "indirect" and "invasive." These uses of language are far from trivial. They show that we do not value our own assessment knowledge. Our unfortunate cultural concern for control, distance, objectification, and quantification . . . does not favor teachers, whose knowledge is often intuitive, usually nonnumerical, more inclined to the narrative, and gained through personal involvement. . . . Detailed knowledge comes from proximity and involvement, not distance. (p. 61)

As I reflect on Johnston's words I agree that the term *informal assessment* has a negative connotation—implying assessment that is sloppy or haphazard—something less worthy compared to *formal assessment*, meaning standardized testing. Thus, I prefer to use the term **indirect assessment** to refer to the standardized, norm-referenced types of tests discussed in this chapter and the term **direct assessment** to refer to performance assessment and the classroom-based, or teacher-based, assessment techniques discussed in Chapter 6. Perhaps you will come to agree with this distinction as well. Meanwhile, the terms *indirect* and *direct* assessment will be used throughout this text to refer to "formal" standardized and "informal" classroom-based assessments, respectively.

Currently, indirect measures, commonly known as standardized tests, although less meaningful to the teacher in terms of instructional planning because of their distance from what happens in the classroom, are likely to be around for some time, because there continues to be a need for large-scale testing in school districts. For example, large-scale testing results remind us that there is an achievement gap for poor and minority children (Raines, 2000). Large-scale testing can provide information about achievement that we need to be aware of, but the increasing reliance on a single test score to make important and substantial educational decisions (**high-stakes testing**) is a disturbing trend.

Go to MyEducationLab and first select the topic *Overview of Reading Assessment.* Then go to the Activities and Applications section, and complete the simulation entitled "Accountability" to learn more about the impact of high-stakes testing on students with disabilities. Next respond to the accompanying questions.

Chapter 5 discusses the basic concepts related to indirect (or formal) assessments, enabling teachers to better decide for themselves how valuable a particular test score may be. Also, the information found here should help teachers better discuss standardized test results with parents.

A review of the basic concepts of assessment and evaluation includes definitions, measurement concepts, a brief discussion of different kinds of scores, and, more specific to the goal of this text, purposes of testing in the literacy domains. After this review, the chapter proceeds with a discussion of particular published literacy tests.

ASSESSMENT AND EVALUATION: BASIC CONCEPTS

Definitions

Both assessment and evaluation are critical to the analytic process. Many educators use the terms interchangeably; however, **assessment** usually refers to the process of gathering data about a learner's strengths and difficulties, and **evaluation** refers to the process of judging achievement or growth, or of decision making. Thus, evaluation implies the need to use assessment techniques to obtain information for making judgments or decisions.

In schools, literacy achievement is frequently evaluated through the use of standardized achievement tests. **Standardized tests** are so called because they have been administered in the same way to a large group of students (who represent students for whom the test was designed) to establish a reference or norm group. The scores of these students become the **norms** and can be used for comparison with the scores of other students taking the test. Thus, the term **norm-referenced test** is also used to describe a standardized test. Part of the standardization procedure involves preparing a standard set of directions for administration that includes directions to students and time allotment for completing subtests. This standard set of directions is another reason these tests are called standardized, and because the directions for administration must be strictly adhered to, the tests have also become known as **formal tests**.

Several other terms associated with standardized testing will be used throughout this chapter. Those related to interpreting standardized test scores will be defined here. Other important terms are defined in the next section. Because a standardized test is norm-referenced, norm tables are included in a test manual to tell you how the raw scores are converted into normed scores. These normed scores include percentile scores, standard scores such as stanines and normal curve equivalent scores, and grade equivalent scores. Each will be defined here. For help in seeing how some of these scores and others relate to the normal curve, refer to Figure 5.1.

Percentile Scores. Percentile scores, converted from raw scores, compare students only with others of the same grade or age. Students who receive a percentile score of 63 have done as well as or better than 63 percent of students in the norm group. The percentile scores do *not* represent the percentage of items answered correctly. Percentile scores can range from 1 to 99 (Figure 5.1) and can be compared directly with other subtests or tests taken previously. Interpretation of percentile scores is limited, however, to comparing students with those in the norm groups or those in the same classroom or school. For example, if fourth-grader Georgia's raw score of 17 converts to the 12th percentile on the reading comprehension subtest, the proper interpretation is that Georgia has done as well as or better than 12 percent of a large sample of fourth-grade children who took this test. If her score on the vocabulary subtest converted to the 6th percentile, the teacher can say that Georgia performed slightly better in reading comprehension than in vocabulary. The

Go to MyEducationLab and select the topic *Formal Assessments*. Then, go to the Activities and Applications section, and watch the video entitled "Standardized Tests" for further explanation of the nature of norm groups, percentile scores, and a comparison of standardized tests to criterion-referenced tests. In addition, this video presents ways to prepare students for test-taking, a topic that will be discussed further in Chapter 14. Next respond to the accompanying questions.

Figure 5.1	Normed Score Distributions for the Normal Curve

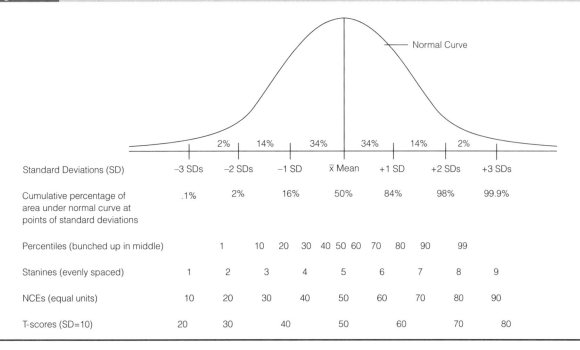

	–3 SDs	–2 SDs	–1 SD	x̄ Mean	+1 SD	+2 SDs	+3 SDs
Standard Deviations (SD)							
Cumulative percentage of area under normal curve at points of standard deviations	.1%	2%	16%	50%	84%	98%	99.9%
Percentiles (bunched up in middle)		1	10 20 30	40 50 60	70 80	90	99
Stanines (evenly spaced)	1	2	3	4	5	6	7 8 9
NCEs (equal units)	10	20	30	40	50	60	70 80 90
T-scores (SD=10)	20	30	40	50	60	70	80

teacher cannot, however, average the two percentiles and say that, overall, Georgia scored at the 9th percentile. That is an inaccurate statement because of the way percentiles bunch up in the middle of a normal distribution; distances between scores are not equal. The teacher may also compare Georgia's score with those of her classmates who took the same test or with her previous scores on this test. That information might help the teacher place Georgia in an initial group for instructional reading purposes, but it is not at all helpful for deeper-level analytic purposes (that is, level 3 analysis). Therefore, the teacher must still rely on other means of assessing reading behaviors to help identify Georgia's specific areas of reading strength and difficulty.

Standard Scores. Standard scores are derived from raw scores in such a way as to obtain uniformly spaced scores. Standard scores indicate an individual score's distance from the average, or mean, score in terms of the variability of the distribution of all scores. A number called the **standard deviation** indicates the degree of variability; that is, the higher the standard deviation, the more variability in the scores. Standard scores allow comparisons to be made among scores on different tests and subtests. Some standardized achievement tests convert raw scores according to an average standard score of 50 with a standard deviation of 10 (see T-scores, Figure 5.1). For example, if Jerry earned a raw score of 52 on a math test and 42 on a reading test, the scores cannot be directly compared because they do not reflect anything about the total distribution of scores for all the students taking the tests. By converting the raw scores to standard scores, each of Jerry's scores can be considered in relation to an average score of 50 and a standard deviation of 10. Jerry's scores convert to a standard score of 80 on the math test and 48 on the reading test. Jerry therefore did much better on the math test than on the reading test, but the raw scores did not indicate such a large difference. Jerry also scored well above average on the math test. The average is 50; thus 80 is 30 points or 3 (30 divided by 10) standard deviations above the mean. On the other hand, Jerry did just about average on the reading test.

There are two commonly reported standard scores, stanine scores and NCE scores. **Stanine scores** are standard scores for which the raw scores have been converted into nine equally spaced parts, with a stanine of 1 being low and 9 being high. A stanine of 5 is considered average, and the standard deviation is approximately 2 (Figure 5.1). Stanine scores are interpreted similarly to percentiles, with the major difference being the number and size of units involved; there are 99 percentile units and only 9 stanines. For interpretation purposes, stanines 1, 2, and 3 reflect poor performance; stanines 4, 5, and 6 reflect average performance; and stanines 7, 8, and 9 reflect good performance on a test.

NCE Scores. NCE scores, or **normal curve equivalent scores**, are based on the normal curve and represent a score that has more recently come into use. NCE scores range from 1 to 99 with a mean of 50, and in this way they are similar to percentile scores. The points in between are different from percentiles, however. Percentile scores tend to pile up around the mean and spread further apart on approaching the extremes; NCE scores are in equal units. Therefore, NCE scores are interpreted just like the T-scores discussed earlier in the example of Jerry.

Grade-Equivalent Scores. Grade-equivalent scores are usually stated in terms of years and tenths of years. For example, if the average raw score of beginning fourth-grade children in the norm group is 33, then 33 is assigned the grade equivalent of 4.1 (fourth grade, first month). Any child who scores 33 raw-score points receives a grade-equivalent score of 4.1.

Grade-equivalent scores appear easy for teachers to interpret because the reference point is a grade in school, but interpretation actually has some serious limitations. The further away a pupil's score is from the average, the greater the chances are that the grade equivalent will be misinterpreted. Grade-equivalent scores for average children are probably accurate, but low or high scores are susceptible to error of interpretation. It is particularly important for teachers of students who are reading poorly to remember this. To continue with the example of the fourth-grader, if Georgia scores 17 raw-score points (a fairly low score), which converts to a grade-equivalent score of 2.1 according to the norm table found in the test manual, the teacher should not conclude that Georgia is reading in a manner similar to a beginning second-grade child. All that can be said is that Georgia is reading poorly compared to her fourth-grade classmates and that she earned the same raw score as the average of second-graders in the first month of second grade.

Grade-equivalent scores do not indicate grade placement for a student. For example, suppose Tommy, a third-grader, takes the test containing second-, third-, and fourth-grade material and receives a grade-equivalent score of 5.3. This does not mean that Tommy is able to handle fifth-grade, third-month material because he was never tested on fifth-grade material. It only means that Tommy can perform second-, third-, and fourth-grade tasks in the test as well as average students in the third month of fifth grade can perform these (below-grade-level) tasks.

Grade-equivalent scores have been so seriously misinterpreted that in 1981 the International Reading Association passed a resolution calling on publishers to eliminate grade equivalents from their tests. Therefore, percentile scores, stanines, or NCEs are recommended for comparing a student's performance to that of the norm group.

Basic Measurement Concepts

Successful assessment and evaluation in the literacy domains depend considerably on the tools teachers use. These tools can be called "tests" in the broadest sense of that term, but tests can range from informal reading inventories, to teacher-made spelling tests, to the highly structured standardized achievement tests. Some concepts are basic to all measurement systems, regardless of how they are constructed or used. Among the more important concepts are validity, reliability, and standard error of measurement.

Validity. The most important of all measurement characteristics is **validity**. A test is valid *if it measures what it claims to measure and does the task for which it is intended*. The critical question for the teacher to ask is, Does this test measure what I have been teaching? Sternberg (1991) reminded us "we need to be considerably more cautious in our use of test scores and that we need at least to think about creating tests that are more realistic simulations of people's behavior in the kinds of situations in which they use the aptitudes and achievements that we measure. . . . Reading tests [are] considerably less valid as measures of real-world reading behavior than most people have wanted to believe" (p. 540).

Test content that matches a teacher's instructional objectives is said to have **content validity**. If the match is poor, the test is an invalid measure of those particular instructional objectives. For example, a teacher has been concentrating on teaching reading comprehension for the past three months and now wants to test the pupils. A test measuring reading comprehension would be valid; a test measuring knowledge of phonics would be invalid because the test would not measure what had been taught. The phonics test is not a bad test in and of itself; rather, it is inappropriate for the purpose intended. Kavale (1979) suggests that teachers can best determine content validity by actually taking the test.

Teachers are unlikely to make an error in situations in which the validity issue is so clearly apparent, as in the preceding example, but occasionally the matter is more subtle. Consider, for instance, the use of a test called "Vocabulary Knowledge" when the match between the test and the lessons taught is a matter of approach. If the teacher has used a modified cloze procedure approach, and the test measures vocabulary from a synonym-matching approach, the test would not be highly valid because it does not assess vocabulary as it was taught. Teachers and school administrators must be jointly responsible for choosing appropriate tests.

Another type of validity, **construct validity**, refers to the degree to which a test measures a certain ability or trait. For example, an intelligence test is said to have construct validity to the extent that it actually measures intelligence. Because most traits cannot be measured directly, tests having construct validity measure behaviors believed to reflect the trait. The titles of some tests imply construct validity without providing empirical information in the test manual to support the existence of the validity (Sax, 1980). Such a practice is misleading to teachers and to others who may not be knowledgeable about measurement concepts. A test on reading comprehension, for example, should provide evidence that the test does, in fact, measure reading comprehension.

Many tests designed to measure word recognition skills have been questioned on the basis of their construct validity. If a syllabication subtest asks students to identify the number of syllables in various words, and the examiner *speaks* the words, the construct validity of the test can be questioned. In the real reading situation, the students *see* and do not *hear* the words that they must syllabicate. Thus the question is whether the behaviors measured by oral presentation measure the same trait required during the process of silent reading.

Construct validity is typically supported by **correlation coefficients**, which indicate how strongly two variables are related. To be of most value for assessment, the subtests involved must be relatively independent, as reflected by low correlation coefficients ranging from 0.00 to 0.70. A high correlation (0.70 to 1.00) indicates a strong relationship between the subtests; in that case, the subtests are too interrelated to measure the different aptitudes they purport to measure.

Reliability. The consistency or dependability of a test and its measurements denotes its **reliability**. If a teacher were to give the same test to a group of students more than once (test–retest) within a short time frame (so that growth isn't being measured), and the scores on the tests are nearly the same for each student, the test is considered reliable because it yields essentially the same score each time it is given.

Reliability is also expressed through a correlation coefficient. The higher the correlation coefficient, the more dependable the scores obtained from the test. A coefficient of 0.90 or more is considered very reliable; if it is below 0.80, the teacher should be cautious in making decisions about individual students. Reliability can be estimated in a number of statistical ways, and each has a different name. Test manuals indicate the type of reliability by using terms such as *split-half reliability, parallel forms reliability*, and *Kuder-Richardson reliability*. In any case, a high correlation coefficient is desirable.

No reading test is perfectly consistent. Some common conditions affecting reliability are objectivity in scoring, needed variability among scores of students being tested, number of items on the test, difficulty level, and standardization of test administration and interpretation (Sax, 1980).

Objectivity in scoring is critical. If different teachers independently score the same test but arrive at different scores, reliability cannot be very high. Multiple-choice tests are relatively free from problems of this type compared to more subjective measures, such as essay tests.

Reliability also depends on the variability of the students taking the tests. If everyone taking a particular test functions at the same level and gets the same score, the reliability of that test is zero, because student variability is lacking.

The easiest and most efficient way to improve reliability is to increase the number of items on the test, provided that the added items consistently measure what the original items measure. This explains, in part, why some tests are so long. For behavioral observation, the teacher must increase the number of times the student is observed performing a specific task.

Difficulty level also affects reliability. A very easy or very hard test does not measure individual differences because all student responses tend to be the same (Sax, 1980). Clearly, such a test cannot be used for analytic purposes.

Standardization of test administration and interpretation or criteria for scoring and interpreting provide more reliable information. Tests and assessment measures that lack such clear guidelines result in interpretations that are highly dependent on the person making the assessment.

Standard Error of Measurement. When a score is obtained for a student, the teacher should ask how much confidence can be placed in it as the student's *true* score. Many test manuals describe a statistic known as the **standard error of measurement** (SEmeas or SEM). This statistic indicates the extent to which an individual's score can be expected to vary each time the test is taken. In other words, standardized tests are not precise instruments, and there is error associated with any score. The *true score* is the score that would result if the same test were taken many, many times and those scores were averaged. Because this isn't possible, the standard error of measurement is reported for the test, and it is used to determine a range within which the true score lies. This range is called the *band of probability* or the *confidence interval*. This band identifies the highest and lowest scores that the true score falls between two-thirds of the time. For example, let's say the SEM is 10 standard score points, and in this example the raw score converts to a true T-score between 60 and 80. The SEM of 10 was added and subtracted from the obtained T-score of 70 to achieve the band of probability for the true score. If we then convert these scores to percentiles (refer to Figure 5.1), the interpretation would be that, for two out of three testings, the true score would fall between the 82nd and 99th percentiles. In one out of three testings, the score could fall below the 82nd (for percentiles the 99th is the highest score; Fry, 1980).

Because the range or band of probability for a test score can be fairly wide, ideally we would like to use a test with high validity, high reliability, and a small SEM. The concept of the SEM is not restricted to standardized tests, however. Teacher observations, surveys and checklists, informal reading inventories, criterion-referenced tests, and text-related tests, which will be defined a little later, also have a potentially large SEM because they have not been given to large groups of students with the intention of revising to lower the SEM. Thus there is considerable potential for error with direct as well as indirect measures. Before making a decision about a student's ability, the teacher must consider a variety of information (test score plus informal observation plus work samples). The nature of assessment is multidimensional, much as literacy is a multidimensional process.

PURPOSES OF TESTING

Testing has many different purposes, and many tests are available, so take care to choose a test appropriate for a specific purpose. As Kavale (1979) said, "If the uses for the test results are not known in advance, the best test to use is none at all" (p. 9).

Test selection should be based on answers to the questions *what, who, by whom*, and *for what* (Merwin, 1973). Kavale (1979) provides some examples of how these questions might be answered. For instance, a test is needed to:

1. Assess reading achievement (*what*) of [an eighth-grade student] (*who*) by the teacher (*by whom*) to help determine the student's instructional reading level (*for what*)

2. Assess word attack skills (*what*) of a [second-grade child] (*who*) by the teacher (*by whom*) to determine whether particular phonics knowledge is needed (*for what*)

3. Assess gain in reading achievement (*what*) of a group of fourth-grade students (*who*) by a curriculum supervisor (*by whom*) to determine the effectiveness of a new set of instructional materials (*for what*) (p. 10)

Using Merwin's guidelines, the answer to the *for what* question represents the specific purpose of testing, but the other questions are equally important in the selection of a test.

Because of the great number of purposes of testing in literacy, all cannot be listed; however, some examples are particularly relevant for classroom teachers:

1. Organizing the class into reading, skill, or interest groups
2. Assessing reading levels of individual students
3. Identifying specific literacy difficulties in areas such as word identification, inferential comprehension, vocabulary development, or writing
4. Evaluating individuals or small groups

ADMINISTERING STANDARDIZED TESTS

Teachers must carefully follow directions when administering standardized tests. Tests are designed to give every pupil, as nearly as possible, the same chance when taking the test. If teachers do not follow the standardized directions, scores cannot be used reliably and validly. Directions should never be rushed or examples omitted. On the other hand, teachers should never give more information to pupils than is specified in the test manual. Deviations from the directions or test time will put the pupils in a context different from the norm group, and norms for the test will not be appropriate. It is imperative, therefore, to follow instructions precisely or note any deviations from the standardized procedures.

Along with the tests themselves, publishers provide examiner manuals and several additional aids, such as scoring keys and record sheets. A test's technical manual or examiner manual contains vital information that must be studied before giving the test. A good test manual contains directions for test administration and scoring as well as information to aid effective interpretation of the scores. Additional information of a statistical and technical nature, such as validity and reliability coefficients and the SEM, is usually found in the technical manual.

The testing environment is an important consideration because classroom conditions affect the reliability of test results. The classroom should be well lit, ventilated, and free from undue noise or interruptions. A sufficient number of tests, answer sheets, and marking pencils should be available. Pupils unaccustomed to taking tests should be briefed beforehand regarding such test-taking behaviors as no talking, no helping, and no drinks of water. In classrooms in which cooperative learning groups and conversation are the norm, these testing requirements can certainly affect results (McAuliffe, 1993). Most students benefit from a practice session using practice booklets, which are often available with standardized tests (see Chapter 14 for more on test-taking strategies). At times teachers have difficulty maintaining the neutral role needed during the testing period, but you should resist the temptation to help students. The roles of teacher and tester are not the same.

Standardized Reading Survey Tests

Standardized tests most widely used in schools today are achievement test batteries such as the *Comprehensive Test of Basic Skills (CTBS), Iowa Tests of Basic Skills (ITBS), Metropolitan Achievement Tests* (e.g., *Metropolitan 8*), and *California Achievement Tests* (e.g., *CAT6*). Designed to sample broad knowledge in a given area, these batteries typically yield two or three reading scores plus scores for other subject areas, such as arithmetic and social studies, and are useful for Level 1 analysis (see Chapter 2). Common areas assessed in reading are vocabulary, comprehension, total reading (often a combination of the vocabulary and comprehension scores), and, less frequently, measures of study skills and rate of reading.

Survey reading tests are similar to the reading subtests on achievement test batteries. When general reading is the focus of testing, a survey test saves time and money because other content areas are not included. These tests help in placement and are often used in pre- and postintervention assessments to determine whether students have benefited from that particular intervention. Two examples of survey reading tests are the *Gates-MacGinitie Reading Tests*, 4th ed. (MacGinitie, MacGinitie, Maria, & Dreyer, 2000), available for K–12 and adult, and the *Nelson-Denny Reading Skills Test* (Brown, Fishco, & Hanna, 1993), for high school, college, and adult, with an electronic version of the survey test made available in 2001. Be aware, however, that scores from these tests probably reflect either maximum or minimum performance on the part of many students. They usually either try hard to do their best on tests of this type or give up altogether and answer questions randomly. In either case, their scores tend to reflect a level of concentration and performance not typical of their day-to-day reading activities.

Although survey reading tests can help teachers with Level 1 analysis, identifying those students who may need assistance in their reading development, and perhaps with

Level 2 analysis, identifying the major domain in which reading difficulties are occurring, they are not designed to do more than this. Other tests and assessment procedures are more helpful for analyzing reading behaviors at Levels 2 and 3 (areas of difficulty), and they can supplement data obtained from survey tests. Also consider that some students are effective readers but never do well on standardized tests.

Most survey reading tests are designed to be administered in one of two ways. The first, called **at-level testing**, uses a single level of the test for a specified grade level. For example, level A of the test is to be used for first and second grades, level B for third and fourth grades, and level C for fifth and sixth grades. A third-grade teacher would administer the level B test to all students in the class.

The second option, called **out-of-level testing**, allows the teacher to select the level of the test that best reflects the average achievement of the class. For example, a teacher of students whose average achievement is atypically low or high could select a level better suited to the students, thus increasing reliability. If out-of-level testing is desired, be sure to check the teacher's manual for further information about the test being used.

Standardized Diagnostic Reading Tests

The major purpose of standardized diagnostic reading tests is to measure discrete reading subskills. Teachers sometimes use these tests to identify students' specific areas of strength and difficulty (Level 2 analysis; refer to Chapter 2). A graphic profile is used to compare subtest scores for individuals and to determine level of ability in areas associated with literacy instruction. Because diagnostic assessment is directed at identifying specific strengths and areas of difficulty, the total test score is much less meaningful than the profile; it represents a composite performance. Reviewing the profile for an entire class can aid appropriate grouping for instruction. In the class summary profile for a fourth-grade urban classroom seen in Figure 5.2, the teacher circled stanines that are in the low range (1, 2, and 3). Such a procedure helps a teacher readily identify students who may need assistance in only one literacy domain (for example, Marcus T., reading comprehension), or several (for example, Irwin J., all domains). The teacher can also begin to form tentative hypotheses for instruction and groupings (see comments in Figure 5.2).

The most common diagnostic reading test used by classroom teachers is the *Stanford Diagnostic Reading Test*, 4th ed. (Karlsen & Gardner, 2003), available online and also in a Braille edition. The *Stanford (SDRT 4)* provides six levels for assessing reading competence, with a single form for the first three levels and two parallel forms for the three upper levels. The six levels are designated by color: (a) red level for grades 1.5 through 2.5, (b) orange level for grades 2.5 through 3.5, (c) green level for grades 3.5 through 4.5, (d) purple level for grades 4.5 through 6.5, (e) brown level for grades 6.5 through 8.9, and (f) blue level for grades 9.0 through 13.0. In addition, *SDRT 4* offers teachers three optional assessment tools: (a) Reading Strategies Survey, for determining which reading strategies students understand and use; (b) Reading Questionnaire, for assessing attitudes, interests, and factors affecting comprehension; and (c) Story Retelling, which uses a scoring rubric (see Chapter 6) to assess either an oral or written retelling.

This newest edition of the *Stanford Diagnostic Reading Test* reflects an effort to respond to current instructional approaches. The *SDRT 4* includes new reading selections written by published authors that parallel the type of literature used in classrooms today. There is also a new focus on assessing reading strategies in addition to literal, inferential, and critical comprehension.

Go to MyEducationLab and first select the topic *Ongoing Assessments*. Then go to the Activities and Applications section, and complete the simulation entitled "Classroom Assessment" to discover more assessment methods. Next respond to the accompanying questions.

Figure 5.2   Graphic Profile for Comparing Subtest Scores

Teacher _____Ms. B._____   Grade _____4_____   Date _____October_____

Pupil's Name	Auditory discrimination	Phonic analysis	Structural analysis	Auditory vocabulary	Literal comprehension	Inferential comprehension	Total comprehension	Comments
Duane B.	(3)	4	5	4	4	4	4	VERIFY AUDITORY DISCRIMINATION
Elizabeth B.	6	4	6	5	5	4	5	COULD PEER TUTOR?
Isaiah D.	5	5	(3)	(3)	4	(3)	(3)	VOCABULARY AND INFERENTIAL COMP.
Rebeka D.	8	6	7	8	7	7	7	COULD PEER TUTOR?
Irwin J.	(1)	(2)	(3)	(3)	(2)	(2)	(2)	COMPREHENSION STRATEGIES 1ST
Austin J.	4	4	4	4	(2)	(1)	(2)	COMP STRATEGIES- FOCUS INFERENTIAL
Brandon M.	5	5	(2)	(2)	4	4	4	COMBINE VOCAB AND AFFIXES
Latasha M.	5	5	4	4	(1)	(1)	(1)	COMPREHENSION, DOES LATASHA RELY
Natasha M.	5	(3)	6	5	5	5	5	TOO MUCH ON HER TWIN, NATASHA?
Kalisha M.	(3)	4	6	(3)	(3)	(1)	(2)	FOCUS ON INFERENTIAL COMP.
Paul M.	5	4	5	(3)	(3)	(3)	(3)	SOME COMP ASSISTANCE
Bichhuy N.	(2)	(2)	4	5	5	5	5	LANGUAGE INTERFERENCE?
Julius P.	7	9	9	9	9	8	8	COULD PEER TUTOR?
David P.	4	(1)	4	(1)	(1)	(1)	(1)	COMP STRATEGIES LEA? VERIFY STRUCT
Eric T.	(1)	(2)	5	(2)	(2)	(2)	(2)	COMPREHENSION 1ST/ VERIFY STRUCTURAL
Marcus T.	5	4	4	4	(2)	(2)	(2)	COMPREHENSION STRATEGIES
Brian T.	4	(1)	5	4	(3)	(3)	(3)	VERIFY PHONIC SCORE
								10/17 NEED
								COMPREHENSION ASSISTANCE

The areas included in the *SDRT 4* are phonetic analysis, vocabulary, reading comprehension, and scanning for information. More specifically, the red level measures phonetic analysis, auditory vocabulary, word recognition, and comprehension of sentences, riddles, cloze paragraphs, and short paragraphs with questions. The orange level measures phonetic analysis, auditory vocabulary, reading vocabulary, comprehension of cloze paragraphs, and paragraphs that represent recreational, informational, and functional types of text. The green level measures phonetic analysis, reading vocabulary, and reading comprehension of paragraphs representing various types of text. The purple, brown, and blue levels measure reading vocabulary, comprehension of various types of text, and scanning to locate information.

Although several of the subskills tests are administered over most levels, the specific subskills are measured differently. For example, the phonetic analysis subtest for the red level measures students' abilities to discriminate among consonant sounds represented auditorily by single consonant letters, consonant clusters, and digraphs in the initial and final positions. The same subtest for the green level measures whether the student can recognize the same consonant sounds represented by the same spelling or two different spellings (for example, *f*ace and *r*ain; *f*oam and gra*ph*; *p*ie and repl*y*; *s*ugar and na*ti*on). The changes in what is measured from level to level are intended to reflect the developmental characteristics of literacy growth. Teachers will have to decide whether these subtests provide valid (content validity) assessments for their students.

Criterion-Referenced Tests

A **criterion-referenced test** measures how well an individual performs a specific task following instruction for that task. Usually a desired level of performance is specified, thus the term *criterion*. Criterion-referenced tests, or skills management systems, are assessment/instructional materials that focus on literacy subskills (Level 3 analysis; see Chapter 2). They are also referred to as **mastery tests** because students are said to have mastered a subskill when they attain the specified criterion. Teachers have actually been using the concept of a criterion-referenced test for years. Any time they develop a test to measure some specific instructional objective and designate a specific grade as passing, they are using the concept of criterion-referenced testing. For example, the content of a criterion-referenced test may be final consonant sounds. To say that Jimmy knows final consonant sounds, he may have to respond correctly to 90 percent or more of the test items. Jimmy's performance is not compared with the group's performance. Teachers set the criterion level to coincide with their expectations for a particular individual.

The assumption underlying criterion-referenced tests and the manner in which they are constructed are different from those for norm-referenced tests. Criterion-referenced tests focus on whether a student (or group of students) has learned a particular set of subskills. This is different from the norm-referenced test that compares learners with a norm group on general ability in the major literacy domains. Table 5.1 compares and contrasts norm-referenced and criterion-referenced tests.

For criterion-referenced or mastery tests, interpretation of the results appears straightforward in that 80 percent indicates passing or mastery of a subskill and less than 80 percent indicates failure or nonmastery. The decision-making process is simplified for teachers. Using the score as a basis, they decide whether a student has learned the subskill; if mastery is attained, the next decision is whether to move on to another subskill or to a higher level of difficulty for the subskill. If the student has not mastered the subskill, the teacher decides either to reteach or to review the particular subskill.

Some students learn their literacy subskills well but still cannot adequately perform literacy tasks. Likewise, some students perform adequately but still fail literacy subskills tests (Jackson, 1981; McNeil, 1974). A pure subskills approach to literacy instruction can result in students who struggle, just as a no-skills approach can.

Table 5.1	Comparison of Norm- and Criterion-Referenced Tests
Norm-Referenced	**Criterion-Referenced**
1. Norm-referenced tests assess the student's knowledge about the particular subject or content being tested.	1. Criterion-referenced tests assess the student's ability to perform a specific task.
2. Norm-referenced tests compare a student's performance with that of the norm group. (During the last phase of test construction, a final draft form is given to a large number of students who are representative of the students for whom the test was designed. This is the *norm group*.)	2. Criterion-referenced tests determine whether students possess the skills needed to move to the next level of learning.
3. Norm-referenced tests can be used annually as pretests and posttests to determine student gain while comparing these gains to those of the norm group.	3. Criterion-referenced tests can be used as pretests and posttests to determine which skills need to be taught and which skills have been mastered.
4. Norm-referenced tests contain items that are considered to be precise, valid, and reliable to discriminate among the weakest and best students.	4. Criterion-referenced tests contain items that determine whether the student is able to use the learned skill in particular situations.
5. Norm-referenced tests have a high degree of validity.	5. Criterion-referenced tests have only content validity; the items assess the ability needed to perform a given behavior.
6. Norm-referenced tests have a high degree of reliability. They consistently measure the same behavior with each administration of the test. This factor is *essential* for norm-referenced tests.	6. Criterion-referenced tests are not concerned with statistical calculations of reliability. If students are retested, they should not make the same score.
7. Interpretation of the student's score on norm-referenced tests depends on the scores obtained by the norm group.	7. Interpretation of the student's score on criterion-referenced tests depends on whether the student is able to perform a specific task.
8. Norm-referenced test scores yield global measurements of general abilities.	8. Criterion-referenced test scores yield exact measures of ability to achieve specific objectives.
9. Norm-referenced test scores are interpreted in terms of norms that have been statistically listed in the test manual by the author or the publisher.	9. Criterion-referenced test scores are interpreted in terms of a score that is considered acceptable by the teacher and by examining specific items that were correct or incorrect.
10. Norm-referenced test items are written to create variability among the individual scores in a particular group.	10. Criterion-referenced test items are designed to assess ability to perform a specific task as stated by a behavioral objective.

Source: From Eddie Kennedy, *Classroom Approaches to Remedial Reading,* 1977, pp. 82–83. Adapted by permission of the publisher, F. E. Peacock, Publishers, Inc., Itasca, IL.

Summary

The chapter begins by reviewing the state of fundamental change in assessment. New ways of thinking about assessment and evaluation are introduced. Several important measurement concepts are discussed, such as content and construct validity, reliability, and standard error of measurement.

The second part of the chapter begins with purposes of testing followed by a description of a published diagnostic reading test that is easily administered by classroom teachers. Criterion-referenced tests are also briefly explained and contrasted with norm-referenced tests.

Recommended Websites

International Reading Association's Position Statement
    www.reading.org/resources/issues/positions_high_
    stakes.html
This site provides a statement on IRA's policies regarding high stakes testing.

National Center for Research on Evaluation, Standards, and Student Testing
    www.cse.ucla.edu
Results of research about educational testing in the United States are presented on this site.

Nation's Report Card
    www.nces.ed.gov/nationsreportcard/
Results of recent research and assessment as reported by the National Assessment of Educational Progress (NAEP) can be found here.

Reading Assessment Database
    www.sedl.org/reading/rad/database.html
Go to this site for descriptions of commercially prepared reading assessment tools for kindergarten through third grade. Most of these tools are indirect measures while others (for example, informal reading inventories) are more direct assessment measures.

Student Assessment Division
    www.isbe.net/assessment
This Illinois State Board of Education homepage for assessment provides an example of how states use standardized measures.

MyEducationLab is a research-based learning tool that brings teaching to life. Go to the Gipe 7th Edition MyEducationLab for Reading Assessment site at www.myeducationlab.com to:

- Engage in multimedia exercises to help you build a deeper and more applied understanding of chapter content.
- Use extensive resources including videos from real classrooms, Praxis and licensure preparation, a lesson plan builder, and materials to help you in your teaching career.

CHAPTER 6

Informal Literacy Assessment
Direct Measures

For many years teachers have felt that standardized tests do not give sufficient information for instructional decision making. The main justification for using performance assessments and classroom-based tests and measures is that they supply useful information for direct teaching applications. Because these assessment tools often involve the actual materials and tasks used in the classroom, the teacher obtains a more realistic view of how the learner functions within the instructional setting.

Direct assessments occur frequently; thus the reliability of such assessments is increased. If standardized tests were administered as often as direct assessments, the process would be extremely time consuming, subtracting substantially from available teaching time, already at a premium in the classroom. Furthermore, the cost would be prohibitive. Also, the information yielded by many standardized tests is not the type that teachers want most; that is, information that tells whether specific strategies have been learned or shows the particular strengths of an individual student relative to his or her curriculum and instructional program.

A number of direct assessment tools that help teachers assess and evaluate students' literacy behaviors will be explained in this chapter. No one technique is sufficient, nor should the results of standardized or criterion-referenced tests be ignored. In the words of Emily Grady (1992), "education needs accountability, but accountability must contribute to the growth of students. . . . Teachers must be central to the assessment process; they must be the documenters and reviewers of their students' learning. Students [also] must enter into the assessment process in order to gain insight and confidence in controlling their own learning" (p. 29).

Additionally, assessments "should accommodate the full spectrum of the intelligences, allowing students choices based on how they feel they can demonstrate that they have mastered the required material" (Lazear, 1994, p. 94). Figure 6.1 provides a variety of suggestions to assist teachers in designing opportunities for all students to demonstrate what they know and what they can do.

Go to MyEducationLab and select the topic *Informal Assessments*. Then, go to the Activities and Applications section, and watch the video entitled "Performance Assessment" to learn more about a wide variety of techniques used for direct assessment. Scoring rubrics are also discussed, and this topic is addressed later in this chapter. Next respond to the accompanying questions.

COMMONLY USED DIRECT ASSESSMENT TOOLS

Text-Related Tests

In addition to core materials found in many classrooms (such as basal readers, workbooks, and teacher's manuals), most publishers provide ancillary materials, including tests, to help assess student learning. These **text-related tests** measure the acquisition of strategies and subskills emphasized in a reading series or text at a particular level. Such tests have the advantage of content validity because they are intended to measure the

Figure 6.1   Multiple Intelligences Assessment Menu

Verbal-Linguistic Intelligence
(Language Arts–Based Assessment Instruments)

- written essays
- vocabulary quizzes
- recall of verbal information
- audiocassette recordings
- poetry writing
- linguistic humor
- formal speech
- cognitive debates
- listening and reporting
- learning logs and journals

Logical-Mathematical Intelligence
(Cognitive Patterns–Based Assessment Instruments)

- cognitive organizers
- higher-order reasoning
- pattern games
- outlining
- logic and rationality exercises
- mental menus and formulas
- deductive reasoning
- inductive reasoning
- calculation processes
- logical analysis and critique

Visual-Spatial Intelligence
(Imaginal–Based Assessment Instruments)

- murals and montages
- graphic representation and visual illustrating
- visualization and imagination
- reading, understanding, and creating maps
- flowcharts and graphs
- sculpting and building
- imaginary conversations
- mind mapping
- video recording and photography
- manipulative demonstrations

Bodily-Kinesthetic Intelligence
(Performance–Based Assessment Instruments)

- lab experiments
- dramatization
- original and classical dance
- charades and mimes
- impersonations
- human tableaux
- invention projects
- physical exercise routines and games
- skill demonstrations
- illustrations using body language and gestures

Musical-Rhythmic Intelligence
(Auditory–Based Assessment Instruments)

- creating concept songs and raps
- illustrating with sound
- discerning rhythmic patterns
- composing music
- linking music and rhythm with concepts
- orchestrating music
- creating percussion patterns
- recognizing tonal patterns and quality
- analyzing musical structure
- reproducing musical and rhythmic patterns

Interpersonal Intelligence
(Relational–Based Assessment Instruments)

- group "jigsaws"
- explaining to or teaching another
- "think-pair-share"
- "round robin"
- giving and receiving feedback
- interviews, question-naires, and people searches
- empathic processing
- random group quizzes
- assess your teammates
- test, coach, and retest

Intrapersonal Intelligence
(Psychological–Based Assessment Instruments)

- autobiographical reporting
- personal application scenarios
- metacognitive surveys and questionnaires
- higher-order questions and answers
- concentration tests
- feelings diaries and logs
- personal projection
- self-identification reporting
- personal history correlation
- personal priorities and goals

Naturalist Intelligence
(Natural World–Based Assessment Instruments)

- classifying leaves
- sorting animal pictures
- planting seeds
- caring for a classroom pet
- developing an ecology project
- matching animal characteristics to human traits
- maintaining a garden or terrarium
- correlating animal sounds to human emotions
- tracking star locations and constellations
- reporting on biological inventions such as cloning or genetically altered foods

Adapted from *Multiple Intelligence Approaches to Assessment,* © 1994 Zephyr Press, Tucson, Arizona. Reprinted with permission.

content learned from the curriculum materials completed. Although carefully constructed, they usually have not been normed, like previously discussed standardized tests. They also measure a smaller number of subskills and objectives. Good students may not have a chance to show what they can do; they often *top the test* (obtain very high scores). The tests can, however, indicate students who need assistance. Thus they can have considerable analytic value for the classroom teacher.

Many basal systems contain **end-of-unit tests** in the teacher's manual or in the student workbooks. These tests provide useful information regarding student accomplishment of relatively small learning segments. Extension procedures are often recommended for students who do not perform well on these tests.

Informal Reading Inventories

The **informal reading inventory (IRI)** is probably the most widely known nonstandardized, direct assessment tool. Major purposes for using an IRI include (a) to help the teacher observe a student's strategic reading behaviors with material of various grade levels; (b) to aid the teacher in choosing appropriate texts, readers, or other reading materials for each student in the class; (c) to aid the teacher in estimating three different reading levels—the independent reading level, the instructional reading level, and the frustration reading level; and (d) to aid the teacher in learning more about each pupil's reading strengths and needs. This individually administered, nonstandardized instrument enables the teacher to assess those reading strategies that can be assessed only through direct observation, such as the ability to monitor and self-correct oral reading miscues. Other advantages include the flexibility to modify or clarify directions for some students and the opportunity to observe other behaviors, in addition to reading, in the context of assessment.

The traditional IRI consists of a series of graded passages that students read and answer questions about. Inventories can be (a) published instruments, in which passages and questions are carefully constructed to reflect reading grade levels accurately; (b) teacher made, with passages selected from the reading materials used in the school; or (c) constructed by a publisher to accompany a particular basal reader series. Lists of words graded by difficulty are often used as quick screening devices to determine a starting point for reading passages. Passages are then read orally, silently, or both, depending on the teacher's purpose. Word recognition errors are recorded for the oral selections, while comprehension is checked for passages read orally or silently. Rate of reading can also be obtained by recording the time spent reading the passages.

Probably the greatest disadvantage of many published IRIs is that they do an inadequate job of assessing reading comprehension—the heart of reading. Some inventories use as few as five test items per level. The reliability of test results can be seriously questioned when so few items are used. IRI questions are not always well written, nor do they necessarily assess higher-level thinking skills. Applegate, Quinn, and Applegate (2002) investigated eight widely used informal reading inventories to determine if the comprehension questions were largely literal (text based) or whether the questions required high-level inferences or responses that call for the reader to discuss or react to the reading in some way. They found that these inventories rely heavily on text-based questions, when it could be argued that comprehension is more about making personal connections with the text or linking previous knowledge with the text. Similarly, some inventories claim to provide information on comprehension subskills (for example, determining main ideas, recalling details, identifying cause and effect, inferring word meanings from context); however, research shows they do not, so IRIs should not be used for this purpose (Duffelmeyer & Duffelmeyer, 1989; Duffelmeyer, Robinson, & Squier, 1989; Schell & Hanna, 1981). Furthermore, comprehension is frequently assessed on oral reading of the passages. This is of particular concern with readers who struggle with decoding and readers in the early elementary grades, who may expend their cognitive abilities trying to perform well reading aloud, thereby diverting attention from constructing meaning. (For a critical analysis of eight IRIs, see Nilsson, 2008.)

IRIs can be time consuming to administer and interpret, especially if administered to an individual to record oral reading behaviors. Average administration time per student is 30 minutes. Interpretation time can be at least as much and probably more. However, not every student needs to be assessed with an IRI.

Many teachers choose published IRIs because of the time required to construct one. Examples of some published inventories are the *Analytical Reading Inventory* (Woods & Moe, 2007), the *Basic Reading Inventory, Preprimer–12* (Johns, 2005), the *Classroom Assessment of Reading Processes* (Swearingen & Allen, 2000), the *Critical Reading Inventory* (Applegate, Quinn, & Applegate, 2008), the *Ekwall/Shanker Reading Inventory* (Ekwall & Shanker, 2000), the *Comprehensive Reading Inventory* (Cooter, Flynt, & Cooter, 2007), the *Informal Reading Inventory* (Roe & Burns, 2007), the *Qualitative Reading Inventory* (Leslie & Caldwell, 2006), the *Bader Reading and Language Inventory* (Bader, 2005), and the *Stieglitz Informal Reading Inventory* (Stieglitz, 2002). As with standardized tests, reliability and validity must be considered. For individual assessment purposes, a desirable reliability coefficient is 0.90. Authors of published IRIs should provide this information in their administration manuals.

The question of validity is most critical. Does the IRI measure what it is intended to measure? To answer this question, you must recall the four major purposes for administering an IRI and remember that the issue of validity differs somewhat for each one. For example, if the purpose is to aid the teacher in placing a pupil in an appropriate reader, then a publisher-constructed or teacher-made IRI based on the reading series being used may be more valid.

Another validity issue is related to the purpose of identifying the three reading levels that IRIs purport to establish. For some time, writers and users of informal reading inventories have chosen to use the arbitrary criteria set up by Betts (1946) to distinguish the independent (99 percent word recognition, 90 percent comprehension), instructional (95 percent word recognition, 75 percent comprehension), and frustration (90 percent or less word recognition, 50 percent or less comprehension) reading levels discussed in the next section. These criteria were based on data obtained from 41 fourth-grade students who read the passages silently before reading them aloud. Not until 1970, when William Powell adjusted these criteria to be dependent on the grade level of the child being tested, were the Betts criteria challenged. Powell (1970) found that children who could comprehend material reasonably well (70 to 75 percent comprehension) achieved average word recognition scores ranging from 83 to 94 percent across grades 1 through 6. Older readers were even more accurate in word recognition. Unfortunately, too little research evidence is available either to support the Betts criteria (Roberts, 1976) or to define appropriate criteria for establishing the three reading levels. (See also the Interpreting IRIs section later in this chapter, specifically Figure 6.4 and Table 6.1.) Published IRIs are generally consistent in using the Betts criteria, with only a few exceptions. Regardless, the scoring criteria are clearly noted in each inventory's administration section.

It is important to remember that IRIs are nonstandardized assessment tools and thus can be used flexibly. Published IRIs provide what sound like rigid procedures for administration; however, teachers using published IRIs understand their own purpose(s) for using the IRI, employ good judgment, and rely on their knowledge of the reading process. For example, Cardarelli (1988) found that when students were allowed to look back at a passage to answer the comprehension questions, more than half of these students increased their scores sufficiently to change frustration reading levels to instructional reading levels. This procedure makes good sense if a teacher normally allows students to look back in their textbooks for answers to questions rather than insisting that the students answer the questions from memory as directed in most IRI manuals. Also, students can look back at text read on standardized tests as well, so learning how to improve their ability to locate answers and clues to answers could help these scores improve.

In any event, teachers must use other direct assessment procedures to supplement results of IRIs on comprehension. For instance, the student can be directed to recall as much about the passage or story as possible before questions are asked. This procedure is called **retelling**. General comprehension questions can be asked if the student does not respond freely. For example:

> Tell me about . . .
> Who was in the story?
> What happened?
> Where did this happen?
> How did it happen?
> Why do you think the story was written?

Teachers may record a student's retelling by making check marks on a previously prepared outline that identifies major points from the passage related to characters, events, plot, and theme (Appendix I; see also Figure 12.1) in the case of narrative material or to informational content in the case of expository material. This outline, record sheet, or **protocol** is also called a *scoring rubric*. Scoring rubrics are discussed later in this chapter. If the student does not mention the items listed, the teacher asks questions, also prepared in advance, to help elicit desired information. This is called *prompting*. Questions about retellings should not supply information or insights the reader did not provide in the retelling. Most questions should be of the *Wh-* variety and refer to information already given by the reader. These questions, when asked following a story, should be keyed toward the elements of a story. For example, as modified from Weaver (2002, p. 193):

Characters:

What else can you tell me about (name of character(s) provided in the retelling)?
Who else was in the story besides (the characters mentioned)?

Events:

What else happened?
What happened after (event provided in the retelling)?
Where (or when) did (event mentioned in the retelling) happen?
How did (event mentioned in the retelling) happen?

Plot:

Why do you think (action[s] mentioned in the retelling) happened?
What was the main problem for (character mentioned in the retelling)?

Theme:

How did you feel when (event mentioned in the retelling) happened?
What do you think the author might have been trying to tell us in the story?

Setting:

Where and when did the story take place?
How was (character or event mentioned in the retelling) important to the story?

These questions can easily be modified for retellings of expository material. For example:

- What else can you tell me about (topic of passage mentioned in the retelling)?
- What else was this passage or section about besides (the topic mentioned)?
- What other information did the author provide about (the topic or important concept briefly mentioned in the retelling)?
- What happened after (event mentioned in the retelling)?
- What do you think the authors are trying to tell us in this section?
- How was (event or fact mentioned in the retelling) important to this passage?
- How do you think you might use this information?
- How is this information like anything you have read about before?

For both narrative and expository passages, teachers also should ask questions related to the reading event. These questions are modified from the *Reading Miscue Inventory: Alternative Procedures* (Goodman, Watson, & Burke, 1987):

Is there anything you'd like to ask me about this (story, passage)?
Were there any (concepts, ideas, sentences, words) that gave you trouble? What were they?
Why did you leave this word out?
Do you know what this word means now?
Were there times when you didn't understand the story? Show me where.
Tell me about those times when you didn't understand.
Remember when you said the kid was a "typeical baby"? What is a "typeical baby"? (Ask about key words that were mispronounced or otherwise miscued to see if the reader understood the concept despite the miscue.)

In addition to demonstrating an understanding of story structure, story retellings reveal the reader's ability to remember facts, make inferences, and recall sequence (Morrow, 1985a, 1985b). To evaluate retellings, a scoring rubric is recommended (refer to Appendix I and Figure 12.1). Many IRIs include retellings in their procedures and provide scoring rubrics. To assess silent reading for groups or for students in the upper grades, try a written retelling (Smith & Jackson, 1985). Also, story frames (see Figure 12.2) or paragraph frames (see Chapters 10 and 13 and Figure 13.11) are useful for this purpose.

The "think-aloud" procedure (Brown, 1985; Kavale & Schreiner, 1979; Olshavsky, 1976, 1977) addresses the criticism that comprehension questions do not assess the process of comprehension. This procedure requires readers to verbalize their thoughts while in the act of reading. These verbalizations provide insights into the ways individual readers derive meaning from text.

Three Reading Levels. Three reading levels relevant to classroom teaching can be estimated from administering and interpreting IRIs. The first level, the **independent reading level**, refers to the difficulty level at which a learner reads comfortably without the teacher's help. Students should be reading library books and other materials for pleasure at this level, with little or no difficulty recognizing words or comprehending. School reading to be done at home should be at students' independent reading levels. Students learn to read for fun and enjoyment when they read easy materials. At this level they develop favorable attitudes toward and positive interests in reading; they are in their "comfort zone."

At the **instructional reading level**, students read with some direction and supervision; they are in their "growth zone." Students are usually placed in basal readers written at their instructional reading levels, but most other materials pupils read should not be this difficult unless a teacher or someone else is available to help them. Without help, students may feel tense, and other unfortunate outcomes may result (Arnold & Sherry, 1975). Too often, a single content-area textbook is used for instructional purposes. This practice assumes that all students in a class have the same instructional reading level.

The **frustration reading level** is one at which reading deteriorates and students cannot continue reading because the material is too hard even with instruction and guidance; they are in their "groan zone." Physical behaviors frequently associated with frustration include frowning, crying, squirming, whispering, or rebelliousness. Teachers should guide students away from this level of reading material.

Constructing and Administering IRIs. The informal reading inventory is constructed using materials typically read in the school, including content-area textbooks. The selections, chosen from the variety of material read, might range from 50 words at the primer level, to 100 to 150 words in grades 1 through 3, to 200 to 250 words or so beyond grade 3. The selections should be well formed and cohesive enough to allow development of diverse types of comprehension questions. These questions should also be **passage dependent**, that is, answerable on reading the passage, and balanced between literal and inferential comprehension, with at least one vocabulary question. Longer selections and more comprehension questions increase the reliability of the results (try for a minimum of 10 questions). For help in writing questions, Dantonio and Beisenherz (2001), Pearson and Johnson (1978), and Valmont (1972) are recommended readings. Finally, prepare the scoring criteria for word recognition and comprehension performance. Based on the number of words in the passage, and on the number of questions, determine how many words read accurately and correct responses constitute the independent, instructional, and frustration reading levels. For listening comprehension, determine how many correct responses are needed for 75 percent accuracy.

To assess retellings, prepare a list of the main points of each selection (refer to Appendix I). Type the selections, list of main points, and questions on separate sheets of paper and duplicate them. These pages become the protocol, record sheet, or rubric used for assessment. With permission from publishers, the teacher may reproduce the pages from the texts and bind them in a notebook. A sample of about 20 words introduced in each text can be placed in list format to be used for "quick" screening purposes. These procedures are time consuming and explain why many teachers prefer published IRIs.

Once the protocols and the student's notebook are assembled, the IRI is given. With a published inventory, begin by asking the learner to read the word lists (most common format) or sentences, if provided, starting with the lowest level available. If the student reads the first list with at least 80 percent accuracy, try the next level. The student continues to read the word lists until she or he fails to meet the 80 percent criterion. At this

Go to MyEducationLab and select the topic *Informal Assessments*. Then, go to the Activities and Applications section, and watch the video entitled "Administering an Informal Reading Inventory" to observe a partial administration with a fourth-grade boy. See if you can evaluate his oral reading performance and comprehension of the story read. Also view the video "Using Assessment to Inform Instruction" to observe the administration of a running record. Next respond to the accompanying questions for both videos.

point, ask the student to read the selection corresponding to the highest-level word list on which he or she scored 100 percent. Beginning at an easier level helps to ensure that the first selection will be read successfully. When using a published inventory, the criteria for determining starting points may vary. You should carefully read the directions for administration found at the beginning of the inventory being used.

The student reads selections of increasing difficulty while the teacher codes behaviors in oral reading and comprehension. There are two popular ways to code passages read orally: by using traditional miscue codes, which are similar to an editor's proofreading symbols, or by using **running records**, a combination of proofreading symbols and check marks (Clay, 2000b). Figure 6.2 provides an example of a coded IRI passage using traditional miscue codes. Figure 6.3 shows the same passage recorded, scored, and analyzed as a running record. Note that the use of running records does not require a protocol. Thus, running records can be used with any material a student is reading, making it a most adaptable method for assessing oral reading behaviors. As long as the teacher has paper and pencil handy while observing the student reading, a running record of that reading can be made and later scored and analyzed. A tape recording allows the performance to be reviewed to verify the codings and scoring estimated during the administration. Reading continues until the student reaches the criteria associated with the frustration level. At this point, in addition to not achieving a minimum level of word recognition and comprehension, the student usually exhibits other symptoms, such as squirming in the chair or making facial contortions.

For novice users of informal reading inventories, all these directions for administration may seem formal and intimidating. Keep in mind, however, that the essential point in all assessment is to learn more about the student as a reader—not merely to determine reading levels. Brozo (1990) makes a case for **interactive assessment**, in which the teacher tries "to discover the conditions under which a student will succeed in reading" (p. 523). Using an informal reading inventory as an example, Brozo illuminates the much less testlike procedures of interactive assessment, which, briefly, include beginning with a diagnostic interview to learn about interests, attitudes, and students' goals and perceptions about reading, and moving through the steps of IRI administration in an instructional manner rather than a test-taking manner. Kletzien and Bednar (1990) support this approach for assessing readers who struggle when they describe the value of what they term *dynamic assessment:*

> When the at-risk reader is made an active participant in the assessment, the reader gains greater confidence and a sense of control over reading strategies. The social interaction between the examiner and the reader is particularly important for these learners. Too often, they simply give up on a standardized test and receive a very low score, further depressing an already low self-concept. [Dynamic assessment/interactive assessment] acknowledges what the reader actually can do, and thus provides a positive experience. (p. 532)

Such views of assessment have led to instructional procedures teachers can use to provide students with feedback about their miscues. One of these procedures is called *Retrospective Miscue Analysis* (Y. M. Goodman, 1996; Goodman & Marek, 1996). You are urged to examine the Goodman (1996) source for more information on RMA.

As teachers gain experience in IRI administration and begin to appreciate the flexible uses of IRIs and other assessment tools, interactive assessment procedures may have more appeal. Remember two important goals of assessment—to learn students' capabilities and to guide instructional planning—as you proceed through the rest of this chapter.

Figure 6.2	Example of a Traditionally Coded IRI Passage

FORM A: LEVEL 1 ASSESSMENT PROTOCOLS

You Cannot Fly! (96 words)

PART I: SILENT READING COMPREHENSION

Background Statement: "Have you ever wished you could fly? A boy named Sam in this story wants to fly. Read this story to find out if Sam gets to fly. Read it carefully because when you're through I'm going to ask you to tell me about the story."

Teacher Directions: Once the student completes the silent reading, say, "Tell me about the story you just read." Check off any answers to the questions below that the student provides during the retelling. Ask all remaining questions not addressed during the retelling.

Questions/Answers	*Story Grammar Element/ Level of Comprehension*
✓ 1. Who was the story mainly about? *Sam* *(Sam)*	character–characterization/ literal
— 2. What was Sam's problem? *he kept falling* *(Sam wanted to fly, but couldn't)* *off his bed*	story problem(s)/literal
— 3. What were two ways Sam tried to solve his problem? *he tried to fly and he* *(jumping off his bed and a box)* *got a letter*	problem resolution attempts/literal
— 4. How was Sam's problem finally solved? *(Sam got to ride on an airplane)* *everybody laughed*	problem resolution/inferential
✓ 5. What did the family and Sam do after reading the letter? *they laughed* *(laughed)*	problem resolution attempts/literal
— 6. Where did the story take place? DK *(Sam's house)*	setting/inferential
— 7. What lesson did Sam learn? *Letters make you* *(responses will vary, accept plausible ones)* *laugh*	theme/evaluative
✓ 8. What words would you use to tell *nice,* someone what kind of boy Sam was? *happy* *(responses will vary, accept plausible ones)*	character–characterization/ evaluative

PART II: ORAL READING AND ANALYSIS OF MISCUES

Directions: Say, "Now I would like to hear you read this story out loud. Please start at the beginning and keep reading until I tell you to stop." Have the student read orally until he/she reaches the oral reading stop-marker (//). Follow along on the Miscue Grid marking any oral reading errors as appropriate. Then complete the Developmental/Performance Summary to determine whether to continue the assessment. (*Note:* The Miscue Grid should be completed *after* the assessment session has been concluded in order to minimize stress for the student.)

continued

Figure 6.2 *continued*

	MIS PRONUN	SUB STITUTION	SELF CORRECT	INSERTION	TCHR ASSIST	OMISSION	MEANING DISRUPTION
You Cannot Fly!							
Once a boy named Sam *want* wanted to	1						
fly. His mother and father said,							
"You can(not) fly." His sister said,						1	1
"You can(not) fly." Sam tried *to jump* jumping	1			1		1	1
off a box. He tried *to jump* jumping off	1			1			
his bed. He fell down each time. *eight times*	1	1					
Sam still tried hard but he *heard* (still)		1				1	1
could not fly. Then one day *The(SC)*	1		1				
a letter came for Sam. The letter							
said, "Come and see (me) Sam, on						1	1
the next airplane." It was from							
his grandfather. Sam went to his							
father family and read the letter. Sam		1					1
said, "Now I can fly." Sam and his							
TA family all laughed together. //					1		
TOTALS	5	3	1	2	1	4	5

Notes:

Student's miscues for the most part aren't serious, but a few were crucial to a lack of understanding this passage. Confidence level was high, but student never made the connection that his grandfather lived somewhere far enough to fly to.

continued

Figure 6.2 *continued*

Examiner's Summary of Miscue Patterns:

PART III: DEVELOPMENTAL/PERFORMANCE SUMMARY

Silent Reading Comprehension   **Oral Reading Accuracy**

_____ 0–1 questions missed = Easy   _____ 0–1 oral errors = Easy

_____ 2   questions missed = Adequate   _____ 2–5 oral errors = Adequate

_5_   3+   questions missed = Too hard   _✓_   6+   oral errors = Too hard

Continue to next assessment level passage?   _____ Yes   _✓_ No

Examiner's Notes: I would like to try RMA procedures with this passage, focusing on the miscue of *can* for *cannot*.

FORM A   LEVEL 1 ASSESSMENT PROTOCOLS

Adapted with permission from Flynt/Cooter, *Reading Inventory for the Classroom.*

Figure 6.3 Level 1 Passage Scored and Analyzed as a Running Record

Name: Louis   Count   Analysis

Page of Text **You Cannot Fly!**	Running Record	E	SC	E MSV	SC MSV
Once a boy named Sam wanted to	✓ ✓ ✓ ✓ _want_ ✓ 　　　　wanted	1		Ⓜ ⓈⓋ	
fly. His mother and father said,	✓ ✓ ✓ ✓ ✓ ✓				
"You cannot fly." His sister said,	✓ _can_ ✓ ✓ ✓ ✓ 　cannot	1		M ⓈⓋ	
"You cannot fly." Sam tried jumping	✓ _can_ ✓ ✓ ✓ _to jump_ 　cannot　　　　　−jumping	3		M ⓈⓋ Ⓜ ⓈⓋ	
off a box. He tried jumping off	✓ ✓ ✓ ✓ ✓ _to jump_ ✓ 　　　　　　−jumping	2		Ⓜ ⓈⓋ	
his bed. He fell down each time.	✓ ✓ ✓ ✓ ✓ _eight times_ 　　　　　　each time	2		M Ⓢ Ⓥ Ⓜ ⓈⓋ	
Sam still tried hard but he still	✓ ✓ ✓ _heard_ ✓ ✓ = 　　　hard　　　　still	2		M S Ⓥ	
could not fly. Then one day	✓ ✓ ✓ _The_ ✓ ✓ 　　　Then		1		Ⓜ ⓈⓋ
a letter came for Sam. The letter	✓ ✓ ✓ R|SC ✓ ✓ ✓ ✓				
said, "Come and see me, Sam, on	✓ ✓ ✓ ✓ = 　　　　me ✓ ✓	1			
the next airplane." It was from	✓ ✓ ✓ ✓ ✓ ✓				
his grandfather. Sam went to his	✓ ✓ ✓ ✓ ✓ ✓				
family and read the letter. Sam	_father_ ✓ ✓ ✓ ✓ family	1		Ⓜ ⒮ Ⓥ	
said, "Now I can fly." Sam and his	✓ = ✓ ✓ ✓ _now_ ✓ ✓ ✓ 　now　　　　　−	2			
family all laughed together.	T ✓ ✓ ✓	1			

Analysis and Summary

Total Words: 96

Total Errors: 16

Error Rate: 96/16 = 1:6

Total Self-Corrections: 1

Accuracy Rate: 100—(16/96 × 100) = 83%

Hard text (frustration level)

Louis tends to rely mostly on visual and structure (syntax) clues. With a low accuracy rate, he is losing the support of the meaning of the text. Once critical errors were made (e.g., *can* for *cannot*), Louis began to invent his own meaning for the text. It is hypothesized that because the invented text made sense to Louis, he felt no reason to self-correct. This level of text is too hard for Louis.

Scoring IRIs. The following guidelines for scoring oral reading accuracy are the most commonly used.

Count the following as one error for each occurrence:

1. Any word used that deviates from the text and disrupts the meaning
2. Any word pronounced by the teacher after the reader has hesitated about five seconds

Count the following as only one error, regardless of the number of times the error is made:

1. Repeated substitutions (one word substituted for another, such as *when* for *then*). Repeated substitution errors of proper names are counted only once (for example, *Bobby* for *Billy*).
2. Repetitions (individual words or groups of words that are said more than once). There is disagreement on counting repetitions as errors. For example, Spache (1976) counts two or more words repeated as a repetition error; Ekwall and Shanker (2000) think *all* repetitions should be counted as errors; Clay (2000b) and Taylor, Harris, and Pearson (1988) do *not* count repetitions as errors at all. In general, I favor noting repetitions but *not* counting them as errors. Repetitions usually occur for a reason and demonstrate that the reader is concerned with maintaining understanding of material read. However, a great number of repetitions may indicate the material is too difficult.
3. Repeated errors on the same word, even though the errors themselves may be different. Again, there is variation among authors of published inventories. For example, Leslie and Caldwell (2006) count once as an error a repeated miscue that maintains meaning (for example, *phone* for *telephone*) but count as errors each miscue on the same word when the pronunciation changes the meaning (for example, *expect* and *export* for *expert* would count as two errors).

Do *not* count the following as errors:

1. Pronunciations or miscues that reflect cultural or regional dialects
2. Spontaneous self-corrections
3. Hesitations
4. Ignoring or misinterpreting punctuation marks

Count all the errors and convert the number to a percent accurate score based on the number of words pronounced correctly and the total number of words in the selection.

In addition to recording oral reading behaviors, record retellings and responses to comprehension questions asked after each selection. Sometimes these responses can be scored as the student answers the questions. More often, however, judgment about comprehension performance can be made only in relation to the nature of the student's oral reading and how the student has responded to the retelling and the questions. Therefore, it is best to analyze these responses carefully at a later time.

Interpreting IRIs

Estimating Reading Levels. Once the teacher has obtained scores on (a) oral reading behaviors and (b) comprehension of silent or oral reading or both for the selections read,

Figure 6.4	Sample Table to Aid Interpretation of Scores for Reading Accuracy and Comprehension

Summary of Results of Informal Reading Inventory
Name: Sandra   Grade: Beginning 4th

Level of Text	Oral Reading		Silent Reading	Reading Level
	Percent Accuracy	Percent Comprehension	Percent Comprehension	
2^1	99	100	100	Independent
2^2	97	80	90	Instructional
3^1	98	100	100	Independent
3^2	94	80	100	Instructional
4	93	80	90	Instructional
5	88	50	70	Frustration

Estimated independent reading level: 3^1
Estimated instructional reading level: 4*
Estimated frustration reading level: 5

*or 3^2 to 4, if a range is desired.

the scores are assembled in a table such as that in Figure 6.4 to aid interpretation of results. All published inventories provide a similar table, usually called a *summary sheet*. When interpreting results of an IRI, remember that these inventories are subject to error of measurement. Thus, the criteria for determining the independent, instructional, and frustration reading levels must be interpreted judiciously. The teacher surveys the assembled scores and makes judgments about the estimated reading levels based on the progression of scores as well as the scores themselves. Powell and Dunkeld (1971) and Cooper (1952) indicate that the student's grade level should also be a consideration (see Table 6.1). As indicated earlier, there is no absolute agreement on the criteria used to estimate reading levels.

Almost always, interpretation requires some estimating and interpolating. In interpreting Sandra's scores (Figure 6.4), chances are good that Sandra's independent reading level is third grade and that the 80 percent comprehension score obtained at the 2^2 reader level for oral reading reflects error of measurement. The instructional reading level is probably fourth grade, the higher of the two sets of scores yielding that outcome, especially in light of the silent reading comprehension score. Notice also that the 94 and 93 percent accuracy scores are slightly below the Betts criterion of 95 percent but are acceptable for the instructional level according to both the Powell and Dunkeld and the Cooper criteria.

Once reading levels have been estimated, the teacher verifies these tentative working hypotheses (that is, independent reading level equals beginning third grade; instructional reading level, fourth grade; frustration reading level, fifth grade). Placing Sandra in fourth-grade-level materials to see if she can deal effectively with the texts and accompanying lessons accomplishes this. Verification of placement in materials is critical to effective analysis and instructional planning. Without verification, all the analytic effort may be for naught.

Student achievement in reading, especially for developing readers, is positively affected if a large portion of instructional time is spent with relatively easy material (error rates of 2 to 5 percent), with regular exposure to more difficult material (Beck, 1981;

Table 6.1	Powell/Dunkeld and Cooper Criteria for Determining Informal Reading Inventory Instructional Reading Levels
Powell and Dunkeld Criteria for Instructional Level	
Grades 1–2	88–97.9% word recognition 70–89% comprehension
Grades 3–5	92–97.9% word recognition 70–89% comprehension
Grades 6+	94.4–97.9% word recognition 70–89% comprehension
Cooper Criteria for Instructional Level	
Grades 2–3	95–98% word recognition 70% minimum comprehension
Intermediate grades	91–96% word recognition 60% minimum comprehension

Berliner, 1981; Gambrell, Wilson, & Gantt, 1981; Jorgenson, 1977). Beck (1981) explained that in this way the reader is allowed "to develop fluent and automatic responses in less difficult text while encountering a challenge to develop new knowledge and strategies in more difficult text" (p. 89).

The best advice might be to be conservative. If reading levels are unclear or other characteristics about a student deserve consideration (immature personality, general academic difficulty, poor work habits, or disruptive home background), the student should be placed in the easier material (Haller & Waterman, 1985). As a result, the reader is able to feel successful and, if placed in material that is too easy, can be moved up to more difficult material without sacrificing self-esteem.

Analyzing Results of the IRI. Analysis of IRI results beyond estimating the three reading levels provides a wealth of information. Oral reading behaviors and comprehension performance can be examined further to find patterns in a student's reading behaviors and shed light on that student's reading strategies. Borrowing heavily from the *Reading Miscue Inventory* developed by Goodman and Burke (1972), coded oral reading behaviors can be thought of as miscues. A **miscue** is defined as an observed response that differs from the expected response—that is, the reader does not say exactly what is written. With this inventory, Goodman and Burke introduced the notion of **qualitative analysis**; rather than simply count errors (**quantitative analysis**), the examiner attempts to analyze the reader's strategies.

The rationale for analyzing miscues is that not all unexpected responses are equally serious. For example, if the reader inserts *very* before the word *happy* in the sentence *Tom was not happy*, the meaning of the sentence has not been seriously altered. The teacher may overlook miscues if meaning is not changed. This kind of qualitative analysis often reveals that students are extracting meaning from what they read despite apparent word recognition errors. This is especially relevant for linguistically diverse learners. If nothing else, the qualitative analysis makes the teacher aware of the language functioning of the student who speaks a dialect variation (see Chapter 3). At its best, the qualitative analysis makes the teacher aware of the student's reading strategies.

Go to MyEducationLab and select the topic *Informal Assessments*. Then, go to the Activities and Applications section, and watch the videos entitled "Running Record" and "Informal Reading Inventory" to observe how retellings are used and to hear how the respective teachers interpret the results of these assessments. Next respond to the accompanying questions for both videos.

A detailed **miscue analysis** is not necessary for every reader, not even for every reader experiencing difficulty. A thorough miscue analysis might be done only for readers who demonstrate especially perplexing reading miscues. For such cases the teacher is referred to Goodman and Burke's *Reading Miscue Inventory Manual* (1972).

To determine the instructional needs of most students, a simple form of miscue analysis is extremely useful. A partial analysis that looks at the use of graphophonic, syntactic, and semantic cues and asks whether the reader views reading as a meaning-making process provides valuable information about areas of strength and need. This underlying philosophy of determining whether the reader is reading for meaning and what strategies the reader uses is essential in miscue analysis.

A brief set of questions can be asked about miscues to provide insight into the reader's use of language cues and reading strategies. These questions should (a) emphasize that reading for meaning is more important than exact reproduction of the surface structure, (b) aid the teacher in identifying both a reader's strengths and needs, and (c) acknowledge the importance of self-corrections of miscues that do not fit the context. Figure 6.5 shows the results of such an analysis.

In a much-abbreviated version of miscue analysis, a teacher might simply ask whether the miscue changed meaning (unacceptable), whether it was acceptable in con-

Figure 6.5	Example of Miscue and Comprehension Qualitative Analyses Based on a Fifth Grader's Oral Reading of Passages from the Woods and Moe *Analytical Reading Inventory*

Student: Jason

Miscue Analysis Chart

Level of Passage	Miscue in Context	Acceptable		Unacceptable	Self-Correction of Unacceptable Miscues	Graphic Similarity			Unknown Words
		Syntax	Semantics			Initial	Medial	Final	
3	Suddenly he dashed home and soon returned with a bucket of yellow (paint) one of black, and several brushes			✓					
3	I thought you might want to paint your and (so) clubhouse yellow with black stripes			✓	✓				
4	Con-di-tion The pony's condition was growing worse as his breathing grew louder and harder	✓	✓			✓	✓	✓	
4	bucket At nightfall Jody brought a blanket from the house so he could sleep near Gabilan	✓		✓		✓		✓	
4	blizzards Looking up he saw buzzards, the birds of death, flying overhead	✓		✓		✓		✓	
4	blizzard perching A buzzard was perched on his dying pony's head.	✓		✓		✓		✓	
		✓	✓			✓	✓		
	Column Total	5	2	5	1/5	5	2	4	0
	Total No. of Miscues Analyzed	7	7	7		7	7	7	7
	Percentage	71%	29%	71%	20%	71%	29%	57%	0%

Figure 6.5 *continued*

Comprehension Analysis Chart

Lower Level		Oral	Silent	Higher Level		Oral	Silent
Level of Passage				Level of Passage			
2	No. Correct	3		2	No. Correct	3	
	Total Possible	3			Total Possible	3	
	Percentage	100%			Percentage	100%	
3	No. Correct	4		3	No. Correct	3	
	Total Possible	4			Total Possible	4	
	Percentage	100%			Percentage	75%	
4	No. Correct	3		4	No. Correct	3	
	Total Possible	4			Total Possible	4	
	Percentage	75%			Percentage	75%	
5	No. Correct	2		5	No. Correct	2	
	Total Possible	4			Total Possible	4	
	Percentage	50%			Percentage	50%	
	No. Correct				No. Correct		
	Total Possible				Total Possible		
	Percentage	LISTENING			Percentage	LISTENING	
6	No. Correct		1	6	No. Correct		2
	Total Possible		4		Total Possible		4
	Percentage		25%		Percentage		50%
5	No. Correct		4	5	No. Correct		3
	Total Possible		4		Total Possible		4
	Percentage		100%		Percentage		75%
	No. Correct				No. Correct		
	Total Possible				Total Possible		
	Percentage				Percentage		
Total No. Correct		12		Total No. Correct		11	
Total No. Questions		15		Total No. Questions		15	
Total Percentage		80%		Total Percentage		73%	

text, or whether it was corrected. A simple form also might be used for periodic assessments of oral reading behaviors (see Appendix J). With this form, the teacher can compare the responses to these questions. If "Yes" is checked for question 3 and "No" or "Sometimes" for question 1, the student may be relying too heavily on graphophonic cues. Instruction in the use of syntactic and semantic context clues would be in order. On the other hand, if "Yes" is checked for question 1 and "No" or "Sometimes" is checked for question 3, the student may be relying too heavily on context clues. Instruction in phonics or structural analysis would be advisable. This instruction might include such facilitating questions as, "Do you see any part of the word that you know?" (for example, *run* in *running*), or, "What word do you know that starts with _____ and would make sense?"

As the miscue analysis and evaluation of comprehension performance are being conducted, factual summary statements for observed reading behaviors and strategies can be made. Instructional goals will become more evident from examination of these summary statements. Examples of summary statements can be found in Figure 6.6. Summary statements can be written for each level of material, the type of material (narrative or expository), listening comprehension, and any other relevant observations such as written language samples and oral language samples (discussed later in this chapter).

Listening Capacity. Another piece of information that can sometimes be estimated by an IRI is **listening capacity**, also called the listening comprehension level. This is the highest level at which the student can understand 75 percent of the material read aloud by the teacher. The teacher reads and asks questions about a selection beginning at the next level above the frustration reading level. This score is sometimes used as an indication of a learner's ability to understand oral language.

Listening comprehension is sometimes considered an estimate of reading expectancy; that is, if the student were able to read the material, the listening comprehension level, or listening capacity, represents the level at which it could be understood. However, listening comprehension is probably not a valid indicator of reading potential for primary-grade children. For other learners, if the listening comprehension level is higher than the instructional reading level, the student may be reading below what can be expected, or the student may need to develop reading comprehension skills.

Similarly, Sticht and Beck (1976) found that listening comprehension surpasses reading comprehension until about grade 7. First-graders are struggling with word recognition. Likewise, second- and third-graders may sometimes be unfairly labeled as under-

Figure 6.6	Summary Statements Based on the Miscue and Comprehension Analysis Charts for Jason

SUMMARY STATEMENTS

Name:	Jason	**Date:**	December
Age:	10	**Level of Material:**	3–6
Grade:	5	**Type of Material:**	Narrative

1. The majority of Jason's miscues (71%) are unacceptable; that is, they change meaning.
2. Jason self-corrected only 20% (1 out of 5) of his miscues.
3. The majority of Jason's miscues (71%) are acceptable syntactically; that is, they maintain the same part of speech as the original text.
4. Jason is aware of context clues but does not use these clues consistently.
5. Jason's substitutions are usually graphophonically similar to the initial and final position of the word in text.
6. Jason's substitutions involve words of more than one syllable (4 out of 5).
7. Jason's substitutions involve words that may not be in his meaning vocabulary.
8. Jason's oral reading comprehension is consistent for both lower and higher levels of questions.
9. Jason's oral reading comprehension level is consistent with his word recognition abilities.
10. Jason's listening comprehension is approximately one year higher than his oral reading comprehension.

achievers if listening comprehension is found to be higher than reading comprehension. As students learn to read, which appears to take longer (grades 6 through 8) than the traditionally designated primary grades (1 through 3), their reading comprehension skills overtake their listening comprehension skills. As stated by Sticht and James (1984), "precisely what is happening that makes this additional time necessary is not certain, though it may be that in the first three or four years of school, children learn the rudiments of reading-decoding . . . while an additional two to three years of practice is required for the automaticity of reading to equal that of auding [listening comprehension]" (p. 307).

Cloze Procedure

Another direct measure used for initially estimating or verifying the instructional reading level is the **cloze procedure**. A cloze passage requires a reader to fill in blanks for words that have been systematically deleted from the written selection; most often, every fifth word is deleted. Cloze passages are more typically administered to groups of students in the upper elementary, middle, and secondary levels to assess suitability of textbook material (see readability websites at the end of this chapter).

Cloze passages are relatively easy and inexpensive to construct, administer, and interpret. Follow these steps to prepare a cloze test passage:

1. Select a passage containing 250 to 300 words (Bormuth, 1975). Be sure the passage does not depend on information presented earlier in the text (that is, a passage with many pronouns). The passage should be representative of the content of the book.

2. Keep the first sentence intact.

3. Beginning with the second sentence, delete words at a consistent interval (for example, every fifth, seventh, or tenth word) for a total of 50 deletions (Bormuth, 1975). Replace the deleted words with blanks of equal length. Duplicate the desired number of copies.

4. If the blanks are numbered, prepare an answer sheet with corresponding numbers for students to use in recording their responses.

5. If desired, students can write their responses directly on the blanks.

Administration of a cloze passage for scoring purposes is fairly straightforward. Students who have never experienced a cloze test should be given some practice with the procedure first. This practice test should use material easy for the students to read and should contain at least 10 deletions (Pikulski & Tobin, 1982).

Instructions for the cloze test *must* direct the students to read through the entire passage before trying to fill in the blanks. Students should also be told that only one word goes in each blank and that misspelled words are not counted as errors. Although the test is untimed, the teacher may want to set a reasonable time limit.

Scoring a cloze test is an often misunderstood procedure. Only exact words should be considered acceptable as correct responses. This decision is not arbitrary; it is based on considerable research (Gallant, 1964; Henk & Selders, 1984; McKenna, 1976; Miller & Coleman, 1967; Ruddell, 1964; Taylor, 1953) in which exact-word replacement scores were compared to synonym replacement scores. The synonym scores were higher than the exact-word scores, but the two scores were highly correlated (0.95 and above). Because students essentially ranked the same using either technique, giving credit for synonyms has no advantage when the purpose of the test is to estimate students' instructional levels. Preparing a list of acceptable synonyms as part of cloze test preparation simply would not be worth the time or effort (Pikulski & Tobin, 1982).

In addition to yielding slightly higher scores, synonym replacements would invalidate the scoring guidelines. Criterion scores have been established for determining independent, instructional, and frustration reading levels using exact word replacement scores. Thus, to allow synonyms would yield an inflated score and the available criteria could not be used appropriately. Pikulski and Tobin (1982) have synthesized the research on criterion scores and suggest the following guidelines:

Independent level: Students who obtain cloze scores of at least 50 percent accuracy should be able to read the material with relative ease. No teacher guidance should be necessary. Consequently, this material should be appropriate for homework assignments and other types of independent projects.

Instructional level: Students scoring between 30 and 50 percent should be able to use the material for instructional purposes. However, some guidance will be necessary to help them master the demands of the material.

Frustration level: Students scoring lower than 30 percent usually find the material much too challenging. Because there is almost no potential for success, the material should be definitely avoided. (pp. 53, 54)

Go to MyEducationLab and select the topic *Informal Assessments*. Then, go to the Activities and Applications section, and watch the video entitled "Informal Reading Assessment" to see how two middle school teachers use writing samples and the cloze procedure as direct assessment tools. Next respond to the accompanying questions.

The disadvantage of the cloze procedure is that its effectiveness as an assessment tool is not clearly established. Carefully constructed cloze tests could potentially provide helpful information regarding a reader's use of syntactic and semantic cues during silent reading. But teachers still need to observe other dimensions of the reading process. In addition to textbook selections, cloze passages can also be constructed from students' own written stories or other familiar materials and used instructionally to show readers how to use the syntactic, semantic, and graphophonic cue systems. Cloze passages can also be completed by small groups of students working collaboratively. When used for instructional purposes, cloze passage construction can be modified in many ways to suit specific purposes. Cloze as an instructional tool is discussed in more detail in Chapter 8.

A variation of the cloze procedure is the **maze technique**. Instead of deleting words from a passage, the maze procedure gives the reader a number of words from which to choose. Although this format may have more appeal for the test taker, construction of the test is more time consuming and more prone to error than the cloze procedure. Guthrie and colleagues (1974) suggest the following guidelines for constructing a maze test:

1. Select a representative passage of about 120 words.

2. Beginning with the second sentence, replace words at constant intervals (for example, every fifth or tenth word) with three word choices. These should include the correct word itself, a word that is the same part of speech as the correct word, and a word that is a different part of speech.

3. Vary the position of the correct word.

4. Duplicate copies.

As of yet, research is lacking on the maze technique, and criterion scores should be considered tentative. Guthrie and colleagues (1974) suggest that 85 percent or higher accuracy reflects an independent level; 60 to 75 percent, an instructional level; and below

50 percent, the frustration level. More research is needed on the maze technique before its use as a placement tool is recommended. As with the cloze procedure, the maze technique can be a most effective tool for improving word recognition (see Chapter 8).

Modifications for Emergent Readers

Emergent readers demonstrate characteristics associated with very young readers. They might be students with learning disabilities or students who are just learning to speak English. It will not yet be possible to administer the informal reading inventory and cloze procedures just discussed to emergent readers. Alternative measures or modifications to the IRI and cloze procedures can yield valuable information, however.

A good starting point would be to learn what the student knows about printed language. A modified *Concepts about Print* (*CAP*) (Clay, 1985, 2000a) assessment can provide this information. This assessment should be administered within the context of reading a real book. The examiner (teacher) sits with the student and asks the student to point to the book's features as listed in Appendix K. For instance, the examiner might indicate a particular page and ask, "Please show me the first word on this page. Can you point to the beginning of that word? To the end of that word?" Likewise, the student can be shown letters of the alphabet in both lower- and uppercase and asked to identify the letters. Letters should be shown in random order so that the assessment actually reveals knowledge of letters and not knowledge of the "Alphabet Song."

Emergent readers can be shown pictures that reveal a story line and asked to tell the story seen in the pictures. The *Comprehensive Reading Inventory* (Cooter, Flynt, & Cooter, 2007), both English and Spanish versions, provides a wordless picture book format for assessing stages of emergent reading. A set of criteria for these stages is provided that can be used as a scoring rubric.

The *Bader Reading and Language Inventory* (Bader, 2005) and the *Basic Reading Inventory* (Johns, 2005) are two published inventories that accommodate emergent readers. These inventories contain several alternative measures for assessing emergent literacy skills. In addition to a section on literacy concepts, similar to *Concepts about Print,* data can be gathered to assess visual and auditory discrimination, letter knowledge, phoneme manipulation (blending and segmenting), hearing letter names in words, syntax matching, syntactic and semantic closure, and spelling through dictation. Emergent readers can also be asked to write as many words as they know (such as, their name, the colors, the numbers, family members, animals) to provide information about their stage of spelling.

Emergent readers can participate in rhyming games to assess their phonemic awareness of like sounds. They can participate in oral cloze exercises to determine their ability to apply syntactic and semantic information in providing a missing word from text read aloud. These students can also be observed in their daily work samples, just like other students, for indicators of literacy development. More information about early literacy assessment can be found in Chapter 7.

Assessment by Observation, Conferences and Interviews, and Performance Samples

Observation. During the first week of school, analytic teachers observe their students and document through anecdotal notes or checklists what they discover about their students' unique talents and intelligences, preferred ways of learning, strengths, and instructional needs. At the same time, analytic teachers notice peer interactions and relationships, students' interests, thinking abilities, and oral language patterns, as well as each student's level of self-esteem and ability to complete assignments. Suggestions for a week of student observation include the following:

1. *Free time.* Who interacts with whom? Who reads and writes independently? Who needs structure or freedom? Who prefers to interact with group members? Who enjoys some time alone? Who enjoys working with computers? Who is sensitive to the moods and feelings of others?

2. *Reading groups (randomly assigned).* Who can identify ideas or words not understood? Who uses background knowledge and context to determine unknown words? Who monitors his reading comprehension? Who understands that the main goal of reading is comprehension? Who identifies with story characters? Who asks questions?

3. *Playground.* Who displays leadership abilities? Who appears to be a follower? Who needs to learn to take turns? Who is able to empathize and get along well with others? Who likes to show others how to do something? Who is particularly well coordinated physically?

4. *Lunchroom.* Who appears overly hungry? Who needs to learn table manners? Who appears lethargic or tired? Who has difficulty staying still in her seat?

5. *Class meetings.* Who speaks in complete sentences? Who has a sense of humor? Who listens carefully? Who understands and participates in problem solving or brainstorming activities? Who has difficulty hearing? Who is shy? Who offers helpful suggestions? (See Glasser, 1969, for a thorough discussion of class meetings.)

6. *Sustained silent reading (SSR) or DEAR (drop everything and read).* Who can choose books on his independent reading level? Who "mouths" words when reading silently? Who becomes easily distracted? Who points to words and sentences and might find a sentence marker useful? Who chooses books that complement her personal interests?

7. *Small groups.* Who completes learning tasks? Who cooperates? Who works to his best abilities? Who helps others learn a skill she has mastered? Who appears to be an auditory, visual, or kinesthetic learner? Who communicates ideas that especially contribute to the group's understanding of difficult concepts? Who is quick at solving a variety of problems?

8. *Visual and performing arts activities.* Who displays exceptional artistic, imaginative, or creative abilities? Who needs to learn how to use visual-art media (tempera paints, watercolors, fine and broad markers, crayons, colored pencils, glue, scissors, chalk)? Whose artistic accomplishments are not commensurate with age or grade level? (See Lowenfeld, 1970, for a discussion of the stages of children's art.) Who is interested in performing plays and puppet productions?

9. *Teacher reading aloud.* Who listens and remembers? Who needs opportunities to develop appropriate background knowledge to comprehend and appreciate stories? Who understands the relationships among **basic story features** (characters, setting, problems, and solutions) and their connections? Who identifies with story characters? Who recognizes how authors portray story characters (Richards & Gipe, 1993; Richards, Gipe, & Necaise, 1994)? Who recognizes and understands inferential language (such as metaphors, similes, and idioms)? Who doodles during this and similar class activities?

10. *Creative writing.* Who is willing to use developmentally appropriate invented, or constructed, spelling? Who is interested in unusual words? Who uses written language in particularly appealing ways? Who uses drawings, "speed writing," semantic maps, outlines, or conversations with peers to help plan her compositions? Who proofreads? Who is ready to learn about punctuation or paragraphing? (Please refer to Chapter 8 for a detailed discussion of student writing, activities, and lessons.)

11. *Independent literacy activities.* Who likes to read stories that are accompanied by recorded book tapes or DVDs? Who demonstrates impulsivity or reflective tendencies? Who likes to work with multisensory materials such as flannel boards and story character cutouts, digital cameras, tape recorders, computers, hand puppets, art supplies, or literacy games? Who enjoys creative bookmaking? Who can remember songs or rhymes easily?

As you can see, a large amount of information about students can be obtained through observation. Instructional decisions should never be made on the basis of one observation, however. Teachers who try to organize the instructional setting specifically to improve and enhance behavioral observation increase the reliability of those observations. For example, the more opportunities students have to show the teacher that they know the initial consonant blend *st* or that they can use word order clues to predict the next word in a sentence, the more reliable the information. *More opportunities* is analogous to *more items* on a test, an important way to achieve reliability.

Observing students, or kidwatching, is a skill that teachers develop over time through practice. According to Yetta Goodman (1996), who popularized the term in the late 1970s, **kidwatching** is "careful and knowledgeable observation of students as they are immersed in their own learning and language use" and "is a conscious process on the part of teachers as they take field notes" (p. 209) or mark miscues. Also, through observation and the use of anecdotal records, teachers can record "learning in action" (Drummond, 1994, p. 89). These records can then be used to (a) identify and understand each student's modes of learning or intelligences, (b) form general ideas or hypotheses about students, (c) plan instruction that meets students' needs and uses their individual strengths, and (d) communicate more effectively with parents about a student's learning. Considering the busy nature of classrooms, the key to successful kidwatching is developing a system for maintaining written records of observations.

Checklists. Many teachers use *anecdotal records* (informal notes to aid recall of observed behaviors; see also Chapter 4) that they later compile for assessment and evaluation purposes (see Figure 6.7). Other teachers prefer to use checklists that they have developed

---

Figure 6.7 Example of an Anecdotal Record

Name: *Keyotta*

12/3/08	Is learning to use her background knowledge and the context of a passage to determine unknown words in text.
1/4/09	Is becoming a motivated, wide reader. She has read three books this week—topics: outer space, baby animals, African Americans of achievement.
1/14/09	Still needs to develop confidence in her abilities to use her background knowledge and the context of a passage to determine unknown words. Appears to use both auditory and visual modalities to process new information.
1/29/09	Has become interested in wild animals and their habitats (assemble literature on this topic). Is especially competent working with musical and spatial (e.g., puzzles) activities.
2/14/09	Created and presented a play to the kindergarten—topic: animals and Africa.

Figure 6.8	Example of a Teacher-Developed Checklist

Name: _____Scotty_____   Date: _____October 10_____

	Yes	No	Comments
Enjoys listening to literature selections	✓		always listens closely and gives opinions on story content
Responds enthusiastically to literature heard or read by creating art projects, writing in literature response journals, creating stories, books, and drama activities	✓		• Created a dinosaur diorama • Writes daily in his literature response journal • Actively participates in our playwriting interest group
Is developing reading independence			
Is learning to use reading comprehension strategies according to need (e.g., word identification, K–W–L, It reminds me of)		✓	still over-reliant on graphophonic cues to determine unknown words (review three-step word identification plan)

Go to MyEducationLab and select the topic *Informal Assessments*. Then, go to the Activities and Applications section, and watch the video entitled "Self-Assessment" to hear a high school teacher discuss the benefits of encouraging student self-assessment. Next respond to the accompanying questions.

or have found in various professional resources (see Figure 6.8 for an example). Checklists are especially helpful for novice teachers who are still developing a strong knowledge base about literacy development. The checklist can provide guidance on what to observe. It is important that checklist usage allows for multiple observations over time and in a variety of contexts. There should be a place for the teacher to note not only the date of the observation, but also the context of the observation—such as the type of material read, the purpose for reading, and whether it was student- or teacher-initiated reading—as well as the instructional conditions (the teacher's instructions or type of program). Appendix L represents one attempt to guide observation of early reading development.

A checklist can also be used to summarize the performance of several students at once. This procedure is useful because teachers are usually working with groups of students functioning at different levels. The checklist in Appendix M can be used to record the progress of a group of students using a particular set of reading materials or receiving instruction at a level different from other classmates. Students can also use checklists for self-evaluation (see Figure 6.9) for an example.

Although observation, anecdotal records, and checklists provide much information about literate behavior, a system must be organized to aid interpretation of what has been observed. Such systems are referred to as rating scales and scoring rubrics.

Rating Scales. Checklists ask teachers to note the presence of a particular behavior on a particular date; rating scales assist in summarizing such data. A rating scale asks the teacher to judge the degree to which or frequency with which a behavior is exhibited. A five-point scale is common, with ratings similar to the following:

1 = not exhibited
2 = rarely exhibited
3 = sometimes exhibited
4 = often exhibited
5 = always exhibited

Figure 6.9   Example of a Student Self-Evaluation Checklist

Name: _Mary Alice_   Date: _May 9_

	Yes	No	My Explanation
I completed my reading goals for this week	✓		_I finished the first chapter of Sarah, Plain and Tall_
I monitored my reading comprehension		✓	_I forgot to write down what I didn't understand_
I learned something new as I read	✓		_Sarah was a mail-order bride. Long ago, people lived very far away from each other, so they didn't get to meet each other. When they wanted to get married, men would sometimes advertise for a bride._
I helped someone with his or her reading	✓		_I gave Angela a suggestion for her creative dinosaur book_
I connected reading with other learning activities	✓		_I created a mural showing Sarah as a mail-order bride. I also used the Internet to find some facts about how farm people lived long ago._

MacLachlan, P. (1985). *Sarah, Plain and Tall.* New York: Harper and Row.

The rating scale in Appendix N can be used to summarize the observations associated with the eight multiple intelligences (Lazear, 1994).

Scoring Rubrics. A **scoring rubric** is a record sheet that indicates a set of criteria used for rating students' performance or writing samples, portfolios, or oral and multimedia presentations. Scoring rubrics communicate the standards used in evaluating students' works to the students themselves, other teachers, parents, administrators, and other interested parties. According to Hart (1994), "a scoring rubric describes the levels of performance students might be expected to attain relative to a desired standard of achievement. These descriptors, or performance descriptions, tell the evaluator what characteristics or signs to look for in a student's work and then how to place that work on a predetermined scale" (p. 70).

The following example of a scoring rubric provides for consistency in evaluating students' written responses to a particular question by establishing five levels for scoring, each defined by a set of characteristic behaviors, or criteria. Scores of 4 and 2 were given for responses that fell somewhere in between 5 and 3 or 3 and 1, respectively. (See also Figure 12.1 for a completed story-retelling scoring rubric.)

5   Focus of response is clear; ideas flow smoothly; supporting details are evident and relevant; references are appropriate and adequate.

3   Response lacks focus but remains on topic; reader can follow flow of thought somewhat; supporting details are not relevant; references are insufficient.

1   Response has no focus and is off topic; little or no flow among ideas; supporting details are not provided; no references provided.

Go to MyEducationLab and select the topic *Ongoing Assessments*. Then, go to the Activities and Applications section, and watch the video entitled "Portfolios as Assessment Tools" to hear two teachers' perceptions of the value of portfolio assessment. Next respond to the accompanying questions.

Teachers of English learners might wish to use an observation matrix (rubric) such as the *Student Oral Language Observation Matrix* (*SOLOM;* see the websites at the end of this chapter for guidelines and a copy of the SOLOM, which is available in the public domain) to classify data regarding their English learners' comprehension, fluency, vocabulary, pronunciation, and grammar usage. These data can also supplement or verify information teachers may have received from standardized measures administered by trained personnel (for example, *Brigance Diagnostic Assessment of Basic Skills, Language Proficiency Test, California English Language Development Test [CELDT],* or *Basic Inventory of Natural Languages*). Checklists, rating scales, and scoring rubrics are good sources of information for planning instruction as well as evaluation.

Conferences, Interviews, and Interest and Attitude Surveys. Even teachers who carefully plan opportunities for observation will have unanswered questions about the progress of some students. Thus the teacher must structure short periods of time to focus more directly on behavioral responses of individual students. These periods are usually called teacher–student conferences, or interviews.

The teacher arranges a conference any time during the day when 5 to 20 minutes can be spared for an individual student. A variety of assessment procedures (IRIs, a written lesson, teacher-made exercises, portfolios) can be used to gather information, but usually the teacher is interested in finding answers to the specific questions that motivated the conference. For instance, if the student has made inconsistent responses (sometimes observing punctuation and sometimes not) during the instructional period or on written work, the teacher will want to know whether meaning is being affected for the student. Or the teacher may wish to help a student see his or her own progress and so will examine several work samples together with the student.

Go to MyEducationLab and select the topic *Ongoing Assessments*. Then, go to the Activities and Applications section, and watch the video entitled "Portfolios and Student Self-Assessment" to observe a student-teacher conference in which the student is comparing her current writing with her earlier writing. Next respond to the accompanying questions.

Conferences and *interviews* between the student and the teacher may reveal potential areas of instructional need. Identifying these areas early enhances the effectiveness of a personalized literacy program. Most learners, including high achievers, falter from time to time in their learning. Brief, timely conferences pay great dividends because they identify areas of difficulty before they become serious problems.

Interests and attitudes are also important student characteristics that are neither easily nor quickly determined by observation. Asking requires the least time and effort. Teachers can gather the information in casual conversations with students or, more efficiently, during an interview through the use of interest and attitude surveys. These surveys can be conducted as oral interviews, in written format, or by some combination of each.

Interest and attitude surveys provide information that may be useful in choosing instructional techniques for working with the student. If interests are known, the teacher uses materials that deal with those interests. If the student has a negative attitude, expected in students having serious reading difficulties, the teacher makes special efforts to motivate the learner and improve attitudes toward reading.

Obtaining information on interests consists of asking a series of questions regarding students' favorite activities, whether they have pets or hobbies, what television programs they watch, and so forth. An example of an interest inventory is presented in Appendix O.

Attitude surveys also ask questions, but of a different nature. Usually students respond "yes" or "no" or indicate some degree of feeling (strongly agree, agree, don't know, disagree, strongly disagree). Appendix P contains representative items from an attitude survey appropriate for primary grades.

Arts Connection

Interest inventories and attitude surveys can be presented in artistic ways that will encourage enthusiastic participation. A group of elementary school teachers crafted three-dimensional interest inventories containing approximately 10 questions designed to help them determine their new students' interests. The questions also provided opportunities for the teachers and their students to become acquainted with one another. For example, one teacher began her school year by showing her students a giant yellow cardboard school bus she had created. The teacher first modeled the interest inventory activity for her students by opening the school bus door and pulling out a question printed on a card designed like a bus tire. "If you could be anywhere in the world right now, where would you like to be?" she read aloud. Continuing to model her thinking for her students, she answered the question by saying, "I'd like to be swimming and sunbathing at the beach." Then each of her students took turns answering this question as the teacher recorded their responses. Next, a student was invited to open the school bus door and choose a second question to read aloud. "What books do you like to read?" he asked. The interest inventory activity continued until all the questions were read.

The teacher carefully took notes on all student responses generated during the interest inventory activity. The dated notes served as the first entry in each student's anecdotal record profile maintained by the teacher throughout the school year. The teacher also studied the interest inventory responses to determine small-group, broadly based themes or thematic units of instruction that allow for all types of explorations (such as, Celebrations; Magic and Mystery; Going Places and Doing Things) and to help form interest groups and gather book selections for literature circles.

Attitude surveys should also address students' perceptions of reading as a process and perceptions of themselves as readers. For example, an interview format can be used to provide relevant information about students' perceptions of themselves as readers and writers. The interview might include some of the following key questions:

- Do you like to read (write)?
- What is your favorite book (or who is your favorite author)?
- When do you read (write)?
- Do you think you are a good reader (writer)? Why or why not?
- Who is the best reader (writer) you know? Why?
- When you get to a word you do not know, what do you do?
- If someone asked you for help figuring out a word, how would you help?
- When you do not understand what you read, what do you do?
- Would you rather read a story or write a story?
- Would you rather read (write) or ride a bike?
- Would you rather read (write) or watch TV?
- Would you rather read (write) or sleep?
- Would you rather read (write) or draw?
- Would you rather read (write) or do arithmetic homework?
- Would you rather read (write) or help do the dishes?
- When you write, what kinds of problems do you have? What do you do about them?
- Do you ever make changes in what you write? What kind of changes?

Open-ended statements are also used to assess attitudes. For example, the student might be asked to complete the following sentences:

Reading is . . .
I think reading . . .
Most books . . .
My parents . . .
Teachers . . .

The entire *Incomplete Sentence Projective Test* (Boning & Boning, 1957) can be found in Appendix G.

Valid and reliable interest and attitude surveys for reading and writing are available for use or modification by teachers. Some of these are listed in Figure 6.10. In addition, a standardized instrument, the *Estes Attitude Scales* (Estes et al., 1981), is available in both elementary and secondary forms. As reviewed in the *Ninth Mental Measurements Yearbook* (Mitchell, 1985), the *Estes Attitude Scales* measures attitudes toward school subjects. The elementary form for grades 2 through 6 includes items for math, reading, and science; the secondary form for grades 6 through 12 includes items for English, math, reading, science, and social studies. The scales take 20 to 30 minutes to administer. Reliability is reported as 0.76 to 0.88 for the elementary scale and 0.76 to 0.93 for the secondary scale, which is quite respectable for measures of this sort. The *Estes Attitude Scales* would be useful for obtaining affective data for comparisons at local levels. This instrument is especially valuable in light of the research that shows the importance of considering attitudes toward content areas at the middle and secondary levels (Alexander & Cobb, 1992). A positive attitude toward reading in a content area undeniably has an impact on achievement in that subject.

Performance Samples. Teachers have many options for regularly assessing literacy development as students complete a variety of school assignments. Any tangible products

Figure 6.10	Sources of Interest and Attitude Surveys for Reading and Writing Available for Use or Modification by Teachers

Bottomley, D., Henk, W., & Melnick, S. (1997/1998). Assessing children's views about themselves as writers using the Writer Self-Perception Scale. *The Reading Teacher, 51,* 286–296.

Gambrell, L. B., Palmer, B. M., Codling, R. M., & Mazzoni, S. A. (1996). Assessing motivation to read. *The Reading Teacher, 49,* 518–533.

Henk, W. A., & Melnick, S. A. (1995). The Reader Self-Perception Scale (RSPS): A new tool for measuring how children feel about themselves as readers. *The Reading Teacher, 48,* 470–482.

Kear, D. J., Coffman, G. A., McKenna, M. C., & Ambrosio, A. L. (2000). Measuring attitude toward writing: A new tool for teachers. *The Reading Teacher, 54,* 10–23.

McKenna, M. C., & Kear, D. J. (1990). Measuring attitude toward reading: A new tool for teachers. *The Reading Teacher, 43,* 626–639.

Pitcher, S. M., Albright, L. K., DeLaney, C. J., Walker, N. T., Seunarinesingh, K., Mogge, S., et al. (2007). Assessing adolescents' motivation to read. *Journal of Adolescent and Adult Literacy, 50,* 378–396.

Tullock-Rhody, R., & Alexander, J. E. (1980). A scale for assessing attitudes toward reading in secondary schools. *Journal of Reading, 23,* 609–614.

such as journals, videotapes, audiotapes, art, drama productions, songs, and graphic organizers can be analyzed for oral and written language development. In this way the teacher has the means to assess students' needs on a continuing basis. Additionally, students have the opportunity to see their own development if they are keeping portfolios (also see Chapter 8 for types of portfolios). Because instruction and assessment overlap to a great extent, the instructional suggestions presented in the following chapters can also serve as direct assessment measures.

One good way to sample students' oral and written language is to ask them to draw, talk, and then write about what they have produced. After the drawing and writing are complete, ask the student to read what was written. If a student seems reluctant, the teacher might invite the student to draw a picture of her family and write something about each member.

Wordless picture books are a good source of oral language samples as well as written samples for any age student, including older and adult students, and English learners (for suggested titles, see Bloem & Padak, 1996; Danielson, 1992; Johnson-Weber, 1989; Neal & Moore, 1991/1992; Polette, 1989; Rutland, 1987; Tiedt, 2000). Oral language samples can be tape recorded for later transcription and written samples, with teacher notations, collected and dated to document growth.

Sulzby (1985) has developed a seven-point scoring rubric for assessing various levels of sophistication in students' attempts at rereading their own written language. For example, a score of 2 is given to the behavior of the learner producing random marks on paper but refusing to reread them; a score of 4 is given for a learner attempting to reread what was written but not keeping eyes on the print; and a score of 7 is given when the learner's eyes are following the print and there is a match between voice and print. This type of assessment not only informs the teacher about a student's understanding of literacy concepts but also promotes students' literacy development by drawing their attention to the distinctions between oral and written language.

Writing also plays an important role in learning our alphabetic system—that is, graphic symbols representing oral language. Writing forces learners to attend to the visual features of print, which in turn helps them become aware of letter–sound patterns and their relationship to words. As young children or English learners hear and see stories read over and over, learn letter names, print or spell words, and try to read and write new words, they will learn, naturally, the written English alphabetic system. Of course, progress can be enhanced with encouragement, modeling, and instruction geared toward the student's current level of understanding about print. An analysis of students' invented spellings reveals development of such phonic skills as segmentation (breaking words into parts), blending (putting sounds together to form words), and letter–sound correspondences. (See Appendix R for a spelling test that can be used to sample students' spelling.)

In addition to analyzing spelling, a more focused analysis of written language samples can reveal students' knowledge of writing. Examination of writing samples should be made with the intention of providing feedback to students that will help them become more skillful writers. A system that looks at the qualities of good writing as well as the process of writing might serve a teacher's needs best. Chapter 8 provides suggestions for instructional and assessment practices that support a reading–writing connection.

Students construct their own rules for oral grammar and written language based on their observations and explorations with print. By listening to students speak and by examining their writing samples, we gain insight into what they have already learned about oral and written language.

Go to MyEducationLab and select the topic *Informal Assessments*. Then, go to the Activities and Applications section, and watch the video entitled "Forms of Assessment" to observe how an eighth-grade teacher uses several of the concepts presented in this chapter. Next respond to the accompanying questions.

DOCUMENTATION AND RECORD KEEPING

Go to MyEducationLab and select the topic *Ongoing Assessments*. Then, go to the Activities and Applications section, and watch the video entitled "Portfolios and Self-Assessment" for a glance at how students can self-assess their work samples. Also recall the video "Portfolios and Student Self-Assessment" in which a young writer compared her current writing to her earlier writing. Next respond to the accompanying questions for both videos.

It is important for teachers to keep records to monitor students' literacy progress and their changing interests. As seen throughout this chapter, documentation includes the nature and content of student–teacher conferences (Figure 6.11), records of teacher observations, examples of students' work, comments and suggestions, and notes on specific reading comprehension and writing strategies students employ. Documentation can be accomplished through checklists, anecdotal records, student self-evaluation, examples of students' work gathered in *working* and *showcase portfolios* (see Chapter 8), tape recordings, videos, photographs, and students' comments about their achievements and instructional needs. Portfolios can be used as assessment tools because they contain artifacts of a student's progress over time, as well as students' own reflections on each chosen artifact and on their learning.

Documentation and record keeping also provide information for evaluating a student's progress. Although continual assessment of each student's literacy progress is essential in determining future instruction, teachers are also expected to evaluate students' efforts and assign grades. Student evaluation should be based on the following:

1. Motivation for reading and writing
2. Growth in ability to read for comprehension and write for authentic purposes
3. Growth in ability to employ word identification strategies
4. Growth in ability to recognize and understand basic story features and their connections
5. Growth in ability to appreciate and judge the quality of literature read or heard
6. Growth in ability to compare and contrast the structure of poetic and expository text

---

Figure 6.11 Example of Student–Teacher Conference Documentation

Name: _Jo Ellen_   Date: _March 12_

Topics of Discussion:	Teacher's comments;
Literature read or heard	Is reading *Cousins* by Virginia Hamilton
Reading comprehension strategies	Explained that she uses prediction strategies often
Achievements	
Problems	
Behavior	
Weekly goals	1. Complete *Cousins* 2. Begin writing a play based on the main characters in *Cousins*
Long-term goals	1. Write and direct a three-act play

Hamilton, V. (1990). *Cousins.* New York: Putnam and Grosset.

7. Growth in ability to use reading comprehension and writing strategies based on need

8. Growth in ability to monitor reading comprehension

9. Development of wide reading interests

10. Growth in ability to write on a wide range of topics using different *voices of composition* (see Chapter 8)

11. Growth in ability to evaluate the quality of personal literacy efforts

It is especially important for students to learn how to evaluate their own literacy achievements and progress. Students who can evaluate their own work in terms of strengths and needs develop responsibility for their own learning (Tierney et al., 1991). Teachers must work to provide the "risk-free environments necessary in order for this to happen" (Glazer, 1993, p. 108).

VIGNETTE   **Putting It All Together**

This vignette demonstrates the analytic process as implemented by one classroom teacher at the beginning of a school year.

The School Context

An urban, public elementary school with a diverse, at-risk, lower socioeconomic student population has 32 students in the third grade.

The Teacher

Ms. Johnson, a dedicated teacher who has helped make the classroom an inviting, exciting place, has been teaching for four years.

Ms. Johnson has collected a wide variety of literature at different grade levels and has created an attractive area for individual silent reading. She displays students' work, including art projects, language experience stories, and students' creative books. Learning centers are interesting, appealing, and orderly. Ms. Johnson believes that reading quality fiction and nonfiction to her students enhances their love of reading, reading comprehension, oral language, and writing abilities. She also supplies multiple copies of literature selections for her students so that she can teach reading using quality fiction and nonfiction. Occasionally she uses basal text stories with her reading group if they are pertinent to a thematic unit being studied.

Ms. Johnson also observes her students carefully and notes their particular talents and literacy instructional needs. She then forms temporary groups according to student needs (for example, helping students understand paragraphing or learn the importance of predicting and hypothesizing about text ideas and events). Ms. Johnson sincerely likes her students and her job. She is energetic, empathic, open to new ideas, and confident in her abilities to influence her students in positive ways and to make sound educational decisions.

Ms. Johnson conducts daily whole class meetings and encourages her students to discuss problems, pleasures, and learning goals.

During the first week of school, Ms. Johnson carefully observed each of the students in her classroom during free time, reading groups, lunch, whole group instruction, art, music, independent reading, and morning class meetings. She placed each student's name on an individual page of a large notebook. She noted peer interactions, language ability, ability to complete assignments, and apparent feelings of self-esteem for each student. She also made tentative notes concerning each student's apparent listening abilities and reading and writing strengths and began to classify observations on the Student Behavior Log of Demonstrated Multiple Intelligences (see Appendix N).

Also during the first week of school, Ms. Johnson asked for her students' help. She explained that she would meet individually with each student to discuss their personal learning goals and interests. She also told her students that she wanted them to experience as much success as possible. Ms. Johnson discussed the reasons for flexible reading groups and student conferences as well.

Jamika

One of Ms. Johnson's students was Jamika. During the first week of school, when Ms. Johnson wrote her initial ideas about students in her notebook, she made the following notes about Jamika:

Jamika (Birthdate: 3/13/2002)

1. Quiet
2. Cooperative
3. Polite
4. Appears to have adequate oral language abilities
5. Appears interested in class activities
6. Appears healthy

Ms. Johnson observed Jamika further and added notebook comments:

7. Does not volunteer to share ideas and opinions about literature heard or read
8. Follows along carefully as teacher reads
9. Understands basic story features and their connections
10. Often doodles and enjoys drawing

Ms. Johnson began to formulate some questions about Jamika. She asked:

- Why does Jamika exhibit apparent passive behavior?
- Does Jamika lack self-confidence and self-esteem?
- Is the reading material too difficult for Jamika?
- What reading comprehension strategies might help Jamika?

Ms. Johnson decided to look at Jamika's cumulative folder and then make additional notebook comments:

11. Youngest of three siblings
12. Above average grades in first and second grades
13. Average and slightly below average standardized test scores
14. Many absences in first and second grade because of illness

Ms. Johnson decided to have a conference with Jamika. Because the teacher was an active, empathic listener and communicated with Jamika in a nonjudgmental manner, Jamika felt comfortable in sharing her thoughts. After the conference Ms. Johnson wrote:

15. Brother and sister both high achievers
16. Believes that she is not as "smart" as her siblings

Ms. Johnson decided to gather some definite information about Jamika's literacy abilities. She wanted some answers to these questions:

- Is Jamika reading to her fullest potential?
- What is Jamika's instructional reading level? Independent reading level? Listening comprehension level?
- Is Jamika in need of supplementary instruction, possibly because of learning gaps due to illness?
- What are Jamika's general writing abilities?
- What writing behaviors does Jamika exhibit?

- What perceptions does Jamika have about reading and writing?
- What perceptions does Jamika have about herself as a reader and writer?
- What are Jamika's interests?

Ms. Johnson decided to get some ideas about Jamika's interests and reading ability using an interest inventory and an informal reading inventory. She worked with Jamika while the class was actively involved in learning center activities. Afterwards she recorded the results in her notebook:

17. Interested in dinosaurs and baby animals
18. Adequate sight vocabulary commensurate with third grade
19. Reading independently at second grade
20. Reading instructionally at third grade
21. Listening comprehension level is fifth grade

Ms. Johnson then invited Jamika to write an informal letter or story of her choice, which she could then illustrate. As Jamika wrote, Ms. Johnson observed her and made notes about her writing behaviors:

22. Jamika wrote in the expressive voice. She wrote about a trip to Disney World.
23. Jamika used standard and transitional spelling commensurate with her age and grade (for example, "Dizneewrld").
24. Jamika wrote legibly and was overly concerned with forming letters correctly.
25. Jamika used appropriate capitalization and punctuation at the end of sentences.
26. Jamika did not use a plan for writing, nor did she reread her work or revise.
27. Jamika appeared to be very anxious as she wrote, but was eager to illustrate her story.

Next, Ms. Johnson interviewed Jamika to determine her perceptions about reading and writing. She asked Jamika questions such as, Do you like to read? Why or why not? What do you do when you come to a word that you don't know? How do you figure it out? Do you think that you are a good reader? Why or why not? Why do people write? How do you decide what to write? What part of writing do you like the most? The least? Why? Are you a good writer? Why? Why not? (See earlier section in this chapter for additional questions.)

After examining Jamika's responses to these questions, Ms. Johnson wrote the following tentative hypotheses in her notebook:

- Needs to develop motivation to read
- Needs to develop confidence in herself as a reader and writer
- Needs to learn word identification plans
- Needs to learn to read for comprehension and actively seek meaning
- Needs to learn some prewriting strategies
- Needs to learn editing techniques

After analyzing and reflecting upon Jamika's IRI results, the Student Behavior Log, writing behaviors, perceptions about writing, oral language abilities, and affective dimension behaviors, Ms. Johnson decided that Jamika probably had far greater reading and writing potential than she demonstrated. Ms. Johnson added the following to her tentative hypotheses:

- Lack of motivation, possibly due to poor self-esteem; lack of confidence; lack of reading and writing success in first and second grades
- Possible feelings of inadequacy because of high-achieving older siblings
- Insufficient knowledge about the processes of reading and writing
- Focus on talent in visual/spatial intelligence

Ms. Johnson decided to plan a program of reading and writing instruction together with Jamika. After the planning conference, she wrote the following instructional alternatives for Jamika:

Literacy Instructional Plan

1. Place in temporary groups focusing on word-identification plans and reading comprehension techniques
2. Assign creative bookmaking
3. Assemble literature that meets Jamika's interests (dinosaurs and baby animals)
4. Teach reading comprehension techniques that help Jamika learn to read for meaning
5. Provide opportunities for Jamika to engage in collaborative writing and bookmaking activities
6. Help Jamika engage in numerous nonstructured writing activities
7. Establish dialogue journal with Jamika to foster a reading and writing connection and provide a risk-free opportunity for Jamika to write
8. Provide teacher-guided writing lessons such as "Writing Cohesive Paragraphs"
9. Arrange physical examination, including visual and auditory acuity
10. Schedule student–parent–teacher conference

Ms. Johnson will continue to observe Jamika's literacy progress throughout the school year. She plans to continue student–teacher conferences and informal communication, teacher support, and providing for Jamika's success as a reader and writer.

Summary

Chapter 6 presents a variety of tools for direct assessment. These classroom-based assessment procedures are valuable to the teacher for gathering information and verifying tentative teaching hypotheses in the analytic process. Appropriate use of both classroom-based and standardized measures is most effective in learning students' literacy needs. The chapter ends with an example of one teacher's implementation of the analytic process. This teacher now has information necessary for providing differentiated instruction.

Recommended Websites

Assessment of Literacy Development in Early Childhood
   http://cela.albany.edu/publication/article/johnrogers.htm
This site discusses the Primary Language Record (PLR), a tool that focuses on what the young child CAN do. It is intended to inform instruction, is cumulative, and involves the parents, the child, and teachers.

Assessment of Oral Language with the SOLOM
   www.cal.org/twi/evaltoolkit/appendix/solom.pdf
   http://coe.sdsu.edu/people/jmora/Pages/solom914.htm
The SOLOM is designed to assess authentic oral language used for real, day-to-day classroom purposes and activities. These two sites provide the matrix and the guidelines for using the SOLOM.

Creative Student Assessment
   www.nald.ca/CLR/csa/contents.htm
A variety of assessment materials related to literacy can be found here.

Assessment in a Constructivist Classroom
   www.ncrel.org/sdrs/areas/issues/methods/
   assment/as7const.htm
Lists of the principles a constructivist teacher uses within the classroom are provided on this site. It discusses how to use assessment to enhance both student learning and teacher understanding of the student's understanding.

Questionnaires for Assessing Interests and Attitudes
   www.nald.ca/CLR/csa/appx_c.htm
This site provides a variety of surveys to include learning style preferences.

Portfolio Assessment
   www.teachervision.fen.com/teaching-methods/
   experimental_education/4528.html?detoured=1
   http://school.discoveryeducation.com/schrockguide/
   assess.html#portfolios
   www.essentialschools.org/cs/resources/view/ces_res/225
Follow the links to view digital portfolio samples.

Literacy Portfolio Cases

    www.prenhall.com/literacy_portfolios/html/
    portfolios.html

Four sample literacy assessment portfolios are shown on this site.

Take a Cloze Readability Test

    www.privacyrights.org/fs/fs24b-ClozeFinancial.htm

Get a feel for a cloze readability test by taking this real-life readability application. Participate and check your answers online.

Fry Readability Graph

    http://school.discoveryeducation.com/schrockguide/fry/
    fry.html

Readability is one factor in deciding if material is suitable for a student.

MyEducationLab is a research-based learning tool that brings teaching to life. Go to the Gipe 7th Edition MyEducationLab for Reading Assessment site at www.myeducationlab.com to:

- Engage in multimedia exercises to help you build a deeper and more applied understanding of chapter content.

- Use extensive resources including videos from real classrooms, Praxis and licensure preparation, a lesson plan builder, and materials to help you in your teaching career.

Early Literacy Skills

OBJECTIVES

After you have read this chapter, you should be able to:
1. Explain the value of oral language development to reading.
2. Discuss the benefits of reading aloud to children for their oral language development and for their understanding about print concepts.
3. Recognize the essential characteristics of phonemic awareness.
4. Appreciate a child's early efforts at writing as a window into their thinking about how print works.
5. Assess a child's oral language, concepts about print, phonemic awareness, and letter knowledge.
6. Provide instruction that enhances a young child's oral language development, awareness of print concepts, phonemic awareness, and letter knowledge.

VOCABULARY ALERT

alphabetic principle	interactive read alouds	shared reading
constructed spelling	interactive writing	telegraphic stage
emergent writers	invented spelling	temporary spelling
grapheme	phoneme substitution	
holographic stage	phonemic awareness	

The Major Domains: Chapter 7–14

These chapters discuss the commonly recognized areas of literacy instruction. Each chapter can stand alone, so the order in which each is studied, or applied within a clinic or field-based setting to address the specific needs of K–12 learners, can be modified from the order presented. However, each chapter does assume the information found in Part 1 of the text. For example, the concepts about assessment apply to each of the Part 2 domain chapters, as does the information about English language learners and physical, psychological, and environmental factors. Most importantly, the analytic process that assists in differentiating instruction can be facilitated because each of the domain chapters contains specific information for assessment and instruction within that literacy area, as well as ideas for integrating the multiple intelligences, the visual and communicative arts, and strategies well suited to the needs of English language learners. When a connection to information in other chapters, in an appendix, or in MyEducationLab is helpful, that connection is noted.

Literacy is described in Chapter 1 as a continuously developing process with several stages of developing readers. This chapter focuses on the early reader stage of literacy acquisition (sometimes called emergent literacy). Certainly literate interactions with supportive adults prior to beginning school will help prepare children for literacy instruction. Such experiences as being read to, being engaged in conversations, and playing with both spoken and written language through rhyming games and writing messages or stories are to be encouraged in the home. Because of these experiences, some children learn to read at home before coming to school; however, many do not. Children who have had few experiences with print or oral language will need explicit instruction in all aspects of literacy development. In addition to oral language development, areas of literacy instruction associated with emergent and early readers are print conventions and book handling; phonemic awareness; letter recognition; basic sight words; and using context clues to make sense of text, construct meaning, and determine word meanings. The areas of oral language development, print conventions and book handling, phonemic awareness, and letter recognition are addressed in this chapter, as they are especially pertinent to instruction for emergent and early readers. Discussion of basic sight words and using context clues occurs in Chapters 8, 9, 10, and 11, as they are a focus of literacy instruction beyond early literacy.

EARLY LITERACY DEVELOPMENT AND EMERGENT READERS

Early literacy skills certainly begin at birth and extend through the first five years of life. A child's early experiences with books and language provide the foundation for later success in literacy learning. However, early literacy does not mean literacy skills are formally taught to the child. All that is needed is an environment that provides many opportunities for the child to talk and be listened to, as well as being read to, sung to, and encouraged to draw and write. Through such interactions with caring adults and family members, the young child will develop her or his oral language as well as key understandings about print conventions and book handling; phonemic awareness; vocabulary, to include basic sight words; letters and their relationship to writing; story structure; and literacy as a meaning-making process.

ORAL LANGUAGE DEVELOPMENT

Starting at birth, every child is ready for positive experiences with language in all forms. Language play is especially helpful for the later development of word recognition and comprehension skills. From the time a child makes his or her first utterances, from birth through 8 months, language is available for the development of thinking skills. Although these early utterances are at first reflexive (for example, cries, burps) and progressive to babbling (such as specific but nonword sounds), by 18 months the child is using the appropriate rhythms, phrasings, and intonational patterns of the native language. Following babbling, the child develops authentic speech, indicating an understanding that the function of speech is to communicate. This understanding may occur at about 12 months and is referred to as the **holographic stage** of language development. A common example is a child's first word of *Mommy* or *Daddy,* spoken when the mother or father is in view. For a period of time, the child then uses one word to represent several ideas. For instance, *doggie* might refer to the family pet, or it might mean any dog seen in the neighborhood. It could also mean the child is asking the dog to come, or the child is commenting on any other action of the dog. Then, between one and two years of age, children add another word to their speaking repertoire indicating particular functions of language; for example, requesting (*Joey cookie*), describing (*good boy*), expressing interest (*see baby*), identifying location (*go home*), suggesting an object and action (*Daddy come*), and giving information (*me hungry*). This two-word stage greatly increases the child's communicative repertoire and is called the **telegraphic stage** of language development.

Beyond two years of age children experience a "language explosion," such that by the time they enter school most children are able to use all the linguistic patterns in their speech with the possible exception of passive voice (for example, "The story was read to the children by their teacher."). It is through active listening and oral reproduction activity that young children become aware of sounds, words, ideas, and how to communicate their ideas prior to entering school.

Assessment Techniques for Oral Language

Vocabulary is an important aspect of oral language. Kindergarten students are often assessed prior to coming to kindergarten using the Peabody Picture Vocabulary Test (Dunn & Dunn, 2006). The PPVT is a highly reliable and valid test of receptive vocabulary and verbal ability, and was designed for persons as young as $2\frac{1}{2}$ years of age. The child does not need to be able to read, as receptive vocabulary is measured by asking the child to point to the one illustration from among four that represents a word spoken orally by the examiner.

The Clinical Evaluation of Language Fundamentals (CELF) is also used to measure oral language proficiency. The CELF-Preschool 4 (Wiig, Secord, & Semel, 2006) measures expressive and receptive language skills through seven subtests: sentence structure, word structure, expressive vocabulary, concepts and following directions, recalling sentences, basic concepts, and word classes. There are also supplementary subtests, including one for phonemic awareness.

Administering a listening comprehension assessment (see Chapter 6) or asking for a retelling of a story (see Appendix I) that the teacher has read can also provide indications of oral language development (see Appendix Q). The teacher notices if the child can answer questions about the material read aloud, or if the child can paraphrase what the text was about and maintains these observations in anecdotal records for later comparisons (see Chapter 4). The use of anecdotal notes and checklists (see Appendix L) helps the teacher to keep track of a student's progress. Students can also be asked to summarize a story or to identify the problem and solution in a story, compare or contrast characters, or compare one story to another similar story.

Oral cloze assessments can provide information about vocabulary and also about syntactic understanding. During the oral reading of a story, the teacher can stop at pre-arranged locations and ask the student what the next word might be. For example, "Chippy Chipmunk put three nuts in his cheek. He also put some nuts in a _____." Or, "Chippy Chipmunk wants to move to an apple _____." Or, "So he could talk to Gray Kitten, Chippy took the nuts out of his _____." (See Chapter 6 for more on cloze assessment.)

Get Ready To Read (GRTR) is a useful screening instrument that takes little time to administer (10 to15 minutes) and has high internal reliability (r = 0.78) (Farver, Nakamoto, & Lonigan, 2007). The GRTR comes in both Spanish and English versions, each containing 20 items that assess print knowledge, letter name and sound knowledge, rhyming, initial sound matching, compound word blending, and knowledge of writing. It correlates highly with more comprehensive instruments, so it serves well as a screening tool to assess the oral language, phonological, and print processing skills of Spanish- and English-speaking children.

Instruction for Oral Language Development

Read Alouds. Reading aloud to students is among the most effective ways of developing oral language for both native and nonnative English speakers. Shared readings and interactive read alouds are two techniques used when reading aloud to young students. **Shared reading** refers to a technique in which the teacher reads aloud from a big book while students listen or follow along using individual copies of the book. The two teachers in the MyEducationLab video clip "Preparing for Learning" are conducting a shared reading using the big book for *Mufaro's Beautiful Daughters*. Notice how the teachers lead the children in a picture walk (see Chapter 9) or book walk to promote readiness for listening. These two teachers then go on to read a story that their students would not be able to read on their own. Another benefit of shared readings is that students can be exposed to more interesting material and hear more sophisticated language than they could read for themselves.

Interactive read alouds refers to a technique in which the teacher reads aloud while students listen, but with the teacher stopping to engage students with the material by discussing vocabulary; making connections between the material and personal experiences, other texts previously read, or to the world; teaching the use of context clues and prediction-making skills; and developing awareness of text features, to include narrative and expository text structures (see Chapters 10, 11, 12, and 13). Interactive read alouds can be quite effective for vocabulary development, especially with English language learners (Dietrich, 2008; McBroom, 2009; Zipoli, 2007). Interactive read alouds are useful not only for oral language development but also for instructing young students in the conventions related to print and book handling as discussed in the following section. For oral language development, the teacher's goal is to encourage students to talk about their thoughts and ideas related to the material they are listening to. Vocabulary instruction is provided directly through interactive read alouds as appropriate contexts are readily available for teacher-facilitated discussion and deeper understanding. For example, during the reading of *Spiders* (Otto, 2002), the teacher might stop at the word *orb* to discuss its meaning because the type of spider explained in the book is an orb spider. *Orb* is another word for *circle,* so the teacher might explain that the orb spider makes a web shaped like a circle or like a bicycle wheel. It is important in vocabulary instruction to make connections between what is familiar to

Go to MyEducationLab and first select the topic *Comprehension.* Go to the Activities and Applications section, watch the video entitled "Preparing for Learning," and respond to the accompanying questions. Then select the topic *Emergent Literacy.* Go to the Activities and Applications section, watch the video entitled "Beginning Reading," and respond to the accompanying questions. Observe the shared reading of *Mufaro's Beautiful Daughters* in both videos.

Go to MyEducationLab and select the topic *Informal Assessments*. Then, go to the Activities and Applications section, and watch the video entitled "Story Time: Large Group" to observe one way to conduct an interactive read aloud when the purpose is on prediction-making skills. Next respond to the accompanying questions.

MI Connection: bodily-kinesthetic; intrapersonal

Go to MyEducationLab and select the topic *Informal Assessments*. Then, go to the Activities and Applications section, and watch the video entitled "Contextual Analysis and Story Dramatization" to observe a read aloud followed by Ms. Murphy's use of stick puppets for story retelling. Next re-spond to the accompanying questions.

MI Connection: interpersonal

the students and the new word or concept (see Chapter 10 for more instructional strategies related to vocabulary). The students in the MyEducationLab video clip "Story Time: Large Group" are engaged in an interactive read aloud in which the teacher is focusing prediction-making skills through the use of an oral cloze technique. By rereading an already familiar story, the teacher is ensuring that students have the context necessary for active participation in this interactive read aloud. Repeated interactive read alouds, such as the one seen in this video clip, offer opportunities to focus on vocabulary development in the first reading, followed by a focus on print conventions in a second reading and a focus on enhancing story comprehension or constructing retellings in a third reading (McGee & Schickedanz, 2007).

Books chosen for read alouds can range from wordless picture books to challenging stories or informational books. Sharing books on a wide range of topics will keep children's attention and also engage them in a variety of ways to respond to literature. Some books will provide many opportunities to learn new words, while others will enhance students' thinking about a character's motivations or introduce them to new cultures. Wordless picture books can be useful for helping students tell a story from their own experiences using the well-crafted illustrations found in the book. Predictable books can engage students in the reading through the rhyming patterns and repetition found in these books. Teachers should make every attempt to include selections from all genres—fiction, nonfiction, prose, poetry, books about ethnic groups, and informational books. By choosing books that contain sophisticated language, teachers are enhancing oral language development while sharing interesting material that is more motivating for students (McBroom, 2009; Santoro et al. 2008).

Informal Drama and Play Centers. Informal drama activities are unrehearsed and often spontaneous, and they allow children to use their imagination, to play with language, and to express their own feelings and thoughts. These drama activities may involve simple movements and props but are not elaborate productions. (See the Arts Connection box.) As students engage in drama activities, they can be encouraged to speak loudly and clearly and to use relevant vocabulary. Providing puppets might be useful for students who are reluctant to speak before an audience. Making a photocopy of pictures from the book and cutting them out for placement on a Popsicle stick is an easy way to construct stick puppets for characters in a story. This is exactly what Ms. Murphy did in the second half of the MyEducationLab video clip "Contextual Analysis and Story Dramatization."

Play centers are commonly found in kindergarten classrooms and provide many opportunities for informal dramatic play. Such centers provide purposeful practice in oral language, which is key for developing proficiency. Dramatic play centers such as kitchen, post office, restaurant, grocery store, and department store encourage spontaneous conversations and interaction with other children and serve to also help develop social skills. Children can take phone messages, prepare shopping lists, use play money to pay bills or write checks, take food orders, prepare menus, create signs, write letters, address and mail them, and converse with the postal worker or the clerks in the grocery store or department store. These centers can also include puppets, flannel boards, simple props (including paper and pencil, nonworking telephones, empty food containers, plastic dishes and utensils), and dress-up clothes. Informal dramatic play provides the stimulation for the oral language practice young learners need and is effective in developing their oral language (Wilson, 2007).

Some students are either reluctant to speak orally or have underdeveloped oral language. These students will need some one-on-one attention that focuses on modeling

Arts Connection

Children of all ages instinctively use the visual arts as a natural means of expression. For example, toddlers spontaneously scribble their ideas on all available surfaces. Kindergarten students enjoy using large pieces of colored chalk to decorate sidewalks. Primary students "come into the classroom drawing pictures" (Blecher & Jaffee, 1998, p. 70). Such willingness to draw will enable teachers to elicit oral language to correspond to the drawing, which can then be written for the child above, below, or beside the drawing.

In addition, the important phonemic awareness skill of rhyming can be enhanced through dramatization. For example, one primary grade teacher linked the dramatic arts with music when she helped her students perform a skit based on the story *Double Trouble in Walla Walla* (Clements, 1997). Modeling the characters in the book, who speak in rhymes, the teacher and student actors also used rhyming words (*nit-wit, okey-dokey, wowie-zowie, jeepers-creepers*). Then, as the book explains, without warning, hundreds of rhyming words began to fill the air. Rather than merely repeating all of these rhyming words, the students had fun and played with language. Beating small drums, stamping their feet, and snapping their fingers faster and faster, they chanted, "Fuzzy-wuzzy, fuddy-duddy, loosey-goosey, lovey-dovey, huggy-huggy, rinky-dinky-doo, ga-ga, rah-rah, go-go, so-so, goo-goo, wooh-wooh, rinky-dinky-doo, arf-arf, woof-woof, boogie-woogie, bow-wow, rinky-dinky-doo, clippity-cloppity, hippity-hoppity, clickity-clackety, rickety-rackety, baa-baa-baa, ha-ha-ha, clip-clop, drip-drop, click-clack, rick-rack, eager-beaver, lucky-ducky, comfy-dumfy, fat-cat, hee-haw, tweet-sweet, chirp-chirp, cheep-cheep, cluck-cluck, quack-quack, rick-rack, hee-haw, rinky-dinky-doo!" Such language play is to be encouraged.

---

conversation and on facilitating conversation. The teacher in the MyEducationLab video clip "Encouraging Conversation: Child with Language Delay" demonstrates the use of a child's magazine with pictures of trains and other items to sensitively expand on the child's language as she also models the use of facilitating questions to maintain the conversation. At such an early stage of oral language development, specifically worded questions seem to be more effective than open-ended questions.

Go to MyEducationLab and select the topic *Informal Assessments*. Then, go to the Activities and Applications section, and watch the video entitled "Encouraging Conversation: Child with Language Delay" to observe how a teacher works one-on-one with a child in need of oral language development. Next respond to the accompanying questions.

Additional Activities. There are many activities teachers can use to encourage oral language. A few are presented here:

1. Following the sharing of a book, students can engage in *flannel board retellings*. The profiles of the main characters in the story can be cut out of felt, along with any other important items that were crucial to the plot (for example, three pigs, wolf, house of sticks, house of straw, house of bricks, cooking pot). Students receive a felt piece and are asked to share in the retelling of the story by placing their felt piece on the flannel board at the appropriate time. These flannel board pieces can then be placed in a learning center for student use at any time.

2. Challenging students to *expand phrases* is an enjoyable way to build oral vocabulary. On chart paper, a chalkboard, or an overhead, write a simple phrase that contains a subject and predicate (for example, *dog ran, bird sings, girl skipped, door slammed, boy jumps*). Read the "phrase of the day" to the children and point to each word as it is spoken. Ask the children to say each word after you until each child can repeat the phrase accurately. Then give the children paper and crayons so they can draw a picture that shows the action they imagine in the phrase. These drawings can be shared and additional words added to the phrase to extend the picture. Then the drawings are given back to the students, and they can add to the original drawing or create a new drawing to correspond

Figure 7.1   Example of an Expanded Phrase

to the expanded phrase. Figure 7.1 shows an example for the phrase *dog ran*. Students might even want to expand their drawings into a story by adding more pictures to show what happens next.

3. Oral language games can increase vocabulary and also phonemic awareness (addressed in a later section). One such game is *I'm Going to Grandma's*. In this game the teacher might begin by saying, "I'm going to Grandma's, and I will take a book." Then the teacher invites the children to join the game, and each child will repeat the sentence; but instead of *book* he or she will replace that word with another word beginning with the same sound (if this is too difficult for most students, then just ask that the word *book* be replaced by any noun). The game can be repeated by focusing on going to a different place or by focusing on a different sound.

PRINT CONVENTIONS AND BOOK HANDLING

When a child has been read to at home, many of the concepts related to print conventions and book handling have been mastered before a child enters first grade. However, children who have not been exposed to books or read to at home will likely be confused by questions such as:

Who can show me the title of the book?
Who can show me where to start reading?
Who can show me where the end of the story is?
Who can point to a word?
Who can show me a capital letter?

These questions are generally included in any assessment of a child's awareness of print conventions and book handling.

Assessment of Print Conventions and Book Handling

Simply by handing a child a book, asking him or her to read the book, and observing what that child does will demonstrate his or her familiarity with book handling. Notice if the child holds the book with the cover in front and right side up. Does the child then open the book and pretend to read from the left to the right? Clay (1985, 1993, 2000a) developed a Concepts about Print assessment as part of a larger battery of observational tools that asks children a few simple questions to determine which students need direct instruction in print conventions and book handling. For example, on handing a child a book, the examiner asks, "Where is the front of the book?" "Where do I start reading?" or "Show me the title of the book." (See Appendix K for a similar early reading concepts assessment.) These print convention and book handling skills are easily taught during read-aloud sessions.

For computer-based assessment, the Waterford Early Reading Program (WERP) provides detailed information on students' knowledge of print concepts, as well as phonemic awareness and letter recognition (Pearson Digital Learning, 2006). WERP can be used to track students' progress on a weekly basis.

Instruction for Print Conventions and Book Handling

In addition to their usefulness in developing oral language, read alouds provide the best opportunity to develop concepts about print. Important concepts that can be taught directly during read alouds include (Clay, 1993):

- A book has a front and back cover, a title page, an author, and an illustrator (for picture books).
- We read text from left to right and from top to bottom.
- We go from the left page to the right page.
- Letters are the marks on the page.
- A word is a group of letters surrounded by white space.
- Punctuation marks help with inflection and meaning.
- The words on a page carry the potential for meaning (we read words, not pictures).
- A story has a beginning, a middle, and an end.

Another technique for reinforcing understanding of print conventions is **interactive writing**, in which the teacher takes students' dictations of sentences to develop a story. Interactive writing is also useful for phonemic awareness instruction as well as for a variety of other purposes as discussed elsewhere in this text (see Chapter 8). When interactive writing is used for teaching print conventions, the teacher must make sure students watch as she begins each sentence with a capital letter and ends with a period. There may be occasions to introduce punctuation other than the period in the case of a question (question mark) or a particularly exciting sentence (exclamation mark). Children should also watch as the teacher forms letters and writes words and see how she uses white space to separate words. They will also observe the teacher moving from the left to the right and from top to bottom. The MyEducationLab video clip "An Interactive

To see the variety of skills that can be taught using the interactive writing technique, go to MyEducationLab and first select the topic *Phonemic Awareness and Phonics*. Go to the Activities and Applications section, watch the video entitled "An Interactive Writing Activity," and respond to the accompanying questions. Then select the topic *Emergent Literacy*. Go to the Activities and Applications section, watch the video entitled "Interactive Writing," and respond to the accompanying questions.

Writing Activity" shows Ms. Klein, a kindergarten teacher, carefully demonstrating the use of a capital letter at the beginning of a sentence and white space between words. In the MyEducationLab video clip "Interactive Writing," the students demonstrate similar understanding of concepts about print in their writing.

PHONEMIC AWARENESS

Phonemic awareness is the ability to hear, identify, and manipulate individual sounds in spoken language. Griffith and Olson (1992) define phonemic awareness as "an understanding of the structure of *spoken* language" (p. 518). Thus, "phonemic awareness is strictly an oral ability and does not involve recognizing or naming letters or knowing which letters make which sounds [i.e., phonics]" (Cunningham, 1999, p. 69). Phonemic awareness also includes such abilities as orally/aurally recognizing and producing rhyming words, matching sounds, blending and segmenting phonemes (/*m*/ + /*ake*/= *make*), splitting syllables (/*cow*/ + /*boy*/ = *cowboy*), and manipulating sounds to create new words, called **phoneme substitution** (Change the /*m*/ in *make* to /*b*/—what is the new word? *Note*: When the backward slash marks contain a letter(s) or word, what is inside the slashes represents that *sound* being made.) While phonemic awareness is *not* the same as phonics (learning letter–sound correspondences), it can be considered a prerequisite to success in phonics instruction (Adams, 1990; Juel, 1988; Mercer, 1997; National Reading Panel, 2000).

Assessment for Phonemic Awareness

Assessment activities for phonemic awareness are essentially the same as instructional activities, but several published assessment tools are available for use with individual students. One that uses colored blocks for showing sequences of sounds in nonsense syllables and is useful for a range from kindergarten to adult is the *Lindamood Auditory Conceptualization Test (LAC-3)* (Lindamood & Lindamood, 2004). A norm-referenced test that provides percentile scores for phoneme awareness, blending, memory, and rapid naming is the *Test of Phonological Awareness, second edition* (Torgesen & Bryant, 2004). There are two forms of this test, one for ages 5 through 6 and another for ages 7 through 18. A valid and reliable measure used with kindergarten and first-grade students for the phonemic awareness area of segmenting is the *Yopp-Singer Test of Phoneme Segmentation* (Yopp, 1995). For blending, the *Roswell-Chall Auditory Blending Test* (Roswell & Chall, 1997) assesses the blending ability of two and three sounds. Second-language learners should be assessed in their native language. The *Preschool Language Scale-4: Spanish* (Zimmerman, Steiner, & Pond, 2002) asks children to respond to direct questions using pictures and common objects (for example, show the child a picture of gloves and ask "¿Por qué nos llevamos guantes?" or, in English, "Why do we wear gloves?"). The *Preschool Comprehensive Test of Phonological and Print Processing* (Lonigan et al., 2002) is available in both English and Spanish as well. A teacher who is aware of instructional activities for phonemic awareness can easily devise tasks that can serve as direct assessments. The screening instrument described earlier, GRTR, also contains seven items on phonemic awareness and is also available in a Spanish version.

Instruction for Developing Phonemic Awareness

Some useful instructional activities for developing phonemic awareness follow. As with oral language development, reading well-chosen children's literature aloud to students is one of the best ways to develop phonemic awareness. Literature that contains specific language elements such as rhyme, alliteration, phoneme substitution, or phoneme segmentation provides occasions for children to attend to the sounds in language in a playful way. While reading such books to students, point to each word as it is read. Once a selection has been completed, go back to interesting words and frame them by cupping hands around the word or by using pieces of poster board cut to surround the word. Many books of poetry and stories written in rhyme (such as Dr. Seuss books) can be read and reread for various purposes such as directing students to listen for words that rhyme and then tell what they are or to listen for words that begin like /sh/ as in *sugar* (McGee & Schickedanz, 2007).

There exists a wealth of children's literature to assist students in alliteration, rhyming, blending and segmenting, and manipulation of phonemes (see Griffith & Olson, 1992, and Opitz, 2000, for further information). Some examples are *Animalia* (Base, 1986), with its "Lazy lions lounging in the local library"; *Sheep on a Ship* (Shaw, 1989), with "It rains and hails and shakes the sails. Sheep wake up and grab the rails"; the *Jamberry* poem (Degen, 1983), containing "Hatberry/Shoeberry/In my Canoeberry"; and *Don't Forget the Bacon!* (Hutchins, 1976), in which "a cake for tea" becomes "a cape for me" becomes "a rake for leaves." Additional activities that foster phonemic awareness using books that emphasize rhyme or alliteration include asking learners to listen for a particular sound during the oral reading and clap when they hear it. Students can also be asked to repeat the sound. Or students can engage in extensions of the book's focus (see the Arts Connection feature for this chapter). Pictures showing words that rhyme can be cut from magazines. Thumbs up/thumbs down as an every-pupil response technique that serves as a quick check of student understanding can be used with rhyming words to indicate yes, the words rhyme, or no, they do not, respectively. Card games showing pictures of rhyming words can be created, and matches can be sought to form pairs. Students can also work in small groups, or in a learning center, to sort objects that rhyme to reinforce the concept of rhyme. The MyEducationLab video clip "Matching Sounds" shows this activity for the rhyming words: *man, pan, van; rat, cat, bat;* and *dog, log, hog.*

The emphasis of these activities is on hearing and reproducing the sounds that students will need to match to printed symbols in order to decode. Once learners understand the concept of *word* ("I am going to say two words, and I want you to tell me which word is longer: *dinosaur* or *dog.*"), recognizing rhymes is the easiest phonemic awareness task, followed by producing rhyming words. Syllable-level tasks are easier than phoneme-level tasks ("Clap the parts of the word *cowboy.*" [/clap/ /clap/ = *cow + boy*] versus "How many sounds do you hear in cowboy?" [4 = /k/ + /ow/ + /b/ + /oy/]). Also, blending syllables and beginning sounds ("Put /st/ and /ick/ together to get the word *stick*") is easier than segmenting sounds as in the previous example. Substituting and manipulating beginning sounds is easier than substituting and manipulating middle and ending phonemes (*make* to *bake* as in a previous example versus *make* to *Mike* or *make* to *man*).

To emphasize the sounds in words, use a "rubber-banding" technique: the teacher stretches out the sounds within the word while keeping the sounds connected (for example, "mmmuuuunnnkkkkeeee"). Have the students count the sounds they hear in these rubber-banded words. Again, an every-pupil response technique can be employed for a group of students by providing them with a set of five cards that have the numbers

Go to MyEducationLab and select the topic *Phonemic Awareness and Phonics.* Then, go to the Activities and Applications section, and watch the video entitled "Matching Sounds" to observe how work with rhyming words can also expand oral language. Next respond to the accompanying questions.

Figure 7.2   Using Elkonin Boxes for Phonemic Awareness

The teacher pronounces a word, stretching out the sounds so the student can determine how many sounds are heard in the word. The student then puts a marker into a box for each sound heard, while repeating the word and stretching out its sounds. For example:

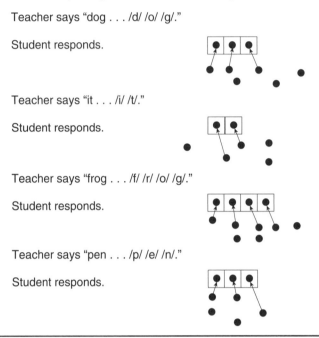

Teacher says "dog . . . /d/ /o/ /g/."

Student responds.

Teacher says "it . . . /i/ /t/."

Student responds.

Teacher says "frog . . . /f/ /r/ /o/ /g/."

Student responds.

Teacher says "pen . . . /p/ /e/ /n/."

Student responds.

1, 2, 3, 4, and 5 on them so they can hold up the appropriate card for the number of sounds they hear.

A variation of counting sounds is the use of Elkonin boxes (named after a Russian researcher). The learner places a marker (a button or a coin) in a box for each sound heard in a word pronounced orally (see Figure 7.2). Pictures can also represent words at first, and eventually the word itself can be used to begin a transition to phonics. This transition will also help the learner realize the **alphabetic principle**: understanding that each speech sound or phoneme has its own distinctive graphic representation, or **grapheme**. The results of the Elkonin boxes activity can be expanded to a graphing activity (see Figure 7.3).

An activity for blending sounds that would engage the bodily-kinesthetic learner is called *arm blending* (Fox, 2000). This refers to the motion of sweeping one arm down the length of the other as the sounds in a word are being pronounced. The motion parallels what the voice does when blending sounds together. Connecting each sound to a placement on the arm also seems to help the learner remember where the sound occurs in the word for spelling purposes. For example, to blend /h/ /o/ /t/, place the hand on the opposite shoulder and say /h/, slide the hand down to the elbow and say /o/, and finally down to the wrist to say /t/. These same activities can be made appropriate for older learners by using song lyrics instead of Dr. Seuss books, or age-appropriate magazine or catalog pictures (see Yopp & Yopp, 1996). For additional activities related to phonemic awareness, go to MyEducationLab and select the topic "Instructional Decision Making." Then analyze the case study, "Early Reading

Figure 7.3   Graphing Sounds Heard in 20 Words Following the Use of Elkonin Boxes

Following the Elkonin box activity seen in Figure 7.2, students can gain additional practice identifying the number of sounds in words by completing a graph. This graphing activity would be especially appealing for the student with a strength in the logical-mathematical intelligence. The 20 words used for the Elkonin box activity were: *dog, it, pen, frog, treat, she, lamb, clock, see, cake, pot, Dad, fish, fly, boat, nest, book, brick, lunch, the.*

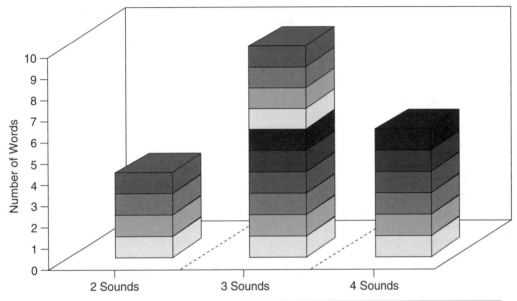

(Level A—Cases 1, 2, and 3)." Be sure to refer to the STAR sheets for strategies related to phonemic awareness.

LETTER RECOGNITION

Regardless of a child's background, all children enter school with a rich store of language experiences on which to build literacy skills. For example, most children entering kindergarten can read their name or can recognize environmental print such as Wal-Mart or the McDonald's golden arches logo. Experts in children's emergent literacy behaviors also note that young children spontaneously engage in pretend reading and writing in their individual and group play. For example, when my friend's granddaughter was 3 years old, she enjoyed role-playing the part of a McDonald's waitress. She "wrote" her family's orders for Big Macs and Happy Meals, "read" the orders, and "served" the food. As described earlier in this chapter, kindergarten teachers commonly set up classroom centers that encourage this kind of role-playing activity (for example, writing telephone messages, preparing a grocery list, writing letters or e-mail messages.). However, to read and write, children need to know the symbols used in English reading and writing. They need to know the letters of the alphabet. In fact, knowledge of the letters of the alphabet remains a strong predictor of future success in reading (Snow, Burns, & Griffin, 1998). Manis, Lindsey, and Bailey (2004) found this to be true not only for native English speakers but for native Spanish speakers as well. In a study of English language learners in kindergarten and first grade, Manis and colleagues found phonemic awareness, letter knowledge, and rapid automatic naming of

Go to MyEducationLab and select the topic *Instructional Decision Making*. Then, go to the Activities and Applications section, read the case study entitled "Early Reading (Level A—Cases 1, 2, and 3)," and respond to the accompanying questions.

letters in both English and Spanish to be significant predictors of early decoding in English. Teachers are responsible for finding out what their young students know about letters and to proceed from there with effective instructional techniques.

Assessment for Letter Recognition

In about 5 to 10 minutes, the teacher can determine which letters the child knows and can identify. All letters, in both upper- and lowercase format, should be assessed. However, the letters should not be presented in the order of the alphabet. All the capital letters should be presented first, then the lowercase letters. The letters could be placed on separate index cards or on a sheet of paper. If presented on cards, the cards should be put into two groups: capital letters and lowercase letters. Prior to showing each card, make sure the letters are not presented in alphabetical order. If presented on paper (see Figure 7.4), be sure the child moves from left to right to identify the letters so that the letters are treated in a random order and the rows that remain can be kept covered by another piece of blank paper.

There are several ways to administer a letter recognition assessment, but in all of them the use of the word *letter* in any questions should be avoided. In other words, when showing a letter card, ask, "What do you call this?" rather than "What letter is this?" When showing the paper, introduce the task by asking, "What do you call these?" while sweeping a hand under a row of letters. Then ask, "Do you see any that you know in this top row?" If a child does not respond, point to a letter and ask from among the following: "What is this one?" "Do you know its name?" "What sound does it make?" "Do you know a word that starts like that?" If a child still hesitates, start with the first letter of the child's name, and then proceed again to the cards or paper presentation. The entire page of letters could also be shown (or all the cards displayed) and the child asked, "Can you find some that you know?" Be sure to prepare a scoring summary sheet that lists the letters along with the possible types of responses (for example, alphabet response, sound response, word, or incorrect) and record the child's responses

Figure 7.4	Format for Presenting Letters of the Alphabet for Letter Recognition Assessment				
A	J	K	T	U	Z
B	I	L	S	V	
C	H	M	R	W	
D	G	N	Q	X	
E	F	O	P	Y	
a	j	k	t	u	z
b	i	l	s	v	a
c	h	m	r	w	
d	g	n	q	x	
e	f	o	p	y	g

as well as the date of administration and any other relevant information or comments (such as letter confusions, unknown letters, knows capitals only, comments on behavior or volunteered information). By the end of kindergarten, most children know all the letters, though some children are confused by *b* and *d*, or *C* and *S* (Mason & Stewart, 1990).

If a standardized measure is preferred, *The Preschool Word and Print Awareness Assessment* (PWPA) (Justice, Bowles, & Skibbe, 2006) measures alphabet knowledge and print concepts. Also, the *Bracken-R* (*BBCS-R*), (Bracken,1998) which measures children's receptive language skills, basic concept acquisition, and preacademic skills through 11 subtests, includes a subtest for letter recognition. (The other subtests are color, numbers/counting, sizes, comparisons, shapes, quantity, direction/position, texture/material, time/sequence, and self/social awareness.) The letter recognition subtest is administered individually and takes about 10 minutes.

Instruction for Letter Recognition

A natural way to begin teaching letters of the alphabet is by supporting the emergent writings of young children. Teachers encourage their **emergent writers** (beginning writers) to write any words, alphabet letters, numbers, or symbols they know, or to convey a message by scribbling or drawing a picture (see Figure 7.5). Such writing samples reveal what students know about letters and words, so they are also useful for assessment purposes. If students are reluctant to write because they say they cannot spell, or if they request help in spelling, their teachers should encourage them to use **invented spelling** or **constructed spelling** (also called **temporary spelling**) by saying, "It's OK to spell words your own way for now. When you are finished writing, we can read your story together. We can then look at how the words are spelled." As discussed in Chapter 8, spelling is important but should not be a major emphasis for emergent writers. By inventing their spellings, children are exploring how the writing and spelling systems work and will be more receptive to learning the letters and how to form them. It would be helpful at this point to examine several writing artifacts produced by emergent writers in preschool through grade 2.

Chapter 8 further discusses the stages of spelling and the connections between reading and writing. Chapter 9 discusses associating printed letters with the speech sounds they represent (that is, phonics).

As children engage in pretend reading and writing they come to focus on individual letters. But there is no reason to wait for children to show this level of readiness before teaching the letters of the alphabet. The individual letters should be directly taught in a variety of ways as soon as possible. Some recommendations follow:

1. Teach the child to become familiar with the letters in his own name, beginning with the first letter, which represents the uppercase form. Using the child's name and the names of classmates is a motivating way to practice recognizing letters. "Your name, Maria, begins with the letter *M*. This is the capital *M*. The other letters in your name are in lowercase. Can you look at our list of classmates' names and find other names that begin with a capital *M*? . . . Yes, there is one more name besides yours. It is Mark. Mark also starts with a capital *M*." To view another way to work with students' names, view the MyEducationLab video clip "*Name Lotto*" in MyEducationLab by selecting the topic "Informal Assessments." Notice how the teacher points to each letter in the child's name as it is said and color-codes in red the capital letters

Go to MyEducationLab and select the topic *Spelling*. Then, go to the Activities and Applications section, and compare the artifacts entitled "Linear Repetitive Stage (Preschool)" and "Linear Repetitive Stage—Advanced (Preschool)" with the artifacts entitled "Random Letter Stage (Preschool)" and "Random Letter Stage with Illustration (K–2)." What makes "Linear Repetitive Stage—Advanced (Preschool)" more advanced than "Linear Repetitive Stage (Preschool)"? What knowledge has the writer developed in "Random Letter Stage (Preschool)" and "Random Letter Stage with Illustration (K–2)"? Respond to the accompanying questions.

To view another way to work with students' names, go to MyEducationLab and select the topic *Informal Assessments*. Then, go to the Activities and Applications section, watch the video entitled "Name Lotto," and respond to the accompanying questions.

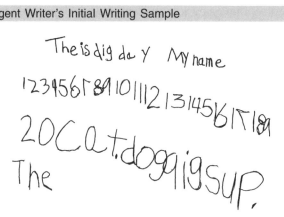

Figure 7.5   Emergent Writer's Initial Writing Sample

---

at the beginning of a child's name and the rest of the letters in black (for example, Emma). Also, notice how the teacher deals with different spellings of the same name (for example, *Nicholas* versus *Nicolas*).

2. Capitalize on any words the child recognizes in his or her environment. Popular culture environmental print can effectively be used to teach letters of the alphabet (Dyson, 2003; Vera, 2007). Children are exposed to many examples of popular culture environmental print (including toys, posters, clothing labels, food and beverage labels, and games, as well as the media—television, video games). These examples can all be used to explicitly teach alphabet letters. For example, the character Nemo can be used in place of Jack in the familiar nursery rhyme: Nemo be nimble, Nemo be quick, Nemo swim over the candlestick. The cartoon character of Goofy can be sung to the tune of B-I-N-G-O (Curtis, 2007). The first letters in characters' names can be taught as capital letters (for example, Aladdin, Big Bird, Cinderella, and the like).

3. Teach the alphabet song while pointing to the letters on a transparency or on the wall. Then provide individual copies of the alphabet for each student to keep at her or his desk or worktables.

4. Play letter-matching games in which a letter is matched with a picture of an object beginning with that letter.

5. Develop word walls (see Chapter 9) with pictures of objects whose first letter represents each letter of the alphabet.

6. Availability of computers and their keyboards will support letter recognition. Invest in software programs that emphasize learning alphabet letters (such as *Dr. Peet's Talk/Writer,* published by Interest-Driven Learning and Software, or MacKiev's adaptation of *Dr. Seuss's ABC* book. For a demo of the Dr. Seuss soft-

ware visit www.mackiev.com/abc.html). Video games are also possibilities for making connections to letters and writing in general (Compton-Lilly, 2007; Gee, 2003)

7. Share the wide variety of available alphabet books (Bradley & Jones, 2007) (see Figure 7.6 for a brief list of some popular alphabet books).

Once the letters of the alphabet are known, emergent readers and writers must also be taught letter formation; so early literacy instruction must include teaching students not only what the letters of the alphabet are but also how to write the letters. By actually forming letters with their bodies, children can learn the shapes of the letters. They can trace sandpaper letters or letters written in crayon so they can feel the shape of the letters they trace. As they learn to write the letters and learn a few words, they can begin to spell those

MI Connection: bodily-kinesthetic

SPOTLIGHT ON ENGLISH LEARNERS

Word Configuration Boxes

Similar to the cheerleader spelling idea presented in Chapter 9, word configuration boxes help English learners (ELs) visualize the orthography of the English language. Useful not only for letter formation but for spelling and for visual patterns that onsets and rimes provide, word configuration boxes draw attention to these visual elements.

Write each word in the correct word box. The first one is done for you.

1. walk
2. judge
3. fasten
4. could
5. knife
6. write
7. bridge
8. half
9. lodge
10. edge
11. should
12. thumb
13. watch
14. sign
15. wrong

| **Figure 7.6** | Short List of Popular Alphabet Books |

Alda, F. A. (1994). *Gathering the sun: An alphabet in Spanish and English.* New York: Lothrop, Lee & Shepard Books. *Through beautiful illustrations, their book celebrates migrant farm workers and their language and culture; a wonderful addition for a multicultural classroom.*

Anno, M. (1975). *Anno's alphabet.* New York: Crowell. *This is a classic alphabet book.*

Dr. Seuss. (1963, 1991). *Dr. Seuss's ABC.* New York: Random House. *This widely popular alphabet book is also available as an interactive software program.*

Ehlert, L. (1989). *Eating the alphabet: Fruits and vegetables from A to Z.* New York: Harcourt. *This book shows both upper- and lowercase letters when labeling drawings of foods and lends itself to follow-up books using many other topics, such as "swimming with the alphabet: creatures of the sea from A to Z."*

Geisert, A. (1986). *Pigs from A to Z.* Boston: Houghton Mifflin. *Pencil sketches of pigs form the letters of the alphabet with their bodies. Geisert has a series of books with pigs as the focus.*

Grover, M. (1998). *The accidental zucchini: An unexpected alphabet.* San Diego: Voyager/Harcourt. *The author provides unusual alliterative two-word descriptions for each letter of the alphabet, such as* apple autos *and* zigzag zoo.

Horenstein, H. (1999). *Arf! Beg! Catch! Dogs from A to Z.* New York: Scholastic. *Alphabet letters are associated with words related to dogs.*

Howland, N. (2000). *ABC drive!* Boston: Clarion. *A boy on a drive with his mother encounters objects along the way in ABC order; an ambulance, a bus, and so forth. A similar pattern book could be created by the class for many topics—ABC zoo; ABC farm; ABC ocean.*

Musgrove, M. (1976). *Ashanti to Zulu: African traditions.* New York: Dial. *This one is a great addition for classrooms of cultural diversity.*

Pallotta, J. (1989). *The yucky reptile alphabet book.* New York: Bantam Doubleday.

Pallotta, J. (1991). *The dinosaur alphabet book.* New York: Dell. *Pallotta has a series of alphabet books, each with themes children love (also, The icky bug book).*

Sandhaus, E. (1999). 26 of the most interesting letters in the alphabet. New York: Paul Sandhaus Associates, Inc. *This author asks children to think about the shapes of the letters.*

Snow, A. (1994). *The monster book of ABC sounds.* New York: Puffin. *This is a nice transition book for moving from letters to the sounds they make.*

Go to MyEducationLab and select the topic *Reading and Writing Connections.* Then, go to the Activities and Applications section, and watch the video entitled "Writing and Reading" to observe how Ms. Gold uses writing to teach her kindergarten students about letters, words, and print conventions. Next respond to the accompanying questions.

words according to whether the letter ascends, descends, or stays within the lines on lined paper (see Cheerleader Spelling in Chapter 9). Daily exposure to writing has a positive influence on print knowledge (Snell, 2007). Ms. Gold, a kindergarten teacher, demonstrates several ways that writing can be used for teaching letters and learning words and print conventions in the MyEducationLab video clip "Writing and Reading." A more thorough treatment of the impact writing has on learning to read is presented in Chapter 8.

Summary

The early literacy areas of oral language development, understanding print conventions and book handling, phonemic awareness, and letter recognition are the focus of Chapter 7. Recommendations for both assessment and instruction are provided for each of these areas. The topics discussed in this chapter form the basis for literacy development and should be considered as potential areas in need of development when a learner struggles with literacy tasks.

Recommended Websites

Emergent Literacy: Synthesis of the Research
  http://idea.uoregon.edu/~ncite/documents/techrep/
  tech19.html
This is a thorough review of the research on the relationship between early childhood literacy experiences and later reading acquisition.

Assessment of Literacy Development in Early Childhood
  http://cela.albany.edu/publication/article/johnrogers.htm
The Primary Language Record (PLR) is discussed at this site.

Using Multiple Methods of Beginning Reading Instruction
  www.reading.org/resources/issues/positions_
  multiple_methods.html
The International Reading Association provides its position statement about reading methodology for beginning readers here.

Center for the Improvement of Early Reading Achievement
  www.ciera.org
This site maintains archival reports about innovative emergent literacy programs.

Topics in Early Reading Conference
  www.sedl.org/reading/topics
Short papers on topics in early reading from the Southwest Educational Development Laboratory can be found on this site.

Between the Lions
  www.pbskids.org/lions
This is the website for the popular PBS literacy program for ages 3 through 7.

Phonemic Awareness and the Teaching of Reading
  www.reading.org/resources/issues/positions_
  phonemic.html
The International Reading Association presents its position of phonemic awareness and reading here.

Patti's Electronic Classroom
  http://teams.lacoe.edu/documentation/classrooms/patti/
  k-1/activities/phonemic.html
Phonemic awareness activities for the kindergarten and grade 1 classroom are on this site.

A Goldmine of Phonics and Phonemic Awareness Worksheets
  www.tampareads.com/phonics/phonicsindex.htm
This site provides links to 56 phonics and phonemic awareness worksheets.

MyEducationLab is a research-based learning tool that brings teaching to life. Go to the Gipe 7th Edition MyEducationLab for Reading Assessment site at www.myeducationlab.com to:

- Engage in multimedia exercises to help you build a deeper and more applied understanding of chapter content.
- Use extensive resources including videos from real classrooms, Praxis and licensure preparation, a lesson plan builder, and materials to help you in your teaching career.

The Reading/Writing Connection and the Writing Process

Janet C. Richards
University of South Florida

OBJECTIVES	*After you have read this chapter, you should be able to:*

1. Explain how reading and writing are mutually supportive processes and how writers gain valuable knowledge about reading.
2. Discuss the importance of a writing program for students who struggle.
3. Define the role of an effective writing teacher.
4. Explain how to implement writing lessons and activities in a comprehensive literacy program.
5. Define and explain the differences and benefits of nonstructured, collaborative, teacher-guided, and creative writing.
6. Explain the relationship between writing instruction and writing assessment.
7. Discuss the value of helping students learn to assess their own writing.

VOCABULARY ALERT

analytic scoring
artifacts
author's chair
collaborative writing
conventional spelling
creative writing
electronic portfolios
genre
holistic scoring

language conventions
nonstructured writing
personal dictionary
portfolios
quickwrites
recursive nature of
   writing
rehearsal
rubric scoring

showcase portfolio
symbol systems
teacher-guided writing
   lessons
voices of composing
working portfolio
writer's workshop
writing process

Connecting the literacy learning modalities of reading and writing makes sense. Both are thinking, meaning-making processes. Each supports, complements, and contributes to the other's development; that is, knowledge of reading does not precede knowledge of writing, and writing promotes reading. Writers read extensively to gain information about writing topics and to revise their writing. They also read when they write collaboratively with a partner and when they share their work with others.

Writers become familiar with different *language functions* (purposes) and **genre** (styles) or **symbol systems** (any form of writing that offers meaning) such as poetry, grocery lists, news articles, personal diaries, letters of invitation, stories, reports, and Web pages. Further, as they write, observe others writing, and read, they construct knowledge about **language conventions** such as spelling, punctuation, capitalization, and paragraphing. For example, as one 6-year-old journaled with her teacher, she commented, "I'm making dots at the end of sentences just like you do." Another student in second grade recently became aware of quotation marks. "I know you don't put these marks around every word," he told his teacher. "I think you only do that when people say something."

Writers are "less likely to be intimidated by written language" (Newkirk, 1982, p. 457). By becoming authors themselves, students learn that written language can be changed, deleted, or expanded. It is not something that is rigid and beyond criticism. Studies show that in classrooms where students write extensively, reading scores go up (Graves & Murray, 1980). "Daily writing promotes and enhances reading" (Dionisio, 1989, p. 747).

It is especially important to connect reading and writing instruction for students who struggle. Many of these learners have had few positive writing experiences, or they are not comfortable enough with the English language to write in English. Because reading and writing develop simultaneously, and strengthen and build on each other, it is imperative that students who struggle have opportunities to write and observe others as they write (Wiseman, 1992). For these (and all) learners, "reading and writing instruction shouldn't be separated, nor should writing instruction be postponed until students are able readers" (Rhodes & Dudley-Marling, 1988, p. 14).

THE ROLE OF TEACHERS IN AN EFFECTIVE WRITING PROGRAM

The role of teachers in an effective writing program is to model writing and writing processes for their students. Good writing teachers are writers themselves (Graves, 1988; Solley, 2000). They are enthusiastic about writing and wholeheartedly believe their students can learn to write well. They know it takes time to move through a **writing process**—deliberate writing that includes prewriting/rehearsal, drafting/composing, revising, editing, and publishing/sharing—so they give their students the time and resources they need to write. These teachers also know that writing creatively is a complex, problem-solving process in which writers move back and forth between planning, composing, and revising their work. They recognize and support the developmental nature of spelling and know where their students are along the developmental spelling continuum. Good writing teachers understand that students learn how to spell in conventional ways by engaging in meaningful reading and writing activities. They understand that the "stage of writing is set by what the teacher does, not by what the teacher says" (Graves, 1988, p. 12). Therefore, teachers learn about writing along with their students. They demonstrate and model the various functions of writing and freely share their writing experiences.

Good writing teachers also understand that students learn about writing by writing for their own purposes and audiences as part of a larger community of language users. Consequently, they never require their students to complete meaningless, isolated writing tasks, such as copying sentences from the board or writing weekly spelling words five times each. Instead, they create a learning context in which students feel free to take risks, experiment with writing, and use writing to communicate meaning (Graham, MacArthur, & Fitzgerald, 2007). Most important, good writing teachers know that "the key to helping readers [and writers] in trouble is to help them revalue themselves as language learners and users" (Goodman, 1982, p. 88).

IMPLEMENTING THE WRITING PROGRAM

Students in an effective writing program begin writing, and thinking and talking about writing, from their first day of the school year. To get an idea about the general writing abilities of each new group of students, their teachers might invite them to write an informal letter or story on a subject of their choice (Figure 8.1). Effective writing teachers never tell students what to write but encourage them to self-select their writing topics, using their own ideas to write about what is important to them. As the students write, their teachers continually reassure them that their daily writing samples will not be graded but will be used to help plan future writing lessons and activities. As discussed later in this chapter, spelling is important but should not be a concern until students are working on final drafts of their writing.

Figure 8.1 Antonia's Story for Assessing General Writing Abilities

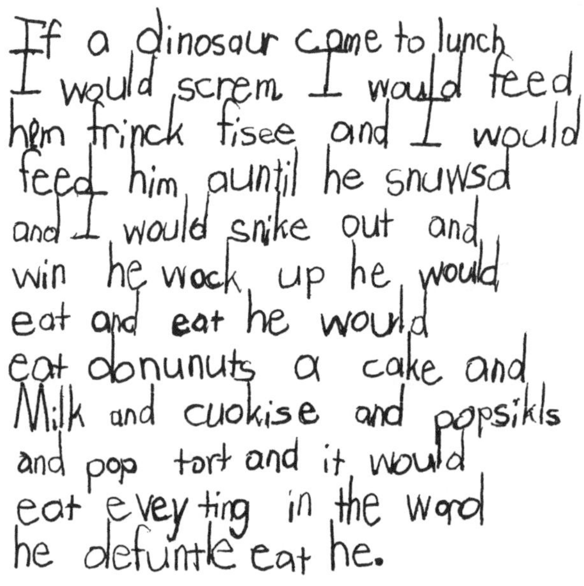
If a dinosaur came to lunch
I would screm I would feed
hem frinck fisee and I would
feed him auntil he snuwsd
and I would snike out and
win he wack up he would
eat and eat he would
eat donunuts a cake and
Milk and cuokise and popsikls
and pop tort and it would
eat evey ting in the word
he defuntle eat he.

Observations, Initial Assessments, and Instructional Decisions

As the students write, their teachers carefully observe and make notes about each student's writing behaviors ("John reread and revised his story"; "Melissa spoke aloud to herself as she wrote"; "Matt erased extensively and used body language indicating that he was anxious and frustrated about writing"; "Andy planned his composition using his artistic abilities. He drew pictures"). Later, teachers analyze the writing samples (Figure 8.2), guided by a developmental writing checklist (Appendix S).

Figure 8.2   Teacher's Analysis of Antonia's First Writing Sample

ANTONIA

Antonia is 8 years old. Her completed composition follows a logical progression and is interesting and enjoyable for the reader. Antonia wrote in both the expressive and imaginative voices. She wrote about herself (that is, "I"), and created an imaginary story about a dinosaur. Antonia used conventional and transitional spelling (e.g., "screm" (scream), "hem" (him), "frinck fisee" (french fries), "auntil" (until), "snuwsd" (snoozed), "snike" (sneak), "wock" (woke), "donunuts" (doughnuts), "cuokise" (cookies), "pop tort" (Pop Tarts), "eveyting" (everything), "word" (world), "defuntle" (definitely). Antonia wrote legibly and formed graphemes correctly. She capitalized the first word of the composition and *I* appropriately.

Antonia did not use a plan for writing. She completed her first draft and did not reread or revise. Antonia did not write for a specific audience. She did not title her composition nor include any punctuation until the end of the composition. The entire piece consists of one long sentence with "and" used as a connector throughout.

INITIAL INSTRUCTIONAL DECISIONS

1. Encourage Antonia to participate in many nonstructured writing activities. She expresses herself well and combines *voices* effectively. Encourage her creativity and help her write for her own purposes and for her own audiences.
2. Develop Antonia's awareness of *audience* (that is, to whom is she writing?).
3. One of Antonia's immediate writing needs is using appropriate punctuation. In structured writing activities, point out the use of punctuation. Explain to Antonia how punctuation helps readers understand an author's writing.
4. Consider initiating a small unit on dinosaurs. Antonia is very interested in this topic.
5. Antonia is a good storyteller. She would probably enjoy participating in *add a paragraph/write a book*.
6. Model use of punctuation in dialogue journal activities.
7. Use teacher dictation to help draw Antonia's attention to punctuation.
8. Antonia would probably enjoy reading about dinosaurs. Assemble a literature collection composed of dinosaur books (fiction, nonfiction, poetry, jokes).
9. Antonia's story could contain two paragraphs (for example, first paragraph: "If a dinosaur came to lunch I would scream. I would feed him french fries and I would feed him until he snoozed"). Use teacher-guided activities and introduce *cohesive paragraphs* to demonstrate the concept of paragraphing.
10. Antonia uses interesting, descriptive vocabulary (such as snoozed and definitely*)*. Compliment Antonia on the use of interesting words. Consider *rephrasing* activities.
11. When reading, draw Antonia's attention to titles of stories and books. Discuss how authors choose titles for their work. Discuss why authors title their compositions, stories, and books.
12. Perhaps Antonia would like to learn the conventional spelling of some of the descriptive words she used in her composition.
13. Continue to observe Antonia daily to revise and extend instructional decisions.

Also on the first day, or early in the school year, effective writing teachers attempt to determine their students' perceptions about writing by recording students' responses to questions on a writing perception survey (Appendix T). The teachers then carefully reflect on the three sources of information (observation notes, writing sample analysis, and students' responses to questions on the writing perception survey) to get a sense of what each student knows and thinks about written language. This information, coupled with data gathered from an informal reading inventory and an interest survey (refer to Chapter 6), gives teachers insight into each student's literacy development, interests, and experiences.

But students' writing abilities and their understanding about writing grow daily. Therefore, ongoing observation is necessary. To ascertain each student's ever-changing writing (and reading) instructional needs, teachers find a rich source of information in paying close attention to students as they respond to instruction.

Nonstructured Writing Activities

MI Connection:
spatial;
interpersonal

There are always personally important reasons to write during the school day. When writing is a natural and purposeful activity, everyone wants to write. For instance, a student may decide to take stock of all the books he has written (Figure 8.3); a group may create a mural illustrating and telling a favorite story; two friends may spontaneously exchange informal notes concerning their feelings (Figure 8.4); or a student may write a list of rules for her friends to follow when they come to her house to play (Figure 8.5). These types of **nonstructured writing** activities are "primarily student-centered with pupils writing about what is of most interest and concern to them" (Templeton, 1991, p. 218). By participating in nonstructured writing activities, students gain knowledge about written language without direct instruction. Nonstructured writing activities also help foster a supportive, risk-free environment that in turn encourages students to write.

Figure 8.3	Student's Writing Record

Here is all my books I wrotin.

Beauty and the Beast.
The Lizrd.
Michelle and the Casle.
The rabbit who had no friends.
The cat who ate all the fish.
Once I was taking a nap.
My bedroom and bed.

All my dogs.

Figure 8.4   Informal Notes between Two Students

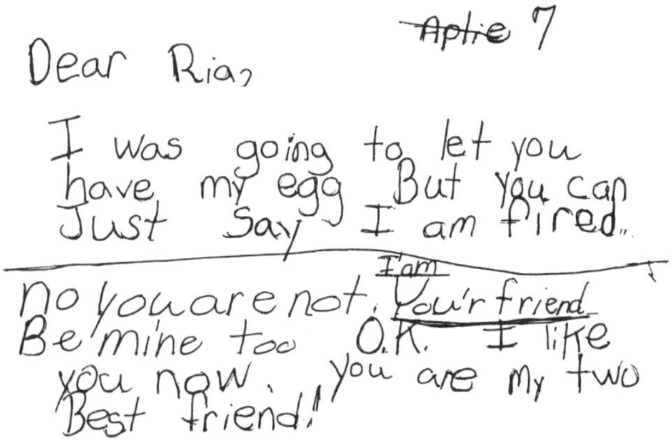

Dear Ria,   Aptie 7

I was going to let you
have my egg But you can
Just Say I am fired...

no you are not. You'r friend
Be mine too O.K. I like
you now. you are my two
Best friend!

Structured Writing Lessons and Activities

Throughout the school year students also engage in more structured writing lessons and activities that can be categorized as (a) collaborative writing, (b) teacher-guided writing, and (c) creative writing. In these more focused writing endeavors, "the [student's] purposes come first but the teacher deliberately creates a setting in which writing in different forms can be perceived as useful" (Nathan et al., 1989, p. 93).

Figure 8.5   Betsy's List of Rules for Her Room

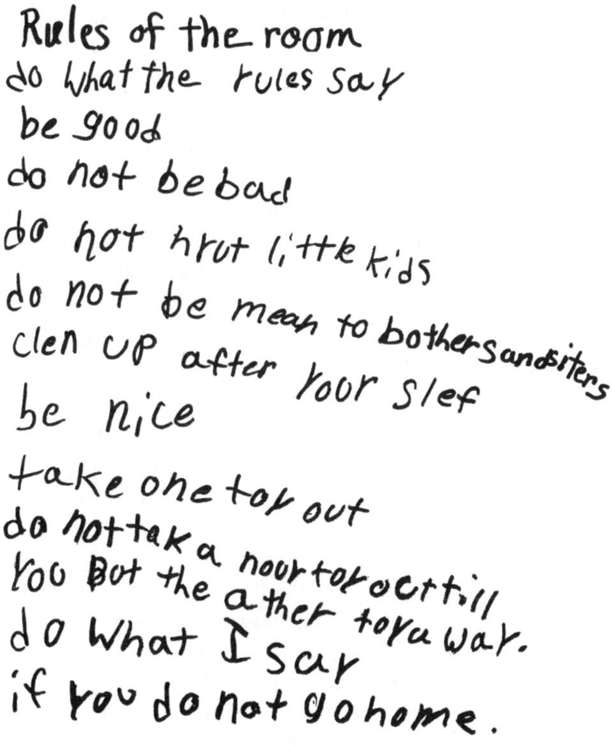

Rules of the room
do what the rules say
be good
do not be bad
do not hrut little kids
do not be mean to bothers and sriters
clen up after your slef
be nice

take one toy out
do not tak a noor toy oer till
You put the ather toy a way.
do what I say
if you do not go home.

Go to MyEducationLab and first select the topic *Assessing Reading and Writing*. Go to the Activities and Applications section, watch the video entitled "Writing Process: Editing," and respond to the accompanying questions. Then select the topic *Reading and Writing Connections*. Go to the Activities and Applications section, watch the video entitled "Writing Workshop Mini-Lesson in 2nd Grade," and respond to the accompanying questions. Observe various portions of Writer's Workshop in action in both videos.

MI Connection: interpersonal

MI Connection: spatial

Go to MyEducationLab and select the topic *Teaching with Literature*. Then, go to the Activities and Applications section, and watch the video entitled "Mini-Lesson: Teaching 1st Graders to Add Detail" to observe how this teacher is introducing young writers to the concept of voice in their writing. Next respond to the accompanying questions.

Any of these structured writing activities can occur within a classroom organization known as writer's (or writing) workshop (Graves, 1983). **Writer's workshop** simply refers to a structured, predictable time for students to become involved in writing and for teachers to provide direct writing instruction, usually through minilessons. When a classroom is organized for writer's workshop, the physical arrangement allows for purposeful movement by the students. For example, some students might meet together to share their drafts and discuss ideas for revision. Other students work alone on writing or explore some reference materials. One or two students might type a first draft at a classroom computer or prepare a final draft. There are many interpretations of writer's workshop, and teachers execute writing workshops in a wide variety of ways.

Collaborative Writing Activities. Language is facilitated in social situations that include genuine conversations (Bloome & Egan-Robertson, 1993; Pappas, Kiefer, & Levstik, 1999). **Collaborative writing** activities give students opportunities to enjoy writing with a partner or a group of friends and sometimes a teacher who serves as a role model (see also the section on interactive writing in Chapter 7). When writers plan, discuss, respond to one another, and write together, they spark one another's creativity and become less anxious about individual performance. Five collaborative writing activities that students particularly enjoy are (a) write a sentence/make a story, (b) add a word/stretch the sentence, (c) change a word/change the sentence, (d) add a paragraph/write a book, and (e) dialogue journaling. Teachers model each of these activities for their students, perhaps during a minilesson, before having their students participate.

Write a Sentence/Make a Story. This activity links reading and writing and helps develop students' understanding of *basic story features* and their connections (characters, setting, problems, and solutions). To begin this activity, three to five students and a teacher, student teacher, or classroom aide sit in a circle around a table. On a large sheet of paper each participant writes his or her idea for the first sentence of an imaginative story. If there are six participants, there are six different sentences (for example, "Joanne got a rabbit for her birthday" or "Shane loved to play baseball"). Participants then pass their papers to the person on their right, who reads the sentence and then adds a second sentence to the story ("One day Joanne took her rabbit to the playground" or "Shane played baseball every day with his friends").

Participants continue passing their papers, adding one additional sentence to each of the stories until they receive their original papers. Group members may pass their papers around the circle a second or third time if they decide that their stories need further development. Emergent writers, those just beginning their writing development regardless of age (see Chapter 7), participate in write a sentence/make a story by drawing sentence pictures or dictating their sentence ideas to their teacher, an aide, or an older child.

At the end of the activity, participants read their collaboratively created stories aloud for everyone's enjoyment. Teachers might also lead a discussion about the characters, setting, problems, and solutions in each story and how these basic story elements connect to one another. Figure 8.6 shows an example of a collaborative story between a classroom tutor and two students.

Add a Word/Stretch the Sentence. This activity promotes a reading and writing connection, helps students construct knowledge about the subtle interplay and interconnectedness of *syntax* and *semantics* (word order in sentences and meaning, respectively), improves students' control of written syntax, and helps students construct more elaborate written sentences in the various **voices of composing** to include the expository voice.

Figure 8.6   Example of a Collaborative Story

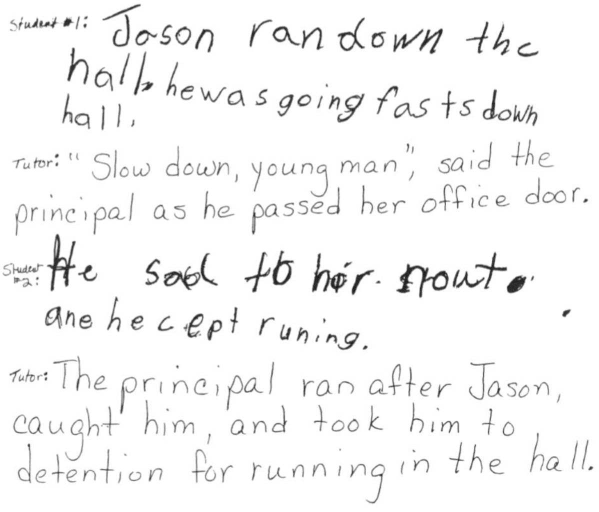

Student #1: Jason ran down the hall, he was going fasts down hall.

Tutor: "Slow down, young man", said the principal as he passed her office door.

Student #2: He said to her. snout. ane he cept runing.

Tutor: The principal ran after Jason, caught him, and took him to detention for running in the hall.

To start the activity, students and the teacher or other helping adult sit in a circle around a table. On a large sheet of paper each participant creates a beginning sentence of a written discourse in any *composing voice*. For example, "I love science class" is written in the *expressive voice;* "The zoo has a dinosaur exhibit" is written in the *expository voice;* "Once there lived three little puppies" is written in the *imaginative* or *poetic voice* (see Britton et al., 1975, for a thorough discussion of voices of composition). Next, participants pass their papers to the person on their right, who reads the last sentence and rewrites it, adding one additional word in any appropriate place in the sentence (for example, "I really love science class" or "The zoo has opened a dinosaur exhibit"). Emergent writers participate in this activity by dictating their original sentence and each of their "stretched" sentence ideas to their teacher, helping adult, or an older child.

At the end of the activity, participants take turns reading aloud their original sentence and each of the "stretched" sentences for the group's enjoyment. They also discuss how the meaning of each original sentence was expanded or changed (Figure 8.7). Teachers also look for opportunities to teach other skills (such as *everyday* versus *every day*).

Go to MyEducationLab and select the topic *Emergent Literacy*. Then, go to the Activities and Applications section, and watch the video entitled "Additional Sentences" to see an example of the Add a Word/Stretch the Sentence technique. Next respond to the accompanying questions.

Figure 8.7   Example of "Stretched" Sentence

Nan can read.
Nan can read Books
Nan can read many books
Everyday Nan can read many books.

Change a Word/Change the Sentence. This activity links reading and writing and helps students develop understanding of parts of speech, synonyms and antonyms, and the relationship and connections between syntax and semantics.

To begin the activity, a small group of students and their teacher sit in a circle around a table. Each participant has a large sheet of paper and a pencil. The teacher and students each write a sentence on their papers, such as, "There was a young boy in Florida who loved to play." Participants pass their papers to the person on their right who reads the sentence and rewrites it, changing one word in any appropriate place. Participants keep passing their papers until they receive their original papers, or they may pass their papers twice, if appropriate. Then, they take turns reading their original and changed sentences aloud for everyone's enjoyment. At this time teachers have opportunities to lead discussions about parts of speech, geographical terms, and other concepts portrayed in the changed sentences. For example, in one group of second graders, the original sentence, "There was a young boy in Florida who loved to play" changed into the following sentences as the students passed their papers twice:

> There was a young boy in <u>Mexico</u> who loved to play.
> There was a young <u>girl</u> in Mexico who loved to play.
> There was a young <u>man</u> in Mexico who loved to play.
> There was a young man in <u>Antarctica</u> who loved to play.
> There was a young <u>dog</u> in Antarctica who loved to play.
> There was a young <u>dinosaur</u> in Antarctica who loved to play.
> There was a young <u>lion</u> in Antarctica who loved to play.
> There was a <u>fat</u> lion in Antarctica who loved to play.
> There was a fat lion in Antarctica who loved to <u>draw</u>.
> There was a fat lion in Antarctica who loved to <u>sing</u>.

As with all good strategies, teachers can use this strategy as a direct assessment to record students' developing understandings about parts of speech, knowledge of synonyms and antonyms, and recognition of the interplay between syntax and semantics.

Add a Paragraph/Write a Book. This activity promotes a reading and writing connection, alleviates writers' anxieties, and helps students construct knowledge about basic story features and their relationships. To initiate this activity, teachers place the first paragraph of an imaginative story at the beginning of a book made from blank pages stapled together. When time permits, individual students add either an anonymous or an author-signed paragraph to the story. As the story progresses, students and teachers take turns reading the partially completed story aloud for the group's enjoyment. They also discuss ideas for further story development. Once the book is completed, participants add visual art to clarify and highlight the story's ideas and stimulate readers' imaginations. Teachers also provide additional opportunities for students to exploit their special intelligences by encouraging them to create dances, songs, or drama productions that accompany and offer new insights about their stories (Armstrong, 2000; Gardner, 1995, 1999). Then they share their collaborative authorship efforts with classmates and students in other classrooms.

Dialogue Journals. *Dialogue journaling* (also referred to as interactive journals) provides a way for teachers and individual students to "carry on a conversation over time, sharing ideas, feelings, and concerns in writing" (Staton, 1987, p. 47). The journal entries are private and are read only by the two journal partners. Dialogue journals also provide an excellent vehicle for risk-free writing. These journals are *never* graded, and since the teacher responds in writing, a model for spelling and handwriting, as well as grammar and sentence structure, is always available to the student. Students write in a bound notebook

MI Connection: spatial

MI Connection: bodily-kinesthetic; musical

to their teacher about anything they want (early or emergent writers may draw pictures to get their message across). The teacher writes back in the same notebook, responding naturally, as in conversation. Some teachers also arrange for e-mail pen pals so students can journal with a student in another location. E-mail journals can be used for the same purpose as dialogue journals and may provide a more motivating venue for upper elementary and older students (Seaborg & Sturtevant, 1996).

Journaling also fosters a reading/writing connection and motivates students to write. Writing collaboratively with an equal partner enhances students' informal writing abilities and writing confidence as well. For instance, because of insecurity with English or lack of writing experience, some students initially choose to convey a journal message by drawing a picture or dictating a message. However, as the school year progresses, these students begin to feel more comfortable using the English language and have learned a great deal about written language. Many students model and imitate the *language functions* (such as reporting facts or opinions, asking questions) and *language conventions* (such as using exclamation marks or closing entries by writing "love") their teachers use in their own journal entries.

As shown in the series of three nonconsecutive days of journaling seen in Figure 8.8, when Tonya, who was working with a university tutor, first began journaling she wrote just a few words and drew hearts to show her feelings. Two weeks later she answered her tutor's question, attempted to write complete sentences, and imitated her tutor's use of question marks. Six days later Tonya wrote a long journal entry in which she shared a considerable amount of information and feelings.

Journal writing is never considered a writing assignment. Therefore, effective writing teachers never correct their students' spelling, punctuation, or capitalization in these journals. Instead they try to be particularly responsive to what their students write. They never ask their students too many questions or write only about their own interests and concerns. Rather, they compliment their students' work ("I liked your story about wolves"), support and affirm their students' efforts ("You really are trying hard, and it shows!"), and write honest, interesting, personal messages that encourage and entice their students to respond (Young & Crow, 1992).

Teacher-Guided Writing Lessons. Many teachers recognize that, to become proficient writers, students usually need to engage in activities that draw their attention to certain aspects of language they may otherwise disregard or overlook. Short, **teacher-guided writing lessons** provide a way to help students focus on and practice writing skills so that they experience success. These types of lessons, referred to as minilessons within the context of writer's workshop, concentrate on discrete aspects of written language such as spelling, punctuation, and capitalization and also include more global aspects of composing such as prewriting strategies, paragraphing, and editing.

Teachers design these teacher-guided writing lessons based on their students' immediate writing needs. Therefore, the students view these types of minilessons as personally useful and meaningful because they are able to immediately apply the concepts they learn in their own independent writing and revision efforts. Three particularly effective teacher-guided writing lessons are teacher dictation, rephrasing, and writing cohesive paragraphs. Features of these three lessons can easily be modified or adapted to suit the writing needs of diverse groups of learners in any educational setting.

Teacher Dictation. This teacher-guided lesson connects the processes of listening, writing, and reading and enhances students' understanding of *language conventions* at the sentence level (spelling, punctuation, and capitalization). Language conventions such as

MI Connection:
interpersonal

Go to MyEducationLab and select the topic *Ongoing Assessments*. Then, go to the Activities and Applications section, and watch the video entitled "Journals" to learn more about dialogue journals and other types of journals as well. Next respond to the accompanying questions.

Figure 8.8 Dialogue Journal Entries

Dear Tonya,   2-25
     How is your book coming
along? I like to write, and
create characters. It is fun
to create a problem and then a
solution. If you need any
help let me know. You'll have
a beautiful book to keep when
you are finished.
                         Your Tutor,
     I The book is coming
find   Mrs. Buchanan

Dear Tonya,   3-4
     Did you get to play with
your friends? My daughters have
the Pretty Princess game too. They
love to play it. Did you like
how your book turned out? I
think you did an excellent job.
I think you are a very good writer.
You should not be afraid to
write because you are very good at
creating story ideas. Tell me about
some of your favorite books.
                         Your Tutor,
     Yes I get to play
     with my friends. Mrs. Buchanan

     I do to?

     I Love to play it to?

     Go sole EB for
     the Oak Bark

Dear Tonya,   3-16
     I'm really looking forward to
my spring break. What do you have
planned?
                    Mrs. Buchanan
     yes I have planned for
springbreak.

     I have a good good

     I hop you have good
     spring break and I
     hop I have a good
     springbreak to.
     My baby brother
     His to go to the
     hospital today
     be caues he
     bart His hand its
     Working good
     but he have iny
     hard time
     what it. My big
     brother is going
     to the race
     out I dot what
     to go because
     I think that
     races or
     broing to go.

punctuation are a particular problem for students having writing difficulty (Norton, 1993). To begin this teacher-guided lesson, students listen carefully as their teacher dictates a sentence that contains particular aspects of language that students are ready to address in their independent writing. For example, if some students are ready to learn about capitalizing the first word of a sentence, the teacher might dictate the sentence "Wild animals live in the zoo." Students then write the dictated sentence. Their teacher also writes the sentences on a large chart or chalkboard while modeling his or her thinking aloud ("I need to begin a sentence with a capital letter"). The teacher then reads aloud the dictated sentence as students follow along.

The next step is a discussion of the particular language conventions pertinent to the sentence ("The word *Wild* begins with a capital letter because it is the first word of the sentence"). To complete the lesson, teachers help their students edit or "fix" any problems in their sentences such as adding a period or editing spelling. As the school year progresses, students take over the teacher's role and dictate sentences to the group. As extensions to this activity, teachers help students focus on the particular patterns, structures, and spelling features of any spelling words they have missed. For example, interactive writing (discussed in Chapter 7) could be used in which the teacher "stretches" individual words students dictate for a sentence so they can distinguish the sounds and letters. Students also enter their "missed" words in their personal dictionaries (see the section on spelling later in this chapter).

Rephrasing. This teacher-guided writing lesson connects listening, writing, and reading; enhances and expands students' vocabularies; and helps students generate language and construct knowledge about how language works. The procedure for this lesson begins with the teacher dictation activity described in the previous section: (a) teacher dictates a sentence; (b) students and teacher write the sentence; (c) teacher reads the dictated sentence aloud as students follow along; and (d) if necessary, students edit their writing with teacher's help.

Following editing of the sentence, students take turns orally rephrasing the sentence by creating variations in vocabulary and attempting to keep the original meaning of the sentence intact. Participants might rephrase the sentence "Today is Tuesday" as "This is the third day of the week"; "This is the day before Wednesday"; "This is the day after Monday"; or "This is the day before the fourth day of the week." Rephrasing can also be done in writing instead of orally. Participants then share all their rephrased sentence ideas and discuss any possible meaning changes that may have occurred. Groups often write and display all their sentence variations on sentence strips or charts to share their work (Figure 8.9).

Writing Cohesive Paragraphs. This lesson provides a strategic plan students can follow independently to improve their abilities to write paragraphs that focus on a central theme. To begin the lesson, teachers help their students develop a prewriting semantic

---

Figure 8.9   Example of Oral Rephrasing

Teacher: The boys and girls cooked a meal.
Pedro: The children fixed cocoa.
Tonya: The kids made a cake.
Brad: The children made a pie.
Chris: The kids made sweet potatoes for dinner.
Jessica: The friends made dinner.
Marian: The kids made biscuits.

MI Connection:
spatial; logical-
mathematical

map on a topic of the student's choice, such as the topic of dogs, in which the student brainstorms what they know about dogs. Next, teachers help their students categorize and link the concepts in the map. Students then rank the categories according to the order in which they might place the information in a composition by developing a simple outline (Figure 8.10). (See also the discussion on K–W–L plus in Chapter 13.)

Teachers go on to help their students think about how to organize the composition into an opening paragraph, subsequent paragraphs, and a closing paragraph. For example, in an expository voice composition about dogs, the student may decide that the opening paragraph might present a short history of dogs. Subsequent paragraphs may equal the number of categories included in the conceptual map (such as dogs' physical

Figure 8.10   Categorizing and Outlining from a Semantic Map on Dogs

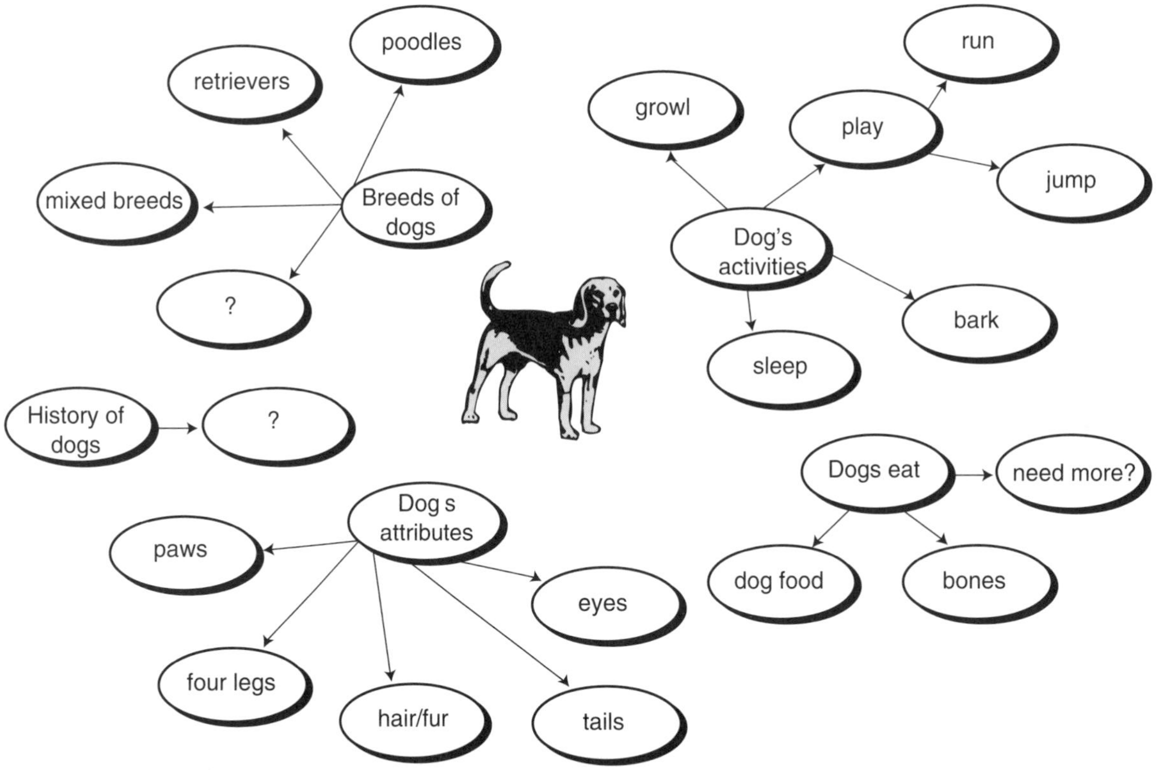

Outline for Dogs (first draft)
I. Miscellaneous Thoughts
  A. History of dogs
    1. ?
  B. Dog's attributes
    1. paws
    2. four legs
    3. hair/fur
    4. tails
    5. eyes
  C. Dog's activities
    1. sleep
    2. growl

    3. bark
    4. play
      a. jump
      b. run
  D. What dogs eat
    1. dog food
    2. bones
    3. need more?
  E. Breeds of dogs
    1. poodles
    2. retrievers
    3. mixed breeds
    4. ?

attributes, dogs' activities, preferred foods of dogs, and paragraphs about the breeds of dogs). A closing paragraph might present a summary of ideas in the composition.

Because writers usually discover new or "just thought of" ideas as they write during a process known as **rehearsal** (the writer mentally tries out several versions of a composition before deciding on the final version), teachers encourage their students to incorporate these new ideas into the appropriate categories of their semantic maps. If necessary, students may decide to create an additional category for a new idea. In this way, they consciously choose to use the new information by inserting these ideas into the appropriate paragraphs in the composition.

One popular approach to helping students write expository paragraphs is step up to writing (Auman, 2002). The step up to writing techniques are color coded, making them visually appealing and helpful to students for distinguishing various parts of expository writing (topic sentences from details, from explanations). With a growing research base, this system is effectively helping teachers teach students of all grade levels and abilities to generate expository text summaries and cohesive, coherent paragraphs.

THE CREATIVE WRITING PROCESS

Recognition of writing as a process began in the early 1970s. Researchers became less concerned with students' final writing products and more aware of the thinking processes students employ as they write (Solley, 2000). Through observations of prekindergarten through twelfth graders, researchers learned that writers ask themselves questions, determine the specific words and sentence structures to use in their compositions, and deliberately change the order of words, sentences, and paragraphs (Elbow, 2000; Emig, 1983). In the early 1980s, models of the writing process were developed that included planning, writing first drafts, and reviewing the developed composition (Harste, Woodward, & Burke, 1984). A second, more detailed model of the writing process evolved in the late 1980s that has great implications for classroom teachers. Termed *social constructivism* (Rhodes & Shanklin, 1993), this model focuses on the **recursive nature of writing** (writers discover "new" or just-thought-of ideas as they write and must go back and work those ideas into previously written material, as mentioned previously). This model also notes that good writing evolves from authentic experiences within a social community of learners where freedom of expression is encouraged (Calkins, 1994; Graves & Kittle, 2005). From this *social constructivist* perspective, earlier views of the writing process were extended to include *rehearsal* (trying out ideas for writing), drafting, revising, and editing (Solley, 2000).

Following social constructivism tenets, we believe that all good writing (authentic, honest, meaning oriented) starts with experiences. Therefore, the starting point in a **creative writing** program is to provide diverse experiences for students that give them topics they can naturally and easily write about. The experiences provided for students should complement their individual strengths and help develop their linguistic intelligence (Gardner, 1983, 1995, 1999). Examples of experiences commonly provided to students include (a) reading, listening to, and discussing quality fiction and nonfiction; (b) inviting guest speakers to talk on wide-ranging topics such as dinosaurs, Great Britain, and rabbits; (c) designing, creating, and flying kites; (d) making and eating cakes and banana splits; (e) preparing a tea party for others; (f) presenting plays and readers' theater productions for others to enjoy; (g) making a substance similar to Play-Doh to use as sculpture material; (h) creating and playing literacy board games; (i) walking outside to view clouds, toads, flowers, rain, or shadows, or to plant seeds; and (j) planning and

MI Connection: logical-mathematical; bodily-kinesthetic; spatial; naturalist; interpersonal

participating in a Literacy Celebration Day at which food is served, students' work is displayed, and students, student teachers, parents, grandparents, and classroom teachers have an opportunity to celebrate students' literacy successes.

Prewriting

Prewriting strategies help students generate ideas for writing and determine what they know or need to know about a creative writing topic. Several prewriting strategies that students especially enjoy are presented here.

SPOTLIGHT ON ENGLISH LEARNERS

The Language Experience Approach

In the language experience approach, the teacher takes advantage of students' experiences to motivate oral expression, develop reading skill, and demonstrate the reading/writing connection. Students, either individually or in small groups, dictate a story about a common experience to a teacher who functions as a scribe, editor, and language expander and interacts with the students to elicit elaborations when appropriate. Once the story is written down, the teacher and students analyze it for specific functions and structures. The first draft becomes an invaluable first step in language expansion.

For example, students can expand the syntax of the first draft. Starting with a sentence such as *The boy ran,* students can be led to add words for various slots and yield a sentence such as *The happy boy ran slowly through the yard.* Students can also expand their sentences by adding other clauses or by applying sentence-combining activities.

Teachers also ask questions that elicit more descriptive words or phrases or alternative ways of expressing thoughts, including standard English equivalents to vernacular dialects. Teachers can also teach vocabulary and comprehension through the use of semantic maps. In this way, the language experience approach is invaluable in literacy instruction for linguistically diverse students. After discussion of an experience, these students can dictate a story in their vernacular that is written down in the native dialect with standard spellings. For example, notice the following hypothetical sample developed through students' experiences with an event, in this case a parade:

My friend, he went to the parade. He don't like the crowd. He climb a tree and he saw the band. And he saw the float.

To elicit a first draft, the teacher asks facilitating questions to lead students to generate thinking and use language in social settings. The teacher could ask questions such as, "Who went to the parade?" "What did he see or hear?" Students should be encouraged to express themselves in their natural language or dialect to generate language for a first draft of an experience story. Then the teacher and students *together* revise the language by rephrasing or expanding on it. This leads the students to learn editing skills as well as develop awareness for edited standard English. The teacher leads the students to produce a revised draft of their emerging text through discussion and questioning. For example, "Does this sound like 'school' language?" "Could we add new sentences or new information?" "Could we add some words or take some out?"

My friend went to the parade. He doesn't like crowds. He climbed a tree. He saw the bands. He saw the floats.

The teacher continues to ask questions to elicit responses for further revision and elaboration. For example, "Who is your friend?" (*Nathan*) "What kind of parade?" (*Mardi Gras parade*) "What kinds of bands and floats?" "Can we say or write some of these ideas in one combined sentence?" This will yield an elaborated text with more description and connective words:

My friend Nathan went to the Mardi Gras parade. Because he doesn't like large crowds, he climbed an oak tree on the street corner. Then he saw the marching bands and the decorated floats.

The language experience approach uses the following five steps: discussing an experience, dictating, accepting without correcting, revising, and follow-up. In each of these steps the teacher engages the students through questioning and dialogue. The teacher may also use various adjunct aids such as webs and maps or visuals and realia to help students organize their thoughts. Students learn their language skills through the writing-reading process in the social context of a classroom community.

Arts Connection

Wearing a sunbonnet, a fluffy apron, and a pair of "old-timey" black lace-up shoes, one teacher played the part of Great Aunt Arizona as she read *My Great Aunt Arizona* (Houston, 1992) to her fourth graders. Because the story depicts Aunt Arizona's imaginary travels, following the reading, the fourth-graders used watercolors, crayons, and fine-line markers to create individual illustrations showing where they wished they could travel. Combining creative writing with the visual arts, they printed the book's title and author on their paintings, included information about the story ("Great Aunt Arizona dreamed about traveling to wonderful places."), and composed short paragraphs about their imaginary travel wishes ("I want to travel to Disneyland because I have never been there and all my friends say it is cool. They have scary rides and Mickey and Minnie Mouse."). The teacher then helped her students mount the drawings and paragraphs on sturdy cardboard. Finally, she bound their work into a large collaborative book. To continue explorations about travels, the students used the Internet to discover places they would like to visit (Australia to see marsupials and the Great Barrier Reef; the Amazon basin to see reptiles and rain forests). The students also read fiction and content text (multiple texts, formats, and genres) that pertained to their dream travels, such as *Verdi* (Cannon, 1997), a story about a young green python, and *The Great Kapok Tree: A Tale of the Amazon Rain Forest* (Cherry, 1990).

In another example, a teacher working with fifth graders read the story *Gregory Cool* (Binch, 1994) to coincide with their theme of "Going Places and Doing Things." In the story, Gregory, who lives in a large U.S. city, visits his grandparents on the small island of Tobago. Gregory initially has great difficulty adjusting to island life and pretends he is so "cool" that he isn't interested in joining his cousin in island activities such as fishing, eating unusual food like *bake* and *buljol* (bread and saltfish), and climbing coconut trees. Following the story, the fifth graders created a large mural that included their letters of advice and solace to Gregory.

1. *Drawing*. Often, students explore ideas for writing and begin the writing process by representing their ideas through drawing. Drawing is a natural, visual prewriting strategy that all students find beneficial. More important, drawing is "especially motivational for youngsters who otherwise might be unreachable" (Sautter, 1994, in Sidelnick & Svoboda, 2000, p. 176). As Blecher and Jaffee (1998) noted, drawing helps support "those students who are still in the margins" (p. 95). Drawing provides opportunities for students with special writing needs to represent what they want to write through another modality or symbol system other than print (Richards & McKenna, 2003). Drawing also allows students to sequence story events and keep track of details.

> **MI Connection:** spatial

2. *Drama enactments*. Drama is another way of preplanning and representing writing ideas that students find helpful. In the classroom, individual students may perform or tell stories they want to write. In addition, small groups of students may collaborate and present a drama enactment that offers multiple perspectives about a single topic. For example, four sixth-graders recently worked together to plan their expository compositions about the November 2008 U.S. presidential debates and national election. Prior to writing, each student took a different perspective and played the part of one of the candidates.

> **MI Connection:** interpersonal

3. *Speed writing*. Speed writing, also known as *free writing* or **quickwrites**, alleviates writers' anxieties about composing, helps writers generate ideas for writing, and frees writers from worrying about language conventions (Norton, 1993).

Participants in speed writing write nonstop for a certain amount of time (for example, two to five minutes) without erasing, crossing out, or requesting help with spelling. The idea is to relax and let ideas emerge. At the end of the designated writing time, authors share their efforts with the group. Listeners ask questions and offer comments and suggestions that may help authors clarify or further develop their work. As an extension to speed writing, the teacher or other students can also write supportive individual notes to students who have shared their speed writing to tell about sad, confusing, or worrisome times in their lives. For example, one student recently wrote about the death of her

> **MI Connection:** interpersonal

pet. When she finished reading her writing to her class group they immediately created sympathy cards to offer her support and express their concern.

4. *Story features and their connections.* This is a prewriting strategy that helps writers plan their imaginative stories in a thoughtful, organized, and interesting way by considering the four basic story features of characters, settings, problems, and solutions. To implement this strategy, teachers help their students fill in semantic maps based on their ideas about the specific feature they might include in a story. The story features map pictured in Figure 8.11 was created by a group of sixth graders. The group decided to portray three characters named Lisa, Chad, and Sam; include three settings (a school, a Florida beach, and a bungee-jumping park); create two problems (a group of students needs money for a trip, and Chad hurts his leg); and offer a solution for each problem.

When the story features map was filled in, the sixth graders brainstormed how their story features might connect to one another, a form of rehearsal. The map shows that the three characters connect to the Florida beach (a setting) because the characters travel to Florida. The map also illustrates how the problem of "needing money" is solved when the three characters earn money by cutting grass. After completing the map and determining the connections among the story features, the sixth graders wrote a first draft of their story and titled it "Bungee Jumping."

Once students have a sound understanding of the four basic story features and their interconnections, their teachers help them focus on other important parts and connections of well-formed stories such as episodes (a series of actions and happenings) and resolution (the final outcome of a story). Teachers might also assist their students in constructing the implied story themes pertinent to their story (the underlying ideas that tie the characters, goals, setting, and episodes together). For example, the students who composed the story "Bungee Jumping" decided that the themes of their story were "Friends are important," "Friends help one another," "Never give up," and "Be a problem solver."

MI Connection: spatial

MI Connection: logical-mathematical

Go to MyEducationLab and select the topic *Reading and Writing Connections.* Then, go to the Activities and Applications section, and watch the video entitled "Writing Process: Prewriting" to see an example of a teacher using a modified story features map to help her young students prepare to write a story. Notice also how the teacher uses children's literature to provide a common and meaningful experience to trigger ideas. Next respond to the accompanying questions.

Figure 8.11   Story Features Map for Trying Ideas for Writing

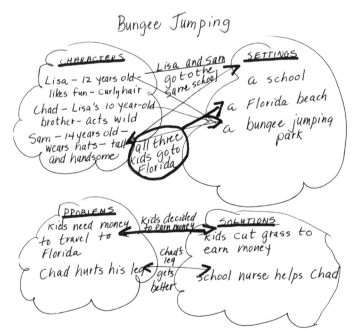

Figure 8.12   Student Letter to a Favorite Author and Student Recipe for Cooking Turkey

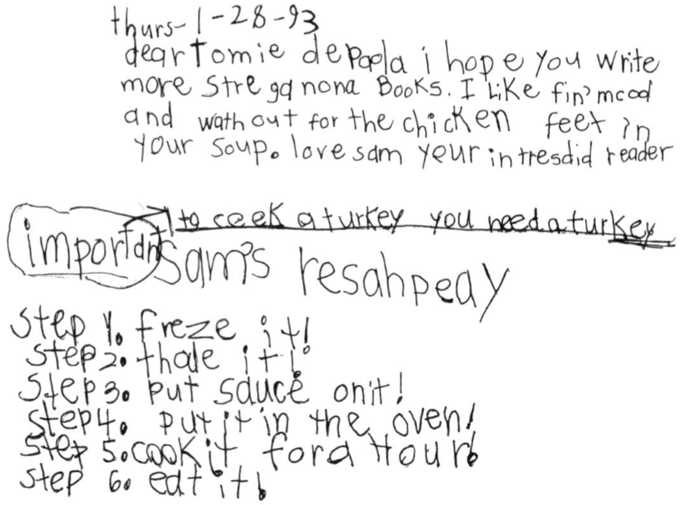

thurs-1-28-93
dear tomie depoola i hope you write
more strega nona Books. I like fin'mcod
and wathout for the chicken feet in
your soup. love sam your intresdid reader

important to cook a turkey you need a turkey

sam's resahpeay

step 1. freze it!
step 2. thade it!
step 3. put sauce on it!
step 4. put it in the oven!
step 5. cook it for a Hour!
step 6. eat it!

Drafting/Composing and Sharing for Feedback

As students write first drafts of their imaginative stories, books, plays, and poems; write letters to favorite authors; and create recipes (Figure 8.12), they are encouraged to concentrate first on their messages and not worry so much about spelling and punctuation at this time. Good writers are seldom concerned about correct language conventions (spelling, punctuation, capitalization, and paragraphing) until they are ready to edit their work. During these composing sessions teachers might circulate and interact among their students, offering encouragement and providing guidance if asked. Teachers also ask their students questions designed to encourage them to experiment with writing and further develop their work (for example, "Tell me more about this new character in your story. I want to know what he looks like so that I could recognize him if I meet him"). In addition, teachers model for their students how to use such reviewer forms as praise, question, and polish (PQP) (Figure 8.13) so that writers can get necessary feedback from others for revision and reviewers learn how to critique writing.

Revising and Editing

Revision is concerned with content; editing is concerned with mechanics. "Overemphasis on the mechanics of writing and neatness in the early stages of writing development often overshadows the ideas students are trying to express" (Searfoss, 1993, p. 12). Therefore, when students' first drafts are completed, each student's evolving literacy development and corresponding ability to complete revision tasks guide editing decisions. It makes no sense to require a student to conduct extensive, personally meaningless revisions if she (a) is anxious and hesitant about writing, (b) has just begun to commit personal thoughts to paper, (c) is developmentally not ready to use conventional spelling or punctuation, or (d) has just begun to believe in herself as a writer.

MI Connection:
interpersonal

Go to MyEducationLab and select the topic *Writing*. Then, go to the Activities and Applications section, watch the video entitled "Peer Editing," and think about what the teacher might have done to prepare her students to be effective peer editors. Next respond to the accompanying questions. Compare this video to the one you will view in the next section entitled "Grammar and Punctuation."

Figure 8.13	Using Praise, Question, and Polish in the Revising/Editing Stage of the Writing Process

---

Praise, Question, Polish (PQP) Form for Peer Feedback

Writer/Author _____

Reviewer/Editor _____

Title of Writing _____

1. PRAISE
   (These are the things I particularly like about what you wrote.)
   I like the part where . . .
   I'd like to know more about . . .
   You used some powerful words, like . . .
   I like the way you explained . . .
   Your writing made me feel . . .
   I like the order you used in your writing because . . .
   Your dialogue was realistic, the way (character) said . . .

2. QUESTION
   (These are the questions I have about what you wrote, or these
   are questions that the writer has for the reviewer.)
   What do you think is the strongest part of my writing?
   What do you want to know more about?
   What part doesn't make sense to you?
   Is there a part I should throw away?
   How can I make my writing clearer?
   Did I use some "tired" words that I should change?
   Are there some sentences I should combine?

3. POLISH
   (These are suggestions to make what you wrote even better.)
   What is your favorite part?
   Could you write a lead sentence to "grab" the reader?
   Do you need a closing?
   I got confused in the part about . . .
   Could you add more to this part because . . .
   Could you leave this part out because . . .
   Could you use a different word for _____?
   Is this paragraph on one topic?
   Are your paragraphs in the best order?
   Could you combine some sentences?

Go to MyEducationLab and select the topic *Assessing Reading and Writing.* Then, go to the Activities and Applications section, and watch the video entitled "Editing Conference with Teacher" for a peek into a teacher-student editing conference. Peer editing can also be a useful approach if the teacher first prepares students for this task. View the video "Grammar and Punctuation" to see a teacher preparing her students for peer editing on the mechanics of punctuation, capitalization, and grammar issues. Next respond to the accompanying questions for both videos.

Students can refer to a set of questions to guide their revising and editing. Some examples follow.

- Did I read my writing to see if it makes sense?
- Did I write several sentences about each topic before I changed to a new topic?

- Did I use details that tell a lot about my topic?
- Do I like what I wrote?
- Did I circle the words that I think I misspelled?
- Does each sentence end with a punctuation mark (. ! ?)?
- Did I use capital letters to begin sentences or to begin names?
- Did I read my writing to someone else for their ideas?

Spelling problems especially "tend to inhibit many students who would otherwise be imaginative, intelligent writers" (Silva & Yarborough, 1990, p. 48). Therefore, many teachers provide private spelling guidance for their students during editing conferences (see the next section on spelling).

Publishing/Sharing

After students complete any developmentally appropriate revision tasks and are satisfied with their work, the teacher invites them to share their writing efforts with peers. In these sharing sessions, often using the format of the **author's chair** where a student reads his or her writing to others for feedback, students and the teacher offer positive feedback to each writer ("I really liked the part in your story where the giant meets the wicked prince"), and each writer's efforts are applauded and celebrated as a literacy accomplishment. Following sharing, final revisions are made and final products are "published" and made available in the classroom library for others to enjoy.

IMPLEMENTING A SPELLING PROGRAM

In developing students' literacy competencies "spelling, although a small piece of the writing process, is of great concern [and presents some confusions] to teachers, parents, and the general public" (Wilde, 1996, p. x; see also Solley, 2000). Children's spelling is an extension of their overall language development and follows a natural progression from nonstandard to **conventional** (or "correct") **spelling** (see Figure 8.14 for stages in spelling development). Students progress at their own pace. Therefore, students' developmentally appropriate *invented spellings* (constructed by listening to the sounds heard in a word and temporary until the conventional spelling becomes known; also called temporary or constructed spelling; see Chapter 7) are an important part of their written language growth. These constructed spellings enable the teacher to assess spelling development and also observe what the student knows about phonemic awareness (Chapter 7) and phonics (Chapter 9).

Teachers who encourage their students to view themselves as writers who are capable of using interesting and dynamic words rather than confining themselves just to the spelling words that they have memorized are more likely to produce students who will write and enjoy writing. Likewise, supporting students' use of individually constructed spellings in their dialogue journals, in their literature and prediction logs, and in initial drafts of their compositions will produce similar results. At the same time, students do need to develop an interest in spelling and learn to value using conventional spelling in their "public" work so that others can read their writing. Thus, teachers need to provide both nonstructured and structured spelling activities and lessons and to offer different strategies for students who have difficulty acquiring spelling naturally and effortlessly.

Go to MyEducationLab and select the topic *Assessing Reading and Writing*. Then, go to the Activities and Applications section, and watch the video entitled "Author's Chair" to observe how a teacher helps peers critique the stories shared, using elements found in the PQP form, Figure 8.13. Notice also how the teacher incorporates mini-lessons into this sharing opportunity. Next respond to the accompanying questions.

Go to MyEducationLab and select the topic *Spelling*. Then, go to the Activities and Applications section, and examine the artifact entitled "Random Letter Stage with Illustration (K-2)" for a look at early invented spelling. Next respond to the accompanying questions.

Figure 8.14	Stages in Spelling Development

The stages represented here should be viewed from a developmental perspective; that is, a student's spelling is likely to change over time so that it resembles the examples seen at each stage. The following stages are those proposed by J. Richard Gentry (1982, 1987, 1996). These stages are also referred to by the names given in parentheses following Gentry's term.

Stage 1: Precommunicative Spelling (also Prephonemic)
Typical of children ages 3 through 5, the learner at this stage uses scribbles, letterlike forms, and letters, showing a preference for uppercase letters. There is no match between letters and phonemes.

Examples: candy $SCOZ]$

went $\exists N^{\circ}C$

(strings of letters) $crtogDok$

Stage 2: Semiphonetic Spelling (also Early Phonemic)
Representative of the spelling of 5- and 6-year-olds, the learner has discovered the phonetic principle—that is, awareness that letters are used to represent sounds. However, letters for only one or two sounds in a word are generally written down.

Examples: My brother was crying all night.

$MBRW\ KLN+$

I like to go to the zoo.

$I\ LK\ +o\ 6++Z$

Stage 3: Phonetic Spelling (also Letter Name)
Six-year-old children are typically phonetic spellers. At this stage the learner represents all essential sounds in spelling a word and chooses letters that show a relationship to the sound heard in the word (for example, *AT* for *eight*; *PEKT* for *peeked*).

Examples: Jackie
I had a apel For lungsh
(I had an apple for lunch.)

bob —
a boy so The man run Awa
(A boy saw the man run away.)

Stage 4: Transitional Spelling
Once a student begins reading, typically around age 7, spelling begins to change as the learner visually notices the spelling of words and relies less on spelling words according to the way they sound. Transitional spelling looks more like standard or conventional spelling as the learner uses silent letters such as e-markers (such as *clime* for *climb*) and vowel letter combinations (including digraphs such as *whair* for *where* and diphthongs such as *zoo*), demonstrating more reliance on how the words look rather than how they sound. Transitional spellers also use a vowel in every syllable and spell many words correctly.

Figure 8.14   *continued*

Examples:

> Can I go see a movee wif
> My fren Susi sed her mom
> sed Oka win We go
>
> (Can I go see a movie with my friend Susie? She said
> her Mom said ok. When can we go?)
>
> Goin To The zoo is fun I
> lik The linz and The big
> burdz wit blue feters
>
> (Going to the zoo is fun. I like the lions and
> the big birds with blue feathers.)

Stage 5: Correct or Mature Spelling (also Conventional or Traditional)
With more exposure to print and more opportunities to write, learners reach this stage around age 8 or 9. The student recognizes when words look misspelled and can consider alternative spellings. Most basic rules of English orthography are applied to include use of silent letters and double consonants, and many irregular words are spelled correctly. Occasionally, spellings may still be constructed for some words.

Nonstructured Spelling Activities

Because writing provides a natural incentive for learning how to spell, spelling lessons should be placed within the context of each student's developmentally appropriate spelling needs addressed during individual writing conferences. These conferences include informal discussions about particular spellings of unusual words and words that do not follow a particular spelling pattern. Thinking and talking about spelling and focusing attention on words help students become more proficient spellers and enhance their oral language and vocabulary as well.

Students also find it useful to record interesting words, words that do not follow a typical spelling pattern, past-tense words, and words and their synonyms and antonyms in a word study notebook or personal dictionary (see the following section). In addition teachers serve as role models, demonstrating to students how they value conventional spelling by proofreading and self-correcting their own spelling, using such resources as a dictionary, a thesaurus, and a computer spell-check system.

Structured Spelling Activities

Some structured spelling activities that students find particularly helpful are *personal dictionaries, word categories* (also called *word sorting*), weekly *spelling meetings,* and word games (such as *"Begins with . . ."*). These activities can easily be altered to suit the spelling needs of different age groups, English learners, or students with special learning needs.

1. *Personal dictionaries.* **Personal dictionaries** provide a place where students can record new and unusual words they have discovered (from reading or listening to

MI Connection: intrapersonal

quality children's literature and interacting with peers, parents, and guest speakers), or words that they "absolutely" must have when they are composing. Personal dictionaries also facilitate students' gradual transitions from invented (or temporary) spelling to standard spelling by developing their awareness of spelling conventions and focusing their attention on the specific features of words such as number of syllables, affixes, medial vowels, and patterns.

You can quickly make personal dictionaries for younger students by stapling 26 blank sheets of paper together and placing one alphabet letter (A to Z) on each blank page. Cover the dictionaries with sturdy paper and print students' names on the front ("Suzie's Dictionary"). Older students prefer to use hardcover notebooks or binders with loose-leaf paper to record their spelling words and organize them alphabetically. If necessary, help students turn to the appropriate page to enter their new words in meaningful sentences in their dictionaries. Have students highlight or underline each new word. For example, during a unit on marsupial animals, some students entered the word marsupials in their dictionaries on the *M* page by writing sentences such as *Marsupials are pouched animals* or *Pandas are marsupials.* To encourage students' explorations of multiple learning modalities, tell your emergent writers to draw illustrations next to each word to serve as a memory aid (see Figure 8.15). Provide time each week when students can share the words they have entered into their personal dictionaries, discussing the meanings of their new words and the various ways to use these words in different contexts. Teachers use many of the words in students' personal dictionaries in the "teacher dictation" lessons described previously.

MI Connection: spatial

2. *Word categories.* Word categories is a word-sorting activity in which students develop a list of weekly spelling words relating to literature or to a thematic unit, then analyze and categorize the words in terms of their similarities, differences, and discrete or unusual aspects. For a list of 15 to 20 words it may be possible to devise 20 to 30 categories. For example, after reading and discussing the story *Too Many Tamales* (Soto, 1993), a story about a Hispanic girl named Maria who takes her mother's diamond ring

MI Connection: logical-mathematical

Figure 8.15 Example of a Personal Dictionary Page

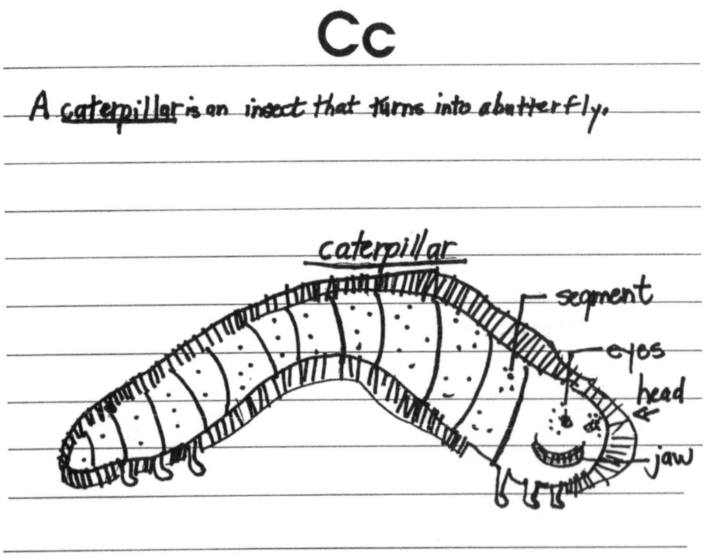

to "wear just for a minute," a group of third graders developed the following list of spelling words: *desperate, tamales, diamond, Christmas, cousins, necklace, Hispanic, confess, stomach ache, bossy, scared, worried, demanding, celebration,* and *multicultural.* With their teacher's help, the students sorted the words into 20 categories: one-, two-, three-, four-, and five-syllable words; words that describe feelings; words that describe people; nouns; adjectives; words for holidays; words for jewelry; synonyms; words containing "silent" alphabet letters; words ending in *-ed;* words ending in *-ing;* compound words; words that begin with a consonant blend; more than one word; words with double consonants; and words for food. Students then chose five of these words to enter into their personal dictionaries.

3. *Spelling meetings.* Scheduled weekly spelling meetings promote a spirit of genuine inquiry about spelling, encourage students "to be curious about words and to have a respect for the language they will use . . . [in their writing]" (Laminack & Wood, 1996, p. 81), and provide opportunities for students to explore the conventional spellings, letter–sound relationships and patterns, and unusual spelling attributes of interesting words they have discovered during the week as they read, write, and interact with peers, tutors, and visitors. In a typical 15-minute weekly spelling meeting, the focus is not on students' spelling errors. Rather, students and teacher explore useful strategies for figuring out how to spell difficult words (see Topping's [1995] cued spelling and Zutell's [1996] directed spelling thinking activity) and talk about words that are spelled in unexpected ways (such as *elephant, broccoli,* and *lettuce*). Students can also be directed to choose five of their longest words, shortest words, words that make them feel happy, or the most unusual words they learned during the week to enter into their personal dictionaries.

MI Connection:
interpersonal

4. *"Begins with."* This game focuses students' attention on beginning components or sounds and spellings of words and expands students' vocabulary. Teacher and students sit in a circle. Then the teacher or a student volunteer says, "Tell me all the words you can think of that begin with *c-a-n*" (or *p-e-n, p-r-e, a-c-t, b-e,* and so forth). Students take turns giving all their ideas. For example, fifth graders responded to words beginning with *c-a-n* with the following single-syllable and multisyllabic words: *can, candle, cannot, canoe, canvas, canopy, cantaloupe, canteen, canary, cancel,* and *Canada.* These words are also written on a word wall for visual inspection.

The goal of spelling instruction is to increase knowledge about how words are spelled and the range of spelling strategies, as opposed to moving students to the next spelling stage. Spelling stages are just a way to facilitate discussion about spelling growth. Figure 8.16 presents five useful strategies for spelling, and also presents instructional guidelines to use with students functioning at the various spelling stages prior to conventional spelling.

WRITING INSTRUCTION AND ASSESSMENT: A CONTINUOUS PROCESS

Most literacy experts agree that "writing is a developmental process that evolves much like oral language" (Glazer & Brown, 1993, p. 47; Pappas et al., 1999). Daily, systematic classroom-based assessment, conducted as students write and respond to literacy lessons and activities, allows teachers to observe and understand the writing behaviors and processes their students employ. This ongoing approach to assessment also helps teachers concentrate on an individual student's progress over time rather than measure one student against another at one point in time.

| Figure 8.16 | Instruction for Spelling Development |

The goal of spelling instruction is to increase knowledge about how words are spelled and the range of spelling strategies, as opposed to moving students to the next spelling stage. Spelling stages are just a way to organize discussion about spelling growth.

Strategies for Spelling
1. Look at word spelled. Does it look correct? Circle if not.
2. Does it sound like another word I know?
3. Is it written anywhere nearby? In a book?
4. Ask somebody.
5. Mark it and check later.

Instruction for Precommunicative (or Prephonemic) Spellers
Learn to represent *some* sounds.
1. LEA (connection between voice and print).
2. Individual help listening for sounds and writing them down.
3. Dialogue journaling—to provide a written model.

Instruction for Semiphonetic (or Phonemic) Spellers
Learn to represent *more* sounds and spell some words conventionally.
1. Model listening to one syllable at a time and ignore some "off" spellings.
2. Minilessons during LEA.
3. Say, "That is how you could spell it in your writing, but it is actually written this way."

Instruction for Phonetic (or Letter Name) Spellers
Moving away from spelling what you hear.
1. Reading environment rich in print and opportunities to read.
2. Students uncomfortable with "invented" letter name spellings are showing growth and will benefit from introduction to several spelling strategies.
3. Instruction should draw attention to visual information contained in conventional spellings. Say, "Think about what the word looks like in books" (as opposed to "Write what you hear," as in earlier stages).
4. Word sort lessons on visual patterns directed to specific needs.

Instruction for Transitional Spellers
Increase expanding knowledge of the regularities in English language orthography.
1. Say, write and say, check, trace and say, write from memory, check.
2. Five or six words of personal interest.
3. Word games (such as Hangman, Boggle, Spill and Spell, Scrabble).
4. Word derivations and words with similar meanings tend to have similar spellings (such as *sign, signal*).
5. Plurals, past-tense markers—spelled same although sound different (*pigs, cups, raked, purred, traded*).
6. Categorize spelling errors over time; infer the rule (inductive learning) (*their, there, they're*).

Classroom-based assessment that takes place within the context of teaching and learning requires teachers to (a) observe their students carefully as they write and interact with one another, (b) celebrate their students' writing strengths rather than concentrate on deficiencies, (c) "note what a student is developmentally ready to learn" (Glazer & Brown, 1993, p. 52), (d) document students' writing progress and the writing processes they employ guided by observation notes and writing checklists (such as the developmental writing checklist in Appendix S), and (e) reflect upon and consider what each student knows about written language. Studying this information provides teachers with direction for future writing lessons. Thus, writing instruction and assessment merge and become a mutually supportive, continuous process. There does come a time when students' writings must be graded. Traditionally, all samples of student writing were graded intensively and negatively with every error being marked. However, such an approach did not produce noticeable improvement in subsequent writing. Now it is accepted that not every piece of writing a student does needs to be formally marked or scored (when students are writing exploratively, or creating drafts, for example). When student writing does need to be evaluated (such as at the end of a marking period or at district benchmarks), the criteria used to score the writing should get at the heart of writing and should not focus solely on mechanical errors.

No one scoring system or approach is best. Ideally, the teacher and student working together construct scoring guides because they can be content specific; that is, focusing on those aspects the teacher and students have identified as important and that need to be developed further. Whatever scoring system is used—holistic, analytic, or use of a rubric—the goal of assessment and evaluation should be to help students improve as writers and feel successful. Briefly, **holistic scoring** refers to judging a piece of writing in terms of the whole instead of its individual parts. The teacher would first read the whole piece, considering certain features, and then immediately assign a score or grade. This approach would not be appropriate if the teacher wants to assess how well students have used a particular writing form or applied specific writing skills. Also, teacher bias can affect the final grade in this type of system. **Analytic scoring** focuses on assessing the writing in terms of its individual parts. Usually the traits of good writing are identified and categorized, as seen in Figure 8.17. Similarly, **rubric scoring** identifies the traits to be evaluated and provides a brief description of the criteria for each level of performance (see Chapter 6). Evaluation of

MI Connection: intrapersonal

Figure 8.17   An Analytic Scoring System

	STRONG	AVERAGE	WEAK
Ideas			
1. Ideas are creative.	_____	_____	_____
2. Ideas are well developed.	_____	_____	_____
3. Audience and purpose are considered.	_____	_____	_____
Organization			
1. An organizational pattern is used.	_____	_____	_____
2. Ideas are presented in logical order.	_____	_____	_____
3. Topic sentences are clear.	_____	_____	_____
Style			
1. A good choice of words is displayed.	_____	_____	_____
2. Figurative language is used.	_____	_____	_____
3. A variety of sentence patterns is used.	_____	_____	_____
Mechanics			
1. Most words are spelled correctly.	_____	_____	_____
2. Punctuation and capitalization are used correctly.	_____	_____	_____
3. Standard language is used.	_____	_____	_____

Comments:

Go to MyEducationLab and select the topic *Assessing Reading and Writing*. Then, go to the Activities and Applications section, and watch the video entitled "Writing Assessment" to observe a teacher working with students on writing a personal narrative through the draft stages. You will also see a student-teacher conference in which analytic scoring is demonstrated. Next respond to the accompanying questions.

writing should be a positive learning experience, not a threatening one. One way to ensure that evaluation is open is to involve the students during instruction in negotiating or jointly developing the criteria for assessment and evaluation, and to stop looking solely for errors.

Similarly, there are alternatives for learning about students' ongoing spelling competencies besides the weekly spelling test. In particular, teachers can learn about students' spelling growth by observing and recording information as their students write. Through careful observation teachers can learn (a) whether students attempt to spell unknown words, (b) whether students use their personal dictionaries as spelling resources, (c) what strategies students use when they attempt to spell unknown words, (d) whether students proofread their work for spelling errors, and (e) students' developmental spelling stages. This type of direct assessment focuses on students' spelling proficiencies and considers what students are ready to learn next about spelling. If a standard for reporting spelling progress is needed, the spelling tests provided in Appendix R can be used.

The importance of helping students learn how to assess their own writing progress also needs to be acknowledged. "By engaging students in self-assessments students learn they are ultimately responsible for their own learning" (Tierney et al., 1991, p. 59). Four different formats to increase students' involvement in self-assessing their writing are shared observations, postwriting questionnaires, spelling questionnaires, and portfolios.

Shared Observations

Students cannot begin to monitor or assess their own writing behaviors and progress until they know something about the processes good writers use, recognize their own composing behaviors, and receive specific feedback that gives them a good sense of their writing success or growth. Therefore, teachers share their observation notes with each of their students in short, informal conferences ("Today I noticed that you reread your story and edited your punctuation and spelling. All good writers edit punctuation and spelling when they are satisfied with the message they have written. Good for you.").

Postwriting Questionnaires

MI Connection:
intrapersonal

Although it isn't expected for every piece of writing, students find it helpful occasionally to respond to a postwriting questionnaire. Postwriting checklists and questionnaires are self-monitoring tools that help emerging writers of any age develop an awareness about their writing behaviors (see Appendix U). (Such self-assessments can also be useful for portfolio assessments if completed at regular intervals (at the beginning, middle, and end of a school year).

Spelling Questionnaires

Questionnaires designed to help students assess their spelling achievements and goals vary according to students' ages, the developmental stages of students' writing, and what teachers consider important about students' spelling. With their teacher's help if necessary, students might fill in the questionnaire shown in Appendix V at least three times throughout the semester.

Portfolios

Portfolios are an organized collection of evidence to demonstrate growth in knowledge, skills, and attitudes. Portfolios also provide a way for students to keep a record of their writing efforts. **Artifacts** (items within a portfolio such as visual art, music tapes, photographs) help complement students' writing and document students' abilities to combine intelligences. Most important, selecting and categorizing work to include in portfolios and making decisions about why the work is important gives students opportunities to assess their writing.

Students are directed to keep all of the writing they accomplish throughout the school year in two different folders labeled "working portfolio" and "showcase portfolio" (Tierney et al., 1991). **Working portfolios** house (a) the student's writing in progress, (b) work that may never be completed, (c) first drafts, (d) revision pages, (e) work generated during writing lessons and activities (such as speed-writing efforts), (f) ideas for possible future writing (such as drawings, notes, concept maps, and pictures), and (g) copies of completed postwriting questionnaires. The working portfolio documents all of the student's writing during nonstructured, collaborative, teacher-guided, and creative writing activities. At regular intervals, students can be asked to self-evaluate their work and suggest possible areas they wish to improve.

Showcase portfolios contain examples of writing chosen by students because the work is special to them in some way. For example, each writing sample included in the showcase portfolio is accompanied by a short statement or caption that explains why the writer chose that particular piece for inclusion ("This is the first story I ever wrote"; "I worked very hard on the ending of this story"; "I want to be a ballerina when I grow up, so I wrote a story about a dancer"; or "This story is very special. I included an audiotape of two songs I created about the characters in my story."). Teachers also encourage students to include pieces in their showcase portfolios that represent their abilities to explore, use, and combine intelligences. For example, students may include samples of their drawings and paintings or photographs of their sculptures, murals, and dioramas that complement their creative writing efforts and combine verbal/linguistic and visual/spatial intelligences (Gardner, 1995, 1999). To further personalize their work, students can decorate the front covers of their showcase portfolios and include a reflective introduction to their portfolio (see Figure 8.18), a table of contents, photographs of themselves, and an autobiography. With the availability of digital technology, students can create **electronic portfolios** that allow for such items as photographs, oral reading samples, art, music, and even video clips to become part of a portfolio. Prior to having the storage options of flash drives and CDs or DVDs, such items would have been cumbersome or impossible to store and present to others. The added ability to connect parts of a portfolio through hyperlinks also allows for the cross-referencing of goals to examples of how those goals have been met (Barrett, 2007).

With the students' permission, portfolios can be displayed during a Literacy Celebration Day or at parent–teacher conferences. Students' artifacts accompanied by written reflections, self-assessment questionnaires and surveys, and even oral readings of selected creative writings provide students, teachers, and parents with concrete evidence concerning individual students' improvements, efforts, personal writing interests, and perceptions about themselves as writers. More important, portfolios provide a way for students to take some responsibility for organizing their work and help them evaluate their achievements and writing instructional needs.

Go to MyEducationLab and select the topic *Assessing Reading and Writing*. Then, go to the Activities and Applications section, and examine the artifact entitled "Self-Evaluation (6–8)" to see how one student felt about her portfolio work. Next respond to the accompanying questions.

Go to MyEducationLab and select the topic *Ongoing Assessments*. Then, go to the Activities and Applications section, and watch the video entitled "Portfolios and Self-Assessment" to see how one teacher works with her students to help them choose artifacts for their portfolios. Next respond to the accompanying questions.

Figure 8.18   Child's Reflective Introduction for a Showcase Portfolio

Introduction*

My name is Arthur. I will be entering the fifth grade at XX School. I created this portfolio during my summer tutoring session at the University of New Orleans. My tutor's name is Marcia L. I began making things for my portfolio on June 21 and completed it on July 20. I began deciding what to include in my portfolio on July 16.

I picked items that were important to me to include in this portfolio. I wanted to show what I had learned, and I put all of my favorite projects in the portfolio. I also wanted to show that I am a hard worker.

The way I decided which things would go first in my portfolio was easy, I picked my favorite thing first. I had a list of everything I wanted in my portfolio, and I just put it in order starting with my favorite item.

This portfolio shows that I kept a book list for my readings. It also shows that I have a prediction log that I use when I am reading stories. My portfolio shows what I learned through reading. I learned about hurricanes and sand dollars. It also shows that there are some things about my reading that I have to work on still.

My portfolio also shows the different types of writing I can do. I included a book that I wrote and illustrated. I also included some comic strips that I wrote the story for as well as a story that uses new vocabulary.

I think that my best items are the comic strips, my hurricane report, and my movie review. These activities were all fun, and I learned a lot from completing each of these.

My portfolio shows the improvements I have made this summer. It shows what I can do. I can write a book if I use my imagination! It shows I can improve with practice and it shows that I am a hard worker.

*All names have been changed for purposes of privacy.

Summary

It makes sense to connect reading and writing instruction. Students' paths to literacy learning differ and the literacy learning modalities of reading and writing support and contribute to each other's development. It is especially important to connect reading and writing instruction for students who struggle, regardless of age. Many of these learners write very little because they have had few positive writing experiences. Because reading and writing develop concurrently, strengthening each other, it is crucial that students with literacy difficulties have opportunities to write.

The role of the writing teacher is to model effective writing strategies. Good writing teachers recognize that writing is a social process and that their students learn about writing by writing for their own purposes and audiences.

Implementing an effective writing program entails collecting information about each student's knowledge and preconceptions of written language. Ongoing observation is also necessary to assess students' ever-changing progress and the processes they employ as they write.

Students enjoy participating in nonstructured writing activities that allow them to write about subjects that interest and concern them. They also benefit from more structured writing lessons and activities categorized as collaborative, teacher-guided, and creative.

Finally, students benefit from learning how to assess their own growth in writing. Through completion of questionnaires and development of portfolios, students will become aware of what good writing is about.

Recommended Websites

Connecting Reading and Writing
   www.literacy.uconn.edu/writing.htm
This site provides an extensive list of writing websites for educators, grades K through 12.

Writing Folders
   www.sasked.gov.sk.ca/docs/xla/ela15c3.html
Basic information about the purpose and contents of writing folders can be found here.

6 + 1 Trait Writing
   www.nwrel.org
A widely used framework is presented for helping students learn traits that make for quality writing.

Developmental Stages of Spelling
   http://coe.west.asu.edu/students/dcorley/writing/wrspel
   .htm
Characteristics of the spelling stages are presented in an easy-to-understand format, one that can help teachers communicate these stages to parents.

Reconceptualizing Spelling Development and Instruction
   www.readingonline.org/articles/art_index.asp?
   HREF=/articles/handbook/templeton/index.html
This article from the *Handbook of Reading Research*, volume III (2000), provides background for and discusses developmental stages of spelling à la Henderson.

Shared Spelling Strategies
   www.readwritethink.org/lessons/lesson_view.asp?
   id=48
A lesson in "constructed" spelling for middle school students is provided here.

Everyday Spelling
   www.everydayspelling.com
Grade–level spelling lists are available, to include troublesome words for the elementary grades.

How to Start a Writer's Workshop
   www.teachers.net/lessons/posts/681.html
Here are some helpful suggestions for getting started with writer's workshop.

Writing Workshop
   http://teacher.scholastic.com/activities/writing/
This is a great site for both teachers and students for example projects (including persuasive writing, research writing, and oral history) that demonstrate all components of the writing process, as well as connections to national literacy standards.

Dialogue Journals: Interactive Writing to Develop Language and Literacy
   www.cal.org/resources/digest/peyton01.html
This article presents the benefits, challenges, and logistics of using dialogue journals.

KidPub
   www.kidpub.com
This site has online stories by kids, plus a chat area and a message center.

Electronic Portfolios in the K–12 Classroom
   www.educationworld.com/a_tech/tech/tech111.shtml
An excellent article discusses more about electronic portfolios and portfolios in general.

MyEducationLab is a research-based learning tool that brings teaching to life. Go to the Gipe 7th Edition MyEducationLab for Reading Assessment site at www.myeducationlab.com to:

- Engage in multimedia exercises to help you build a deeper and more applied understanding of chapter content.
- Use extensive resources including videos from real classrooms, Praxis and licensure preparation, a lesson plan builder, and materials to help you in your teaching career.

CHAPTER 9

Word Recognition

OBJECTIVES   *After you have read this chapter, you should be able to:*

1. Explain the difference between products of word analysis instruction and the process of word recognition.
2. Describe the five major skill strands for word recognition.
3. Develop a sequence for instruction of a word unknown in print.
4. Choose and develop materials and exercises appropriate for instruction in the process of word recognition.
5. Devise an instructional program in word recognition for a student struggling in this area.

VOCABULARY ALERT

analytical vocabulary	onsets	psychological set
automaticity	outlaw words	readers' theater
context	perceptual unit of	reading vocabulary
decodable text	analysis	rimes
expectancy clues	phonics	scriptal information
fluency	phonological awareness	sight vocabulary
key words	picture clues	sight words
listening vocabulary	picture walk	structural analysis
meaning clues	predictable text	visual synthesizing
meaning vocabulary	productive language	word walls

Figuring out words unknown in print is only one of many processes used in constructing meaning from written text. These processes are dynamic and ever changing as a student's knowledge and skills increase. They are also symbiotic, reciprocal, and interactive. For example, word analysis and word identification influence a reader's ability to understand what is read in a passage or sentence, which influences the ability to decode other unknown words. In this chapter, word recognition is conceptualized as an interaction among the skills learned (the *product* of word analysis instruction) with the way the student analyzes the unknown words (the *process* of word recognition). The more knowledge and skills readers have, the easier and more efficient word recognition will be and the more fluent their reading will become. Further, the more background and understanding readers bring to the reading passage, the better able they will be to use contextual analysis to decode words.

Reading instruction has a long methodological history, with method being closely related to the **perceptual unit of analysis** (the size of the visual stimuli used for word analysis). Different methods have emphasized teaching symbol–sound correspondence using letters of the alphabet, syllables, whole words, sentences, or whole stories. Students have learned to read successfully with each method.

Likewise, some students have trouble learning to read with each method, and different methods tend to yield different types of reading difficulties. You will find teaching ideas in this chapter that focus on small units of analysis, such as word parts, but you will also find suggestions for teaching that use larger analytical units typically associated with a holistic or psycholinguistic view of teaching reading. Invariably, the goal of all decoding instruction is to develop independent readers who not only comprehend what they read but who also choose to read. We do not want to make decoding instruction so boring or laborious as to "turn kids off" to reading.

I believe that students with word recognition difficulties profit from learning a variety of analytic units, depending largely on the individual's specific strategy needs. I also believe that many, if not all, beginning readers must learn to analyze words but that this analysis is only effective when they already know the words' meanings. If a word's meaning does not exist in the student's listening (or understanding) vocabulary, all the effort to analyze the word is pointless because it does not trigger a meaningful response. Unfortunately, beginning readers and many others (including ELs and learners with learning disabilities [LD]) do not know whether the word exists in their understanding vocabularies until after they have worked to analyze the word. Only when they are sure their efforts have identified the correct word do they feel the possibility of success.

Sadly, these students have no sure way of determining whether they have mistakenly analyzed a word or if the word is new to them in terms of meaning. This dilemma facing the young or struggling reader disappears or lessens only with maturity in reading.

The best defense is to develop in the student, from the very beginning, the need to demand meaning from what is read and to seek help if meaning does not result from analytic effort. Further, students should have a balanced set of word analysis strategies and varied techniques to allow them to solve the problem of decoding words with flexibility.

Teachers are advised to focus word recognition instruction on three long-term goals: (a) building a listening vocabulary, (b) building a sight vocabulary, and (c) building a balanced set of word recognition strategies. As a prerequisite for building a set of word recognition strategies, teachers need to be sure their students develop phonological awareness abilities. **Phonological awareness** refers to an awareness that words are made up of syllables; word parts, such as onsets and rimes, prefixes, and suffixes, as well as individual phonemes. This concept is slightly different from phonemic awareness, which only relates to spoken words (see Chapter 7).

LISTENING VOCABULARY

All teachers wish to support students in gaining knowledge. Frequently this means teaching new concepts and elaborating on more basic ones. Words reflect these concepts. When students have opportunities to experience new areas of knowledge, they learn new words and their meanings, thereby expanding their **meaning vocabulary**. There are two mandatory components of meaning vocabulary: (a) **listening vocabulary**—the word is heard and understood in speech—and (b) **reading vocabulary**—the word is pronounced and understood in printed form. A word cannot be considered part of one's meaning vocabulary until it is in *both* the listening and the reading vocabulary.

Many students come to school with good listening vocabularies; they continue to add to their store of concepts and word meanings as they proceed through the curriculum. Some students, however, have limited knowledge of the world or nontraditional knowledge that is at odds with traditional or cultural expectations. World knowledge affects a student's attempts to analyze words unknown in print. *No matter how hard students try to analyze a word, and no matter how accurate their analytical skills may be, they cannot trigger a meaningful response if the word is not in their listening vocabulary.* To illustrate the point, try to pronounce the following words: *miscreant, putative, egregious*. If you have previously heard these words, chances are good that you will feel secure pronouncing them. If not, chances are equally good that your pronunciation will be incorrect. Make several guesses (hypotheses) about the pronunciation of the words. For fun, if you don't know the meanings of these words, try to guess the meanings from the words provided.

miscreant	*putative*	*egregious*
mistake	reputed	helpful
hero	punishable	dreadful
degenerate	ugly	powerful
relapse	childlike	tolerable

If you still feel insecure about their meanings, read the following sentences, which may help clarify them.

The *miscreant* defaced Michelangelo's *Pieta*.
Charles's terrier is the *putative* sire of the litter of pups.
Crashing into the train was an *egregious* mistake.

If you knew all the other words in the sentences, you may have used the context to identify the *meaning* of each word and thus you were able to understand the sentence. Sometimes, however, the context may not be sufficient. Regardless, you *still* do not know how the word is pronounced because it is not yet in your listening vocabulary. You need to have someone pronounce the word for you while you are seeing the word in context. Nor is the unknown word in your reading vocabulary because you cannot pronounce the word. All you can do is speculate about its meaning from context. But outside of a textual presentation you are not able to associate a meaning with the word until you hear it used in a context from which you can derive its meaning. On encountering such words while reading, mature readers attempt to use context and apply their graphophonic (symbol/*graph*–sound/*phon*) knowledge and do whatever is necessary to maintain the meaning of the passage. Sometimes the word is not important to the overall understanding of the passage and so mature readers skip it. If it turns out the word is important, mature readers consult a dictionary or ask someone. This kind of thoughtful behavior, a strategy or plan, is something we need to teach students.

Assessment

Limitations in listening vocabulary are often detectable during oral reading. Typically, when asked to figure out a word, readers with a listening vocabulary limitation can demonstrate knowledge of word analysis, blending skills, and use of context clues, coming close to an acceptable pronunciation, but they still cannot come up with the word. This suggests that they are not associating the meaning of the word with its attempted pronunciation. Frequent occurrence of this behavior suggests that these students are meeting too many words with meanings they should but do not know.

Using standardized test results, teachers can compare vocabulary subtest scores and subtest scores that assess word recognition skills. When vocabulary knowledge is considerably weaker than other word analysis skills, a limitation has been identified. The *Stanford Diagnostic Reading Tests* (Karlsen & Gardner, 2003) is one of the few group standardized tests available for this purpose. Another assessment procedure is to ask students directly if they know what a word means. Assessment of receptive vocabulary, an indicator of oral language development, is discussed in Chapter 7.

Instruction

Following are examples of activities recommended to expand listening vocabularies. These activities encompass many areas of the curriculum, so they are appropriate for any age or grade level:

1. Provide many and varied firsthand experiences.
   a. Arrange field trips, preceded and followed by discussions that are deliberately planned to use and review relevant vocabulary. As Durkin (1978) stated, "Experience and vocabulary do not grow together automatically. . . . Teachers should have made some decisions beforehand about the concepts and words that ought to come alive as a result of the experience" (p. 380).
   b. Develop interest centers in the classroom, arranged and maintained by both teacher and students, using appropriate charts and labels. Such interest centers also provide discussion topics.

2. Provide vicarious experiences.

   a. Invite speakers to talk about relevant areas of study. Before and after the presentation, initiate discussion and elaborate on important concepts and vocabulary.

MI Connection:
spatial

   b. Make full use of carefully selected appropriate media—for example, films, video clips, transparencies, tapes, models, and computer simulations.

3. Provide increased opportunities for silent reading of relatively easy materials and for reading aloud to students. Explanations and elaborations by authors frequently add dimensions of meaning. This activity is particularly important for more mature readers who lack experience in a particular area; such an activity could be conceptualized as learning about the world through books. Authors often help by giving context clues that define words or terms and elaborate meanings.

4. Guide the development and use of dictionaries that relate either to a topic of special interest to the student or to a group project or thematic unit.

MI Connection:
spatial

   a. Have young children construct personal picture dictionaries.
   b. Have students construct personal spelling dictionaries (see Chapter 8).
   c. Have students construct personal vocabulary notebooks.
   d. Have students prepare alphabet books for a particular topic. Many alphabet books on a wide variety of topics are available to serve as models (for example, see *Animalia* [Base, 1986], suitable for upper grades, or *The Icky Bug Alphabet Book* [Pallotta, 1986], suitable for younger students).

5. Guide the direct study of words through such activities as listing synonyms, antonyms, or affixes and searching for word derivations.

MI Connection:
musical

6. Read aloud books emphasizing sensory impressions (selected children's literature can provide the stimulus, for example, *Click, Rumble, Roar: Poems about Machines* [Hopkins, 1987] and scores of books about animals).

SIGHT VOCABULARY

Sight vocabulary refers to words in print that are recognized instantly and effortlessly. Mature readers perceive most words they encounter in this fashion. Most children entering school, on the other hand, begin with few or no words that they can read quickly with ease. As sight vocabulary increases, the number of unrecognized words decreases. Eventually, the student encounters few unknown words; when they are encountered, they are probably not in the student's meaning vocabulary. Analytical techniques seldom help mature readers who encounter unknown words because the issue is lack of meaning rather than lack of appropriate word recognition facility.

Students seem to learn words in three phases. At first encounter, they do not recognize the word in print, although it may exist in their listening vocabularies. Then, with repeated exposure, they recognize it partially but still need to analyze its representation in graphic form. (These words make up the **analytical vocabulary**; the student says the word correctly but not quickly.) Finally, after several encounters, the word is recognized instantly. Every word that students read should be considered a candidate for their sight vocabularies, with the possible exception of rare, unusual, or foreign words. As a student reads more and more, words accumulate in the student's sight vocabulary and need no further study because they are recognized automatically (LaBerge & Samuels, 1974). The concept of **automaticity** is emphasized at both the word and word-element levels because the efficient reader must learn these units so thoroughly that little effort is needed to recognize a new word or word part. Of course, automaticity is best achieved by practice in reading whole, meaningful texts, not by isolated word drills.

The term *sight vocabulary* should not be confused with that of **sight words**. The latter term refers to a relatively small set of words in our language that do not conform to rules of pronunciation (also known as **outlaw words**) or to analytical techniques learned by children beginning to read but that need to be made a part of one's sight vocabulary. Examples of these basic sight words are *to, of, are, come,* and *you*. Also included are words that appear so frequently that they must be thoroughly learned as soon as possible. The Dolch (1953) list of 220 words and the first 300 high-frequency words of Fry's Instant Words (Fry & Kress, 2006) account for more than 50 percent of the words found in reading materials for children (and adults).

Basic sight words should be given high priority for every young child's sight vocabulary, but they should not be considered the only words to be learned to the point of instant recognition. Because sight words are usually words whose function is to connect other words, they often have no concrete referent. For this reason, use of phrases rather than isolated words provides a more meaningful presentation (for example, *be good; here is a(n) . . .; there are . . .*). For a list of phrases based on the Dolch word list, see the Web links at the end of this chapter. Teachers should also make a point of including words associated with the computer age as an essential part of sight vocabulary (see Figure 9.1 for a short list of computer and Internet terms).

Figure 9.1	A Sampling of Useful Computer Terms

access	links
alt key	memory
archive	menu
backspace	monitor
bit	mouse
bookmark	Mozilla
boot	multimedia
bug	network
byte	online
click	operating system
clip art	password
cookie	Pentium
crash	save
cursor	search engine
database	server
desktop	software
disc	spam
download	spreadsheet
enter	upload
ESC (escape)	URL
Google	virus
hard disk	web page
hardware	word processor
icon	worm
Internet	Yahoo
laptop	zip

Assessment

Students who have not committed words to their sight vocabularies are relatively easy to spot. They do not recognize many words on a page. They frequently are word-by-word readers. When reading orally they analyze nearly every word, sounding out words or word parts with painful slowness. By the time they reach the end of the sentence they often have forgotten much, if not all, of what they read.

A sight vocabulary word can be recognized in about one-half second or less. The classroom teacher can assess this speed in several ways. A good source for words is the glossary found in the student's present texts, one of the high-frequency word lists, or words the student has been working on recently, such as words used in a language experience story or in a new thematic unit.

The following is a good group procedure for screening purposes. Construct a test using words from the texts available for student use, from a sight word list such as the Dolch 220 or Fry's instant words, or from graded word lists such as those found in a published informal reading inventory. On each line, type three or four words (depending on the maturity level of the group) of approximately the same difficulty level. Test item difficulty increases by using words that are visually similar (*though, through, thought*) and decreases by using visually dissimilar words (*though, paper, statue*). Make copies for each member of the group and one for you to use as a key. A practice test is always a good idea, especially with young children, to help them know what to do when the test is given.

To prepare students for a speed test, tell them the following:

1. This is a speed test and not like real reading when you can look back and forth as much as you want.

2. You will have to hurry your looks (fixations). You may have time only to glance once at each word, then mark the one I say.

3. Some of you may have trouble with this test, but don't worry. If you do, we'll schedule some time to practice these and other words. It's OK if you don't do as well as you would like. You will get better.

4. If you miss a word, be ready to go on to the next line.

In administering the test the teacher says the stimulus word twice, then allows about five seconds for pupils to respond before proceeding to the next item.

Scoring procedures are straightforward; the number of correct items indicates the performance level. More important for screening purposes, however, is locating the stragglers in the group. Those who have done poorly on the group test should be further observed individually.

To assess individual students, make two typewritten copies of the words in list format (one word per line) and give one copy to the student. Ask the student to read the words to you as quickly as possible while you check accuracy and rapidity from your copy (this reading might be tape-recorded for later analysis). Remember, accurate but slow is *wrong* for sight vocabulary. Words must be read accurately and quickly. For differentiation, words read correctly but slowly are referred to as being in a student's analytical vocabulary.

A second procedure is to make small typewritten or neatly printed flash cards from the word list and show them for about one-half second, allowing the student a moment to respond. If necessary, record the response on your copy of the word list from which the flash cards were made. These words can be used in sentences on the back of each card to test for recognition in context.

Instruction

Repetition and practice are key concepts for the improvement of sight vocabulary. Many students attain speed and accuracy simply by reading often and meeting the words in their books. Probably the most natural way of meeting common words repeatedly is through extensive recreational reading of relatively easy materials or materials chosen by the students, as in a literature-based program. This type of reading exposes the student to many known words that will assist recognition of those that are unknown. Books with **predictable text** (such as Eric Carle's *The Very Hungry Caterpillar*, 1987, or Bill Martin's *Brown Bear, Brown Bear*, 1983) contain a lot of repetition and provide an excellent source of easy reading, as do language experience stories and multimedia storybooks such as the *Living Books Library* available from Edmark. The value of predictable language to reading fluency is further discussed later in this chapter. Predictable books are more like real language, whereas books with **decodable text** restrict the language used to words that are easily decoded (phonetically regular). There are relatively few examples of decodable books that provide meaningful text, which young readers need in order to learn how to use all the language cue systems together. Dr. Seuss books and the Scholastic Phonics Chapter Books for grades K–2, which include *Fun with Zip and Zap* (Shefelbine, 1998), are examples of meaningful decodable books. Cunningham (1999) made the point,

> It is very hard to make much meaning if the text you are reading can only contain words you can decode and if you have only learned a few elements . . . "Dan is in the van. Jan is in the van. The van is tan. Dan ran the van. Jan fans Dan." Children learned to read this and did apply their decoding, but what did it mean? . . . If a child is just learning to read and the text being read makes no sense but is just there to practice decoding, some children will get in the habit of turning the meaning-making part of their brains off when they read. (p. 71)

Although there is sometimes a need to use decodable books to support a reader struggling with matching visual patterns with sounds, decodable books must be supplemented frequently with real literature so students do not lose sight of the purpose of reading.

A more direct approach may be needed for students with more serious sight vocabulary deficiencies. Often these students have had an unfortunate experience with a reading program or a teacher who overemphasized analytical techniques or synthetic phonics (decoding a word letter by letter from left to right). These students acquire the bad habit of looking for parts in all words rather than just unknown words. They try to sound out everything. Exercises that ask them to analyze words into smaller units *should be avoided*. Techniques that promote fluent reading, such as neurological impress, echo reading, repeated readings, and readers' theater (see the "Fluency" section in this chapter) are recommended.

Direct teaching of sight vocabulary words might proceed as follows. The teacher recites a sentence containing the word to be learned and then writes the word, followed by several more sentences using the word, on the chalkboard, on the overhead transparency, or on sentence strips.

Teacher: "I *heard* you were sick."

(teacher writes)

> heard
>
> Mary *heard* a new joke.
>
> Have you *heard* anything else?
>
> John said he *heard* what you said.

Next, the teacher draws attention to the word in isolation by asking questions about it and providing practice in writing it, such as:

What letter does the word begin with?

What's the last letter in the word?

How many letters are in this word?

Spell the word.

Trace the word in the air.

Spell, say, spell, write the word.

Go to MyEducationLab and select the topic *English Language Learners*. Then, go to the Activities and Applications section, watch the video entitled "Introducing Words to Young Readers," and notice how the teacher uses individual white boards to help students learn new words. Next respond to the accompanying questions.

Following this focus on the word's graphic form, students must read the word in a phrase or sentence or use it in a phrase or sentence they create. Students should also practice reading the word in whole text. The text might be one developed by the teacher or a book, poem, or language experience story.

Finally, independent practice must be provided. The word might become part of a game, or the student could be asked to find the word used in other printed material such as books, magazines, or newspapers.

Three effective methods for increasing sight vocabulary are the language experience approach (LEA), Fernald's (1943) VAKT (visual, auditory, kinesthetic, tactile) approach, and intensive word practice (Moe & Manning, 1984). Although the LEA can also be used to teach a word recognition strategy, the VAKT approach and intensive word practice are used specifically to help students learn *troublesome* sight words.

The Language Experience Approach. Many learners, including ELs, are motivated to increase their knowledge of the word recognition process when material that they have dictated is written down or typed for them. Using the LEA, the teacher is also assured that the words used in follow-up activities are part of the student's listening vocabulary.

Any language experience material should be the result of a direct experience of the learner (or learners, in the case of a group production; see also the "Spotlight on English Learners" feature in Chapter 8). In addition to developing stories and accounts about field trips, an unusual classroom event, or the actions of a classroom pet, teachers plan many interesting experiences for students to write about, such as reading an exciting book to the students, working with clay or Play-Doh, making no-bake cookies, painting pumpkins for the fall season, performing a science experiment, or sharing family pictures. In the example that follows, the teacher gave each student a marshmallow and directed the students to think about how it looks, feels, smells, and tastes. Then a group account was dictated.

The Marshmallow

A marshmallow is soft, white, and fluffy. It is shaped like a drum. It looks like a pillow. It's too small for a pillow. It can roll. The marshmallow smells sweet, airy, and delicious. It's squeezable. It's sticky. There is powder on the outside of it. It tastes like a sponge. It makes you want another one.

Following dictation, the teacher reads the entire account back to the students as they follow along. Any changes students wish to make to the account should be made at this time. This step also provides many teaching opportunities. For example, students may notice many uses of *it* and *it's*. If not, the teacher should point them out. The teacher can then ask about the referent for *it* and discuss the nature of pronouns in a real and meaningful context because the students themselves created the account. In this particular example, a discussion of adjectives would also be appropriate. Additionally, the teacher might want to point out features of words, such as (in this example) compound words, syllabication between two consonants, the vowel-consonant-silent *e* pattern, and the vowel-consonant pattern. The teacher can also take this opportunity to expand conceptual knowledge by introducing material that discusses the marshmallow plant (try typing in the words "marshmallow plant" in Google for information).

Once material has been dictated and read by the teacher, the student reads it. Even if the material is just a caption for a picture drawn by the student, the words from the material are used in many ways to ensure repeated exposures. First, the student should write each word in a personal dictionary with a self-generated sentence or picture or both. In this way, if the student comes across one of the words again and cannot remember it, the teacher can direct the student to his personal dictionary to find the word. The sentence or picture will provide the needed help. Not only are new words learned through this approach, but also alphabet knowledge (see Chapter 7) and dictionary skills (see Chapter 14) begin to develop, as does a strategy for becoming an independent reader.

Additional activities might include matching words from students' stories put on cards to words found in other printed material (such as basal readers or storybooks) and playing sight vocabulary games such as a vocabulary version of bingo. The teacher should insist that the word be pronounced each time it is matched or encountered in the game. Arranging word cards to form sentences also reinforces recognition of the words in other contexts. Any teacher concerned that the words students use in their language experience stories will not help them in other reading tasks need only compare those words to a word list such as Fry's instant words.

As soon as possible, students should write their own stories. Students' efforts at writing will not only help them learn the nature of written language but also focus their attention on the visual features of print, aiding letter and word recognition.

Students with very limited sight vocabularies can be provided sentence starters to get them going. Initially, high-frequency words can be used to create *pattern books*, which are merely sheets of paper stapled together. For instance, the teacher might provide several sheets of paper with "I like to eat _____." written on each. The student then draws a picture of the food, and the teacher writes the word for the food item on the blank line, one on each page. When the book is completed, a cover with a title such as "Things I Like to Eat by Kalisha" can be created and attached to the stapled sheets. Of course, Kalisha then reads the book. Many words can be taught this way. Other examples of sentence starters are:

I like to play _____.
I like to go _____.
_____ are big.
_____ are little.
My favorite _____ is _____.

The Visual, Auditory, Kinesthetic, Tactile Approach. The VAKT approach begins with the teacher eliciting a word from the student that the student wants to learn. The teacher writes or prints the word in crayon (for the tactile sensation) on a strip of paper in letters large enough for the learner to trace by direct finger contact (sometimes students are asked to trace in salt or on sandpaper). The student is then shown how to trace the word and told how to pronounce it at the same time. Following the teacher's example, the student traces and pronounces the word. This continues until the student feels ready to write the word from memory. If the student is successful, the session ends. If not, tracing continues. Words successfully written from memory should be checked for recognition later in the day or the next day.

After a period of time that varies from learner to learner, the student reaches a point at which tracing can be eliminated. Instead, someone pronounces the word, and the student looks at it and repeats it as often as necessary until she can write it from memory. If the written word is incorrect, the student looks at the word more carefully while pronouncing it and tries once more to write it from memory. Strict use of the VAKT approach, which includes charting the number of times a word needs to be traced before it is learned, is probably not necessary for most students. Usually the tracing technique itself is sufficient.

Intensive Word Practice. Intensive word practice (Moe & Manning, 1984) also uses a multisensory approach. Usually, three to six new or troublesome words are randomly placed among other words in each of four sections on a word practice sheet (Figure 9.2). Sentences using the new words in a meaningful context are placed beneath the four

Figure 9.2   Example of an Intensive Word Practice Sheet for Three New Sight Words: *this, was, in*

1			2		
	boy	was		this	on
	on	in		was	the
	the	this		in	boy
3			4		
	on	in		boy	on
	the	was		in	was
	this	boy		the	this

1. My milk is in this cup.
2. Mother was in the house.
3. This is the dog I like.

sections. The procedure emphasizes listening skills and following directions as well as practicing troublesome words, and it can be used with a group.

First, direct the students to fold the paper on the bottom line to separate the sentences from the word boxes. They should see only the numbered boxes. Next, instruct the students to fold the paper again on the line that separates boxes 1 and 2 from boxes 3 and 4. Finally, tell the students to fold the paper on the vertical line so they can only see box 1.

The teacher has previously prepared large word cards, each containing one of the new words to be learned; for this example, cards are needed for *this, was,* and *in.* The teacher gives the directions for box 1, instructing the students to mark each of the new words in some way while the teacher pronounces the word and shows the word card. Two repetitions of the word should be sufficient. For example, while showing the word card for *this,* the teacher might say, "I want you to draw a circle around *this.* Draw a circle around *this.*" While showing the word card for *was,* the teacher might say, "Put a line under *was.* Put a line under *was.*" Likewise, for the word card *in,* the teacher might say, "Draw a box around *in.* Draw a box around *in.* Now turn your paper over so you just see box 2."

The directions for box 2 also instruct the students to mark the new words. This time, however, the teacher shows but does not pronounce the word. It is hoped that the students are mentally pronouncing the words as they look back and forth from word card to paper. The directions proceed as follows: "Put a line under _____" (while showing *was*). "Draw a box around _____" (while showing *this*). "Draw two lines under _____" (while showing *in*). Students are then directed to refold their papers so only boxes 3 and 4 can be seen.

For box 3 the teacher pronounces the word but does not show it. All directions are oral: "Put a line under *this.*" "Draw a circle around *in.*" "Draw a box around *was.*"

For box 4 the students are simply told to circle the three words practiced in the lesson. Success with box 4 indicates that the student has at least visual memory for the words taught. Not until the sentences are read at the bottom of the page can the teacher judge whether the students have learned to pronounce the words as well. Students are asked to underline the new words in the sentences and to read the sentences.

The following exercises, and many like them found in developmental texts, activity books, and computer software, are used to develop the habit of looking at words rapidly and can readily be developed into learning game formats:

1. Read along with interactive, multimedia stories (also referred to as e-books or "talking books"). Many excellent interactive animated stories are available that highlight the words while they are being read aloud for students to follow, but it is important for teachers to first evaluate the books available (see the guidelines provided by Shamir and Korat, 2006). High quality CD-ROM storybooks can increase the sight vocabulary of young children (Lewin, 2000), assist readers in constructing meaning (Doty, Popplewell, & Byers, 2001), increase reading motivation, especially in readers who struggle (Glasgow, 1996, 1996/1997), and "enhance literacy acquisition, especially for [ELs] and students experiencing difficulties with the code" (Nikkel, 1996). Labbo (2000) lists 12 things to do with a talking book in a classroom computer center.

   MI Connection: spatial

2. Use exercises emphasizing expectancy or context clues:

   a. A snowman melts in the _____.

   sun   cold   man

b. The bird is in the _____.

boy   tree   table

3. Use exercises requiring quick scanning of a group of words:

a. See how fast you can find the word that does not belong in each list. Put a line through it.

1	*2*	*3*
boy	dog	pie
girl	look	cake
pipe	bird	much

b. Put an *X* by the things you can find in the food store.

meat	soup	dogs
house	candy	cans
eggs	truck	milk

4. Present activities and games using individual words:

MI Connection:
spatial

a. *Fish pond.* Make word cards with a new (or review) vocabulary word on one side and an easy sentence on the other side with the word underlined. Affix a paper clip to each. Attach each card to one of multiple varieties of paper fish created by students. Put these in "fish pond." Attach a small magnet to the end of a fishing pole. A player who fishes out a word and reads it correctly and quickly scores 2 points; if the sentence helps the player say the word, 1 point. Any number of students can play.

b. *Star Trek.* Invite students to create a large poster board with slots to hold cards placed at appropriate intervals representing the route of a space trip to a worm hole (or wherever). Make a stack of cards, writing a sentence on each one containing the word being practiced. The word should be underlined and in isolation above the sentence. Students take turns drawing from the stack of cards. If they read the word correctly, they put the card in the appropriate slot marking the next step in a trip through the galaxy. This game is best played with two to five students, depending on the number of slots; if more than one poster is created, teams could compete.

c. *Bang.* Make a "bang" card for every five word cards. The word cards have the word of interest on one side and a sentence using the word on the other. (This 5-to-1 ratio can be changed depending on how long you want the game to last: the more "bang" cards, the longer the game will last.) Place the cards in a bag or box and have students take turns drawing them out one at a time. If a word card is drawn and the word is pronounced correctly within two seconds (one student acts as a timekeeper in charge of the stopwatch), the card is kept. If the sentence needs to be read to pronounce the word, that one card is returned to the bag. If a "bang" card is drawn, *all* word cards collected up to that point are placed back in the bag. This element of chance enables learners of different abilities to play together and also provides the necessary repetition of new words. The first player to collect five (or three or ten) words is the winner. Several students could play together on teams.

| Figure 9.3 | Cheerleader Spelling for the Word *They* |

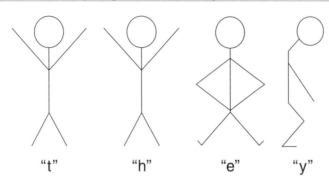

"t"   "h"   "e"   "y"

d. *Cheerleader spelling.* Cheerleader spelling involves using the entire body in learning to spell conventionally. In cheerleader spelling (Rogers, 1999), students position their hands and arms either above their heads, at their waist, or toward the floor to correspond to each letter in the word according to whether, when written on lined paper in lowercase form, it is an ascender (*b, d, f, h, k, l, t*), between lines (*a, c, e, i, m, n, o, r, s, u, v, w, x, z*), or a descender (*g, j, p, q, y*). (See Figure 9.3 for the cheerleader spelling of the word *they*.) This activity requires students to look carefully at the word, think about the letters and how they are written, and engage in the physical movements that match each letter formation. Through cheerleader spelling, the form of the word can literally be felt, and the visual patterns of the words spelled in this way are more readily recalled.

MI Connection:
bodily-kinesthetic

5. *Activities for adolescent readers.* The Bang game may be suitable for any age, but students in upper elementary and middle school generally require more age-appropriate activities for practicing words, even though their abilities may be closer to those of much younger students. Curtis and McCart (1992) present several gamelike activities using words that are more challenging both linguistically and cognitively (such as *flammable, combustible, rayon, crayon, mayonnaise*). Their suggestions often have students working in pairs, which further encourages the students to want to work hard. One of their examples is Beat the Clock, a speeded word recognition activity. Student pairs record the time it takes them to read through the words. Timings at the beginning and end of the week give a gauge of progress. Points can be awarded.

FLUENCY

Fluency refers to more than just smooth, automatic reading or a quick reading rate. It also includes the "ability to read in expressive rhythmic and melodic patterns" (Richards, 2000, p. 535). As such, there are three interactive aspects to fluency: rate or pace, smoothness or automaticity with accuracy, and *prosody,* or reading with expression, natural intonation and appropriate phrasing (Rasinski, 2003). One common goal of literacy instruction is to develop fluent readers.

The instructional methods provided here are intended to increase reading fluency, which in turn should enable the ineffective decoder of any age or grade level to focus more on meaning than on individual words (Samuels, 1988). The increased amount of practice in reading whole text should also increase the automatic recognition of words.

Predictable Language Method

The predictable language method takes advantage of the rhythmic, repetitive, and re-dundant language structures in children's storybooks and nursery rhymes (Walker, 2003). It assumes that word identification is facilitated by the predictive nature of the material. Choose a book that contains a predictable pattern, such as Bill Martin's *The Haunted House* (1970) ("One dark and stormy night I came upon a haunted house. I tiptoed into the yard. No one was there. I tiptoed onto the porch. No one was there. . . ."). First read the material aloud to the students so they can hear the whole story. During this reading, emphasize the predictable parts using an enthusiastic voice. Now the students are ready for a second reading. During the second reading, ask the students to join in whenever they feel they know what to say. During subsequent readings, an oral cloze procedure (omitting particular words) can be used to give students practice in predicting upcoming words in text. Finally, students are ready to read the book on their own, using the pre-dictable language pattern and picture clues to aid them. Students can also be asked to write their own story, using the same predictable pattern found in the book but chang-ing the characters or setting. For example, the haunted house might become *The Haunted School* with a whole new set of spaces and rooms to tiptoe through.

Neurological Impress Method (NIM)

In the neurological impress method (NIM), the student and teacher read orally in unison (Heckelman, 1969, 1986), sitting side by side, with the teacher slightly behind on the right side to read into the student's right ear. The teacher's voice will actually be a bit ahead of the student's, especially if the student has a limited sight vocabulary. The teacher thus models fluent and expressive reading and allows the student to experience the way that feels. The teacher does not stop when the student falters. The student is directed to con-tinue to read with the teacher as much as possible. The teacher should move a finger along the line of print being read so the student can follow more easily. This method does take some getting used to. Using short, rhythmic, and repetitive materials, such as poems or song lyrics, might prove helpful.

Bedsworth (1991) reported impressive gains for three middle school students who used NIM only 10 minutes a day for nine weeks. All three students made significant gains—three and a half years in nine weeks for silent reading. In addition, the students' attitudes and perceptions about their reading became more positive. Bedsworth specu-lates that NIM works because it provides a nonthreatening reading experience; it is a novel approach; the attention of the learner is focused through visual, auditory, and kinesthetic-tactile modalities; and students read in units rather than word by word. Modifications of NIM include *dyad reading* or buddy reading (paired reading activities in which students take turns reading aloud and listening so they can summarize what their partner read).

Audiobooks also provide an opportunity for students to read or follow along with an expert reader. In addition to freeing the teacher to work individually with a larger number of students, audiobooks have many other benefits, especially in the secondary classroom (Baskin & Harris, 1995). Audiobooks enable older students to experience age-appropriate literature as well as enhance their reading fluency if they attempt to read along with the recording.

Repeated Readings

In repeated readings, a self-selected passage is reread orally until it is read accurately and fluently (Samuels, 1979/1997). Repeated readings encourage the use of contextual meaning and sentence structure to predict upcoming words and to correct miscues. The teacher should make a copy of the passages used for repeated reading so that, as the student reads, the teacher can record errors and speed. Afterwards, the teacher and student together will chart these numbers on a graph. The student then practices rereading the material silently. (During this time the teacher can work with another student.) The student rereads the passage aloud for the second time while the teacher records errors and speed using a different ink color. Again these numbers are charted and any progress noted. This procedure is followed until the student achieves a speed of 85 words per minute. A substantial amount of research shows that the process of repeated readings can help students recall more of what they read, comprehend more, and increase their reading rate, accuracy, and oral reading expression (National Reading Panel, 2000; Therrien, 2004). Additionally, a modification that supports a cooperative learning approach using partners, called *paired repeated reading* (Koskinen & Blum, 1986), also seems to be effective and easy to manage in regular classrooms.

Echo Reading

Echo reading is similar to both the neurological impress method and the repeated readings procedure in that the student is following a teacher's model and may need to repeat the reading that is being imitated. In echo reading (Walker, 2003), the teacher reads one sentence of text aloud with appropriate intonation and phrasing. The student then tries to imitate this oral reading model. The text reading continues in this fashion until the teacher feels the student can imitate more than one sentence at a time. This technique allows students to read text fluently that they otherwise might not have been able to handle. This technique can also be used in conjunction with repeated readings or the neurological impress method to model particularly troublesome sentences. Echo reading is quite helpful for the student who needs a model of fluent reading—for instance, students who focus too much on the words in a passage rather than the meaning or those unconcerned about whether their oral reading sounds like fluent language.

Readers' Theater

Readers' theater provides a realistic opportunity for students to read orally and practice their use of intonation, inflection, and fluency. In readers' theater, students present a dramatic interpretation of a narrative passage through an oral interpretive reading. Character parts are assigned or selected by participating students, and appropriate parts for oral reading are identified and then practiced silently. Following practice, the students read their scripts orally for an audience. (Props and costumes are not necessary.) The mood of the story is conveyed through proper intonation and phrasing. This technique is especially helpful not only for fluency but also for comprehension. When deciding what should be included in the script, the students must decide what dialogue and narration is important to the understanding of the story. Once again, there is an opportunity for repeated readings. Research by Corcoran and Davis (2005) and Martinez, Roser, and Strecker (1998/1999) demonstrated that use of readers' theater increases reading rate. Readers' theater can also be adapted for use with expository material (see Chapter 13).

WORD RECOGNITION PROCESSES

The following word recognition processes give students the needed flexibility to identify and analyze unknown words. Sometimes students need to use only one of these processes. At other times, two or more are needed and are used either separately or together as parallel processes. The five word recognition processes are:

1. Context clues
   a. Expectancy clues
   b. Picture clues
   c. Meaning clues
2. Knowledge of word parts
   a. Phonic analysis
   b. Structural analysis
3. Visual analysis
4. Blending and synthesizing
5. Dictionary skills (discussed in Chapter 14)

Parallels can readily be seen between these word recognition processes and the major skill strands recognized by many reading instructional systems today: namely, sight vocabulary, contextual analysis, phonic analysis, structural analysis, and dictionary skills. The skills are usually sequenced from easy to difficult, according to an author's or a curriculum committee's logic and experience. Thus, skill sequences vary from one school district to another, with differences ranging from slight to considerable. When a student changes from one district to another that is quite different, the teacher must monitor progress carefully to ensure that the student does not experience learning gaps during the transition.

Most reading curriculum guides indicate a scope and sequence of word recognition skills (Figure 9.4). Teachers must know the scope and sequence used in their school, particularly the skills taught in immediately preceding and subsequent years. If a school system does not provide scope and sequence information, teachers must do their own analyses and assume that, in general, the students have received skills instruction randomly or on a basis other than that represented here.

Use of Context Clues

Expectancy and Picture Clues. Two important context clues, **expectancy clues** and **picture clues**, relate directly to understanding what is about to be read. Expectancy clues are related to **psychological set**; that is, when a person is introduced to a topic, certain related concepts rise to the threshold of the mind. These ideas, especially the words associated with them, become more readily available from memory storage. In essence, the reader's nonvisual information, or schemata, for a topic is activated. When teachers

SPOTLIGHT ON ENGLISH LEARNERS

Choral Reading and Readers' Theater

Children's literature books are very useful in reinforcing standard English word patterns. For example, with Gag's *Millions of Cats* (1928), students can perform a choral reading of "Hundreds of cats, thousands of cats, millions and billions and trillions of cats" (practicing plural suffixes) while experiencing an interesting parable that also teaches values. Students can practice *-ed* and *-er* suffixes while doing choral readings of parts of *Drummer Hoff* (Emberly, 1967) as part of a thematic unit on military history. Although teachers should focus on the aesthetic, meaningful experience that literature allows, the acquisition of standard structures can be an important by-product of an authentic literary experience. Students who use only workbooks are deprived of the richness of language, culture, and thinking that literature provides. Choral reading activities with various predictable plot books or books with rhymes are useful for facilitating the literacy development of English learners especially.

The following stories contain repetitive lines and predictable patterns. Choral reading allows students to read within the safety of a group; thus, they are more likely to take risks. Students who cannot read independently can participate successfully by orally "reading" the lines of repetition they recall from memory:

dePaola, Tomie. (1975). *Strega Nona*. Upper Saddle River, NJ: Prentice Hall.

Martin, Bill Jr. (1983). *Brown Bear, Brown Bear, What Do You See?* New York: Holt.

Martin, Bill Jr. (1991). *Polar Bear, What Do You Hear?* New York: Holt.

Peek, Merle. (1985). *Mary Wore Her Red Dress (and Henry Wore His Green Sneakers)*. New York: Ticknor & Fields.

Soule, Jean Conder. (1964). *Never Tease a Weasel*. New York: Parents Magazine.

In addition, readers' theater can be of special benefit to English learners. **Readers' theater** has been defined as the oral presentation of drama, prose, or poetry by two or more readers. Students begin by reading a story, then transform the story into a script, formulate and refine their interpretations, and finally perform their reading for an audience.

The steps for preparing a readers' theater production follow:

1. Select a story or part of a story. Good sources of materials are children's books with lots of dialogue or plays that can be used without the proscribed stage directions. Other sources include folk tales, myths, fantasy or fairy tales, and even poetry. Also see Aaron Shepard's website, and others, listed at the end of this chapter for prepared scripts, some of which come in a variety of languages.

2. Once the selection has been read, begin writing the script. Students can include their own ideas about the characters and events as they write the dialogue.

3. Rehearsal of the script includes repeated readings to help the students use techniques such as intonation and characterization to bring their reading roles to life. A good technique is to ask them to "become" the character and use their imaginations to answer questions not only about the character's personality but also about what is happening to the character in the story. These "who," "what," "when," and "where" questions help to develop thoughts, intentions, and feelings for what is happening and where the action is occurring.

4. Performance is the fun part. It can be as simple as a brief presentation for the class or as elaborate as a stage production for other classes and parents. Parts are always read, not memorized.

5. Evaluation of the experience and follow-up commentary often reveal greater understanding of the characters, setting, and plot development because the students have not only read the material but have also experienced it.

introduce new material to develop background and experiences, they promote the use of expectancy clues. For example, when students know they will be hearing a selection about how birds build their nests, the words they expect to hear are quite different from those expected in a story about a fire in the basement. Teachers might begin by asking students what they already know about birds building nests and then writing these ideas down so the students can see the words they have used.

Pictures also function as clues to readers, suggesting certain sets of words that might occur in the story. Recognizing the value of pictures as an important context clue is the

Figure 9.4   One Curriculum's Scope and Sequence for Word Recognition Behaviors

Emerging Abilities
1. Learning letter names
2. Developing awareness of letter–sound relationships
3. Hearing similarities and differences in beginning and ending phonemes
4. Recognizing rhyming sounds
5. Demonstrating left-to-right orientation
6. Tracing, matching, and copying letters and words
7. Demonstrating awareness of word boundaries in writing
8. Pointing to known words while being read to

First Grade
1. Begin alphabetizing skill (picture dictionary)
2. Begin using initial consonants in a modified cloze (use of context)
3. Begin consonant digraphs with context
4. Begin consonant blends with context
5. Begin short vowels with context
6. Begin spelling patterns
7. Begin final consonants with context
8. Begin initial and final consonant substitution with context
9. Begin common inflectional endings with context
10. Begin long vowels with context
11. Begin common suffixes with context
12. Begin compound words with context

Second Grade
1. Review previous letter–sound correspondences
2. Begin unusual consonants and consonant digraphs (*c, g*, silent *h*) with context
3. Begin unusual vowels *(y)* with context
4. Begin vowel digraphs and diphthongs with context
5. Introduce schwa with context
6. Begin *r*-controlled and *l*-controlled vowels with context
7. Introduce concept of syllabication (# of vowel sounds = # of syllables)
8. Continue compound words
9. Continue suffixes
10. Begin prefixes with context
11. Begin spelling changes involved in suffixes and inflected endings

Third Grade
1. Review previous letter–sound correspondences
2. Begin difficult consonant blends (triple letters)
3. Begin unusual and difficult vowels and vowel clusters
4. Introduce structural analysis (concept of roots and affixes, compounds)
5. Introduce more complex spelling patterns
6. Introduce two- and three-syllable words (syllable patterns)
7. Begin inductive teaching of consistent phonics rules and their application
8. Begin dictionary skills using diacritical markings and pronunciation spellings

Go to MyEducationLab and select the topic *Comprehension.* Then, go to the Activities and Applications section, and watch the video entitled "Preparing for Learning" to observe a version of the picture walk technique. Next respond to the accompanying questions.

basis for the **picture walk** technique used by primary grade teachers where the text illustrations are previewed before reading to get a sense the story. For example, a picture of two youngsters playing on a raft in a pond elicits many words in the mind that are different from those provoked by a picture of the same children working to build a raft for the pond. Thus, the concepts of expectancy and picture clues are closely related to ideas regarding a reader's ability to mentally organize the material about to be read. Obviously, this ability is also related to background and experience, or **scriptal information** (Pearson & Johnson, 1978), and is further discussed in Chapter 11. Some students who have difficulty using context clues often do not have the conceptual development for dealing with the ideas found in many classroom reading materials. Understanding is thus unlikely, and decoding such content has little value. More familiar material must be used in these cases. Students' own language experience stories are an appropriate beginning.

Assessment. Students will have problems with expectancy and picture clues if they cannot anticipate what may happen (what words may be present) in a story about a given topic, a given set of illustrations, or both. A good way to directly assess a student's ability to use these clues is to ask questions before reading:

> "The selection we are going to read today is about Neil Armstrong, the first man on the moon. What special words do you think we will meet in this selection?"
> "This paragraph will tell us how the pioneers kept warm in the winter. Before we read, let's guess how they might have done it."
> "You're right, Shayne. This is a picture of the wolf in bed waiting for Little Red Riding Hood. What words do you think we will need to know in this part of the story?"

Notice that these questions are to be answered orally; although the teachers have no objective measures of expectancy, still they can identify those who are having considerable trouble anticipating forthcoming events and the words possibly associated with them. The difficulty may be the result of not being able to use expectancy clues adequately or inadequate experiential, conceptual, or language background. The best way to differentiate among these is to sample behavior across a wide variety of content.

Instruction. Techniques to improve the use of expectancy clues generally give the stimulus (the subject or topic of concern or a picture portraying it) and call for **productive language** from the student—that is, generating or identifying possible words that may appear. This process differs from reading the words, which is a receptive language process. The following activities are suggested:

1. Activities to develop use of expectancy clues
   a. Have small groups or individuals prepare to write a story about a given topic of interest. Before students begin writing, the teacher promotes a discussion of words to be used in the story, writing some words on the chalkboard as the discussion proceeds. For beginning readers, use techniques involved in the LEA, in which the teacher does the writing; or conduct an interactive writing activity (see Chapter 7).
   b. Use exercises requiring knowledge of a particular topic. For example: "These words are about cars, airplanes, or both. Mark the words about cars with a *C*; mark the ones about airplanes with an *A*; and mark those about both with a *B*."

____hood	____landing	____engine
____wings	____wheels	____garage
____body	____bumper	____tail

2. Activities to develop expectancy through use of picture clues
   a. Display a picture showing several different items, such as the produce in a market, candies in a store window, or a barnyard scene. Ask the students to name the items; write them down for further reference. Or use students' own drawings prior to writing about them.

MI Connection:
spatial

    b. Show a set of two to four pictures (comic strips are a good source). Tell the students the pictures can be arranged to tell a story. Ask them to arrange the pictures. Then have them choose partners and tell each other (or the teacher) their stories.

    c. Before reading a story, conduct a picture walk where illustrations are surveyed and students tell what they think is happening or what will happen. In this way, words that might be used in the story will be suggested. Verify predictions after reading the story.

Meaning Clues. Meaning clues are more specific to the content being read than expectancy and picture clues. **Context**, as related to meaning clues, is defined as the words surrounding a target word, which is the word to be decoded. Meaning clues often exist within the sentence being read, but they can also exist within phrases or other sentences. Context usually restricts alternative words that fit meaningfully into the slot represented by the target word. Consider the following examples:

> As the _____ began to rise into the air, his pole bent.
> She put the cake mix in the bowl, then _____ one-half cup of water.

Meaning clues can be used effectively for analyzing words unknown in print only if the surrounding words are easily read and understood, and the unknown word in print must be part of the student's listening vocabulary. When the reading matter is too difficult, the reader becomes discouraged and may guess more and demand less meaning from the passage.

Assessment. Students who do not use meaning clues might lack scriptal data or have poorly developed language skills, but more likely they have not been shown how to use such clues. These students can be identified by comparing their analysis of words in isolation to their analysis of words in context. Analysis of a word in context should be easier than analysis of the same word in isolation because language and context limit the word choices that fit meaningfully. If students have learned to *demand meaning* from every sentence they read, they are more likely to be aware of their difficulty and of words unknown in print. If not, a major teaching task has been identified (see Chapter 10 for strategies to teach use of context clues to infer word meanings).

Teachers should suspect inadequate use of context when a student makes wild attempts at a word not recognized in print form. Wild guessing indicates misuse of context and lack of word analysis skills. Also, many substitutions that graphically resemble the actual word but are semantically incorrect (for example, *horse* and *house*), and substitutions that are not self-corrected indicate inadequate use of meaning clues.

Teachers can structure a set of tasks to evaluate the student's ability. Select a few words the student does not know in print, using one of the methods discussed earlier in this chapter. Present the words first in isolation, then in context. If trouble with the words occurs consistently *in both settings,* the student probably is not using context as an aid to word recognition. The following illustrates the two settings, words in isolation and words in context:

Words in Isolation	*Words in Context*
train	We heard the whistle as we walked along the _____ tracks.
night	It was very dark that _____.
stone	Tim felt a sharp _____ under his foot.
wrong	The car was going the _____ way down the one-way street.

Instruction. Techniques for developing the use of meaning clues should be presented in larger discourse units to take advantage of all available language clues. It is advisable to begin with easy materials. Initially, an oral cloze procedure can be used during a read aloud. Story clues provide the context for predicting a word, which will be part of the process used for identifying a word unknown in print. A first-grade teacher demonstrates this technique in the first half of the MyEducationLab video clip "Contextual Analysis and Story Dramatization."

With print material, if the student has to guess too many words, language clues will be obscured. I recommend using a modified cloze procedure (see Chapter 6), beginning with a ratio of about one target word for every 15 to 20 words. Once students understand how the process works and what they are supposed to do, the ratio can be decreased.

The standard deletion ratio of one deletion every fifth word suggested for *assessing comprehension* (Bormuth, 1967, 1968a, 1968b; Rankin & Culhane, 1969) is inappropriate for teaching the use of context clues as an aid for analyzing words because it distracts from the analytical task at hand and asks the student to guess too frequently. The task can be discouraging for readers who are already frustrated with the reading task. Alternatives to reduce this frustration include using a sentence or two with one word deleted, using a multiple-choice format (maze), and adding letters or other word parts to the slot. Another option would be to use a group cloze procedure so that students can help each other figure out what words might best fit each blank.

The following are representative cloze activities:

1. Exercises using thought units of a paragraph
   One day when the lion was looking for food, he walked into a trap. The trap was made of strong _____, and the lion couldn't get out. The lion jumped this way and that way. He tried and tried. All day _____, the lion worked to get out of the trap. But he couldn't get _____.

2. Riddles with meaning clues that give the answer

   It has four legs.
   It has a back.
   You sit on it.
   It is a _____.
   dog   cat   chair

3. Exercises using a maze technique and the meaning of a sentence
   a. He climbed it to paint the ceiling.

                            lake   looking   ladder

   b. The car is in the _____.

                            house   church   garage

4. Modified cloze exercises using context and word parts of the target word
   a. The car is in the g_____.
   b. He is cl_____ing the ladder.

For all of these exercises, the most important aspect is incorporation of teacher-led discussion (Valmont, 1983). This discussion points out the clues that lead to suggesting a certain word. For example, in the riddle exercise, the first two clues (four legs, a back) also describe a dog, cat, or other animal. You must have the third clue (something to sit on) before *dog* and *cat* are eliminated and *chair* becomes the answer. Any unknown word can be approached the same way. The context provides certain clues, and several

Go to MyEducationLab and select the topic *Informal Assessments.* Then, go to the Activities and Applications section, watch the video entitled "Contextual Analysis and Story Dramatization," and respond to the accompanying questions.

Go to MyEducationLab and select the topic *Comprehension.* Then, go to the Activities and Applications section, and watch the video entitled "Word Analysis Strategy" to see how one teacher uses a group cloze procedure. Next respond to the accompanying questions.

words are suggested. The teacher leads a discussion of what the clues are, why some words fit better than others, and which words are equally acceptable.

Using context and other meaning clues alone is not enough for effective, efficient word recognition, however. Both younger readers and readers having difficulty may rely too heavily on context (Gough, 1984; Nicholson, Lillas, & Rzoska, 1988; Stanovich, 1980; [Yoon] Kim & Goetz, 1994). Overemphasizing context and neglecting other decoding skills can lead to unfortunate learning outcomes. When this happens, students guess too often when they encounter words unknown in print, resulting in a distorted or misunderstood message. This outcome must be addressed immediately; if it is allowed to continue, the student may develop the bad habit of *not* expecting meaning from the passage.

Knowledge of Word Parts: Phonics and Structural Analysis

Go to MyEducationLab and select the topic *Phonemic Awareness and Phonics*. Then, go to the Activities and Applications section, and watch the video entitled "Teaching Phonics" to get an overview of the nature of phonics instruction. Next respond to the accompanying questions.

When students cannot figure out a word unknown in print from context clues alone, they must resort to analysis. Essentially, this means they must look for a word part that they already know. Using the pronounceable word part strategy, ask students, "Is there any part of this word that you know?" (Gunning, 1995, p. 488; see also Gunning, 2001, pp. 50–51). Common word elements are presented in Figure 9.5. Two major instructional units concerned with this knowledge are phonics and structural analysis. **Phonics** deals with letter–sound relationships or word parts that do not necessarily have meaning. Examples of phonic elements include consonants, consonant blends, consonant digraphs, vowels, vowel clusters (digraphs and diphthongs), and many syllables (phonograms or rimes). **Structural analysis** deals with such meaningful word parts as derivatives (affixes, or prefixes and suffixes), variants (word endings), and compounds and is also referred to as morphemic analysis. With phonics, students focus on learning what various word parts say, whereas with structural analysis the focus can be twofold: what the word part says and what it means.

The goal of instruction in phonics and structural analysis is for common word parts to become so well known that students can recognize them instantly and automatically (LaBerge & Samuels, 1974). When this level is attained, students do not have to spend an unusually long time analyzing unknown words. With practice, students continually add word parts to their *instant recognition* repertoires. Notice the similarity of the concept to that of sight vocabulary—words that have become so familiar they can be recognized instantly and automatically.

Practice is the key to automaticity. Some students quickly achieve instant recognition, but others need much practice with written language before these word parts become second nature. Teachers must be diligent in providing ample practice that does not become a deadly dull drill. The best solution may be to provide many opportunities to write for authentic purposes (for example, pen pal letters, journals, lists, messages; refer to Chapter 8) and to read easy and interesting material (such as SSR or DEAR, literature circles, book clubs; refer to Chapter 12).

Assessment. Teachers must answer three questions about students learning word parts:

1. Does the learner know the word part?
2. Can the learner recognize the word part quickly?
3. Can the learner identify the element embedded in a word unknown in print?

Knowledge of word parts is assessed directly through examining writing samples, observing oral reading during individual conferences, or using the subtest of the SDRT (Karlsen & Gardner, 2003).

Figure 9.5   Common Word Elements

1. Consonants
a. *one sound (usually)*
b, d, f, h, j, k, l, m,
n, p, q, r, t, v, y, z
b. *more than one sound*
c: cat, city
g: get, gem
s: sit, his, sure
x: box, exam, xylophone

2. Consonant blends
bl, br
cl, cr
dr, dw
fl, fr
gl, gr
pl, pr
sc, sch, scr, shr, sk,
sm, sn, sp, spl, spr,
st, str, sw
thr, tr, tw

3. Consonant digraphs
a. *one sound (usually)*
ck, gh, ng, nk, sh
b. *more than one sound*
th: thing, they
wh: when, who
ch: chair, chorus, choir

4. Vowels (long, short, or controlled)
a, e, i, o, u, (y)

5. Vowel clusters
†ai: mail, said
†ay: say
†ea: heat, head
†ee: sheep
ei: receive, weigh
ie: believe, tie
ew: few
ey: key, they
†oa: road, broad
oe: hoe
oi: boil
oo: book, moon
ou: though, bough, bought
ow: mow, now
oy: toy
ue: blue

6. Prefixes
ab, ad, ante, anti, auto,
be, bi, com, con, co,
de, dis, em, en, ex, fore,
il (meaning "not"), im, in, inter, ir,
mid, mis, non, op, out, over,
per, post, pre, pro,
re, semi, sub, super,
trans, un, under

7. Suffixes
able, age, al, ance, ate, ble, ence,
er, est, ful, ible, ise, ize, ish,
ist, ite, ity, ly, less,
ment, ness, our, ship, some,
tion, ure, ward

8. Phonograms (rimes)

a	e	i	o	u
ab		ib	ob	ub
ack*	ear	ice*	ock*	uck*
	eat*	ick*		
		icle		
ad	ed	id	od	ud
		ide*	ode	
		if		
ag	eg	ig	og	ug*
		ight		
ain*		ike	oke	
ake*		ill*		
all*	ell*			
ale*				
am	em	im	om	um
ame*			ome	upm*
an*	en*	in*		un
		ine*		ung
		ing*		
ank*		ink*		unk*
ap*		ip*	op*	up
are		ir*	or*	
			ore*	
ash*	est*	is		us
at*	et	it		ush
ate*				ut
awe				
aw*	ez	iz	ow	
ay*				

9. Variants
ed, es, ing, s, 's

*Especially useful phonograms, or rimes
†Most reliable vowel clusters

Arts Connection

Drama activities support many aspects of students' language and literacy development. Because the benefits of dramatizations are so wide ranging, it is not surprising that some scholars consider drama the nucleus of oral and written language expansion for all students, including those who struggle with literacy tasks and those who are linguistically and culturally diverse (Edminston, Encisco, & King, 1987). For example, drama encourages a variety of meaningful communication skills, including oral language, listening abilities, creative writing, and interpretations of authors' works. Drama enactments also provide a venue for students to experience and understand how characters feel and think and to participate in imaginary, desired adventures. In addition, dramatizations increase students' motivation for learning because they get to experience the social aspects of language. Further, peers, teachers, and parents recognize, appreciate, and applaud their efforts and talents. Because of the wide-ranging benefits of drama activities, many teachers strive to integrate reading and writing lessons with readers' theater (see the spotlight on English Learners in this chapter), choral reading, puppet shows, scripted plays, improvisational scenes, and videotaped "television shows" whenever possible. Drama activities do not necessitate complex extravaganzas. They can range from simple, spontaneous story enactments and dramatic play to formal productions that require scripts, rehearsals, and costumes.

Automaticity requires accuracy as well as alacrity. To assess knowledge of word parts with a group of young students, try an exercise similar to the one that follows, which provides three or four word elements per line. The teacher gives the stimulus, silently counts to three, and goes on to the next element without giving students time to be analytical:

Teacher	*Student marks element*		
1. mm—man—mm	h	m	b
2. ing—laughing—ing	ed	s	ing
3. tion—motion—tion	tion	ilk	ton

With practice in this type of exercise, students soon learn to work as quickly as they can. Those who have difficulty with this activity should be further observed. The stimulus in this exercise is the sound and not the symbol; therefore it is not exactly like real reading. Measurement specialists are critical of assessment techniques of this nature, citing lack of construct validity; however, if the student can match the written version to the oral version, the teacher can be more certain that given multiple exposures to the written form the student can also produce the oral equivalent for the written word.

The easiest and most accurate way to determine speed is to give the student a list of words containing elements recently explored and ask for the list to be read as quickly as possible. If the elements on the list can be pronounced quickly, one after another (about one-half second per unit of analysis), the student has attained the desired level of instant recognition. Such elements are easy to incorporate into a learning game format.

The teacher must observe a student reading orally to assess the use or application of knowledge of word parts embedded in unknown words. This is best done in situations enabling the teacher to note when a student comes to a word that should be easy to analyze but is not. This may occur during a reading lesson or any other time when oral reading is done. Similar behavior occurs when the student comes to the teacher to ask for a word that is not known but should be. If frequent, this behavior may suggest ineffective knowledge of word parts, inability to use meaning clues, or both.

Tests or subtests assessing knowledge of word parts are available, such as the *Stanford Diagnostic Reading Test* (Karlsen & Gardner, 2003). This test assesses accuracy but not speed. Teachers must use their own judgment regarding this ability, or they can assess this knowledge using the revised version of the *Names Test* (Duffelmeyer & Black, 1996; Duffelmeyer et al., 1994).

Instruction. A natural way to support students in their developing knowledge of the graphophonic system is through the use of children's literature. Trachtenburg (1990) proposes a three-step whole-part-whole strategy in which the first step is to read a literature selection, such as *Bringing the Rain to Kapiti Plain* (Aardema, 1981), that contains many examples of a particular graphophonic element. In the second step, the teacher draws attention to that particular phonic or structural analysis element. Refer to Figure 9.6 for the

---

Figure 9.6	Useful Phonic and Syllabication Generalizations

1. The *c* rule. When *c* comes just before *a, o,* or *u,* it usually has the hard sound heard in *cat, cot,* and *cut.* Otherwise, it usually has the soft sound heard in *cent, city,* and *bicycle.*
2. The *g* rule. When *g* comes at the end of words or just before *a, o,* or *u,* it usually has the hard sound heard in *tag, game, go,* and *gush.* Otherwise, it usually has the soft sound heard in *gem, giant,* and *gym.*
3. The *VC* pattern. This pattern is seen in words such as *an, can, candy,* and *dinner.* As a verbal generalization it might be stated as follows: In either a word or syllable, a single vowel letter followed by a consonant letter, digraph, or blend usually represents a short vowel sound. (Note that *C* stands for a letter, digraph, or blend, e.g., *bat, bath, bask.*)
4. The *VV* pattern. This pattern is seen in words such as *eat, beater, peach, see, bait, float,* and *play.* As a verbal generalization it might be stated like this: In a word or syllable containing a vowel digraph, the first letter in the digraph usually represents the long vowel sound and the second letter is usually silent. According to Clymer (1963/1996), this generalization is quite reliable for *ee, oa,* and *ay* (e.g., *fee, coat, tray*) and works about two-thirds of the time for *ea* and *ai* (e.g., *seat, bait*), but it is not reliable for other vowel digraphs such as *ei, ie,* or *oo,* or diphthongs such as *oi, oy, ou,* and *ow.*
5. The *VCE* (final *e*) pattern. This pattern is seen in words such as *ice, nice, ate, plate, paste, flute, vote,* and *clothe.* As a generalization it might be stated this way: In one-syllable words containing two vowel letters, one of which is a final *e,* the first vowel letter usually represents a long vowel sound and the *e* is silent. If the vowel is not long, try the short sound.
6. The *CV* pattern. This pattern is seen in one-syllable words and syllables such as *he, she, go, my, cry, hotel, going,* and *flying.* As a generalization, it might be stated this way: When there is only one vowel letter in a word or syllable and it comes at the end of the word or syllable, it usually represents the long vowel sound.
7. The *r* rule. This rule applies to words such as *far, fare, fair, girl, fur, her,* and *here.* As a generalization it might be stated as follows: The letter *r* usually modifies the short or long sound of the preceding vowel letter.
8. The *VCCV, VCV,* and *Cle* patterns are three syllabication rules worth knowing. For the *VCCV* pattern, the rule is to divide between the two consonants. This pattern is represented in words such as *blanket, happy,* and *represent.* For the *VCV* pattern, the rule is to divide before or after the consonant. Words representing this pattern are *robot, robin, divide,* and *before.* For the last pattern, *Cle,* the rule is to divide before the consonant. Words representing this pattern are *Bible, uncle, table,* and *example.*

(*Note:* Phonics generalizations should be taught inductively. Known words in a meaningful context should be used to illustrate a letter–sound relationship. When teaching something new, use words familiar to children. To learn whether children can apply what has been taught, use words they cannot read. Practice applying phonics knowledge in context whenever possible. Once a generalization has been taught inductively, concentrate on unknown words in the context of a sentence or brief passage.)

phonic generalizations that are most consistent and thus worth teaching. (In *Bringing the Rain to Kapiti Plain* this might be the long sound of *a* as represented by the *ai* [VV] and *aCE* [VCE] spelling patterns.) The third step involves reading another literature selection that contains examples of the element introduced in step two (such as *The Lace Snail,* Byars, 1975), so students make the connection that these graphophonic patterns occur throughout all reading material. (See Trachtenburg, 1990, for a list of trade books that repeat long and short vowel sounds.) Similarly, Moustafa and Maldonado-Colon (1999) support starting phonics instruction with a story and the use of familiar language. They remind us that although English can be analyzed into phonemes, onsets and rimes, or syllables, Spanish is not an onset/rime language; the unit in Spanish is the syllable (for example, *ca* + *sa* = *casa*). They also support the use of analogies between familiar and unfamiliar words, predictable text, and word walls (discussed later in this chapter). For a summary of useful phonic and syllabication generalizations, see Figure 9.6. To test your own knowledge of phonic elements, see Appendix W.

The activities for practice with word parts that follow are organized around the scope and sequence chart in Figure 9.4. Teachers designing lessons for word parts should present them within the context of familiar, meaningful language. Initial instruction in specific phonic or structural analysis elements should follow inductive, or inquiry, procedures (see Chapter 2).

1. Activities to support learning of initial consonants

MI Connection: spatial

   a. *Personal dictionaries.* As young children use and select new or interesting words from their language experience stories or journals, or come across them in reading their storybooks, place these words on alphabetically ordered pages to create a dictionary. A sentence and a picture should accompany each word. Even older students can create personal dictionaries for specialized topics. For example, seventh graders studying the Middle Ages could create a medieval dictionary based on a literature selection such as *Illuminations* (Hunt, 1989) with words such as *Normans, portcullis, troubadour,* and *zither.*

   b. *Alphabet books.* Students of all ages can create alphabet books on a particular topic of interest or as part of a content area unit. For example, one student created an alphabet book on "Life in the Sea" and located a sea creature for each letter of the alphabet (*a* = anemone, *b* = barnacle, *c* = clown fish, and so on), illustrated each page, and provided a brief commentary for that creature. These books can become quite involved and sophisticated.

   c. *Choosing the beginning letter.* Instruct students to read the sentence and then write in the missing letter. The source material has been read to the students and they are familiar with it.

The cow jumped over the _____oon.
   r   n   m
Humpty Dumpty sat on a _____all.
   w   t   c

   d. *Practice with rimes.* Instruct students to read the sentence before writing in the missing word. Again, the material is familiar.

Sam ate the _____.
   ram   ham   slam
Jack and Jill went up the _____.
   bill   will   hill

2. Activities to support blending of initial consonant clusters
   a. *Use these letters to make a word for each sentence.*

br sl cl	ch wh sh
The _____ock struck one.	_____icken Little said, "The sky is falling!"
He _____oke his crown.	Mary's lamb was _____ite as snow.
Don't _____am the door.	Cinderella lost her _____oe.

   Half the students receive the initial consonant cluster, and half receive the partial sentence. Students then try to find their "partner," the person who needs the piece they hold. Once partners have found each other, they work together to act out their sentence for the rest of the class.

   b. *Make a word for the one missing in each sentence that starts like the word that has a line under it.*
   We have a good <u>place</u> to _____.
   Let's <u>try</u> to _____ the squirrel.
   I <u>think</u> he is in _____ grade.
   <u>When</u> did the bicycle _____ break?

MI Connection: interpersonal

Students can create similar activities for classroom learning games or for other students.

Instruction using retrospective miscue analysis (RMA; Goodman, 1996) is most helpful for encouraging readers to explore their own reading processes, and to revalue themselves as readers. Teacher and student together examine reading miscues for their quality and patterns that reveal the reader's strategies and knowledge of the language cue systems. Questions like these are common: "Did the miscue make sense?" "Why did you make the miscue?" "Does the miscue look like the word in the text?" "Did the miscue affect your understanding of the text?" "Should it have been corrected?" "Did you correct the miscue?" "How did you figure it out?" Goodman and Marek (1996) stated, "When readers are in environments that encourage risk-taking with teachers who respect them as knowledgeable about their own reading, they begin to depend on themselves as the most important resource to answer their questions as they read" (p. 205).

MI Connection: intrapersonal

Visual Analysis

During the course of reading, students may become aware that they cannot pronounce a word after they have looked at it. The symbol (word) has not cued a meaningful response, and the context has not been a sufficient aid; therefore, they must figure out the word some other way. First, they must visually inspect the word and try to recognize smaller parts or spelling patterns that they can pronounce. Thus, visual analysis precedes any application of phonic or structural analysis, although it is possible that the "smaller parts" might also be structural elements. *Phonic exercises that emphasize "sounding it out" as a first step fail to communicate to students that they have to segment visually before they sound out.* Also, when sounding a word from left to right, the initial vowel sound is often distorted because the sound of the vowel is dependent on what follows the vowel, not what comes before the vowel. For example, if the word being sounded is *robin,* the reader might sound /rrrrr . . . ohhhh . . . buh/ which will not be helpful to pronouncing the word. Visual analysis will help the reader form chunks (syllables) that will be pronounceable, such as /rob/ and /in/. In addition, use of the visual analysis process assumes phonemic awareness on the part of the reader (see Chapter 7).

Visual segmentation of a word embedded in a sentence providing no helpful context clues presents especially difficult analytic problems, much like when reading words in isolation as in a list. Durkin (1978) claimed that decoding in such circumstances occurs at the syllable level, where only visual clues can be used. She identified eight syllabication generalizations that help decode syllables. A problem with this procedure is that the students must memorize and be able to apply all of the rules before attaining precision—an unrealistic expectation for students already in difficulty. The following might be a simpler, although less precise, set of *content rules* to help students begin visual segmentation of words into syllables:

1. Every syllable has one vowel sound.
2. Syllables contain *about* three letters (plus or minus two letters).
3. Syllables are often divided between two consonants (*plan-ter, pic-ture*).
4. In a syllable with more than one vowel letter, the final *e* or the second vowel is often silent.

These four content rules, plus basic knowledge of letter–sound correspondences, are needed before students can begin to analyze words independently. (For a listing of the more consistent phonic and syllabication content rules, refer again to Figure 9.6.) However, these four content rules are useful in that they capture patterns of spelling. Productive use of these rules lies in relevant experiences, not in rote memorization.

Visual analysis that uses an analogy strategy is also effective. By accessing memory for **key words**, or familiar words containing patterns that resemble the new word, the reader can figure out the word. For example, if the new word is *screen* and the reader already knows and can access _green_ and _scream_, the new word can be more readily pronounced. Some readers will have difficulty doing this and must be directly shown, whereas students with a strong naturalist intelligence may notice the patterns very quickly. Visual analysis will help support both word recognition and spelling because it focuses on examining textual features and linguistic patterns in words (Strickland, 2000).

Visual Analysis of Monosyllabic Words. Students can be helped to apply at least three basic phonic process rules. The following process rules are adapted from Durkin's (1978) discussion on blending syllables. They are included in this section on visual analysis because they may be helpful to students who have unsuccessfully tried to use the *initial consonant plus context clues* strategy and are unaware of how to continue. The next step in an analytical strategy must begin with visual segmentation of unknown words and then proceed to sounding and blending. The basic phonic process rules are as follows:

1. Separate the beginning consonant(s) from the rest of the word.
2. Say the sounds indicated by the spelling pattern, or rime, to include any final consonant(s).
3. Add and say the sound for the beginning consonant(s), or onset.

This strategy is illustrated in Figure 9.7 for monosyllabic words, where only the first syllabication content rule is needed.

Visual Analysis of Polysyllabic Words. As students become adept at analyzing unknown monosyllabic words, the focus of the strategy changes to polysyllabic words. The remaining three syllabication rules must then be learned. This process is quite difficult

Figure 9.7	Applying the Process Rules in Analyzing Unknown Words

Step	Analyzing Monosyllabic Words	Example Words				
1.	Separate the beginning consonant(s) from the rest of the word.	l - ed l	fl - ame fl	c - art c	g - o g	w - ait w
2.	Say the sounds indicated by the spelling pattern, or rime, to include any final consonants.	led ↓↓ ĕd ↓	flame ↓↓↓ āme ↓	cart ↓↓ art ↓	go ↓ ō ↓	wait ↓↓ āit ↓
3.	Add and say the beginning consonant(s), or onset.	lĕd	flāme	cart	gō	wāit
4.	Check if the word makes sense in the sentence.	It fits.	It fits.	It fits.	It fits.	It fits.

Step	Analyzing Polysyllabic Words	Example Words			
		vccv	vcv	v cvc cvc	vcv cc vccv
		penguin ↓ ↓	visit ↓↓	apartment ↓ ↓ ↓	caterpillar ↓ ↓ ↓↓
1.	Find the vowels.	e ui	i i	a a e	a e i a
2.	Try to make syllables.	pen - guin	vis - it	a - part - ment	cat - er - pil - lar
3.	Say the trial syllables.	pen - guin	vis - it	a - part - ment	cat - er - pil - lar
4.	Blend the trial syllables.	pen‿guin	vis‿it	a‿part‿ment	cat‿er‿pil‿lar
5.	Check if the word makes sense in the sentence.	It fits.	It fits.	It fits.	It fits.

for some students, and they simply give up when asked to analyze polysyllabic words. They must be encouraged to use the following process rules:

1. Find the vowels.
2. Try to make syllables using the consonants before and after the vowels (apply process content rules 2 and 3 for monosyllabic words to each syllable).
3. Say the trial syllables.
4. Blend the trial syllables.
5. Verify with the meaning of the sentence.

This strategy, although helpful, is not precise, and students must be cautioned that, if the word they come up with does not fit, they must try to segment the syllables in another way or try different possible vowel sounds. However, after several unsuccessful efforts it is likely the word is not part of the student's listening vocabulary. The word should then be pronounced for the student and recorded for discussion of its meaning following the reading of the text.

Once a student begins using the steps, another word or word part may be recognized, and the steps may be short-circuited somewhat. The identification of vowels and addition of consonants frequently trigger this recognition. For example, a student may easily recognize *ment* in *apartment* once analysis begins. Such short-circuiting should be encouraged. Notice, also, that the division of *apartment* in step 2 is technically incorrect (*a* versus *ap*), but the student comes up with the word anyway.

As students develop a word recognition strategy, they are constantly adding to their skills repertoire. Consider the following possible strategies for figuring out a new word as a student adds analytical units (the products of instruction) to the memory store. In the example, replacing an *x* with letters implies that the student can visually identify and say that word part.

Target sentence:

I want something to eat.

When a child can read a few words but does not yet have any word analysis skills:

I want xxxxxxxxxx to eat.

(Child skips word or stops at unknown word.)

Add visual segmentation and ability to sound beginning consonants:

I want sxxxxxxxx to eat. "I want spaghetti to eat."

(Child fails, but the guess is sensible.)

Add knowledge of common word endings:

I want sxxxxxxing to eat. "I want s-s-s-ing to eat."

(Child fails.)

Add knowledge of one common word:

I want somexxing to eat. "I want some-ing—something—to eat."

(Child succeeds by approximation.)

Add knowledge of two common words:

I want something to eat. "I want some-thing to eat."

(Child succeeds.)

Another form of instruction is for the teacher to demonstrate and model the most appropriate word analysis process to use. For example, the teacher might model for students by beginning with one of the following statements:

1. This word is best decoded by its syllables.
2. This word is best decoded by using phonics.
3. This word is best decoded by looking for a prefix and/or suffix (structural analysis).

Two important abilities develop when visual analysis skills are learned, discrimination and memory. Visual discrimination training helps the learner see differences between letters, word parts, and words; memory helps the learner recall these differences quickly without having to resort to a slower, more analytical approach. (For more information on visual discrimination, refer to Chapter 4.)

Assessment. Assessment activities for visual analysis rely on observing what readers do when they are reading a word list, or when they meet a word unknown in print while they are reading orally. These oral reading behaviors can be assessed during an administration

Figure 9.8	Common Visual Analysis Errors	
Stimulus Word	Pupil Response	Possible Reason for Error
clock	chalk	Overdependence on general configuration
flag	flash	Visual dependence on initial clues
show	grow	Visual dependence on final clues
peep	sleeve	Visual dependence on medial clues
now	no	Nonrecognition of diphthongs
drop	drope	Confusion with final *e* principle
hope	hop	Confusion with final *e* principle
meat	met	Nonrecognition of digraphs
pad	paid	Confusion of digraph with short vowels
pit	pet	Confusion of short vowels
chew	shew (shoe)	Confusion of initial consonant digraphs
watch	wash	Confusion of final consonant digraphs
pat	bat	Static (letter) reversal
saw	was	Kinetic (word) reversal
chew	ch-we	Partial reversal
cat	at	Omission
at	sat	Addition
is the where under beyond who	in this when over before what	These are all structural or function words, not content. They have meaning only as they relate to other words. The words should be taught as sight words. Then they need to be practiced within the context of phrases where they have meaning (e.g., under the table, beyond this week, and so on)
horse boat board simple	house boot broad sample	The decoding is not so bad. Show the student the importance of context. These words would likely be read correctly in context.

of an IRI (see Chapter 6) or by having the student read orally during a student-teacher conference. Figure 9.8 shows some common visual analysis errors and a possible reason for each error.

Students having problems with visual analysis often have been taught letter–sound correspondences but cannot visually identify them when they are embedded in new words or in other materials. Sometimes this is inappropriately considered a lack of ability to apply phonics skills when, in fact, it reflects inability to visually segment word parts. For example, Damien has learned several consonant sounds as well as some words. He has just successfully completed an exercise in consonant substitution (*onsets*) with the following phonograms (*rimes*): *an, et,* and *ill.* His efforts to read orally proceed as follows for the sentence *Will you let Dan go with me?*

> *Damien:* No response. Then, "I don't know the first word."
> *Teacher:* "Think about our lesson this morning."
> *Damien:* No response.
> *Teacher:* "What is the first letter?"
> *Damien:* "*W.*"
> *Teacher:* "Good! Now what does the rest of the word say?"
> *Damien:* "*Ill.*"
> *Teacher:* "What sound does the first letter make?"
> *Damien:* "*Wah,* as in *want.*"
> *Teacher:* "Now sound them together."
> *Damien:* "*Wah-ill—will.* Will you . . ." Student does not continue.

The teacher returns to the original strategy, noting that Damien had done his earlier lesson satisfactorily but cannot independently segment the initial consonant or phonogram from the whole word. Practice in this ability is considered advisable as it may represent a lack of phonemic awareness (see Chapter 7).

Another indication of a need for visual analysis practice is continued use of inappropriate word parts even when they do not work. Trying a word element is acceptable, but if it does not work, it should be rejected and another tried. Inflexibility may suggest rigid instructional procedures. Teaching a sound-switching strategy (Vogt & Nagano, 2003) encourages students to try alternative sounds. The following is an example of applying flexibility in an effort to analyze a word, trying different word parts:

> *Target sentence:* Yes, you may go with father.
> *Student's first trial:* "Yes, you may go with fat-her." (Student rejects this trial because sentence does not make sense.)
> *Student's second trial:* "Yes, you may go with fa-ther, no, father." (Student accepts this trial because the sentence makes sense.)

(*Note:* This example indicates an opportunity to teach a minilesson on consonant digraphs, specifically *th.*)

Instruction. Instruction in visual analysis encourages students to look for known parts embedded in unknown words and then try to segment other *reasonable* word parts—elements that may represent a word part. (Recall the content and process rules described earlier and begin instruction by helping learners discover these rules if needed.)

Daily events in most classrooms provide ample opportunity for visual analysis practice in a meaningful context. In Tim O'Keefe's classroom (Mills, O'Keefe, & Stephens, 1992), students made the following "discoveries" simply from examining their student attendance sign-in sheets:

> *Chiquita* and *Charles* both have the letters *ch* at the beginning of their names.
>
> Justin noticed that *O'Keefe* has two *e*'s together, as in *Kareem*'s name. Then he looked around the room and saw the color words collage. He added *green* to his list of words that have two *e*'s together.
>
> Amanda noticed that she, Justin, and Vania all have *r*'s in their last names (p. 5).

A more direct approach can be taken to help students identify the structural features of words containing prefixes and suffixes; thus the term *structural analysis.* Compound words are also a structural form, as well as inflectional endings (such as plurals, past-tense endings, possessive form). Students might be asked to help create a class

Figure 9.9	Words from the "At the Beach" Word Wall	
cetacean	submarine	sand shark
fin	dolphins	trench
monk shark	conch	oil tankers
pail	sun	beach
moon jellyfish	lifeguard	water
common sand dollar	sand	jellyfish
mackerel	schooners	flying fish
octopus	pontoon bridge	blowfish
medusa	raft	nurse shark
whales	sand crabs	sand dollar
blubber	sea snakes	sea
plankton	surfing	arrowhead sand dollar
starfish	dogfish	sailboats
cod	five-hole sand dollar	dunes
tsunami	sea turtle	yellow sting ray
hotwater vent	crab	beach ball
continental shelf	seaweed	kelp
submersible	continental slope	cowrie
shark	whelk	reef
seagulls	coral	seahorse

dictionary of words they encounter in their reading that contain a structural element. Such a dictionary can be maintained on a computer, as it would be updated frequently. The entry words should be alphabetized, written in syllables, pronunciation indicated, the structural element highlighted, and a meaning given. In this way students not only gain practice in recognizing the structural elements but also practice other word analysis skills as well. Because these elements are also meaning-bearing—that is, affixes have a meaning (*pre* means *before* or *er* means *one who, s* means *more than one,* or *landslide* means *earth that has moved*)—instructional strategies for these elements are further discussed in Chapter 10.

Similarly, the words that students encounter on a daily basis as part of their ongoing reading, writing, and content learning are candidates for word walls (Cunningham, 1999, 2005). **Word walls** are charts or bulletin boards on which words of interest or for learning are placed for reference during word analysis activities or during writing tasks. The words from a word wall developed during a thematic unit entitled "At the Beach" can be seen in Figure 9.9. Because students of varying literacy needs contributed words to the word wall, a wide variety of purposes exist for word study. For example, words beginning with single consonants could be grouped (*fin, pail, cod, kelp, sand*), as could words beginning with consonant blends (*blubber, trench, crab*), or consonant digraphs (*whales, shark*). In addition to many other phonic elements, words could be grouped in various ways related to their meaning (animals, plants).

The following activities can also aid instruction in visual analysis:

1. Give students sets of unknown words that contain word parts they already know.

   a. After a lesson on word endings, or variants, provide exercises such as the following:

      Draw a circle around the word endings you see. Then use each word to complete the sentences.

      look   looks   looking

   Johnny _____ very tired today.

Go to MyEducationLab and select the topic *Vocabulary.* Then, go to the Activities and Applications section, and watch the videos entitled "Creating Word Walls" and "Word Walls" to observe different ways word walls can be used. Next respond to the accompanying questions for both videos.

MI Connection:
naturalist

"_____ out!" shouted Susan as the car came speeding toward them.

"What are you _____ for?" asked Mother.

b. After lessons on initial consonant blends, provide exercises such as this: Here are some words. If they start with a consonant, mark a *C* and circle the consonant. If they begin with a consonant blend, mark a *B* and circle the blend.

_____	cat	_____	slip
_____	bring	_____	sing
_____	try	_____	wall

c. After lessons in various structural analysis (also called morphemic analysis) elements, ask students to look for the relevant unit in the unknown words.

1. Put a line between the two words in each of these compound words.

   sweetheart   playground   nighttime

   Then write a sentence for each of these compound words in your notebook.
2. Draw a circle around each affix. Then complete each sentence using the base (or root) word.

   rewrite   careful   happiness

   The little boy touched his new baby sister with _____.
   I will _____ a letter to grandmother.
   Dad told me I did a good job and that made me _____.

Students soon learn that if they segment the word in the wrong place, they may not be able to sound the "odd" word parts. They should be encouraged to try again and break the word apart in a different place, always keeping the context in mind.

"Here are some words that have been divided for you. Which one helps you most to sound it out? Put an *X* on that word."

t/hi/nk	th/in/k	th/ink	Be sure you *think* before you speak.
spr/ing	s/pri/ng	sp/ri/ng	Today is sunny and warm and feels like *spring*.

This exercise has no right or wrong answer, especially if the student arrives at the correct pronunciation. This type of practice is probably best done individually, so the teacher can encourage the learner to resegment the word if it was inappropriate on the first trial.

Blending and Synthesizing

As students learn to segment words visually and say the word parts, they also learn to reassemble the parts to form a recognizable word, a process referred to as *blending and synthesizing*. *Auditory blending* refers to a sounding process: The student says the word parts and blends them together to cue a meaningful response. This is what emerging readers do when they are first learning to read, and it is a very important skill at that level of learning. **Visual synthesizing** is a more mature process, used by readers who can analyze words mentally without having to resort to overt sounding and blending. For typical learners, a gradual shift from auditory blending to visual synthesizing occurs as the analytical techniques and word parts become automatic. Visual synthesizing is faster than auditory blending and should be the ultimate goal.

Some students have trouble with blending and synthesizing because their reading program has overemphasized learning word parts in isolation. A few students may not be able to blend sounds orally and must learn to rely solely on visual synthesizing.

Assessment. A learner who cannot yet pronounce various word parts or remember a sequence of sounds obviously cannot blend these sounds together. Assuming that the word parts are known, students who are having difficulty with auditory memory or auditory blending can be identified relatively easily. The teacher says the word parts slowly, with a one-second interval between parts, and asks the student to respond by saying the whole word. Following is an example of auditory blending:

Objective	*Teacher*	*Student*
letters	s–a–m	sam
letters and phonogram	s–am	sam
syllables	sam–ple	sample
combination	s–am–pling	sampling

Both the stimulus and response are at the oral level; a student who does this task successfully still may not be able to do it effectively while reading. Therefore, a stimulus must also be provided in printed form, separating the letters or word parts with dashes and spaces. Following is an example of auditory blending when the stimulus is in print:

Student reads and says	*Student says*
tr–ack	track
d–an–cing	dancing

When the student says the parts out loud and blends them together, the process is auditory blending. When the student simply looks at the word parts and rather quickly says the whole word aloud without sounding out the parts, the process is visual synthesizing.

Instruction. Instruction in auditory blending should begin at the level of the syllable (Ericson & Juliebo, 1998). Slow and exaggerated pronunciation of the syllable or phoneme is helpful. Practice in segmentation of sounds is also helpful for combining individual sounds to form words, or auditory blending. Start with compound words like *football* and *raincoat* before blending words of two syllables, like *sister* or *baby*. Move from this syllable level to blending initial consonants with the rest of the syllable in a one-syllable word. For example, "I am going to make some sounds and I want you to tell me what word I am trying to say. Listen: */m/-/an/, /m/-/an/*. What word is that?" Continue development by increasing the number of phonemes spoken in isolation (see the section on assessing auditory blending). This instruction can take the form of a guessing game ("I am thinking of a word that is the color of Cory's pants. It is */b/-/l/-/ack/*."). Songs can also be adopted as blending activities, such as the song "Bingo."

Adams (1990) stated, "because children have special difficulty analyzing the phonemic structure of words, reading programs should include explicit instruction in blending" (p. 126). The use of **onsets** (single consonants, consonant blends, and consonant digraphs occurring at the beginning of words or syllables) and **rimes** (the vowels and consonants that follow the initial consonant, consonant blend, or consonant digraph in a syllable, also called phonograms or word families) may be most helpful in this regard (Goswami & Mead, 1992). The biggest advantage in using rimes lies in the relatively high

MI Connection: musical

stability of vowel sounds within most end rimes (that is, -*ean* as opposed to *bea-*). Rimes are far more generalizable than isolated vowels or even vowel teams. Of 286 phonograms appearing in primary-grade texts, 95 percent were pronounced the same each time they were met (Durrell, 1963). In fact, nearly 500 early elementary words can be derived from the phonograms marked by an asterisk in Figure 9.5 (Fry & Kress, 2006; Wylie & Durrell, 1970).

Gunning (1995) described a word-building strategy for teaching phonic elements within the context of naturally occurring text that relies on adding onsets to rimes. He suggests that students are more likely to recognize pronounceable word parts if phonic elements are taught in natural clusters, such as onsets and rimes.

Use of rimes will mediate the following obstacles to blending:

1. Analyzing rimes into component parts
2. Being unaware that different onsets can be placed before the same rime to make many different words
3. Analyzing complex onsets (such as *tw, cl, wh, squ, sch, thr*) into individual phonemes

Go to MyEducationLab and select the topic *Phonemic Awareness and Phonics*. Then, go to the Activities and Applications section, and watch the video entitled "Word Chunking" to see how words containing rimes are learned. View the video "Onsets and Rimes" for additional ideas for using these word parts. Next respond to the accompanying questions for both videos.

With initial instruction, model the following procedures for students. Present separated word parts containing rimes to the student to reassemble. Maintain a vertical listing of the words so that the rime can be easily recognized, such as the teacher does in the "Word Chunking" video clip in MyEducationLab. Begin with known word parts in known words so that the learner understands the task:

m–eat   meat
sh–ell   shell

If the teacher pronounces the word parts and the student responds by saying the whole word, this is auditory blending, with the stimulus and the response both at the oral level.

Perceptual unit	Teacher says	Student says
syllables	bask–et	basket
structural elements	some–thing	something
phonic elements	p–ain–ter	painter

It is best to begin with natural word divisions represented by syllabic utterances, as found in rimes, and then proceed to more artificial phonic elements. Students need practice with these elements because they are likely to segment words into elements other than the correct syllables (for example, mo–ney, rob–ot, fat–her); therefore, they must be able to blend them to cue an appropriate response.

When the stimulus is changed from word parts spoken by the teacher to written word parts read by the students, the task is considered either auditory blending or visual synthesizing, depending on whether the response is primarily auditory or visual. The following exercises develop both skills:

1. When the words are in isolation:

Print	Student reads
gra vel	gravel
gr avel	gravel
gr av el	gravel

2. When the words are in context:

   a. The men walked toward the <u>gra</u> <u>vel</u> pit.

   b. Add the right word part.
      The men walk____ toward the gravel pit.

   c. End-of-line segmentation
      The men walked <u>to</u>-
      <u>ward</u> the gravel pit.

Children's books, such as the Dr. Seuss series, that contain many examples of phonograms can provide much needed practice with blending in a meaningful context. *Green Eggs and Ham* (Seuss, 1960), available as an interactive CD-ROM storybook (The Learning Company), provides good aural reinforcement of several useful rimes.

Work in visual synthesizing can also help students with their spelling. As one teacher (A. Gex, personal communication, April, 2004) related,

> I needed to give my students information to help them blend sounds and spell words. Onsets and rimes seemed like a logical choice because my students were very good at recognizing rhyming words. After reading them the book *Alphabet Soup,* I did a minilesson using a pocket chart to visually manipulate many different words for the rimes *–at, –et,* and *–all.* Most students made some great words, even some words that I hadn't thought of. However, they still need to transfer this skill to their independent writing. For instance, just the other day when I was working with one of my students, he was having difficulty spelling two words that rhymed. He had picked the words *cat* and *mat* to write into a poem. I asked him to write his words down for me. "I can't spell them," he said. "Can you spell *cat?*" I asked. He quickly wrote the word *cat,* correctly. Then I said, "Listen to the word *mat,* it ends just like *cat* but the first letter is different." I then rubber-banded the word *mat, mmmmmmmmmat,* so he could listen to the beginning of it. "Can you spell it now?" I asked. I can't tell you how exciting it was when he wrote immediately after. That was when I really knew that this strategy was working.

Summary

Word recognition is presented as an interaction between the *process* of figuring out words unknown in print and the *products* of instruction, such as individual word parts. Several factors influence this interaction. One of the most important is that the word exists in the reader's listening vocabulary; another factor is the size of the student's sight vocabulary. The text also must be sufficiently easy to permit the reader to use context clues. Readers cannot use their understanding of language when material is too difficult, and they are forced to resort to more artificial analytical techniques.

Context clues such as expectancy, or anticipation of words likely to occur in the selection, play an indirect but vital part in the word analysis process. Meaning clues, or knowledge of the language surrounding an unknown word, also contribute immeasurably to an analytical strategy.

For the beginning reader, however, knowledge of word parts is an important way of relating visual symbols to words that are already in the meaning vocabulary. Disregarding context clues for the moment, the process of word recognition can be summarized by the following steps or stages:

1. The reader knows by looking that he or she does not recognize the word.
2. The word is segmented visually into parts.
3. Some of the parts may be recognized.

4. The reader attempts to analyze the remaining unknown parts. The more techniques the reader has for doing this, the more successful the outcome.

5. The word is reconstructed by auditory or visual means or both, to approximate the word and cue a meaningful response.

6. The word is confirmed or rejected based on the meaning of the sentence when the word choice is made.

Students *without* reading difficulties probably use bits and pieces of this process intuitively. However, students *with* reading difficulties often need direct instruction to clarify the process at points where their strategy breaks down. The teacher must use the analytic process to help identify areas of strength and need. Ultimately, students assume responsibility for analyzing words independently, always checking for sentence sense and understanding of the passage being read.

Recommended Websites

Dolch Word Lists—Preschool through Grade Three
   www.kidzone.ws/dolch/
The word lists and activity ideas for using the Dolch words can be found on this site.

Dolch Phrases
   www.createdbyteachers.com/dolchphrases.html
This site has phrases using the Dolch words.

Fry's Instant Words
   www.nifl.gov/readingprofiles/Instant_Words.pdf
   http://rbeaudoin333.homestead.com/sightvocab_1.html
These sites provide lists and activities for Fry's instant words.

ESL Vocabulary Lists
   http://iteslj.org/links/ESL/Vocabulary/Lists/
This site has an extensive list of links to a wide variety of word lists.

Language Experience Approach
   www.sasked.gov.sk.ca/docs/ela/e_literacy/
   language.html
Detailed information on the LEA is provided here.

What Is Decodable Text?
   www.nrrf.org/features.htm#dt
A concise definition and related links are on this site, one being decodable words versus predictable text.

Using Decodable Text
   www.auburn.edu/~murraba/decodable.html
This site defines the concept of decodable text and provides an example book to read.

Fluency Activities
   http://literacy.kent.edu/eureka/strategies/fluency_activities
   .pdf

   www.rocksforkids.com/FabFours/duet_reading.htm
   www.auburn.edu/~murraba/fluency.html
   www.readingcenter.buffalo.edu/center/research/tmgrr.html
These sites include discussions of repeated readings and NIM.

Readers' Theater Scripts
   www.aaronshep.com/rt/RTE.html
   www.cdli.ca/CITE/langrt.htm
   www.teachingheart.net/readerstheater.htm
   www.storycart.com
These sites provide access to many scripts.

The Role of Phonics in Reading Instruction
   www.reading.org/resources/issues/positions_phonics.html
The International Reading Association's position statement on phonics and reading instruction is posted on this site.

National Right to Read Foundation
   www.nrrf.org/aboutphonics.htm
This site provides important information about phonics.

Puzzlemaker: Word Games and Puzzles
   www.puzzlemaker.com
For fun with words, create computer-generated word searches, cryptograms, and more at this site.

Using Think-Alouds to Analyze Decision Making During Spelling Word Sorts
   www.readingonline.org/articles/art_index.asp?
   HREF=/articles/fresch/index.html
This article provides information for how to make word sorting a useful activity.

Making and Writing Words
   www.readingonline.org/articles/words/rasinski_index.html
An activity is shared that is helpful in developing proficiency in word recognition and spelling.

MyEducationLab is a research-based learning tool that brings teaching to life. Go to the Gipe 7th Edition MyEducationLab for Reading Assessment site at www.myeducationlab.com to:

- Engage in multimedia exercises to help you build a deeper and more applied understanding of chapter content.
- Use extensive resources including videos from real classrooms, Praxis and licensure preparation, a lesson plan builder, and materials to help you in your teaching career.

CHAPTER 10

Meaning Vocabulary

OBJECTIVES

After you have read this chapter, you should be able to:

1. Explain why direct instruction of meaning vocabulary is needed.
2. Develop assessment activities for word meanings.
3. Explain the connection between schema theory and vocabulary instruction.
4. Describe strategies that effectively teach word meanings.
5. Devise an instructional program in vocabulary development for students with limited meaning vocabularies.

VOCABULARY ALERT

associative words	homographs	open word sorting
clarifying table	homonyms	specialized vocabulary
closed word sorting	homophones	structured overview
concept ladder	list-group-label	word-learning strategies
context clues	morpheme	word map
directive context	morphemic analysis	word wall

There is a reciprocal relationship between meaning vocabulary and comprehension; as one grows it enhances the other, and the result is a cycle of growth in both areas. This relationship holds true for both native English speakers and English learners (Carlo et al., 2004). Competent readers know many words, whereas students with limited vocabularies often struggle with reading (Biemiller, 1999).

The importance of having a large meaning vocabulary increases for learners in the upper and middle grades. Here, the emphasis on content-area learning and more sophisticated works of literature requires a rich vocabulary base. Students will be learning new words for already familiar concepts as well as new words for entirely new concepts almost on a daily basis.

Vocabulary growth is not an area that should be left to chance. While it is true that many new words are learned incidentally through wide reading, direct instruction has an important role in vocabulary acquisition. Teachers cannot assume that students will read widely enough to encounter a variety of new words or learn them. Likewise, being able to determine a word's meaning from context implies both having the skill to infer the word's meaning and that the context will be informative to the word's meaning (Beck, McKeown, & Kucan, 2002). Thus, in addition to teaching new words and concepts explicitly, direct instruction can also provide strategies that will assist readers, even capable decoders, in figuring out new word meanings as they are encountered during independent reading (Farstrup & Samuels, 2008). Instruction for meaning vocabulary is an important and sometimes neglected area of focus in literacy education, and vocabulary instruction will be "most effective, and most likely to influence students' comprehension when it is rich, deep, and extended" (Graves, 2006, p. 6). This chapter informs classroom teachers about assessment and instructional strategies for acquiring a large meaning vocabulary.

ASSESSING KNOWLEDGE OF WORD MEANINGS

When assessing knowledge of word meanings, the degree of word knowledge should be considered. According to Dale (1965) and Dale, O'Rourke, and Bamman (1971), levels of familiarity with a word proceed from total ignorance ("I never saw it before"), to awareness ("I've heard of it, but I don't know what it means"), to general knowledge ("I recognize it in context—it has something to do with . . ."), and finally to accurate knowledge ("I know it"). Dale and colleagues (1971) suggest that in a vocabulary program, it is probably best to move the *almost known* words into the category of *known* words. Therefore, when assessing students' vocabulary knowledge for the purpose of discovering their vocabulary needs, identifying words that are at least at an awareness level is recommended.

| **Figure 10.1** | Degrees of Word Knowledge |

Goal: To shrink the interior circles until *all* words are known words.

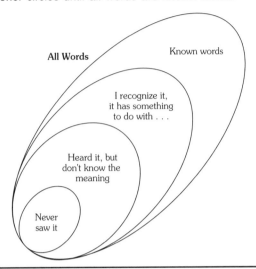

Figure 10.1 shows the relationship for the degrees of word knowledge with the goal being to eventually move as many words as possible into the category of known words.

Dale and colleagues (1971) proposed four methods for assessing awareness vocabulary that are easily adaptable by classroom teachers for direct assessment:

1. *Identification.* In this simple, most direct method, the student is asked to indicate orally or in writing whether the meaning of a word is known as it is used in specific text. The meaning is identified according to its definition or use or by an associated word.

2. *Multiple choice.* The student selects the correct meaning of the tested word from three or four definitions or examples.

3. *Matching.* The tested words are presented in one column, and the matching definitions are presented, out of order, in another column.

4. *Checking.* The student checks the words that are known or not known. (p. 20)

Within these four methods are a variety of techniques teachers can use to assess and test meaning vocabulary. Some examples follow.

Identification

A list of words, preferably related to material the student will be asked to read, is constructed in an easy-to-read sequence. The students are later asked to define (orally or in writing) only words checked as unknown. In preparation for a selection on skydiving, the following list might be used:

_____	sport	_____	hover
_____	speed	_____	harness
_____	target	_____	daredevil

_____ parachute   _____ coordination
_____ ripcord   _____ plummet

Multiple Choice

Words are presented in context and several answers are provided. The student selects the best response. For example:

A. Mary was <u>hungry.</u> She wanted her _____.
   (flower, coat, snack)

B. He bought an <u>expensive</u> gift.
   1. very beautiful
   2. did not cost too much
   3. cost a lot

Matching

Several types of matching exercises evaluate vocabulary development. Examples of three useful types follow:

A. Matching words with definitions

   1. _____ census   a. A town near a large city
   2. _____ suburb   b. Areas where people live close together in towns and cities
   3. _____ urban   c. Where people live on the surface of Earth
                       d. A count of people
                       e. The study of where people live and carry on their activities

B. Matching affixes with definitions

   1. _____ pre   a. three
   2. _____ es   b. someone who
   3. _____ er   c. not
   4. _____ bi   d. against
   5. _____ un   e. two
                    f. more than one
                    g. before

C. Matching words with related words or phrases. These are matches of associations and not definitions. Lines are drawn to the matches. (The first match is done for you.)

   1. owl   flies high
      eagle   called wise
   2. canine   puppy
      feline   kitten
   3. lions   pride
      geese   gaggle
   4. carat   diamond
      caret   editing

Checking

The fourth method involves checking by the student. This alerts both the student and the teacher to vocabulary strengths and needs. Two types of self-checking tests follow.

A. If the underlined word in the sentence is used correctly, the student puts a check beside it. If both sentences in the unit are incorrect, the student checks "neither" (Gipe, 1977).

1. a. _____ The gooey <u>bramble</u> stuck to the roof of his mouth.
   b. _____ The <u>bramble</u> caught on Mary's coat.
   c. _____ Neither
2. a. _____ <u>Graphite</u> will erase the mark Jim made with his pencil.
   b. _____ <u>Graphite</u> will leave a mark on the paper.
   c. _____ Neither
3. a. _____ The cat's cries were <u>luminous</u> in the night.
   b. _____ The cat's eyes were <u>luminous</u> in the night.
   c. _____ Neither
4. a. _____ Our friend brought good <u>impede</u>.
   b. _____ We bought some <u>impede</u> from our friend.
   c. _____ Neither

B. The student indicates on a chosen list of words how well each word is known. The code to use might be:

+   means "I know it well."
✔   means "I know it somewhat."
0   means "I've seen it or heard of it."
−   means "I don't know it at all."

For example, the following type of list, drawn from a science book, is best used analytically before new material or a unit of study is introduced:

___0___ hypothesis
___+___ experiment
___✔___ interact
___−___ substance
___0___ element

These assessment methods are primarily intended to help the teacher determine strengths and gaps in students' vocabularies. They should also serve as a source of motivation for students. Once students are sensitized to words and recognize that they can expand their vocabularies, they develop a sense of excitement about words. A teacher who is enthusiastic about developing vocabulary will also enhance students' enthusiasm. Many exercises on word meanings are found in classroom materials and teachers' manuals accompanying basal readers. These exercises also serve as tools for assessing vocabulary at an awareness level.

For assessment of full conceptual knowledge of vocabulary, however, the tasks required must be more sensitive to the specific dimensions of the vocabulary items than those used for assessing an awareness level. Simpson (1987) proposed a hierarchy of four processes that, in turn, suggest formats for assessing full conceptual knowledge:

1. Students should be able to recognize and generate the critical attributes, examples, and nonexamples of a concept. . . .

2. Students should be able to sense and infer relationships between concepts and their own background information. . . .

3. Students should be able to recognize and apply the concept to a variety of contexts. . . .

4. Students should be able to generate novel contexts for the targeted concept. (p. 22)

Simpson also provided examples of alternative formats for these four processes. Similarly, Nagy and Scott (2000) focused on the complexity of word knowledge as having five aspects: *incrementality* (each encounter with a word leads to deeper and more precise meaning); *multidimensionality* (there are different types of word knowledge such as nuances between words like *diminutive* versus *miniature*); *polysemy* (many common words have multiple meanings such as "*Run* to the store" compared to "*Run* the store while I am gone."); *interrelatedness* (schematic associations among words such as *cats meow* or *lions roar*); and *heterogeneity* (a word's meaning will differ depending on how it is functioning in context demonstrating range in its application—*spilled* the soup [clean the floor] versus *spilled* the beans [get ready to apologize). While these dimensions of word knowledge have implications for both instruction and assessment, studies have not been conducted to examine them in any systematic way (Scott, Lubliner, & Hiebert, 2006). Pearson, Hiebert, and Kamil (2007) have challenged the research community to develop vocabulary measures that will allow the empirical relationship between vocabulary and comprehension to be strengthened.

EFFECTIVE INSTRUCTION FOR WORD MEANINGS

Although meaning vocabulary is certainly learned incidentally through experience and reading (Nagy, Anderson, & Herman, 1987), there are far too many words to be learned in this way, and incidental learning is not at all predictable (Dale, O'Rourke, & Barbe, 1986), especially for students who do not read well or often. Readers with limited meaning vocabularies, a category that includes many English learners, must receive direct and intense instruction focused on vocabulary expansion. Planned lessons for vocabulary development can focus on providing rich and varied experiences, such as field trips, in-class demonstrations, or laboratory activities in math or science where the key vocabulary words are used before, during, and after the experience; teaching individual words that need to be learned for success with grade level materials; or developing strategies for independent word learning that is focused on teaching skills such as using context, morphemic analysis, and dictionaries and on developing an interest and awareness in words and their meanings. Effective vocabulary instruction helps students (a) relate new vocabulary to what they already know, (b) develop a broader understanding of word knowledge in a variety of contexts, (c) become actively involved in learning new words, and (d) develop strategies for independent vocabulary acquisition (Carr & Wixson, 1986; Gipe, 1977; Kibby, 1995). Marzano (2003) suggested clear principles for vocabulary instruction:

1. Wide reading and language-rich activities should be the primary vehicles for vocabulary learning. Given the large number of words students encounter in written and oral language, general language development must be encouraged as one of the most important vocabulary development strategies.

2. Direct vocabulary instruction should focus on words considered important to a given content area or to general background knowledge. Because effective direct

vocabulary instruction requires a fair amount of time and complexity, teachers should select words for instruction that promise a high yield in student learning of general knowledge or of knowledge of a particular topic of instructional importance.

3. Direct vocabulary instruction should include many ways of knowing a word, as well as multiple exposures to new words, and provide for the development of a complex level of word knowledge. Because word knowledge is stored in many forms (mental pictures, kinesthetic associations, smells, tastes, semantic distinctions, linguistic references), direct vocabulary instruction should take advantage of many of these forms and not emphasize one to the exclusion of others. This particular principle is consistent with multiple intelligences theory, suggesting the linking of learning new concepts, skills, and tasks to as many different intelligences as possible (Armstrong, 1993). For example, to learn a new word, spell the word aloud; visualize the word and then write the word; form the word or a representation of its meaning in clay or with paints; create a song that explains the word and its meaning; relate the word and its meaning to a personal experience; think about the word's origin or the spelling rules it might follow; and have another person "test" you on the word by asking questions that require you to explain the new word.

Choosing Words to Teach

Choosing which words to teach is not a straightforward task. There are over 180,000 different words contained in the reading materials students will use while in school (Graves, 2006). Thus, it is critical for teachers to select "words that are most important for understanding a specific reading selection or concept, [and] words that are generally useful for students to know and are likely to encounter" frequently in their reading (Hiebert, Lehr, & Osborn, 2004, p. 10). In addition, select words that represent key concepts to teach fewer words in depth and to connect them to known concepts (Ellis & Farmer, 2000).

Words should be taught that help students comprehend material at their instructional reading levels and understand content-area class discussions. These words are found in the books and content-area materials being used in the classroom. Beck and colleagues (2002) emphasized the importance of teaching what they refer to as "tier two" words. According to them, tier two words include:

1. Words that are characteristic of mature language users and appear frequently across a variety of domains (that is, importance and utility)

2. Words that can be worked with in a variety of ways so that students can build deep knowledge of them and of their connections to other words and concepts (that is, instructional potential)

3. Words for which students understand the general concept but provide precision and specificity in describing the concept (that is, conceptual understanding) (p. 19)

Consider the following selection from *The World of the Sea Otter* (Paine, 1993) as an example of applying Beck and colleagues' criteria for selecting words to teach. In this Sierra Club work, readers are informed of the sea otter as a legally protected ocean mammal. Referring to the criteria above, decide if you agree with the underlined words selected as important and useful words to teach directly. Also decide if there are additional words you would teach.

The underlined hairs of the sea otter's fur can only form a waterproof barrier if they are absolutely clean. If hairs are soiled and stick together in clumps, the waterproofing is lost, the barrier leaks and the underfur is wetted. Then the animal becomes chilled and dies. There is little wonder that sea otters are fastidious in their grooming. Every centimeter of the sea otter's coat must be attended to. The coat is scrubbed, licked clean and combed. The air layer is renewed by drying and blowing. Like a toddler's blanket sleeper, the sea otter's coat is large and loose so that every part of it can be pulled around the otter's mouth and paws to be groomed. (p. 12)

The criteria suggested for choosing words to teach are useful, but teachers must also apply these guidelines with the specific needs of their students in mind. The words finally chosen for teaching are up to the judgment of each teacher but should reflect a decision made with thought and care.

Teaching Individual Word Meanings

Typically, teachers present new vocabulary words by writing sentences on the board containing the new words. Definitions are given, meanings are discussed, and the material is then read. However, according to Goodman (1994), word meaning is built through the context of its use, both in the course of language use and through reading. It makes more sense, then, to discuss most new vocabulary after material is read or at least during the reading as in an interactive read aloud (see Chapter 7) (Dietrich, 2008; Hair, 2009; Wasik & Bond, 2001), so the reader has access to the word's appropriate use within its natural context (Beck et al., 2002). If a new word is especially crucial to the understanding of the material to be read, as is often the case with content-area material, introduce it before reading and discuss it further both during and after the reading. It would not be wise to introduce too many words before reading, however, as interest in the material may wane.

Results of vocabulary studies indicate that about eight to ten words per week can be taught effectively (Stahl & Fairbanks, 1986). To teach individual words, the nature of the word itself must be considered. Some words require little explanation (such as *waterproof*) or can be easily shown or demonstrated (such as *coat* or *leak*). Such words do not require much elaboration. Words that are more abstract, such as *fastidious*, require more explanation, discussion, and use. Such words can be acted out or graphically represented so their relationship to other words can be made clearer. Use of a graphic organizer like a semantic map (see the word map discussion later in this section) or a clarifying table can be helpful. A **clarifying table** is an organizing template that can be used to anchor the meanings of new terms, especially terms used in content areas (Ellis & Farmer, 2000). Figure 10.2 illustrates how to construct a clarifying table using the word *fastidious*.

Even though the focus may be on teaching a new word, associating the new word to words already known will facilitate learning. Thus, the easiest vocabulary exercises employ simple associations. Students use knowledge already in their schemata to work with synonyms, antonyms, homophones, and **associative words** that often occur together (*green/grass, bacon/eggs*), and to classify (*animal: dog, cat, horse*). The following activities can be used as the core of lessons, as practice activities, or as learning games designed to promote vocabulary development. For these activities to be considered instructional, student and teacher must interact. If they are done independently, they become practice activities.

Synonyms. Students are often taught that synonyms are words that have the same meaning. This is not exactly true, however. Synonyms have *similar* meanings, which allows us to express the same idea in a variety of ways or discriminate among different nuances.

Go to MyEducationLab and select the topic *Vocabulary*. Then, go to the Activities and Applications section, and watch the video entitled "Vocabulary Strategies" to hear about some general strategies teachers use to help students with new vocabulary. Next respond to the accompanying questions.

Go to MyEducationLab and select the topic *English Language Learners*. Then, go to the Activities and Applications section, watch the video entitled "Teaching Diverse Learners," and observe how this teacher helps her English learners relate a familiar term in their first language to a new term in English. Next respond to the accompanying questions.

Figure 10.2	A Clarifying Table for the Word *Fastidious*

WORD (select a word critical to understanding a text selection):   *Fastidious*

CORE IDEA (a simple definition):   Having excessively demanding standards so as to be difficult to please; picky; perfectionist

CLARIFIER (students brainstorm descriptors for the word):
Someone who finds fault with our work regardless of how hard we tried.
Someone who is very particular.

EXAMPLES (after discussion, brainstorm examples and write down one or two that reflects the essence of the word's meaning):
Sea otters are constantly grooming their fur. They never stop.
Leroy keeps tearing up his drawings whenever he makes a small mistake.

CONFUSED WITH (brainstorm concepts that are easily confused with the new word but discuss ways they are substantively different):
Neatness. Susan likes to make her bed each morning, but she does not obsess over a wrinkle or two in the bedspread.

KNOWLEDGE CONNECTIONS (brainstorm common examples of how/when the word is used and list these):
Teachers might be when they grade our papers!
Critics who review movies.
My mom when she inspects my room.

EXAMPLE SENTENCE (Have small groups of students develop a sentence for the word that demonstrates they understand its meaning. Then have the groups share their sentences and come to a consensus on one sentence that best reflects the meaning of the word.):   The boy was so fastidious about the food on his plate that if one food item touched a different food item he would not eat any of his food.

The study of synonyms is probably the easiest and most efficient place to start expanding students' vocabularies because it starts with a familiar word. The student already has a schema for the known word; by comparing synonyms the student sees the relationships between words and is able to further generalize and classify words, thus enhancing the current schema. Some characteristic synonym activities follow:

1. Underline the word that means about the same as the word underlined in the sentence. (Note that this activity encourages the use of context clues.)

   We almost missed Sue's name because she wrote so <u>tiny</u>.

   large   small   big   hot

2. Match the words that have about the same meaning. (Note how the structural clue, the prefix *un-*, can help with this task.)

   a. _____ large   1. unhappy
   b. _____ tiny   2. big
   c. _____ hen   3. chicken
   d. _____ sad   4. small

3. Circle the *two* words that could complete each sentence.

   a. The clown did a _____ right in front of us.
      treat   stunt   trick

b. The neighborhood kids play baseball in the _____ lot.
empty   vacant   full

c. A large tree _____ blew down in the storm.
branch   leaf   limb

4. Use the words in the box to complete the paragraph. Each word will be used twice, and it will have a different meaning each time. A synonym has been provided in parentheses for each space.

> keen   slim   serious

The hikers were (eager) _____ to reach the cabin. The approaching storm could be (dangerous)_____. Already, a (sharp) _____ wind was blowing, and the possibility of finding a cave to shelter in was (unlikely) _____. "Come on," said the guide, a tall, (thin) _____ woman. Her expression was (solemn) _____.

These formats are easily adapted to language experience stories or other creative writings with the use of a thesaurus (see Chapter 8 for additional ideas).

Comparing synonyms helps students see the relationships among words of similar meaning and also recognize that fine distinctions often should be made. Before these fine discriminations are possible, however, gross discriminations, as in the first three exercises, must be mastered. For example, the word *tiny* from the first set of exercises has many synonyms (*little, small, minute, diminutive, miniature, microscopic,* and so on), but not all of these terms are interchangeable. The use of contextual clues, a dictionary (see section on "Word Learning Strategies"), and discussion will help students determine the most appropriate shade of meaning for the following sentences:

1. We all agreed that Mary's feet were _____ but
   small   tiny

smaller yet were Sue's _____ feet.
small   tiny

2. The doll was an exact _____ of a real British soldier.
   miniature   diminutive

The meanings of synonyms, although similar, are not exactly the same. Choosing a synonym depends on how the word is used. Dale and colleagues (1986) provided an excellent example for synonyms of the word *get*. The student is directed to write the best word to use in place of *get. Buy, catch,* and *win* are the synonyms:

1. I will *get* the ball you throw.

2. The fastest runner will *get* a prize.

3. Will you *get* a new sweater at the store? (p. 85)

This type of activity is especially valuable during editing of students' written compositions. Laframboise (2000) suggested the use of webs for "tired" words as a way to expand vocabulary growth toward ownership of new words with the side effect of enhancing written compositions and calls such a web a "said web" because of the greatly overused word "said" in children's written stories. A group of students is asked to brainstorm words that are related to the "tired" word. These words do not have to be restricted to synonyms because synonyms often trigger antonyms as responses as well. All these words can be accepted during brainstorming; their relationships will become part of the

Figure 10.3   Chart Posted for Alternate Words for *Said*

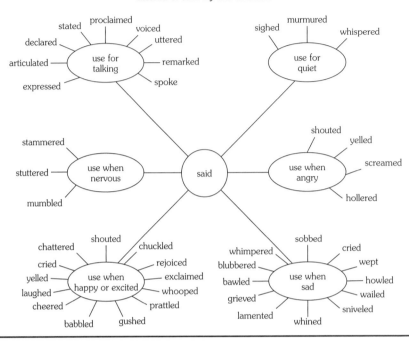

Instead of *said* try one of these:

follow-up discussion. The words that are listed are then categorized according to relationships, and charts are created. These charts can be posted in the writing center for reference (see Figure 10.3).

A group cloze activity (Jacobson, 1990) can be used to help students fine-tune their
knowledge of synonyms and language use in general. The cooperative completion of a
cloze passage can enhance each student's understanding and retention of the material
read in addition to providing practice with the vocabulary and language patterns used by
skilled writers. Basically the steps are as follows:

1. Each student individually completes the cloze passage (see Chapter 6 for construction of cloze passages).

2. In groups of three (triads), students discuss the reasons for one another's sup-
   plied words. Each student tries to convince the others that her choice is best, but
   if the others are convinced of another word there is no problem (or penalty) for
   changing words.

3. One triad then meets with a second triad to discuss word choices. Changes can
   be made if reasons are clear.

4. Results are shared with the whole class. The teacher might show the original passage on an overhead transparency for whole-class discussion.

Certain authors of children's literature are very aware of the opportunity they have
to increase vocabulary through the use of synonyms (for example, Franklyn Branley,
Vicki Cobb, Joanna Cole, Ron and Nancy Goor, Kathryn Lasky, Patricia Lauber, Bianca
Lavies, Molly McLaughlin, Hershell and Joan Nixon, Dorothy Patent, Laurence Pringle,

Revisit the use
of group cloze
by going to
MyEducationLab
and selecting
the topic
Comprehension.
Then, go to the
Activities and
Applications section,
and watch the video
entitled "Word
Analysis Strategy" to
better understand
how a group cloze
activity can help stu-
dents' comprehen-
sion of the material
read. Next respond
to the accompanying
questions.

Helen Roney Sattler, Jack Denton Scott, Millicent Selsam, and Seymour Simon). A good example is Molly McLaughlin's *Dragonflies* (1989). Numerous synonyms are used to help readers understand vocabulary related to dragonflies:

> "This larva, or nymph, is quite different from its colorful flying parents." (p. 16)
> "This remarkable lip, or labium, is one of the tools that make the 'pond monster' such a fearsome hunter." (p. 19)
> "As the time for the big change, or metamorphosis, comes closer, the nymph's behavior changes, too." (p. 22)

Antonyms. Just as no two synonyms are exactly alike in meaning, no two antonyms are exact opposites. To develop the concept of opposites, however, antonyms can be grouped according to their general meaning. Most activities suggested for synonyms can be modified for antonyms:

1. The student is instructed to change the underlined word so the sentence will have almost the opposite meaning.
   Jack <u>hates</u> to read.
   Spot is a <u>fat</u> dog.
   It is a <u>hot</u> morning.

   The study of antonyms is readily adapted to the use of structural analysis clues (see the "Word Learning Strategies" section that follows). The teacher can purposely present pairs of words to illustrate how opposites result from the addition of certain prefixes and suffixes (happy/unhappy; fear/fearless).

2. Antonym trees are a useful visual to help study the formation of antonyms (Figure 10.4). Given a root word at the base of the tree, students prepare "leaves"

MI Connection:
naturalist

Figure 10.4	Antonym Tree. Students Make "Leaves" with Words Opposite in Meaning to the "Root" Word at the Base of the Tree

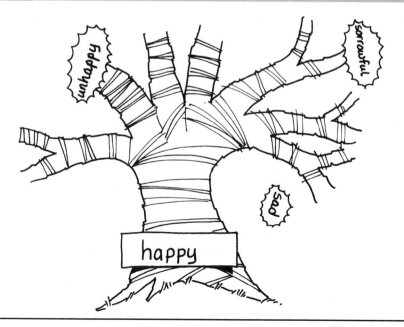

for the tree by writing words that mean the opposite of the root word. Students soon discover the use of prefixes and suffixes in forming antonyms. Some antonyms formed from prefixes and suffixes are listed here (Dale et al., 1971, p. 57).

Prefixes Forming Antonyms

*in*doors	vs.	*out*doors	*in*hale	vs.	*ex*hale
*pre*paid	vs.	*post*paid	*sub*ordinate	vs.	*super*ordinate
*in*flate	vs.	*de*flate	*under*fed	vs.	*over*fed
*post*test	vs.	*pre*test	*pro*gress	vs.	*re*gress

Suffixes Forming Antonyms

worthy	vs.	worth*less*	widow	vs.	widow*er*
lion	vs.	lion*ess*	use*less*	vs.	use*ful*
beard*less*	vs.	beard*ed*	hero	vs.	hero*ine*

3. The student is directed to read the sentence and choose the word that best completes the sentence.
   <u>Cowardly</u> means the opposite of a person who is _____.

   timid   courageous   fearful

   Was the bread <u>fresh</u>, or had it become _____?

   burned   stale   delicious

To help students see how knowledge of prefixes, suffixes, synonyms, and antonyms can help them increase their vocabulary, try the following exercise:

Build Your Vocabulary From 6 to 24!

<u>Word</u>	<u>Synonym</u>	<u>Antonym</u>	<u>Prefix</u>	<u>Suffix</u>
teach (example)	instruct	learn	reteach	teacher
build	_____	_____	_____	_____
safe	_____	_____	_____	_____
agree	_____	_____	_____	_____
patient	_____	_____	_____	_____
work	_____	_____	_____	_____
polite	_____	_____	_____	_____

Homophones. Words that sound alike but are different in spelling and meaning are called **homophones** (*dear* versus *deer*). Related terms are **homonyms**, words that sound alike and are spelled alike but have different meanings, such as *row* (a line) versus *row* (move a boat); and **homographs**, words that are spelled alike but do not sound alike and have different meanings, such as *bow* (and arrow) versus *bow* (as in curtsy). Homophones may confuse encoding and decoding tasks (distinguishing between *reed* and *read*) but may help the comprehension task (the reader knows *reed* refers to a tall grass), as opposed to homonyms and homographs, which are spelled alike. With homonyms and homographs, the reader must use context to infer the appropriate meaning. As with synonyms and antonyms, the student needs much practice discriminating between one homophone and another. The activities that follow present several approaches. Many of these activities can be performed as pantomimes using body language and signs for "sounds like."

MI Connection:
bodily-kinesthetic

SPOTLIGHT ON ENGLISH LEARNERS

Homophones, Homographs, and Idioms

Many young English learners have trouble understanding common English expressions, and they take many idioms literally. For example, "It's raining cats and dogs!" would bring looks of amazement at the thought of cats and dogs falling from the sky. In Spanish, for instance, there aren't any words that have multiple meanings, and there are no homonyms. Therefore, the following books are especially important to discuss with the learner whose first language is Spanish.

Cox, James. (1980). *Put Your Foot in Your Mouth and Other Silly Sayings.* New York: Random.

Gwynne, Fred. (1970). *The King Who Rained* (also *A Chocolate Moose for Dinner,* 1976). New York: Prentice-Hall.

Hunt, Bernice Kohn. (1975). *Your Ant Is a Which.* New York: Harcourt Brace Jovanovich.

Terban, Marvin. (1990). *Punching the Clock: Funny Action Idioms* (also *Eight Ate: A Feast of Homonym Riddles,* 1982; *In a Pickle and Other Funny Idioms,* 1983; *Mad as a Wet Hen and Other Funny Idioms,* 1987). New York: Clarion.

In addition, it would be helpful for English learners to participate in vocabulary role play (Herrell, 1998). Vocabulary role play encourages learners to connect their past experiences with the content being studied and the new vocabulary in that content. Students and the teacher discuss the vocabulary, and then students are asked to create a skit that uses the new vocabulary.

Dave's ESL Café is a useful website for teachers of English learners. You can find the URL, along with other helpful instruction for EL websites, at the end of this chapter.

1. Students practice exercises in which they are given a word and asked to supply its homophone. This task begins simply by giving letter-space clues.

       bear, b a r e   stare, s t a i r
       cite, s i g h t   hour, o u r

2. Students choose the correct homophone using context clues.

   a. They met on the (*stairs, stares*).
   b. They spent a (*weak, week*) at the beach.
   c. We stayed for the (*hole, whole*) game.
   d. (*Meet, Meat*) me at six o'clock.

3. Students supply the correct homophone using definition clues.

   a. It stops a bike. It sounds like *break.* __ __ __ __ __
   b. It's an animal skin. It sounds like *fir.* __ __ __
   c. Boats stop here. It sounds like *peer.* __ __ __ __
   d. It's taking what doesn't belong to you. It sounds like *steel.* __ __ __ __ __

Associative Words. Unexpected responses for associative activities are not uncommon. The teacher must be flexible regarding acceptable responses for association activities.

A. Students underline the word that best fits the sentence. Discuss why one choice is better than another.

   The sky is so _____ it looks like the ocean.
     blue   orange   red

B. Students match the word in the first column with one from the second column that is usually associated with it.

1. _____ tall   a. tiger
2. _____ electric   b. buildings
3. _____ green   c. energy
4. _____ ferocious   d. sky
5. _____ blue   e. fields

Classifying or Categorizing Activities. Instruction in classifying and categorizing develops an understanding of word relationships. Once a new word is identified as belonging to an already familiar category, all attributes of the known category can be assigned to the new word, and the new word becomes known. This is also an example of how schemata are expanded. Consider the familiar category of colors and take *azure* as the unfamiliar word. Once azure is identified as a color, it receives all the attributes that may be associated with color (hue, shade, brilliance). Further, once azure is identified as the color of the blue sky, it takes on the additional attributes of the already familiar word *blue*.

A teacher can present classification or categorization activities in many ways. The following general formats can be modified to accommodate many categorizing needs. The same formats provide the basis for classification games:

1. *Direct categorization.* Given a work sheet with category titles and a set of words to be categorized, the student lists the words under the appropriate category title. This would be an example of **closed word sorting** because the category titles are provided. A higher level of difficulty would be a **list-group-label** (Taba, 1967) activity. Given a list of words (25 is sufficient) such as those found on the word wall in Figure 9.9, students examine the list for ways to group words that have something in common. This is an example of **open word sorting** because students can choose to sort the words in a variety of ways. Each group should have at least three words in it. Words can be used in more than one group. Then students re-sort the list and label the groupings to indicate the relationship of the words in each grouping. The teacher records the categorized listings on the board, on an overhead transparency, or on poster paper. Students are asked to orally explain why they have grouped the words in these ways. For example, the words *lava, ash, rocks, dust,* and *smoke* were grouped together, and students explained that these words are all things emitted from a volcano. Groupings developed by students using the words from Figure 9.9 included: things that float on top of the water (*schooners, raft, oil tankers, sailboats*); kinds of sea shells (*cowrie, whelk, conch, five-hole sand dollar, arrowhead sand dollar, sand dollar, common sand dollar*); and plants that live in the sea (*plankton, seaweed, kelp*).

MI Connection: naturalist

Word sorting is also used to involve students in categorizing. For example, a group (or individual) may be given a set of words that represent several different common elements:

ray	tangent	rhombus
triangle	octagon	dodecagon
hexagon	pentagon	trapezoid

MI Connection: interpersonal

The group sorts the words (for example, *rhombus, trapezoid; ray, tangent; rhombus, trapezoid, triangle, pentagon, octagon, hexagon, dodecagon*) and reads the words in one group to the rest of the class. Those listening must determine the category title (such as quadrilaterals; lines; polygons). Discussion follows that focuses on essential characteristics of the categories.

2. *Categorizing by omission.* Students are shown a set of words (such as *four, too, six, eight*) and asked to indicate the word that does *not* fit the category represented by the majority of the words. Subsequent discussion reveals the category title.

3. *Structured vocabulary overview.* In preparation for or in review of a unit of study it is helpful to fit words into categories. For example, a unit on algae might call for the categories of *microscopic* and *nonmicroscopic.* The specialized vocabulary items to be classified might be *desmids, Irish moss, brown kelp,* and *diatoms. Freshwater* and *seawater* are two additional categories for classifying these same words.

MI Connection:
naturalist

4. *Looking for common elements.* Given a group of words that all have something in common, the student decides what that something is. For example, given the words *buffalo, prairie dog,* and *eagle,* the student may conclude that all these make their habitat in the Great Plains.

5. *Word maps.* The Frayer model of concept attainment (Frayer, Frederick, & Klausmeier, 1969) provides a basis for word map activities. This model offers a structure that encourages the independent learning of new word meanings. Briefly, a **word map** is a graphic organizer in which concepts are presented in relation to relevant and irrelevant attributes; examples and nonexamples; and superordinate, coordinate, and subordinate aspects of the concept. Using the Frayer model leads readily to thinking about new words in relation to known, related words. Following discussion, a new concept can be *mapped* using the structures illustrated in Figure 10.5.

MI Connection:
spatial

Similarly, Schwartz (1988) presents a concept definition word map that describes four types of relationships: (a) the general class to which the concept belongs (what is it?); (b) the primary properties of the concept and those that distinguish it from other members of the class (what is it like?); (c) examples of the concept (what are some examples?); and (d) comparison of the new concept with an additional concept that belongs to the same general class but differs from the target concept (comparisons). An example of a concept definition word map is displayed in Figure 10.6.

One additional example is the *concept circle* or *concept wheel* (Rupley, Logan, & Nichols, 1998/1999). In this technique, students use their background knowledge to suggest words that they associate with the target word. Consider the previous example of the new word *polygon*. Students are asked for words they think of when they hear the word *polygon* and to explain why they thought of that word. Some suggestions might include *hexagon* because it has the same ending sound; *triangle* because it is a geometric figure; and *rectangle* because it is a geometric figure that has four sides. Students continue to make suggestions until it is apparent that no new information is forthcoming or that the students are moving off track. The teacher then produces a list of words that appropriately reflects the word *polygon,* including as many of the students' suggestions as possible. At this point, the definition of the new word is read to the students, and the list is compared to the definition. Finally, the teacher asks the students to narrow the list down to three words that will help them remember the new word (see Figure 10.7).

MI Connection:
intrapersonal

Teaching Word Learning Strategies

Teaching word meanings is the major goal of vocabulary instruction, but helping students become independent word learners is an aspect of vocabulary development that cannot be ignored because there are far too many words for students to learn, and they cannot all be taught directly. A vocabulary instructional program should include teaching

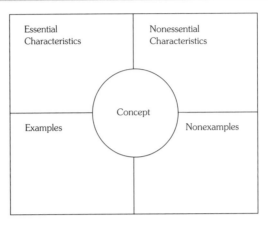

Figure 10.5   The Frayer Model of Concept Attainment Encourages Thinking about New Concepts in Relation to Known, Related Concepts

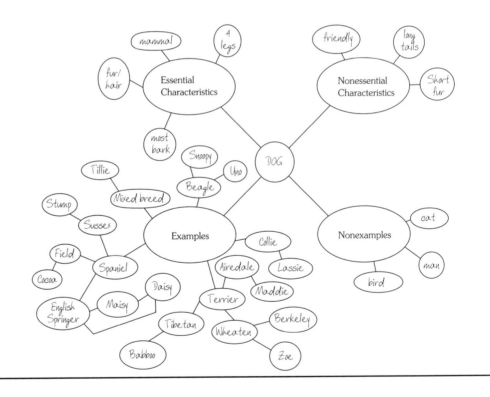

strategies students can independently apply to words they meet in varied contexts. Such strategies will help students use prior knowledge in ways that allow the benefits of direct vocabulary instruction to go beyond the words actually taught. Teachers can model and teach word-learning strategies explicitly to show students how to determine the meanings of unknown words. Three important **word-learning strategies** for vocabulary growth are

Figure 10.6 Concept Definition Word Map

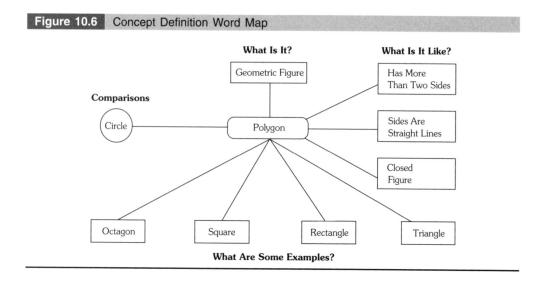

(1) using context clues to comprehend word meanings; (2) using word parts (morphemic analysis) to decipher word meanings; and (3) using the dictionary (Graves, 2006).

Using Context Clues. Context clues refer to other words, definitions, examples, or illustrations within text that provide clues to the meaning of the unknown word. However, not all texts provide helpful context clues for determining a word's meaning. For example, using a sentence seen earlier, "The air layer is *renewed* by drying and blowing," demonstrates a context not helpful in determining the meaning of *renewed,* other than to know it is an

Figure 10.7 Concept Circle for *Polygon*

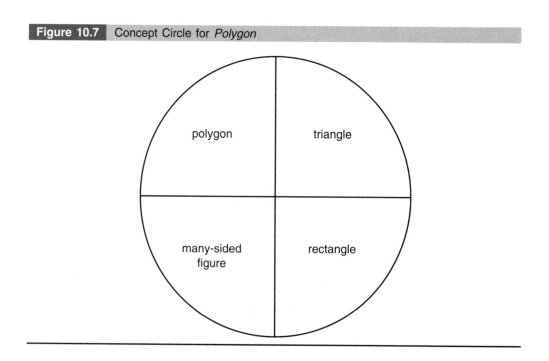

Arts Connection

Integrating the arts can enhance students' comprehension and understanding of text concepts. By creating murals, scripts, dioramas, drama improvisations, or skillfully illustrated concept maps, as seen here, students portray their understandings about what they have read.

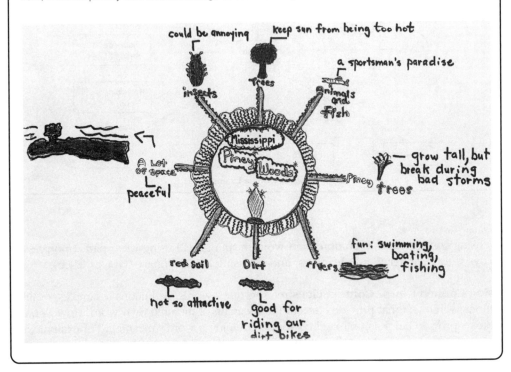

adjective describing what happens to the air layer after drying and blowing. Such contexts are referred to as *nondirective contexts* (Beck, McKeown, & McCaslin, 1983).

Research by Gipe (1978/1979, 1980) indicated that new word meanings are effectively taught by providing a familiar and **directive context**; that is, a context created specifically to provide enough information to determine a word's meaning. Gipe developed a four-step layered-context procedure. The teacher prepares a passage for students in which the first sentence uses the new word appropriately, thereby providing valuable syntactic and semantic information. The context is composed of familiar words and situations. The second sentence of the passage describes some of the attributes of the new word. As with the first sentence, terms are already familiar to the students. The third sentence defines the new word using familiar concepts. The last sentence gives students an opportunity to relate the new word to their own lives by asking them to write an answer to a question about the word's meaning, to complete an open-ended statement that requires application of the word's meaning, or to draw a picture representing what the word means to them. An example of a complete passage follows:

> The boys who wanted to sing together formed a *quintet*. There were five boys singing in the *quintet*. *Quintet* means a group of five, and this group usually sings or plays music. If you were in a *quintet*, what instrument would you want to play?

Talk Through (Piercey, 1982) is another technique that recognizes the importance of helping students relate what they already know to a word that is unfamiliar or has multiple meanings. In "talk through," the teacher identifies key concept words, perhaps prior to a content-area reading selection, that students are likely to find difficult. These words may be totally new, may have been introduced previously, or may possess a different meaning from the common meaning. The teacher begins by using the word in a sentence on the chalkboard:

The frog has gone through a complete *metamorphosis* from its days as a tadpole.

Then the teacher helps relate the meaning of the new word to students' own lives and personal experiences. The teacher asks students for input, as opposed to telling them what the word means. For example:

Teacher: "James, remember when you brought in a tree branch that had a cocoon attached to it? What made that cocoon?"

James: "The caterpillars in the trees in my backyard made that cocoon."

Teacher: "Class, does anyone remember what happened to the cocoon? Lisa?"

Lisa: "One day a butterfly came out of it."

Teacher: "Yes, and right after that happened, remember I read you the story of *The Very Hungry Caterpillar* by Eric Carle. What happened to that caterpillar? Tony?"

Tony: "The caterpillar ate one bite out of lots of different things, leaves, apples, tomatoes, and then it went to sleep inside a cocoon. Then one day it became a butterfly."

Next the teacher writes the word of interest in isolation:

metamorphosis

Then the teacher writes:

meta + morphe
(over) (shape or form)

and says, "*Metamorphosis* comes from two Greek words—*over* or *beyond* and *shape* or *form*—combined to mean that the shape or form of something changes over to a different shape or form. Our experience with the cocoon and the story of *The Very Hungry Caterpillar* showed us that the *shape* or *form* of a caterpillar changed *over* to the shape or form of a butterfly. That is what *metamorphosis* means."

Then the teacher seeks to further relate the new word to students' lives.

Teacher: "What else goes through a metamorphosis that you are familiar with?"

Possible responses:

"We had some mealworms once to feed our pet chameleon. They changed into beetles."

"I think some caterpillars change into moths."

"My mom told me that flies lay eggs that hatch out little white worms. And then later on those worms turn back into flies."

"I saw a movie once where a man turned into a wolf."

"Frogs must change—it's in the sentence on the board."

And so it goes! The concept of metamorphosis is more meaningful now than if the students were simply told what it meant and then told to read the text containing the subject matter.

Students also must be taught a process for how to use the natural context of new words to help them determine the meanings of unknown words or some reasonable possibilities for a word's meaning (Beck et al., 2002). As Blachowicz and Zabroske (1990) pointed out, students need to be aware of the kinds of clues provided by context. "Context can clue you to—what a word is (what it's like); what a word isn't (what it's different from); what it looks like; something about its location or setting; something about what it's used for; what kind of thing or action it is; how something is done; a general topic or idea related to the word; other words related to the word; and so forth" (p. 506).

Buikema and Graves (1993) field-tested a vocabulary instructional unit with seventh- and eighth-grade students to help them learn to use descriptive context cues to infer word meanings. After beginning instruction using "What am I?" word riddles to introduce the idea of *descriptive* context cues, they introduced students to this same notion in text passages. Students could refer to a posted definition of descriptive context cues that read, "Descriptive cues give us clues as to the *sensual* aspects of an unknown word (its appearance, smell, taste, feel, or sound) or the *action* the word indicates or the *purpose* the word has" (p. 452). Following modeling and group work with sample passages for several days (instruction lasted for five consecutive 50-minute periods), students learned the strategy.

Students were then given many opportunities to use the strategy with their reading materials. A sample practice work sheet to accompany this strategy is presented in Figure 10.8. The work sheet was modified to show this strategy as an adaptation of Gipe's (1978/1979) context strategy discussed earlier.

Any vocabulary instruction can include the hypothesis/test strategy steps used by Blachowicz and Zabroske (1990). The steps should be modeled in stages for students. They are as follows:

Look—before, at, after the word

Reason—to connect what you know with what the author tells you

Predict—a possible meaning

Resolve or redo—decide whether you know enough, should try again, or should consult an expert or reference (p. 506)

Students can be encouraged to keep a vocabulary notebook while they read to practice the use of these steps. A suggested format is shown in Figure 10.9.

These hypothesis/test strategy steps can also be applied during literature circle discussions or literature study groups (see Chapter 12) by using the "vocabulary enricher" job sheet (Daniels, 2002). The role of the vocabulary enricher is to select new, important, or interesting words from the assigned reading, determine a definition for these words, and teach these words to the other group members. There are a variety of ways to share the words with group members (see Harmon, 1998).

Using Word Parts. Students also must be taught a process for how to use word parts, or structural analysis clues (see Chapter 8), to help them determine the meanings of unknown words or some reasonable possibilities for a word's meaning (Beck et al., 2002). **Morphemic analysis** (also known as structural analysis) focuses attention on word parts; root words, prefixes, derivational suffixes, and inflectional suffixes. A **morpheme** is the smallest element having meaning in a word. For example, words such as *skill* and

Figure 10.8 Inferring Word Meanings from Context

PRACTICE WORKSHEET

Name: _____ Date: _____

Strategy Practice: Using the descriptive cues strategy, do all the following for the short paragraph below.

1. Underline the unknown word(s).
2. List in the space the descriptive cues that give hints for the word's meaning.
3. List any thoughts, experiences, or statements that helped you decide on the word's meaning.
4. Using your cue list, write a possible definition for the word.

The boys who wanted to sing together formed a <u>quintet</u>. There were five boys singing in the <u>quintet</u>. This group of five boys often sings and plays music together. If you were in a <u>quintet</u> would you want to sing or play a musical instrument?

1. quintet

2. to sing together
    five boys
    sings and plays music together

3. I heard my dad talk about a barbershop quintet
    being at the mall on Saturday.

4. I think a quintet is five people singing or
    playing musical instruments together.

---

hair are morphemes (that is, root words), and so are word parts such as *–ful*, as in *skillful* (that is, a derivational suffix), and *–s*, as in *hairs* (that is, an inflectional suffix). Knowing word parts plays an important role in learning word meanings as more than 60 percent of new words students meet contain identifiable morphemes (Nagy et al., 1989).

Students need direct instruction in morphology, especially in the upper grades (Carlisle & Stone, 2005). Once students can recognize the structural element (root word, affix, endings, compounds), they can be shown how to use these meaning-bearing elements to decipher a word's meaning. In addition to the class dictionary activity mentioned in Chapter 9, graphic organizers such as word walls and mapping activities are useful. For example, a word wall showing words containing the prefix *bi-* can be presented, the words and their meanings discussed, and students invited to add words to the word wall as they locate additional candidates. As a new word is added it should be discussed as well. Such a word wall might include the words *bicycle, binoculars, bifocal, biannual,* and *bimonthly* to start. "Spider" maps can be constructed by small groups of students with each group being given a root word or Greek and Latin roots for differentiating instruction, according to the learners' ability levels. Then each group provides as many words as they can that contain the root. Students should share what they know about each word's meaning, as not every student in the group might know the word. These maps can be posted on the classroom walls

Figure 10.9   Sample Format for Vocabulary Notebook

Book Title: _The Secret Garden_

Word	Page Found	Predicted Meaning	Actual Meaning
Coax , "saves a bit o' his bread to coax his pets"	_33_	_feed_	_Persuade, to try to get his pet to do something_

MI Connection: spatial

for further discussion. Figure 10.10 shows a collection of spider maps for a variety of root words.

Sports terms include many compound words. Why not use these familiar terms to study compound words? Have the class create a chart of sports terms such as the one in Figure 10.11 (Chant & Pelow, 1979). Many words may be categorized under two headings. For instance, _center_ refers to a position played in football or basketball. _Yards_

Figure 10.10   Spider Maps for Root Words

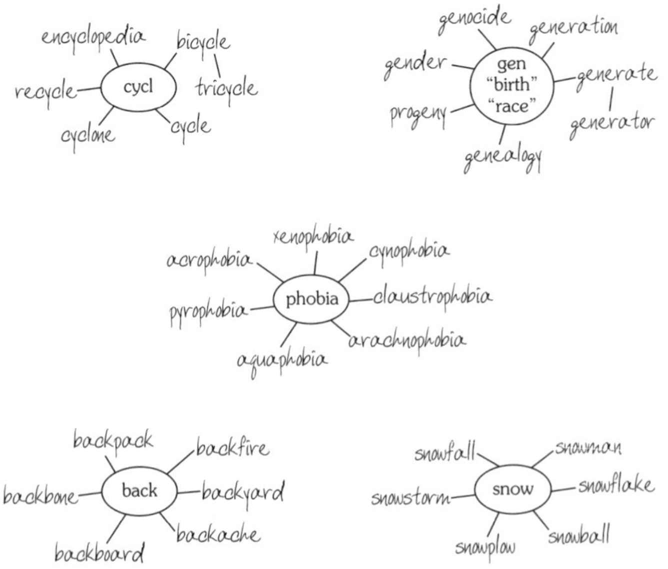

Figure 10.11   Sports Terms Include Compound Words and Can Be Used to Study Them

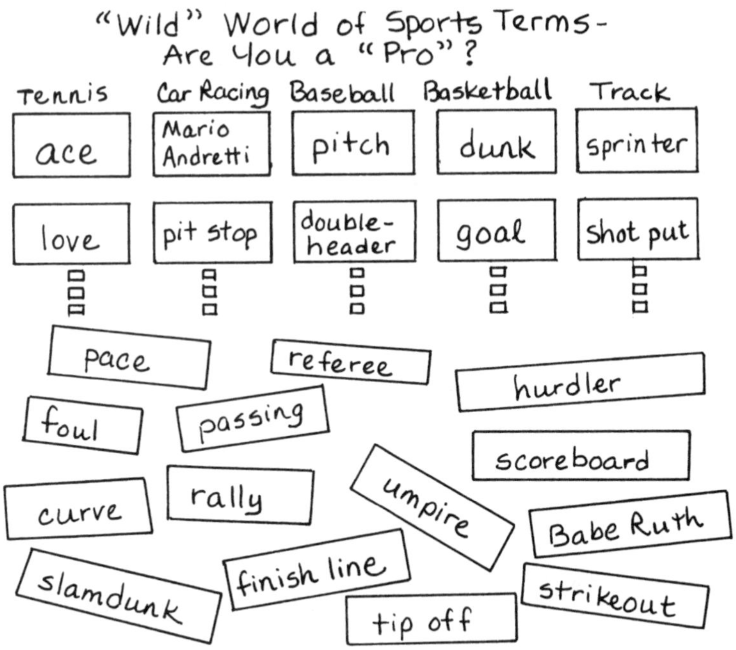

"Wild" World of Sports Terms-
Are You a "Pro"?

Tennis	Car Racing	Baseball	Basketball	Track
ace	Mario Andretti	pitch	dunk	sprinter
love	pit stop	double-header	goal	shot put

pace   referee
hurdler
foul   passing
scoreboard
curve   rally   umpire   Babe Ruth
slamdunk   finish line   strikeout
tip off

relates to the number of yards on a golf drive or the number gained or lost on a particular play in football. Make duplicate word cards for those terms that refer to more than
one sport (there may need to be several cards prepared for *scoreboard*).

Using the Dictionary. Dictionaries can also be valuable resources for learning word
meanings. But instruction using dictionaries is seldom helpful if students are asked only
to look up definitions and then use the word in a sentence (Gipe, 1978/1979; Scott &
Nagy, 1997). Effective dictionary instruction requires that the teacher model the use of a
dictionary and how to select the most appropriate meaning for a word (see Chapter 14).
Additionally, teachers should consider the appropriateness of the dictionaries available to
their students. For example, collegiate dictionaries are not the most appropriate for students
in middle grades or for English learners. Rather, learners' dictionaries that include fewer yet
more high frequency words and definitions, written in accessible language with age-
appropriate sample sentences, should be used. For example, the *Collins COBUILD Learner's
Dictionary* (2003) provides explanations rather than definitional phrases: "Something that is
sparse is small in number or amount and spread out over an area." Such a dictionary would
be an excellent choice for a classroom dictionary. Students also need instruction in using online dictionaries, glossaries, and the thesaurus (see the websites at the end of this chapter).

Developing Word Awareness

Developing a curiosity and interest in learning new words is also critical to vocabulary
instruction. Activities focused on raising the level of word awareness include (1) learning
to value the use of words to bring text to life through rich descriptions (for example, "joy
jiggling inside" from *Bridge to Terabithia* [Paterson, 1977, p. 101] or "Jack was a long

Word riddles like Hink Pink help to increase meaning vocabulary, but they can also increase phonemic awareness because students must either develop or solve the riddles with words that both rhyme and have the same number of syllables. The one-syllable Hink Pinks are the easiest format. The more advanced Hinky Pinkys and Hinkity Pinkitys have two and three syllables, respectively.

Hink Pinks

What is a (an):

seat that is uncovered?	(bare chair)
unhappy parent?	(sad dad)
dance of a hog	(pig jig)

Hinky Pinkys

What is:

a humorous rabbit?	(funny bunny)
an attractive cat?	(pretty kitty)
work done for the person living next door?	(neighbor labor)

Hinkity Pinkitys

What is a (an):

preacher who is evil?	(sinister minister)
dog that is happier than the other dogs?	(merrier terrier)
leader who waits too long?	(hesitant president)

string bean of a man"); (2) learning figurative uses of words (such as idioms, puns, tongue twisters); (3) engaging in word play (for example, word riddles such as Hink Pink or jokes: "What do you call it when a pig loses its memory? Answer: Hamnesia!" from Blachowicz and Fisher, 2004, p. 229); and (4) participating in word games (such as crossword puzzles, jumbles or anagrams, Scrabble) or competitions (like the *Reader's Digest National Word Power Challenge*).

Learners of all ages enjoy the rhyming game of Hink Pink (similar to the "Rhyme Time" category on *Jeopardy*), a game good for vocabulary development (for example, "What is the dance of a hog? A pig jig"). Hink Pinks are two words that rhyme and that both have one syllable. There are also Hinky Pinkys and Hinkity Pinkitys, for two- and three-syllable words, respectively (see Figure 10.12 for more examples).

Instruction for Specialized Vocabulary

The **specialized vocabulary** of content areas must also be addressed directly. Content-area materials may introduce 10 or more technical (a meaning of a common word form specific to a content field) or unfamiliar words on a page. These words usually are not repeated often, nor are they unimportant in understanding the subject matter. They are usually labels for important concepts being discussed. For example, in the area of social studies, abstract words such as *culture, technology,* and *adaptation* may be unfamiliar but extremely important to understanding the material. Not all words in content-area materials are new in terms of pronunciation, however. Common words such as *mouth, matter, suit,* or *recess* may be confusing if a specialized meaning is attached to them. Whereas most students associate the word *recess* with time out to play, a different meaning is presented in the following sentence: "When it was time to do his homework, Bob hid in the *recess* hoping that his mother would not find him." *Mouth* may refer to the facial cavity,

For two examples of activities that enhance word awareness and vocabulary, go to MyEducationLab and first select the topic *Teaching with Literature*. Then, go to the Activities and Applications section, and examine the artifact entitled "Journal Assignment (6–8)." Select the topic *Writing*, go to the Activities and Applications sections, and examine the artifact entitled "Creative Activity (3–5)." Respond to the accompanying questions.

to a part of a musical instrument, or to the place where a stream enters a larger body of water. Content-area materials abound with words that have multiple meanings.

Under most circumstances, assessment of specialized vocabulary for a content area is not necessary. Instead the teacher may safely assume that the specialized words are unknown and proceed with teaching procedures.

Most teachers at all levels agree that specialized vocabulary representing a *crucial* concept is best introduced before the lesson, although research by Memory (1990) indicates no superior time of presentation (before, during, or after) for technical vocabulary. Before reading, the teacher may (a) give the students a sentence using the new word and show how the context implies the meaning, or (b) give students a brief list of words (perhaps as part of a study guide or simply to copy from the board or into notebooks as seen in Figure 10.9) and direct them to look up each word's meaning in the book's glossary and copy it down for later reference while they are reading. After reading, the teacher must also discuss new word meanings using the context of the material read, along with glossary definitions. Multiple encounters with a new word and its meaning will enhance learning of that new vocabulary word (Stahl & Fairbanks, 1986).

Vocabulary techniques are essentially useless without discussion. New words can be discussed in many ways that greatly enhance understanding of their meaning and, in turn, understanding of the material read. The new concept should be related to something already familiar to the students (Gipe, 1980). For example, the students may be studying history and about to confront the word *tariff,* which is unfamiliar. But the word *tax* is probably not. Thus, any discussion about the new word should include mention of taxes and experiences students have had with them, such as having a dollar but not being able to buy a 99-cent item unless they have more money for the tax. Another example implemented with first-grade students involved the introduction of content-specific words through interactive read alouds, with young students then discussing the word along with a visual representing the meaning of these words. Students could also create their own drawings for the new words in a vocabulary notebook. These visuals were then placed on word walls to provide a visual reminder of the word and its meaning, or to assist in writing tasks (Dietrich, 2008).

New terms are probably best taught as new concepts. In addition to relating the new word to familiar concepts, the specific characteristics of the new concept must become part of the students' understanding as well. Eventually the students must be able to distinguish examples and nonexamples of the particular concept. The technique of the concept circle, discussed earlier, would be appropriately used for relating new words to familiar concepts. The **concept ladder** is another technique for thinking of the meaning of one word in relationship to the meaning of other words. For instance, meanings of words often have hierarchical relationships with other words. A dog is not just a four-legged animal that barks and has fur; it is also a kind of mammal. And there are different kinds (breeds) of dogs as well as stages of development (puppies grow up to be dogs). In order to complete a concept ladder, Upton (1973) proposed a set of questions to be asked when pursuing more depth in understanding a word's meaning: What is it a kind of/what are the kinds of it? What is it a part of/what are the parts of it? What is it a stage of/what are the stages of it? What is it a product or a result of/what are the products or results of it? At least three of these four pairs of questions should be asked as part of the concept ladder activity. Sometimes both parts of the question are not relevant. In those cases, just answer the questions that are relevant. Figure 10.13 shows how one student completed a concept ladder for the concept of *cetacean.*

It is also important to provide students opportunities to identify and discuss words new to them that may not have been selected by the teacher for discussion. Haggard (1986) suggests the *vocabulary self-collection strategy* (VSS) to help students learn to identify important words and concepts and to use passage context to determine meaning.

Go to MyEducationLab and select the topic *Vocabulary*. Then, go to the Activities and Applications section, and watch the video entitled "Teaching Vocabulary" to observe one middle school teacher conducting a vocabulary lesson for economic concepts. View the video "Vocabulary Instruction" for an additional example of vocabulary instruction at the middle and high school levels. Next respond to the accompanying questions for both videos.

Figure 10.13 Concept Ladders for Vocabulary Development

Concept Ladder for *Cetacean**

What kinds of cetaceans are there?	What is a cetacean a part of?	What is a cetacean a product of?
toothed whale	marine mammals	other male and
baleen whale		female cetaceans

What are the kinds of cetaceans?	What are the parts of a cetacean?	What are the products of a cetacean?
whales	flippers	oil
dolphins	flukes	whale blubber
porpoises	dorsal fins	waste products

POSSIBLE ANSWERS:

whales	flippers	calves	baleen whale	waste products	the sea
dolphins	food	oil	whale blubber	humpback whale	flukes
blowhole	blue whale	manatees	toothed whale	porpoises	dorsal fins
	marine mammals		other male and female cetaceans		

*Any one of an order of aquatic (mostly marine) mammals including the whales, dolphins, porpoises, and related forms with large head; fishlike, nearly hairless body; and paddle-shaped forelimbs.

Following the reading of a content-area selection, teams of two to five students select a word they feel is important to understanding that content. A spokesperson nominates the word before the entire class and states where the word occurred in the text, the team's definition for the word, and why the team feels it is important for the class to learn. Classmates discuss the word's value and definition. Finally, with teacher guidance, words are narrowed to only those that the class wishes to learn. These words and their final agreed-upon definitions are written in learning logs or vocabulary notebooks and used in follow-up activities. This strategy can be readily adapted to any content area. Chase and Duffelmeyer (1990) developed a modification for use in English literature called *VOCAB-LIT* and found it an effective tool for helping students recognize that knowledge of literary elements is essential to understanding and appreciating novels.

MI Connection: interpersonal

A specific technique developed not only for introducing new vocabulary but also for introducing overall organization of a selection, including important concepts, is the **structured overview**. This particular technique, developed by Richard Barron (1969), uses a graphic representation of terms that are indispensable to the essence of the selection to be read. The graphic representation makes this technique doubly attractive for reviewing the material. The steps for developing and using a structured overview are as follows:

MI Connection: spatial

1. List the vocabulary words that are important to understanding the selection. (This analysis could include both familiar and new words.)

2. Arrange these words so they show the interrelationships among the concepts represented.

3. Add to the diagram vocabulary that the students understand and that further helps to show relationships.

4. Evaluate the diagram. Does it clearly depict the major relationships? Can it be simplified and still communicate the important ideas?

5. Introduce the lesson by displaying the diagram (perhaps as a transparency for an overhead projector). Explain why you arranged the terms the way you did. Encourage the students to contribute any information they have. Give each student

Figure 10.14   Example of a Structured Overview for Social Studies

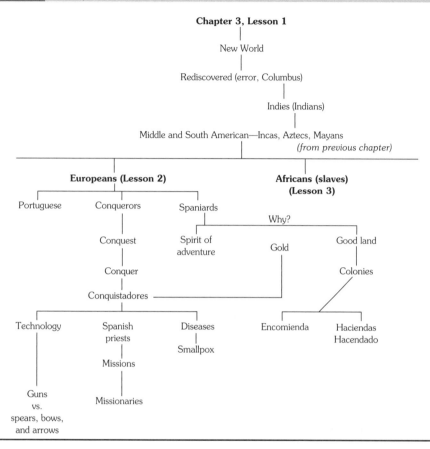

familiar vocabulary terms on slips of paper. As you discuss the overview, the students help construct it by placing their vocabulary terms in logical positions.

6. As the selection is read, continue to relate the new information to the structured overview.

An example of a structured overview was developed for a section of a social studies text dealing with explorers coming to the New World (Figure 10.14). Students had previously studied the Incan, Aztec, and Mayan cultures.

Burmeister (1978) presents teaching techniques for words that have both common and specialized meanings. She suggests a two-part activity: Part 1 demonstrates the common meanings, and part 2 uses sentences with blanks for the unique meanings. The students must fill in the blanks in part 2. Burmeister provides examples for several content areas; a few items follow for clarification:

Mathematics

Part 1

Term	Common Use
1. difference	You know the *difference* between right and wrong.
2. root	The tree *root* was growing through the sidewalk.
3. base	Jim ran as fast as he could to get to first *base*.

Part 2

1. The subtraction operation finds the (difference) between two numbers.
2. Find the square (root) of 9.
3. The (base) of the triangle is 10 cm long.

Activities that reinforce the idea that words may have several meanings are worthwhile and easily developed for any lesson. Simply use a dictionary and put together a list of sentences directly from the material of interest.

Some excellent general formats for specialized vocabulary instruction and practice follow. Each activity is easily modified to fit the needs of the teacher in any content area.

Word Pairs (Stevenson & Baumann, 1979). Use a table that allows students to show the relationship of various word pairs. Students may add word pairs to the list. Discuss the relationships among the words.

Word Pair	Almost the Same	Opposite	Go Together	Not Related
land/sea		X		
ship/galleon	X			
merchant/commerce			X	
pirate/bread				X

Semantic Mapping (Heimlich & Pittelman, 1986; Johnson & Pearson, 1984).

1. Select a word central to the material to be read (for example, *transportation*) or from any other source of classroom interest. Write it on the chalkboard.
2. Ask the class to think of as many words as they can that are related in some way to the word you have written and to jot them on paper.
3. Have individuals share the words they have written. As they do, write the words on the board and attempt to put them into categories.
4. Number the categories and have the students name them:
   a. Kinds of transportation
   b. Places we can travel to
   c. Reasons for transportation
5. Discuss the words. This is crucial to the success of semantic mapping. Students learn meanings of new words and new meanings for known words, as well as seeing relationships among words. (A completed semantic map for the "tired" word *said* can be seen in Figure 10.3.)
6. If time permits, select one word from the existing semantic map and begin to develop a new one (for example, start a new map with the word *exploration*).

Constrained Categorization (Stevenson & Baumann, 1979). Give students a chart with relevant category titles listed across the top and various letters listed along the side.

Have students fill in the chart using a word that fits the category and also begins with a certain letter. Some of the words should be found in the material read. Groups or individuals can research other words.

	Solids	Liquids	Gases
S	salt		
C		coffee	carbon dioxide
I	ice		
E		ether	ethylene
N			neon
C		cleaning fluid	
E	earth		

Semantic Feature Analysis (Pittelman et al., 1991).

1. Select a category (*vehicles*).
2. List some words in the category (*car, train*) in a column.
3. List some features shared by some of the words (*engine, wheels*) in a row.
4. Put pluses or minuses for each word beneath each feature (*? means uncertain*).
5. Add additional words.
6. Add additional features.
7. Complete the expanded matrix with pluses and minuses.
8. Discover and discuss the uniqueness of each word. (*Try to eliminate ?s through research.*)
9. Repeat the process with another category.

	engine	4 wheels	steering wheel	handlebars	runners	carries people
car	+	+	+	−	−	+
train	+	−	?	−	−	+
bus	+	?	+	−	−	+
truck (semi)	+	−	+	−	−	+
bicycle	−	−	−	+	−	+
sled	−	−	−	?	+	+

Some beginning categories:

games	vegetables	pets
occupations	food	clothing
tools	buildings	animals
plants	transportation	

More advanced categories:

moods	sizes	entertainment
feelings	shapes	modes of communication
commands	musical instruments	

A student who is successful with these basic vocabulary activities will be ready for instruction in some of the more difficult aspects of vocabulary development (analogies, connotative and denotative meanings, figures of speech, word origins). These aspects of vocabulary are not easily learned without a firm vocabulary base. In turn, a strong vocabulary base is essential for effective reading comprehension.

Summary

One goal of this chapter is to impress upon the reader the importance of direct instruction in meaning vocabulary. Vocabulary instruction is an overlooked area in many school curricula, but its importance to comprehension is undeniable. Teachers who are enthusiastic about new and interesting words will pass on this enthusiasm to their students. The chapter presents many techniques for assessing and teaching word meanings that students will find engaging. Beginning with the recognition that one can know a word at different levels of understanding can be a motivating factor in helping students move totally unknown words to a stage of awareness, then to a fair understanding, and finally to in-depth knowledge. Strategies used for concept development are presented that assist in this in-depth understanding of new words. Attention is also given to the specialized words found in all content areas. The following graphic organizer represents a summary of the content of this chapter.

Summary Graphic Organizer for Chapter 10

Recommended Websites

Student Online Dictionary
www.wordcentral.com
This excellent dictionary, thesaurus, and rhyming words resource for students includes daily buzzwords and games. Students can even create words to share (such as "dudify: to make something extra cool").

Little Explorers Picture Dictionary
www.enchantedlearning.com/dictionary.html
This multilingual picture dictionary with links contains over 2,400 entries that young children can use. For full use of this extensive site a subscription is now required. Prospective subscribers can sample pages to see what is available on the site.

Online Dictionary
www.allwords.com
Geared to use in upper grades, this site allows students to query words, hear words pronounced in one of five languages, and read definitions and related information. Also provides links to other sites for etymology, puns, speeches, word games, and jokes.

Heinle's Newbury House Dictionary of American English
http://nhd.heinle.com/home.aspx
Especially useful for English language learners, this site provides definitions and a wealth of sample sentences and idioms.

Online Thesaurus
http://www.thesaurus.com
Type in a word and receive a list of synonyms and antonyms.

Word Spy
www.wordspy.com/index.asp
This site is devoted to "lexpionage," the sleuthing of new words and phrases.

Oh My Words!
www.education-world.com/a_curr/curr096.shtml
This article by Sharon Cromwell in *Education World* includes links to some of the best wordplay sites on the Internet.

Worldwide Wordplay
http://teacher.scholastic.com/fieldtrp/lanarts/wordplay.htm
Scholastic has put together an enticing introduction to some of the best wordplay sites in this Internet fieldtrip.

Roget's Thesaurus Search Form
http://humanities.uchicago.edu/orgs/ARTFL/forms_unrest/ROGET.html
This site is useful for enhancing vocabulary and writing that contains too many tired and overused words.

The Word Detective
www.word-detective.com/
This is the online version of a newspaper column answering readers' questions about words and language written by Evan Morris.

Quizzes for English Learners
http://a4esl.org/
Quizzes and puzzles in many languages on grammar, vocabulary, idioms, homonyms, scrambled words, and places can be found here.

Fact Monster Dictionary
http://dictionary.Factmonster.com
This is a fun-filled site for word lovers and fact seekers.

Word Power Challenge
www.wordpowerchallenge.com
This national competition involving words is sponsored by *Reader's Digest*.

MyEducationLab is a research-based learning tool that brings teaching to life. Go to the Gipe 7th Edition MyEducationLab for Reading Assessment site at www.myeducationlab.com to:

- Engage in multimedia exercises to help you build a deeper and more applied understanding of chapter content.
- Use extensive resources including videos from real classrooms, Praxis and licensure preparation, a lesson plan builder, and materials to help you in your teaching career.

Reading Comprehension:
Foundations

VOCABULARY ALERT

abstract referent	phonological system	schema
attentive listening	process of comprehension	scriptally implicit
auditory comprehension	question–answer	semantic system
concrete referent	relationships (QARs)	semantic webbing
directed reading-thinking	reciprocal question–	structured comprehension
activity (DRTA)	answer relationships	syntactic system
graphic organizers	(ReQARs)	text organization
listening	repeated words	textually explicit
mapping	replaced words	textually implicit
phase-out/phase-in strategy	scaffolds	transactional model

oncern for understanding reading comprehension is not new. Historically, reading experts have tried to explain reading comprehension by identifying what successful comprehenders do. A classic study by Davis (1944) listed nine skills considered basic to successful comprehension:[1]

1. Knowledge of word meanings
2. Ability to select appropriate meaning for a word or phrase in the light of its particular contextual setting
3. Ability to follow the organization of a passage and to identify antecedents and references in it
4. Ability to identify the main thought of a passage
5. Ability to answer questions that are specifically answered in a passage
6. Ability to answer questions that are answered in a passage, but not in the words in which the question is asked
7. Ability to draw inferences from a passage about its contents
8. Ability to recognize the literary devices used in a passage and to determine its tone and mood
9. Ability to determine a writer's purpose, intent, and point of view—that is, to draw inferences about a writer (p. 186)

These skills and similar listings are considered products of comprehension. Traditional skills-centered approaches to reading comprehension deal predominantly with the products of comprehension. These products are described by terms such as *literal, inferential, critical* (analyzing text), and *creative* (synthesizing or applying text) thinking skills.

Consider the following example. Through an assessment technique Banetta is found to have difficulty drawing conclusions from a passage, a *product* of comprehension. The usual procedure is to give Banetta additional practice in drawing conclusions. Unfortunately, whether such practice affects the *process* of drawing conclusions is not certain. On the other hand, if the underlying tasks involved in drawing conclusions were known, the procedure would be to determine the stage at which the process broke down and proceed with appropriate instruction from that point. What is really needed, then, is a better understanding of comprehension processes. What does the reader have to do to draw a conclusion or to predict an outcome? The answer represents the underlying abilities involved in the process of comprehension.

---

[1]From F. B. Davis, "Fundamental Factors of Comprehension in Reading." *Psychometrika, 9* (1944): 186. Used with permission.

FACTORS AFFECTING THE COMPREHENSION PROCESS

The **process of comprehension** is best examined in light of the strategies used by skilled comprehenders. In this way, areas of difference between skilled and less skilled comprehenders will be easier to recognize. The ultimate goal is to design appropriate reading comprehension instruction so less skilled comprehenders can become skilled comprehenders. Key factors affecting the comprehension process are best grouped into three categories: (a) factors within the reader, (b) factors within the written text, and (c) factors within the reading environment (Pearson & Johnson, 1978). Table 11.1 summarizes these factors and provides an *advance graphic organizer* (a visual representation of the text's concepts presented in advance of the reading to aid in comprehension) for the following three sections.

Factors within the Reader

Some factors within the reader that affect reading comprehension are linguistic competence, decoding ability, prior knowledge or experience including knowledge of key vocabulary and text structure, and interests and attitudes.

Linguistic Competence. *Linguistic competence* refers to what the reader knows about language. Three systems are involved in learning language: phonological, syntactic, and semantic. The **phonological system** refers to knowledge of individual sounds in the language, knowledge of how these sounds are blended together to make words, and knowledge of stress, pitch, and juncture. Briefly, stress refers to such differences as:

> The DOG broke the cup. (not the cat)

> The dog BROKE the cup. (as opposed to just knocking it over)

Table 11.1	Key Factors Affecting the Reading Comprehension Process	
Factors within the Reader	Factors within the Written Text	Factors within the Reading Environment
• Linguistic competence	• Word difficulty	• Home influences on prior knowledge (conceptual development) and on language base
• Decoding ability	• Word imagery (abstract vs. concrete)	• Reading models available
• Prior knowledge or experience	• Sentence structure	• Risk-free classroom atmosphere
• Interests and attitudes	• Paragraph relationships	• Direct instruction
• Knowledge of key vocabulary	• Text organization (narrative vs. expository)	• Appropriate materials
• Ability to recognize text structures		• Well-planned teacher questions
		• Ample opportunities to read

Pitch refers to intonation differences:

We'll leave in an hour.

We'll leave in an hour!

We'll leave in an hour?

Juncture refers to the differences between *nitrate* and *night rate* or between *icing* and *I sing*.

K. S. Goodman (1996) termed this first important system the *graphophonic system*, which includes the orthographic and phonic systems as well as the phonological. Because the cues in reading are also visual, the reader must have knowledge of the particular orthography of the language being read. In English this is an alphabetic system, as compared to Japanese, for instance, which uses a combination of Chinese characters and syllabic orthography. Additionally, the reader must have knowledge of the relationships between oral and written language using an alphabetic system, better known as phonics.

The **syntactic system** refers to word order in sentences, punctuation, and the use of capital letters. Syntactic knowledge helps the reader determine whether a string of words makes a grammatically acceptable English sentence. For example:

The dog chased the cat.

    or

Chased dog the cat the.

Syntactic knowledge, sometimes called "sentence sense," also helps the reader know that two different word orders have the same meaning:

The dog chased the cat.

    or

The cat was chased by the dog.

His friend said, "The doctor is ill."

    or

"The doctor," said his friend, "is ill."

Knowledge of syntax even enables the reader to use context clues to read and answer questions on material that has no real meaning:

The ill zoo was a bab. That forn, the sossy ill zoo larped and was mitry.

What was the ill zoo? When did the sossy ill zoo larp? Who was sossy?

In short, syntax is the primary means by which the reader determines relationships between words.

Simply being able to pronounce words and answer certain questions correctly does not ensure that understanding has occurred. Because the sentences about the ill zoo had no real meaning (readers are not able to relate the nonsense words to anything already available in their minds), the importance of the semantic system becomes obvious. The **semantic system** refers to knowledge of word meanings, the underlying concepts of words, and the interrelationships between concepts. Semantic knowledge enables the reader to organize the text into a coherent structure and determine the relative importance of the various concepts found in text (for example, main ideas versus supporting details).

Pragmatic knowledge is sometimes considered a part of this system along with schematic knowledge. Pragmatic meaning is always partly found in the text and partly found in the context of the literacy event. The reader's schemata must be called on to achieve pragmatic comprehension (such as understanding the humor in a comic strip).

In summary, if the phonological, syntactic, and semantic information provided for the reader on a page of print closely matches the phonological, syntactic, and semantic abilities in the reader's mind, understanding is likely.

Decoding Ability. When a reader approaches text to construct meaning, decoding occurs naturally. However, constructing meaning will be difficult if the reader cannot readily pronounce many of the words in the passage or is overly concerned with accurate word pronunciation. The reader who has to devote too much attention to decoding or to correct pronunciation, as in the case of oral, round-robin reading, cannot also attend to processing the meaning of the material (LaBerge & Samuels, 1974; Opitz & Rasinski, 1998; Stanovich, 1980). Readers who identify words quickly and automatically, on the other hand, do not have to focus on decoding and can give their full attention to comprehension, especially when reading silently.

Difficulty with decoding does not imply, however, that comprehension cannot occur. In fact, comprehension must be the goal for decoding to occur more readily. Consider the following argument presented by Pearson and Johnson (1978):

> Comprehension helps word identification as much as word identification helps comprehension. That is, having understood part of the message helps you to decode another part. In short, context can help to short-circuit the amount of attention you have to pay to print. (p. 15)

Decoding ability is discussed in detail in Chapter 9, but you may conclude from this brief discussion that decoding is made easier if the reader is reading for meaning. Concern with comprehension instruction is important at every stage of reading development. The reader must *expect* and *demand* that material read *makes sense*.

Prior Knowledge or Experience. What readers bring to the reading task is critical to their understanding of what is read. A reader's background gives personal meaning to the printed page; thus not all readers comprehend material in exactly the same way. For example, if a young reader who has never been out of the city tries to read a book about life on a farm, so many words and events will be unfamiliar that the reading will probably become more of a word-calling situation. Even if this reader uses all of his linguistic competence to make predictions about what will occur in print, words such as *silo, harvester,* and *trough* and events such as birthing a calf or hauling hay will have little or no meaning. Adult readers experience the same frustrations if they try to understand material in an area they are unfamiliar with, such as a physics text, a medical journal, or legal documents. This does not imply that the reader cannot understand material concerning something not experienced but rather that a reader must have a repertoire of relevant concepts to interpret the printed page. Consider another young reader who has always lived in the Deep South and has never experienced heavy snows. This reader is asked to read a story about a blizzard. Even though she has never experienced a blizzard, some relevant concepts available to her might be ice, the wind of a hurricane, and the possible tragedy of its aftermath.

In summary, for maximum comprehension to occur, the reader must be able to relate the printed material to personal experiences. Direct, firsthand experiences are usually best. At the very least, vicarious or secondhand experiences must be provided, such as listening to stories on a variety of concepts, seeing relevant pictures, and watching films or video clips.

Interests and Attitudes. Closely related to prior knowledge and experience are interests and attitudes. Shnayer (1969) reported that interest in a topic enables readers with reading ability from two years below grade level to one year above grade level to read beyond their measured ability. Thus, a reader will better understand a book about explorers if she has an interest in history and the concept of exploration. Readers' attitudes are closely related to their interests. Attitudes are learned and probably reflect previous experiences. A reader with a poor attitude toward reading on any subject has little motivation to pick up a book and read, much less comprehend. Because attitude is influenced as much by factors within the reading environment as by factors within the reader, interests and attitudes are addressed further in Chapters 4 and 6.

Factors within the Written Text

As Smith and Johnson (1980) stated, "Reading comprehension is not entirely dependent on the reader" (p. 133). Text features can affect the difficulty of the material. The size of the print, whether there are pictures or other visual aids, the use of color, and the amount of white space on the page can make a difference. Most importantly, elements in the written message must be considered, including the words themselves, sentence complexity and length, paragraph structure, and the organization of longer units of discourse, such as stories.

Words. What makes some words easier to learn than others? The most researched characteristics of words are frequency and imagery. Frequency refers to how often a word occurs in the language. Several studies (Ekwall & Shanker, 1988; Jorm, 1977) have demonstrated that passages containing words that occur frequently in the language are more easily comprehended than passages containing words that do not occur frequently.

Imagery refers to how easily a word is visualized. A word with a **concrete referent**, such as *dog,* is probably easier to learn than a word with an **abstract referent**, such as *way.* Passages containing a heavy concentration of words with low imagery (abstract words) will probably be more difficult to understand than passages containing a large number of words with high imagery (Thorndyke, 1977).

The results of a study by Jorm (1977) are particularly relevant. Jorm analyzed the effects of word imagery, length, and frequency on the reading ability of good and poor readers ages 8 through 11. Although word length had little effect on either type of reader, Jorm found that high-frequency words were easier to read for both good and poor readers. He also found that imagery facilitated word recognition only for poor readers. Jorm explains that ineffective readers are more likely than good readers to use a whole-word method for word recognition, and visual imagery is an aid for this type of learning. On the basis of this information, teachers are advised to carefully examine materials to be used with readers who struggle for the occurrence of high-imagery words.

Teachers must also be concerned with the difficulty of material. The ratio of known words to unknown words is most important. In fact, the ratio of difficult words in a text is the most powerful predictor of text difficulty (Anderson & Freebody, 1981), and a reader's knowledge of key vocabulary predicts comprehension of text better than reading ability or achievement (Johnston, 1984). (See Chapter 10 for a discussion of meaning vocabulary and its relationship to comprehension.) When students are provided material at their *instructional reading level,* the number of known words approximates 95 out of 100. Students are often taught the *five-finger method* to determine whether a library book is easy enough for them to read. This idea is analogous to the instructional reading level criterion: If the student counts more than five unknown words on a page, the book is probably too difficult (see also the Goldilocks Strategy in Chapter 12).

Sentences, Paragraphs, and Longer Units. Comprehension of written material demands much more than understanding each word in the selection. Words must be understood in relation to other words. Likewise, readers seldom read isolated sentences, but they must comprehend relationships within sentences if they are to comprehend a paragraph. Just as sentence comprehension is more than understanding each word, paragraph comprehension is more than understanding individual sentences. Paragraphs are structured to function in longer units of written discourse. To understand a paragraph, the reader must recognize who or what the paragraph is about. The reader must also recognize the relations existing within and between paragraphs, such as cause and effect, question and answer (or problem and solution), sequence, enumeration, description, or comparison and contrast. Englert and Thomas (1987) reported that for instructional purposes, sequence is the easiest relationship to recognize, followed by, in order of difficulty, enumeration, description, and compare–contrast.

As with sentences, a reader does not often read isolated paragraphs. Paragraphs exist in the context of longer selections and serve specific functions: introductory, expository, narrative, descriptive, definitional, persuasive, transitional, or summary and concluding. The skilled comprehender recognizes how paragraphs function within the total context of the selection.

Specific relationships also exist within narratives (stories) and expository material (nonfiction). Stories are usually organized in consistent, predictable patterns. The reader expects relationships that specify themes, setting, characters, goals, and resolutions. Thorndyke (1977) suggested that some story structures (such as fairy tales and fables) become more familiar with experience and that stories with several cause–effect relationships are easier to comprehend than those without causal relationships. (Chapter 12 provides more information specific to the comprehension of narrative material.) Similarly, expository material also uses the writing patterns of problem–solution and cause–effect but includes as major patterns time order, compare–contrast, listing of facts, and enumeration as well. (Chapter 13 presents information specific to the comprehension of expository material.)

In summary, recognizing text organization is key to understanding written material. The reader must identify who or what the material is about, discover the relationship between actors or agents and actions, and determine the function or purpose of the material.

Environmental Factors

Essentially two environments affect reading comprehension—the home and the school. The preceding emphasis on prior knowledge and experience explains the important role of the home environment in providing the language base necessary for reading comprehension. The student with an extensive language base comes to school better equipped for the comprehension process than a student who has not been spoken to frequently, read to, taken on trips, or involved in other concept-developing activities.

The school environment refers, for the most part, to the student's classroom, teacher, and peers. However, the atmosphere of the entire school and the attitude of administrators and other teachers also affect reading comprehension, even if only in a general, indirect sense.

Although the classroom teacher has the most direct influence on reading comprehension, classmates provide a source of competition or approval or a standard for comparison. Unfortunately, classmates may also have an emotionally negative influence as sources of ridicule or harassment.

Teachers can do much to affect comprehension both instructionally and emotionally. Teachers influence comprehension in a positive way through the following practices:

1. *Establishing a comfortable, risk-free atmosphere in which students do not fear ridicule or penalty for failure.* Teachers should provide the kind of feedback that encourages curiosity, risk-taking, and creativity.

2. *Providing a model for their students.* Reading is perceived as a valuable, enjoyable, and relevant activity when students see their teachers reading and are read to by their teachers.

3. *Providing direct instruction.* This includes preparing students for reading by discussing backgrounds and essential vocabulary of text and by helping students establish purposes for reading with appropriate follow-up activities.

4. *Choosing appropriate materials for instruction.* Teachers must know their students' strengths, needs, and reading levels. Frustrating material does nothing to help comprehension.

5. *Planning the type of questions they will ask.* Teachers' questions are often poorly planned with respect to the objectives of the lesson (Bartolome, 1969) and do not demand much thinking beyond a literal level (Bartolome, 1969; Cecil, 1995; Dantonio & Beisenherz, 2001; Durkin, 1981; Guszak, 1967). Instructional techniques in this chapter and those that follow emphasize this important aspect of comprehension instruction.

6. *Providing ample opportunities and time to read.* Students need large blocks of time to just read, at least 20 minutes each day. The benefits go beyond enhancing reading comprehension to improving writing, self-esteem, and attitude toward school (Block & Cavanaugh, 1998; Elley, 1991; Krashen, 1993). Block (1999) refers to this type of comprehension instruction as "Type 1 lessons," whose purpose "is to provide enough time for students to not merely read but to live within a book . . . students select their own books and reading goals . . . and have time to read without having to perform a task about what they comprehended" (pp. 101–102). Students, especially those who are struggling with comprehension, need more practice reading whole text, not less. Classroom organizational patterns that include activities such as book clubs or literature circles and DEAR time (see Chapter 12) are desirable.

THEORIES AND MODELS OF THE COMPREHENSION PROCESS

Schema Theory

Linguists, cognitive psychologists, and psycholinguists have used the concept of **schema** (pl. *schemata*) to understand the interaction of key factors affecting the comprehension process. The term *schema* itself is not new (Bartlett, 1932; Kant, 1787/1963), but the recognition of its importance to reading is more recent (Rumelhart, 1975, 1980, 1994).

Simply put, schema theory states that all knowledge is organized into units. Within these units of knowledge, or schemata, is stored information. A *schema,* then, is a generalized description or a conceptual system for understanding knowledge—how knowledge is represented and how it is used.

According to this theory, schemata represent knowledge about concepts: objects and the relationships they have with other objects, situations, events, sequences of events, actions, and sequences of actions. A simple example is to think of your schema for *dog.* Within that schema you most likely have knowledge about dogs in general (bark, four legs, teeth, hair, tails) and probably information about specific dogs, such as collies (long hair, large, Lassie) or spaniels (English Springer, docked tails, liver and white or black and white, Millie; or Field, solid brown or black, Cocoa). You may also think of dogs within the greater context of animals and other living things; that is, dogs breathe, need food, and reproduce. Your knowledge of dogs might also include the fact that they are mammals and thus are warm blooded and bear their young as opposed to laying eggs. Depending on your personal experience, the knowledge of a dog as a pet (domesticated and loyal) or as an animal to fear (likely to bite or attack) may be a part of your schema. And so it goes with the development of a schema. Each new experience incorporates more information into one's schema.

What does all this have to do with reading comprehension? Individuals have schemata for everything. Long before students come to school, they develop schemata (units of knowledge) about everything they experience. Schemata become theories about reality. These theories not only affect the way information is interpreted, thus affecting comprehension, but also continue to change as new information is received. As stated by Rumelhart (1980),

> Schemata can represent knowledge at all levels—from ideologies and cultural truths to knowledge about the meaning of a particular word, to knowledge about what patterns of excitations are associated with what letters of the alphabet. We have schemata to represent all levels of our experience, at all levels of abstraction. Finally, our schemata are our knowledge. All of our generic knowledge is embedded in schemata. (p. 41)

The importance of schema theory to reading comprehension also lies in how the reader uses schemata. This issue has not yet been resolved by research, although investigators agree that some mechanism activates just those schemata most relevant to the reader's task. Although theories try to explain the comprehension process, related models have been developed to describe and represent literacy processes. Five classifications of models are termed cognitive-based, sociocognitive, transactional, transactional-sociopsycholinguistic, and attitude-influence, and they are further described in the following sections.

Reading Comprehension as Cognitive-Based Processing

There are several models based on cognitive processing. For example, the LaBerge-Samuels' model of automatic information processing (Samuels, 1994) emphasizes internal aspects of attention as crucial to comprehension. Samuels (1994) defined three characteristics of internal attention. The first, *alertness,* is the reader's active attempt to access relevant schemata involving letter–sound relationships, syntactic knowledge, and word meanings. *Selectivity,* the second characteristic, refers to the reader's ability to attend selectively to only that information requiring processing. The third characteristic, *limited capacity,* refers to the fact that the human brain has a limited amount of cognitive energy available for use in processing information. In other words, if a reader's cognitive energy is focused on decoding and attention cannot be directed at integrating, relating, and combining the meanings of the words decoded, then comprehension will suffer. "Automaticity in information processing, then, simply means that information is processed with little attention" (Samuels, 1994, p. 823). Comprehension difficulties occur when the reader cannot rapidly and automatically access the concepts and knowledge stored in the schemata.

One other example of a cognitive-based model is Rumelhart's (1994) interactive model. Information from several knowledge sources (schemata for letter–sound relationships, word meanings, syntactic relationships, event sequences, and so forth) are considered *simultaneously*. The implication is that when information from one source, such as word recognition, is deficient, the reader will rely on information from another source, for example, contextual clues or previous experience. Stanovich (1980) termed the latter kind of processing *interactive-compensatory* because the reader (*any reader*) compensates for deficiencies in one or more of the knowledge sources by using information from remaining knowledge sources. Those sources that are more concerned with concepts and semantic relationships are termed *higher-level stimuli;* sources dealing with the print itself— that is, phonics, sight words, and other word-attack skills—are termed *lower-level stimuli*. The interactive-compensatory model implies that the reader will rely on higher-level processes when lower-level processes are inadequate, and vice versa. Stanovich (1980) extensively reviews research demonstrating such compensation in both good readers and readers who struggle.

Reading Comprehension as Sociocognitive Processing

A sociocognitive processing model takes a constructivist view of reading comprehension by viewing comprehension as a process that involves meaning negotiation among the text, the reader, the teachers, and other members of the classroom community (Ruddell & Unrau, 1996). Schema for text meanings, academic tasks, sources of authority (residing within the text, the reader, the teacher, the classroom community, or some interaction of these), and sociocultural settings are central to the meaning negotiation task. The teacher's role is one of orchestrating the instructional setting and being knowledgeable about teaching and learning strategies and about the world.

Reading Comprehension as Transactional

The **transactional model** takes into account the dynamic nature of language and both aesthetic and cognitive aspects of reading. According to Rosenblatt (1994),

> Every reading act is an event, or a transaction involving a particular reader and a particular pattern of signs, a text, and occurring at a particular time in a particular context. Instead of two fixed entities acting on one another, the reader and the text are two aspects of a total dynamic situation. The "meaning" does not reside ready-made "in" the text or "in" the reader but happens or comes into being during the transaction between reader and text. (p. 1063)

Thus, text without a reader is merely a set of marks capable of being interpreted as written language. However, when a reader transacts with the text, meaning happens.

Within the transactional model, schemata are not viewed as static but rather as active, developing, and ever changing. As readers transact with text they are changed or transformed, as is the text. Similarly, "the same text takes on different meanings in transactions with different readers or even with the same reader in different contexts or times"

(Rosenblatt, 1994, p. 1078). This model explains how a reader can reread material at a later date and interpret the material differently from the earlier reading.

Reading Comprehension as Transactional-Sociopsycholinguistic

Building on Rosenblatt's transactional model, K. S. Goodman (1994) conceptualized literacy processing as including reading, writing, and written texts. He stated,

> Texts are constructed by authors to be comprehended by readers. The meaning is in the author and the reader. The text has a potential to evoke meaning but has no meaning in itself; meaning is not a characteristic of texts. This does not mean the characteristics of the text are unimportant or that either writer or reader are independent of them. How well the writer constructs the text and how well the reader reconstructs it and constructs meaning will influence comprehension. But meaning does not pass between writer and reader. It is represented by a writer in a text and constructed from a text by a reader. Characteristics of writer, text, and reader will all influence the resultant meaning. (p. 1103)

In a transactional-sociopsycholinguistic view, the reader has a highly active role. It is the individual transactions between a reader and the text characteristics that result in meaning. These characteristics include physical characteristics such as orthography—the alphabetic system, spelling, punctuation; format characteristics such as paragraphing, lists, schedules, bibliographies; macrostructure or text grammar such as that found in telephone books, recipe books, newspapers, and letters; and wording of texts such as the differences found in narrative and expository text.

The reader's schemata, however, limit understanding, making what the reader brings to the text as important as the text itself. The writer also plays an important role in comprehension. In addition, readers' and writers' schemata are changed through transactions with the text as meaning is constructed. Readers' schemata are changed as new knowledge is assimilated and accommodated. Writers' schemata are changed as new ways of organizing text to express meaning are developed. According to K. S. Goodman (1994):

> How well the writer knows the audience and has built the text to suit that audience makes a major difference in text predictability and comprehension. However, since comprehension results from reader–text transactions, what the reader knows, who the reader is, what values guide the reader, and what purposes or interests the reader has will play vital roles in the reading process. It follows that what is comprehended from a given text varies among readers. Meaning is ultimately created by each reader. (p. 1127)

Reading Comprehension as Influenced by Attitude

Mathewson's (1994) "Model of Attitude Influence upon Reading and Learning to Read" is derived from the area of social psychology. This model attempts to explain the roles of affect and cognition in reading comprehension. The core of the attitude-influence model explains that a reader's whole attitude toward reading (prevailing feelings and evaluative beliefs about reading and action readiness for reading) influences the intention to read, in turn influencing reading behavior. *Intention to read* is proposed as the primary mediator between attitude and reading. *Intention* is defined as "commitment to a plan for achieving one or more reading purposes at a more or less specified time in the future" (Mathewson, 1994, p. 1135). All other moderator variables (extrinsic motivation, involvement, prior knowledge, and purpose) are viewed as affecting the attitude-reading relationship by influencing the intention to read. Therefore, classroom environments that include well-stocked libraries, magazines, reading tables, and areas with comfortable chairs and lamps will enhance students' intentions to read. Mathewson stated, "Favorable attitudes toward reading thus sustain intention to read and reading as long as readers continue to be satisfied with reading outcomes" (p. 1148).

SKILLED VERSUS LESS SKILLED COMPREHENDERS

An early review of the literature by Golinkoff (1975/1976) that looked at "good" and "poor" comprehenders reveals that good comprehenders are adaptable and flexible. They seem to be aware that reading is a process for gaining information or expanding one's knowledge about the world. More specifically, in terms of three comprehension subskills that Golinkoff used to compare good and poor comprehenders, the skilled comprehender is a master at decoding, accessing single word meanings, and extracting relationships between words in sentences and larger units of text.

Less skilled comprehenders, on the other hand, are not as adaptive and flexible in their reading style. They make more decoding errors and take more time to decode. They tend to read word-by-word, which implies one of three things: They are unfamiliar with the printed words (decoding), they are unaware of the clues to proper phrasing (syntactic aspects), or they are unaware that reading involves using what they already know about the concepts and contextual constraints found in the text to construct meaning (semantic aspects). This last characteristic is also supported by research on the acquisition of word meanings from context (McKeown, 1985).

Although such characterizations have led to the conclusion that poor comprehenders are more concerned with pronouncing words correctly than with getting meaning from the printed page, this is not necessarily the case. Stanovich (1980) gave evidence that in some situations poor readers rely more on contextual information than good readers. To cope with a large number of visually unfamiliar words, some poor readers depend too much on the syntactic and semantic clues available. This phenomenon, referred to as the interactive-compensatory hypothesis, has been tested and supported by (Yoon) Kim and Goetz (1994).

Kolers (1975) presented evidence that such dependence on syntactic and semantic clues to avoid decoding may be a common source of reading difficulty. Kolers's subjects—good and poor readers ages 10 through 14—read sentences in normal and reversed type. The poor readers made 10 times as many substitution errors as the good readers. Also, the reversed type had less effect on the reading speed of the poor readers than that of the good readers. The poor readers guessed frequently and paid relatively little attention to the typographical (graphemic) aspects of the print. These results were interpreted as indicating an overreliance on syntactic and semantic clues.

Stanovich (1980) distinguished between two types of contextual processing when discussing differences between good and poor comprehenders. The first type involves relating new information to known information and imposing structure on the text (text organization). The second type is the contextual hypothesis-testing strategy that allows previously understood material to help with ongoing word recognition. Good readers use both types of contextual processing, whereas poor readers are more adept at the second type. In itself this is not a problem; however, if processing is being used to aid word recognition, the reader is depleting valuable cognitive resources that could otherwise be employed for making inferences or relating new information to old. Stanovich views the comprehension problem as a direct result of slow and nonautomatic word recognition skills that require the poor reader to draw on the wrong kinds of knowledge sources. As stated by Stanovich (1980):

> Given that the ability to use prior context to facilitate word recognition is not a skill that differentiates good from poor readers, there appear to be two general types of processes that good readers perform more efficiently than poor readers. Good readers appear to have superior strategies for comprehending and remembering large units of text. In addition, good readers are superior at context-free word recognition. There is some evidence indicating that good readers have automatized the recognition of word and subword units to a greater extent than poor readers. However, good readers recognize even fully automated words faster than poor readers. . . . In short, the good reader identifies words automatically and rapidly. . . . The existence of this rapid context-free recognition ability means that the word recognition of good readers is less reliant on conscious expectancies generated from the prior sentence context. The result is that more attentional capacity is left over for integrative comprehension processes. (p. 64)

A study by Kletzien (1991) looked at the comprehension strategies used by good and poor comprehenders with expository material at the secondary level. Results support earlier findings (see Golinkoff, 1975/1976) that good comprehenders are more flexible in their use of strategies. By means of student self-reports, Kletzien found that both good and poor comprehenders are aware of a variety of strategies, but attention to vocabulary, rereading, making inferences, and using prior knowledge were the most frequently used strategies for both groups. More strategies were used with easier material. Poor comprehenders used fewer strategies as the difficulty of the material increased. Kletzien suggested that poor comprehenders need to know when, how, and why to use a particular strategy.

Poor comprehenders apparently do not effectively use the strategies that good comprehenders do. Research by Olshavsky (1976/1977) revealed that poor readers are not proficient in using context to aid reading fluency or in using their knowledge of the language to add information that is not in the text but would help in understanding the material (making inferences). Olshavsky concluded that, in general, poor readers use fewer strategies than good readers, but Kletzien's research indicated that this may be due to uncertainty about when to use a strategy rather than lack of awareness of the strategies themselves.

Rumelhart (1980) offered additional explanations of failure to comprehend a selection, assuming that the words are automatically recognized:

1. The reader does not have the appropriate schemata necessary (lack of conceptual background).
2. The reader has the appropriate schemata, but clues provided by the author are insufficient to suggest them.
3. The reader interprets the text but not in the way intended by the author. (p. 48)

These breakdowns are likely when reading something in a new field of study or something abstract, vague, technical, or too difficult.

In conclusion, comprehension demands that the reader be active, attentive, and selective while reading. As Tierney and Pearson (1994, p. 497) advocated, "teaching procedures that encourage students to monitor their own processing strategies—how they allocate attention to text versus prior knowledge, how they can tell what and that they know (such as metacognition), and how to apply fix-up strategies when comprehension is difficult" should be adopted. (See Figure 11.1 for a T-chart summarizing the comparison of skilled and less skilled comprehenders.)

Figure 11.1   T-Chart Comparing Skilled and Less Skilled Comprehenders

Skilled Comprehenders	Less Skilled Comprehenders
• Adaptable and flexible	• Less adaptable and less flexible
• Aware that reading is a process that uses known concepts or context clues to construct meaning	• Unaware of reading as a process or unable to use known concepts or context constraints to construct meaning
• Masters at decoding	• Make more decoding errors and take more time to decode
• Readily access single word meaning and relationships between words, sentences, paragraphs	• Tend to read word-by-word for reasons not clearly established (poor decoding skills or not aware of syntactic clues)
• Relate new information to known and use text structure	• Possible overreliance on syntactic or semantic information due to weak decoding skill
• Use previously understood text to help with ongoing word recognition	• Use previously understood text to help with ongoing word recognition
• Aware that reading increases knowledge	• May or may not be aware that reading increases knowledge
• Proficient and effective use of strategies	• Less proficient use of strategies

ASSESSMENT AND INSTRUCTION FOR GENERAL COMPREHENSION

Reading comprehension, as discussed in this text, includes three major areas: comprehension of individual word meanings (vocabulary); comprehension of stories (narrative); and comprehension of informational text (expository). And because there are strategies that are particularly well suited for each of these areas, three separate chapters are devoted to each of them—Chapter 10 (meaning vocabulary), Chapter 12 (strategic reading for narrative text), and Chapter 13 (strategic reading for expository text), respectively. The following reading comprehension strategies are effective for any type of text. I am calling these general comprehension strategies, and they are appropriately used with either narrative or expository material.

Reading comprehension requires a number of thinking and reasoning skills. No longer is it sufficient to consider material "comprehended" if the reader can recall elements of the text. As Pearson (1985) has stated, "no longer do we regard text as a fixed object that the reader is supposed to 'approximate' as closely as possible as s/he reads. Instead we now view text as a sort of blueprint for meaning, a set of tracks or clues that the reader uses as s/he builds a model of what the text means" (p. 726). It is only when readers actively construct logical connections among their own prior knowledge, ideas in the text, the specific task at hand, and the situation they are in and can express these ideas in their own words, that the text is considered comprehended.

Teachers also need to recognize the importance of prior knowledge and writing to reading comprehension. "Writing is one of the most powerful tools for developing comprehension because it can actively involve the reader in constructing a set of meanings that are useful to the individual reader" (Irwin, 1991, p. 24). Because writing activities help develop reading comprehension, many of the assessment and instruction techniques discussed in Chapter 8 are also relevant here.

In addition, **listening**, or oral language comprehension, is an area in which much assumptive teaching occurs. Many teachers associate listening with hearing and assume listening is simply a matter of either paying attention or not paying attention. This is not true. After extensive study, Lundsteen (1979, p. 15) concluded that listening is "the process by which spoken language is converted to meaning in the mind" and, as such, involves the same processes as reading comprehension.

Briefly, listening comprehension involves both **attentive listening** (attending to the message) and **auditory comprehension** (constructing meaning from an oral message). Auditory comprehension includes literal understanding of the message and also critical evaluation of what is heard. Both auditory comprehension and attentive listening are prerequisites to academic success because as much as 70 percent of a student's time in school requires following oral directions and listening to teachers or guest speakers (Goodlad, 2004). Because of their prerequisite connection to abilities associated with academic learning, such as note taking, techniques for assessment and instruction of attentive listening and auditory comprehension are presented in Chapter 14.

In summary, instruction in reading comprehension involves helping learners with such processes as predicting, visualizing, inferring, self-questioning, monitoring, summarizing, and synthesizing.

Assessing the Ability to Organize Text

Reading comprehension requires that readers make connections between their own prior knowledge and the organization of the text, also referred to as text-to-self connections (Harvey & Goudvis, 2000; Tovani, 2000). **Text organization** refers to the relationships between words, sentences, paragraphs, and longer units. As such, it is key to reading comprehension. In constructing relations between words, the reader must be able to construct meaning at (a) a sentence level, (b) a paragraph level, and (c) a level involving longer passages or series of paragraphs. For example, using a single sentence, can the student tell who or what the sentence is about (subject), what the action is (verb or predicate), and where or when the action is taking place? Does the student understand pronoun referents? Does the student appreciate how punctuation can affect meaning? Can the student recognize that different sentences can have the same meaning?

These same questions can be asked about paragraphs and are best asked directly during reading. For example, assume the following paragraph is being read:

> Andrew was being very selfish. He did not want to share his toys. Because of this, he played alone.

The teacher can ask:

- Who is the first sentence/paragraph about? (Response: Andrew)
- What is Andrew doing in this sentence (or in this paragraph)? (Response: being selfish, playing alone)
- Who is the "he" in the second sentence? (Response: Andrew)
- Why did Andrew play alone? (Response: he wouldn't share his toys)
- What does "this" refer to in the last sentence? (Response: he didn't share his toys)
- What is another way to say the last sentence (or "Is this another way . . ." depending on child's response). (Response: Andrew played alone because he would not share his toys.)

This last question is really asking for a main idea. Determining the main idea of a paragraph is analogous to determining a category title for a set of words. Pearson and Johnson (1978) discussed several types of main idea organizations that are useful for both assessing and teaching. Knowledge of each of these organizations can be observed by asking the student to locate the sentence that best expresses the main idea of the paragraph. The material used should correspond to the student's instructional level.

1. *Explicit main idea is stated at the beginning of a paragraph.* Polar bears are well adapted to life in the Arctic. Their color makes them hard to see against a snowy background. A jacket of fat keeps them warm and helps them float in the water. Hair on the soles of their paws gives them good footing on ice.

2. *Explicit main idea is stated at the end of the paragraph.* The color of polar bears makes them hard to see against a snowy background. A jacket of fat keeps them warm and helps them float in the water. Hair on the soles of their paws gives them good footing on ice. Polar bears are well adapted to life in the Arctic.

3. *Main idea is implicit—that is, not stated.* The color of polar bears makes them hard to see against a snowy background. A jacket of fat keeps them warm and helps them float in the water. Hair on the soles of their paws gives them good footing on ice.

Recognizing explicit main ideas is easier than determining implicit main ideas. Both tasks are simplified by providing multiple-choice responses. Example choices should include the four types of distractors shown in the following example:

Polar bears are fat, hairy, and white. (*too specific*)

Polar bears are good swimmers. (*not mentioned*)

Life in the Arctic. (*too general*)

Polar bears are well adapted to life in the Arctic. (*right level of generality*)

For assessing text longer than a sentence or a single paragraph, the student can be asked about cause-and-effect relationships, enumeration, and sequence, as well as compare-and-contrast, question-and-answer, and generalization organizational frameworks. This does not mean the reader is required to label the function or purpose of a series of paragraphs but should be able to recognize the characteristics or key words for each type. One effective way of assessing comprehension of these organizational frameworks is with paragraph frames (see also Chapter 13). A paragraph frame uses common key words to signal the relationships among paragraphs. For instance, cause-and-effect relationships are signaled by key words such as *because, since, for, hence, so, therefore, if . . . then,* and *as a result.* Look for key signal words (in italics) in the following series of paragraphs:

Expository example

In the early years of our country the Mississippi River was important for both trading and travel. First it was used by the Indians, then by the Spanish explorers. Finally French fur traders used the river.

Later, the river helped many settlements get started. But *because* the railroads came, river traffic almost disappeared. Then came World War I.

As a result the United States was shipping so many goods to help fight the war, river traffic once again became important. The railroads could not carry all the goods. Today the river remains busy.

Go to MyEducationLab and select the topic *Content Area Literacy.* Then, go to the Activities and Applications section, watch the video entitled "Literature and the Reading Process," and observe how a middle school teacher uses both fiction and nonfiction text to address main ideas. Next respond to the accompanying questions.

Ask: What caused Mississippi River traffic to almost disappear? Why did river traffic once again become important?

Narrative example

> *If* she [Mary] had been friends with Colin she would have run to show him her presents at once, and they would have looked at the pictures and read some of the gardening books and perhaps tried playing games, and he would have enjoyed himself so much he would never once have thought he was going to die or have put his hand on his spine to see if there was a lump coming. He had a way of doing that which she could not bear. It gave her an uncomfortable frightened feeling *because* he always looked so frightened himself. He said that if he felt even quite a little lump some day he should know his hunch had begun to grow. (from *The Secret Garden*, Burnett, 1962, p. 150)

Ask: Were Mary and Colin friends? What did Colin do that made Mary feel frightened?

A paragraph frame for assessment of cause-and-effect relationships would ask readers to supply the missing information in their own words. For example,

> In the early years of our country the Mississippi River was important for both trading and travel. First it was used by the Indians, then by the Spanish explorers. Finally French fur traders used the river.
>
> But because _____.
>
> As a result, _____.
>
> Today, _____.

Common key words for other paragraph relationships are:

Enumeration: one, two, three, another, more, also, most important, to begin with
Sequence: first, second, third, last, before, after, while, then, later, finally
Compare-and-contrast: but, however, although, yet, even though, on the other hand
Question-and-answer: why, how, when, where, what
Generalization: for example, for instance, characteristics are, in fact

Instruction for General Comprehension

No single, easy way has been found to improve comprehension skills. Because of the complex interrelationship between the many factors operating during comprehension, better understanding cannot be assured simply by having a student experience a certain activity. However, if the teacher is aware of the factors within the reader, the text, and the learning environment that affect comprehension and tries to account for these factors in instruction, the chances for improvement appear greater.

The instructional techniques that follow are organized according to the three major text organization categories: sentence level, paragraph level, and longer units. Underlying all comprehension instruction is the assumption that the teacher is aware of and uses good questioning techniques. Facilitating questions must be asked at the right times to help both the teacher and the student further understand the comprehension process. A good questioning technique models appropriate strategies and teaches students to ask themselves questions while reading; this ensures active participation and helps students realize that the material being read should and must make sense to them (Dantonio & Beisenherz, 2001).

Instructional Techniques Using Sentences. The main purpose of instruction at the sentence level is to teach students how to note the important details of a sentence, how to use word order and punctuation to indicate the meaning of the sentence, and to realize that the same thing can be said more than one way. According to Kamm (1979), focusing on the details of a sentence is an analysis task that should begin with simple sentences such as *The dog ran*. (Language experience and students' creative stories provide an excellent source for such sentences.) This sentence is read aloud, and the student is asked to identify the action. If the response is "running" or "ran," the sentence is shown to the student and the specific word representing the action underlined. The next question asks who or what ran, and if the student responds "the dog," the word *dog* is underlined twice. The student then sees "The <u>dog</u> <u>ran</u>."

Through sentence expansion (see also add a word/stretch the sentence in Chapter 8), the student is shown that the action (verb, predicate) and agent (subject) do not change even if words are added. For example, the sentence may be expanded to *The brown dog ran down the street*. The following sequence then applies:

- What is the action? (*ran*) Underline once.
- Who or what ran? (*dog*) Underline twice.
- What color is the dog? (*brown*)
- Where did the dog run? (*down the street*)
- How else could you describe the dog? (*black, spotted, lost, frightened*)
- Where else could the dog have run? (*away, into the house, across the street*)

A follow-up activity for this type of instruction is to transform sentences into telegrams, teaching the reader that recognition of just the important words still gives the meaning of the sentence.

Sentence expansion also allows instruction in word order. Using just the form *The brown dog ran down the street,* the student is asked, "Why might the dog run down the street?" In most responses a prepositional phrase will be added. All forms of open-ended sentences or sentence fragments aid teaching word order. For example:

The brown dog _____.

The brown dog ran _____.

Down the street _____.

The writing technique of sentence combining and collecting (Speaker & Speaker, 1991) can help students gain knowledge of more complicated syntactic structures—an ability that transfers to reading. For example, the sentences *The dog ran down the street* and *The dog is brown* can be combined as *The brown dog ran down the street*. (See Chapter 8 for additional ideas.) Hughes (1975) observed that training in sentence combining was most effective for lower- and middle-ability students. Similarly, Neville and Searls (1991) reported that sentence combining has more impact on reading comprehension for elementary students.

Another aspect of sentence comprehension is synthesis (Kamm, 1979). At this stage the learner is involved in paraphrasing sentences (see the section on "Rephrasing" in

Chapter 8). This paraphrasing takes two forms: rearranging the words in the sentence or substituting appropriate synonyms.

One way to begin teaching paraphrasing is to give students a set of four to seven sight words taken from students' personal word banks, then show them how to form as many different sentences as possible using each word only once. For example, *Bob-what-Mary-does-says* can become:

1. Bob does what Mary says.
2. Mary does what Bob says.
3. What Mary says Bob does.
4. Mary says what Bob does.
5. Bob says what Mary does.
6. What Bob says Mary does.

Once the sentences are developed, the teacher instructs the student to find those that mean the same thing and asks questions as follows. "What action goes with *Bob* in sentence 1?" Response: *does*. "What action goes with *Mary* in sentence 1?" Response: *says*. "Find any other sentences where *Bob does* and *Mary says* are together." Response: sentences 3 and 4. The conclusion to be drawn is that sentences 1, 3, and 4 mean the same thing even though the word order is different. "What about sentences 2, 5, and 6?" Response: *They have the same meaning because in all three Mary does and Bob says.*

After this kind of explicit instruction, students practice with a new set of sentences or sentence pairs. This practice can consist of role playing or dramatizing the action in the sentences to help those whose strengths are bodily-kinesthetic.

Instruction in comprehension should also provide the student a strategy for constructing meaning. Therefore, the teacher must ask questions that the students should ask of themselves when the time comes to work independently: Who or what is this sentence about? What is happening in this sentence? When? Is there missing information? What seems to be missing? Discuss incorrect responses as well as correct responses so that the students understand which features are important.

Comprehension instruction that focuses on making meaning from single sentences or pairs of sentences is also discussed by Durkin (1978/1979). She suggested providing a sentence and asking students to name everything it tells. Her example, *The little kindergarten boy was crying,* elicits the responses that tell about the boy. All the facts of the sentence are written on the board. If a student speculates on why the boy was crying, this response leads into a list of what the sentence does not tell. This latter step is an application of "negative type questions" (Willford, 1968). Such questions represent an attempt to move away from the "right answer syndrome" (Caskey, 1970) to more speculation and predicting. As an example, Willford (1968) related:

> Watch a five or six year old. You put a picture up and say, "Okay, what can you do with a horse?" Out of a group of 10, five of them have had an experience. The others don't know what you can do with a horse. We turn it completely around and say, "What can't you do with a horse?" You ought to see the different responses we get. Every child can tell you what you can't do with a horse. "What can't you do?" "Well you can't take a horse to bed with you." Someone else might say, "You can too if you live in a barn." This kid never thought about this. So now we find, what can you do with a horse? You can take a horse to bed with you if you live in a barn. You can flip the thing over by using a negative question as a stimulus to get a variety of answers. Kids love to do this. You may get more conversation from a single picture than any single thing you can do. (p. 103)

Sentence-level instruction should move from a literal level of understanding to an implied or inferred level. Heilman and Holmes (1978), in *Smuggling Language into the Teaching of Reading,* give two excellent activities for this level of instruction. To help students understand the reasoning involved, the directions and questions here have been modified.

1. *Choose the best meaning for the following sentence:* The moving van stopped in front of the empty house.

   a. The truck was probably empty.
   b. The truck was there to pick up furniture.
   c. The truck contained furniture for the people moving into the house. (p. 68)

Questions: Why did you make the choice you made?

What clues were in the sentence?

2. *Fill in the blank.* Only one word makes sense. Put two lines under any words that helped you decide what the one word had to be.

   a. The score was <u>tied</u> <u>seven</u> to <u>(seven)</u>.
   b. The <u>right</u>-hand <u>glove</u> will <u>not fit</u> on your <u>(left)</u> hand.
   c. The <u>umpire</u> said, "<u>(strike)</u> <u>three</u>, you're <u>out</u>!"

(Note how important background knowledge is at the implied or inferred level.)

At all levels of comprehension instruction, students should be directed to form mental pictures of what they are reading and to attend to text illustrations if they are present (Gambrell & Jawitz, 1993). Although an imagery strategy may not benefit all readers having comprehension difficulty, imagery instruction may help readers whose reading vocabulary is adequate but whose comprehension is poor (Gambrell & Bales, 1986; Wilhelm, 1997).

Imagery instruction begins by having students "make a picture in their heads" for specific things, such as a favorite animal or a place they have visited. These pictures are then shared so that each student can respond and listen to others' descriptions. The students are now ready to form mental pictures about the reading material. For example, if the reading contained the phrase, *As I was walking alone on that cold winter afternoon,* appropriate questions would be: "Where are you walking?" "What does the sky look like?" "How do you feel?" "How are you dressed?" Selections used for imagery instruction should not have overly elaborate descriptions. Material already rich in imagery leaves nothing for the student to visualize. Some students may wish to draw their images either as a pre-reading activity or as a follow-up activity (Whitin, 1996).

Instructional Techniques Using Paragraphs. Instruction in comprehension must include helping the reader see the relationships between ideas in a paragraph. Marvin Cohn (1969) developed **structured comprehension**, a technique that moves quite well from the sentence level to the paragraph level. Cohn suggested that material selected for this technique be somewhat difficult for students to read in their usual fashion. Passages from content-area materials are recommended. Only a selection of two or three sentences is needed for this technique because instruction proceeds sentence by sentence and can become tedious if the selection is overly long.

Once the sentences are selected, some background is given to the students to put the sentences into their appropriate context. The next step is for the students (or the teacher) to read just the first sentence aloud. Any decoding errors are simply corrected.

MI Connection:
logical-mathematical

MI Connection:
spatial

The students are then directed to ask themselves, "Do I know what this sentence means?" They may ask the teacher as many questions as necessary to understand the sentence. Once the students' questions have been answered, the teacher asks several questions about each sentence. These questions must be prepared in advance because Cohn recommended that certain questions always be asked if the opportunity presents itself (see the next paragraph). Students may look back to the text for answers, but the answers must be written. The questions asked should require only two or three words to answer; questions requiring longer answers are put in a multiple-choice format.

Questions always to be asked seek the following information:

1. Clarification of the referent for a pronoun

2. Clarification of meaning when a word has multiple or unusual meanings

3. The meaning of figurative expressions

4. Definition of causal or other relationships left implicit

Answers for each question are discussed. For incorrect answers, the teacher demonstrates why they are incorrect and explains the reasoning behind the correct answer. Correct answers, when put back into the text, make sense; incorrect answers do not. This cross-checking procedure also helps students *demand* that material read be meaningful.

Initially Cohn recommended that literal meanings be stressed more than relationships or implied information. Beginning with emphasis on the literal meaning provides more success for students and also allows them the opportunity to develop appropriate questioning techniques. The passive reader may become more actively involved through this process. Possible teacher questions can be seen in the "Andrew" paragraph discussed earlier in this chapter. For an example of a structured comprehension lesson used with expository material, see Figure 13.6.

A useful strategy for helping the reader identify who or what a paragraph is about uses the concepts of repeated and replaced words. **Repeated words** are those found in almost every sentence of the paragraph. Given the following paragraph, the student should be able to recognize the repeated word and tell what (or who) the paragraph is about:

> The city of Bern, Switzerland, starts its holiday season each year with *onions*. The fourth Monday in November is *Onion* Market Day. On this day farmers display *onions* in the public square. Red, yellow, and white *onions* are piled in colorful mounds. Wreaths and garlands of *onions* are on view. Visitors can sample free *onion* cake and hot *onion* soup.

Replaced words are substitutes for words that would normally be repeated. The pronoun is the most common substitute. Given the following paragraph, the student should be able to mentally substitute each replaced word with its referent and thus recognize who (or what) the paragraph is about:

> Two *scientists* "camped" for a week at the bottom of the sea. *Their* underwater home was a cabin shaped like a barrel. The *men* did not spend all *their* time in *their* underwater bubble. *They* went out to explore the sea bottom.

In addition to recognizing who or what a paragraph is about, the reader also must be able to identify significant details. Newspaper articles are a ready source of material that lends itself to the kind of questioning involved in teaching students to look for details. The following questions may be asked regarding the article in Figure 11.2.

Figure 11.2   Example of Newspaper Article That Helps Students Look for Details

The Times-Picayune   **Sunday, September 23**

Nursing Home Hit in Arson?

By JOHN LUNDQUIST

MINNEAPOLIS (AP)—Police said they believe the nursing home fire which claimed the life of one elderly resident and injured three others Saturday was the work of an arsonist.

A 38-year-old female resident of the Bryn Mawr Nursing Home, who was not identified, was taken into custody about 3½ hours after the blaze broke out, police said.

Charges were not filed immediately, police said.

Teams of firemen who responded to the three-alarm blaze helped many of the elderly at the home to safety from second floor windows. The residents were carried down ladders in rescue baskets or down stairways in their wheelchairs.

One fireman, Jeff Bartholomew, about 30, suffered smoke inhalation when he took off his mask and put it over the face of a woman he helped out of the two-story building, said Capt. Cecil Klingbile, one of the station fire chiefs on the scene.

"He took a lot of smoke when he did that," said Klingbile, who aided in the rescue.

Bartholomew was treated and released.

The Hennepin County medical examiner identified the dead woman as Fanny Anttila, 85.

Two elderly women in serious condition suffering from smoke inhalation were identified as Rose Seiger, 80, and Esther Cotter, 79.

A 75-year-old man, whose identification was being withheld until relatives had been notified, was in critical condition with second-degree burns.

Twenty-five other people were taken to hospitals but they were not admitted. David Lesperance, associate administrator, said they were "disposition cases," meaning the hospital was arranging accommodations for them.

One of the displaced residents was Richard Fobes, 71, who sat in a waiting room with his two sons.

"I was sitting in the recreation room on the first floor when the fire broke out," he said. "They (nursing home workers) told us to get in our rooms, and pretty soon they came and got us outside."

Fire Capt. Ronald Knoke said 44 firefighters from nine engine and four hook-and-ladder companies answered the alarm.

He said the fire was discovered at 9:54 a.m. (CDT) in the closet of a resident room, then spread down the hall to other parts of the second floor. Firefighters had the blaze under control at 10:28 a.m.

Knoke said most of the danger was from smoke, because of the age of the residents.

Source: From *New Orleans Times-Picayune.* Used with permission of AP Newsfeatures, New York.

1. Who was involved in this event? (*residents of the nursing home, police officers, firefighters*)

2. What took place? (*a fire*)

3. Where did it take place? (*Bryn Mawr Nursing Home in Minneapolis, Minnesota*)

4. When did it take place? (*Saturday, September 22*)

5. How or why did it take place? (*Police believe the fire was caused by arson.*)

Menus, recipes, and directions are additional sources of written materials rich in details for one main idea.

Main-idea instruction easily follows from here. Instruction in main ideas begins by using material with a topic sentence that explicitly states the main idea. Using the paragraph about polar bears discussed earlier, the student is first directed to find the key words or significant details, words that occur more than once, and a sentence that summarizes these details. The following questions might be asked:

> What do most of the key words seem to point out?
> What key words occur more than once?
> What do these words relate to?
> Is there a sentence that summarizes these ideas?

> <u>Polar</u> <u>bears</u> are well adapted to life in the <u>Arctic</u>. Their <u>color</u> makes them hard to see against a <u>snowy</u> background. A jacket of <u>fat</u> <u>keeps</u> them <u>warm</u> and <u>helps</u> them <u>float</u> in the water. <u>Hair</u> on the soles of their paws gives them <u>good</u> <u>footing</u> on <u>ice</u>.

The first step is to underline key words, as shown in the paragraph. These key words aid in determining the significant details. In searching for recurring words, students are first led to discover the pronoun referents. Ask: "Who or what is the first sentence about?" Response: *polar bears*. Ask: "Who or what does the word *their* refer to in the second sentence?" Response: *polar bears*. "In the same sentence you see the word *them*. What does *them* refer to?" Response: *polar bears*. In actuality, the term *polar bears* occurs quite frequently in this paragraph, which is a clue to the main topic of the paragraph. Significant details about polar bears should then be discussed by asking, "What does this paragraph tell us about polar bears?" A diagram may be used, such as that shown in Figure 11.3, and compared to students' maps used for prewriting to demonstrate how reading and writing are connected. Color-coding for main ideas and details might also be used (Auman, 2002).

MI Connection: spatial

Going back to the paragraph, ask, "Can you choose one sentence that includes all of the supporting details or summarizes those details?" Elicit the response that the first sentence does this. Explain why this sentence summarizes the others if students have difficulty (a) recognizing that the first sentence describes the main idea of the paragraph or (b) determining why polar bears are well adapted to life in the Arctic.

The usefulness of activities such as the structured comprehension lesson for teaching paragraph understanding should now be apparent. Instruction in this area helps the student know what to look for in a paragraph to determine its meaning. After instruction, the following activities should be easier for students:

Figure 11.3   Diagram for Denoting Main Ideas and Supporting Details in the Polar Bear Paragraph

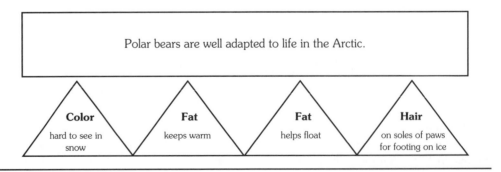

1. *In this activity, the student must find the sentence that does not belong in this paragraph:*

   Tommy was baking a cake for Mother's birthday. He sifted flour, added two eggs, and put it in the oven to bake. It seemed to take forever to be done. At last the potatoes were ready. The frosting was chocolate with marshmallows. (Heilman & Holmes, 1978, p. 65)

   Possible questions to ask regarding this paragraph are:
   - What is this paragraph about?
   - Which sentence doesn't seem to belong? Why?

2. *In this activity, the student attempts to determine implied information.*

   Tomorrow is the big day. John has been practicing ever since school started. Now is his chance to show all his friends his special tricks. This is the time of year when spooky things are really popular. He doesn't even need to wear a costume to scare people. After the parade the older kids get to put on a show for the little ones. Gee! It will be great fun to see their faces turn white. It's a good thing it will be on the last day of the school week. They will have the weekend to recover from their fright. (Heilman & Holmes, 1978, p. 70)

   Possible questions to ask regarding this paragraph are:
   - What day of the week will something important take place?

     a. Saturday   b. Sunday   c. Friday

   To help students answer this question, the teacher directs their attention to the appropriate sentences. "What sentences in the paragraph mention the word *day?*" Response: *first and eighth sentences.* "Does the first sentence help us to know what day it is?" Response: *no, only tomorrow.* "What about the eighth sentence?" Response: *yes, the last day of the school week is Friday.*

   - What holiday do you think it is?

     a. Halloween   b. Fourth of July   c. Easter

   Once again the relevant sentences are discussed. First, the teacher elicits key words associated with Halloween, Fourth of July, and Easter. Next, the students look for key words in the paragraph. Once the words *spooky, costume, trick, scare,* and *fright,* elicited for Halloween, are also found in the paragraph, the holiday becomes apparent.

   - How long has John been practicing?

     a. about two weeks   b. about two months   c. about two hours

   Ask: "What sentence mentions practicing?" Response: *the second sentence.* "When does school start?" Response: *late August or early September.* "When is Halloween?" Response: *late October.* "How much time is between late August or early September and late October?" Response: *about two months.*

As noted before, prior knowledge and experience are important for success in implied-information activities. Most of the guiding questions require the readers to think about something they already know or have experienced. Additional activities and discussion of implicit main ideas can be found in Pearson and Johnson's (1978) *Teaching Reading Comprehension,* Chapter 5.

The questions in the foregoing examples represent the direction that instruction in paragraph comprehension should take. Students must be shown explicitly how to deal with paragraph information. Teachers instruct best by modeling or thinking out loud with their students to reveal the strategies they themselves use. Once shown the strategy, students can practice and finally apply this type of thinking to material read independently. They can write their own paragraphs and plan a lesson for transmitting the main idea to other students. This also gives students the opportunity to practice the question-asking strategies involved.

Sometimes the problem of not understanding material can be attributed to inappropriate phrasing. Even material used in a structured comprehension lesson can be rewritten into phrase units to aid the reader. This technique, referred to as *chunking* (Walker, 2000), "facilitates comprehension and fluency by using thought units rather than word-by-word reading" (p. 200). An example from Heilman and Holmes (1978, p. 127) follows.

> This material
> is written
> in short phrases
> so that you
> can practice
> seeing words
> in thought units.
> This helps you
> read faster.
> However,
> remember also
> that reading
> in phrases
> or thought units
> helps the reader
> get the meaning.

Some commercial materials intended for use with readers with special language needs or with learning disabilities use chunking or phrasing in their printed books. One example page of text from *Reading Milestones* (Quigley et al., 1998) is printed as:

The bus	stopped	near the woods.
The boys	looked	at the trees.
The girls	looked	at the trees, too.

Echo reading (discussed in Chapter 9) can also be used to model appropriate phrasing.

Instructional Techniques Using Longer Units. When teaching reading comprehension for units of discourse longer than a single paragraph, it is useful to think of a comprehension framework for strategic reading. One common framework consists of three phases: prereading, active reading, and postreading. During the prereading phase, students access their prior knowledge or build background knowledge for the upcoming reading and focus on the intent of the strategy being taught or used by the teacher. In other words, students should be informed of the purpose of the strategy, what it is, and why it is being used. During the active reading phase, students set purposes for reading, monitor their reading, and interact with the text in some way. During the postreading phase, the student responds to the reading either independently or within a group. This might include a retelling activity, a written response, a

---

Figure 11.4   Teaching Active Comprehension

The Hare and the Fox

A small, brown hare was sitting near a creek sunning himself, when he saw a fox. The fox was getting a drink in the small stream.

The hare ran from his nest, but the fox saw him hopping in the grass. Quick as a wink, the fox was running to catch the hare.

The brown hare ran into a hole in an old log. The hole was too small for a fox.

As the hare ran from the hole, he saw the fox digging to get into it.

When the fox got inside the old log, he did not find a hare. All he saw was a hole as long as the log.

Source: "The Hare and the Fox." From *Basic Reading,* Book C. © J. B. Lippincott Company, 1975, p. 37. Used by permission.

---

drawing, or some other extension activity such as a presentation or a self-assessment. Guided reading is one approach that closely follows this framework (Fountas & Pinnell, 2001). The strategies that follow are all applicable to this three-phase comprehension framework.

Prereading. The ultimate goal of all reading instruction is to develop independent readers. Comprehension instruction, then, must bring the reader to the point of being able to independently and actively interact with the text. What occurs *prior* to reading the text can be the most important step toward being an active reader. The teacher helps this process by encouraging students to *ask themselves* questions about what they are about to read and also to continue to ask themselves questions while they read. Teacher-posed questions, such as those in the structured comprehension lesson previously discussed, provide models of questioning behavior for students. However, a gradual transfer from teacher-posed to student-posed questions is desirable to develop independent readers (Gillespie, 1990/1991). This transfer, described by Singer (1978) in his **phase-out/phase-in strategy,** promotes active comprehension.

The most important procedure in promoting active comprehension is to *ask a question that requires another question as the response.* Using "The Hare and the Fox" (Figure 11.4), a lesson may proceed as follows, with the teacher asking questions to elicit initial student questions. (Even though the example is for narrative text, this strategy is equally effective with expository text.)

Teacher: "Look at the title. What questions could you ask about this story after reading just the title?"

Possible student questions:

"What will the hare and the fox be doing?"

"What is a hare?"

Go to MyEducationLab, first select the topic *Comprehension,* and go to the Activities and Applications section. Watch the videos "Before and During Reading Strategies," "During Reading," and "After Reading" to observe the three phases being implemented by a primary grade teacher using an expository book. Then select the topic *Emergent Literacy,* and go to the Activities and Applications section. Watch the video "Guided Reading" for a look at how this approach uses the three-phase framework. Next respond to the accompanying questions.

"What will happen to the hare?"

"What will happen to the fox?"

"Will the fox chase the hare?"

"Will the fox catch and eat the hare?"

"Will the hare get away?"

The teacher then asks questions paragraph by paragraph.

Teacher, paragraph 1: "What else would you like to know about the hare? What else about the fox?"

Possible student questions:

"Is it a baby hare?"

"Is the hare a fast runner?"

"Is the fox a fast runner?"

"Is the fox hungry?"

Teacher, paragraph 2: "What would you like to know more about when the fox starts running to catch the hare?"

Possible student questions:

"Will the fox catch the hare?"

"Will the hare get away?"

Teacher, paragraph 3: "Is there anything you'd like to know when the hare runs into the log?"

Possible student questions:

"Will the hare be safe?"

"Will the fox get into the log?"

"Will the fox wait for the hare to come out of the log?"

Teacher, paragraph 4: "What would you like to ask when the hare runs from the log?"

Possible student questions:

"Why did the hare run from the log?"

"Is the fox waiting outside to catch the hare?"

"Where will the hare run to next?"

"Will the fox be able to catch the hare?"

Teacher, paragraph 5: "After you read the last paragraph, what questions about the hare and the fox do you still have?"

Possible student questions:

"Did the fox run out of the log to chase the hare some more?"

"Where did the hare go?"

"Did the hare get away from the fox?"

"What happened to the fox and the hare next?"

SPOTLIGHT ON ENGLISH LEARNERS

The Experience-Text-Relationship Method

Because reading comprehension requires that readers integrate information in the text with their previous experience, teachers must expand students' background knowledge, especially if there are cultural variations in background knowledge affecting comprehension.

The *experience-text-relationship method* (Au, 1979) allows the teacher to motivate students to talk about their experiences relevant to the central focus of a story or content chapter (the *experience* step); read natural segments of text (the *text* step); and relate the content of a story with the prior experiences discussed in the story (the *relationship* step). The sample lesson transcript from Au (1979) that follows illustrates the teacher–student interaction in developing reading of culturally diverse students. Techniques like this one allow the teacher and students to bridge the knowledge gap between learners' experiences and the text. Likewise, the experience-text-relationship method allows students to become actively involved with the text and permits culturally compatible styles of interaction between teacher and students. Au and Kawakami (1985) found that a focus on comprehension, rather than on word identification, and a culturally compatible style of interaction greatly improve the quality of reading by sociolinguistically diverse students. Teachers need to recognize that students from various cultures possess culturally unique communication routines that often contrast with the verbal discourse routines of the school (Au, 1993; Barnitz, 1994; Cazden, John, & Hymes, 1972; Heath, 1983; Hiebert, 1991; Tharp & Gallimore, 1988).

Experience Step

Teacher:	. . . Okay, let's think if we could do anything else with a frog. What would you do, Shirley?
Ann:	I wouldn't touch the legs. Yuck.
Shirley:	I would put it in a bucket.
Teacher:	You would put it in a bucket. Okay, that's something different. What would you do with it?
Shirley:	*(Inaudible)*
Ann:	Yeah, you eat the legs?
Teacher:	Okay, Shirley might even eat it. Good, you can eat frog, can't you?

Text Step

Teacher:	. . . Shirley, why did you say Freddy laughed? Okay, read the part that you said— when Freddy laughed.
Shirley:	*(Reading)* "I would take it fishing. Freddy laughed."
Teacher:	Okay, who says, "I would take it fishing"?
Nathan:	Mr. Mays.
Teacher:	Mr. Mays. And why did Freddy laugh?
Ann:	Because maybe he didn't—maybe he didn't know that he was going to use the frog.
Teacher:	No, he laughed for another reason. Ellie? Who can read that?
Ellie:	Because—'cause Mr. Mays didn't know what to do with the frog. That's all he could think was—he didn't know that he could use frogs was—was a bait. That's why Freddy laughed.
Teacher:	Okay, wait a minute. That's not the reason Freddy laughed.
Nathan:	Frogs can't fish.
Teacher:	Right. Okay, Mr. Mays says, "I don't have a frog, but if I did, I'd take it fishing," and Freddy thinks, hah, going fishing with the frog sitting down with the fishing pole?

Relationship Step

Teacher:	. . . Did you know before this that fish like to eat frogs?
Group:	Nooo.
Teacher:	I didn't—I never heard of using frogs for bait. Do you think they really do?

continued

Spotlight on English Learners (*continued*)

Nathan:	Yeah.
Teacher:	You think so.
Ann:	My daddy—my daddy—use bread.
Teacher:	Yeah, some people use bread. What else do you use for bait?
Shirley:	Fish.
Teacher:	Sometimes you use smaller fishes.

From "Using the Experience-Text-Relationship Method with Minority Children," by Kathryn Hu-Pei Au, *The Reading Teacher,* March 1979. Reprinted with permission of Kathryn Hu-Pei Au and the International Reading Association.

This lesson sequence supplies example questions for each paragraph to provide ample explicit practice for the learner. This procedure is not necessary for every lesson, however. The teacher may receive such a variety of questions at the initial stage that the students will be motivated enough to read the rest of the story or expository text material. When students are able to find answers to their own questions, they become active comprehenders. By seeking answers to their own questions, the students become involved in the reading; situations or problems are identified and further understandings are sought while reading. Comprehension is the result.

Other recommended prereading instructional techniques are Hennings's (1991) essential reading, in which students survey text to predict the main idea of the selection before reading, similar to a picture walk (see Chapter 9) where illustrations are surveyed and students tell what they think is happening or what will happen; *I Wonder . . .?* (Richards & Gipe, 1996), in which students wonder aloud based on the cover and title of the text what they might find out or what might happen; and the K and W steps of the K–W–L strategy (Ogle, 1986), in which students first tell all they know already about a topic and then propose questions for what they would like to find out.

Active Reading. A major goal of comprehension instructional techniques is to help students become more actively involved with text. Instruction focuses on encouraging flexibility, risk taking, and deep thinking. Questions mold the student's thinking, rather than test for right and wrong answers. As Schwartz and Sheff (1975) stated, "Instruction should provide a type of questioning that consciously directs the reader to become involved in understanding what he reads" (pp. 151–152).

Stauffer's (1975, 1981) **directed reading-thinking activity (DRTA)**, a teaching technique that focuses on enhancing the reader's comprehension through active involvement with the text, actually incorporates all three aspects of the comprehension framework. The goal of the DRTA strategy is to enhance reading (or listening) comprehension through a cycle of prediction making on the part of the reader. This prediction cycle ensures active reading as the reader (or listener) is checking to see whether predictions made prior to and during reading are confirmed. The sample lesson (see Figure 11.5) focuses on helping students learn to use both their prior knowledge and the context of the material to make predictions throughout the text and ultimately to understand the value of the common earthworm (a content goal). This strategy is equally effective with both narrative and expository material and with very young students or nonreaders if modified to a directed listening-thinking activity (DLTA). The only difference between

Figure 11.5 Sample Lesson Using Directed Reading-Thinking Activity (DRTA)

A DRTA lesson usually contains the following components, which will be highlighted in the example.

I. Building Background for the Reading Selection
II. The DRTA Cycle
    a. Students set purposes, make predictions
    b. Silent reading (or listening if a DLTA)
    c. Students verify predictions, satisfy purposes
III. Comprehension Check
IV. Rereading Parts of the Selection for Specific Purposes
V. Enrichment or Follow-Up Activities (or Evaluation)

DRTA Lesson
Teacher Goals:
1. To help students discover how to use both prior knowledge and the context clues in text to anticipate the following text
2. To expose students to a more expository (informational) writing style

Student Objectives:
1. Each student will participate in the lesson by:
    a. offering answers to the opening riddle
    b. making predictions about what (who) the text will be about
    c. verifying their predictions by citing evidence in the text
    d. answering comprehension questions following the silent reading and verification of predictions
    e. writing their own "first person" riddle

Materials:
Text: *A Not So Ugly Friend* by Stan Applebaum and Victoria Cox. This text is from *The Satellite Books* published by Holt, Rinehart, and Winston and is a Level 10 book, meaning it is intended for use with second-semester second-grade readers. The text begins in a riddle format, each page providing clues for the reader about what is being described—in other words, who is the "not so ugly friend." For example, from the first page: "I can't see you. I have no eyes, but I can feel you walking. I have no nose, but I have a mouth and I can taste. Do you know what I am?" Midway through the book the answer to the riddle is revealed, and then the book becomes informational about the earthworm and how valuable earthworms are to us—why we should consider them friends.

Procedures:
To develop *background* for this lesson, introduce the idea of "first person" riddles, as the text is written in this format. It may be an unusual format for the students. These "practice" riddles should relate to people and things very familiar in the students' lives. In teaching new concepts it is much better to relate the unfamiliar to the familiar. For example, one practice riddle is: "I am something you drink. I come from a cow, and I'm white. Babies really like me a lot. Do you know what I am?" Write the riddles on individual index cards so that students can take turns reading them. After each riddle is solved, students must tell what the important clues were in the riddle that helped them solve it. At this point, students should be eager to solve yet one more riddle, the one in the text.

    The *DRTA cycle* begins by introducing the title of the selection. Tell students that this text is written like the riddles they just solved. The cover of the text may also be used if desired. Predictions will be made based on the key question, "What or who do you think is the not so ugly friend?" Write students' predictions on the chalkboard. Once all predictions are made, ask

continued

Figure 11.5 *continued*

each student to choose one they think will answer the question. Their purpose for reading is to verify whether their prediction is supported by the text. With this text, proceed one page at a time, reading silently. After each page, students will reevaluate their predictions and make changes, although they must be able to use the clues to justify their changes or new predictions. Once the answer is revealed in the text, discuss the clues as a group. At this point introduce a new key question: "What does the earthworm do for us?" Again, write their ideas on the board. Students again read the rest of the selection silently to verify their predictions. Discuss their predictions, which ones were supported, and what new information they discovered.

The questions for the *comprehension check* include vocabulary items that may be new or are important for understanding the text. Sample questions are:

1. Who is this book about? (earthworm) *textually explicit*
2. Who is telling the story? (earthworm) *textually implicit*
3. Can earthworms *really* talk? (no) *scriptally implicit*
4. What is soil? (dirt, earth) *scriptally implicit; possibly textually implicit*
5. What does it mean to make the soil richer? (better for plants, helps plants grow better, provides nutrients) *scriptally implicit*
6. Why does the earthworm come out of the ground when it rains? (because the water fills the earthworm's underground hole) *textually implicit*
7. Why doesn't the earthworm like to be out in the sun? (because the sun dries out its skin) *textually implicit*
8. Where do earthworms come from (or how are they born)? (eggs) *textually explicit*
9. What did you learn about earthworms that you did not know before? (answers will vary) *textually explicit, textually implicit*
10. Can we think of earthworms as our friends? (yes, no, give reasons) *scriptally implicit, textually implicit, textually explicit*

Following the questions, ask students to *reread for the specific purpose* of completing a semantic map of the selection to help them organize what they have read. The core question of the map is, "What does an earthworm do?" Allow the students to look back to the text since this is a rereading activity. Each idea can be read aloud if desired.

The *enrichment* activity for this lesson should be done individually. Have the students write three "first person" riddles that ask "Who Am I?" or "What Am I?" as their last line. These riddles can be posted later for other students to solve. (This activity could also serve as an evaluation activity.)

---

a DRTA and a DLTA is who does the actual reading of the material. When the student reads, it is a DRTA; when the teacher reads, it is a DLTA because the student will be listening while thinking.

Students who begin their reading with a set of questions about the material to be read, or a set of "I Wonders . . .," are poised to read more actively to satisfy their own purposes. Active reading ensures comprehension. The use of scaffolds can help guide students to focus on the important aspects of the material and to read actively. **Scaffolds** are support mechanisms that enable students to accomplish a more difficult task than they might be able to achieve without assistance. One example of a scaffold for reading comprehension is use of a study guide. Study guides are typically associated with content-area material, but they can be developed for narrative material as well. Three examples of study guides that serve as scaffolds for active reading are three-level study guides, concept guides, and structured question guides. Three-level study guides address comprehension at the literal, inferential, and critical/creative levels. Figure 11.6 shows examples for primary grades, upper grades, and algebra to demonstrate the versatility of the three-level study guide. Concept guides help students organize ideas, actions, events, characters, and

Figure 11.6	Examples of Three-Level Study Guides

Example 1. Little Red Riding Hood
Level 1 (Literal Level): What did the author say? Check two.

- Red Riding Hood met a wolf in the woods.
- Red Riding Hood visited her aunt.
- Red Riding Hood recognized the wolf immediately when she entered Grandma's house.
- The woodsman killed the wolf.

Level 2 (Inferential Level): What did the author mean? Check two.

- The wolf only wanted the goodies meant for Grandma.
- The wolf appeared to be a lot like Red Riding Hood's grandmother.
- Red Riding Hood was a gullible little girl.
- Red Riding Hood was a trusting little girl.

Level 3 (Critical/Creative Level): How can we use the meaning? Check two.

- Don't walk in the woods alone.
- Don't speak to strangers.
- Look more carefully at sick grandmothers.
- All's well that ends well.
- Don't send a little girl to do a nurse's job.

Example 2. "The Open Window," by Saki (H. H. Munro)
Level 1: What are the facts in the story? Check six.

- Vera is 12 years old.
- Framton Nuttel is a horse doctor.
- Mrs. Sappleton is Vera's aunt.
- Framton did not know any people in the town.
- One of the hunters wore a red coat.
- Ronnie was singing, "Bertie, Why Do You Bound?"
- The hunters always come in through the window after they hunt.
- Framton needs plenty of rest and relaxation.
- Vera spoke to Framton about the window.

Add any other facts that you wish.

Level 2: What did the story mean? Check six.

- Framton Nuttel was a very smart man.
- Framton was trying to be polite.
- Vera liked to make up stories.
- Mrs. Stappleton was crazy.
- Framton did not like talking to strangers.
- Mrs. Stappleton did not know why Framton was nervous.
- Framton hated hunting.
- Mrs. Stappleton was heartbroken over the death of the hunters.
- Vera was a good storyteller and actress.
- Framton was a victim of his own credulity.

Add any other things you can think of that the story meant but did not specifically say.

Figure 11.6 *continued*

Level 3: How can we use these meanings? Check one.

- A person sees what she or he wants to see.
- People who live in the country are strange.
- Never believe anything a girl says.

Add at least one more interpretation.

Example 3. Algebra I—Distance Problems

A ship must average 22 miles per hour to make its 10-hour run on schedule. During the first four hours bad weather caused it to reduce its speed to 16 miles per hour. What should its speed be for the rest of the trip to keep the ship to its schedule?

Level 1: Complete the following statements.

1. The scheduled length of time for the run is _____.
2. The ship's average speed for the run is to be _____.
3. The ship was forced to travel at a reduced speed for _____ hours.
4. During the bad weather, the ship averaged _____.

Level 2: Circle the correct answers.

1. The entire trip will cover
   a. 64 miles   b. 160 miles   c. 220 miles

2. During the first four hours, the ship traveled
   a. 88 miles   b. 64 miles   c. 22 miles

3. After the bad weather, the time remaining to complete the trip on schedule will be
   a. 10 hours   b. 6 hours   c. 4 hours

4. The distance still to be traveled after the bad weather is
   a. 60 miles   b. 156 miles   c. 160 miles

Level 3: Use the answers to the questions above to solve the problem here. Then answer the questions below.

What can you say if the ship's maximum speed is 25 miles per hour?

If the ship went 25 miles per hour for the first four hours, could you say anything about the answer to the problem before you begin to calculate an answer?

---

words in a reading assignment into categories that serve as a more efficient means for remembering the basic themes and relationships in what was read. Through the concept guide students are made aware of the details of the material from which they can then group these details and associated inferences into broader, more abstract, yet understandable, units of thought. To prepare a concept guide the teacher must first read the material to determine the major concepts students need to understand after reading. These concepts will be used in Part 2 of the guide (see Figure 11.7 for an example of a concept guide). Then the teacher rereads the material to choose statements or phrases that exemplify or illustrate the major concepts identified for emphasis. These are listed in Part 1. Students respond to the statements in Part 1 and then categorize responses into appropriate conceptual groups in Part 2. The students will be expected to justify their choices. A structured question guide focuses on a single question but one that represents a major concept students are expected to understand after the material is read. Figure 11.8 shows a structured question guide for the concept of "progress." The structured question guide should be completed prior to reading the material to ensure active reading.

Postreading. Students are often asked questions about what they have read as a way of checking their understanding. Thus, learners would benefit from direct instruction in how to answer questions. They need to know about the different sources of information

---

Figure 11.7   Example of a Concept Guide

Concept Guide for "Auto Wreck," by Karl Shapiro

Part 1. In the space provided below check the words or phrases used in the poem (do not check any that were not used). In a phrase or two, tell what the checked words describe or refer to in the poem (e.g., ambulance, policeman, observer, auto wreck, victims).

- quick soft silver bell _____
- pulsing out red light like an artery _____
- the zodiac _____
- wings in a heavy curve _____
- the mangled _____
- we are deranged _____
- making notes under the light _____
- the hand that held my wrist _____
- husks of locusts _____
- our throats were tight as tourniquets _____
- common sense _____
- our richest horror _____
- by hands _____
- flower _____
- wicked stones _____

Part 2. Below are several words that reflect some feelings or ideas suggested by the poem. Write the words or phrases from Part 1 under the word(s) to which they apply. You may use words or phrases more than once, and you may use other words from the poem as well. Compare and defend your choices with the other members of your group.

Innocence   Life   Sanity   Insanity   Death   Guilt

Figure 11.8	Structured Question Guide

Problem: How can a person tell if the society in which he or she lives is making progress?

To Find Out:

Part 1. In column A below you will find a list of relatively new products and developments in American society. In column B list the advantages of these products and developments. In column C list the disadvantages of these products and developments. Then give the product or development a rating from 1 to 5 (1 is Poor; 5 is Excellent) regarding its contribution to the progress of American society. Part 1 is to be done on your own. Part 2 will be done with a group.

A	B	C	D
New Products and Developments	**Advantages**	**Disadvantages**	**Rating (1 2 3 4 5)**
Internet			
Medical marijuana			
Electric cars			
Cloning			
Border fence between the U.S. and Mexico			
Assisted suicide			
iPhones			
Gay rights			
Global warming			
Kindle			

Part 2. Compare your answers with the members of your group.

1. What features of these items did several members of your group give as advantages?
2. What features of these items did several members of your group give as disadvantages?
3. If there were few or no repetitions for questions 1 and 2, why do you think this occurred?
4. How did your ratings in column D compare with those of other members of the group?
5. Why do you think there were differences in ratings?

What is your solution to the problem?

---

available for answering questions (Raphael & Pearson, 1985). As Raphael (1982) has pointed out, many students who struggle with comprehension do not realize that it is both acceptable and necessary to use their prior knowledge about the world to answer some types of comprehension questions. For this reason, instruction in **question–answer relationships (QARs)** is especially helpful.

Raphael's classification scheme for QARs is based on Pearson and Johnson's (1978) question taxonomy of **textually explicit** (the answer to the question is directly stated in one sentence in the text), **textually implicit** (the answer to the question is in the text but requires some integration of text material, as the answer might span several sentences or paragraphs), and **scriptally implicit** (the answer must come from the reader's prior knowledge).

In Raphael's original scheme, the first QAR was termed *right there* because the answer is directly stated in a single sentence. The second QAR was termed *think and search* because the answer requires information that spans several sentences or paragraphs. The third QAR was termed *on my own* because readers must rely totally on their own background knowledge for the answer.

After conducting several research studies, Raphael (1986) revised her classifications to include a fourth QAR, *author and me,* which recognizes that for some questions the answer comes from the reader's background knowledge, but only in connection with information provided by the author. The revised classification scheme now consists of two main categories, *in the book* and *in my head; right there* and *putting it together* (formerly *think and search*) falling under *in the book;* and *author and me* and *on my own* falling under *in my head.* Figure 11.9 provides an organizational chart for these QARs. Note that these question types are also analogous to literal, inferential, critical, and creative thinking levels.

Figure 11.9   Organizational Chart for Question–Answer Relationships (QARs)

Text: Steve's Lizard
Steve's pet is a lizard. It lives in a cage. Every day Steve feeds his pet bugs. The lizard's name is Lil.

In the Book (or Textually Based)	In My Head (or Scriptally Based)
Right There Explicit, directly stated in the text, usually within the same sentence.	**Author and Me** Implicit, not available in the text, but within one's schema. The response must fit with what the author tells in the text.
Who has a pet? (Steve)	*Does Steve keep his pet lizard in his room? Explain your answer.* (Steve probably keeps his pet in his room because he has a cage for it and he likes to watch it while he is in his room.)
Putting It Together (Think and Search) Implicit; the answer is in the text, but not in one place. Parts of the answer come from different places in the text.	**On My Own** Implicit; the answer is not in the text at all. In fact, you can often answer the question without even reading the text. The answer is totally in your head.
What does Lil eat? (Lil is the name of the pet lizard and Steve feeds his pet lizard bugs, so Lil eats bugs.)	*Do you think boys should have pets?* (Yes, I think boys should have pets so they can learn how to care for helpless creatures and learn responsibility.)

Arts Connection

A first-grade teacher read *Snow White and the Seven Dwarfs* (a Brothers Grimm fairy tale retold by Gag, 1938) to his students. Recognizing that 6- and 7-year-olds cannot sit still for long periods of time, the teacher stopped at appropriate places in the book and used visuals (an apple, a computer-generated illustration of Snow White, and small ceramic figures of the seven dwarfs) to help his students predict what might happen next in the story, an important element of the DLTA strategy being taught. As the story progressed, the teacher and his students created clay and tempera paint representations of Snow White. Further on in the story, they used large pieces of colored chalk to illustrate their ideas about how the story might end. As a culminating, after reading activity, the students created large papier-mâché "poison" apples. Then they wrote to Snow White, offering advice about being careful when eating strange foods and not to eat food offered by strangers.

An introductory lesson in QARs must first define all the question types. Using the nursery rhyme *Little Miss Muffet,* consider the following questions as examples of each type:

> Little Miss Muffet sat on a tuffet,
> Eating her curds and whey.
> Along came a spider that sat down beside her,
> And frightened Miss Muffet away.

1. What did Miss Muffet sit on?
   Response: A tuffet
   QAR: Right there (textually explicit, literal level)

2. Why did Miss Muffet get up from the tuffet?
   Response: A spider sat beside her and frightened her away
   QAR: Putting it together (textually implicit, inferential level)

3. What are curds and whey?
   Response 1: Something to eat
   QAR: Right there (textually explicit, literal level)

   Response 2: In making cheese, the milk is allowed to sour. The curds are the thick part that separates from the whey, the watery part. The curds are something like cottage cheese.
   QAR: On my own (scriptally implicit)

4. What do you think Miss Muffet did when she first saw the spider?
   Response: She probably threw her curds and whey up in the air, screamed, and jumped up as fast as she could to get away.
   QAR: Author and me (textually implicit, critical level)

Depending on the age and ability of the students, follow-up lessons will be needed for practice in recognizing the category types and using this knowledge in answering comprehension questions. Raphael (1986) suggested beginning QAR instruction with first- and second-grade students by introducing only the two-category distinction: *in the book* and *in my head.* Middle-grade students can learn all four QARs in one lesson, although the types can still be distinguished by the two headings *in the book (right there* and *putting it together)* and *in my head (author and me* and *on my own).* The teacher presents sample text with the questions, responses, and QAR provided and discusses the reasons for each classification with the students. Once students understand category differences, the teacher provides other samples of text, questions, and responses so students can identify the QAR. Finally, when provided text and questions only, students will have learned to recognize the key words in questions that cue them as to whether the answer lies in the text or in their heads. At this point, students are well on their way to using text organization as an aid to comprehension.

Helfeldt and Henk (1990) suggested a combination of ReQuest procedure (Manzo, 1969, 1985) and QAR instruction in a technique they term **reciprocal question–answer relationships (ReQARs)**. Intended for middle- and upper-grade students, particularly those with word recognition difficulties, the technique helps these readers anticipate the nature of teachers' questions, focus on informative parts of text, and learn how to construct appropriate responses to questions. Essentially, the goal of ReQAR is to assist students in viewing comprehension as the goal of reading. The instructional sequence is outlined in the original source, and the reader is encouraged to consult that source.

Teachers should not overlook the value of group discussion. Goldenberg (1992/1993) discussed "instructional conversations" as discussion-based lessons intended to support and enhance students' conceptual and linguistic development. The teacher's responsibility becomes one of weaving students' prior knowledge, experiences, and discussion comments and contributions into the conversation. Similar ideas include "grand conversations," or dialogue among readers about their interpretations of a book or story they have read in common to co-construct meaning (Peterson & Eeds, 1990), and the student-led small group discussions and closing "Community Shares" that are part of book club programs (McMahon & Raphael, 1997).

MI Connection:
interpersonal

Questioning and discussion are not the only postreading activities that students can participate in to enhance comprehension. Visual structures or **graphic organizers** such as maps, charts, webs, grids, matrices, and diagrams provide a visual representation of the facts and concepts in the material read. These visual structures help make content information more accessible to English learners because they summarize text in fewer words, thus converting complex information into manageable chunks.

MI Connection:
spatial

Different visual structures suit a variety of purposes. **Semantic webbing** (also called **mapping**) specifically aids readers in organizing what they read, thus improving comprehension (Freedman & Reynolds, 1980; Reutzel, 1985; Sinatra, Stahl-Gemake, & Berg, 1984). In semantic webbing, a visual display is constructed representing relationships in the content of a story or expository selection (Davidson, 1982; Freedman & Reynolds, 1980). The technique visually demonstrates how main ideas are logically related to subordinate ideas (Sinatra et al., 1984).

MI Connection:
logical-mathematical

Four steps are basic in constructing a web or map:

1. Answer the *core question*.
2. Use the answers to the core question as *web strands*.
3. Provide *strand supports*—facts, events, inferences, and generalizations taken from the text that distinguish one web strand from another.
4. Decide what *strand ties* exist—that is, how strands are related to each other. (Dotted lines may be used to indicate strand ties, or locations on the map itself, such as grouping.)

Before using a semantic web with students, the teacher must organize the content of the selection conceptually. For instance, in step 1, the core question, the focus of the web for *The Three Little Pigs,* is chosen by the teacher (Figure 11.10) and placed in a central position. Answers to the core question elicited through discussion (the eight characters) become the web strands. The strand supports are facts, events, inferences, and generalizations that distinguish the characters from one another. Strand ties in this example are represented by placing the man with straw beside Pig #1, the man with

Figure 11.10   Semantic Web for *The Three Little Pigs*

twigs beside Pig #2, and so forth. Placement in sequential order also indicates the repetitive pattern in this story. The relationship between Pig #3 and the wolf is actually more complex than the strand supports in the figure indicate, however. The story contains a series of episodes in which the wolf tries to trick the pig and the pig outsmarts the wolf. If the teacher thinks further exploration of a part of the web would be beneficial, a section such as the relationship between the wolf and Pig #3 may be enlarged to examine the more complex relationships.

Figure 11.11   Using Semantic Webs as Advance Organizers

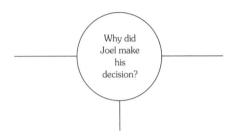

Although described here as postreading activities, semantic webs may also be introduced in incomplete form as organizers *before* reading or writing. In an example suggested by Cleland (1981) and seen in Figure 11.11, three distinct responses are indicated; students reading the selection will know to look for three major reasons for Joel's decision. A similar approach but one that provides more detail from the story is the cloze story map (Reutzel, 1986).

The real benefit of using semantic webs and charts comes from the discussion that the teacher directs. The teacher guides the students in constructing the web or chart by pointing out relationships between ideas and characters and events in the material read. Such techniques are not reserved for stories but, like DRTAs, work as well with expository material. In using content-area material, Davidson (1982) observed that "as students interact with one another by sharing maps and asking questions about various elements in each other's maps, they gain insights about the various reasoning processes used by others" (p. 56). For detailed examples of a wide variety of mapping ideas, refer to Heimlich and Pittelman's (1986) *Semantic Mapping: Classroom Applications.*

MI Connection: interpersonal

Reutzel (1985) summarized the ways maps, webs, and charts help teachers and students to:

- plan and execute more purposeful, focused reading lessons;
- organize readers' efforts toward specific comprehension objectives;
- focus questions and discussion on the important aspects of the text;
- create a workable structure for storage and retrieval of important information learned from the text;
- provide a visually coherent summary of the text;
- furnish a structure for guiding prereading experiences;
- supply students with a model for organizing and integrating text information in the content areas;
- present events and concepts in divergent visual patterns designed to emphasize specific types of relationships;
- experience a visual representation of text arrangements to encourage sensitivity to varying text patterns;
- summon the correct collection of background experiences and knowledge to facilitate comprehension of the text; and
- encourage students to think about and monitor their reading. (p. 403) (See Chapter 12.)

Additional types of visual structures for aiding comprehension appear in subsequent chapters.

Summary

Readers who comprehend text well generally approach reading as a meaning-making task; therefore, comprehension instruction for all learners must emphasize understanding as the paramount purpose of reading. Direct instruction includes use of short selections, concrete words and examples, and appropriate questions. It must be explicit—involve teacher–student interaction. Teachers should verbalize and model for their students the strategies they themselves use while trying to comprehend text. These strategies might include finding the main idea, predicting an outcome, or self-questioning. Comprehension instruction is not limited to intermediate grades and beyond; it *must* be taught from the first grade. Many techniques presented in this chapter can be adapted as listening activities to accommodate emergent readers or those who struggle with word identification. To be good comprehenders, students must first realize that written materials should make sense. Until the student has internalized this realization, no instruction in comprehension is likely to help.

Recommended Websites

Ten Research-Based Principles for Improving Reading Comprehension
 www.ciera.org/library/instresrc/compprinciples/index
 .html
CIERA provides a draft of guiding principles for improving the reading comprehension of America's children.

Reading for Understanding: Toward an R&D Program in Reading Comprehension
 www.rand.org/multi/achievementforall/reading/
 readreport.html
The RAND report focuses on middle and secondary students' comprehension.

Reading Comprehension
 http://muskingum.edu/~cal/database/general/reading
 .html
A learning strategies database created by the Center for Advancement of Learning at Muskingum College can be found on this site.

Teaching Readers Who Struggle: A Pragmatic Middle School Framework
 www.readingonline.org/articles/art_index.asp?HREF=ash
Ash describes an extension to reciprocal teaching that engages students in critical evaluation of text.

Comprehension Strategies
 http://literacy.kent.edu/eureka/strategies/read_with_
 understanding.html
This site provides a wealth of links to many comprehension strategies.

Guided Reading
 www.discover.tased.edu.au/english/guide.htm
This site provides details of guided reading lessons with a focus on enhancing comprehension skills as conducted by Janet Seymour and Carmel French at Lindisfarne North Primary School.

Reading Comprehension Articles
 www.readingonline.org
Use the search functions; to gain access to many excellent articles; for example, "Reading Comprehension on the Internet: Expanding Our Understanding of Reading Comprehension to Encompass New Literacies," by Julie Coiro, published February, 2003.

The Graphic Organizer
 www.graphic.org/
 www.eduplace.com/graphicorganizer/
A nice collection of resources and examples of graphic organizers, some ready-to-print, can be found here.

How Readable Are Your Texts?
 www.readability.biz/Indices.html
This is a brief explanation of readability.

Factors Affecting Text Readability
 www.nald.ca/fulltext/readab/readab.pdf
This comprehensive treatment by William Dubay discusses factors affecting readability and a thorough scrutiny of many readability formulas.

MyEducationLab is a research-based learning tool that brings teaching to life. Go to the Gipe 7th Edition MyEducationLab for Reading Assessment site at www.myeducationlab.com to:

- Engage in multimedia exercises to help you build a deeper and more applied understanding of chapter content.
- Use extensive resources including videos from real classrooms, Praxis and licensure preparation, a lesson plan builder, and materials to help you in your teaching career.

CHAPTER 12

Strategic Reading for Narrative Text

OBJECTIVES	*After you have read this chapter, you should be able to:*
	1. Describe the characteristics and structure of narrative text.
	2. Assess comprehension of narrative material using retellings.
	3. Provide instruction for story retellings.
	4. Use graphic organizers for teaching story structure.
	5. Recognize the relationship between writing and reading comprehension of narrative text.

VOCABULARY ALERT			
	book club	graphic novels	story frames
	double entry journal	literature circles	story grammar
	Goldilocks strategy	novel study	story impressions

In addition to vocabulary knowledge, reading comprehension requires the use of thinking and reasoning skills. Different types of text (such as narrative or expository) require different kinds of thinking and reasoning. As mature readers, we approach narrative and expository text differently because their internal structures are different. We need to teach our students about these differences. This chapter and the next present strategies best suited for narrative and expository text, respectively. Taken together, Chapters 10 through 13 provide a large repertoire of strategies that will positively affect comprehension.

ASSESSMENT FOR NARRATIVE TEXT: RETELLINGS

Reading comprehension requires that readers make connections between their own prior knowledge and the organization of the text. Text organization for narrative text includes a setting or settings, characters, and a goal, followed by some problem(s), events, and a resolution. These elements, essential to any well-formed story, result in a structure referred to as **story grammar**. In general, narrative text is easier for children to recall and comprehend than expository text (Leslie & Cooper, 1993). This could be due simply to greater familiarity and exposure at early ages to narrative text, or it could be due to the fact that narratives are about people engaged in goal-oriented action, thought to be the building blocks of cognition (Mandler, 1984; Nelson, 1986). Another factor relates to the consistent structure of the narrative as opposed to expository structures (compare–contrast, description, enumeration, sequence; see Chapters 11 and 13). Although narrative text is generally easier to comprehend, not all readers find narrative text easy. Many readers can decode words easily yet do not make the connections to texts that are necessary for comprehension. One of the critical connections is between the reader's prior knowledge and the content of the story. The more prior knowledge, the better the comprehension. One easy way to assess prior knowledge for narrative text is through a free-association task (Leslie & Cooper, 1993). Simply ask readers to tell what they think of, or are reminded of, or what is meant by either several well-chosen words from the story, or the title, or the cover of the book before it is read. Another way to assess prior knowledge is to ask for a prediction about the story based solely on the title or book cover.

A story-retelling rubric is a commonly used tool for assessing the extent of a reader's awareness or understanding of the structure or features found in a particular narrative text. The generic retelling form found in Appendix I was used to assess Matt's retelling of Aesop's "The Lion and the Mouse" (see Figure 12.1). Note that this scoring rubric provides a percentage score that can be loosely interpreted using the same criteria for reading comprehension scores derived from an IRI administration (see Table 6.1 for

Figure 12.1   Story Retelling Scoring Rubric for Matt's Retelling of an Aesop Fable

Name: *Matt*   Grade: *4*   Date: *9/16*

Story Title (and Author): *The Lion and the Mouse   (Aesop)*

Context: Story Read by Child _✓_ Silently ____ Orally _✓_ Story Read to Child ____

Main Points for Retelling		Unprompted		Prompted
CHARACTERS (_6_ points each)	⑫			
1. *lion*		✓		____
2. *mouse*		✓		____
3. *hunters*		____		____
4. ____		____		____
5. ____		____		____
SETTING (_6_ points each)				
1. *lion's den*	⑥	____	⑥	✓
2. *forest*		✓		____
3. ____		____		____
4. ____		____		____
EVENTS/PLOT (_6_ points each)				
1. *lion asleep in den*	㉚	____	⑫	✓
2. *mouse wakes lion*		____		✓
3. *lion catches mouse to kill*		✓		____
4. *mouse begs for life*		✓		____
5. *mouse promises to repay lion*		✓		____
6. *lion lets mouse go free*		✓		____
7. *lion caught in hunters' net*		✓		____
8. *lion roars loudly*		____		____
9. *mouse recognizes lion's roar*		____		____
10. ____		____		____
RESOLUTION/THEME (_6_ points each)				
1. *Mouse chews through rope*	⑫	✓		____
2. *lion freed by mouse*		✓		____
3. *Moral: Even small acts of kindness are important*		____		____

TOTAL POINTS: _78_/100 = _78_ %   _60_/100   +   _18_/100

Evaluative Comments: *Matt read the story fluently and seemed comfortable during the retelling. He recalls major points of the plot. His overall comprehension of 78% is adequate — this material is at his instructional reading level. He demonstrated understanding of the moral. Matt said, "Just because you're small doesn't mean you can't help somebody." Maybe compare to silent reading recall.*

comprehension percentages). In the scoring rubric, point values out of 100 are determined by the total number of items to be recalled. In this example, there were 17 items; therefore $100/17 = 5.88$. Rounding off meant each item recalled was worth approximately 6 points. The student received two scores, one for unprompted and one for prompted recall. These scores can be interpreted separately or combined for a total percentage recall score.

Retellings can be either oral or written. In the case of oral retellings, a tape recorder should be used to capture the retelling for later analysis. It is difficult to listen to a retelling and at the same time make notations of all points recalled. A tape recorder also allows students to record their own retellings while the teacher works with other students. Written retellings can take a variety of forms. One form, **story frames**, is useful for assessing knowledge of story structure and also the degree to which the story is recalled (Cudd & Roberts, 1987; Fowler, 1982). Story frames provide the key words or phrases representing the organizational pattern of the text. See Figure 12.2 for an example.

INSTRUCTION FOR NARRATIVE TEXT

Questions and activities based on story grammar may improve students' comprehension by enhancing their schemata for narrative material (Fitzgerald & Spiegel, 1983) and their level of involvement during reading (Dimino et al., 1990). In Mandler and Johnson's (1977) story grammar, the story elements are described as a setting (who, where, and

---

Figure 12.2   A Story Frame

Title: *Petronella.*
Directions: Look over the entire story frame, then go back and fill in the missing parts.

In the kingdom of _____ there lived _____
_____.
One problem in this story was that Petronella was a _____ instead of a prince.
But Petronella did not let that stop her from seeking her fortune. The first thing that happened
to Petronella and her brothers was _____
_____
_____
_____.
After that Petronella _____
_____
_____.
Then Petronella had to _____
_____
_____.
After Petronella left with Prince Ferdinand _____
_____
_____
_____.
The story ends _____
_____
_____.

when); a beginning or initiating event (the problem for the hero); a reaction (what the hero says or does in response to the problem); a goal (what the hero decides to do about the problem); an attempt (the effort or efforts to solve the problem); an outcome (the consequence or result of what the hero does); and an ending (a brief wrap-up of the whole story).

Dimino and colleagues (1990) investigated the use of story grammar as a framework for improving at-risk high school students' comprehension and recall of short stories. Four categories of story grammar components were modeled, explained, and practiced: conflict/problem, character information, attempts/resolution/twist, and reaction/theme. Student engagement in lessons approached in this way was high. As a result, these researchers concluded that "it is unfair to deprive low-track students of the potentially rich and stimulating experiences of analyzing and discussing works by authors such as Nathaniel Hawthorne, Dorothy Parker, Toni Morrison, or Guy de Maupassant simply because their reading ability is not as high as their peers" (p. 19).

Sadow (1982, p. 520) suggests five generic questions to ask about stories:

1. Where and when did the events in the story take place, and who was involved in them? (setting)
2. What started the chain of events in the story? (initiating event)
3. What was the main character's reaction to this event? (reaction)
4. What did the main character do about it? (action: goals and attempts)
5. What happened as a result of what the main character did? (consequence, outcome)

A format such as the story map seen in Figure 12.3 can help students see the structure of stories. A story feature chart can also be provided, as shown in Figure 12.4. These activities can help prepare a student for either oral or written retelling assessments. Gambrell, Pfeiffer, and Wilson (1985); Gambrell, Koskinen, and Kapinus (1991); and Morrow (1988) have found that retellings significantly improve comprehension and sense of story structure. But retelling is a skill in and of itself that needs to be practiced (see Hoyt, 1999). The prompting provided by the story map, story feature chart, and checklists containing questions such as those suggested by Sadow (1982) are effective scaffolds for developing the skill of retelling for readers struggling with comprehension and English learners alike.

MI Connection:
spatial

Semantic webbing, also called *mapping* (discussed in Chapter 11), results in a visual display representing relationships in the content of a story; that is, a graphic organizer. Carefully planned questions based on story grammar and asked in conjunction with developing story maps help students see the underlying organization of ideas and relationships in a story (Beck & McKeown, 1981). For instance, in *The Three Little Pigs* (refer back to Figure 11.7), once the web strands (characters) were identified, the teacher asked about the initiating event to begin eliciting information about each strand: "What caused the three pigs to go out on their own?" The responses provided strand supports for the old sow. Likewise, the reaction (in this example, three separate reactions for each pig) were elicited by asking: "What does each pig decide to do?" The goals, attempts, and outcomes followed by asking: "What does Pig #1 (Pig #2, Pig #3) decide to build?" "What is the first problem for the pigs?" "What happens to Pig #1?" "What is the next problem for the pigs?" "What happens to Pig #2?" "What is the problem for Pig #3?" "What happens to Pig #3?" "How is Pig #3 different from Pig #1 and Pig #2?" The ending was addressed by a question regarding a theme or a moral, such as, "Which pig is the hero, and why?" These questions helped construct the story map; however, questioning in the form of extension or enrichment can continue once the map (web) is completed.

| **Figure 12.3** | Story Map for *Goldilocks and the Three Bears* |

Character(s) and Setting: Goldilocks, Papa Bear, Mama Bear, Baby Bear Bear's house in the woods

Problem: Goldilocks goes into bears' house while they are out.

Goal: Goldilocks decided to make herself right at home.

P L O T

Event: She tasted the bears' porridge and ate Baby Bear's.

Event: She sat in the bears' chairs and broke Baby Bear's.

Event: She lay down on the bears' beds and fell asleep in Baby Bear's.

Resolution: The 3 bears came home, found their porridge tasted, their chairs sat in, and Goldilocks in bed. She woke up and ran away.

A strategy that shows students how story features relate to each other is to *find the features and connect them* (Richards et al., 1994). The teacher first familiarizes students with the basic story features of character, setting, problem, and solution. Then, by using a familiar story and discussing the way two elements are connected, the teacher introduces the connection strategy. Figure 12.4 shows one way in which this discussion might be recorded for students to examine. Students can also use such a chart or graphic organizer for prewriting or planning their creative stories or as a reader response activity.

Figure 12.4   Example of a Story Feature Chart

Student's Name _David_   Story Title _Goldilocks and the Three Bears_

FIND THE FEATURES AND CONNECT THEM

Story Feature: Characters	Story Feature: Setting	The Connection
Mama Bear Papa Bear Baby Bear Goldilocks	the woods	The bears lived _in_ the woods. Goldilocks lived _near_ the woods. Goldilocks walked _in_ the woods.

Story Feature: Problem	Story Feature: Solution	The Connection
The porridge was too hot to eat.	The bears went for a walk.	Some of the porridge got cool while the bears were gone.

Too often, many young readers and readers who struggle with comprehension have trouble relating to the human element in stories. Although they may be able to name the characters in a story, these students cannot identify with the characters or understand their feelings, goals, or motives. Comprehension is certainly affected in these cases. Developing a *getting to know my character map* (Richards & Gipe, 1993; Tompkins & Hoskisson, 1991) may help students better understand stories they read, as well as develop broader social understanding in general. Through modeling and explanation of the teacher's own thinking, both descriptive and inferred information about a main character is discussed and placed on a map (see Figure 12.5).

Several other useful graphic organizers help students focus on story features. Some of these are the *story structure chart* (Worthy & Bloodgood, 1992/1993), used for charting similarities and differences among story features for several versions of the

Figure 12.5 Example of a Character Map

GETTING TO KNOW MY CHARACTER

Story ___Fox Song___   My Character ___Jamie___

FACTS ABOUT MY CHARACTER

1. Jamie's Grama Bowman has died.
2. Jamie lives with her family on the Winooski River.
3. Jamie did many things with Grama Bowman, her great-grandmother.

WHAT I KNOW ABOUT MY CHARACTER'S ACTIONS

1. Jamie would not get out of bed.
2. She stayed in bed with her eyes closed so her mother would think she was asleep.
3. Jamie saw pictures in her mind of all the things she did with Grama Bowman.
4. Jamie ran to the tree where she sat with grama.
5. Jamie sang the song Grama taught her.

WHAT I KNOW ABOUT MY CHARACTER'S FEELINGS

1. Jamie felt so alone.
2. Jamie loved doing things with Grama Bowman.
3. Jamie loved her parents for letting her stay in bed to remember Grama Bowman.
4. Jamie missed her grama.

WHAT I KNOW ABOUT MY CHARACTER'S THOUGHTS

1. Jamie could not imagine being in the woods without her grama.
2. Jamie understood why her grama gave her her bone awl.
3. Jamie wondered if she had really seen the fox.
4. Jamie knew she would never be alone.

Figure 12.6   Story Structure Chart for Several Versions of a Story

TITLE	Little Red Riding Hood	Lon Po Po	Little Red Riding Hood	Little Red Riding Hood
COUNTRY	France	China	United States	Canada
AUTHOR	Perrault	Young	Hyman	Lang (Editor)
ILLUSTRATOR	Holmes	Young	Hyman	?
CHARACTERS (with a one word description)	Mother (loving) Little Red (naive) Wolf (shrewd) Grandma (kindly)	Mother (trusting) Shang (clever) Tao (plump) Paotze (sweet) Wolf (stupid)	Mother (prim) Little Red (free-spirited) Wolf (shrewd) Grandma (sickly) huntsman (brave)	Mother (loving) Little Red (pretty) Grandma (sickly) Wolf (tricky)
SETTING	village	country house	forest, Grandma's house	forest
EVENTS (list the major events)	1. LRRH goes to Grandma's 2. Meets wolf 3. Wolf pretends to be Grandma	1. Mother leaves to go to Po Po's house 2. Wolf comes to house as Po Po 3. Children trick wolf to come to the gingko tree 4. Wolf is killed	1. LRRH takes food to Grandma 2. Meets wolf 3. LRRH picks flowers 4. Wolf eats Grandma 5. LRRH arrives 6. Wolf eats LRRH 7. Huntsman comes	1. LRRH goes to Grandma's 2. Meets wolf 3. Wolf races to get to Grandma's house first 4. Wolf eats Grandma 5. Wolf eats LRRH
ENDING	Wolf eats both	Children go back inside and to bed	Wolf is killed and the huntsman frees Grandma and LRRH	Wolf eats both
THEME	Deception	Symbolism	Magic	Deception

Go to MyEducationLab and select the topic *Reading and Writing Connections*. Then, go to the Activities and Applications section, and watch the video entitled "Graphic Organizer: Venn Diagrams" to observe a teacher directing her students to develop a Venn diagram for the characters in The *Scarlet Letter*. Next respond to the accompanying questions.

MI Connection: spatial

same story (see Figure 12.6), and *Venn diagrams* to compare and contrast story elements (see Figure 12.7). When only contrasts are of interest, a *T-chart* works better than a Venn diagram (see Figure 12.8). Worthy and Bloodgood (1992/1993) presented an interesting version of the traditional Venn diagram for comparing story plots. This technique, called a *circle graph,* allows students to draw representative sketches of important plot elements as well as list the elements (see Figure 12.9). Finally, the Somebody/Wanted/But/So *plot relationships chart* helps students look at each story feature from the perspective of the characters in the story. The column headings, in order, each relate to the characters, goals, problems, and solutions found in the story. See Figure 12.10 for a completed chart.

Additional forms of reader-response activities include double-entry journals (see Figure 12.11) or other types of response journals, as well as writing letters to the author, or Wacky Want Ads that demonstrate key understandings of the narrative read (see Figure 12.12). Bromley (1993) defined a **double-entry journal** as "one in which students keep two separate entries related to the same topic, idea, or activity" (p. 71). Students can be asked to make connections between the material they are reading and their own lives (text-to-self), another text they have already read (text-to-text), or to world issues and current events outside the school community (text-to-world). It is easiest to introduce double-entry journals using personal connections (that is, text-to-self connections) as a way of responding to text. The teacher introduces the double-entry journal by first

| **Figure 12.7** | Venn Diagram Comparing and Contrasting *Little Red Riding Hood* and *Lon Po Po* |

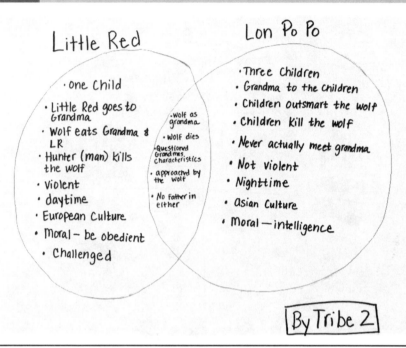

By Tribe 2

| **Figure 12.8** | Reader Response Example: T-Chart for Contrasting Two Versions of *Little Red Riding Hood* |

Little Red Riding Hood	*Lon Po Po*
Mother stays home and sends Red Riding Hood to Grandma's house	3 children, Shang, Paotze, and Tao, stay home, and Mother goes to Grandma's house
Red Riding Hood is trusting of Wolf	Oldest child, Chang, is clever and discovers Wolf is a wolf
Wolf is clever	Wolf is easily tricked
Grandma and Red Riding Hood are eaten by Wolf (violent death)	Children kill Wolf (subtle death)
Huntsman is the hero and saves Grandma and Little Red Riding Hood	Children are the heroes who outsmart the wolf
Grandma is a main character	Grandma, Lon Po Po, is only a name in the story, as well as the title
Foods mentioned are bread, wine, sweet butter	Food mentioned is gingko nuts

Figure 12.9	Circle Graph Summarizing the Stories *Little Red Riding Hood* (Outer Circle) and *Lon Po Po* (Inner Circle)

Figure 12.10	Plot Relationships Chart for *Goldilocks and the Three Bears*

SOMEBODY	WANTED	BUT	SO
Goldilocks	to sit	chair was too soft	tried another chair
Goldilocks	to sit	chair was too hard and big	tried another chair
Goldilocks	to sit	chair was too small	chair broke
Goldilocks	to eat	food was too hot	tried another bowl
Goldilocks	to eat	food was too cold	tried another bowl
Goldilocks	to eat	food was just right	ate all the food
Goldilocks	to sleep	bed was too hard	tried another bed
Goldilocks	to sleep	bed was too soft	tried another bed
Goldilocks	to sleep	bed was just right	She fell asleep until the bears came home and they woke her up. Then she ran away.

Figure 12.11	Example Page from a Double-Entry Journal for Reader-Response Connections

Book Title: *Al Capone Does My Shirts (Gennifer Choldenko)*	**Connections** Text-to-Me/Text-to-Another Text/Text-to-World
Date: <u>3/13</u> Page(s): <u>5</u> *"When I was five, I was kind of a runt. … Natalie was the first person to call me "Moose." I swear I started growing to fit the name that very day. Now I'm five foot eleven and a half inches" [at 12 years] …*	Me <u>√</u> Another Text __ World __ *I remember this boy in 7th grade who everyone called "Shorty" because he was shorter than most of the girls. Then over the summer before 8th grade, he spurted up to about six feet, three inches! "Shorty" no more.*
Date: <u>3/15</u> Page(s): <u>39</u> *"Do not speak to any outsiders about what goes on in here. Don't go shooting your mouth off about Al Capone. You say his name and hordes of reporters come crawling out of the woodwork ready to write stories full of foolish lies."*	Me __ Another Text __ World <u>√</u> *I think the media likes to exaggerate things like some of the stuff they write about celebrities. Who really knows what is true and what isn't?*
Date: <u>3/18</u> Page(s): <u>75-79</u> *"Once in a lifetime opportunity. Get your clothes laundered by Al Capone … only costs 5 cents … When class ends, two lines form outside the bathrooms. One by one Miss Bimp's students come out, sweaters over bare chest … as they hand Piper their clothes and their money."*	Me __ Another Text __ World <u>√</u> *This reminds me of how some people just have to be the first to see a new movie, or buy the latest electronic gadget. These kids wanted to be able to say they had their clothes laundered by Al Capone.*
Date: <u>3/20</u> Page(s): <u>189</u> *"Hey, Natalie, did you know your birthday is four months and ten days after Al Capone's," Annie says as my mom cuts the cake.*	Me __ Another Text <u>√</u> World __ *Everyday the newspaper prints a list of famous people's ages because that date is their birthday, so you could figure out how close your birthday is to some famous person by reading this list.*

dividing a journal page into two columns and then selecting a quote from an assigned reading. The quote is written in the left column, and the teacher models a personal response in the corresponding right column. Students then read a portion of the material until they find a quote that reminds them of a particular event in their own life. They proceed to write the quote in the left column and their personal connection in the right column. Discussion that follows the journaling is also important because this discussion supports the students in understanding the impact of their own life experiences on the way text is interpreted.

MI Connection:
logical-mathematical

Dramatizing material read can also enhance comprehension. In addition to the reading and rereading required to prepare a readers' theater script and drama production, activities that accompany these productions—such as preparing backdrops, deciding on props, and conducting library research to verify content—help comprehension (see various "Arts Connection" features throughout this text for examples). Bidwell (1990) listed several ideas and ways to use drama in the classroom for the purposes of increasing motivation, comprehension, and fluency. The reading/writing connection is also made clear in preparing these productions through writing the plot, developing characters, and revising and editing the final script.

MI Connections:
intrapersonal; interpersonal; spatial; bodily-kinesthetic

Figure 12.12 Wacky Want Ads

1. Lost! Several young rams and ewes. No idea as to whereabouts. If seen, call Meadow at 444-2884.
2. Am seeking plastic surgeon to shorten extremely long nose. Desperate! It is still growing longer.
3. For sale: Cradle, slightly damaged in fall from broken tree limb. Useful for very breezy days.
4. Wanted: To rent very solid house for three brothers. Must be able to withstand strong winds.
5. Son: Please come home. Your mother misses you. The girls forgive you. The Piper
6. Wanted: Loggers to work in large lumber camp. Must have unusual skill. We work fast! $500 per week salary!!
7. Desperately need to rent 27-bedroom house. Present home as tight as an old shoe.
8. Lost! Three small pairs of woolen mittens. Owners greatly upset by loss. Please return if found.
9. Will pay for information leading to arrest of a small girl who loves porridge and breaks chairs. She wrecked our small son's bed and chair.
10. Warning: The sky is falling! The world is coming to an end! There's still time to flee! Contact ME!!

Answer key:
1. Little Bo-Peep
2. Pinocchio
3. Rock-a-Bye Baby
4. The Three Little Pigs
5. Tom, the Piper's Son
6. Paul Bunyan
7. The Old Woman Who Lived in a Shoe
8. Three Little Kittens
9. Goldilocks and the Three Bears
10. Chicken Little

Writing stories also helps reading comprehension. Reluctant writers are greatly assisted by **story impressions** (McGinley & Denner, 1987), a strategy that introduces a list of words or phrases (no more than three words) to be used in their written story, with order of use indicated by arrows.

Stories can be written by individuals or by groups. The words and phrases are selected to designate characters, setting, and key elements of the plot. Depending on the age of the student, limit the number of words and phrases listed to 10 to 15. Figure 12.13 shows the word list followed by a group story.

A strategy related to phase-out/phase-in for active comprehension (see Chapter 11), but one better suited to narrative text, and one very simple for students to grasp, is called *I Wonder . . . ?* (Richards & Gipe, 1996). Beginning with the title and cover of a book, students are encouraged to ask "I wonder" questions. For example, using the book *Fox Song* by Joseph Bruchac (1993), some questions might be:

"I wonder if the fox will sing?"
"I wonder where the fox is?"
"I wonder why the fox is alone?"
"I wonder what the fox is looking at?"

Figure 12.13	Group Story

Story Impressions

Directions: Use these words in your story in the order listed.

Grandma and me
↓
beach
↓
windy
↓
hot dogs
↓
seashell
↓
deep water
↓
fins and mask
↓
sand castle
↓
home

Grandma and me whent to
the beach by Brittany Williams
   illustrator by Ridge Petes, illustrator by
One day Grandma and me whent some   Aubry
where on Friday. We whent to the
beach. It was windy and cold the water
was whavy. We whent to get hotdogs,
And we font seashells. The sun came
out and we whet into the deep water.
A diver came to swim whith a mask
and fins. And we got out of the
water and we dig a hole in the
sand and we biled a sandcastler
And we wint home becuse we
was tirde.

SPOTLIGHT ON ENGLISH LEARNERS

Generating Stories

Wordless picture books are especially beneficial to linguistically different readers because they can easily provide a successful interaction with text (Cassady, 1998). Such books can be used to develop prediction strategies, plot story maps, develop vocabulary, and make connections between written and spoken language. English learners can initially "read" the book in their native language to stimulate oral communication and a sense of accomplishment. Then, working with a partner, they can create a story to accompany the book and share the story with the class. Variations in either or both languages can be prepared. Partners could be directed to work together as follows:

"Read" the story silently first.

Discuss interpretations with your partner.

"Read" the story into a tape recorder (to be typed later).

Cut apart the typed sentences and paper clip them to the appropriate pages in the picture book.

Read the story to another person.

Teachers can assist learners by using culturally relevant children's literature to motivate both reading and writing.

For example, Cynthia Rylant's (1982) book *When I Was Young in the Mountains* can be used to help students learn about mountain culture as well as to motivate reflection on students' own lives while writing their own memoirs: *When I Was Young in* _____. In doing so, the students can make their own individual books or a class book with one page written and illustrated by each student. The students will be integrating their writing with their reading in a social context so that all learners (from various cultures and neighborhoods) can share stories about themselves and their self-generated language. Moreover, in the context of this activity, the students are developing their awareness of complex sentence structure (for example, subordinated adverbial clauses) and story structure while using the language of the author and themselves for a real audience.

In a culturally diverse classroom, children's literature about various ethnic cultures can enhance cross-cultural understanding as well as empower learners to read books that relate to their own cultures. Further, teachers can encourage parents to use literature activities as part of their children's lives in family and community contexts (Barnitz & Barnitz, 1996). In recent years, family literacy programs and parenting programs have been established to facilitate literacy development in the community (Morrow, 1995; Rasinski, 1995; Thomas et al., 1999a, 1999b).

This process can occur at other points in the story as well. Students then read (or listen) to satisfy their own purposes, a process that facilitates comprehension.

Perhaps the most effective way to increase readers' abilities to comprehend narrative text is to allow them large blocks of time to read. As introduced in Chapter 11, a minimum of 20 minutes each day for silent reading should be a goal; more time would be even better. Other ways to ensure that students get a large amount of silent reading time are a **book club** program (McMahon & Raphael, 1997) in which students choose the books they wish to read, discuss them with others in a small group, and later come together in a "community share" to share and hear about other books that other clubs have read; and the use of **literature circles**, similar to book clubs with the added feature of students fulfilling specific job responsibilities such as "vocabulary enricher," "passage master," and "summarizer" (Daniels, 2002). Even very young readers can participate in literature circles with proper guidance and scaffolding from the teacher.

Book clubs and literature circles are especially beneficial for English learners as they engage in comfortable talk about books. They hear natural oral language when native English speakers talk about the books read. They pay closer attention to the way their English-speaking classmates use English within the relaxed setting of the literature circle (Hadaway, Vardell, & Young, 2004). Feelings of anxiety about speaking before the whole class are diminished. Because everyone in the literature circle has a turn to speak, English learners gain much needed practice in using academic English. For students in transition

MI Connection:
interpersonal

Arts Connection _____

Art activities such as painting, singing, dancing, and engaging in spontaneous or scripted drama en-actments offer opportunities for students to share their ideas about story characters' goals and actions and portray their thinking about what might happen next in a story. It is common for students to be authors and visual artists by writing and illustrating their own stories and books and reading them aloud for peers' and younger students' enjoyment. The visual and communicative arts provide other options as well. Because dancers use their bodies to communicate nonverbally, harmonizing literacy events with dance improvisations and more structured dance enactments are ideal alternatives for inspiring and liberating students who may struggle with oral and written language. Dancing provides freedom for students to take risks, use their imaginations, and express themselves with confidence and joy. Dancing offers a way for students to internalize and convey complex ideas, emotions, and thinking through movement. In fact, "the expression of personal thoughts and feelings is central to creative dance" (Drewe, 1998, p. 41).

In addition to facilitating personal expressions and confidence, dance as an alternative language provides students with a venue for portraying complicated ideas about literature. For example, accompanied by appropriate music, students can communicate encompassing moods depicted in stories, such as Jamie's deep sadness about her grandmother's death in the Native American story *Fox Song* (Bruchac, 1993), or the feistiness and gumption of Margaret, the physically challenged primary student in *The Balancing Girl* (Rabe, 1981). Dance also provides opportunities for students to portray characters' goals and actions and to use their imaginations and bodily-kinesthetic intelligence to communicate alternative resolutions and endings to fairy tales, fables, folk tales, and chapter books.

Unfortunately, dance is excluded from educational curricula in many schools. Yet a significant amount of research indicates that kinesthetic movement such as dance is central to language development (Bruner, 1966; Piaget & Inhelder, 1969; Vygotsky, 1978). In addition, dance and movement enhance students' problem-solving abilities, concentration, memory, and imagination (Eisner, 1981; Gardner, 1983; Greene, 1988; Jensen, 1998; Montessori, 1967; Vygotsky, 1978). Dancing also can serve to unite students' motor and cognitive understanding (Cecil & Lauritzen, 1994). Further, as a distinctive mode of expressing knowledge and feelings, dance provides an alternative way for students from diverse cultures and heritages to successfully contribute to class projects and group collaborations.

who need direct support during reading, a buddy system or paired reading can be implemented, along with the use of visuals or realia.

Book selection is critical for ensuring vibrant and meaningful discussions. Books that relate to students' lives and their interests are important, but the books offered for student choice must also encourage positive discussion strategies (Clarke & Holwadel, 2007). Table 12.1 presents a brief sample of books that inspire good discussions.

For help in choosing quality literature, and for a lesson example, visit the related websites at the end of this chapter. For book clubs or literature circles, students will often be selecting their own books to read, so they also need to know how to select an appropriate book for their ability level. Recall that a high interest level can sometimes allow readers to stretch and read beyond their actual ability. But how to select a book needs to be discussed, especially with younger students. In addition to the five-finger method described in Chapter 11, the **Goldilocks strategy** (Ohlhausen & Jepsen, 1992) is an effective way of helping young readers select an appropriate book. Relating to the story sequence in *Goldilocks and the Three Bears,* students together with their teacher describe what might make a book "too easy," "too hard," or "just right." These characteristics can then be listed and posted in the library section of the classroom. "Just right" books might have the following characteristics:

- I want to read this book; it looks interesting.
- I can decode most of the words.
- My teacher or someone I know has read this book to me before.

Go to MyEducationLab and first select the topic *Teaching with Literature.* Go to the Activities and Applications section, and watch the video "Literature Circles." Select the topic *Informal Assessments,* go to the Activities and Applications section, and watch the videos "Engaging in Reading" and "Thinking in Young Students." Then select the topic *Comprehension,* go to the Activities and Applications section, and watch the video "Checking Comprehension." Observe how one teacher accomplishes literature circles with her young students, but also helps these students compare two versions of the Cinderella story (*Mufaro's Beautiful Daughters* by Steptoe and *Cendrillon: A Caribbean Cinderella* by San Souci) as a way of checking for comprehension. Next respond to the accompanying questions.

- I have read other books by this author before.
- I already know something about this topic.
- My reading buddy can help me if I need it.

Table 12.1	Short List of Books That Promote Meaningful Discussions		
Title/Date	Genre/Theme	Author/Publisher	Annotation
Monster (2001)	Realistic fiction/social acceptance	Walter Dean Myers/Amistad	This book provides a close-up look at the real struggles, fears, and choices for kids living in the inner city.
Speak (2001)	Realistic fiction/identity	Laurie Halse Anderson/Puffin	This suspenseful story is about choices and the need to fit in.
Freedom Summer (2001)	Fiction/social justice/friendship/racism/prejudice/	Deborah Wiles/Atheneum Books	Despite the societal attitudes against Black people in the 1960s, Joe and John Henry become friends.
Hana's Suitcase (2002)	Biography/Holocaust	Karen Levine/Albert Whitman & Co.	Fumiko Ishioka, curator of a children's Holocaust museum, tells the story of Hana, and her own research process, through alternating chapters.
Locomotion (2003)	Juvenile poetry/self-discovery/African American boys/orphans	Jacqueline Woodson/ G. P. Putnam's Sons	Lonnie deals with the death of his parents and separation from his sister by discovering his poetic voice.
Al Capone Does My Shirts (2004)	Historical fiction/family problems and responsibility	Gennifer Choldenko/ G. P. Putnam's Sons	This book provides a look at life on Alcatraz during the 1930s through the eyes of 12-year-old Moose Flanagan.
The Curious Incident of the Dog in the Night (2004)	Realistic fiction/autism and coping with loss	Mark Haddon/Doubleday	This mystery novel explores an autistic boy's reactions to emotional losses.
Something about America (2005)	Poetry/immigrants/national characteristics/children of immigrants	Maria Testa/Candlewick	Told in simple verse, this is a tale of fear, starting over again, hope, and challenge.
The Time Hackers (2005)	Science fiction/space and time/computer games	Gary Paulsen/Wendy Lamb Books	Dorso Clayman, a seventh grader, journeys through space and time to stop pranksters using futuristic technology to play practical jokes.
Hearts of Stone (2005)	Historical fiction/U.S. Civil War/family/personal cost of war/sacrifice	Kathleen Ernst/Dutton Juvenile	This is the story of 14-year-old Hannah and her siblings' 200-mile journey to a relative's house following the death of her mother and her father joining the Union forces.

Table 12.1 *continued*

Title/Date	Genre/Theme	Author/Publisher	Annotation
Crossing the Wire (2006)	Realistic fiction/illegal immigrants/survival/ Mexicans/friendship	Will Hobbs/HarperCollins	To support his family, 15-year-old Victor must cross the Arizona border to work in the United States.
Travels of Thelonious: The Fog Mound (2006)	Fiction/adventure	Susan Schade and Jon Buller/Simon & Schuster	A chipmunk, a bear, a porcupine, and a lizard set out to prove that humans once inhabited Earth. Alternating chapters of prose and graphic novel appeal to reluctant readers.
Sand Dollar Summer (2006)	Realistic fiction/coming of age/family	Kimberly K. Jones/Simon & Schuster	Twelve-year-old Lise is forced to face personal and environmental obstacles.

ADOLESCENT LITERACY

Recent attention to adolescent literacy has led to a shift in thinking about how adolescents learn best and demands greater appreciation for the sociocultural influences brought about by an increasingly diverse student population and the widespread use of digital media by adolescents (Alvermann, 2002; Lewis & Fabos, 2005; Phelps, 2005). Teachers need guidance in developing instructional strategies that are responsive to the particular needs of the adolescent learner. For example, adolescence is a time of identity exploration. Therefore, literacy development and identity development need to be intertwined. The use of novels, films, and song lyrics as instructional media offer teachers opportunities for their adolescent learners to explore and evaluate their developing identities. To illustrate, adolescents have created "teen zines" on their own time as a way of representing and exploring their changing identities (Guzzetti & Gamboa, 2004). An alternative high school teacher found that students who wrote rap lyrics demonstrated sophisticated understanding of figurative language, voice, and rhythm (Weinstein, 2007). Schools and teachers that reject such creations as inappropriate can impede the literacy development of adolescents. (See also the topic of media literacy in Chapter 13.)

Similarly, curriculum based on teacher-selected books may limit students' reading. Ivey and Broaddus (2001) found more than 60 percent of a group of 1,800 economically and culturally diverse sixth graders preferred free reading and teacher read alouds, while less than one-third preferred reading novels. Thus, providing large blocks of time for free reading is especially important for the adolescent learner. Book clubs and literature circles might be more effective if students were allowed to make their own reading choices. Also, character study using film rather than novels or using graphic novels for conducting novel studies as opposed to using the traditional list of classics may be more effective approaches to literacy development. **Novel study** refers to the in-depth reading and interpretation of a novel, addressing both efferent (reading for information) and aesthetic (reading for enjoyment) dimensions. While typical goals of novel studies are to (1) introduce students to quality literature, (2) help students interpret literature and see meaning and relevance in a variety of genres, and (3) familiarize students with the various literary awards, the use of alternative materials such as graphic novels does not thwart these goals. In fact, the use of graphic novels could assist students in reaching these goals as well as examining their own identity issues. **Graphic novels** are book-length comics usually published in soft cover and containing between 130 and 150 pages. They often contain highly visual, action-oriented story lines, and they can serve to increase student interest. "A student *reads* the words, *sees* the action, *comprehends* the meaning, and is motivated to read more" (McTaggert, 2006, p. 2). In addition, "the visual art . . . can illuminate such devices as character development, elaboration, mood, point of view, irony, and satire" (Kiefer, 1995, p. 184). See the websites at the end of this chapter for examples of novel studies and graphic novels that would meet these goals.

Teachers can readily modify novel study to focus on positive themes depicted in fiction, such as acceptance, caring, compassion, and bravery. Quality literature is also useful for meeting the demands of content area text that includes social studies, media literacy, and the visual arts. In addition, the strategy of novel study can be refashioned to provide a critical analysis framework for examining diverse issues related to engagement in a democratic society that include identifying authors' points of view, comparing text messages written on the same issue, challenging the destruction of our natural resources, detecting powerful, advantaged story characters, and recognizing the silenced voices of those who have been marginalized, not only in literature, but also in films, music, visual art, television sitcoms, and advertisements. In short, novel study can be a most effective strategy for teaching critical thinking.

A strategy developed specifically for helping students read and think critically is the question, connect, transform (QCT) strategy (J. Richards, personal communication, June 2008). The strategy should first be modeled for students. For example, after reading passages from the true story, *Baseball Saved Us* (Mochizuki, 1993), demonstrate how to *question (Q)* the unfair internment of Japanese American citizens during the Second World War (for example, "I *question* why the U.S. government separated Japanese American families who were loyal American citizens, and placed them in internment camps. I think that was illegal and against our Constitution.").

Then, demonstrate how students might *connect (C)* their personal experiences to the lives of interned Japanese Americans (for example, "I never had to live in a camp because of my ethnic or cultural background, or my religious affiliation, or political views. But, I *connect* to Shorty's experiences in the story *Baseball Saved Us* because when I was a young girl, my mother became ill and could not take care of me. I was sent to my aunt's house to live. I remember feeling scared and lonely and I missed my neighbors and friends from school just as Shorty did.").

Finally, model, and brainstorm with students, ways one might have worked to *transform (T)* the unfair treatment of Japanese American citizens and to take action to promote social justice in our world now (for example, "I can think of many ways I might have worked to *transform (T)* the unjust treatment of Japanese American citizens during the Second World War. I could have written letters of complaint to newspapers or displayed signs in my yard that said, 'Release Japanese American Citizens Now,' and 'Please Unite Japanese American Families.' I could have written letters of disapproval to the president of the United States and my congressional representatives. I could have organized neighborhood meetings to protest this tragic event. I could have hired a lawyer to work toward releasing the Japanese Americans. At the very least, I could have sent food, money, clothing, and books to the Japanese American people. I could even have tried to visit the people in the camps. In today's world, we all have opportunities to take a compassionate stand and challenge and *transform (T)* what we believe is unfair and undeserved treatment of others. Who can name some individuals, or groups of people who have been treated unjustly? What might you do to make a positive difference in their lives?").

MI Connection:
spatial

Go to MyEducationLab and select the topic *Teaching with Literature*. Then, go to the Activities and Applications section, and watch the video entitled "Teaching with Literature" to observe a guided reading lesson for *Sarah, Plain and Tall* that uses visuals and realia to place the story in its historical context. Next respond to the accompanying questions.

Adolescent learners are anxious to tackle the "weightier" issues that adults face. They need the opportunity in school to explore these issues through multiple literacies and multiple texts, to critique, and to receive guidance, feedback, and encouragement from both peers and adults (Phelps, 2005). As adolescent learners are developing their critical literacy abilities, they can work with a partner or in small groups employing multiple literacies to enhance their thinking and ways of knowing. For example, according to their varied expressive language abilities, students might write a poem, e-mail a letter to a story author, or develop a script that contains their questions about issues depicted in historical fiction, such as the Holocaust described in the true story, *One More Border* (Kaplan, 1998). Students might also collaborate and take photographs or create sketches, videos, Venn diagrams, dioramas, murals, graphic novels, or illustrated books that portray their connections to story characters' experiences such as Shorty in the story *Baseball Saved Us* (Mochizuki, 1993). In addition, they might devise an informal dramatic enactment, a dance, a musical composition, or an online chat in which they share ways they might work to transform inequities presented in literature and in their world.

> *MI Connection:* intrapersonal; interpersonal

It behooves teachers of adolescent learners also to continue the search for ways to incorporate digital literacy into the classroom. In light of its extreme popularity with adolescents, modalities such as instant messaging (IM) present opportunities to engage these youth in literate activities. Reading and writing are central to IM, and so students could be more motivated to engage in decoding, writing, interpretation, and critical analysis simply by using this technology. Chapter 13 addresses the topic of expository reading and the Internet and includes further discussion of media literacy.

> *MI Connection:* spatial; bodily-kinesthetic

Summary

Direct instruction includes use of short selections, concrete words and examples, and appropriate questions. It must be explicit, that is, involve teacher–student interaction. Teachers should verbalize for their students the strategies they themselves use while trying to comprehend narrative text. These strategies might include predicting an outcome or charting the story features. Comprehension instruction is not limited to students who have mastered decoding; it must be taught from the very beginning to everyone. Many techniques presented in this chapter can be adapted as art activities so that a reader who is not yet fluent in responding to text in writing can respond through visual representations. To be good comprehenders, students must first realize that written materials should make sense. Until students have internalized this realization, no instruction in comprehension is likely to help. The needs of adolescent learners, in particular, require that schools accept digital literacy as a viable path to their future literacy development, both in school and in their communities.

Recommended Websites

Booklists for Children's Literature
   www.reading.org/resources/tools/choices.html
   www.ala.org/ala/yalsa/yalsa.cfm
To learn about books that are recommended by both teachers and students, visit these sites developed by two professional organizations.

The Read-Aloud Handbook
   www.trelease-on-reading.com/
Extensive information about Jim Trelease's efforts to engage children in books, and excerpts from his read-aloud handbook can be found here. Be sure to read his retirement letter!

Guidelines and Student Handouts for Implementing Read-Aloud Strategies in Your Classroom
>   http://teacher.scholastic.com/reading/bestpractices/comprehension/strategies.htm

This is a collection of guidelines, checklists, and assessment tools for think-aloud strategies.

Literature Circles Resource Center
>   www.litcircles.org

This site provides guidelines for establishing literature circles for both elementary grades and middle school as well.

Literature Circles Build Excitement for Books
>   www.education-world.com/a_curr/curr259.shtml

This reader-friendly article explains literature circles and provides links to other relevant sources.

Bookfinder
>   www.literatureplace.com/awards/book_finder_ by_subject.asp

Use this site to find book titles related to particular themes, authors, or awards.

Lesson Example: "Give Them a Hand: Promoting Positive Interaction in Literature Circles"
>   www.readwritethink.org/lessons/lesson_view.asp?id=1078

This lesson teaches students skills for engaging in productive discussions.

Lesson Example: "Guided Comprehension: Visualizing Using the Sketch-to-Stretch Strategy"
>   www.readwritethink.org/lessons/lesson_view.asp?id=229

This lesson teaches students to interpret texts through drawing.

Lesson Example: "Creating a Class Pattern Book with Popular Culture Characters"
>   www.readwritethink.org/lessons/lesson_view.asp?id=1010

Young students take photos of popular culture characters and create a digital pattern book.

Author Study
>   http://teacher.scholastic.com/fieldtrp/

This Internet field trip links to many valuable ideas.

Author Studies
>   www.eric-carle.com/
>   www.tomie.com
>   www.janbrett.com

These three sites are wonderful for planning author studies.

Novel Study Links
>   http://edselect.com/novel_studies.htm

This site provides links to a wide variety of novel studies.

Teacher's Guide for the Novel Study, A Company of Fools
>   www.fitzhenry.ca/download/guides/CompanyofFoolsTG.pdf

Teachers have permission from the author and publisher to make copies of this guide for personal classroom and student use.

Rainbow Horizons Publishing
>   www.rainbowhorizons.com

The publishers will send one free unit study of choice.

Graphic Novels
>   www.noflyingnotights.com

This site is devoted to presenting reviews for graphic novels that kids of all ages will find useful, as well as those who work with them, to include teachers, librarians, and parents.

Guidelines for Selecting Kid-Safe Graphic Novels
>   www.graphicnovels.brodart.com/selection_criteria.htm

Selection criteria are presented in three age groups: 7 to 12, 10 to 14, and 12 to 19.

Explore Pop-Ups
>   www.robertsabuda.com/popmakesimple.asp

To integrate art with creative writing, follow the precise instructions for making simple pop-up books.

Stories on Stage
>   www.aaronshep.com

Go here for scripts for readers' theater performances; how-to tips for scripting, staging, and performing; and links to related Internet sites.

Script Packages
>   http://scriptsforschools.com

Annotated descriptions of scripts for readers of all levels can be purchased at this site.

MyEducationLab is a research-based learning tool that brings teaching to life. Go to the Gipe 7th Edition MyEducationLab for Reading Assessment site at www.myeducationlab.com to:

- Engage in multimedia exercises to help you build a deeper and more applied understanding of chapter content.
- Use extensive resources including videos from real classrooms, Praxis and licensure preparation, a lesson plan builder, and materials to help you in your teaching career.

CHAPTER 13

Strategic Reading for Expository Text

OBJECTIVES	*After you have read this chapter, you should be able to:*
	1. Identify ways to determine whether students know about and are able to use strategies for reading expository text.
	2. Describe the unique characteristics of expository reading and the Internet.
	3. Explain the value of media literacy for participation in a democratic society.
	4. Give examples of skimming versus scanning.
	5. Explain what happens in comprehension monitoring.
	6. Describe techniques for teaching self-questioning skills and postreading organizational skills.

VOCABULARY ALERT			
	comprehension monitoring	problem-based learning	skimming
	content-area literacy	(PBL)	studying
	during-reading stage	productive questioning	text-based collaborative
	K–W–L	reciprocal teaching	learning
	media literacy	ReQuest procedure	think-links
	metacognition	(reciprocal questioning)	understanding questions
	postreading stage	scanning	WebQuest
	prereading stage		

How do you intend to read this chapter? The steps you follow make up your plan, or strategy. If you are a good strategic reader you might proceed in the following manner:

1. *Look through the entire chapter and ask questions.* How long is this chapter? How much time will I need to read it? Do the headings refer to familiar ideas, or does this material seem difficult? Do the figures (tables or graphs) appear helpful?

2. *Decide on purposes for reading.* I want to know more about some of the terms used. The figures appear interesting. I want to know more about the techniques they represent.

3. *Read the material.* At the same time try to paraphrase sections (note taking) and continue asking questions. Do I know what this means? Do I see how I can apply this with students? Decide what needs further clarification from the instructor.

4. *Question yourself after reading the material.* Can you go to the objectives listed at the beginning of the chapter and honestly say you have met them? Can you outline, from memory mostly, the important points? Can you explain the meaning of the terms listed at the beginning of the chapter?

If you have never tried to read expository text, such as this textbook chapter, strategically, why not try it now, using the preceding list if you like? See whether employing a strategy helps you remember more. If you are convinced that using some kind of strategy helps you remember more of what you read, you will be more likely to teach expository reading strategies to your students.

Strategic readers understand that, when the purpose of reading includes the expectation of learning or remembering specific information, a different set of strategies is needed from what they use when reading for enjoyment. Expository reading, also known as **content-area literacy**, requires readers to use the following strategies: (a) think about what they already know about the topic; (b) clarify their purpose for reading; (c) focus their attention on the content; (d) monitor whether they are understanding what they read; (e) use fix-up strategies (look back, reread, read ahead, consult a dictionary) when they do not understand; (f) fit new material into what they already know; (g) take notes; (h) think aloud to be sure of their understanding; (i) create mental images to aid understanding of difficult concepts; (j) summarize what they have read by mapping or using some other form of graphic organizer; (k) evaluate their understanding of what they read and whether or not their purpose was achieved; and, (l) if necessary, seek outside sources for additional information.

In addition, expository text presents some unique challenges that differ from narrative text (Fang, 2008). The language of expository text reflects specialized knowledge about a topic. Thus, words that do not occur frequently in everyday language are used. The

Go to
MyEducationLab
and select the topic
*Content Area
Literacy*. Then, go to
the Activities and
Applications section,
and watch the video
entitled "Content
Area Literacy" to
hear Donna Ogle,
the developer of the
KWL strategy, talk
about the nature of
content area literacy
and expository text
features. Next re-
spond to the accom-
panying questions.

language is often technical and abstract. The density of concepts is high, which can lead to cognitive overload. The grammar structures in expository text differ as well, with passive voice commonly being used. Students need help in coping with the challenges presented by expository text through exposure and work with sentence expansion and rephrasing (see Chapter 8) and sentence completion using modified cloze techniques (see Chapter 9).

Skill in expository reading is also a prerequisite to **studying**, or learning information to demonstrate understanding of that information. An important characteristic of studying is that it is student-directed instruction. In other words, a teacher is not usually available to ask guiding questions, point out or clarify important concepts, or help with decisions about what to do next when material is not understood. Nevertheless, teachers need to demonstrate, or model, the variety of strategies available for reading expository text so that students can become independent learners. (Additional information about specific study skills can be found in Chapter 14.) Garner (1987) proposed the following six guidelines for developing strategic readers of expository text:

1. Teachers must care about the processes involved in reading and studying and must be willing to devote instructional time to them.

2. Teachers must do task analyses of strategies to be taught.

3. Teachers must present strategies as applicable to texts and tasks in more than one content domain.

4. Teachers must teach strategies over an entire year, not in just a single lesson or unit.

5. Teachers must provide students opportunities to practice strategies they have been taught.

6. Teachers must be prepared to let students teach each other about reading and studying processes. (pp. 131–138)

For teachers to effectively follow these six guidelines, they need to take the time to analyze the content material students will be expected to use. With the technique referred to as a content analysis, the teacher will examine the content material to determine the major concepts presented, noticing if there are technical terms and if the concepts are accompanied by visual aids (illustrations, graphs, photos). Then the teacher must determine which words are essential to understanding the content. Vocabulary can be general, specialized, or technical (see Chapter 10). Next, the teacher will establish the predominant organizational pattern of the material. The material may use a chronological pattern, listings or numbered paragraphs, comparison/contrast, cause/effect, or some combination of all these. If there are chapters, they are likely divided into sections. Questions might be provided at the beginning, interspersed throughout, or at the end of chapters. Once the material has been carefully scrutinized, the teacher identifies the skills students will need to unlock the meaning of the essential vocabulary, follow the organization and understand the concepts presented, or make connections to concepts already understood. Sometimes skill lessons may need to be taught prior to reading the material. The teacher might also think of interesting ways to present the material to enhance understanding of the concepts. Use of media, a guest speaker, simulations, or field trips could be arranged. At this point the teacher is ready to plan the lesson or unit and prepare students for the reading (see Chapter 2).

Go to
MyEducationLab
and first select the
topic *Overview of
Reading Assessment*.
Then go to the
Activities and
Applications section,
and complete the
simulation entitled
"The Reading Blues"
to learn more about
strategies that can
help upper elemen-
tary students achieve
success with exposi-
tory material.
Respond to the ac-
companying
questions.

ASSESSING AWARENESS OF STRATEGIC READING FOR EXPOSITORY TEXT

One quick way to determine whether students are aware of and use strategies for reading expository text is to administer a questionnaire similar to the one found in Appendix X. If you worry about students answering honestly, you can give the questionnaire on an anonymous basis to the entire group. A tally of the responses to each item indicates areas in which students as a whole need instruction.

Another way to assess students' strategic reading abilities is through observation. After directing a group of students to read some expository materials for later class discussion, observe their behavior. Some type of survey of the material should be apparent, such as a quick perusal of the title and headings or looking at pictures, charts, or graphs. Often, in a survey of the material, a strategic reader quickly reads the first and last paragraph in the various sections of the material or the introductory and summary passages.

After a survey of the material, most students start reading from the beginning. Observable behaviors, such as note taking, underlining, highlighting or marking material with Post-it notes, looking back at previously read text, or rereading, indicate that the reader is engaging strategically with the material.

A number of behaviors are possible when readers complete their reading. Some readers go back and try to outline the material. Others choose to go back and take notes or mark certain information.

Both the questionnaire and the observable behaviors indicate three phases in the process of strategic reading. A student may consistently exhibit behavior for one of the phases but not for all three. These phases will be discussed in detail in the next section.

INSTRUCTIONAL TECHNIQUES FOR DEVELOPING STRATEGIC READING FOR EXPOSITORY TEXT

A Framework for Strategic Expository Reading

As introduced in Chapter 11, when reading longer discourse, it is useful to apply a three-stage framework: prereading, during reading, and postreading. These three stages have specific characteristics when applied to expository, or content-area material.

Briefly, the **prereading stage** is characterized by attention to the overall theme of a selection. The student prepares to read the selection by considering what is already known about the topic. Headings, subheadings, graphs, tables, and new vocabulary words are typical items of concern at this stage. The student also clarifies a specific purpose for reading that helps in focusing attention on the content to be read.

The **during-reading stage** is more difficult to briefly describe because of the wide variety of possible behaviors. Ideally, this stage is characterized by active involvement with the print. The term *comprehension monitoring* has been used to describe one behavior that should be occurring at this stage (this topic will be discussed further in a later section). Readers who monitor their comprehension continuously ask themselves, "Do I understand this material?" (Baker, 1979). If material is not understood, fix-up strategies must be used. The reader also tries to relate any new information to what is already known and to recognize the organizational structure of the text (see also Chapter 11).

In the **postreading stage**, students engage in activities that help them retain information. The most commonly used activities are organizational (outlines, maps), translational (paraphrases, annotations, formulating questions), and repetitional (recitations, rehearsals). Following are instructional techniques for each stage.

Prereading. Throughout this text I have emphasized analyzing the processes involved in the various reading domains. Even for the domain of strategic reading for expository text, task requirements, or underlying processes, are important considerations. When the purpose is to learn and remember information, students must look over the material: titles, headings, illustrations, tables, introductions, summaries, and topic sentences. The prereading stage thus demands that students be proficient in **skimming** and **scanning**. "*Skimming* and *scanning* both refer to rapid reading during which the reader does not direct attention to all of the information on the page. *Scanning* is fast reading to obtain answers to specific questions. . . . *skimming* is rapid reading to find out what something is about or a general idea" (Schachter, 1978, p. 149).

Flexibility in rate of reading is a skill that every student can and should practice. Even young children can be asked to skim or scan pictures for particular objects or colors. They can scan magazines or newspaper articles for a specific letter of the alphabet or catalogs for objects beginning with a specific sound. Just about any type of printed material can be used to teach skimming and scanning, including telephone books (both yellow and white pages), menus, catalogs, newspapers, or textbooks.

Direct instruction for skimming and scanning. Developing readers often demonstrate a tendency to read every word. As students progress through the grades, teaching them when and how to vary their reading rate takes on increasing importance. An introduction to skimming and scanning uses a technique that shows the student what is meant by flexible reading rate, or skimming and scanning. For example, ask a student to look up a classmate's phone number in the telephone book (father's name: William Jenkins). Point out that the student would not start at the beginning and read the whole book or even start at the beginning of the *J*s and read through all the names beginning with *J*. Instead, using alphabetizing skills, the student finds the general location and then scans to locate *Jenkins, William*. If asked, students are usually able to identify other situations from real life in which they skim or scan material; for example, scanning the TV schedule to decide what channel to watch or a recipe to see if the needed ingredients are available.

In direct instruction, students are taught to skim and scan for a variety of purposes. Initially, directions are simple, with activities chosen specifically to teach the concepts of skimming and scanning. Eventually, activities are more directly related to what students will be expected to do on their own as strategic readers of expository material. Here are some specific activities:

1. Direct the students to scan a passage that is easy to read and underline 10 verbs. You might set time limits on this task and gradually decrease the time allowed.

2. Direct the students to locate five items on a menu that sell for less than three dollars.

3. With the librarian's help, give students copies of brand-new book arrivals. Have each student skim a book (consider a time limit) and briefly share the general idea of the book.

4. Give students a list of questions to answer from the classified ads: How much does the 2008 Mustang cost? What breed of cat was lost? Where can you call to buy a used dishwasher? How much does a 30-foot sailboat cost?

5. Questions similar to those in activity 4 can be used with content-area material. Tables of contents and indexes are ready sources for similar questions. Here are some sample question starters: Find the place at which . . . Locate the page on which . . . List the chapters that . . .

6. More directly related to studying is an activity that uses a content-area textbook and question guide. Tell students to look specifically for the answers to the questions and *not* to read every word. Sample directions:

   • Look at the paragraph headings for pages 17 through 24. After reading *just the headings,* write a sentence or two that tells what this section is about.

- List the steps that tell how a bill is passed.
- Read the section "The President Wears Many Hats" to find out how many different jobs the president has.

Accessing prior knowledge. Ineffective readers often start reading without first thinking about the subject of what they are reading. They fail to realize that they may already know something about the material and that this knowledge can help them during their reading. Teachers can demonstrate several useful strategies that will help these readers focus on what they already know about a subject.

An uncomplicated procedure discussed by Ogle (1986) for use with any content or grade level, individually or with groups, is the **K–W–L** strategy. The *K* step requires that students identify what is already *known* about the subject. If a group is applying the strategy, this step involves brainstorming information the group already knows about the subject. (This information is then categorized.) The *W* step requires students to reflect on what is already known and determine what they still *want* to learn. Thus, the *W* becomes a question: "What do I want to find out?" The *L* step actually occurs *after* the material is read. Each student writes down what was *learned*. Students should make sure that any questions they identified at the *W* stage have been answered. A chart similar to that found in Figure 13.1 can provide an organizational structure for the reader.

Modifications of the K–W–L strategy have also been developed. The *What Do You . . .* chart (International Reading Association, 1988) seen in Figure 13.2 combines aspects of the K–W–L and DRTA (see Chapter 11) formats. Such a chart serves as a graphic organizer and encourages the student to focus on the subject, the title, the cover of a book, or the illustrations within a text chapter and distinguish between what is known for certain and what is predicted.

Depending on the age and ability of the students, a simplified version of such organizational charts might focus only on accessing prior knowledge and making predictions. Such a version is *What do you know?/What do you think?* (J. Richards, personal communication, Oct., 1988). Given a topic, title, or book cover, the student states what is known ("just the facts") before stating what is predicted. When introducing any new strategy, such as *What do you know?/What do you think?*, begin by keeping all other aspects of the lesson familiar. For example, because the strategy is new, a well-known

Go to MyEducationLab and select the topic *Content Area Literacy*. Then, go to the Activities and Applications section, and watch the video entitled "Building Background Knowledge" to see how to implement the KWL strategy. Next respond to the accompanying questions.

Go to MyEducationLab and select the topic *Content Area Literacy*. Then, go to the Activities and Applications section, and watch the video entitled "Reading for Information" to gain a better appreciation for the value of graphic organizers for use with expository text. Next respond to the accompanying questions.

Figure 13.1   Chart for the K–W–L Strategy

———— K ————	———— W ————	———— L ————
What Do I **KNOW?**	What Do I **WANT** to Learn?	What Did I **LEARN?**
Categories of information I expect to use: A. B. C. D.		

Figure 13.2   What Do You . . .

Know You Know?	Think You Know?	Think You Will Learn?	Know You Learned?

familiar narrative should be used to introduce the strategy before moving to use with expository material. Thus, given the title and cover of the story *Goldilocks and the Three Bears,* the stated facts might include the following:

This is a story about a girl, Goldilocks, and three bears.
The bears have a house in the woods (based on cover illustration).
The girl has yellow hair (based on cover illustration).
There are two big bears and one small bear (based on cover illustration).

Predictions are then based on the known facts and also on the reader's familiarity with other stories of a similar nature. Responses to the question "What do you think?" might include the following:

I think this story will tell about what happens to Goldilocks and the bears.
I think the bears will scare the girl.
I think Goldilocks visits the bears in their house in the woods.
I think that Goldilocks will make friends with the little bear.
I think that the bears will help Goldilocks.

When a book cover or illustration is used, the first question can be changed to "What do you see?" and a three-column map can be prepared for written responses, as seen in Figure 13.3. In this way, even very young students can learn to be strategic readers by beginning with familiar narrative material and moving into more difficult, expository material. See Figure 13.4 for an example of the three-column map applied to an expository science selection on whales.

Additional modifications of the K–W–L include the K–W–W (where I can learn this)–L (Bryan, 1998), the K–W–L–Q (more questions; Schmidt, 1999), and the K–W–L–S (what I still need to learn; Sippola, 1995). K–W–L modifications have even been incorporated into reading guides (Massey, 2007). For example, using questions from the end of a chapter, or even an informal reading inventory, one guide proceeds from "Questions" to "What I think . . . because," to "What the book says," and finally to "Was I right?" This format would also work well when introducing QARs (see Chapter 11).

Richek (1987) discussed a variation of the DRTA (see Chapter 11) that focuses on accessing prior knowledge related to the expository material to be read. The variation, DRTA

| **Figure 13.3** | Three-Column Map for *Goldilocks and the Three Bears* |

What Do You See?	**What Do You Know?**	**What Do You Think?**
a girl with yellow hair	Goldilocks is a girl	The bears will scare Goldilocks
two big bears, one little bear	There are three bears	Goldilocks will hide from the bears
house in the woods	This is a fairy tale	The story will begin "Once upon a time . . ."

| **Figure 13.4** | Three-Column Map for Expository Material about Whales |

What Do You See?	**What Do You Know?**	**What Do You Think?**
a big gray fish	This is about a gray whale.	The gray whale is the biggest fish in the world.
some spots on the fish	A whale spouts water.	A whale can stay under water a long time.
a tail that has two fins	Whales eat smaller fish.	Whales have to eat a lot.

SOURCE, helps students recognize that readers use both the text and their prior knowledge when making predictions. In DRTA SOURCE, students stop after making predictions and identify which part of each prediction was based on something in the text and which part on prior knowledge. The value of this strategy is that it helps students become aware of how important their own prior knowledge is, even when reading expository material.

During Reading. A wide variety of behavior is seen in the during-reading stage of strategic expository reading. After previewing the material, good strategic readers generally start at the beginning and read through the material, engaging in what is termed **comprehension monitoring**. Through this process, students constantly evaluate their level of understanding of what is being read. The ability to monitor one's own comprehension is so critical to expository reading that this topic deserves further elaboration.

Comprehension monitoring. Research in the area of comprehension monitoring is part of a larger area of study called **metacognition**. Instruction in metacognitive strategies can be very effective for readers having difficulty:

> Metacognition refers to one's knowledge concerning one's own cognitive processes and products or anything related to them, e.g., the learning-relevant properties of information or data. For example, I am engaging in metacognition (metamemory, metalearning, metaattention, metalanguage, or whatever) if I notice that I am having more trouble learning *A* than *B*; if it strikes me that I should double-check *C* before accepting it as a fact; if it occurs to me that I had better scrutinize each and every alternative in any multiple-choice type task situation before deciding which is the best one; if I sense that I had better make a note of *D* because I may forget. (Flavell, 1976, p. 232)

Metacognitive activities of interest for the during-reading stage include keeping track of the success with which one's comprehension is proceeding and, if comprehension breaks down, taking action to remedy the failure (Baker, 1979; Baker & Brown, 1984; Brown, 1980; Garner, 1987; Markman, 1979, 1981; Wagoner, 1983). Research in this area yields ample evidence that poor comprehension-monitoring ability is characteristic of ineffective readers (National Reading Panel, 2000). Additionally, comprehension-monitoring ability is not likely to develop simply with maturity; it depends on knowledge, experience, and instruction (Brown & DeLoache, 1978).

Beginning readers and those who struggle with comprehension are often deficient in evaluating their understanding of text (Baker & Brown, 1984; Garner, 1980; Markman, 1979; Paris & Myers, 1981; Winograd & Johnston, 1980). If the reader does not recognize whether the text has been understood, teaching techniques for correcting comprehension breakdowns would be premature. Thus, teachers must first help students develop their own comprehension awareness.

For readers to be able to monitor their own comprehension, they need to be actively involved with what they are reading. Emergent and beginning readers and other readers having difficulty demonstrating monitoring behaviors would benefit from the "Yes/No . . . Why?" and "It Reminds Me of . . ." strategies (Richards & Gipe, 1992). These two strategies easily involve students by encouraging them to use their background knowledge to make decisions about their understanding of the material. In the "Yes/No . . . Why?" strategy, the teacher and students both read silently (or orally if desired) an agreed-upon portion of the text. This might be a page or a paragraph.

Following the silent reading, the teacher models a *yes* and a *no*. A *yes* is something that the reader likes or understands about the passage. A *no* is something not liked or not understood about the passage. A reason for the *yes* or *no* is also provided. Then a student shares a *yes* and a *no* with reasons. For example, the teacher might introduce and model the strategy by reading the familiar nursery rhyme *Jack and Jill* and then say, "My *yes* is that I like the way Jack and Jill were doing their chores because it tells me they are helpful to their mother. My *no* is that I didn't like that they fell because they got hurt." Then a student might respond with, "My *yes* is that I like the name Jill because my cousin's name is Jill. My *no* is that I don't know what Jack broke. I never heard that word before." After a period of sharing *yes/no's,* with the teacher modeling a variety of responses to expository text, the students will become more involved with the material and will become better able to summarize, clarify, predict, and identify main ideas about the material.

To be able to say what a passage "reminds them of," students have to make a connection between the material and their own background, especially when the material being read needs to be learned or remembered, such as with expository text (Carver, 1992; Harvey & Goudvis, 2000). Again with teacher modeling, students can tell or write their responses about what they are reminded of following the reading of a brief portion of text. For example, after reading a paragraph in a newspaper article that talks about flooding along the Mississippi River, the teacher might say, "This reminds me of the story of Noah's ark." The teacher may choose to elaborate further, depending on the needs of the students. Then students are given the opportunity to respond to the same paragraph. As students become more comfortable with these techniques, they will be better able to identify points at which they are not understanding what they read and will then be receptive to learning what to do to improve that situation (strategic reading behaviors combined with fix-up strategies).

Teaching strategic reading behaviors to all learners is especially important because it puts them in control of their own learning. Instruction in strategic reading behaviors for expository text requires that students learn and use comprehension-monitoring skills. Because one of the first steps in comprehension monitoring is recognizing whether the

Figure 13.5   Example of a Thinkalong Self-Monitoring Checklist for Strategic Reading Behaviors

SELF-MONITORING SHEET—THINKALONGS

Thinkalong	Always	Sometimes	Never
I know when I don't understand something.		√	
I ask myself questions to understand the text.		√	
I make a picture in my mind to help me understand the text.		√	
I reread to help myself understand.	√		
I personalize the ideas and relate them to my own experiences. I think about something I know that fits into the new information.		√	
I reread when I don't know what a word means.	√		
I predict what I will read about next in the text.		√	

Name: _Louis_

Date: _October 15_

Source: From Susan M. Glazer, *Reading Comprehension: Self-Monitoring Strategies to Develop Independent Readers.* Copyright © 1992 by Scholastic, New York, NY. Reprinted with permission.

text has been understood, that seems a logical place to begin instruction. Therefore, when students are comfortable with strategies such as "Yes/No . . . Why?" and "It Reminds Me of . . .," they are ready to develop strategies to use during reading.

Glazer (1992) presented a *"Thinkalong"* strategy accompanied by a self-monitoring checklist (see Figure 13.5) for use during reading. Students could complete these self-monitoring sheets on a regular basis for inclusion in student portfolios as evidence of comprehension-monitoring skills. The types of strategic behaviors that are individually modeled for students are listed here. Teachers can use think-aloud procedures (Davey, 1983) to model each of these strategic behaviors:

MI Connection: intrapersonal

1. Making a picture in one's mind about the text
2. Predicting from pictures, subtitles, and words during reading
3. Asking oneself questions about the text
4. Going back and rereading when the text doesn't make sense
5. Personalizing the text based on one's own experiences
6. Guessing the meanings of words during reading (p. 64)

Self-Questioning. Research examining self-interrogation ability reveals that this is a promising area of instruction for improving comprehension-monitoring skills (Andre & Anderson, 1978/1979; Frase & Schwartz, 1975; Schmelzer, 1975). Results from these studies indicate that when reading expository text students remember more if they formulate questions by either writing them down or verbalizing them to a friend. Nolan (1991) found that a "self-questioning with prediction-making" strategy was more effective than self-questioning alone because readers then must monitor not only whether questions are answered but also whether predictions are supported. The following steps are learned in this strategy:

1. Identify the main idea.
2. Write down the main idea.
3. Think of a question based on the main idea and write it down.
4. Answer your question.
5. Predict what will happen next. (p. 135)

Anderson (1980) recommended the use of **understanding questions** to help students monitor their comprehension. Because obstacles to comprehension may occur at the word, sentence, or paragraph level, understanding questions check all three. Some examples are: Does this sentence have any new words? Is a word I know being used in a new way? Did this sentence make sense? Does this sentence fit with what I already know about the topic? What was this section about? Can I explain this in my own words? What were the important facts? Have I read something similar to this before?

Self-generation of questions may be an effective strategy because the student is forced to pause frequently, deal with the effort to understand, determine whether comprehension exists, and finally, become concerned about what to do if comprehension has not been achieved. However, students do not automatically generate important questions just because they are asked to do so. Their teachers must model questioning skills and use productive questioning during instruction (Dantonio & Beisenherz, 2001). **Productive questioning** is concerned with both the process of thinking and learning the content of the text. Open question stems and thoughtful feedback to students' answers will help guide the way students think about the content of their text as they read. Open question stems include phrases such as *what can you, in what way, how*, and *why*. Such stems encourage meaningful discussion compared to closed question stems that imply a "right" answer, such as *do you know, can you, will you*, or *are you*. Notice the difference in changing the question, *"Can you tell me the causes of the Civil War?"* compared to *"What can you tell me about the causes of the Civil War?"*

Instructional techniques for explicitly teaching students how to use understanding questions and read expository text strategically are not taught directly or modeled often enough. Nevertheless, it is clear that "helping poor readers become strategic readers demands modeling of mental processes" (Duffy, Roehler, & Herrmann, 1988, p. 766). Duffy and colleagues (1988) emphasized the importance of the teacher modeling the mental processes (as opposed to procedural steps) that would otherwise be invisible to the students. In this way, the students will have heard examples of appropriate reasoning they can then use to read strategically for themselves (for examples of modeling using shared reading, see Fisher, Frey, & Lapp, 2008).

A few promising techniques for training self-questioning behaviors are presented in the literature. Collins and Smith (1980) recommended a modeling technique in which the teacher demonstrates the various types of understanding questions the students could ask themselves. The teacher tries to think aloud for the students, showing them where and when they would appropriately ask questions. The actual instructional method suggested by Collins and Smith (1980) proceeds in three stages similar to Singer's (1978) active comprehension lesson (see Chapter 11). Initially, the teacher models self-questioning by reading a passage aloud, pausing, and asking relevant understanding questions along the way. The second stage includes the students by asking them to pose the understanding questions, gradually lessening the teacher's involvement. In the third stage students read silently with teacher input only if they encounter difficulties.

Recall structured comprehension (Cohn, 1969), introduced in Chapter 11, as a sentence-by-sentence technique that uses a particular set of questions to help students clarify their understanding of what they are reading. See Figure 13.6 for an example of a structured comprehension lesson used with a social studies selection.

Another technique similar to structured comprehension is the **ReQuest procedure** (**Reciprocal Questioning**) developed by Anthony Manzo (1969, 1985). This procedure, which is used with individuals or small groups, aids students in setting their own purposes for reading. The teacher guides the students through the silent reading of as many sentences

---

Figure 13.6   Structured Comprehension Lesson

Background: The student is told that the Constitution is a list of the rights that the American people have. Soon after the Constitution was written, the people wanted to add more rights. These additional rights are called the Bill of Rights.

Passage: "The Bill of Rights says that every person can speak freely. A person can criticize the government or its officials if he believes that they are not doing a good job. We call this freedom of speech."

—Herbert H. Gross et al., *Exploring Regions of the Western Hemisphere*

Questions

Sentence 1
1. Does "speak freely" mean you won't have to pay before speaking?
2. Is the Bill of Rights a person?
3. How can the Bill of Rights "say" anything?
4. This sentence means:
   a. the Bill of Rights thinks no one should have to pay to speak
   b. an important right of all people is to be able to say whatever they think is important to say
   c. a new law was passed that has cured people who couldn't speak, so that now they can speak

Sentence 2
1. What does "criticize" mean?
2. What does "its" refer to?
3. Who does "he" refer to?
4. Who does "they" refer to?
5. This sentence means:
   a. if the government or the people who are leaders in the government are not doing a good job, anybody can say that they aren't
   b. when the government does not do a good job, the people must believe that they are doing a good job anyway
   c. it is impossible for the government to do a bad job

Sentence 3
1. Who does "we" refer to?
2. What does "this" refer to?
3. "Freedom of speech" means no one can charge to hear a speech. True or false?
4. This sentence means:
   a. all people have the right to speak out if the government does not do what it's supposed to do
   b. the Bill of Rights is also called freedom of speech
   c. the government can say anything it wants to for free

SPOTLIGHT ON ENGLISH LEARNERS

GIST—Generating Interaction between Schemata and Text

GIST (Cunningham, 1982) is a particularly effective strategy for English learners because the participants have a chance to discuss and clarify meaning with the help of a strong English language user as they decide on the best summary sentence for a selection from an expository text. The teacher identifies a section of text that is likely to cause difficulty for the English learner and decides to summarize this text paragraph by paragraph (or other logical stopping points). The class is divided into groups so that there is at least one strong English language speaker or reader in each group, as well as other students of the same language background as the English learner(s) who may be able to provide language support if needed. The goal of GIST is to facilitate understanding of expository text material through discussion and negotiation of a best summary sentence consisting of no more than 25 words. This summary can be completed first in the student's native language and then translated to English. However, if the teacher's purpose includes facilitating English communication, then the discussion and summary sentence generated should be done solely in English. As each group completes their summary sentence, they can share the sentences with the whole class for further discussion. The teacher acts as a facilitator, making sure the summary sentences do indeed capture the "gist" of the material read, by asking appropriate questions or further supporting students' understanding of the material. Once the entire text selection has been read, the groups read and compare all of their summary sentences, maintaining a 25-word maximum as additional material is read and summarized. By the end of the paragraph, all students should have an effective and concise summary of the material and clarification of previous misconceptions.

of a selection as are necessary to enable them to complete the passage independently. Once again, as in structured comprehension, student and teacher exchange questions sentence by sentence. Every question asked by a student or teacher must be answered from recall, or an explanation must be given for why it cannot be answered. The teacher's questions serve as models for the kinds of questions students should ask themselves while reading. Also, when responding to students' questions, the teacher gives reinforcement, such as "That was an excellent question" or "You might want to reword the question in this way . . ." or "I think your questions are really improving." When the teacher thinks students are ready to proceed independently (no more than three paragraphs should be handled reciprocally), a general purpose-setting question is asked: "Did we raise the best question or purpose for which to read this selection?" (Manzo, 1985). At this point, the rest of the selection is read silently.

A technique born of Manzo's original ReQuest procedure, and which proceeds paragraph by paragraph, is called **reciprocal teaching** (Palincsar & Brown, 1984, 1986). In this interactive procedure, students are taught to summarize sections of text, anticipate questions that a teacher may ask, make predictions about upcoming text, and clarify unclear sections of text. Initially, the teacher plays a major instructional role by modeling these behaviors and helping students in a collaborative effort with the wording of summaries and questions. Working with seventh graders who were described as adequate decoders but poor comprehenders,[1] Palincsar and Brown were able to train the students to use comprehension-monitoring behaviors after only 15 to 20 sessions. They also trained classroom teachers to use the technique with similar success.

Reciprocal teaching can be used with either individuals or small groups. (For best results with poor comprehenders, use small groups of two or three students.) The adult teacher takes turns with each student participant role-playing "teacher" and leading a dialogue on a section of text read, usually a paragraph. After each section, the "teacher"

---

[1]The students decoded at least 80 words per minute with a maximum of two words per minute incorrect and were two grades or more behind on a standardized reading comprehension test.

asks a main idea question. If this is difficult, a summary is attempted. A clarification of some aspect of the text may be asked for, or a prediction about upcoming text may be given. Feedback and praise are given by the adult teacher whenever appropriate. In group sessions, feedback also comes from other students.

MI Connection:
interpersonal

Early training sessions require much guidance from the teacher. As students become better able to summarize and ask main idea questions, the teacher's level of participation decreases. Sessions should last about 30 minutes. Although Palincsar and Brown worked with expository passages of about 1,500 words, any type or length of reading material can be used.

Another way to help students develop their self-questioning ability is to provide study guides that list the kinds of questions students should ask themselves. The revised extended anticipation guide (Duffelmeyer & Baum, 1992) is a good example (see Figure 13.7). Part 1 is a prereading activity in which students activate their schema for the topic by reflecting on their beliefs and perceptions and agreeing or disagreeing with teacher-developed statements about the topic. Class discussion following Part 1 will reveal student differences and provide further motivation for reading the selection, in addition to reading to verify choices made in Part 1. Part 2 is completed *during* reading. Here students are constantly asked to question their choices in Part 1. If the reading supports a choice, the student checks the *yes* column and writes evidence or justification in the space provided. Likewise, if a choice is *not* supported, the student checks the *no* column and writes a paraphrase of what was stated in the material to refute the choice.

Once students have reached a level of awareness regarding comprehension monitoring, they can deal with the question of "what to do next" (Anderson, 1980) when they do not understand what they have read. Anderson provides the following guidelines:

1. If a reader reads something that he or she does not understand, the reader may decide to take some strategic action immediately or may store the information in memory as a pending question.

2. If the reader stores it as a pending question, he or she may formulate a possible meaning (usually one) that is stored as a tentative hypothesis.

3. If the reader forms a pending question, he or she usually continues to read.

4. If a triggering event occurs after the reader forms the pending question (that is, too many pending questions or repetitions of the same pending question), the reader may take some strategic action.

5. If the reader takes some strategic action, he or she may:

   a. *Reread* some portion of the text in order to collect more information that will either answer a pending question or form a tentative hypothesis related to a pending question

   b. *Jump ahead* in the text to see if there are headings or paragraphs that refer to the pending question and might answer the pending question

   c. *Consult* an outside source (such as a dictionary, glossary, encyclopedia, or expert) for an answer to some pending question

   d. Make a *written record* of a pending question

   e. *Think/reflect* about the pending question and related information that the reader has in memory

   f. *Quit* reading the text

6. If the strategic action is successful, the reader usually continues to read from the point at which the comprehension failure was last encountered.

7. If the strategic action is not successful, the reader usually continues to read by taking some other strategic action. (pp. 498–499)

Figure 13.7 Example of a Revised Extended Anticipation Guide

Part 1: Before Reading

Directions: Before you begin your reading assignment, *Understanding Autism*, read each of the sentences below. If you think the sentence is true, put a check in the Agree column. If you think the sentence is false, put a check in the Disagree column. You will be asked to explain your choices.

Autism	Agree	Disagree
1. People with autism lack normal language ability.	☑	☐
2. Mental retardation is a characteristic of autism.	☐	☑
3. Autism is a more common disorder than Down syndrome.	☐	☑
4. Autism is believed to be the result of poor parenting.	☐	☑
5. Hans Asperger is close to finding a cure for autism.	☑	☐
6. The essential characteristic of autism is mindblindness, or an inability to understand what other people are thinking or feeling.	☑	☐

Part 2: During Reading

Directions: If the information you read supports your choices in Part 1, put a check in the "Yes" column below. Then write what the text says in your own words in Column A under "Why is my choice correct?" If what you read does NOT support your choices, put a check in the "No" column. Then write what the text says in your own words in Column B under "Why is my choice incorrect?"

Support?		A	B
Yes	No	Why is my choice correct?	Why is my choice incorrect?
1. ☐	☑		True only for "classic" autism. Mild versions still have high language function.
2. ☑	☐	Many with autism test in the normal range for intelligence.	
3. ☐	☑		Autism affects 1 in every 150 American children, more common than Down syndrome or childhood cancer.
4. ☑	☐	Autism is brain-based; suspected causes are: genetic mutations, viruses, toxic chemicals.	
5. ☐	☑		H.A. is the pediatrician who identified a mild version of autism (called Asperger Syndrome).
6. ☑	☐	Research suggests mindblindness is the core of all autism. Even those with mild forms cannot interpret facial expressions or emotions, and have difficulty with social interaction.	

An instructional technique described by Babbs (1984) is appropriate for this area. Using a reading plan sheet and comprehension-monitoring cards, readers are first taught to be aware that they may have a comprehension problem while reading (the plan sheet) and then are taught strategies for dealing with comprehension failure (the cards).

The reading plan sheet asks five questions: "(1) What is reading? (2) What is my goal? (3) How difficult is the text? (4) How can I accomplish my goal? (5) How can I check on whether or not I accomplished my goal?" (Babbs, 1984, p. 201). The questions presented on this plan sheet represent a strategy, and you may see similarities between these questions and the strategy presented at the beginning of this chapter. Students should practice using the plan sheet so that they ask these questions automatically before beginning to read expository material.

The comprehension-monitoring cards encourage readers, in a step-by-step fashion, to evaluate their own understanding of the text read and also aid readers in knowing what to do when a comprehension problem occurs. The nine cards and their identifying numbers are as follows: "(1) Click—I understand. (2) Clunk—I don't understand. (3) Read on. (4) Reread the sentence. (5) Go back and reread the paragraph. (6) Look in the glossary. (7) Ask someone. (8) What did it say? (to check comprehension at the paragraph level) (9) What do I remember? (to check comprehension at the page level)" (Babbs, 1984, pp. 201–202).

MI Connection: logical-mathematical

A modeling procedure is recommended to teach students to use the cards. The teacher reads a sentence of text and then asks, "Did I understand that?" If the answer is "yes," the teacher raises the Click card and goes on to the next sentence. If the answer is "no," the teacher raises the Clunk card and selects cards 3 through 7. If the problem is with a word, the order of the strategy cards is 4–3–6–7. If the problem is with the whole sentence or with a pronoun referent, the order of the strategy cards is 4–5–3–7. The teacher models all of these possibilities using a variety of sentences.

After a complete paragraph has been modeled, the teacher looks away from the page, holds up card 8, and answers that question. If the question cannot be answered, the paragraph is reread without further use of the strategy cards. Likewise, after a complete page has been modeled, the teacher again looks away from the text, holds up card 9, and answers the question. If the question cannot be answered, the page is reread using card 8 after each paragraph.

Once the teacher has modeled the process, Babbs (1984) recommended that each student have a turn modeling before going on to individual practice. She also stated that 15 sessions of 22 minutes each were allowed for learning both the reading plan sheet questions and the use of the comprehension-monitoring cards. At that point the students could describe details of both of these elements from memory.

A similar format is described by Klingner and Vaughn (1999) and is called **collaborative strategic reading** (CSR). CSR includes four comprehension strategies that students apply in small collaborative groups. The four strategies are previewing (prereading), click and clunk (active reading), get the gist (active reading), and wrap-up (postreading). Found to be especially helpful for English learners, the four Clunk cards direct students as follows: "(1) Reread the sentence with the clunk and look for key ideas to help you figure out the unknown word. Think about what makes sense. (2) Reread the sentences before and after the clunk looking for clues. (3) Look for a prefix or suffix in the word that might help. (4) Break the word apart and look for smaller words that you know " (Klingner & Vaughn, 1999, p. 742). For more information about CSR, visit the website listed at the end of this chapter.

Text-based collaborative learning is another small group technique for helping students work with expository material (Klingner et al., 2004; Langer, 2001). In **text-based collaborative learning**, students work with one or two other students to discuss, question, clarify, and prepare written outlines involving expository text. After the teacher has introduced the text material by providing sufficient background information, students work together to notice how the text information is organized (for example, subheadings within chapters, sequential or chronological progression, a proposition with supporting paragraphs). They can determine questions (such as who, what, when, where, why, how) and prepare general outlines using the headings and subheadings in the text material before even beginning the reading. Students will then begin their reading with a purpose. As students read silently, they write notes about unknown words, confusing parts, or answers to their questions and start to fill in their general outlines. Following the reading, students return to the text with their partner or small group and discuss their notes in an effort to clarify the text.

Such activities will help students form habits of (a) thinking about what they know and believe about a topic *before* reading, (b) questioning their understanding of material *during* reading, and (c) focusing on clarifying new information *after* reading.

Postreading. In the postreading stage of strategic expository reading, activities that help the student organize and remember important information are appropriate. Outlining, paraphrasing, and reciting, or rehearsal of information, are common activities for this last stage. These activities can be difficult for students to master, however.

Mapping. *Mapping* (also called *semantic webbing*) aids the learner in linking ideas together (see also Chapters 10, 11, and 12). As discussed here, mapping is intended as a substitute for the organizational activity of outlining. Hanf (1971) discussed three basic steps for designing a map: (a) identify the main idea, (b) identify principal parts that support the main idea (called secondary categories), and (c) identify supporting details. The skeleton of a map may be completed during the prereading stage (the title of the selection becoming the main idea or central theme and the headings becoming secondary categories that support the main idea). However, the map itself should be completed from memory during the postreading stage. The student must add the supporting details. If the map cannot be completed, the student knows to go back and reread the material. Thus there is a built-in feedback device. If the student can complete some parts of the map but not others, the map has provided feedback on categories needing further review. An example of a map for the study of a science chapter entitled "Power for Work"[2] is found in Figure 13.8.

When the K–W–L strategy discussed earlier is combined with mapping and summarization, the technique helps students construct meaning from the text in an independent fashion. This modification of K–W–L, called *K–W–L Plus* (Carr & Ogle, 1987), has been used successfully with secondary readers who have reading and writing difficulty. Basically, students must think critically about what they have read in order to organize, restructure, and apply what they have learned to the formation of a map and a written summary. Figure 13.9 shows how a ninth grader went from the K–W–L listings to a concept map. The map can then be used as an aid for preparing a written summary and also preparing for exams.

Think-Links. Wilson (1981) referred to another organizational strategy called **think-links**. On completion of the during-reading stage of study, the teacher directs the students to think about what they have read. The following steps are then taken (Figure 13.10):

1. Write the name of the person the chapter is about (Lincoln) and some words that describe his early life.

2. Ask students for examples that show that Lincoln's early life was hard and record them.

3. Repeat Step 2 using other descriptive words.

---

[2]From *In Your Neighborhood* (pp. 91–96) by A. O. Baker, G. C. Maddox, and H. B. Warrin, 1955, New York: Rand McNally.

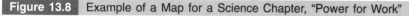

Figure 13.8   Example of a Map for a Science Chapter, "Power for Work"

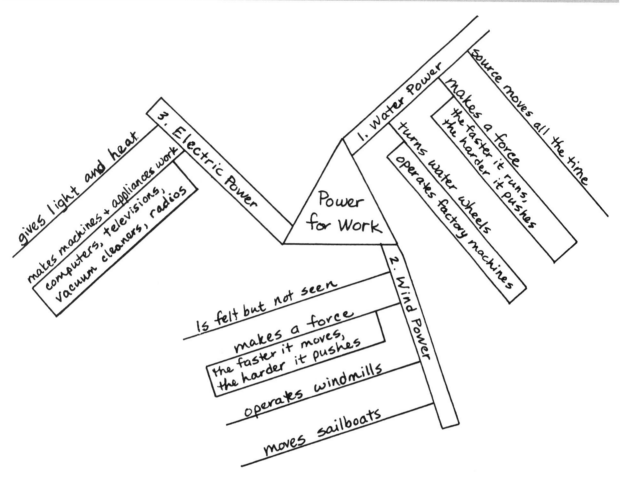

Mapping is thinking: constructing and creating the organizational design of ideas, selecting the information that is relevant, sorting this into its proper place, relating all facts to the whole and relating facts to other facts, and finally responding with personal reaction to the material. (Hanf, 1971, p. 229)

After all of the words have been used, the students have actually reconstructed, graphically, the important parts of the material read.

Once the teacher has helped students develop several think-links, they can start to develop them on their own. Think-links are used to summarize any content-area reading material and should be constructed during the instructional process with the students so they can see a variety of formats.

Paragraph frames. As discussed in Chapter 11, paragraph frames provide a useful in-structional tool for helping students write about what they learn in content areas (Cudd & Roberts, 1989). Intended for students of all grade levels, the introduction of paragraph frames is easiest with sequentially ordered material. A cloze format provides sentence starters focusing on the organizational pattern of the text. The teacher might write a brief paragraph based on a content-area topic just read, using such key words as *first, next, then, now, finally,* and *after this.* The individual sentences are put on sentence strips;

MI Connection: spatial

Figure 13.9 Example of a Ninth-Grader's K–W–L Work Sheet and Resulting Concept Map

A ninth-grade disabled reader's K–W–L work sheet on killer whales

K (Know)	**W** (Want to know)	**L** (Learned)
They live in oceans.	Why do they attack people?	D — They are the biggest member of the dolphin family.
They are vicious.	How fast can they swim?	D — They weigh 10,000 pounds and get 30 feet long.
They eat each other.	What kind of fish do they eat?	F — They eat squids, seals, and other dolphins.
They are mammals.	What is their description?	A — They have good vision underwater.
	How long do they live?	F — They are carnivorous (meat eaters).
	How do they breathe?	A — They are the second smartest animal on earth.
		D — They breathe through blowholes.
		A — They do not attack unless they are hungry.
Description		D — They are warm-blooded.
Food		A — They have echo-location (sonar).
Location		L — They are found in the oceans.

Final category designations developed for column L, information learned about killer whales:
A = abilities, D = description, F = food, L = location

The ninth grader's concept map

Abilities (2)
kill for food
detect pebble-sized aspirin tablet in 30 feet of water
find food in cloudy water
echo-location

Description (1)
warm-blooded
dolphin family
second smartest animal next to man
born alive
10,000 lbs.
30 feet long
blow holes

Killer whales

Location (4)
all oceans
sea worlds

Food (3)
small dolphins
carnivorous (meat eaters)
400 lbs. salmon daily

(1) through (4) indicate the order of categories the student chose later for writing a summary.

Source: Adapted from Carr, Eileen M., & Ogle, Donna M. (1987, April), "K–W–L Plus: A Strategy for Comprehension and Summarization," Journal of Reading, 30(7), 626–631. Reprinted with permission of Eileen Carr and the International Reading Association.

and, as a group, students are asked first to review the topic read and then to arrange the sentence strips in the logical sequence of events. The resulting paragraph is read for "correctness." Following the group work, individual students reorder the sentences on their own, write the paragraph, and illustrate the important parts. Figure 13.11 provides an example of a completed paragraph frame.

Figure 13.10	Think-Links Are Used to Summarize Graphically the Important Parts of Any Type of Reading Matter

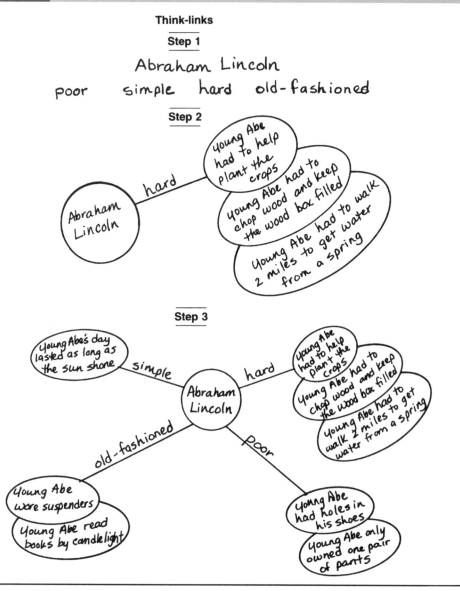

Dramatization. As presented for narrative text, dramatization can enhance comprehension. A similar response can be made to expository material. Fennessey (1995) described how to integrate literature, drama, music, and dance to make history more meaningful for her fifth-grade students. Cooter and Chilcoat (1990) focused on the use of melodramas to build understanding of expository text. "Melodrama, as applied to historical instruction, is an expository text response activity that uses sensational action, exuberant emotions, and somewhat stereotyped characterization to present a message about history" (p. 274). Readers' theater productions can also be created using nonfiction texts. For example, Gail Gibbons's book *Whales* (1993) provides information about the various types of whales. The following represents a partial script developed from a portion of her informational book.

MI Connection: bodily-kinesthetic

Figure 13.11 Example of a Completed Paragraph Frame, Including Illustrations

Sea Otters

The mother sea otter worked hard for almost two hours to take care of her newborn pup. First, while floating on her back, she licked it hard and rolled it over to lick it everywhere. Next, she chewed at the fur, scrubbing it and blowing on it without stopping. Finally, the pup was a dry and fluffy ball of soft brown fur. After that, the mother floated on her back with the pup high on her chest under her chin so the pup could sleep and she could rest.

Reader 1: A beluga, also called a white whale, lives near the North Pole. It is about 18 feet long.

Reader 2: A sperm whale can stay under water for a very long time. It can be 65 feet long. It can dive down more than a half mile.

Reader 3: Toothed whales have only one blowhole.

Reader 4: The teeth are only for catching their food. They gulp down their food without chewing.

Reader 5: A killer whale, also called an orca, has sharp teeth. It eats fish, penguins, seals, and even some of the bigger whales! It can be 30 feet long.

Reader 6: The other main group of whales has no teeth. Instead, they have long, fringed blades hanging from their upper jaws that strain their food from the water. The blades are called baleen, or whalebone.

Reader 7: Baleen whales eat fish and a mixture of tiny plants called plankton. In the plankton are shrimplike creatures called krill.

Reader 8: A pygmy right whale is the smallest baleen whale. It's about 25 feet long.

A *Jeopardy*-type skit could be developed to correspond with a particular content-area unit of study. To prepare the skit, students work with a partner to produce a set of questions and answers, as well as appropriate categories and point values. Or the teacher may provide the answers and categories based on curriculum goals, and the student partners may generate corresponding questions for a selected category, as well as point values. The entire class can take turns participating as contestants and as audience.

MI Connection:
interpersonal

Expository Reading and the Internet

With increasing numbers of young people using the Internet on a regular basis as a source of information (Lenhart, Madden, & Hitlin, 2005), classroom teachers must address the topic of expository reading and the Internet. Helping students comprehend expository material has become even more challenging because of the complexities of *new literacies* (O'Brien & Bauer, 2005). In other words, "Instant messaging, book tapes, cell-phone text messaging, speech translation software, interactive hypertext, and the facility with which text and image (moving or still) are fused" (Johnston & Costello, 2005, p. 257). As a result, the boundaries and the conventions for spoken and written words have been essentially eliminated. Thus, these new technologies (literacies) require new skill sets, but how to analyze and teach these new skills are areas still being explored (RAND Reading Study Group, 2002). In addition, technological tools change so rapidly that teachers themselves and school systems are faced with the continual need to learn and provide for these new digital literacy skills and new literacy practices. However, unless teachers and schools meet this challenge, their students might become less motivated and engaged in school practices (*the digital disconnect*); one example being the recent practice of online publication of one's opinion on topics of interest called *blogging* (or blogs). Blogs definitely embody literacy acts, as they

Arts Connection

The visual and communicative arts can enhance students' comprehension and recall of informational text. By adopting both an efferent and aesthetic stance,[3] students can identify important ideas in their textbooks or nonfiction books and then create murals, scripts, dioramas (visual art within a shoebox), drama improvisations (stage presentations), or skillfully illustrated concept maps that portray their opinions and thinking about what they have read (see Arts Connection box in Chapter 10 for an example of an illustrated concept map).

As part of theme-based activities centered on a specific period in U.S. history, four teachers united their groups of fifth-grade students to read about the Revolutionary War. Determined to culminate the reading lesson with a music activity, prior to the lesson, the teachers and their students accessed the Internet to locate a song that was popular during that time period. To ensure the lesson's success, the teachers carefully planned what each of their responsibilities would be during the actual teaching session. One teacher introduced the lesson by modeling the PreP before reading strategy (Langer, 1981) and then having the students participate. A second teacher modeled the SQ3R expository reading comprehension strategy (Robinson, 1970) and then helped the students to survey, question, read, recite, and review during the reading assignment. (See Chapter 14 for more information on PreP and SQ3R.) A third teacher served as the scribe, writing the students' questions and responses on an overhead projector. The fourth teacher was responsible for the after-reading music activity. She prepared copies of the song "Yankee Doodle" and served as song leader. After singing "Yankee Doodle" through once, the students spontaneously decided to add their own choreographed[4] movements to the music. They held hands and circled left and right, moved into the center of their circle, marched, bowed, jumped, and stamped their feet. Then they performed the song with their original choreographed actions for all program participants to enjoy.

Another very successful dance exploration culminated a thematic unit that focused on how animals grow and change. To initiate the unit, three teachers and their sixth-grade students collaborated

(Continued)

in assembling a very extensive fiction and informational text set about all types of animals. Students used the Internet to research answers to questions: How are animals classified? How do animals grow and change? How do individual animals move? What are the differences among birds, reptiles, and mammals?

As the students read, discovered, and discussed information, they also generated and recorded questions that arose during their study: How can you tell if turtles have backbones? If birds' feathers keep birds warm, why do tropical birds have so many feathers, and why don't birds lose their feathers in the summer? If reptiles are cold-blooded, why don't they freeze in the winter in cold climates?

After locating the answers to their questions through considerable inquiry and exploration, the students created murals that depicted how animals could be classified. They also produced a student newspaper as a venue for sharing their knowledge about animals. As a culminating activity, the sixth graders voted to present a "Dance of the Birds, Reptiles, and Mammals" for all program participants. The students each chose an animal he or she wished to represent. Then they brought in music that sparked their imaginations and helped them formulate ideas for their individual mammal, bird, or reptile dance. Soaring, free music represented birds. Mysterious, slow music exemplified cold-blooded animals. Happy, graceful music portrayed dolphins and whales. During the dance presentation, students wore costumes they created from crepe paper and cardboard. Following the performance, as a special treat, they served "animal" food to the audience, such as animal crackers, "spiders" made of chocolate-covered marshmallows with licorice legs, jellied candy "worms" and "fish" suspended in green Jello, and a "dolphin" cake made with blue icing.

---

[3]An efferent stance occurs when readers concentrate on retaining facts and details commonly presented in informational text. A predominately aesthetic role is generally adopted when readers interact with fiction. This stance stirs up feelings and generates strong personal perceptions, opinions, and attitudes (Rosenblatt, 1983).

[4]Originally created by Raoul Fuillet in 1701, choreography is the detailed planning and "writing down" or coding of a dance. "The word *choreography* comes from the Greek *khoros*, meaning dancing, and *graphia*, meaning writing" (Piazza, 1999, p. 133).

require participants to interactively respond to its content. Teachers in both elementary and secondary classrooms are using blogs to engage their students in responding to material they have read (Boling et al., 2008; West, 2008). Clearly, blogging can present opportunities for changing literacy practices in schools (Lankshear & Knobel, 2003). (See the websites at the end of this chapter for literacy-related blogs.) As Coiro (2003) summarized,

> . . . reading on the Internet is different, and our definition of reading comprehension needs to reflect those differences. Our job now is to envision new constructs of reading comprehension that introduce students to strategies for interacting with these new literacies. We must help students appreciate the distinctions of each one and also be willing to explore digital information environments together in more thoughtful ways. (p. 464)

The RAND Reading Study Group (2002) defined reading comprehension as "the process of simultaneously extracting and constructing meaning through interaction and involvement with written language" (p. 11). While the definition seems similar to the traditional notion of reading comprehension, the description of "written language" includes electronic text and multimedia documents as well as conventional print. "Electronic text can present particular challenges to comprehension, such as dealing with the non-linear nature of hypertext, but it also offers the potential for supporting the comprehension of complex texts, for example, through hyperlinks to definitions or translations of difficult words or to paraphrasing of complex sentences" (p. 14). These "complex texts" are expository in nature; thus the use of electronic text requires not only skills related to reading expository text but also skills and abilities different from those required for conventional, linear print (Coiro & Schmar-Dobler, 2005). Leu and colleagues (2004) have identified the following important electronic text skill areas: "identify important questions, locate information, analyze the usefulness of that information, synthesize information to answer those questions, and then communicate the answers to others" (p. 1570). Azevedo and Cromley (2004) also suggested that instruction in comprehension monitoring (discussed earlier) transfers well to learning in hypermedia. Henry (2006) further suggested the most critical skill for online reading is the ability to search for and locate information. Henry proposed SEARCH as an instructional framework for the critical skill of searching and locating information on the Internet. The elements of the SEARCH framework are as follows:

1. **S**et a purpose for searching.
2. **E**mploy effective search strategies.
3. **A**nalyze search-engine results.
4. **R**ead critically and synthesize information.
5. **C**ite your sources.
6. **H**ow successful was your search? (p. 618)

More information about the use of technology and specific strategies for locating information and Internet search skills can be found in Chapter 14.

WebQuests are good examples of content-area learning that uses the Internet. A **WebQuest** challenges students to explore the Internet for information related to a particular problem or inquiry. Content-area teachers certainly have access to the wealth of relevant information required to design interesting and informative WebQuests. These online adventures offer students access to a variety of resources at a variety of difficulty levels for a particular topic or unit of study. But some teachers feel they lack the technological skill to develop a WebQuest. For a template to assist in developing WebQuests and for examples of good and poor WebQuests, visit the websites provided at the end of this chapter. Students might also be invited to engage in the WebQuest development process, as they are likely to have the technology skills needed.

WebQuests could be considered special examples of project-based learning. A term often used interchangeably with project-based learning is *problem*-based learning. While very similar approaches, project-based learning is more closely aligned with thematic teaching, while problem-based learning is more focused on suggesting solutions to real-world problems. **Problem-based learning (PBL)** provides students with real-world problems or carefully designed problems that mirror real-world problems. Such an approach is consistent with democratic teaching, as it will help prepare students for active roles in a democratic society. One PBL example is a middle-school science class that sought solutions to restore the environmental health of a local stream. Even the school grounds can provide opportunities for PBL (such as enhancing or maintaining the playground area; developing school gardens and attracting wildlife; fund-raising) (Broda, 2007). In PBL, the teacher, acting as a facilitator, helps students develop not only problem-solving skills but also critical thinking, decision-making, and collaborative skills as they work together to ask relevant questions, form hypotheses, identify resources, conduct data searches, and evaluate possible solutions to a real-world problem.

The benefits of problem-based learning are many (Torp & Sage, 1998). Using authentic literacy projects can capture the interest of reluctant learners in ways not possible with the standard curriculum. Students learn to work together in small groups and gain interpersonal skills. They learn to gather information and apply knowledge from multiple disciplines. In addition to improved research, problem-solving, and critical thinking skills, students gain a deep understanding of the subject matter. Increased motivation and self-directedness result, along with effective oral and written communication skills. In summary, problem-based learning enables students to embrace complexity, find relevance and joy in their learning, and enhance their capacity for creative and responsible real-world problem solving. For more information and examples for both project-based and problem-based learning, see the websites at the end of this chapter.

Also, in this digital information age, skill in becoming discriminating users of mass media is required. This skill, referred to as **media literacy**, enables students to "access, analyze, evaluate, and create messages using media in various forms" (Hobbs, 2005, p. 58). The importance of becoming media literate is apparent for a democratic society because a media-literate person thinks critically about what he or she sees and hears on television, the movies, in music, radio talk shows, and what they read in books, newspapers, magazines, advertisements, on the Internet and other emerging technologies (Hobbs, 2001).

One example of a media literacy lesson is to engage students in reading reviews or critiques of movies they might typically see. Then show a small portion of the movie and ask students to critically evaluate its cultural authenticity and the values portrayed. Mo and Shen (2000) provided such an example using the Disney movie, *Mulan*, to discuss with students the distortions and stereotypes of the Chinese culture portrayed in the film. When students learn to recognize how the mass media influences information and to analyze and critically think about the messages the creators of mass media send, they become savvy consumers and informed participants in a democratic society. For additional information on teaching media literacy, see the websites at the end of this chapter.

Summary

The techniques and topics presented in this chapter were chosen because they stress student involvement with text and appear in the professional literature as important considerations for expository reading. Teachers must be concerned with developing strategic reading of expository text, even for the young reader. At the early stages, this may simply involve scanning printed material for a specific word or being taught to question material while reading it; that is, asking, "Do I understand this?" Teacher modeling of the types of questions to ask while reading is one direct way of providing instruction in the area of self-questioning. Also, students at all levels, when given appropriate materials, can be taught to organize what they have read to aid them in both understanding and remembering that material. Because of their graphic form, mapping and think-links are especially promising techniques for students who demonstrate spatial intelligence, and also for English learners. With increased use of the Internet, special attention is given to the topic of expository reading and the Internet. WebQuests and problem-based learning are discussed as viable approaches to content area literacy. The chapter closes with a discussion of media literacy as an important topic for democratic teaching.

Recommended Websites

Monitoring Comprehension: Teaching Comprehension Strategies to Students
www.ed.gov/teachers/how/tools/initiative/
summerworkshop/lewis/index.html
This U. S. Department of Education site has the PowerPoint slides from a summer workshop on comprehension monitoring.

Guided Comprehension: Monitoring Using the INSERT Technique
www.readwritethink.org/lessons/lesson_view.asp? id=230
Go here for a complete lesson plan for teaching intermediate and middle-grade students the INSERT technique.

Guidelines and Student Handouts for Implementing Read-Aloud Strategies in Your Class
http://teacher.scholastic.com/reading/bestpractices/
comprehension/strategies.htm
A collection of guidelines, checklists, and assessment tools for think-aloud strategies can be found on this site.

Reading Comprehension
http://muskingum.edu/~cal/database/general/reading.html
This site has a learning strategies database created by the Center for Advancement of Learning at Muskingum College.

Collaborative Strategic Reading (CSR): Improving Secondary Students' Reading Comprehension Skills
www.ncset.org/publications/researchtopractice/
NCSETResearchBrief_1.2.pdf
This article applies CSR to secondary students with disabilities and concludes that this approach works well in mixed-ability classrooms to improve comprehension.

Reciprocal Teaching General Information
http://ncrel.org/sdrs/areas/issues/students/atrisk/at6lk38
.htm
Palincsar describes the concept of reciprocal teaching.

Reflections on Classroom Use of Blogs
www.jsiporin.motime.com
A third-grade teacher shares her experience blogging with her students.

Links to Various School Bloggers
www.supportblogging.com/Links+to+School+Bloggers
This is a site to locate other educational bloggers.

Will Richardson's Blog
www.weblogg-ed.com
An extensive network of educational blogging opportunities can be found here.

WebQuests
http://webquest.org/index.php
www.spa3.k12.sc.us/WebQuestTemplate/
webquesttemp.htm
http://webquest.sdsu.edu/webquestwebquest-ms.html
These sites offer valuable information, including a template for creating WebQuests, and provide samples of good and poor examples to help novice developers appreciate the power of a well-designed WebQuest.

Best WebQuests
http://bestwebquests.com
WebQuests are inquiry-oriented activities that use the power of the Internet and a scaffolded learning process to assist learning.

Problem-Based Learning (PBL)
www2.imsa.edu/programs/pbln/problems/

Project-Based Learning and Its Benefits
http://pblmm.k12.ca.us/PBLGuide/WhyPBL.html
A strong case is made for the use of project-based learning.

Project-Based Learning Examples
http://pblmm.k12.ca.us/examples_main.htm
View examples at a variety of grade levels and subject areas.

Project-Based Learning
http://pblchecklist.4teachers.org
This site provides assistance for teachers in creating checklists for project-based learning activities.

The Smithsonian
www.si.edu
The Smithsonian provides an important website for use in theme-based and content-area teaching.

Cleveland Rock and Roll Hall of Fame Museum
http://rockhall.com/teacher
This site offers lesson plans that integrate music with history and literature.

7th Grade Science Blog
http://newliteracies.typepad.com/science_exchange
Consider the literacy opportunities of this blog.

RAND Study Group
www.rand.org/multi/achievementforall/reading/
readreport.html
The full report of the RAND Study Group is available at this site.

Center for Media Literacy
www.medialit.org
This is a source for sample lessons in media literacy.

Action Coalition for Media Education
www.acmecoalition.org
Information from an emerging global coalition run by and for media educators is provided here.

PEARSON
myeducationlab
The Power of Classroom Practice
www.myeducationlab.com

MyEducationLab is a research-based learning tool that brings teaching to life. Go to the Gipe 7th Edition MyEducationLab for Reading Assessment site at www.myeducationlab.com to:

- Engage in multimedia exercises to help you build a deeper and more applied understanding of chapter content.
- Use extensive resources including videos from real classrooms, Praxis and licensure preparation, a lesson plan builder, and materials to help you in your teaching career.

Study Skills and Test-Taking Strategies

OBJECTIVES

After you have read this chapter, you should be able to:

1. List and describe the major study skills.
2. Identify prerequisite skills for a given study skill.
3. Identify sources of material other than stories for teaching study skills.
4. Develop assessment activities for any study skill.
5. Develop instructional activities for study skills and test-taking strategies.

VOCABULARY ALERT

arrays
assignment mastery
collaborative listening-
   viewing guide
content words
equal-status relationships
expository material
GRASP (guided reading
   and summarizing
   procedure)

guided reading
   strategy (GRS)
herringbone technique
information literacy
locational skills
main ideas
paraphrase
PORPE
study skills

SQ3R strategy
subordinate relationships
summarizing
superordinate
   relationships
synthesizing
test-taking strategies
thought units
topic

Study skills refers to the tool aspects of reading that allow a reader to extend and expand knowledge as well as literacy abilities. Any discussion of study skills assumes that the reader has some basic word recognition and comprehension ability—one cannot "extend and expand" something that is not present. Only minimum reading ability is necessary, however, as word recognition, comprehension, and study skills are all interrelated. Growth in one area aids growth in another. **Test-taking strategies** are not directly related to subject matter knowledge; the term refers to how one prepares for and approaches the taking of a test, to include psychological aspects. When test-taking strategies are employed, higher test scores may result. Instruction in study skills and test-taking strategies, like strategic reading for expository text, should *not* be delayed until the learner demonstrates well-developed word recognition and comprehension abilities.

The material used to teach study skills is distinctly different from that used to teach word recognition and comprehension strategies. The narrative material of the basal reader, fiction book, or language experience story does not provide an opportunity to learn and apply study skills. For example, the various uses of book parts to locate information cannot be taught when a book's table of contents lists only titles of stories. Being able to use a table of contents is an important study skill, although other book parts typically found in content-area textbooks (such as the title page, index, and glossary) more readily help students realize that specific parts of books can help them locate specific kinds of information. Other study skills, such as using the computer cataloguing system in the library or interpreting a bar graph, simply cannot be learned most effectively by relying on narrative material. Likewise, the internal structure of expository material is different from that of narrative material.

An increasing number of middle-grade and secondary teachers complain that "students can't read the textbook" or that "students don't know how to find information for their research projects." A student who may otherwise be a good reader or one who was thought *not* to have literacy difficulties during elementary school often cannot deal independently with middle/secondary-level textbooks and assignments. At present, direct teaching of study skills seems to be overlooked or ignored during the elementary school years. Part of the problem may be that the elementary-level teacher judges a student's progress in the areas of comprehension and word recognition only with narrative material. The teacher then assumes that the student can apply this ability with narrative material to the material found in content-area textbooks. Thus, an otherwise good reader suddenly has difficulties on entering the grades in which content-area reading increases, generally grades 4 through 6.

Figure 14.1   Basic Study Skills

Study Skill

I. Locating information
   A. Alphabetizes by first letter
   B. Alphabetizes by second letter
   C. Alphabetizes by third letter
   D. Knows and uses book parts (e.g., table
      of contents, index, glossary)
   E. Knows and uses reference materials
      (e.g., dictionary, thesaurus,
      encyclopedia, directories)
   F. Uses the library (card catalog or
      computer system, Dewey
      decimal system)

II. Organizing information
   A. Knows and uses specialized vocabulary
   B. Categorizes information
   C. Recognizes main ideas and supporting
      details
   D. Sequences events
   E. Summarizes and synthesizes information
   F. Takes effective notes
   G. Outlines effectively

III. Interpreting graphic and pictorial materials
   A. Uses pictures
   B. Uses graphs
   C. Uses tables
   D. Uses maps

IV. Has and uses a study strategy

In summary, study skills are tools that enhance the learner's understanding of content-area textbooks and other informative materials. The rest of this chapter presents specific assessment and instructional techniques for the four basic study skills categories listed in Figure 14.1.

STUDY SKILLS AND PREREQUISITE ABILITIES

Study skills differ from other areas of reading in that there are identifiable prerequisite skills or underlying abilities that will assist the learner in the effective use of a particular study skill. For example, Rosa must have certain prerequisite abilities to use an index. The underlying study skills seen in Figure 14.1 are arranged within each category in a hierarchy so that these prerequisite abilities can be easily identified. In other words, for Rosa to use an index effectively, she must be able to alphabetize by first, second, and third letters. The study skills seen in Figure 14.1 have also been developed as a checklist for use as an assessment tool (see Appendix Y).

To provide appropriate instruction, not only must the target area be identified and directly assessed, but also the prerequisite abilities. For example, if the teacher observes that Jackie has difficulty using reference materials, the teacher might suspect that Jackie may not be able to alphabetize properly or know how to use the various book parts. Being asked to use reference materials without first learning these prerequisite abilities will be frustrating. The teacher needs to provide instruction with the underlying prerequisite skills that are causing the difficulty.

Chapter 14 stresses the need to consider underlying abilities. An emphasis on the prerequisite skills is especially relevant for the English learner, who typically would not have experience in these skills without direct instruction.

ASSESSING LOCATIONAL SKILLS

Most standardized achievement tests include subtests on a limited range of **locational skills**, usually termed *work-study skills*. The most common skills tested are interpretation of tables and graphs and use of reference materials (for example, *Iowa Test of Basic Skills* and the *Comprehensive Test of Basic Skills*). Because the range of skills tested is small and the yield is simply a percentile, stanine, or other standard score reflecting a general level of achievement, the teacher obtains only minimal information for instructional purposes. The standardized test may indicate low achievement, but direct assessment will be needed to pinpoint specific teachable units.

Teacher-made tests, if constructed with some thought, are a valuable source of information for instructional decision making. In the study skills checklist (Figure 14.1 or Appendix Y), the ability to locate information has the prerequisite knowledge of alphabetizing by first, second, and third letters and beyond. Most teachers will have no difficulty devising an instrument to determine whether students have these prerequisite subskills.

Alphabetizing

Here are some sample exercises for assessing the ability to alphabetize. They are presented in order of increasing difficulty.

1. Present letters and have students provide the letter that comes immediately before and after.

   __(q)__ r __(s)__   _____ f _____   _____ c _____

2. Present a random listing of letters to students and have them arrange the list in alphabetical order.

   x, c, r, j, d, s, u, t, a, m

3. Provide students a random listing of familiar words that begin with different letters. Ask them to arrange the list alphabetically or place words alphabetically in their word banks or personal dictionaries.

   the, dog, cat, me, house, baby

4. Provide students a random listing of words that begin with the same letter but have different second letters. Ask them to arrange the list alphabetically.

   cat, come, cup, city, cent

5. Provide students a random listing of words that are sometimes different in the first or second letter. Ask them to arrange the list alphabetically.

give, bed, foot, jump, gave, bad

6. Provide students a random listing of words that are alike in the first and second letters, but differ in the third. Ask them to arrange the list alphabetically.

bowl, boat, boy, bottle

7. Provide students a list of words that vary to any extent. Ask them to arrange the list alphabetically.

such, as, to, try, come, camp, look, like, boy, road, read

Book Parts

Simply asking the student to locate a particular book part and then describe its purpose or how it might be used can check knowledge of book parts. Appendix Z shows an example of a skills test for assessing knowledge of book parts in a written format. Book parts that students should be tested on are the title page; copyright page; table of contents; lists of tables, graphs, maps, illustrations, or diagrams; preface or foreword; glossary; index; appendix; and bibliography or references.

Reference Materials

The ability to recognize and use a variety of reference materials, to include the Internet, needs to be assessed. Activities for assessing the more common information sources should come first. For example, use of a text-based dictionary or an encyclopedia can be assessed by the following activities. Even though dictionaries are available online, instances remain when only a text-based version of a dictionary is available, so knowing how to use a dictionary continues to be a useful skill.

Dictionary.

1. Students must be able to alphabetize and interpret diacritical marks to use a dictionary or glossary. An exercise similar to the following, containing words that the students already know how to pronounce, is recommended. Give about 10 items.

   Directions to students: Use the following pronunciation key and circle the correct dictionary respelling of the numbered words. The first one has been done for you.

   ### *Pronunciation Key*

fat	āpe	cär	ten	ēven
hit	bīte	gō	yü as in few	to͞ol
book	up	für	ə = a in ago	

   1. dad

      dād   (dad)   däd   dəd

   2. look

      lo͝ok   look   lōk   lok

3. main

   man   män   mān   māĭn

4. cute

   cute   kute   kut   kyüt

2. Provide students sets of guidewords from the dictionary (such as *mill/mind*). Ask questions about the sets: Which word will be found at the bottom of the page? Why is *mill* written before *mind*? Where will you find *mill* on this page?

3. Provide students guidewords from two pages of the dictionary. Then give them other words and ask them to identify the page on which the word will be found, or whether it cannot be found on either page. For example:

domain/door	***downcast/drain***
dragon	double
doze	doorway
donkey	downstairs
dog	dome

4. Have students write in the guidewords for the pages in their personal dictionaries.

5. Provide students a list of words and have them write the guidewords of the page on which they found each word.

6. Provide the students several dictionary entries. The students should study each entry and be able to answer the following questions. Try to include a variety of parts of speech, accents, syllables, and diacritical marks. Note that dictionary activities assume knowledge that is typically taught as a decoding skill. For example, students must be able to recognize syllables, accents, and diacritical markings before a task like the following can be assigned.

Example:

freight frāt, *n.* 1. a load of goods shipped by train, ship, truck, airplane, or the like 2. the cost of shipping such goods. *v.* 1. to load with freight. 2. to send by freight.

   a. What is the vowel sound heard in this word? ___(long a)___
   b. How many syllables does this word have? ___(one)___ If more than one, on what syllable is the accent? _____
   c. The letter *n* means ___(noun)___.
   d. The letter *v* means ___(verb)___.
   e. If the guidewords on a page of the dictionary were *framework* and *free,* would *freight* be on that page, on a page before, or on a page after? _(after)_
   f. Which definition and part of speech for *freight* is being used in the following sentence? The *freight* for the package was $2.75. _(second; noun)_

Encyclopedia. Today students have access to a tremendous amount of information through a variety of text-based encyclopedias, encyclopedias on CD-ROM (for example, *Encarta, Grolier*), and the Internet. To use encyclopedias and the Internet effectively, students need to know the types of categories and classifications used for storing information (see the section in this chapter on classifying words) as well as how to use Internet search engines. Students will need to know about keywords used for searching, how to refine their searches, how to gain access to information, and how to use the information they find.

To use information from a text-based encyclopedia effectively, a reader must be able to use the encyclopedia index, information on the spine of each volume, guidewords, cross-references, and bibliographies at the end of articles. Each of these items needs assessing. In a skills test for assessing encyclopedia knowledge, for example, the teacher might begin by providing students a set of encyclopedias and asking questions such as the following:

1. How many volumes are in this set of encyclopedias? _____

2. To find out more about the climate in Alaska, which volume would you use? _____

   a. How would you proceed? _____
   b. What would you look for in the index? _____
   c. On what page is the information you need? _____

3. What number and letter(s) are on the volume you would use to find information about each topic in the following list? Which pages give you information about each topic?

Topic	Number	Letter(s)	Pages
climate			
polar			
bees			
Eskimos			
whales			
zebras			

This last task can be easily adjusted to reflect use of the Internet. In place of column headings for number, letter(s), and pages, use the column headings "Search Engine" and "URL."

In addition to the dictionary, encyclopedias, and the Internet, students should be able to use the thesaurus, directories (such as the Yellow Pages), almanacs, and periodicals. Assessment tasks are just as easily constructed for these materials as for the dictionary and encyclopedia.

Reference Skills

This major area dealing with locational skills includes use of the library—helping students go beyond the dictionary, encyclopedia, and the Internet as reference materials and recognize that information can be found in many other resources. To use the library effectively the student must be able to use its computer cataloguing or reference system, its particular classification scheme (most likely the Dewey decimal system or Library of Congress classification), and its special collections (periodicals; records, tapes, and CDs; filmstrips and videos; trade books).

Figure 14.2 Possible Sources of Information for a Research Project

Student Name(s): _____

Project Title: _____

Information sources we might be able to use for this research project are indicated with a check.

_____ almanac	_____ Internet	_____ photographs
_____ art	_____ interviews	_____ posters
_____ atlas	_____ magazines	_____ records, tapes, or CDs
_____ biographies	_____ maps	_____ slides
_____ dictionary	_____ microscopic slides	_____ television programs
_____ encyclopedia	_____ museum exhibits	_____ thesaurus
_____ filmstrips	_____ newspapers	_____ video, video disks, DVDs
_____ history books	_____ nonfiction books	

Others: _____

An effective way to help students learn reference skills and, in turn, identify those needing assistance is to create an authentic need for information to be found in the library. Greenlaw (1992) recommended providing students opportunities to research topics of their own choice. She suggested the use of a "curiosity" sheet at the beginning of a new unit of study. On this sheet students list topics they are curious about, related to the subject of the unit. Once topics are identified and shared with the whole class, there are sure to be several students interested in the same topic. These students can work together on a collaborative research report—although the following steps work for individual students as well. At this point, students working together can brainstorm questions they would like to have answered and identify possible sources of information for answers to those questions (see Figure 14.2). A map or a data chart (see Figure 14.3) can then be developed to aid in gathering and organizing information. Such a chart lends itself to the paraphrasing of information because space is limited. By using several sources, students also learn to synthesize information.

MI Connection: logical-mathematical

Once students have their questions ready, they then have a real need to visit the library or explore the Internet. If the school library is not well equipped, arrange a field trip to the local public library. The librarian, advised earlier of the nature of the trip, will give a thorough tour that includes use of the cataloguing system, location of the various materials that will be helpful, and assistance when students are attempting to locate the information for their data charts. When they have obtained the information, students use it to write a report. In this way students also learn about and practice expository writing.

Observing all stages of this process, the teacher will see those students having difficulty. Once again, the study skills checklist (Appendix Y) serves as a record of observations for the teacher. As checklists are marked, the teacher can consider ad hoc groupings of students needing explicit instruction in related locational skills.

Go to MyEducationLab and select the topic *Content Area Literacy*. Then, go to the Activities and Applications section, and watch the video entitled "Curiosity and Interest in Science" to observe how the teacher leads his students to develop questions about earthworms for use in a data chart. Next respond to the accompanying questions.

INSTRUCTION FOR DEVELOPING LOCATIONAL SKILLS

Teachers want to provide students lessons that are motivating and relevant to their experiences. Rather than just using the students' textbooks and workbooks, consider using more unusual materials. Following are some items that are atypical, yet make good sources for work in the entire area of study skills.

catalogs	newspapers
TV program guides	globes
diaries	*Guinness Book of World Records*
job applications	how-to-make-it books
maps	ingredient labels
menus	advertisements
travel brochures	driver's manual
thesauruses	insurance forms
encyclopedias	weather maps and reports
magazines	police reports
Yellow Pages	cookbooks

Figure 14.3 Research Map and Data Chart for Organizing Research Information

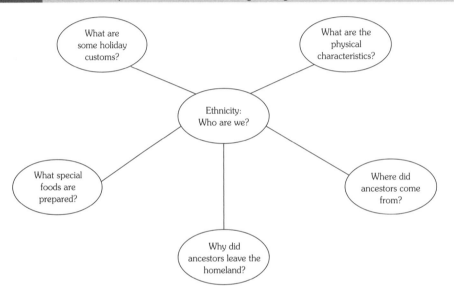

DATA CHART

Researcher _____ Ethnic group _____

Source	What are the physical characteristics?	Where did ancestors come from?	Why did ancestors leave the homeland?	What special foods are prepared?	What are some holiday customs?
1					
2					
3					

Use of such materials also addresses the area of **information literacy**; that is, knowledge about how to locate, acquire, and use information. Students who are familiar with a wide variety of information sources will be more likely to know how to make future decisions about affordable insurance, health care for their families, purchasing a car or securing a loan, or any other type of real-world situation. They will know how to find out what they need because they will know how information is organized, how to locate it, and how to use it.

General Teaching Procedures for Direct Instruction

With some modifications, the exercises used for assessment can also serve as the basis for a lesson. First students should understand the purpose of learning locational skills: allowing them to use such valuable resources as the dictionary, telephone directory, and the Yellow Pages. Once the purpose of the lesson is established, some motivation for pursuing the lesson may be necessary. For example, to play a new game, such as an alphabetizing relay, participants must know how to alphabetize.

The teacher is now ready to teach a minilesson to the students directly, usually demonstrating how a random list of words can be arranged alphabetically. After explaining the actual process used to alphabetize, the teacher invites student feedback to see if the explanation was clear. This may mean simply asking a student to explain the procedure again.

Once the students demonstrate they understand the explanation, the teacher gives them a chance to practice the new skill with no penalties for errors. This practice stage also allows the teacher to clarify any misunderstandings. When the teacher is satisfied the students understand the process, they can begin the alphabetizing relay. After the relay, the teacher may evaluate each student with a worksheet exercise on the same material.

An important part of direct instruction is to give students many opportunities to apply the newly learned skill in appropriate situations. For example, soon after the alphabetizing minilesson, perhaps later in the day or week, a new science term might be introduced. The teacher asks the students how they can find out what the word means and also check on its pronunciation. If no one says the dictionary or textbook glossary, the teacher simply suggests using the dictionary or glossary and reemphasizes the skill taught in the alphabetizing minilesson (how the word would be found in the dictionary using the first letter as a guide).

Another planned application is development of a classroom directory. The students list their names, last names first, on the chalkboard one at a time. Then, using the skills taught in the initial alphabetizing minilesson, they alphabetize the list. Looking up the names in the telephone directory and copying the address and telephone information completes the classroom directory. This particular activity would also provide a good database activity for using technology in the classroom. Periodic checks with similar activities should be planned to ensure that the skill is being maintained.

Thus, the steps of the minilesson are as follows:

1. Establish the purpose of the lesson.
2. Provide motivation for the lesson.
3. Teach the skill directly.
   a. Demonstrate and explain the process.
   b. Check students' understanding of the explanation.
   c. Allow opportunities for students to practice the new skill.
   d. Review the purpose and complete the original task (motivation).

4. Allow independent practice (for example, a follow-up work sheet).

5. Provide application opportunities.

6. Plan for distributed practice (periodic checks).

Specific Activities

This general format can be used in planning lessons to develop the locational skills and many other study skills. Following are some especially worthwhile activities for students needing instruction for locational skills.

Alphabetical Order. As students enter new words in personal dictionaries or vocabulary notebooks (see Chapters 8 and 10), they will need to decide where to write each new word in relation to the words already written. This provides an opportunity for activities such as the following:

1. *Directions:* Fill in the blanks using the words *before* and *after*. The first one has been done as an example.

   g is _(after)_ **e** and _(before)_ **h**   **re** is _____ **ra** and _____ **ro**
   t is _____ **u** and _____ **s**   **se** is _____ **sc** and _____ **sl**
   p is _____ **o** and _____ **q**   **br** is _____ **bu** and _____ **bl**

2. *Directions:* Circle "Yes" or "No" to answer the following questions.

Would *margin* come before *marker*?	Yes	No
Would *alligator* come after *allow*?	Yes	No
Would *picnic* come before *pickles*?	Yes	No

3. *Directions:* Circle the one word on the right that would come between the two words on the left.

beam—beauty	beaver	bean	beak
disk—display	disappear	distance	dislike
drift—drip	drink	driveway	dried

4. *Directions:* Look at each row of words. For each row, circle the word that would come first in the dictionary. Underline the word that comes last in the dictionary.

Example:	grew	*grade*	*go*	(gasp)
1. boy	down	city	over	
2. little	lot	lake	letter	
3. dance	date	days	dark	

Parts of Books. Have the students locate the table of contents in any content-area textbook. Ask questions such as the following:

1. On what pages do you find the chapter called "The Founding of Our Nation?" _(173–202)_

2. On what page does the chapter called "The Civil War Divides the Nation" begin? _(263)_

3. Does this book include a chapter on what the United States is like today? _(yes, Chapter 13)_

4. If you wanted to read about the settlers moving westward across the Appalachian Mountains, which chapter would you go to? _(Chapter 8, "Exploring the North Central States")_

5. How many pages are in the chapter called "Exploring the New World"? _(24)_

6. Does this book have an index? _(yes, begins on page 463)_

Using an Index. Have the students locate the index in any content-area textbook and use the index to find answers to questions. Students write the answer, the page on which they found it, and any heading from the index that helped them.

Choosing Resources. Give the students a variety of resource materials. Ask them to decide which resource would be most appropriate for locating information to answer questions the teacher either asks or has written for them to answer independently. For example, ask whether a dictionary, telephone book, thesaurus, almanac, atlas, or encyclopedia would be used to find the following:

1. Address of a friend
2. Words that mean the same
3. Information about a certain animal
4. Population of the United States
5. Winner of the World Series in 1980

Online Search Skills. The ability to perform online searches is a skill students need to develop as they increasingly use the Internet for completing school assignments. Because there is so much information available on the Internet, students also need to critically evaluate the websites they find to ensure they gain useful and high-quality information (Baildon & Baildon, 2008).

Before beginning online searches, students should have a good grasp of the organization of various search engines so they can employ effective search strategies. To sort through many Internet sites, students need to know about suffixes on URLs that indicate reputable sources, such as the suffixes .edu, .gov, and .mil. Sometimes the suffixes .org and .net are valid sources, but not always. Teachers also need to introduce students to the way search engines are organized (for example, text matching, categories) and the way they work (for example, word frequency, sponsored links) (Henry, 2006). Consider the following activity, whose purpose is to help students understand how to determine which Internet link to follow when they are provided with a long list of choices. This on-paper activity, can be used with the data chart seen in Figure 14.3 to show students how to make predictions about which Internet links to explore (Coiro, 2005):

1. The teacher first conducts a search on the Internet for information relevant to the study of ethnicity, for example, and captures the first few entries from the search with a screen-capture program and then prints them out (see Figure 14.4).

2. The teacher provides small groups of students a handout that includes the first few results of the Internet search and a set of guiding questions that help students critically examine each entry on the list, such as website addresses and file extensions (see Figure 14.5).

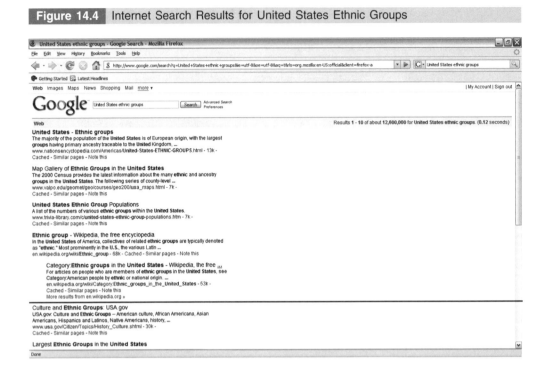

Figure 14.4 Internet Search Results for United States Ethnic Groups

Figure 14.5 Guiding Questions for Analyzing Internet Search Results Using "United States Ethnic Groups" as Search Terms

Questions and answers	How do you know?	Why is this important to know?
1. How many websites were found using these search key words? Answer: 12,600,000	The line at the top of the page says, "Results 1–10 of about 12,600,000"	12,600,000 sites are too many to look at. Try using different search terms to make the results list shorter. Maybe try cultures and nationalities as additional search terms
2. Which website contains information about the topic you are studying? Answer: Culture and Ethnic Groups: USA gov	The description lists the major ethnic groups that we have talked about in class, and the website's suffix is gov so it is a reliable site.	Reading the description saves time because it gives clues about what is in the website and what the website is mostly about. Noticing the suffix helps in knowing if the site is a good one
3. Which site appears to be least helpful? Answer: United States Ethnic Group Populations	There is only a link to scholarly articles, and their titles do not sound helpful for students	Sometimes the results will include a site that might include information on only one aspect of the topic, like "populations." This site will be limited to information about populations as it is only 7K in size. I need more information than this site provides
4. Which URL seems most likely to be available over the next several months? Answer: www.usa.gov/Citizen/Topics/History_Culture.shtml	The URL gives me the website's suffix. It is gov so it is a reliable site, and it is probably going to be around longer than a URL like trivialibrary.com	Looking carefully at the URL can give clues about who developed the site and whether it is a reliable source

Figure 14.6   Guiding Questions for Evaluating Websites

User Friendliness

1. Do the use of graphics and color make the site visually appealing?
2. Do the graphics download quickly (within about 30 seconds)? Or is there a text only alternative offered?
3. Is it easy to move around within the site?
4. Are the links clear and easy to find? And do the links work?
5. Can I read the text and understand it?
6. Are there pictures that help to make the text understandable?

Credibility

1. Is an author or a contact person given, or the host school, institution, or organization identified as the website developer?
2. Is there a way to contact the website developer (e.g., e-mail address)?
3. Does the URL seem official and reliable?
4. Does the site tell when it was last updated? Does the information seem current?
5. Does the information in the site seem to be consistent with what I know already or have read in other sources?

Content Usefulness

1. Does the title of the site match the information contained within?
2. Does the site contain the information I am looking for and need?
3. Are additional resource links included?

---

3. Small groups of students discuss their answers to each guiding question and exchange strategies for deciding how to navigate the Internet. A set of website evaluation questions (see Figure 14.6) should also be used to further analyze the websites once they are opened.

MI Connection: interpersonal

Another activity could be to ask students to locate information using a particular search engine and record the steps they took for later discussion. See the "Search Engines by Category—Source" website at the end of this chapter for help in using the best search tool for both you and your students' particular needs.

ASSESSING FOR ORGANIZING INFORMATION

The study skill area of organizing information is closely related to comprehension ability, as discussed in Chapters 11, 12, and 13. However, although such skills as finding main ideas, sequencing, summarizing, and synthesizing are end products in the reading of class material, they are prerequisite to the more commonly recognized study skills of note taking and outlining. Thus, to be able to take effective notes and develop good outlines, the student must be able to apply the notions of main ideas, sequence, and supporting details to content-related material through listening, viewing, reading, speaking, visually representing, and writing.

The best and most direct way to assess the ability to organize information is simply to ask students to make an outline (or map) or to take notes from a short written selection or video. Any written selection should be easy for the students with regard to word identification and comprehension to ensure that the study skill itself is actually what is assessed.

If a student has difficulty in outlining or note taking, additional practice may not necessarily be the solution. The student may be having difficulty with prerequisite knowledge: attentive listening; classifying words, phrases, or sentences; main ideas; sequencing; summarizing or synthesizing; listening, or auditory comprehension; or knowledge of specialized vocabulary (see Chapter 10). This prerequisite knowledge should therefore be assessed before providing instruction that the student may not be ready for.

Attentive Listening

Assessing the ability to pay attention is complicated; a student may be attending to the speaker without being able to understand the speaker (Norton, 1993). Therefore, Otto and Smith (1980) suggested that procedures designed to assess attention should *not* stress the student's ability to process ideas.

According to Norton (1993), "ability to follow oral directions explicitly demands attentive listening" (p. 129). Because idea processing is not the target of the assessment, directions must be simple. For example, a young child may be told: "Take out your blue crayon, your green crayon, and your red crayon. Pick up the red crayon and show it to me." Or for older students: "Take out a piece of paper and a pencil. Put the point of your pencil on the top center of the paper and draw a circle the size of a quarter. Draw a larger circle below the first circle. Draw a smaller circle inside the first circle." The older the student, the more complicated the oral directions might be.

Classifying Words, Phrases, and Sentences

Being able to distinguish main ideas from supporting details is a prerequisite to summarizing, outlining, or drawing inferences from **expository** (explanatory, content-area) **material**. However, before students can identify main ideas in paragraphs, they must be able to distinguish **superordinate** (general or main idea), **subordinate** (specific or supporting details), and **equal-status** (equally general or equally specific) **relationships** between words, phrases, and sentences. For instance, if Othell has trouble categorizing *hammer, axe,* and *lathe* as specific examples of tools, he will have difficulty identifying the main idea and supporting details in paragraphs discussing the role of tools in a social studies technology unit.

Some assessment techniques for classifying words, phrases, and sentences follow:

1. In one format, students are given a list of category titles such as *birds, mammals, planets,* and *reptiles.* Test items group the members (specific, subordinate relationships) of each category title (general, superordinate relationships), and the student must identify the correct category for the series of items. For example:
   a. deer, whale, dog (mammals)
   b. Mars, Saturn, Venus _____
   c. robin, oriole, blue jay _____
   d. alligator, chameleon, salamander _____

2. Another format combines the specific examples with the general topic. Students are directed to circle the word that represents the general topic. For example:

a. deer	(mammal)	whale	dog
b. Mars	Saturn	planets	Venus
c. birds	robin	oriole	blue jay
d. alligator	chameleon	reptiles	salamander

3. A third format provides the specific items at the top of the page, followed by the skeleton of an outline format. Students must place the specific items under appropriate general headings to complete the outline. For example:

butterfly	dog	beetle	sandpiper	sparrow
Mrs. Jones	firefly	iguana	mouse	haddock
trout	frog	terrapin	swallow	herring

I. Insects   II. Reptiles

    A. butterfly   A.

    B.   B.

    C.   C.

III. Mammals   IV. Fish   V. Birds

    A.   A.   A.

    B.   B.   B.

    C.   C.   C.

Phrases and sentences are assessed in much the same way. Some examples follow:

4. Students are instructed to circle the phrase or sentence that describes all the other items in the list.

    a. cows and pigs   farm animals

       ducks and chickens   sheep and goats

    b. Streets fell apart.   Cars were lost.

       Windows rattled.   An earthquake occurred.

    c. Scientists dig up fossils.

       Scientists learn about dinosaurs.

       Scientists look at the size and shape of bones.

       Scientists study where the bones were found.

    d. They wanted to have their own church.

       They were Separatists.

       They were Englishmen.

       They had secret church meetings.

Main Ideas and Supporting Details

When the student is able to classify words, phrases, and sentences, the next area to be assessed is that of locating the main idea (superordinate topic) and supporting details (subordinate topics) in a single expository paragraph (Aulls, 1978). As discussed in Chapter 11, **main ideas** may be explicit or implicit, and some paragraphs have no main idea at all. For assessment, use paragraphs with stated main ideas because students must be able to recognize stated main ideas before being asked to determine an implicit main idea. Recall from Chapter 11 that main ideas may be stated in the first or last sentences of a paragraph or somewhere in between. Students should be given paragraphs with the main idea stated in each of the three positions and asked to underline the appropriate sentence. Teachers might use the content-area materials adopted in their schools as a source for assessment paragraphs; however, the students should be assessed with material at their instructional or independent reading level. To achieve this, the teacher might have to use a content-area text from a different grade level than the one the student is in currently.

Sequencing

Sequencing is important prerequisite knowledge for outlining because outlines reflect a chronological, forward-moving summary of material read. Sequencing is especially important in studying history and conducting science experiments, because time order (first, second, third, and so on) may be critical to understanding the material. The easiest way to assess this ability is to give the student pictures, phrases, or sentences that relate a sequence of events. The items are out of order, and the student must sequence the items. For example:

Directions: Put a 1 in front of the event that would come first, a 2 for second, and a 3 for third.

a. ____ The air becomes warm.
____ Ice and snow cover the ground.
____ Green leaves appear on the plants.

b. ____ Put the pan on the burner.
____ The water boils.
____ Pour the water into the pan.

Paragraph frames can be readily adapted for use in sequencing (see earlier discussion in Chapter 11 and see Chapter 13 for examples).

Summarizing and Synthesizing

The primary difference between **summarizing** and **synthesizing** is that a summary usually contains the essential ideas of *one* selection, whereas synthesizing summarizes information from several sources into a whole discourse that connects the information. Thus, students must be able to summarize before they can synthesize. The most obvious application of these skills is in writing a report or term paper. Summarizing and synthesizing relate to the ability to paraphrase material read. Specifically, readers must be able to locate the main idea and supporting details, apply literal and inferential thinking skills, and interpret the information in their own words.

Methods that involve retelling of material read (not to be confused with recall) are appropriate for assessment. A retelling assesses the reader's ability to interact with, interpret, and draw conclusions from the text. Other assessment procedures might include questions that ask about main ideas and inferred information. These questions may take the following general form:

What is this section about?
What was learned from this experiment?
What was the purpose of the article?
How would you describe this period of history?
Could this poem mean something else?
Explain that in your own words.

Most teachers' manuals contain questions that ask students to summarize or synthesize information at the end of chapters or units. When some students consistently have difficulty with these questions, an analysis should be made in the areas of main ideas, supporting details, and paraphrasing (Chapter 11).

Listening or Auditory Comprehension

Classroom teachers often rely on observation and the use of checklists or anecdotal records to make listening assessments. One additional technique is the informal reading inventory (see Chapter 6). Instead of the student reading the graded passages, the passages are read to the student and comprehension questions asked or a retelling requested. The listening comprehension level is attained when the student can correctly answer at least 75 percent of the questions or recall about 80 percent of the material. Activities used to teach more specific listening skills, such as listening for main ideas, sequence, details, and so forth, can also be used for assessment.

INSTRUCTION FOR ORGANIZING INFORMATION

The techniques suggested here demonstrate how teachers can provide both instruction and practice in using materials that require students to apply these study skills independently. Many of the instructional techniques presented in Chapter 11 can be adapted for use in content areas. I suggest techniques for the most commonly taught content areas, in which reading difficulty may be the prime cause of poor achievement. The most valuable instructional methods employ the concepts and specialized vocabulary found in the content-area material the students are or will be using.

Attentive Listening

Students are not naturally good or poor listeners. Listening skills can and should be taught. All too often students ask for directions to be repeated or are scolded for not following directions. Often, the teacher may have to take some responsibility for this inattentiveness. Otto and Smith (1980) suggested four factors of inattentiveness: "(1) poor motivation to hear the speaker's message, (2) too much teacher talk, (3) excessive noise and other distractions, and (4) lack of a mental set for anticipating the speaker's message. By careful attention to these four factors, a teacher can help students become more attentive listeners" (p. 307).

Specific activities and methods help students develop attentive listening. The game "Simon Says" requires careful listening to directions. A leader gives an oral command, and the group must do as told if the "magic" words "Simon says" precede the command. If "Simon says" does not precede the command, those students who obey the command are eliminated from the game.

MI Connection: bodily-kinesthetic

To encourage students to listen, give oral directions only once. When a student requests a repetition, ask other students to recall and restate the directions. Learning centers for listening can easily be developed. Listening center supplies may include commercial audiobooks or teacher-made tapes, records, cassettes, CDs, radios, and accompanying printed materials (Baskin & Harris, 1995). Furness (1971) claimed that it is especially appropriate for students with listening comprehension difficulties and learning difficulties in general to number the steps of the oral directions, repeat the number of steps involved, and relate each step to its number.

Classifying

Aulls (1978) suggested that teaching the classification skills of superordinate, subordinate, and equality relationships, which are so important to main ideas and supporting details, involves

(1) an introductory teacher directed lesson; (2) a teacher directed reinforcement lesson which reviews the introductory lesson but uses different examples; (3) a pupil directed review

activity where pupils work individually, in pairs or in small groups using worksheets, games, or learning centers; (4) an application to one of the weekly content area reading assignments; and, (5) a post test of ten to twenty test items. . . . Approximately 80 percent accuracy is suggested as a criterion. (p. 95)

The introductory lesson concentrates on the meaning of general (superordinate), specific (subordinate), and equal word, phrase, and sentence relationships. The discussion involves the students in making decisions, first about pairs of items. For example, the teacher might ask:

"Is *beetle* the general or specific word in the pair 'beetle–insect'?" (*response*)
"How can you tell? Use the rule: Is the (*specific*) a type of (*general*)? If beetle fits the first blank, it is the specific word. The word that fits the second blank is the general word."

Responses should compare "beetle, a type of insect" and "insect, a type of beetle" to conclude that *beetle* is the specific word. Many examples should follow. For phrases or sentences the rule may vary:

Does (*specific*) describe (*general*)?

For example, the teacher might ask:

"Does *Englishmen* describe *Separatists,* or does *Separatists* describe *Englishmen?*"

Gradually introduce the equal relationship concept by comparing three items instead of pairs. For example:

"Wanted to have their own church" (*specific*) describes "Separatists" (*general*).
"Secret church meetings" (*specific*) describes "Separatists" (*general*).

These two sentences demonstrate that "wanted to have their own church" and "secret church meetings" both describe "Separatists," so they are *equally specific*. Continue these lessons until students achieve 80 percent accuracy with four items.

Categorization activities similar to those found in Chapter 10 and the activities included in the assessment section in this chapter for classifying words, phrases, and sentences can also be used as bases for lessons. In addition, many learners need some real-life application to demonstrate how skills that help them read and learn better can also help them outside the classroom in their daily lives. An example of one such activity follows.

The Yellow Pages lists, alphabetically, categories of services available in the area. The companies providing those services are listed alphabetically under their particular heading; for example, Ed's Moving Company would be found under "Movers," along with a telephone number and possibly additional information. As in a dictionary, guidewords give the first and last service listed on a page. Give students hypothetical situations and ask them to determine what service is needed; this is a classification task. Similar activities can be devised using tables of contents, indexes, almanacs, and newspapers (Cheyney, 1992; Olivares, 1993; Short & Dickerson, 1980).

Main Ideas and Supporting Details

Students who can distinguish general, specific, and equal word, phrase, and sentence relationships are ready to learn how to identify main ideas and supporting details. Aulls (1978) suggested moving from lessons in classifying to identifying the general topic of a picture. A **topic** differs from a main idea in that it is usually a word or phrase that represents the major subject of a picture, paragraph, or article. *Main ideas* are statements that give the most important ideas regarding the topic. Thus, the topic must be identified before an important idea about it can be identified.

Direct teaching is essential before asking students to practice a new skill. The teaching sequence suggested for classifying skills also applies here. Initial lessons involve pictures and paragraphs with one topic and several details supporting that topic. For example:

> There are many kinds of seeds. There are small seeds and large seeds. There are seeds with wings that can fly through the air. There are seeds with stickers that catch on your clothes. There are seeds that can float on the water.

After they read the paragraph, ask students to identify the topic of the paragraph from some listed words.

	MI Connection:
	naturalist

> wind   wings   <u>seeds</u>   stickers

Based on the previous discussion about classifying words, phrases, and sentences as general, specific, and equal, the students are often helped with the rule, "Does _____ describe _____?" Specific to the example are the questions: "Are (small seeds) specific kinds of seeds?" "Are (seeds with wings) specific kinds of seeds?" Practice should follow with more paragraphs of the same simple structure.

Finally, students who can identify the topic of a paragraph are ready for instruction in main ideas. Students learn that the main idea is the most important thing that the author wants the reader to understand about the topic (Aulls, 1978).

Instruction proceeds from the writer's point of view. The teacher may suggest a topic and one important piece of information about it. For example, the teacher writes *Water is moving all the time* on the board and says that this statement is the main idea the writer wishes to make in a paragraph. Then the teacher invites students to supply some specific statements that describe the main idea. Some possible responses might include:

> Water moves in the ocean.
> It runs over rocks in streams.
> It falls over waterfalls.
> It ripples on the lake.

If students can understand main ideas from the writer's point of view, they may better understand main ideas from the reader's point of view.

Instruction proceeds to paragraphs with the main idea stated in the first sentence, followed by paragraphs with the main idea stated last, and finally to paragraphs with the main idea stated somewhere in between.

Content-area textbooks can be used to help students apply what they have learned. The teacher may use an illustration that summarizes one of the written sections particularly well. Science and social studies textbooks are best for this type of activity. For example, a section may discuss the concept of the water cycle, while an accompanying illustration clearly shows the whole process. Students are asked to think of a sentence that explains the main idea of the picture and thus the concept of the water cycle and then to find supporting, or specific, details in the text and to list them as brief items below the sentence (Figure 14.7).

| Figure 14.7 | Example of an Illustration That Helps Students Identify the Main Idea and Supporting Details |

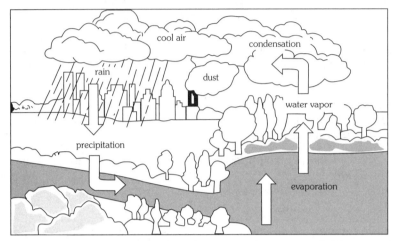

Main Idea: The evaporation and condensation of water over and over again is called the water cycle.
Supporting Details: When water evaporates, it changes into a gas called water vapor. Water vapor is cooled as it is carried up by warm, rising air. The cooling changes it back into a liquid. The vapor condenses into a cloud. Clouds bring precipitation.

Source: From Joseph Abruscato et al., *Holt Elementary Science,* p. 126. Copyright © 1980 by Holt, Rinehart and Winston, Publishers. Used with permission.

Sequencing

Many activities are suitable as bases for sequencing lessons other than the more common exercises that ask the student to put comic strip frames in the proper sequence. The teacher wants to encourage students to think logically. By first relating sequencing to events in their daily lives, the teacher helps students realize that events usually occur in a sensible step-by-step fashion. Initially, activities take a very simple form.

Example: What would you do first?

1. Put the cake in the oven to bake or combine eggs and water with the mix?

2. Put on your shoes or put on your socks?

3. Get dressed or get out of bed?

Having students follow simple written directions to make or cook something also reinforces the idea that certain steps precede others. Remind students to look for key words *(first, second, third, next, then, finally, last)* and other hints of sequence or enumeration. For example, if a science selection deals with the growth stages of insects, the word *stages* is a hint that a sequence of events is going to be related. Students must be made aware of these hints. Many times the stages are listed, giving a numerical hint of what comes first, second, and so forth. (Be careful, though; not all listings are sequential.) Having students write directions for making something so that other students can follow them also reinforces the importance of proper sequencing.

Students can also be invited to create meaningful sentences to help them remember otherwise difficult sequences, such as the order of historical events or a particularly long and troublesome spelling word. For example, a fourth-grade student from Montana submitted the winning sentence for helping others to remember the order of the planets in the 2008 National Geographic planetary mnemonic contest: "My Very Exciting Magic Carpet Just Sailed Under Nine Palace Elephants." The 11 recognized planets, *Mercury, Venus, Earth, Mars, Ceres, Jupiter, Saturn, Uranus, Neptune, Pluto,* and *Eris,* are represented in the sentence according to their order from the sun. Ceres, Pluto, and Eris are considered dwarf planets. One of my own memories for help with spelling the word *arithmetic* is the sentence "A rat in the house might eat the ice cream" in which the first letter in each word represents the spelling of the word.

MI Connection:
logical-
mathematical

Summarizing and Synthesizing

Often techniques used to teach summarizing skills do not differ very much on the surface from activities requesting identification of main ideas. However, in summarizing, instead of the main idea being explicitly stated, the learner is asked to infer a main idea or draw a conclusion about what has been read (or heard).

One method to help students learn to summarize is teaching them to **paraphrase**, or restate a discourse in their own words. Instruction in paraphrasing begins at a sentence level. Initially, two sentences are compared for meaning. For example:

"Do the following sentence pairs have the same meaning?"
The harbor was safe for small boats.
Small boats were protected in the harbor.

To get to the New World, the Pilgrims needed a ship.
The Pilgrims needed a ship to take them to the New World.

Most of the Pilgrims were farmers, weavers, or shopkeepers.
The Pilgrims were farmers.

At this initial level of instruction, the student must simply recognize one sentence as a paraphrase of another sentence.

The next stage in the instructional sequence moves from recognition of paraphrased sentences to production of paraphrased sentences. One method is to have students give synonyms for the **content words** (nouns, verbs, adjectives, adverbs) in a sentence, as in the following examples.

Gasoline engines operate automobiles, airplanes, and dirigibles.
Gasoline engines run cars, planes, and blimps.

When students can paraphrase sentences with ease, instruction proceeds to short paragraphs. Again synonyms are used. However, instead of trying to substitute one word for another, one thought unit is substituted for another. The following word problem demonstrates this procedure.

"Oranges are priced at three for 90¢. How much would you pay for four oranges?"

The first step is to divide the paragraph into **thought units**, or short phrases that contain only one idea. The thought units for this example might be listed as:

oranges are priced
three for 90¢
how much (would you pay)
for four oranges

The next step is to paraphrase each thought unit. One student might suggest:

oranges cost
30¢ each
How much will four oranges cost?

The paraphrases may vary; the concern is that all the thought units in the original paragraph be represented in the paraphrase.

The last step is to compare various paraphrases for meaning changes. If the meaning is the same, the paraphrase is acceptable. No personal translation is incorrect as long as the meaning is the same. For example:

"Oranges cost 90¢ for three. How much will I have to pay for four?"
"Three oranges cost 90¢. Four oranges will cost how much?"

In paraphrasing, other skills such as sentence combining (Chapters 8 and 11) can be applied. In fact, many comprehension skills are involved in paraphrasing: vocabulary knowledge (synonyms), literal understanding of words and sentences, sentence combining, and sentence expansion. The following example demonstrates the use of sentence combining to paraphrase.

> *MI Connection:*
> naturalist

Original: There is a plant that helps people tell the time. The plant has flowers that may be white, red, yellow, or pink. These flowers open in the late afternoon. The flowers close in the morning. The plant is named the "four-o'clock."[1]

Paraphrase: There is a plant, called the "four-o'clock," that helps people tell time. Its flowers, which can be white, yellow, red, or pink, open at about four o'clock in the afternoon and close in the morning.

> *MI Connection:*
> logical-mathematical

As noted previously, synthesizing both paraphrases and combines information from more than one source. To teach synthesizing, at least two different sources must be used. The easiest way to introduce the concept of synthesizing is to give the students two different versions of the same story and have them look for similarities and differences. Children's stories, such as *Goldilocks and the Three Bears, Jack and the Beanstalk,* and *Cinderella,* are available in several different versions. Summaries that use topics and specific details for each version can be listed on the board and then compared (see the story structure chart in Figure 12.6).

The next step is to apply this idea to content-area material. Choose a topic that is presented in different ways (usually different texts or different levels of the same textbook series). As an example, here are two versions of difficulties the Pilgrims faced:

Version 1

Sickness. There was terrible sickness in Plymouth that first winter. There were some days in February when only six or seven people were well enough to take care of the ones who were sick.

By spring, about half of the Pilgrims and sailors were dead. Three whole families died during this terrible time.[2]

---

[1]From *Specific Skill Series, Primary Overview, Drawing Conclusions—Booklet C* (level 3) by Richard Boning, 1985, Baldwin, NY: Barnell Loft.
[2]From . . . *if you sailed on the Mayflower* (p. 48) by Ann McGovern, 1969, New York: Scholastic Book Services.

Version 2

Hard times. New England winters are long and cold. Icy winds blow across the land. The Pilgrims were not used to such cold weather, nor did they have proper clothing. They got wet going to and from the Mayflower. So many became sick that at one time only six or seven settlers were well enough to look after the others. They moved the sick to the Common House and used it as a hospital. By the end of the winter, half the Pilgrims had died.[3]

Guide the students to summarize each version using topics and specific details. Paraphrasing should be encouraged. Example summaries follow for each version:

Version 1

Sickness in Plymouth (*topic*)
terrible sickness (*detail*)
first winter (*detail*)
February—only six or seven people well enough to care for others (*detail*)
by end of winter, half the Pilgrims and sailors died (*detail*)
three whole families died (*detail*)

Version 2

Hard times for Pilgrims (*topic*)
long, cold New England winters (*detail*)
icy winds (*detail*)
Pilgrims not used to such winters (*detail*)
Pilgrims didn't have the right clothes (*detail*)
they got wet (*detail*)
so many became sick (*detail*)
at one time only six or seven settlers well enough to care for others (*detail*)
moved sick to Common House (*detail*)
Common House used as hospital (*detail*)
by end of winter, half the Pilgrims died (*detail*)

Students then compare the summaries and put a checkmark by the details that occur in both versions. The teacher may wish to point out that details found in both versions are probably important and should be included in any written synthesis of the information.

Depending on the teacher's purpose and the students' needs, the teaching sequence may proceed to a written synthesis of the two versions. Sentence-combining strategies (Chapters 8 and 11) are useful at this stage. For example, the Pilgrims' "first winter" from version 1 can be described with details from version 2 such as "long, cold, New England, icy winds" and result in the following sentence:

The Pilgrims' first New England winter was long and cold with icy winds.

Instruction in summarizing and synthesizing also helps prepare students for writing reports that reflect more understanding of a subject than copying information from resource material. Hayes (1989) developed an extension of the guided reading procedure (Manzo, 1975) to show students how to group details into a prose summary. His strategy is referred to as **GRASP (guided reading and summarizing procedure)**. Briefly,

---

[3]From *Exploring Regions of the Western Hemisphere* (pp. 120–121) by H. H. Gross et al., 1966, Chicago: Follett.

students read for information and are directed to remember all they can. After reading, students tell all they remember, and the teacher lists all recollections, no matter how trivial or inaccurate. Following this listing, students reread the material to add to, delete, or correct information on the list. At this, point the teacher shows students how to organize the information by grouping details that belong together. Discussion about how information in each group relates to other information leads to an outline or map (see also Hill, 1991, for use of concept maps in summarizing). Once the relationships are displayed, a prose summary is developed, revised, and refined into a final summary.

Jeanne Day (1980) suggested the following basic rules of summarizing:

1. Delete trivial or unnecessary details. (For instance, a detail found in only one version in the previous example—"the Pilgrims got wet"—could be omitted.)

2. Delete redundant material.

3. Use a category heading for items mentioned within a single category. (For example, if the text mentions *roses, lilies,* and *petunias,* substitute the word *flowers.*)

4. Combine component actions into one encompassing action. (For example, instead of noting that James ate 5 doughnuts on Monday, 10 doughnuts on Tuesday, 5 more doughnuts on Wednesday, and so on, say James ate 50 doughnuts in one week.)

5. Identify a topic sentence or what seems to be the author's summary.

6. If a topic sentence is not apparent, make up your own.

Any summarization strategy involves teacher modeling and discussion of students' ideas and responses. In teaching the strategy, first use material that students find easy (independent level).

Listening or Auditory Comprehension

In addition to gathering information through reading, students also need to understand information heard, as in listening to a lecture or audiotape. Students with listening or auditory comprehension difficulties need help in defining the purposes for their listening. For example, to help students listen to oral directions, stress key words such as *first, second,* and *finally.* Have students close their eyes and visualize themselves carrying out each step of the directions as they hear it. Then ask them to describe each step. Finally, have them physically perform the activity.

Some activities for developing listening follow:

MI Connection: bodily-kinesthetic

- Using "Pin the Tail on the Donkey," direct the blindfolded student to move to the right, to the left, and so on.

- Using a cassette tape, provide a series of numbers *once,* such as 8–5–2–6–9. Ask which number is closest to the sum of 2 plus 2.

- Have each student prepare a two-minute talk on "How to Make a Peanut Butter Sandwich." As the directions are spoken, ask the listeners to visualize themselves following the directions. Next, ask some volunteers to do exactly as the speaker directed. (This activity can be just as valuable for the speaker.)

- To help students listen attentively and for details, play simple listening games with increasingly difficult instructions given to one student and then another. For example, "Jim, take the book from the second shelf and carry it to the windowsill." "Bill, you take it from the windowsill to the library corner and then to my desk." "Janet, you take it from the desk and walk around the desk twice with it, then carry it to the library corner and then to the windowsill, and finally back to the second shelf." And so forth.

An effective listener must be able to follow a sequence of ideas, perceive their organization, recognize the main ideas and important details, predict outcomes, and critically evaluate what is heard. The same can be said for an effective comprehender. Thus, most comprehension activities can be used, with only slight modifications, for instruction in auditory comprehension. The following techniques and activities are recommended:

1. *Listening for main ideas and supporting details.* The teacher selects paragraphs in which the main idea is stated (easiest) or inferred (more difficult). These paragraphs should also state several supporting details. The difficulty level of the paragraphs conforms to the students' ability level. One easy example follows:

I have a new puppy. It is little. It can run and jump. My puppy can do tricks. The puppy is funny.

The teacher reads the paragraph and asks the students to listen carefully for the main idea. After they have suggested a main idea, they should tell why. A request for a "good title" might be substituted for the phrase *main idea* in case students are unfamiliar with this term. In either circumstance, the students are told that the main idea or title can be turned into a question to find the supporting details. For example:

What is a new puppy like?
Why is the puppy funny?

After students hear the paragraph read once more, they are asked to identify supporting details. The "main idea" question will be answered by the supporting details. In other words, of the two questions suggested, one will be answered by the supporting details. For example:

It is little.
It can run and jump.
It can do tricks.
It is funny.

These details best answer the first question, so the first sentence, "I have a new puppy," represents the main idea. If working with titles, "A New Puppy" or "My Puppy" is an appropriate suggestion. Descriptive paragraphs are especially helpful for this activity.

2. *Listening for details that do and do not support the main idea.* Further development of listening skills includes weighing information for its importance to the topic. The teacher reads a paragraph in which one detail does not relate to the rest of the paragraph or to the main idea. The students then state the main idea, the supporting details, and the nonsupporting detail. For example:

Bob and Mary do not know what to do. They don't want to watch TV. They looked for a game to play but could not find one they liked. Mother went to visit her friend.

3. *Listening for sequence.* Activities to develop this skill first stress listening for key words that signify sequences, such as *first, second,* and *finally.* Once the students have been alerted to these key words, they listen to an oral presentation that emphasizes the usefulness of such words. For example:

I have a picture of three monkeys. The first monkey is covering his eyes. The next one is covering his ears. The third one is covering his mouth with his hands. On the bottom a sign says, "See no evil, hear no evil, speak no evil."

Point out to students how the key words signal a certain sequence. This can be demonstrated by rearranging the order of the paragraph to make less sense. Also help students discover the usefulness of the introductory statement, "I have a picture of three monkeys," and show how each of the monkeys is then identified by a signal word: *first, next, third*. This type of activity can be easily adapted to develop understanding of paragraph structure in preparation for writing paragraphs.

Other activities include cutting up comic strips into their individual frames, whiting out the words, mixing up the frames, and then reading the original comic strip aloud while the students put the strip back in order. A flannel board provides the opportunity for students to listen to a story, hear its sequential organization, then retell it via pictures or main idea statements in proper sequence.

4. *Listening to predict outcomes.* The procedure is much like that of a directed reading-thinking activity (Stauffer, 1981). The teacher reads the title of a story to the students and asks them to write a prediction or suggest to the teacher what they think they will hear about in the story. The teacher discusses the reasons for these predictions with the students and then reads the story. Some stories lend themselves to breaks where repredicting can occur. This activity motivates students to listen carefully to see if their individual predictions are correct. Films can also be used in this manner, or a talk or lecture can be stopped at certain points to have students predict what the speaker will say next. The level can be very easy (predicting the next word in a sentence) or more difficult (predicting the possible content or conclusion).

5. *Listening to evaluate.* Students are aided in this area by learning to develop questions to be answered by listening and to listen for cause-and-effect relationships, propaganda, or persuasive statements. As for any lesson, students must be prepared, in this case by being given something to anticipate. For example, after the topic of the talk or lecture is previewed, the students are asked to list three questions they would like to hear answered. A planned study guide helps students use what they already know and alerts them to information particularly important to understanding what they will hear. Devine (1981) suggested that an effective listening guide should include the following:

    a. A preview of the talk, including a statement of its purpose and perhaps even an outline

    b. A list of new words and concepts

    c. Questions for students to think about as they listen

    d. Space for students to write questions they want answered as they listen

    e. Provision for *anticipation* (that is, some problem, question, or student concern that students can look forward to learning about as they listen)

    f. Questions to help the student-listener personalize what is being said—for example, "Have you ever had an experience like this?" or "In what way does this affect your own life?"

    g. Space for students to write such things as main ideas and supporting details

    h. Appropriate visuals that can be duplicated in the guide (such as graphs or tables)

    i. Follow-up activities (including possible test questions or related readings) (pp. 24–25)

Activities for evaluative listening may include identifying cause and effect and discriminating information from propaganda.

For *identifying cause and effect,* a cause is stated, followed by the reading of a series of consequences, some of which are results of the cause and others that are not. Students are to identify any matching cause–effect relationships. For example:

MI Connection: logical-mathematical

Cause

It was the hottest summer that had ever been recorded.

Effects

The greatest danger was the possibility of frostbite. (*No match*)
The hospital reported large numbers of cases of heatstroke. (*Match*)
After a while, a bad water shortage developed. (*Match*)
Most people dressed carefully, wearing many layers of clothes. (*No match*)
It was uncomfortable to leave your home to go outdoors. (*Match*)

For *discriminating information from propaganda,* television commercials provide a never-ending source of material (see also the topic of media literacy in Chapter 13). Prepare tapes to be analyzed and later placed in listening centers to give practice in listening for persuasive statements. A speaker whose purpose is to persuade also provides information while trying to convince the listener of something. Listeners are constantly exposed to such situations. Examples other than TV commercials include campaigning politicians at all levels of government, salespeople (cars, magazines, appliances), and very often our friends. The listener must be able to distinguish statements that inform from those that are intended to persuade. The listener then examines and evaluates only the information before deciding what to do. Students are first instructed in the differences between informative and persuasive statements. For example:

Information tells you about the item being sold.

1. This bicycle comes with a headlight and a rear light.
2. This bicycle is lightweight (20 pounds) and has hand brakes.

Persuasion tries to make you think you want to buy what is being sold.

1. This bicycle is only for people who want the best.
2. Famous stars prefer this bicycle.

A list of statements is then read to students, and they determine which inform and which persuade. For example:

- These knives are made of stainless steel. (*Information*)
- Our gum contains no sugar. (*Information*)
- Why not use what the pros use? (*Persuasion*)
- The jackets come in three sizes. (*Information*)
- Just what you've been waiting for! (*Persuasion*)
- The rubber sole will keep you from slipping. (*Information*)
- This is a nonalkaline-pH shampoo. (*Information*)
- This is a special gift for that special person. (*Persuasion*)
- This dish will not chip or crack. (*Information*)
- Everyone thinks _____ is the best. (*Persuasion*)

Listening must be considered a vital aspect of comprehension ability, although it is often overlooked. It may be mistakenly assumed that a student who hears well also listens well. Instruction in listening must begin in the early grades to help students prepare and develop independence for such tasks as note taking and class discussions.

The lack of listening materials places even greater responsibility for the development of instructional practices on the classroom teacher. The following questions (Burns, 1980) alert teachers to their responsibilities:

1. Do I provide a classroom environment (emotional and physical) that encourages good listening?
2. Am I a good listener, and do I really listen to the pupils?
3. Do I use appropriate tone, pitch, volume, and speed in my speaking?
4. Do I vary the classroom program to provide listening experiences (films, discussions, debates, reports) that are of interest to the students?
5. Am I aware of opportunities for teaching listening throughout the day?
6. Do I help pupils see the purpose of listening in each activity?
7. Do I help students see the importance and value of being good listeners?
8. Do I build a program in which listening skills are consistently taught and practiced? (p. 113)

Other listening strategies may be found in professional literature. One of the most complete collections is still *Listening Aids through the Grades* (Russell & Russell, 1979), which includes almost 200 teaching ideas, ranging from general to specific and from simple to complex.

Note Taking

Instruction in the previous skills of summarizing and synthesizing leads directly to instruction in note taking. In essence, when taking notes on printed material, the student is summarizing the material. If notes are being taken on material presented orally, the process assumes the additional skill of auditory comprehension; if notes are taken on material that is both oral and visual, additional kinds of processing skills may be needed. In any case, the ability to summarize and translate information into one's own language is imperative.

Note taking is a complex skill, as evidenced by the prerequisite skills already discussed. Research by Dunkeld (1978) on taking notes while reading offered some helpful suggestions. First, students are introduced to note taking while reading or listening to a familiar story (such as *Goldilocks and the Three Bears*). Second, in the early stages of note taking, a textbook with subheadings is used. Third, the teacher demonstrates the format of good notes on the chalkboard or overhead using students' own examples. Fourth, students are encouraged to use their notes during class discussions.

Simpson and Nist (1990) suggested a textbook annotation strategy as a way to study and take notes from texts. Students can be given a packet of sticky notes so they can jot down their ideas for annotations as they are reading and place them at the pages they wish to return to when they develop the annotation. Simpson and Nist concluded from their research that the special elements of the strategy—actively involving students in constructing ideas and monitoring their own learning—are what make this strategy effective. Additional support for an annotation strategy is provided by Strode (1993) in her adaptation of the REAP strategy (see later section on study strategies). She noted the following major benefits:

SPOTLIGHT ON ENGLISH LEARNERS

Dictoglos

Originally developed for use with high school students by Ruth Wajnryb (1990), *dictoglos* is a particularly valuable strategy for teachers of English learners of any age because it involves and integrates the four skills of listening, speaking, reading, and writing along with collaboration. It is intended to help students develop a knowledge base in a specific content area such as science or social studies but, more important for the English learner, to have an opportunity to use the language modeled in textbooks.

To start, students are directed to "just listen carefully" as the teacher reads a text passage two or three times at normal reading speed. The passage is then read again, but this time students are asked to write down key words or key phrases they recall. The passage is read once again, and students are asked to again write down additional key words or phrases they recall. Next, students work in pairs to discuss their notes and to recreate as much of the text as they can by expanding on their notes. Each pair then joins with another pair to form a foursome. The group of four works together to recreate as much of the text as they can from their combined notes. This should lead to a fairly accurate version of the original text. Finally, the group attempts to produce a coherent written text that is as close to the original as possible. Follow-up discussion can include analyzing the sections in the text that were especially difficult to recreate. The use of dictoglos with various content-area texts can help the English learner begin to appreciate the ways in which the choices of words and phrasing in English are influenced by the purpose of the writing and the audience for which the writing is intended.

- There is more active involvement in reading because writing will occur afterward.
- Information is processed more thoroughly and has more meaning as a result of the writing component.
- Students write more succinct summaries as a result of learning to write annotations.
- Students attend to often overlooked aspects of text.

This adaptation of REAP is an effective strategy for note taking as well as for enhancing comprehension, specifically for main ideas, and for clearer writing.

Stahl, King, and Henk (1991) presented "a four-stage instructional sequence of modeling, practicing, evaluating, and reinforcing activities for developing student-directed note taking strategies" (p. 614). Teachers first model and provide opportunity to practice any one of a number of suggested note-taking procedures, some of which follow:

- Draw a margin and keep all running lecture notes to one side; use the other side for organization, summarizing, and labeling.
- Skip lines to show change of ideas.
- Use numbers, letters, and marks to indicate details.
- Paraphrase.
- Use underlining, circling, and different colors of ink to show importance.

Smith and Tompkins (1988) presented the structured note-taking strategy that uses graphic organizers for representing information. Using a visual framework that corresponds to a particular text structure (problem/solution, compare/contrast, cause/effect), the teacher initially provides the frame language. For example, text material dealing with environmental issues (a problem/solution structure) may best be presented as a web framework (see Figure 14.8). The first issue discussed in the text is pollution. As students read, they select information to answer the questions within the web framework. Students can work with a partner during the reading to discuss their choices or in small groups

Figure 14.8   Structured Note Taking for Text Selection on Pollution

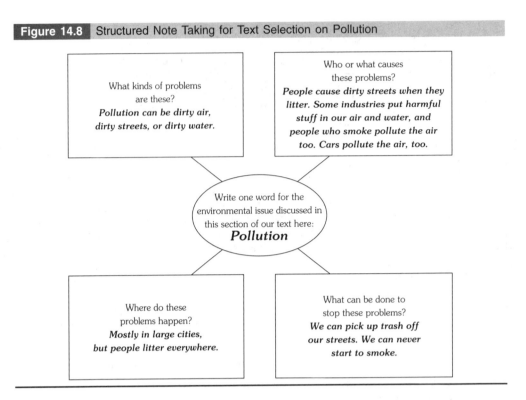

following the reading to justify their responses. With practice, students will be able to develop their own organizers.

With the increased use of video presentations and locating information on the Internet, students also need to be able to take notes while processing all types of information: written, oral, and visual. Flood and Wood (1998) offered a format for guiding students in their note-taking efforts when the information presented is on videotape. Figure 14.9 provides an example of the **collaborative listening-viewing guide** as used with a group of university students viewing a video on differentiating instruction.

Effective note-taking instruction provides students many short practice sessions with the clear purpose of improving their skills. At the end of each session students share their notes, so that the variety of note-taking styles (use of key words, phrases, full sentences) can be discussed.

Outlining

The underlying abilities needed for note taking and outlining are similar. As with note taking, outlining involves identification of main ideas and specific details. With outlining, however, these elements must be properly related. Outlines use any of the following formats: phrases or topics; sentences; paragraphs; or graphic representations. Instruction in outlining begins with easy material and much teacher guidance, discussion, and practice.

The first sessions in outlining should provide a completed outline of the material for the students on a work sheet, chalkboard, or overhead transparency. Students will better understand the function of outlining if they can see how the writer organized the selection. After students have read the material, the reasons for selecting certain topics as main ideas and others as supporting details for the outline are discussed. For example, if the selection being read is about bees and how they communicate, the outline may appear as follows:

Figure 14.9	Example of a Collaborative Listening-Viewing Guide

Collaborative Listening-Viewing Guide (CLVG)

Course: ____ED 309____   Date: ____9/18/06____   Topic: Differentiated Instruction

Name: ____Linda M____   Group Members: __Karen K, Cheryl S, Joanne R__

We know that: the intent is to meet individual student needs, concepts taught are the same but children learn them in different ways

My notes	Our group notes

1. 2, 3, 4 learning options, not 20
   —content (concepts, skills to learn)
      match with readiness
   concrete vs abstract
   simple to complex
   few directions to many
   —activities (the way they explore)
      alternate ways to manipulate ideas
      multiple paths
   —products (demonstrate what is learned)
      modified grading, rubrics
2. grouping-flexible
   —readiness (except-change)
   —learning profile (multiple intelligences)
   —student interest (relevance)
	Key is flexibility and dynamic grouping. Teacher role is redefined—be open minded, a facilitator. Be careful not to just give brighter students more work—make all levels seem the same in terms of work load. Lots of hands-on, not just lecture, or reading

We learned that: The teacher is not the center of the classroom when differentiated instruction is used. Groups change often. DI is valuable at <u>any</u> grade level. Teaching is more effective.

We will find out:

How challenging it will be to implement DI.

If the politics of education today (e.g., the emphasis on standardized testing) will interfere with a teacher's ability/desire to differentiate instruction

    I. Bees communicate with each other.
      A. One bee discovers honey.
      B. Other bees soon appear.
    II. Bee gives message.
      A. Scout bee returns to hive.
      B. Scout bee begins to dance.
      C. Dance tells story.

The discussion emphasizes that the major headings represent the main ideas in the selection. The subheadings provide more specific details that explain the major headings. The outline could be used before the actual reading to help students anticipate the selection's content. Through these activities, students eventually recognize the ways in which written material follows an outline. The teacher is responsible for choosing material that is simple and well organized.

A later stage may provide students with the supporting details and instruction for filling in the main headings. Then a complete skeleton outline can be provided with a few random topics filled in and instruction for completing the outline. Eventually only the structure of the outline is given. Finally, after much practice at each stage, students will be able to formulate outlines without assistance. Examples of outlines for early instruction can be found in Figures 14.10 and 14.11.

Figure 14.10 Selecting Main Headings for an Outline

Paris

Many people think of Paris as one of the most beautiful cities in the world. It has been called the City of Light because of the beauty of its lights at night. Colorful flower beds and famous statues line paths through lovely public gardens throughout the city. Children in Paris go to the parks to enjoy puppet shows and to sail their toy boats in the ponds.

Over the years Paris fashions have been famous throughout the world. When women want to know the latest in fashion, they look to the fashion shows in Paris. Many well-known designers of women's clothes live and work in Paris.

The city of Paris is also famous for its art. Priceless art treasures are on display in several museums. Paintings and statues are among the most popular kinds of art seen in Paris. Many people from all over the world come to Paris each year to study in the outstanding schools of art.

Put the main headings where they belong.

City of fashion
City of art
City of beauty

I. City of beauty
   A. Lights
   B. Gardens
   C. Parks

II. City of fashion
   A. Worldwide fame
   B. Fashion shows
   C. Fashion designers

III. City of art
   A. Museums of art
   B. Kinds of art
   C. Schools of art

Plan 17, Pages 127-130

Comprehension: Selecting main headings for an outline

Directions: Have pupils read the selection and complete the outline.

Exploration: On the board write cleaning a cut, treating with medicine, and bandaging. Have pupils list the materials needed under each heading.

Source: From *Mysterious Wisteria Activity Book,* p. 56. Copyright © 1972 by The Economy Company, Oklahoma City. Reprinted with permission.

MI Connection:
spatial

In addition to the preceding techniques, the strategies of mapping (Hanf, 1971), semantic webbing (Freedman & Reynolds, 1980), and the herringbone technique (Tierney, Readence, & Dishner, 1990) are useful for developing outlining skill. Semantic webbing (mapping) and the *herringbone technique* are graphic representations of the relationships of ideas in a selection. The visual result clearly reveals the major topic, main idea, and supporting details. Such graphic representations have also been called **arrays** (Hansell, 1978). Hansell provided a definition: "An array is essentially a free form outline which requires that students decide how to arrange key words and phrases to show how the author fit them together" (p. 248). Therefore, in maps, webs, and arrays, the student constructs an organizational design of ideas by selecting relevant information, sorting this into its proper place, and relating all facts to the whole and to the other facts. Figure 14.12 shows an example of an array for the African folktale *Anansi the Spider* (McDermott, 1986). In this folktale, Anansi buys all the stories in the world from the Sky God. To pay for the stories, Anansi captures and gives to the Sky God a hive of hornets, a leopard,

Figure 14.11 | Outlining by Relating Subheadings to the Main Heading

Make an Outline

If you wanted to use the following ideas in a report about the ocean, how would you set up an outline?

Use these words for the main headings in the outline.

Bottom of the ocean
Movement of the ocean
Life in the ocean

Put these words under the main headings in the outline.

Seaweeds
Tides
Shelves
Waves
Slopes
Fish
Floor
Shellfish
Whales
Currents

The Ocean

I. Bottom of the ocean
  A. Shelves
  B. Slopes
  C. Floor

II. Movement of the ocean
  A. Tides
  B. Waves
  C. Currents

III. Life in the ocean
  A. Seaweeds
  B. Fish
  C. Shellfish
  D. Whales

(Arrangements under each heading may vary.)

Plan 31, Pages 230-234

Study Skills: Outlining by relating subheadings to main headings

Directions: Have pupils read the instructions and complete the page independently.

Exploration: Have pupils write an article with content based on these headings and subheadings.

Source: From *Mysterious Wisteria Activity Book*, p. 100. Copyright © 1972 by The Economy Company, Oklahoma City. Reprinted with permission.

Figure 14.12 | Example Array Showing Interrelationship of Character and Events

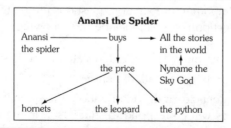

Source: From Hansell, T. Stevenson (1978). "Stepping up to outlining." *Journal of Reading, 22:* 248–252. Reprinted with permission of T. Stevenson Hansell and the International Reading Association.

MI Connection:
logical-
mathematical

and a great python. The diagram shows how these events fit together by the arrangement of key words and arrows designating direct relationships.

Hansell's research suggested certain steps in teaching students how to prepare arrays. First, the teacher selects 10 to 20 key words or phrases (assuming passages of 400 to 800 words) from the material. Next, the teacher develops questions that require students to organize what they already know about the passage—for example, "How would you capture a leopard?"

Next, the students are assigned to small groups. Each group receives several strips of paper that contain the key words and phrases from the passage. This step allows the teacher to pronounce and explain any of the key words or phrases if necessary. After the paper strips have been distributed, the teacher asks the organizing questions. At this point the students actually read the passage, but they are now reading for two very definite purposes: (a) to check their answers to the organizing questions against what is stated in the passage and (b) to find out how the key words and phrases are related.

MI Connection:
interpersonal

The students, still in groups, compare the strips of paper to select the most important idea. This strip is placed at the top or the center to stress its importance. The other strips are positioned around it in a way that reflects the relationships in the material. This positioning must be done with teacher guidance; the teacher asks appropriate questions, encourages, and makes suggestions while moving from group to group. When the group is satisfied with the position of all the paper strips, one member copies the array onto a piece of paper, drawing arrows to show connected ideas and the direction of relationships.

The last step is for the groups to share their arrays and discuss reasons for the arrangement and placement of arrows. The teacher asks extending questions at this time.

Hansell recommended that at least four teacher-guided arrays be constructed before expecting students to do an unguided array. In an unguided array, students select the key words and phrases themselves. Eventually, by moving from free-form arrays to skeletal outlines, students are ready to prepare individual outlines. The array approach is useful because it focuses on the primary reason for outlining in the first place, that is, to identify relevant ideas and fit them into a meaningful pattern. Unfortunately, the focus of most instruction in outlining is on the format, which assumes that students understand the relationships presented in the material—a "cart before the horse" approach. Instruction in array formation puts the horse back in front of the cart. In addition, the Inspiration (and Kidspiration) software (see Chapter 8) has the potential to lead students to a better conceptual understanding of outlining.

The **herringbone technique** (Tierney et al., 1990) is a structured outlining procedure useful for helping students organize information from text. This strategy uses six basic comprehension questions to obtain the important information: who, what, where, when, how, and why.

As with arrays, the teacher must make some specific preparations for teaching the herringbone technique. Important preparation questions for the teacher to ask, especially when differentiated instruction is a goal, include the following:

1. What are the major concepts my students should understand from this material?

2. What are the important vocabulary items?

3. How will my students learn this information? (There will be more than one way because responses will correspond to students' learning profiles.)

4. Which concepts do I expect *all* my students to master, and which do I expect only my better students to achieve?

Figure 14.13   The Herringbone Form

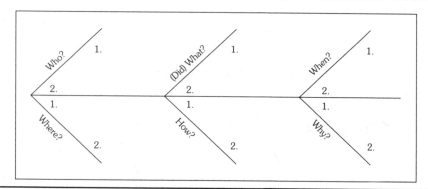

The teacher introduces the lesson as usual, with concern for developing motivation and conceptual background. Then the herringbone technique is introduced. The herringbone form (Figure 14.13) can be provided as a photocopied handout. Students are told they will be seeking answers to the questions on the form. The answers themselves can also be written right on the form. The first few lessons that involve the herringbone technique are walked through with teacher guidance, using an overhead transparency.

As students read the assigned material they will be noting answers to the following questions:

1. Who (person or group) was involved?
2. What did this person or group do?
3. When was it (the event from question 2) done?
4. Where was it done?
5. How was it done?
6. Why did it happen?

The answers to these questions help the student recognize the important relationships in the material. For example:

For a chapter in a social studies textbook entitled "Europeans Rediscover the Western Lands," the students were instructed to read the topic "Columbus Tries to Get Help from Portugal" and to answer the six key questions. The answers to be recorded on the herringbone form were as follows:

Who?   Columbus, king of Portugal, king's experts
What?   Columbus went to the king to ask for ships and supplies to sail west to reach the Indies. King's experts thought Columbus was wrong.
When?   _____
Where?   Portugal
How?   _____
Why?   Columbus wanted to prove (a) that it was possible to sail straight west to reach the Indies because Earth is round and (b) that this route was shorter than going around Africa. King's experts knew Earth was round but thought the distance was much greater than Columbus thought.

As seen in this example, texts do not always contain all the information needed to answer the six key questions. The teacher must decide whether the missing information is

MI Connection: logical-mathematical

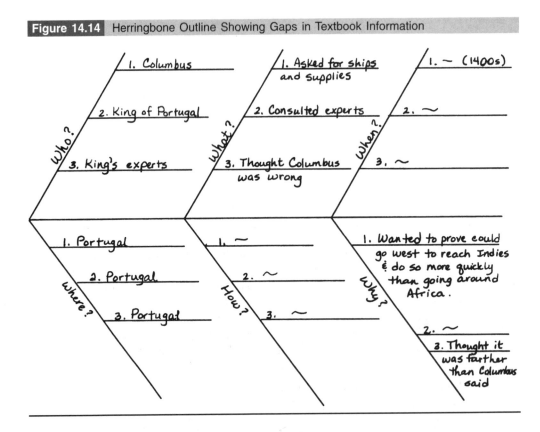

Figure 14.14 Herringbone Outline Showing Gaps in Textbook Information

important enough to look for elsewhere. The herringbone technique readily reveals these information gaps. The teacher can also use the textual answers as springboards for further discussion and research. Figure 14.14 shows the information recorded on the herringbone form.

Mapping, webbing, array tasks, and the herringbone technique use processes employed in both note taking and outlining. More important, they give students a structure for observing relationships in text that further enhance comprehension and retention of information. When these techniques are also used as prewriting strategies, students will quickly begin to understand text organization. Once students are familiar and comfortable with mapping activities, it would be appropriate to introduce the software program Inspiration (Inspiration Software, 1998–1999). This software provides a powerful electronic tool for mapping alternatives (referred to as the diagram view) and also allows these maps to be converted to outlines (referred to as the outline view).

ASSESSING FOR INTERPRETATION OF GRAPHIC AND PICTORIAL MATERIALS

The skills to be discussed in this section differ considerably from those discussed in the previous sections. Whereas the previous skills overlapped with the comprehension skills discussed in Chapters 11, 12, and 13, the reading of graphic and pictorial materials requires a unique set of skills.

As stated early in this chapter, the interpretation of tables and graphs is a subtest commonly found on standardized achievement tests. However, if the information from such a test is not readily available to the teacher (tests are machine scored), the instructional benefits are minimal. Direct measurements developed by the teacher will provide a readily available source of information.

Graphic and pictorial materials help students understand text by explaining, clarifying, or providing additional information. A learner must have skill with the following materials:

1. *Pictures*. Students must be able to use pictures that present or clarify concepts, afford new experiences vicariously, or stimulate discussion. Political cartoons are included in this category.

2. *Time lines*. Students should be able to recognize time lines as graphic presentations of events in chronological order. Both the time and the event are presented on a time line.

3. *Tables and charts*. Students must be able to read the variety of facts presented in a table or chart. These may be in single-column or multicolumn formats.

4. *Graphs*. Many types of graphs clarify and illustrate comparisons. Students should be able to read and interpret circle graphs, line graphs, bar graphs, and picture graphs.

5. *Maps and globes*. Students must be able to interpret a legend and its symbols; the scale indicated; the directions of north, south, east, and west; and the lines of latitude and longitude to read maps and globes effectively.

To assess whether students can use these five types of materials, the teacher simply has to develop a set of questions that can be answered only if the picture, time line, table, chart, graph, map, or globe has been read properly. These measures are quite easily constructed.

INSTRUCTION FOR INTERPRETING GRAPHIC AND PICTORIAL MATERIALS

General Teaching Procedure

Interpretation of pictorial and graphic material, an important aspect of visual literacy, is best taught according to a five-step procedure (Cooper et al., 1979):

1. Explanation of the use or purpose of the material being taught.

2. An understanding of the meanings of the words used to describe the material being learned.

3. The teaching of the specific skills needed for use of the material.

4. A demonstration of the use of the material.

5. The guidance of the students through the initial usage of the material. (p. 259)

The activities described in the remainder of this section point out how the teacher can follow each of the five steps. Because a large amount of visual information is available through multimedia resources as well as textbooks, teachers soon discover that learners who master interpretation of pictorial and graphic materials greatly enhance their understanding of content-area materials.

MI Connection:
spatial

Figure 14.15   Pictures Drawn by a 7-Year-Old Boy *(Left)* and an 8-Year-Old Girl *(Right)* Showing a Rolling Ball Hitting a Tree

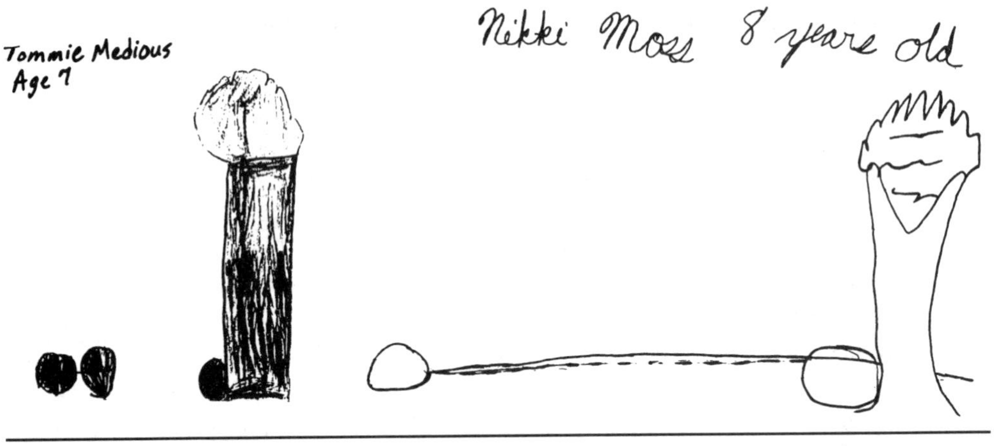

1. When explaining the use and purpose of pictures, examples must be available for students to view during the lesson. For instance, to explain the purpose of arrows, dotted lines, or other directional markers in diagrams found in texts, some actual text pages should be shown. Then, for follow-up practice, students might be directed to produce a similar diagram. The explanation may begin by giving students a sentence describing a scene that can be easily sketched. For example, the students may be asked to draw a picture to correspond to the following sentence:

The ball rolled down the street and hit a big tree.

The resulting drawings are shared, with a discussion of the techniques used to indicate "rolled" and "hit" (refer to step 3). Students should experience a need to indicate the passage of time in their drawings. Some may resolve this problem by showing several pictures that indicate the ball getting closer to the tree; others may use dotted lines to show the ball moving toward the tree (Figure 14.15). Both solutions are found in content-area material.

2. An example from a textbook is appropriate for demonstrating how important it is to understand the key words used. The following sentence was taken from a science text:

The paramecium pinched in the middle and split in two.

First, this sentence may be difficult to visualize if the important words are unfamiliar *(paramecium, pinched, split)*. Therefore, step 2, understanding or at least recognition of the key words, is important. The picture itself attempts to clarify concepts in the text that would otherwise be difficult to understand, as the picture associated with the example sentence clearly demonstrates (Figure 14.16). In this case, the picture provides the learner with a better understanding of the sentence than the words themselves. The whole illustration shows how a paramecium reproduces itself. This kind of concept is best illustrated by a series of pictures (recall the "rolling ball" sentence). Other concepts are better described using arrows or dotted lines if direction or distance is involved (Figure 14.17).

3. Some illustrations have legends that the learner must use to understand the concepts involved. Students must be taught how to use these legends for pictures, maps, and titles and column headings in tables and how to relate the pictorial or graphic information

Figure 14.16   Illustration Clarifying the Concept of a Paramecium Splitting in Two

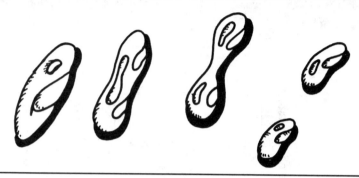

back to the text. Show students where to find the legend on a map and how to interpret the symbols for state roads versus interstate highways, for example. Then have students develop a map of their neighborhood, including symbols for houses, stores, mailboxes, traffic lights, stop signs, and other features unique to their neighborhood. These maps can be posted in the classroom for other students to interpret.

4. The *TV Guide* provides a real-world example to demonstrate the use of legends. In the "movies" section of the guide there is a key to the symbols used for movie ratings and parental guidance. Programs are rated using stars for appeal and letters and numbers for content ratings. Four stars means excellent, three stars means good, two stars means fair, and one star means poor. A *G* refers to general audience; *PG,* parental guidance; *PG-13,* programs unsuitable for children under age 13; and *R* or *NC-17,* mature audiences only or no one under 17. *NR* means not rated. Students can be shown how to locate these symbols and determine the film's appropriateness for viewing.

5. Guidance is essential initially and can be given only by direct instruction. A variety of pictorial and graphic materials with questions relevant to interpretation is the basis of such instruction. Figure 14.18 is a familiar example. The following questions would be appropriate to use with this graph:

a. What kind of graph is this? Circle one.

  bar graph   circle graph   picture graph

b. This graph shows that 30 fifth graders like (hamburgers) best.

Figure 14.17   Use of Arrows to Aid the Reader in Understanding the Concepts Involved

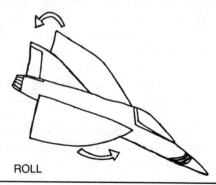

ROLL

Figure 14.18   Students Can Be Instructed in Interpreting Graphic Materials by Being Asked a Series of Relevant Questions That Relate the Graphic Information to the Question Responses

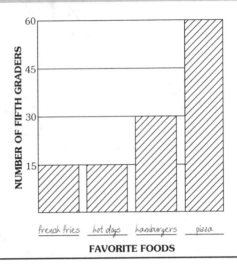

c. Two foods are liked the same. What are these two foods? (french fries) (hot dogs)

d. How many fifth graders like pizza best? (60)

e. How many fifth graders were asked what their favorite food was? (120)

To maintain their competence in this area, students must have many opportunities to use and apply these skills.

Real-World Usage

The best support for developing graphic and pictorial skills is real-world usage. For instance, to learn about the bar graph, the class could collect its own data and construct its own graph. The teacher will be enhancing not only graph skills but math skills as well.

Teachers must be alert to the many opportunities in daily life that help students appreciate the need for learning graphic and pictorial skills. Bus schedules, newspaper weather maps, TV guides, and city street maps are obvious items that can be brought into the classroom. Students who have been taught to graph their own progress on spelling tests could also use this skill to graph progress in a weight-loss program. Who hasn't been asked to draw a map giving directions from "my house" to "your house"? Students can help make maps "from classroom to cafeteria" or "from school to the ice-skating rink." Most large shopping malls have maps that locate the stores. In the Southeast and on the East Coast, hurricane-tracking maps are free to teachers in large quantities during the hurricane season.

Knowing the students and the community in which they live broadens the opportunity to practice graphic and pictorial skills. The least we can do for our students is to give them skills needed for daily life.

Go to MyEducationLab and first select the topic *Study Skills*. Go to the Activities and Applications section, and watch the video entitled "Food Survey Lesson" to see how first graders can be engaged in constructing bar graphs. Then select the topic *Content Area Literacy*. Go to the Activities and Applications section, and watch the video entitled "Promoting Literacy" for another example of students working with bar graphs. Next respond to the accompanying questions.

GENERAL STUDY STRATEGIES

As students gain familiarity with the study skills of locating information, organizing information, and interpreting graphic and pictorial materials, they can also benefit from instruction in a variety of study strategies. Having knowledge of several study strategies will help students become more aware of their own abilities to learn independently from expository material. Several study strategies are presented here with the intent that students and teachers explore their possibilities and consider modifications that may better suit personal preferences.

SQ3R

The best-known study strategy recommended for helping students make optimum use of study time is Robinson's (1970) **SQ3R** (survey, question, read, recite, review) **strategy**. This strategy is designed to (a) provide specific purposes for reading, (b) provide self-comprehension checks, and (c) fix information in memory. Briefly, in the *survey* step, the student reads the title, introductory statement, and main headings; surveys the illustrations; reads the chapter summary; and tries to mentally construct an outline of the chapter. In the *question* step, the student again looks at the main headings and uses them to formulate questions to be answered in the next step. The *read* step has the main purpose of finding answers to the questions formed in the question step. In the *recite* step, the student literally recites the answers aloud to the questions. At this point the student should also be concerned about the quality of the answers; for example, does the author provide answers that satisfy the question? The last step, *review,* is done from memory, with the entire chapter or selection being reviewed in survey fashion. The mental outline is reconstructed. The author's main ideas are recalled, and new ways to use these ideas are considered. A second and even a third review should take place over as many days.

However, several investigations of SQ3R have shown it not to be as effective as expected for students with reading difficulties (McCormick & Cooper, 1991). Instructional adaptations to SQ3R suggested by these studies are as follows:

- Providing shorter selections (300 words) because students did better when reading passages of this length. This presents students with an easier task.
- Having frequent discussion sessions to allow for direct teacher input if reading longer selections.
- Integrating discussion questions at short intervals throughout the selection, rather than asking all questions at the end of a reading.

Edward Strickland (1975) developed a technique called **assignment mastery**. The steps themselves closely parallel those in SQ3R: scanning, preparation for reading, reading, recitation and review, and reading review. The biggest difference from SQ3R is that specific questions are developed for students to ask themselves during the scanning, preparation, and reading stages:

Scanning
- How difficult does the work appear to be?
- Is it a relatively large amount of work?
- Will I have to alter my schedule to get it done?
- Are the terms generally familiar?
- What is the main theme of the assignment?

- What main headings and subheadings are there?
- What words are stressed (in italics or bold print)?

Preparation for Reading (with the help of a dictionary or glossary)

- Are there related terms that I use?
- Have I learned something that changes the meaning of the term from what I thought it was?
- Does the theme of the material appear to challenge or support my ideas?

Reading

- What is the meaning of what I am reading?
- What illustrations of that meaning are given?
- Can I recall any examples from my own experience that would clarify the meaning of the material?
- What questions should I ask my instructor that will help clarify the meaning of this material?

Strickland also stressed underlining or outlining main themes and illustrative examples while reading.

GRS

The **guided reading strategy (GRS)** (Bean & Pardi, 1979), developed specifically for struggling readers, is a modification of the guided reading procedure (Manzo, 1975). Briefly, the steps of a GRS are as follows:

1. Survey the chapter or chapter sections, reading only the chapter title, subtitles, vocabulary lists, graphs, maps, and chapter questions.
2. Close the book and orally state everything remembered from the survey. The teacher records what is remembered on the board.
3. Students recheck the chapter for any missing information; this is added to the board.
4. A crucial step: The teacher and students discuss the results of the chapter survey and organize this information into a topical outline on the board. This organizing highlights the structure of the information and enhances the ability to remember it later.
5. Students read the chapter or selection silently.
6. Students complete a 10-item true/false quiz.
7. About a week later, students take a 10-item pop quiz.

Of the general study strategies, the teacher may find that using the GRS as an introduction to the other strategies is most helpful.

PORPE

A less teacher-directed strategy intended for secondary- and college-level students uses writing as the main learning strategy for planning, monitoring, and evaluating the reading of any content-area material (Simpson, 1986). **PORPE** (*P*redict, *O*rganize, *R*ehearse, *P*ractice, *E*valuate) is especially useful for students preparing to take essay examinations.

Once the five steps of PORPE are modeled and mastered, it becomes a learning strategy that gives the student complete independence and control. The five steps are briefly presented here, but interested readers are urged to refer to Simpson's (1986) detailed description of the steps and how to teach them to students:

1. *Predict.* Students are asked to generate possible essay questions on the material read.

2. *Organize.* Students summarize and synthesize the important ideas in the material. Charts, maps, or outlines are all possible ways for organizing the material.

3. *Rehearse.* Students recite the overall organizational structure of the chart, map, or outline, eventually adding important ideas and examples to this recitation. The purpose is to place these important ideas and organizational structure into long-term memory.

4. *Practice.* Students practice writing answers to the predicted essay questions from recall.

5. *Evaluate.* Students judge the quality of their responses from the perspective of the instructor. An evaluative checklist might be developed to aid in this process.

Two validation studies (Simpson, Stahl, & Hayes, 1989) show PORPE to be a practical and robust strategy for long-lasting learning and student independence. Integrating the arts as part of the study process can also help students recall information (see Arts Connections box).

Arts Connection

A more formal drama enactment materialized when sixth graders discussed how they might better prepare for the unit test on their thematic unit on "Space and Spaces." They decided to create a television newsroom complete with a weather forecaster, two news anchors, and three news reporters reporting "live" from outer-space assignments. To add authenticity to the newsroom, their teacher videotaped the production over several weeks. At the end of the unit they invited all the students and teachers in grades 4 through 6 to view the edited tape that ended with scenes of the numerous, humorous "bloopers" that occurred during the taping. In addition, the teacher arranged for newscasters from the local television news channel to visit the viewing and then later share with the sixth graders information about how the daily news is produced and directed. Not surprisingly, students performed quite well on their unit test after so much active engagement with the topic.

A group of fourth-grade teachers decided that dance would serve as the perfect vehicle for enhancing their students' knowledge following a unit about the solar system. Combining the visual arts with writing and dance, the teachers created and labeled cardboard models of the planets, sun, and moon (for example, "This is Venus"; "Here is Mars"; "Jupiter has 16 moons"). Then, with directions and questions from the teachers, the students held up their models and moved according to their particular sun, moon, or planet positions in the solar system. After a few practice sessions, the group added "outer-space"–type music to the activity, which helped to optimize their learning. The students began to move gracefully in time to the music. They became so captivated by the activity that they created their individual interpretations of a planet, sun, and moon dance. Some students twirled slowly in circles. Others moved their outstretched arms high and low. A few soared dramatically into "outer space." Of course, all the students enhanced their knowledge about the movements and positions of the sun, moon, and planets by engaging their bodily-kinesthetic intelligence along with their readings about the solar system.

Additional Acronyms for Study Strategies. There are many other valuable study strategies, but space constraints do not allow for their thorough explanation. The following listing is intended to alert you to several of these other possibilities, some of which are content-area specific. Interested readers are referred to the sources cited for more information:

AIM (Author's Intended Message)—a metacognitive strategy for constructing the main idea of text (Jacobowitz, 1990).

FLIP (Friendliness, Language, Interest, Prior knowledge)—a framework for helping middle school and secondary students estimate the difficulty of their content-area reading assignments (Schumm & Mangrum, 1991).

PLAE (Preplan, List, Activate, Evaluate)—emphasizes the self-regulatory processes involved in planning, monitoring, and evaluating; field-tested with college developmental reading students (Nist & Simpson, 1989; Simpson & Nist, 1984). Three validation studies conclude that (a) planning is significantly related to performance on tests (Nist et al., 1989); (b) PLAE positively affects both test performance and metacognitive abilities (Nist & Simpson, 1989); and (c) students using PLAE outperformed those using traditional time management on four content-area examinations (Nist & Simpson, 1990).

PLAN (Predict, Locate, Add, Note)—a study-reading strategy that involves mapping before, during, and after reading, helping students from middle school through college develop an active role in comprehension (Caverly, Mandeville, & Nicholson, 1995).

PQRST (Preview, Question, Read, Summarize, Test)—developed to help students read physical science texts (Spache, 1963).

REAP (Read, Encode, Annotate, Ponder)—intended to help readers synthesize an author's ideas and use writing as an aid for future recall and study of ideas (Eanet & Manzo, 1976).

SCAIT (Select key words; Complete sentences; Accept final statements; Infer; Think)—intended for high-school students; uses cooperative learning to help students learn how to select important information from text and develop higher-level thinking skills (Wiesendanger & Bader, 1992).

SQRQCQ (Survey, Question, Read, Question, Compute, Question)—developed to help students solve mathematical reading and reasoning problems (Fay, 1965).

TEST-TAKING STRATEGIES

Test-taking strategies are not related to subject matter knowledge but instead refer to how one approaches the taking of a test, to include attitudes toward tests and knowledge of different kinds of test formats. Learning test-taking strategies helps students become familiar with the conventions of tests and more comfortable in the testing environment. Developing and using test-taking strategies may lead to higher test scores, assuming of course that students have learned the content knowledge being tested (Bangert-Drowns, Kulik, & Kulik, 1983; Scruggs & Mastropieri, 1992). The major areas described in test-taking strategies are:

1. Approaching a test with a good attitude
2. Knowing the different kinds of test formats and how the test will be scored and graded
3. Following directions
4. Managing time
5. Having a strategy for dealing with difficult questions/guessing

Approaching a Test with a Good Attitude

To perform well on a test requires positive thinking and physical alertness. A certain amount of nervousness is natural and perhaps even helpful. Teachers can prepare students by modeling positive attitudes and expecting good results. Motivation to do well on a test may sometimes require incentives, such as an extra recess period or extra time in the computer lab. Discussing the purpose of the test, addressing test anxiety, and involving parents by asking their cooperation in making sure their children get a good night's rest, providing a good breakfast, and ensuring their children do not drink an excess of fluids on the day of the test are important steps to take. To address test anxiety, have students practice turning negative statements like *"I'll never make it through this test"* into positive statements like *"I'm going to do the best I can."* Some classroom activities can also take the form of a test so students become familiar and comfortable with the various formats of test items. For example, work sheets that require students to fill in oval shapes to indicate their response will familiarize students with the type of computer-scorable answer sheets many tests employ. Just prior to test taking, engage students in some relaxation exercises such as deep breathing and stretching and remind them to breathe deeply during the test if they begin to feel stress. Finally, a quiet, orderly testing environment will help students focus on the task of taking the test.

Knowing the Different Kinds of Test Formats

The five most common kinds of items used on tests are multiple-choice, true/false, sentence completion or fill in the blank, matching, and essay. Students need to learn the steps provided in the following sets of guidelines to deal with each of the five types of items. And they should be made aware of which of the five kinds of items will be included on any particular test and how the test will be graded. For example, is guessing on a multiple-choice response a good idea? How much is each question worth? What will count and what won't count when the test is graded? For example, will spelling count on a social studies test? Do you have to show your work on a math test? Will capitalization and punctuation count on a science essay exam? The teacher can model these questions during test preparation so students can better anticipate how they will study for the test and the types of behaviors required during the test. Following are sets of guidelines to be shared and discussed with students for multiple-choice, true/false, sentence completion and fill in the blank, matching, and essay tests.

Guidelines for Answering Multiple-Choice Questions

1. After reading the question stem, formulate an answer before reading the available choices. If you can think of the answer without the help of the options provided, you can be more certain your response is correct when you locate a matching option.

2. Eliminate unlikely answers first. By eliminating two alternatives, chances of a correct answer have increased to 50/50. Then use the true/false methods described in the next set of guidelines to find the incorrect alternative.

3. Select numbered answers from the middle range, not the extremes. For example, if the height of a mountain is requested, eliminate 40,000 feet (high), and 1,000 feet (low). Then choose between 9,000 feet and 12,000 feet.

4. Select answers that are longer and more descriptive. Descriptive detail is given to help you identify the truth, making the answer longer. Shorter (false) answers are created quickly as throwaway items.

5. Similar answers give a clue! One of them is correct, and the other is disguised. Read them carefully.

6. Watch out for the words *"not true."* Remember to reverse your procedure and eliminate truth.

Guidelines for Answering True/False Questions

1. When you are not sure of the answer, mark it true! It is difficult to make a false statement look true, so there are generally more true questions on true/false exams than false questions. Specific detail in the statement may also tend to make it true. For example, the statement "Michael Phelps won eight gold medals in Beijing" has specific detail and is more likely to be true.

2. Look for any part that will make a statement false. It is easy to add a false part to an otherwise true statement. Students often read the question and see some truth and quickly assume that the entire statement is true. For example, "Water boils at 212 degrees in Denver." Water does boil at 212 degrees, but not at Denver's altitude.

3. Extreme modifiers tend to make the question false. Look for extreme *modifiers* like:

all	none	best	absolutely
always	never	worst	absolutely not
only	nobody	everybody	certainly
invariably	no one	everyone	certainly not

4. Qualifying words tend to make a question true. Here is a list of *qualifiers*:

usually	frequently	often	sometimes
some	seldom	many	much
probably	a majority	apt to	most
might	a few	may	unlikely

5. Negative words or prefixes complicate the statement. Double negatives make a positive. For example "not uncommon" actually means common. Some prefixes (un-, im-, miss-) will alter the meaning of the statement.

6. Items that state a reason tend to be false. Words that cause justification or reason (since, because, when, if) tend to make the statement false. Also, the reason that is given may be incorrect or incomplete.

7. There is no substitute for the truth. Many concentrated hours of study to fix facts into your memory are the best way to prepare for true/false questions.

Guidelines for Answering Sentence Completion or Fill in the Blank Questions

1. Notice the number of blanks in the sentence and the length of the space. The test maker might provide clues to the answer by adding spaces or making them longer.

2. Provide a descriptive answer when you cannot think of the exact word or words. Partial credit might be given for your effort.

Guidelines for Answering Matching Questions

1. Look completely through both lists to become familiar with the items, build your confidence, and enhance your memory of key words or phrases. Then examine both lists to determine the types of items and their relationships.

2. Use one list as a starting point and go through the second list to find a match. But move through the entire list before selecting a match because a more correct answer may follow. As you become familiar with the second list, you will be able to go straight to a match that you saw when looking through the lists a previous time.

3. Cross off items on the second list when you are certain that you have a match.

4. Avoid guessing until all absolute matches have been made because you will likely eliminate an answer that could be used for a later choice.

Guidelines for Essay Questions

1. Organize your thoughts before you begin to write. A short outline on a separate piece of paper that includes the main topics and key introductory words will improve your answer.

2. Paraphrase the original question to form your introductory statement. Restating the question also allows the test grader to see how you understood the question. Perhaps you understood it to mean something other than what the test maker intended. This process will help you get the question straight in your mind.

3. Form a clear statement of purpose and place it as near to the beginning of the response as possible. Provide clear explanations to back up the main concept. A complete answer usually has a main idea, supporting details, and illustrative examples.

4. Write or print clearly and legibly, using a dark-colored erasable ballpoint pen. Making teachers or test graders work hard to read your answer might lower your grade. Avoid crossing out words or sentences and don't smudge your paper. Remember to save some space for a brief summary.

5. Use lists or bullets wherever possible.
   - Numbers or bullets allow the teachers to easily see your points.
   - Never bury your lists or key points in the middle of a paragraph.
   - If you must use a long paragraph, underline your key points.

6. Key verbs or words in each question describe the task you are expected to complete. Circle the direction words in the question to make sure that you are focusing on the desired task. Sample direction verbs or adjectives, and their generally intended action or task, are listed below.

   Direction *verbs* that ask you to *review an idea or concept* in your own words:

   summarize,   survey,   discuss,   explain

   Direction *verbs* that ask for a *set of items or ideas* that were presented in class or in reading material. These action words generally require more precise wording of items by giving numbers or steps:

   trace,   outline,   list,   diagram,   solve

   Direction *verbs* that ask you to *speak in favor* of a concept or give the reasons why it should be accepted as valid:

   defend,   argue,   debate,   contend,   justify

Direction *verbs* that ask for a *specific meaning* or picture of a concept:

define,   clarify,   describe,   depict,   illustrate

Direction *verbs* that ask you to show *differences* in several ideas or situations:

contrast,   compare,   distinguish,   differentiate

Direction *adjectives* that ask for *specific information* the test writer considers important:

significant,   critical,   key,   important,   major,   principal,   essential,   vital

Following Directions

It is critical that students understand the importance of reading the directions or listening carefully to the directions given for a test and that they ask questions about any that are not understood. Sometimes words used in directions can be confusing. Students need to know exactly what each word in the directions means. If they do not, direct them to ask for the meanings of any words in the directions they are not sure about. Students also need to notice the details within the directions. A key detail may require that students answer only three out of the five essay questions, or that more than one answer may be possible on a multiple-choice test. Also be sure students know exactly how to mark machine-scored answer sheets. They could receive a lower score if the ovals (bubbles) are not filled in completely. Also, leaving stray marks on a machine-scorable answer sheet could cause the computer to pick up these marks as errors.

Managing Time

Timed tests are a major cause of test anxiety. It is quite common for students to panic when they feel they are running out of time on a test and may not finish. Usually spending too much time on difficult questions causes this problem. Suggest to students that they quickly look over the whole test before beginning. Then they can plan how to use the allotted time. First, try to estimate how many minutes it will take to finish each test section. Then determine a pace that will ensure completing the test within the time allowed. Also build in some time for looking back over the test for skipped items or to review a response. Students should be reminded to start with the section they think is easiest to build confidence or pick out the easy and hard questions without trying to answer them right away and do the easy items first. In other words, students need to know they do not just automatically have to proceed from question #1, then #2, and so on. However, the decision to skip an item should be made very quickly, not after several minutes of attempting to answer. If there is no penalty for guessing, then they can make a guess, mark the item, move on, and come back to the item later. Letting more difficult questions steal valuable time will raise test anxiety. Students should be advised to move on and find success with other questions. When moving through a test, this advice is probably the most important idea to remember. (Note that if an answer sheet is used, and an item is skipped on the test, direct students to lightly mark the skipped item on the answer sheet. This will keep the student from answering the next item in the wrong answer space. Also, with multiple-choice tests, tell students to avoid looking for patterns. Noticing that the last four answers were choice "c" is not a good reason to stop, go back, and break concentration.)

Once students have begun the test they might benefit from first reading the questions that accompany an item before reading the text of the question itself. In this way they will know what information is being requested prior to reading the test material. If there are pictures or diagrams, they should be examined carefully. Usually, the first answer that comes to mind is often the correct answer. Nervously reviewing questions and changing answers may do more harm than good. Change an answer only if the question had been misread initially and the correct answer becomes obvious on review. As students finish the test, remind them to return to any difficult questions that were marked for review. Once the response is complete, erase any stray marks to avoid misinterpretations. Check to make sure all questions have been answered. More than one student has failed to notice questions that might be on the back side of the paper or on a second page. Finally, students should be in a habit of proofreading written essays and attending to grammar and spelling.

Having a Strategy for Dealing with Difficult Questions

Teachers can help greatly in assisting students to develop a plan for dealing with difficult test questions. There is little doubt that students will sometimes guess on an exam. However, if they are taught to make educated guesses, the result could be higher test scores. To make an educated guess, some knowledge about the content on the test must exist. Much of what forms an educated guess is test-wiseness (review the guidelines for each of the five test formats).

Raphael and Au (2005) described the potential for QARs (see Chapter 11 for a discussion of QARs as a framework for comprehension instruction) in helping students with dealing with high-stakes test questions. By identifying the comprehension strategies associated with each of the four types of QARs, Raphael and Au provide guidance for teachers in alerting students to the task demands of the questions on the high-stakes tests they must take. As with any comprehension task, when taking standardized tests students need to be reminded of the importance of using their background knowledge to answer some of the questions. For example, not all multiple-choice questions are "right there" questions. In fact, the trend in national assessments is away from a heavy emphasis on locating and recalling information and toward the integration of ideas across texts, making inferences, critiquing, and evaluating.

Raphael and Au analyzed 12 items from a sample test passage for the format of the questions and their corresponding QARs. They found that "right there" (Where do wombats live?; Describe the sleeping area of wombats.), "think and search" (This passage mostly describes how . . .; Describe one way these two animals are similar and one way they are different.), and "author and me" (Choose an animal, other than a koala, that you know about and compare it to the wombat.; Give two reasons why people should not have wombats as pets. Use what you learned in the passage to support your answer.) QARs were represented in the multiple-choice questions as well as the constructed essays. Teachers who want their students to perform well on high-stakes tests would be wise to provide instruction in all the QARs and the reading strategies associated with them (such as scanning, identifying main ideas, summarizing, making inferences, visualizing, using text organization, predicting, note taking, making text-to-self connections). Through QAR instruction, teachers do not need to teach to a particular test, as is too often the case in preparing students for testing. Instead, teachers can teach students the task demands of different types of questions and alert students to these demands as appropriate to the different test formats students face.

Summary

This chapter addressed the topic of how to help students who are considered to be successful readers but are often at a loss when given assignments such as "Report on one of the following topics" or "Take notes on Chapter 6 in your history book for homework." Such assignments assume the student can locate and organize information and interpret graphic or pictorial information. In short, the student must be an independent reader *and learner*—not just a student who can recognize words in print and understand the message.

Knowing *how* to learn is what study skill instruction is all about. This chapter provides examples of study skills and how they can be taught directly. Teachers must "extend and expand" reading to include a variety of material. Also, study skills must be taught from the beginning. If students are to be independent learners, they must know how to find information they need, how to organize information, and how to interpret the visual aids accompanying information ("reading to learn"). Teachers therefore must provide this instruction using content-area materials in which students can see the application of the study skills.

The general study strategies discussed are most easily learned if the students have previously received instruction for all three stages of strategic expository reading because these strategies address all three phases. Strategic expository reading does not simply develop—it must be modeled, explained, and practiced. The topic of test-taking strategies is also addressed, and guidelines for helping students do their best on tests are provided.

Recommended Websites

Online Reference Materials
   http://encyclopedia.com
A basic encyclopedia and dictionary are provided here.
   http://encarta.msn.com
This extensive site has access to an encyclopedia, a dictionary, and an atlas.
   www.yourdictionary.com
This one is a lexicographer's delight.
   www.atlapedia.com
An online atlas can be found here.
   www.infoplease.com
Go here for access to almanacs and more.

Best WebQuests
   http://bestwebquests.com
WebQuests are inquiry-oriented activities that use the power of the Internet and a scaffolded learning process to assist learning.

So You Have to Do a Research Project?
   www.ri.net/schools/East_Greenwich/research.html
Although not updated recently, this site provides a great collection of resources to help intermediate and middle-school students with a research project.

Harriet Tubman and the Underground Railroad
   http://www2.lhric.org/pocantico/tubman/tubman.html
This website, developed by and for second graders, demonstrates an example of a source for housing an extensive collection of ideas and resources for studying any topic or person.

Search Engines by Category—Source
   www.noodletools.com/debbie/literacies/information/5locate/adviceengine.html
This one is helpful for locating the best search tool for particular information needs.

Skills for Today's Workforce
   http://khake.com/page3.html
This site provides links to a large number of life-skill sites.

The Five-Paragraph Essay
   www.geocities.com/SoHo/Atrium/1437/index.html
If writing a clear and concise essay is a skill you want students to develop, this site will give you multiple ways to achieve that goal. Exemplars are provided.

Writing a Biography
www.bham.wednet.edu/bio/biomaker.htm
http://teacher.scholastic.com/writewit/biograph/index.htm
These are two wonderful guides for helping students learn
to write biographies.

Writing a Book Review
http://teacher.scholastic.com/writewit/bookrev/index.htm
This workshop from Scholastic walks students through the
process of writing a book review.

Paradigm Online Writing Assistant
www.powa.org/
This site helps upper-grade students engage in the writing
process.

NEWSEUM
www.newseum.org/
This site has an interactive news museum.

MyEducationLab is a research-based learning tool that brings teaching to life. Go to the Gipe 7th
Edition MyEducationLab for Reading Assessment site at www.myeducationlab.com to:

- Engage in multimedia exercises to help you build a deeper and more applied understanding of chapter content.
- Use extensive resources including videos from real classrooms, Praxis and licensure
preparation, a lesson plan builder, and materials to help you in your teaching career.

Assessment Resources

This set of appendixes is focused on various forms of assessment, from teacher self-assessments and student assessments, to student self-assessments. Each Appendix can be reproduced as needed. Go to MyEducationLab and click the Resources tab. Then go to the Assessment Resources section to view and print these individual appendixes.

Appendix A   Instructional Environment Survey for Teachers

Directions: This checklist is intended to help you critically examine your classroom environment. Check *Yes* if the item is currently true; check *Maybe* if you are interested in pursuing this item further; check *No* if the item is not true. Reflect upon the results of the survey after it is completed.

	Yes	Maybe	No
1. I know my students' interests.	___	___	___
2. I know my students' attitudes and perceptions about reading and writing.	___	___	___
3. My classroom has its own library including:	___	___	___
a. trade books	___	___	___
b. reference books	___	___	___
c. student-authored books	___	___	___
d. alternative textbooks	___	___	___
e. audiobooks	___	___	___
4. I encourage my students to read and write recreationally by providing time for them to do so.	___	___	___
5. There are places for small groups to work cooperatively on reading and writing activities.	___	___	___
6. There are places for individuals to work quietly.	___	___	___
7. I share what I am reading and writing with my students.	___	___	___
8. I encourage students to share their reading through:	___	___	___
a. art	___	___	___
b. drama	___	___	___
c. speaking	___	___	___
d. writing	___	___	___
9. I tell students what I like about their work.	___	___	___
10. I do not use reading as a punishment.	___	___	___
11. I do not use writing as a punishment.	___	___	___
12. I know some ways to integrate literature with reading and writing.	___	___	___

(Continued)

	Yes	Maybe	No
13. I know some ways to use trade books with pupils who have special needs or are from a culture diverse from my own.	_____	_____	_____
14. My classroom contains:	_____	_____	_____
a. typewriters and/or computers	_____	_____	_____
b. chalkboard space for group writing	_____	_____	_____
c. large sheets of paper on wall for composing	_____	_____	_____
d. transparencies/overhead projector	_____	_____	_____
e. videotaping equipment (VCR/DVD and camera)	_____	_____	_____
f. Internet access	_____	_____	_____
g. scanner or digital camera	_____	_____	_____
15. My classroom has a listening center with tape or DVD recorders and headsets.	_____	_____	_____
16. A variety of writing instruments are available to students, including:	_____	_____	_____
a. pencils/pens	_____	_____	_____
b. crayons/colored markers	_____	_____	_____
c. chalk/erasers	_____	_____	_____
d. computers/color printer	_____	_____	_____
17. A variety of supplies are available to students, including:			
a. lined paper	_____	_____	_____
b. construction paper	_____	_____	_____
c. tissue paper	_____	_____	_____
d. crepe paper	_____	_____	_____
e. yarn/fabric	_____	_____	_____
f. scissors	_____	_____	_____
g. glue/paste	_____	_____	_____
h. tape, all types	_____	_____	_____
i. stapler/hole punch	_____	_____	_____
j. needle/thread	_____	_____	_____

Reflections/Plan of Action:

Appendix B Levels of Analysis and Correlative Diagnostic Questions: A Checklist

Student's name _____ Date _____

Directions: Put a check in the box for a "yes" answer.

Level 1: Determining Lack of Success in Literacy

☐ Is the learner experiencing a lack of success in literacy?
Under what conditions or in what situations?

(Note: This question should be asked after *every* diagnostic question that follows.)

Level 2: Determining the Domain(s) in Which Difficulty Occurs

☐ Does the learner demonstrate underdeveloped oral or written language ability?
☐ Does the learner have difficulty with word recognition?
☐ Does the learner have difficulty with comprehension of narrative text?
☐ Does the learner have difficulty with strategic reading of expository text or with study skills?

Level 3: Determining the Area(s) within the Domain(s)

Oral and Written Language Ability

☐ Does the learner demonstrate underdeveloped oral (that is, speaking or listening) and written language ability, to include spelling?

Word Recognition

☐ Does the learner have a limited sight vocabulary and a word recognition strategy?
☐ Does the learner have difficulty in the area of word analysis (that is, visual analysis and decoding)?
☐ Can the learner reassemble (or blend) word parts that have been visually or auditorily analyzed?
☐ Does the learner have knowledge of word morphology (structural analysis)?
☐ Does the learner have difficulty using context clues?
☐ Can the learner use a dictionary to assist word recognition?

Reading Comprehension and Strategic Reading for Narrative Text

☐ Does the learner have a limited meaning vocabulary?
☐ Does the learner have difficulty with thinking or problem-solving skills associated with comprehension of narrative text, such as identifying story features, predicting events, or evaluating a character's actions?
☐ Does the learner have difficulty recognizing his or her own inability to understand what was read?
☐ Does this apparent comprehension problem result from difficulty with word recognition?
☐ Does the learner's apparent comprehension problem result from difficulty in strategic reading for expository text or study skills?

Strategic Reading for Expository Text and Study Skills

☐ Does the learner have difficulty with content-specific vocabulary?
☐ Does the learner have difficulty with content-specific skills, such as reading visual displays, formulas, or other unique symbols?
☐ Does the learner have difficulty recognizing whether the text is meaningful to him or her?
☐ Does the learner have difficulty locating information?
☐ Does the learner have difficulty organizing information?

Physical, Psychological, and Environmental Factors

☐ Does this learner demonstrate the influence of a physical factor?
☐ Does this learner demonstrate the influence of a psychological factor?
☐ Does this learner demonstrate the influence of an environmental factor?
☐ Has this learner had opportunities for reading and writing related to his or her needs and interests?
☐ Does the learner have a negative attitude toward reading/writing?
☐ Does the learner lack interest in reading/writing?
☐ If someone asked this learner, "What is reading?" or "What is writing?" would the response be one that would please me?
☐ Is my curriculum so skills oriented that this learner never has the opportunity to read or write for his or her own purposes?
☐ Have I examined my own beliefs and attitudes about the way this learner might need to learn?
☐ Have I explored alternative instructional approaches that might benefit this learner?

Appendix C   Self-Assessment Questionnaire for Teachers of English Learners

Role One: Involve the English Learner in Content Learning

☐ How do I specifically introduce new concepts through comprehensible input to prepare my ELs for content-area lessons?

☐ How do I modify my teaching so my ELs can understand the content and complete their assignments?

☐ How do I provide peer support for my ELs?

Role Two: Facilitate English Language Development

☐ How do I provide structured opportunities for ELs and native English speakers to speak English with each other?

☐ How do I avoid correcting the English errors made by my ELs and instead provide con-structive feedback on their English use by expanding or extending what they have said?

☐ How do I help students learn the language associated with the content I am teaching?

Role Three: Help the English Learner Socialize and Acculturate to the Mainstream School Community

☐ How do I help my ELs understand the expectations of the mainstream school culture?

☐ How do I make use of my ELs' language and cultural knowledge in my teaching?

☐ How do I find ways to involve ELs' parents in my classroom or in the school community?

Role Four: Collaborate and Advocate for English Learners

☐ How do I collaborate with my colleagues at school to ensure that my ELs' needs are made a part of all curricular, instructional, and assessment decisions?

☐ How do I try to identify what my ELs bring to the classroom that can be used in all students' learning as well as their own learning?

Reflections: If I am dissatisfied with any of my responses to these questions, what do I plan to do?

| **Appendix D**   Educator's Checklist: Observable Clues to Classroom Vision Problems |

Student's name _____ Age _____ Date _____

1. Appearance of eyes:
One eye turns in or out at any time _____
Reddened eyes or lids _____
Eyes tear excessively _____
Encrusted eyelids _____
Frequent sties on eyelids _____

2. Complaints when using eyes at desk:
Headaches in forehead or temples _____
Burning or itching after reading or
   desk work _____
Nausea or dizziness _____
Print blurs after reading a short time _____

3. Behavioral signs of visual problems:

A. *Eye movement abilities (ocular motility)*
Head turns as reads across page _____
Loses place often during reading _____
Needs finger or marker to keep place _____
Displays short attention span in reading
   or copying _____
Too frequently omits words _____
Repeatedly omits "small" words _____
Writes up or downhill on paper _____
Rereads or skips lines unknowingly _____
Orients drawings poorly on page _____

B. *Eye teaming abilities (binocularity)*
Complains of seeing double (diplopia) _____
Repeats letters within words _____
Omits letters, numbers, or phrases _____
Misaligns digits in number columns _____
Squints, closes, or covers one eye _____
Tilts head extremely while working
   at desk _____
Consistently shows gross postural
   deviations at all desk activities _____

C. *Eye–hand coordination abilities*
Must feel things to assist in any
   interpretation required _____
Eyes not used to "steer" hand movements
   (extreme lack of orientation placement
   of words or drawings on page) _____
Writes crookedly, poorly spaced, cannot
   stay on ruled lines _____
Misaligns both horizontal and vertical
   series of numbers _____
Uses hand or fingers to keep place
   on the page _____

Uses other hand as "spacer" to control
   spacing and alignment on page _____
Repeatedly confuses left–right directions _____

D. *Visual form perception (visual comparison,
   visual imagery, visualization)*
Mistakes words with same or similar
   beginnings _____
Fails to recognize same word in next
   sentence _____
Reverses letters and/or words in writing
   and copying _____
Confuses likenesses and minor differences _____
Confuses same word in same sentence _____
Repeatedly confuses similar beginnings
   and endings of words _____
Fails to visualize what is read either
   silently or orally _____
Whispers to self for reinforcement
   while reading silently _____
Returns to "drawing with fingers" to
   decide likes and differences _____

E. *Refractive status (nearsightedness, farsightedness, focus problems, and the like)*
Comprehension reduces as reading
   continues; loses interest too quickly _____
Mispronounces similar words as
   continues reading _____
Blinks excessively at desk tasks and/or
   reading; not elsewhere _____
Holds book too closely; face too close
   to desk surface _____
Avoids all possible near-centered
   tasks _____
Complains of discomfort in tasks that
   demand visual interpretation _____
Closes or covers one eye when reading
   or doing desk work _____
Makes errors in copying from chalkboard
   to paper on desk _____
Makes errors in copying from reference
   book to notebook _____
Squints to see chalkboard or requests
   to move nearer _____
Rubs eyes during or after short periods
   of visual activity _____
Fatigues easily; blinks to make
   chalkboard clear up after desk task _____

Appendix E   Checklist of Symptoms of Hearing Difficulties

	Yes	No
Inclines one ear toward speaker when listening	____	____
Holds mouth open while listening	____	____
Holds head at angle when taking part in discussion	____	____
Reads in unnatural tone of voice	____	____
Uses faulty pronunciation on common words	____	____
Has indistinct enunciation	____	____
Often asks to have instructions and directions repeated	____	____
Breathes through mouth	____	____
Has discharge from ears	____	____
Frequently complains of earache or sinusitis	____	____
Has frequent head colds	____	____
Complains of buzzing noise in ears	____	____
Seems to be inattentive or indifferent	____	____
Does poorly in games with oral directions	____	____
Has trouble following trend of thought during oral discussions	____	____

Source: Reproduced by permission of the publisher, F. E. Peacock Publishers, Inc., Itasca, Ill., from Eddie C. Kennedy, *Classroom Approaches to Remedial Reading,* 1977, p. 391.

Appendix F   Checklist of Symptoms Associated with Emotional Maladjustment

General Traits or Behavior

	Yes	No
1. Displays signs of excessive shyness	____	____
2. Displays signs of introversion	____	____
3. Displays signs of lack of confidence	____	____
4. Gives up easily on school tasks	____	____
5. Plays alone	____	____
6. Daydreams	____	____
7. Displays signs of overdependence	____	____
8. Seeks approval excessively	____	____
9. Has numerous unexplained absences	____	____
10. Displays signs of nervousness	____	____
11. Does not work cooperatively with classmates	____	____
12. Argues and fights with classmates	____	____
13. Constantly disrupts class	____	____

Reading-Related Traits or Behavior

	Yes	No
14. Shows fear of the reading task	____	____
15. Refuses to read orally	____	____
16. Displays antagonism toward reading	____	____
17. Does not get along with others in reading group	____	____
18. Does not attend during reading lesson	____	____
19. Does not complete reading assignments	____	____
20. Displays fear or nervousness during recitation	____	____

Appendix G   Incomplete Sentence Projective Test

The Incomplete Sentence Projective Test (Boning & Boning, 1957) that follows allows each student to write (or provide orally) information regarding how he or she feels about the item in question (Figure G.1). Responses may be more honest if the teacher tells students the information will be used to provide materials and activities they will enjoy. Any interpretation should be modified and verified by observations over time.

Before administering the incomplete sentences, decide whether oral or written responses are most appropriate. Directions for an oral administration might be: "I will begin a sentence with a few words and then stop. When I stop, you tell me the very first thing that you think of to finish the sentence. I will write down just what you say. Let's do a practice sentence. I think pizza tastes _____. Are you ready to begin?" Directions for a written administration might be: "Finish each sentence with the first idea that comes to your mind. Don't worry about spelling. Let's try the first one together."

Figure G.1   Incomplete Sentence Projective Test

1. Today I feel . . . .
2. When I have to read, I . . . .
3. I get angry when . . . .
4. To be grown up . . . .
5. My idea of a good time is . . . .
6. I wish my parents knew . . . .
7. School is . . . .
8. I can't understand why . . . .
9. I feel bad when . . . .
10. I wish teachers . . . .
11. I wish my mother . . . .
12. Going to college . . . .
13. To me, books . . . .
14. People think I . . . .
15. I like to read about . . . .
16. On weekends I . . . .
17. I'd rather read than . . . .
18. To me, homework . . . .
19. I hope I'll never . . . .
20. I wish people wouldn't . . . .
21. When I finish high school . . . .
22. I'm afraid . . . .
23. Comic books . . . .
24. When I take my report card home . . . .
25. I am at my best when . . . .
26. Most brothers and sisters . . . .
27. I don't know how . . . .
28. When I read math . . . .

29. I feel proud when . . . .

30. The future looks . . . .

31. I wish my father . . . .

32. I like to read when . . . .

33. I would like to be . . . .

34. For me, studying . . . .

35. I often worry about . . . .

36. I wish I could . . . .

37. Reading science . . . .

38. I look forward to . . . .

39. I wish . . . .

40. I'd read more if . . . .

41. When I read out loud . . . .

Source: From Boning, T., and Boning, R. "I'd Rather Read Than . . ." *Reading Teacher,* April 1957, p. 196. Reprinted with permission of the International Reading Association. To interpret the results, the following areas have been identified by item number:

Overall attitudes and self-concept: 1, 3, 4, 5, 8, 9, 14, 16, 19, 20, 22, 25, 27, 29, 30, 33, 35, 36, 38, 42

Family relations: 6, 11, 26, 31

School attitudes: 7, 10, 12, 18, 21, 24

Reading process: 2, 28, 32, 34, 37, 40, 41 (Boning and Boning [1957] found that the most revealing responses were to item 40.)

Reading interest: 13, 15, 17, 23 (Use item 17 to get clues for helping direct children toward increased recreational reading.)

Responses to the overall attitudes and self-concept area are very important to evaluate. They often provide insight into a student's academic problems. Some supplementary questions for the reading process and reading interest areas follow. To determine attitudes and interests toward writing, simply substitute the word *writing* for *reading* in most of the items.

1. *Supplementary reading process questions:*

    a. Reading is . . .

    b. I cannot read when . . .

    c. When reading new words I . . .

    d. Reading out loud . . .

    e. I read better when . . .

2. *Supplementary reading interest questions:*

    a. I like reading about . . .

    b. I don't want to read about . . .

    c. The best thing about reading . . .

    d. I laugh when I read about . . .

    e. The best book I know about . . .

Appendix H Weekly Progress Report for Keeping Parents Informed

Directions: Circle the number that best describes each item. A 4 means always, 3 means usually, 2 means sometimes, and 1 means never. Include comments to explain any item further.

Student

I come to school/class on time	4	3	2	1
I stay on task/pay attention	4	3	2	1
I do my best	4	3	2	1
I read and write each day	4	3	2	1
I use new strategies	4	3	2	1
I cooperate with my teacher	4	3	2	1

Teacher

Gets to school/class on time	4	3	2	1
On task/pays attention	4	3	2	1
Does his or her best	4	3	2	1
Reads/writes each day	4	3	2	1
Applies new strategies	4	3	2	1
Cooperates with me	4	3	2	1

Student comments: _____

_____

_____

_____

Teacher's comments: _____

_____

_____

Parent comments: _____

_____

_____

_____

Date: _____   Signatures: _____   _____   _____

(student)   (teacher)   (parent/guardian)

Appendix I	General Scoring Rubric for Story Retellings

Name: _____ Grade: _____ Date: _____

Story Title (and Author): _____

Context: Story Read by Child _____ Story Read to Child _____

Main Points for Retelling	**Unprompted**	**Prompted**
CHARACTERS (_____ points each)		
1. _____	_____	_____
2. _____	_____	_____
3. _____	_____	_____
4. _____	_____	_____
5. _____	_____	_____
SETTING (_____ points each)		
1. _____	_____	_____
2. _____	_____	_____
3. _____	_____	_____
4. _____	_____	_____
EVENTS/PLOT (_____ points each)		
1. _____	_____	_____
2. _____	_____	_____
3. _____	_____	_____
4. _____	_____	_____
5. _____	_____	_____
6. _____	_____	_____
7. _____	_____	_____
8. _____	_____	_____
9. _____	_____	_____
10. _____	_____	_____
RESOLUTION/THEME (_____ points each)		
1. _____	_____	_____
2. _____	_____	_____
3. _____	_____	_____

TOTAL POINTS: _____ /100 = _____ %   _____ /100 + _____ /100

Evaluative Comments: (for example, awareness of story features; story structure; understands story theme[s], and the like)

Appendix J	Short Form for Assessing Oral Reading Behaviors

Student _____ Date _____

	Yes	No	Sometimes
1. Do the reader's miscues make sense in context?	_____	_____	_____
2. Does the reader correct unacceptable miscues?	_____	_____	_____
3. Does the reader pay too much attention to graphophonic cues and not enough to syntactic or semantic cues?*	_____	_____	_____

*A miscue may be graphically similar in the initial, medial, or final position (or some combination) and be unacceptable in terms of meaning. For example, a reader paying more attention to graphophonic cues than semantic or syntactic cues might substitute *his* for *this* in the sentence *This time it was ready.*

Appendix K	Assessing Emergent Reading Concepts

Name _____ Date _____

BOOK CHARACTERISTICS

_____ Can point to the front of the book

_____ Can point to the back of the book

_____ Can hold the book upright with the front facing forward

_____ Can point to the title of the book

_____ Can distinguish illustrations from print

PRINT ORIENTATION

_____ Can point to where text/print begins

_____ Can show directionality of print from left to right

_____ Can point to the end of the text/print

_____ Can show word boundaries (the beginning and ending of words)

PRINT TERMINOLOGY

_____ Can identify the top and bottom of the page

_____ Can point to a letter

_____ Can point to a word

_____ Can point to a specific letter on request

_____ Can point to a specific word on request

_____ Can point to a lowercase letter

_____ Can point to an uppercase letter

_____ Can point to specific punctuation marks on request

Appendix L	Checklist for Appraising Early Reading Development

Student _____ Age _____ Grade _____

CHARACTERISTICS	Date Observed	Context	Date Observed	Context
Cognition				
1. Understands grade-level material read aloud	_____	_____	_____	_____
2. Remembers new words used in class	_____	_____	_____	_____
3. Remembers content of stories discussed in class	_____	_____	_____	_____
Language				
1. Speaks in complete sentences	_____	_____	_____	_____
2. Speaking vocabulary is adequate	_____	_____	_____	_____
3. Speaking vocabulary is advanced	_____	_____	_____	_____
4. Speech is normal	_____	_____	_____	_____
5. Hearing is normal	_____	_____	_____	_____
General Reading	_____	_____	_____	_____
1. When being read to, the child:	_____	_____	_____	_____
a. sometimes finishes the sentence (anticipates what is next)	_____	_____	_____	_____
b. sometimes follows along with finger	_____	_____	_____	_____
c. pays attention	_____	_____	_____	_____
2. Recognizes signs (such as stop signs), labels (such as "Wheaties"), or logos (such as "McDonald's")	_____	_____	_____	_____
3. Recognizes his/her name	_____	_____	_____	_____
4. Recognizes letters in *(state what context)*	_____	_____	_____	_____
5. Recognizes words in *(state what context)*	_____	_____	_____	_____
6. Remembers words taught as whole words	_____	_____	_____	_____
7. Attempts to blend sound units	_____	_____	_____	_____
8. Can guess new words from context	_____	_____	_____	_____
9. Skips words when reading in order to use context	_____	_____	_____	_____
10. Skips unknown words totally in order to maintain comprehension	_____	_____	_____	_____
11. Reads fluently	_____	_____	_____	_____
12. Reads with little or no transposing of letters/words	_____	_____	_____	_____
13. Observes punctuation in oral reading	_____	_____	_____	_____
14. Reads silently with little or no finger pointing to text	_____	_____	_____	_____
15. Reads silently with little or no subvocalizing	_____	_____	_____	_____
16. Recalls facts of material read	_____	_____	_____	_____
17. Can summarize main points of material read	_____	_____	_____	_____
18. Can locate answers to questions	_____	_____	_____	_____
19. Comprehends narrative material	_____	_____	_____	_____
20. Comprehends expository material	_____	_____	_____	_____
21. Adjusts reading speed according to reading purpose or difficulty of material	_____	_____	_____	_____
Motivation				
1. Enjoys being read to	_____	_____	_____	_____
2. Knows that books have a top and bottom and turns pages front to back	_____	_____	_____	_____
3. Talks about books he/she listened to or read	_____	_____	_____	_____
4. Looks at books on his/her own	_____	_____	_____	_____
5. Has favorite book(s)	_____	_____	_____	_____

Additional Comments and Observations:

Appendix M Checklist of Oral Reading Characteristics for a Group of Students

Date: Names:						
Comprehension						
Recalls facts						
Makes inferences						
Word Recognition/Decoding						
Has adequate sight vocabulary						
Needs few or no words pronounced						
Mispronounces few words						
Omits few or no words						
Inserts few or no words						
Uses context adequately						
Uses strategies in addition to context						
Knows high-utility words						
Analyzes word visually						
Knows symbol–sound associations						
Can blend sounds						
Fluency						
Has few or no hesitations						
Has few or no repetitions						
Phrases appropriately						
Reads phrases or groups of words						
Pays attention to punctuation						
Reads at an appropriate rate						
Usually or always keeps place						
Demonstrates proper use of voice						
Demonstrates proper enunciation						
Demonstrates proper expression						
Uses proper volume						
Observations						
Seldom shows signs of tension						
Reads with little or no finger pointing						
Holds book at appropriate distance						
Concentrates on task at hand						
Comments:						

Appendix N   Student Behavior Log of Demonstrated Multiple Intelligences

Student Name: _____ Age: _____ Date of Observation: _____

Indicate the degree to which you observe the stated behavior or characteristic in each student, using the following scale: 0 = uncertain; 1 = does not fit at all; 2 = fits slightly; 3 = fits moderately; 4 = fits strongly

Verbal-Linguistic Behaviors

Loves talking, writing, and reading almost anything	0	1	2	3	4
Precisely expresses self both in writing and talking	0	1	2	3	4
Enjoys public speaking	0	1	2	3	4
Is sensitive to impact of words and language on others	0	1	2	3	4
Understands and enjoys plays on words and word games	0	1	2	3	4

Logical-Mathematical Behaviors

Is good at finding and understanding patterns	0	1	2	3	4
Is quick at solving a variety of problems	0	1	2	3	4
Can remember thinking formulas and strategies	0	1	2	3	4
Likes to identify, create, and sort things into categories	0	1	2	3	4
Is able to follow complex lines of reasoning and thought processes	0	1	2	3	4

Visual-Spatial Behaviors

Frequently doodles during class activities	0	1	2	3	4
Is helped by visuals and manipulatives	0	1	2	3	4
Likes painting, drawing, and working with clay	0	1	2	3	4
Has a good sense of direction and understanding of maps	0	1	2	3	4
Creates mental images easily; likes pretending	0	1	2	3	4

Bodily-Kinesthetic Behaviors

Has difficulty sitting still or staying in seat	0	1	2	3	4
Uses body gestures and physical movement to express self	0	1	2	3	4
Is good in sports; is well coordinated physically	0	1	2	3	4
Likes to invent things, put things together and take them apart	0	1	2	3	4
Likes to demonstrate to others how to do something	0	1	2	3	4

Musical-Rhythmic Behaviors

Hums quietly to self while working or walking	0	1	2	3	4
Taps pencil, foot, or fingers while working	0	1	2	3	4
Can remember songs and rhymes easily	0	1	2	3	4
Likes to make up tunes and melodies	0	1	2	3	4
Senses musical elements in unusual or nonmusical situations	0	1	2	3	4

Interpersonal Behaviors

Has an irresistible urge to discuss almost everything with others	0	1	2	3	4
Is good at listening and communicating	0	1	2	3	4
Sensitive to the moods and feelings of others	0	1	2	3	4
Is a good, effective team player	0	1	2	3	4
Is able to figure out the motives and intentions of others	0	1	2	3	4

Intrapersonal Behaviors

Is highly intuitive and/or "flies by the seat of pants"	0	1	2	3	4
Is quiet, very self-reflective, and aware	0	1	2	3	4
Asks questions relentlessly; has avid curiosity	0	1	2	3	4
Is able to express inner feelings in a variety of ways	0	1	2	3	4
Is individualistic and independent; is not concerned about others' opinions	0	1	2	3	4

Naturalist Behaviors

Is sensitive to things in nature	0	1	2	3	4
Enjoys caring for classroom pets or plants	0	1	2	3	4
Likes animals and talks about own pets	0	1	2	3	4
Knows about plants, animals, and living things	0	1	2	3	4
Is concerned with the environment; is ecologically aware	0	1	2	3	4

Multiple Intelligence Approaches to Assessment, © 1994 Zephyr Press, Tucson, Arizona.

Appendix O   Sample Interest Inventory

Inventory of Pupil Interests and Activities

Name _____ Age _____ Grade _____

School _____ Date _____ Interviewer _____

1. What is your favorite TV show?

2. Who is your favorite TV character?

3. If you could make up a TV show, what would it be about?

4. Do you have a favorite movie?

5. Do you have any pets?

6. What is your favorite animal?

7. If you could be any living thing, what would you be?

8. Where have you traveled? Name three places.

9. Name all the different types of transportation you have experienced (train, bus, auto, boat, wagon, airplane, jet, truck, buggy, subway, bicycle, ship).

10. If you received two airplane tickets for anywhere in the world, where would you go?

11. If you had a time machine for any time and place in the past or future, where would you go and when?

12. What is your favorite subject?

13. What is the latest book you've read? Did you enjoy it? Why or why not?

14. What kind of books do you read at home?

15. If it were a rainy day at home, what would you do? If it were a sunny day at home, what would you do?

16. What is your favorite sport?

17. What is your favorite hobby?

18. If I gave you $100 to buy whatever you wanted, what would you do with the money?

Appendix P   Primary Grades Attitude Survey

(Teacher: Before administering this survey, be sure children can distinguish the three faces as feeling happy, don't care, and feeling sad, respectively. You might want to ask a few practice questions, such as "How do you feel about Christmas?" or "How do you feel about going to bed early?" Feel free to add items to the survey. For group administration, students can either color in or mark the face that represents the way they feel about each question. Individuals can either point to or hold up individual face cards to indicate their feelings.)

1. How do you feel when your teacher reads a story to you?

2. How do you feel about reading out loud in class?

3. How do you feel about going to the library?

4. How do you feel when you come to a new word in your book?

5. How do you feel about your reading group?

6. How do you feel about getting a book for a present?

7. How do you feel when you read at home?

8. How do you feel when you read to your mom, dad, or a friend?

9. How do you feel about reading a story before bedtime?

10. How do you feel when you don't understand what you read?

Child's Name: _____

For frequency of the observed characteristic, circle the most appropriate number using the following scale.

5 = Always

4 = Most of the time

3 = Sometimes

2 = Rarely

1 = Never

Oral Language Characteristic	Date	Frequency	Date	Frequency	Date	Frequency
Does the child speak in complete sentences?		5 4 3 2 1		5 4 3 2 1		5 4 3 2 1
Does the child include new words when speaking?		5 4 3 2 1		5 4 3 2 1		5 4 3 2 1
Does the child include new sentence patterns when speaking?		5 4 3 2 1		5 4 3 2 1		5 4 3 2 1
Does the child express ideas clearly?		5 4 3 2 1		5 4 3 2 1		5 4 3 2 1
Does the child clearly express relationships between personal events and event in stories?		5 4 3 2 1		5 4 3 2 1		5 4 3 2 1
Does the child respond appropriately to questions or requests for information?		5 4 3 2 1		5 4 3 2 1		5 4 3 2 1
Does the child use extended language in settings other than the classroom (such as playground or cafeteria)?		5 4 3 2 1		5 4 3 2 1		5 4 3 2 1

Comments:

To accurately assess spelling development, students must write words they have not been taught or memorized. If a student is willing to write freely, then those words can be assessed for spelling development. However, some students are unwilling to write freely because they are not confident of their spelling ability. For these students a more structured approach is needed. Following are recommended word lists for spelling assessment. Directions, scoring, and a scored example for the K–2 list are provided. The same procedures would be followed for the list for grades 3 and up.

Directions:

1. Explain to students that they are not expected to know how to spell all of these words. You want to know how they think the words should be spelled. They should do their best, but this exercise will not be graded.
2. If they are stumped by a word, they should first try the beginning of the word, then the middle, then the end.
3. The teacher will read the word, then the sentence, then read the word again, twice. (Do not exaggerate any of the parts—just say the word normally.)

Spelling List (Grades K–2)

1.	late	Kathy was *late* to school again today.
2.	wind	The *wind* blew hard last night.
3.	shed	The wind blew so hard it blew down our *shed*.
4.	geese	The *geese* fly over Texas every fall.
5.	jumped	The frog *jumped* into the river.
6.	yell	We can *yell* as loud as we want on the playground.
7.	chirped	The bird *chirped* when it saw a worm.
8.	once	Jim rode his bike into a creek *once*.
9.	learned	I *learned* to count in school.
10.	shove	Try not to *shove* your neighbor when you line up.
11.	trained	I *trained* my dog to lie down and roll over.
12.	year	Next *year* you'll have a new teacher.
13.	shock	Electricity can *shock* you if you aren't careful.
14.	stained	The ice cream spilled and *stained* my shirt.
15.	chick	The egg cracked open, and a baby *chick* came out.
16.	drive	Bob's sister is learning how to *drive*.

Spelling List (Grades 3 and up)

1.	setter	Her dog is an Irish *setter*.
2.	shove	Don't *shove* when you line up.
3.	grocery	I'm going to the *grocery* store.
4.	button	Did you lose a *button* from your shirt?
5.	sailor	My cousin is a good *sailor*.
6.	prison	The criminal will go to *prison*.
7.	nature	We enjoyed our walk on the *nature* trail.
8.	peeked	He *peeked* at the answers to the test.
9.	special	Your birthday is a *special* day.
10.	preacher	The *preacher* talked for over an hour.
11.	slowed	We *slowed* down on the bumpy road.
12.	sail	The sailboat had a torn *sail*.
13.	feature	We saw a double *feature* at the movies.
14.	batter	The first *batter* struck out.

Scoring

The words are scored according to the stage of spelling they reflect. The word is scored:

1. if it is precommunicative.
2. if it is semiphonetic.
3. if it is phonetic.
4. if it is transitional.
5. if it is correct.

(Continued)

For example, from spelling list (Grades K–2):

1. Lat	3	9. Zud	3
2. wnd	3	10. suf	3
3. sead	4	11. trad	3
4. Gees	4	12. t er	3
5. Bout	3	13. Sock	4
6. uL	3	14. sad	3
7. cutp	3	15. cek	3
8. Los	3	16. drif	3

The mode should be determined. The mode is the single score that occurred most often. (The average can be distorted by the possibility that the student had memorized some of the spellings.) In the preceding example, the mode is 3, meaning that most of the student's spellings were in the phonetic (letter name) stage (Temple et al., 1988, pp. 105–107).

Appendix S Developmental Writing Checklist

Name: _____ Date: _____

UNDERSTANDS THE WRITING PROCESS

1. Developed and used a plan for writing (for example, semantic map, lists, outline, drawings, notes) (Circle which apply.) YES NO
2. Referred to a plan when writing YES NO
3. Reread first draft and revised writing YES NO
4. Rearranged words, sentences, and paragraphs YES NO
5. Revised vocabulary to include descriptive words and a variety of verbs YES NO
6. Wrote for a specific audience (such as teacher, family, friend) YES NO
7. Completed composition follows a logical progression YES NO
8. Completed composition is interesting and enjoyable for the reader YES NO
9. Used expressive *voice;* imaginative *voice;* expository *voice* (Give examples.) (Circle which *voices* apply.) YES NO
10. Combined *voices* appropriately (Give examples.) YES NO

DEVELOPMENTAL STAGE OF SPELLING

(Circle which stage most applies and give examples.)
1. prephonemic
2. early phonemic
3. letter name
4. transitional
5. conventional

KNOWLEDGE OF MECHANICS

1. Titled the composition YES NO
2. Used periods appropriately YES NO
3. Used question marks appropriately YES NO
4. Used commas appropriately YES NO
5. Used exclamation marks appropriately YES NO
6. Used quotation marks appropriately YES NO
7. Used appropriate capitalization YES NO
8. Indented paragraphs YES NO
9. Wrote in complete sentences YES NO
10. Wrote legibly YES NO
11. Formed graphemes correctly YES NO

Name: _____ Date: _____

1. Why do people write?
2. How can you learn to write stories?
3. What stories would you like to write? Why?
4. What is the difference between writing a story and writing a composition that explains, describes, or tells somebody how to do something?
5. If you were teaching someone to write well, what would you tell them to do?
6. When you write, what do you do first?
7. How do you decide what to write?
8. What part of writing do you like the most? Why?
9. What part of writing do you like the least? Why?
10. When you are writing and get stuck, what do you do?
11. How do you know if your writing is any good?
12. If you were writing your own books, what would you write about?
13. Do you think you are a good writer? Why? Why not?

Appendix U   A Self-Assessment Postwriting Questionnaire

Name: _____ Date: _____

This Piece of Writing
1. What part of the writing process was most successful for you (for example, brainstorming ideas, composing, editing)?
2. What writing strategies did you use (such as "Story Features and Their Connections," semantic mapping, speed writing)?
3. What part of the writing process was least successful for you (for example, brainstorming ideas, first draft, editing)?
4. What pleases you most about this piece of writing?
5. In which *voice* did you write?
6. Are you comfortable with this *voice* of composing? Did you choose to write in this voice?
7. What is the topic of this piece? Have you written before on this topic? Why did you choose to write on this topic?
8. How did you organize your writing?

9. What type of mechanical errors caused you the most trouble in this piece (for example, capitalization, paragraphing, punctuation, spelling)?

Your Next Piece of Writing
1. What topic interests you for your next piece of writing? Why?
2. For which audience will you write this next piece? Why?
3. How do you plan on gathering information for this topic?

4. How do you plan on organizing this piece of writing?

Or consider the following set of questions for younger writers:
1. What's good about this writing? Do you like what you wrote?
2. What problems did you have as you wrote?
3. What strategies did you use before you started writing? Did you make a graphic organizer to show your title or main idea? Did you think about your characters? Your setting? A problem and a solution?
4. What strategies did you use after you wrote? Did you reread to see if you had a beginning, a middle, and an end? Did what you wrote make sense?
5. What would you like to try in your next piece of writing?

Appendix V   Spelling Questionnaire

Name: _____ Date: _____

Teacher: _____

_____ I will try to spell a word even if I don't know how to spell the word.

_____ I use invented spelling in my first drafts of compositions.

_____ I know how to spell (some) (many) easy words. (Circle one word.)

_____ I know how to spell (some) (many) difficult words. (Circle one word.)

_____ I write down interesting and unusual words in my personal dictionary.

_____ I am interested in learning how to spell words.

_____ I participate in our weekly spelling meetings.

_____ I try to edit my writing so that others can read my work.

_____ I try to notice how unusual words are spelled.

_____ I care about being a good speller.

Comments:

SELF-TEST FOR ESSENTIAL PHONICS TERMS

Directions: Choose the one item that best illustrates each term. Write a definition for the term in the space provided to the right of the item. An answer key is available at the end of this appendix.

1. Consonant letter
   a. u _____
   b. th _____
   c. b _____
   d. cl _____
   e. oi _____
   f. oa _____

2. Grapheme
   a. ill _____
   b. ight _____
   c. ch _____
   d. ed _____
   e. re _____
   f. boy _____

3. Consonant blend
   a. /t/ _____
   b. /sh/ _____
   c. /ght/ _____
   d. /scr/ _____
   e. /at/ _____
   f. /a/ _____

4. Consonant digraph
   a. a _____
   b. oy _____
   c. p _____
   d. br _____
   e. sh _____
   f. ea _____

5. Vowel letter
   a. a _____
   b. sh _____
   c. v _____
   d. sn _____
   e. oa _____
   f. oy _____

6. Vowel digraph
   a. i _____
   b. m _____
   c. ck _____
   d. bl _____
   e. at _____
   f. oa _____

7. Diphthong
   a. /e/ _____
   b. /wh/ _____
   c. /n/ _____
   d. /st/ _____
   e. /oi/ _____
   f. /ill/ _____

8. A rime (or phonogram) is represented by which boldfaced word part?
   a. **thr**ash _____
   b. thr**ash** _____
   c. **thr**ash _____
   d. thra**sh** _____

9. Phoneme
   a. /it/ _____
   b. /ing/ _____
   c. /igh/ _____
   d. /bl/ _____
   e. e _____
   f. /st/ _____

10. Morpheme
   a. er _____
   b. wh _____
   c. ou _____
   d. ng _____
   e. z _____
   f. kn _____

Answer Key for Self-Assessment

1. **Choice c (b)** A consonant letter is any letter except for *a, e, i, o,* and *u*. However, sometimes *y* and *w* act as vowels as in the words *try* and *cow*. Consonant letters represent consonant sounds that are made by the blockage of air in the breath channel. This blockage of air can be made by the lips (/m/), by the teeth (/t/), or by the tongue (/g/).

2. **Choice c (ch)** A grapheme is a letter or combination of letters that represents one speech sound (or phoneme). The phoneme /ch/ in *chicken* is represented by the grapheme *ch*. The phoneme /f/ in *telephone* is represented by the grapheme *ph*. The phoneme /z/ in *was* is represented by the grapheme *s*.

3. **Choice d (scr)** A consonant blend is two or three consonant letters blended together that retain their own identity. Each letter in the consonant blend maintains its own sound. The /scr/ in *scream* retains the /s/, the /k/, and the /r/ sounds. The /b/ /l/ in *black* and the /t/ /r/ in *trick* are also examples of consonant blends.

4. **Choice e (sh)** A consonant digraph consists of two consonant letters that represent a single sound (phoneme). *Di-* means two and *graph* in this word stands for *grapheme*, or a written symbol for a single phoneme. Remembering these word parts may help you remember the term. Some other examples are /wh/, /th/, /ch/, /ph/, /gn/, /kn/, /wr/, /ng/, /ck/, /mb/, /gh/ as in *ghost* or *tough*.

5. **Choice a (a)** A vowel letter is one of the graphemes *a, e, i, o, u,* and sometimes *y* and *w*. Vowel sounds are made without any blockage of air through the breath channel. There is no one-to-one correspondence between a vowel letter and the sound it may represent. The sound is determined by the letters that surround the vowel (refer to the generalizations in this appendix).

6. **Choice f (oa)** A vowel digraph consists of two vowel letters (*di-*) + (*graph*) that represent a single sound (phoneme) and that retains the sound of one of the letters involved in the digraph. Thus, the *oa* in *boat* sounds like the name of the letter *o*, or /ō/. Other examples are *ee, ea, ai,* and *ay* (see also the fourth generalization in this appendix).

7. **Choice e (/oi/)** The term *diphthong* describes the new, unique vowel sound created when two vowels blend together to form a sound different from the individual sounds of either vowel. The *oi* in *boil* does not sound like /ō/ or /ī/, or /ŏ/ or /ĭ/. It is its own unique sound. Other examples of diphthongs are *oy, ou, ow, au, aw,* and *oo* as in *look* and *moon*.

8. **Choice b (ash)** A rime (or phonogram) refers to part of a syllable that starts with the vowel sound and includes all the consonant sounds that follow. The term *rime* refers to the sounds made; the term *phonogram* refers to the graphemes for these sounds, or the written version of the rime. In other words, *-ash* is the phonogram and /ash/ is the rime. In the word *cake*, *-ake* is the phonogram and /ake/ is the rime. The words *in* and *at* also represent phonograms, with the rimes being /in/ and /at/. See Figure 8.8 for a list of useful phonograms.

9. **Choice c (igh)** If you chose "e" you would have been correct *if grapheme* had been the term to define. However, when we represent sounds in print form, we must use the slash marks around the letters (graphemes) to indicate the sounds made by those letters. Thus, /igh/ makes only one sound, that of the long "i" as in the word *night*.

10. **Choice a (er)** Although not technically a phonic term, the word *morpheme* is in a family of terms represented by *phoneme* and *grapheme*. The *-eme* ending means "smallest unit of" and knowing this could help you to remember each term. Phoneme means smallest unit of sound (*phon*); grapheme means smallest written (*graph*) unit for a single sound. A morpheme, then, is the smallest unit that represents meaning (*morph*). In the word *teacher,* the *-er* is a morpheme meaning "one who." So *teacher* is one who teaches. Similarly, we have *painter, boxer, swimmer,* and many other words. Other examples of morphemes are *-s* and *-es* (meaning more than one), *re-* (meaning do again), and most prefixes, suffixes, and inflectional endings (see Figure 9.5 and Chapter 10, Meaning Vocabulary).

Name _____

Appendix Item 69
Skill Test for Study Skills and Habits

Directions:
Put a check mark (√) in the column that describes how often you do the following. Be honest. I shall help you learn to study if needed.

	Never	Sometimes	Usually
1. Do you look over what you are going to read before you read it?			
2. Do you form questions about the selection before you read it?			
3. Do you use a slower rate when you are reading your textbooks?			
4. Do you try to pronounce and define words that are in bold print or italics?			
5. Do you read the tables, graphs, and diagrams in your textbooks?			
6. Do you answer questions as you go along?			
7. Do you outline the important ideas and facts as you read?			
8. Do you reread the materials you do not understand?			
9. Do you review what you have read when you have finished?			
10. Do you set a time for study?			
11. Do you have a place to study at home or near your home? Are your supplies ready?			
12. Are you able to concentrate when studying?			
13. If you are doing math problems, do you read them carefully and then reread them to see if your answer is correct?			
14. If you must turn work in to your teacher, are you proud of it? Is it neat and well organized?			

Source: From *The Reading Corner* by Harry W. Forgan, Jr. Reproduced by permission of Scott, Foresman and Company. © 1977.

Appendix Y Study Skills Checklist*

Student's Name:				
Study Skill	**Knows**	**In Progress**	**Does Not Know**	**Not Assessed**
I. Locating information				
A. Alphabetizes by first letter				
B. Alphabetizes by second letter				
C. Alphabetizes by third letter				
D. Knows and uses book parts (such as table of contents, index, glossary)				
E. Knows and uses reference materials (such as dictionary, thesaurus, encyclopedia, directories)				
F. Uses the library (card catalog or computer system, Dewey decimal system)				
II. Organizing information				
A. Knows and uses specialized vocabulary				
B. Categorizes information				
C. Recognizes main ideas and supporting details				
D. Sequences events				
E. Summarizes and synthesizes information				
F. Takes effective notes				
G. Outlines effectively				
III. Interpreting graphic and pictorial materials				
A. Uses pictures				
B. Uses graphs				
C. Uses tables				
D. Uses maps				
IV. Has and uses a study strategy				

*Note to teacher: Place dates rather than checkmarks in boxes to provide a chronology of skill development.

Appendix Z   Skills Test for Assessing Knowledge of Book Parts

Name: _____

KNOW YOUR BOOK

Directions:

Use your _____ book to answer these questions.

  1. What is the title of this book?

_____

  2. Who are the authors?

_____

  3. When was the book copyrighted?

_____

  4. What is a copyright?

_____

  5. What company published the book?

_____

  6. What edition is this book?

_____

  7. What kind of information is in the preface?

_____

  8. Why do some books have more than one edition?

_____

  9. Give an example of how the table of contents can help you.

_____

10. Is there a list of tables, maps, or diagrams?

_____

11. How can this help you?

_____

12. How are new words shown?

_____

13. Is there a glossary?

_____

14. How can the glossary help you?

_____

15. Where is the index located?

_____

16. When will you use the index?

_____

17. Is there an appendix?

_____

18. What information is presented in the appendix?

_____

Source: From *The Reading Corner,* by Harry W. Forgan, Jr. Reproduced by permission of Scott, Foresman and Company. © 1977.

Glossary

abstract referent The concept behind words that do not evoke a clear visual image (*way, there, democracy,* and so forth).

academic literacy Instructional literacy; literacy to gain knowledge or information.

action research Systematic inquiry conducted by teachers for themselves to gather information about how their schools and classrooms function, how well they teach, and how well their students learn.

ADD/ADHD A biological disorder with primary symptoms of hyperactivity, impulsivity, and distractibility, effectively treated with medication and behavior modification.

aesthetic reading A type of reading focused on the affective dimensions of reading.

affect The psychological domain of the brain that is connected with feelings.

African American Vernacular English (AAVE) A variation of standard English dialect spoken by the people in many African American communities across the United States; based on its own set of phonological patterns and rules.

aliterates People with the ability to read who choose not to do so due to a lack of positive attitudes, habits, and interests.

alphabetic principle A principle by which each sound or phoneme in our language has its own distinctive graphic representation.

analytic process In reading, a methodical system designed to assist teachers in their observation and assessment of students' engagement of the reading process, allowing them to identify strengths and weaknesses and plan appropriate instruction no matter what the involved domain, method of teaching, or curriculum.

analytic scoring Focuses on assessing writing in terms of its individual parts.

analytic teaching A way of observing and assessing students' literacy development that recognizes, respects, and appreciates students' abilities.

analytical vocabulary Words that students identify correctly in reading, but only after careful examination of the word's graphic image.

anecdotal records Carefully prepared short notes that objectively describe student behavior and aid in the recollection of observations over time.

arrays Outlines of relationships between topics, ideas, and details in graphic form; examples include semantic webs, mapping, and the herringbone technique.

artifacts Items chosen for inclusion in a portfolio.

assessment The process of gathering information (data) about students' strengths, abilities, and need for further instruction.

Assignment Mastery A reading strategy designed to teach readers self-monitoring techniques through the asking of specific questions during each of the various phases of reading (such as scanning, preparation for reading, recitation and review, and reading review).

assistive technology devices Equipment, products, or electronic devices designed to improve the functional capabilities of persons with severe communication disorders, or other disabilities.

associative words Words that often occur together in reading (for example, *happy birthday,* or *bacon and eggs*).

assumptive teaching Instruction resulting from teachers' improper assumptions about what students can and cannot do, which leads to a disharmony between the instructional program and the learner.

at-level testing A survey reading test using a single level of test for each specific grade level so that the same level of test is given to all students in a specified grade.

at risk The state of a student for whom two or more nonreading factors (such as low SES level, health considerations) are believed to threaten the student's chances for success in reading.

attentive listening The act of attending to sounds in spoken language and concentrating on acquiring the message being transmitted.

attributional retraining The act of instructing students to accept responsibility for their own learning in the case of both their failures and their successes; includes teaching students that failure can often be defeated through diligent attempts and perseverance.

auditory acuity The degree of one's ability to distinctly hear sounds.

auditory blending The sounding process, usually employed by emerging readers, by which the student says the word parts and blends them together to cue a meaningful response; the blending of phonemes to form a word.

auditory comprehension The ability to make meaning from oral language, ranging from very literal comprehension to the ability to critically evaluate the spoken message.

auditory discrimination The ability to differentiate sounds.

auditory memory The ability to recall a series of sounds.

auditory perception The ability to determine sounds, combined with auditory memory and the ability to blend sounds.

author's chair A "chair of distinction" that students sit in to share their writing with classmates.

automaticity The act of perceiving and comprehending units of print so thoroughly that almost no effort is needed to recognize new words or parts of words.

Basic Interpersonal Communicative Skills (BICS) A term for the ability more often referred to as conversational language.

basic story features Those parts essential to the making of a real story (i.e., characters, setting, problem, and solution).

best practices Recommendations from research that provide a knowledge base for improving literacy instruction.

bibliotherapy A process by which students are matched with books containing a character or situation with which they can identify, allowing them to better understand themselves through the reading event.

book club An instructional framework developed by Susan McMahon and Taffy Raphael that relies on students choosing books they wish to read, discussing them in small groups, and learning and sharing with the entire group.

brain-based learning Instructional environment created to make the brain more receptive to learning.

civic literacy Knowledge of how to actively participate and initiate change in one's community and in society.

clarifying table A graphic organizer used for teaching the meaning of complex terms.

closed word sorting A technique for grouping words that relies on particular criteria provided by the teacher.

cloze procedure A method for determining a student's instructional reading level; requires the student to fill in a series of blanks that have been systematically deleted from a passage; often used to determine the suitability of a particular text.

cognition Thinking; the ability to design concepts and to organize acquired information; the nature of knowing and of intellectual development.

Cognitive Academic Language Proficiency (CALP) Refers to the ability to engage in the formal language used in school, or academic language.

Collaborative Listening Viewing Guide A type of study guide useful when information is obtained from a video, TV program, or web-based video clip.

collaborative writing Facilitated instruction allowing students to experience writing within a social context, which includes a partner or partners and a university tutor serving as role models.

communicative competence The ability to use language proficiently within a wide variety of social situations.

comprehensible input Presenting information in a way that English learners can more easily understand. For instance, use of graphic organizers, visuals, and physical actions are techniques that make difficult content more accessible to English learners especially.

comprehension monitoring The act of continuously evaluating and monitoring one's understanding while engaged in the act of reading.

comprehensive view A view of literacy instruction that supports providing the proportion of skills, strategies, materials, and social and emotional support that learners need.

concept ladder A technique for examining the relationships among words.

concrete referent The clear visual image evoked by certain words (such *dog, table,* or *blue*).

construct validity The degree to which a test measures a particular trait or ability, usually by measuring the behaviors believed to reflect the trait or ability involved.

constructed spelling The developmentally appropriate form of spelling a word (precommunicative, semiphonetic, phonetic, or transitional). Also called *invented* or *temporary spelling.*

content area literacy Use of reading, writing, speaking, listening, viewing, and visually representing that focuses on the academic curriculum.

content validity The degree to which a test measures what it is supposed to be measuring; how well it matches the teacher's instructional objectives.

content words Words holding the meaning in a particular passage or text.

context A cue system for decoding unknown words in which the student uses the words surrounding an unknown target word to trigger recognition or meaning.

context clues The clues within the surrounding words, sentences, paragraphs, and illustrations that provide syntactic and semantic information.

conventional spelling Correct spelling.

correlation coefficients The number indicating how strongly two variables are related; the higher the number, the stronger the relationship.

creative writing Writing that stems from the writer's experiences; includes fiction, drama, and poetry.

criterion-referenced tests Tests that measure how well a learner performs a particular task as compared to a specified desired level of competence.

decodable text Text using sequenced sound-spelling correspondences based on both frequency and phonic principles.

deductive teaching A didactic style of teaching in which a teacher presents a generalization or rule to students and expects them to apply the rule to specific examples.

diagnosis Identification of reading difficulties based on gathering and evaluating information about student reading behaviors.

dialects Surface variations in the way that a particular language is spoken in different parts of a country or among different ethnic groups; these are still completely rule-governed, fully developed systems of speaking.

dialogue journals (also interactive journals) Collections of daily written conversations over time between students and teachers wherein students are free to express their opinions and feelings about topics of their choosing without fear of judgment or reprisal.

didactic teaching A transmission style of teaching by which a teacher presents certain material to students and expects them to learn it.

differentiated instruction Instructional and management strategies chosen or developed to address content, process, or products that accommodate the interests, readiness, and learning profiles of students.

diorama Visual art created within a box (for example, a shoe box), usually depicting the major elements of a story.

direct assessment Assessment measures used within classrooms and by individual teachers, as opposed to the prepared, standardized type of test given to large groups of students.

direct instruction A highly structured, teacher-directed style of teaching whereby teachers share planned "strategy lessons."

directed reading-thinking activity An instructional strategy developed by Russell G. Stauffer to enhance reading comprehension through a prediction-making cycle.

directive context A context created specifically to provide enough information to determine a word's meaning.

discourse Meaningful language units larger than a sentence; also, a component of communication relating ideas to a particular subject for a specified purpose.

discovery teaching Also called *inductive teaching,* a style of teaching in which students are provided with an appropriate environment and encouraged to seek generalizations for themselves.

double-entry journals Journals that have a two-column format for two types of student response to text.

dramatic play Informal, spontaneous drama among young children.

during-reading stage The second stage of reading, characterized by a reader's direct interaction with print.

dyslexia A persistent, hereditary neurological disorder manifested by difficulty in reading at the word level.

early reader A reader just beginning to use word recognition and comprehension strategies.

ebonics The rule-governed, systematic set of phonological, syntactic, semantic, and discourse characteristics used in African American communities.

efferent reading   A type of reading focused on gaining information.

EL   English learner

ELD   English language development

ELL   English Language Learner

electronic portfolios   Use of multimedia for storing artifacts that provide evidence of literacy development.

emergent literacy   The belief that reading and writing begin at birth and gradually emerge over time through frequent interactions with literacy events.

emergent reader   Young readers just beginning to interact with books and print through pretend reading.

emergent writers   Beginning writers; young children in the process of experimenting with written language through scribbling in the attempt to communicate a written message.

emotional maltreatment   Inappropriate parenting that may include, but is not restricted to, neglect, constant belittling, or verbal abuse.

end-of-unit tests   Tests in the teacher's manual or student workbooks of many basal reading systems; may contain useful information regarding student accomplishments on small segments of material.

entry point   An activity chosen specifically to engage and connect a learner with a desired literacy task.

equal-status relationship   The relationship of words or sentences that describe equal associations between concepts.

ESL (English as a second language) students   Students whose first language is not English.

evaluation   The process of judging student growth and making decisions regarding student achievement through the analysis of collected student data.

evaluation activity   The direct assessment of a lesson's effectiveness and the accuracy of the teacher's hypothesis through teacher-made activities directly related to the tasks involved in the lesson; used to determine whether additional practice is needed by the student or whether a new hypothesis should be formed by the teacher.

expectancy clues   The concepts, and the words that go with them, that rise to mind when a topic is introduced; the schema that is activated from memory storage when new material is encountered.

experience-text-relationship method   A reading strategy designed to help students relate personal experiences to the central events in a story through a cycle of discussing experiences (experience step), reading the text (text step), and relating the experiences to the story (relationship step).

expository material   Material that is explanatory, such as that found in content-area reading.

facilitating questions   Questions designed to encourage continued thinking on the part of the learner, to make the discovery of the solution to a particular problem easier.

fluency   Smooth, expressive, and rhythmic reading or writing.

fluent reader   A reader who reads easily with both accuracy and comprehension at levels beyond normal expectations.

formal tests   Also called *standardized tests,* tests that have been administered in the same way to a large group of students for the purpose of establishing a reference (also called *norm*) group to which all future groups of students can be compared.

frustration reading level   The level at which a student's reading deteriorates to the point whereby continuation is impossible because the material is too difficult even with the guidance of an instructor.

genre   (see *literature genre*) Written works with similar characteristics, such as fairy tales, historical fiction, nonfiction, poetry, mystery.

Goldilocks strategy   A method used to help young readers select material at an appropriate level of difficulty.

grade-equivalent scores   A type of standardized test score, usually stated in terms of years and tenths of a year, that uses as its reference point a grade in school; is often misinterpreted.

grapheme   A written or printed symbol for a phoneme (speech sound). Some examples are *f* for /f/ or *ph* for /f/ and *oy* for /oi/ as in *boy.*

graphic novels   Book-length comic books.

graphic organizer   A visual representation of academic concepts within an organized framework, such as a concept map, Venn diagrams, T-charts, structured overviews, and so forth.

graphophonic cue system   The reading cue system pertaining to sound and symbol clues, or letter/sound relationships.

GRASP (Guided Reading and Summarizing Procedure)   A reading strategy in which students under teacher guidance read for information and are instructed to remember as much as they can; list all recollections following reading; reread to add, delete, and correct information; and then organize information by grouping details.

guided practice   An activity that allows students to apply recently learned information while teacher assistance is still available.

guided reading strategy (GRS)   A modification of the GRASP strategy that contains the following steps: survey of the chapter or section, orally stating everything remembered from the survey; rechecking the chapter for missing information; discussion between teacher and student about the results of the survey and organizing the information into a topical outline; careful silent reading of the chapter or selection; immediate 10-item true-or-false quiz; and, finally, about one week later, an additional 10-item pop quiz on the material.

herringbone technique   A strategy designed to help students organize information from text in the form of a structured outline, using six basic comprehension questions to obtain the important information: who, what, where, when, how, and why.

high-stakes testing   Reliance on a single test score to make important and substantial educational decisions.

holistic scoring   Writing is assessed with an overall rating for the entire piece.

holistic view   A viewpoint that holds that literacy instruction should encourage experimentation and approximation, as in learning to talk, but using whole text; also called top-down.

holographic stage   In oral language development, the earliest stage in which one word is used to represent a concept.

homographs   Words that are spelled alike but do not sound alike and do not have the same meaning (for example, *sow* seeds versus *sow* as a female pig).

homonyms   Words that sound alike and are spelled alike but have different meanings (such as *run* a race, a dog *run, run* in your stocking, and so on).

homophones   Words that sound alike but have different origins and meanings and are often spelled differently.

independent practice   An opportunity for students to apply what they have learned without teacher assistance, which gives the teacher further information regarding the accuracy of the hypothesis and effectiveness of the given lesson.

independent reading level   The level at which a learner can read and comprehend comfortably without teacher assistance.

indirect assessment   Assessment obtained from standardized, norm-referenced testing.

inductive teaching   Also called *discovery teaching,* a style of teaching in which students are provided with an appropriate environment and encouraged to seek generalizations for themselves.

informal reading inventory (IRI) A nonstandard, direct measure, consisting of a series of graded passages that students read and answer questions about to help the teacher (a) observe students' reading tactics, (b) choose appropriate reading material, (c) identify students' three levels of reading, and (d) learn more about students' strengths and needs.

information literacy The ability to locate, obtain, and use information.

instructional reading level The level of reading that is challenging, but not frustrating, for students to successfully read during normal classroom instruction.

interactive assessment The action by which a teacher attempts to determine situations under which students will have the most successful reading experiences.

interactive view Viewpoint that reading comprehension results from the interaction between the reader and the text, with cognitive processing using both whole text and parts of text as necessary.

interactive read alouds A method in which adults read aloud and engage the learners in the reading by discussing new concepts or vocabulary.

interactive writing A mediated writing experience used to assist emergent readers and writers. Children dictate sentences and the teacher verbally stretches each word to help children distinguish sounds and letters. Children then write the letters or words on large chart paper while repeating the sounds.

invented spelling The developmentally appropriate form of spelling a word (precommunicative, semiphonetic, phonetic, or transitional).

key word A familiar word used to represent a particular phonic element.

kidwatching Conscious observation of students by teachers; includes use of field notes.

K–W–L A reading strategy designed by Donna Ogle to assess students' prior knowledge and help them to set purposes for reading; in the K step, students list everything they know about a topic; in the W step, students generate questions about what they want to know about the topic; in the L step, students list what they have learned about the topic and what they still want to learn.

language The system through which meaning is expressed; communication in either oral, written, or visual form.

language comprehension The act of receiving or decoding a written or oral message.

language conventions The rules governing written and oral language.

language cue systems The cues provided by the semantics, syntax, and graphophonic systems of the language for help in both word recognition and comprehension.

language experience approach (LEA) An approach to reading instruction by which the teacher makes use of the children's experiences through the children's dictation of stories to the teacher, who then analyzes the material and follows up with the students by helping them expand on the language through discussion and questioning; as students read and reread their own words, sight vocabulary, language knowledge, and graphophonic awareness are increased and developed.

language functions The purposes for communication in oral or written language.

language production The act of sending an oral or written message.

learning center An actual location within a classroom, or simply a manila folder, that contains clearly defined objectives and instructions; is equipped with appropriate instructional materials for meeting the learning objectives.

learning disability A severe discrepancy between achievement and intellectual ability in one or more academic areas that is not the result of vision, hearing, motor handicaps; mental retardation; emotional disturbance; or environmental, cultural, or economic disadvantage.

learning profile The combination of factors such as gender, culture, developed multiple intelligences, and learning style that affect the way a student learns best.

learning style A preferred modality for learning (such as visual, auditory, or kinesthetic).

lexicon The total vocabulary of a language, speaker, or subject.

linguistic awareness The internalized knowledge of the phonological and syntactic structures of language.

linguistic competence Knowledge that a reader has about language; proficiency in the standard system of language.

List-Group-Label A categorizing strategy developed by Hilda Taba intended to enhance vocabulary and concept development.

listening The action by which oral language is mentally transformed into meaning.

listening capacity Also known as *listening comprehension level;* the highest level at which a student can understand 75 percent of the material read aloud; sometimes used as an indication of a reader's ability to understand oral language or as an estimate of reading expectancy.

listening vocabulary Words understood at the level of oral language.

literature circle A group of students who choose to read and discuss the same book; usually employs guidelines for fulfilling a particular "job," such as summarizer or discussion director.

literature genre A classification of literature surrounding a particular topic (including adventure, animal, detective, fairy tales, fantasy, mystery, romance).

locational skills Also known as work-study skills; the small areas of proficiency tested on many standardized achievement tests.

main ideas The statements in a passage that provide the most significant ideas concerning the topic.

mapping Also called semantic webbing; a visual display of the relationships in the composition of a story or expository selection.

mastery tests Criterion-referenced tests or skills management systems that attempt to assess or instruct through focus on reading subskills.

maze technique A variation of the cloze procedure that offers several possible selections in place of the missing word; a multiple-choice item.

meaning clues The meaning in the context that allows students to decipher unknown words through recognition, where only a limited number of word choices can sensibly be used without altering the intended meaning of a passage.

meaning vocabulary The words that a person understands, whether in written or oral language.

media literacy The ability to think critically about what is seen, heard, and read on the television, radio, newspaper, or through the Internet.

metacognition Self-knowledge regarding one's ability to think; in reading, the ability to self-monitor for comprehension and the ability to recognize when difficulty occurs.

miscue Any deviation by a reader from what is written in print.

miscue analysis An examination of deviations from print made by a reader; gives the teacher insight into whether a reader is reading for meaning, as well as into the reader's use of graphophonic, semantic, and syntactic cues.

morphemes   The smallest meaningful structures in language.

morphemic analysis   Structural analysis, or analyzing words by noticing their meaning-bearing parts, such as prefixes or suffixes.

morphology   The study of meaningful word structures in language.

multiliteracies   Communication beyond traditional reading and writing, including the literacies of music, dance, visual art, drama, and computer technology.

multimedia materials   (see also *visual arts media*) Materials that make use of computers, CDs, film, overhead transparencies, and the like.

multiple intelligences   A theory proposed by Howard Gardner that there are at least eight relatively autonomous intelligences (intellectual competencies or talents) indicating a need to expand our framework for thinking about intelligence; the intelligences are linguistic, spatial, musical, logical-mathematical, bodily-kinesthetic, interpersonal, intrapersonal, and naturalist.

narrative ability   A set of sociolinguistic competencies that includes linguistic competence, sociolinguistic competence, fluency of expression, and the ability to sequence ideas.

nondirective teaching   A teaching model designed to help students set personal goals through facilitated teaching.

nonstructured writing   Student-centered writing activities that allow students to write about whatever interests them as a natural, purposeful activity whereby students learn about written language without direct instruction.

normal curve equivalent (NCE) scores   A type of standard score based on the normal bell curve with scores ranging from 1 to 99 with a mean of 50, differing from percentiles in that the scores are in equal units rather than piling up around the mean.

norm-referenced tests   Standardized tests; standardization requires the preparation of a standard set of directions, a specified amount of time, and sample administration to a large group of students to establish a reference to which subsequent administrations of the test can be compared.

norms   The scores obtained from a large group of students to whom a standardized test is administered, which establish the reference that is then used for comparison in subsequent administrations of the test.

novel study   In-depth reading and interpretation of a novel or group of related stories.

onsets   Single consonants, consonant blends, and consonant digraphs coming before the first vowel in a syllable.

open word sorting   A technique for grouping words that allows for a variety of classifications determined by the sorter(s).

oral interaction   A fundamental societal skill that consists of such competencies as initiating discourse, changing the topic of a conversation, taking turns, using tact, and basic pragmatic abilities such as knowing what to say (or what not to say), pertinence, directness, and so forth.

orthography   The conventional use of written symbols in a given language; the writing system, or correct spelling, for a given language.

out-of-level testing   An indirect measure of assessment used when the average achievement of a class is either high or low; allows the teacher to select the test level best suited to the class to increase the reliability of the test.

outside influences   Elements not directly relating to literacy but affecting all learning, such as physical factors, visual acuity and perception, auditory acuity, neurological factors, poverty, and so forth.

outlaw word   A word that does not conform to rules of pronunciation (such as *to, come,* or *have*).

paradigm   A pattern or process.

paraphrase   To summarize or restate in one's own words by using synonyms in place of the existing words, rearranging existing words, or a combination of the two measures.

passage dependent   The state of questions that can be answered either literally or inferred by reading a particular passage.

percentile scores   Scores obtained by converting the raw scores of a standardized test into numbers from 1 to 99 to compare students with others of the same age or grade either through a norm group or directly with others in the same classroom or school.

perceptual unit of analysis   Size of the visual stimuli used for analysis in reading instruction (such as letter, syllable, word, sentence, or whole passage).

performance assessments   Methods of assessing student knowledge by having students read, write, and solve problems under circumstances like those in the instructional environment.

personal dictionary   A place where each student can record interesting new words from stories, LEAs, journals, or other learning experiences by writing down the word under the appropriate letter of the alphabet, writing a sentence with the word, and drawing a picture to further reinforce the meaning.

phase-out/phase-in strategy   The gradual transfer from teacher-posed to student-posed questions to promote independent reading.

phonemes   The sound structures of language.

phoneme substitution   An oral task in which one sound within a word is replaced by another.

phonemic awareness   Awareness of sounds that make up spoken words; the capacity to distinguish and manipulate sounds in words.

phonics   Letter–sound relationships; phonemes and their corresponding letters.

phonological awareness   Awareness of words: that words are made up of syllables, word parts such as onsets and rimes, and individual sounds.

phonological system   An understanding of individual sounds in language, an understanding of how these sounds are combined to make words, and an understanding of the effects of stress, pitch, and juncture on language.

phonology   The sounds and sound processes of a language.

physical abuse   Deliberate injury of a child that results in bruises, burns, broken bones, or internal injuries.

physical neglect   Abandonment or a lack of provisions such as clothing, shelter, food, or supervision.

picture clues   The pictures in a book that provide clues to the text by bringing certain words to mind.

picture walk   A technique used to survey the pictures in a text prior to reading for the purpose of clarifying concepts or predicting storyline.

PORPE   A student-directed learning strategy for secondary- and college-level students to help them plan, monitor, and evaluate their reading by proceeding through the following five steps: predict, organize, rehearse, practice, and evaluate.

portfolios   A collection of artifacts chosen and reflected upon to show abilities, growth, or development across time.

postreading stage   The final stage of studying, characterized by the use of any number of organizational, translational, or repetitive activities for reinforcing learned information (including graphic organizers, paragraph frames, annotations, recitations, K–W–L charts, think links).

pragmatic cue system Rules connecting the interpretation of language within the social context.

pragmatics The ability to use language in a variety of social settings.

predictable text Text that contains rhythmical, repetitive, or cumulative patterns that assist emergent and early readers to easily predict what the author will say.

prereading stage The first stage of reading, characterized by scanning or skimming text and previewing such information as titles, headings, summaries, illustrations, and topic sentences in preparation for reading to activate schema and increase comprehension.

problem-based learning (PBL) An approach consistent with democratic teaching because students are provided with real-world problems or carefully designed problems that mirror real-world problems.

problem-solving questions Questions designed to assist students in dynamic thinking by (a) making them aware that not knowing an answer is acceptable to the teacher and (b) prompting the students to figure out the strategies necessary to come up with the answer.

process of comprehension The thinking and integration of information sources used by the reader in constructing meaning while reading.

productive language The process by which students generate or identify possible words in the prereading period that may appear in the text, to improve their use of expectancy cues.

productive questioning Carefully crafted questions for guiding conceptual thinking based on student responses.

proficient reader A reader who demonstrates skills, strategies, and reading achievement appropriate for age and grade level.

protocol In the administration of IRIs, the list of main points expected for free recall and questions based on the passages that are typed in advance on separate sheets of paper and duplicated to serve as the record sheet; any record sheet for assessment data.

psycholinguistic processing Using various thinking processes to compose or comprehend meaning of oral and written language.

psychological set The ideas, and the words associated with them, that are retrieved from memory storage upon the introduction to a topic; the activated schemata.

qualitative analysis In IRIs, the analysis of the kinds of miscues made by a reader to determine a pattern and to discover whether the miscues affect the meaning of the text.

quantitative analysis Determination of the number of errors a reader makes without regard to kind or effect on meaning.

question–answer relationships (QARs) A reading strategy designed to assist students in determining the difference between questions whose answers are textually explicit ("right there"), which can be found directly in the text; textually implicit ("putting it together"), which can be found in the text but require some synthesis of the text material; and scriptally implicit ("on my own" and "author and me"), which require the reader to use prior knowledge.

quickwrite A writing activity that requires students to write nonstop for 5 to 10 minutes, usually focused on a topic, also used as a prewriting activity to generate ideas or to clarify thoughts about a topic.

readers' theater The oral presentation of a script.

reading vocabulary Words in meaning vocabulary that are read and understood in print.

reciprocal question–answer relationships (ReQARs) A reading strategy that combines the elements of the ReQuest and QAR strategies to assist middle- and upper-grade students in word recognition, anticipate the nature of teachers' questions, focus on informative portions of text material, and construct appropriate responses to questions.

reciprocal teaching An interactive learning strategy designed to teach children to summarize sections of text, anticipate possible questions, predict, and clarify difficult portions of text; students initially observe the teacher model the target behaviors and then gradually take the instructional role from the teacher.

recreational literacy Independent literacy activities that foster positive attitudes and interests as well as good literacy habits.

recursive nature of writing The back-and-forth nature of writing: as writers think of changes they wish to make in their work while they are writing, they often go back to reword or add new information to previously written material.

readiness A student's level of preparedness for learning a certain skill or concept.

reflective thinking The act of continuous questioning about past events in a purposeful attempt to solve educational problems and improve one's approach to teaching.

regional dialects A thoroughly developed linguistic system identifiable to a particular geographic location.

rehearsal The stage in the writing process in which the writer mentally tries out versions of a composition before choosing the final version.

reliability In standardized testing, the level of consistency of scores when the same test is given to a group of students more than once within a short frame of time.

repeated words Content words found in almost every sentence of a paragraph.

replaced words Substitutes for content words that would normally be repeated in a passage (for example, pronouns).

ReQuest Procedure (Reciprocal Questioning) A procedure used with individuals or small groups to aid students in setting their own purposes for reading; the teacher guides the students as they silently read as many sentences of a selection as it takes for them to be able to read the selection independently, with the teacher and student exchanging questions sentence by sentence as they go along, until finally a general-purpose question is asked and the students begin reading alone.

resiliency The capacity to bounce back from adversity.

retelling A measure of comprehension providing insight into the reader's ability to interact with, interpret, and draw conclusions from text; the process of describing what was just read.

rimes Phonograms; the parts of rhyming words that are the same; the vowel and any consonants after the initial consonant in a syllable.

rubric scoring Use of a set of criteria for rating students' performance in various literacy tasks.

running records A way of coding passages for miscue analysis using a combination of proofreading symbols and check marks without need for a preprinted copy of the material being read by the student.

scaffolding Supporting learning through teacher modeling and assistance as needed.

scaffolds Support mechanisms that enable students to accomplish a more difficult task than they might be ble to achieve without assistance.

scanning A type of fast reading used when a reader is seeking answers to specific questions.

schema A general description for background knowledge; a conceptual system for understanding knowledge.

schematic cue system The use of information from a reader's prior knowledge or personal association with the content or structure of the text.

scoring rubric A set of evaluation criteria used for rating a student's performance on a specific task.

scriptal information Background knowledge; schemata.

scriptally implicit In QARs, the state of answers to questions from which the knowledge must come from the student's own background knowledge.

SDAIE (Specially Designed Academic Instruction in English) Instruction that recognizes and provides for the specific needs of English learners.

semantic cue system What a reader knows about meaning in language, including the meanings of words, the underlying concepts of words, and how those concepts are related, thus allowing a reader to organize concepts and make determinations about the importance of various concepts.

semantic system See *semantic cue system*

semantic webbing Also called *mapping;* a visual display of the relationships in the composition of a story or expository selection.

semantics Meaning in language.

sexual abuse The sexual exploitation, molestation, or prostitution of another individual.

shared reading The teacher reads aloud while students listen and follow along with a Big Book, individual copies of the book, or from a class chart.

showcase portfolio A portfolio displaying evidence concerning a student's literacy development that contains examples of writing chosen by the student with an attached statement as to why that sample has been selected.

sight vocabulary Those words that students encounter in print, which are instantly and effortlessly recognized.

sight words The small set of words in our language that do not conform to traditional analysis methods, which must be learned by sight (for example, *are, to, of, have, come*)

sign systems Any and all forms of communication.

skills-based view Viewpoint that important subskills related to reading and writing must be learned before proficiency can be achieved.

skimming A type of fast reading used when a reader is attempting to obtain a general idea as to what a passage might be about.

social dialects Surface variations of standard English among cultural groups or social classes.

sociolinguistic competence The use of language to accomplish some goal.

specialized vocabulary Common word forms specific to a content field.

SQ3R strategy A reading strategy designed by Robinson to help students make the best use of their study time by using the steps of *survey, question, read, recite,* and *review* to set purposes for reading, provide self-comprehension checks, and fix information into memory.

standard deviation In standardized testing, the measure of distribution that indicates variability; the higher the standard deviation, the greater the variation in the scores.

standard dialect The variety of a language accepted as formal and used in commerce; the variety of language used by the well educated or by people in higher income brackets.

standard error of measurement In standardized testing, also referred to as *SEmeas* or *SEM,* the statistic that denotes the degree to which a person's score can be predicted to fluctuate each time the test is taken.

standard scores In standardized testing, uniformly spaced scores derived from the raw scores; indicate how far an individual score is from the mean in terms of the variability of the distribution.

standardized tests Also called *formal tests,* tests that have been administered in the same way to a large group of students for the purpose of establishing a reference (also called *norm*) group to which all future groups of students can be compared.

stanine scores In standardized testing, equally spaced scores derived from the raw scores such that the lowest score is 1 and the highest 9, with a stanine of 5 representing the mean, and having a standard deviation of 2.

story frames A listing of key words used to guide students' organization of written story retellings by providing a structure through enumeration, generalization, comparison or contrast, sequencing, or question and answer, allowing students to express their awareness of story structure.

story grammar The arrangement that outlines the essential elements of a complete story, including the setting, initiating event, a reaction, a goal, an attempt, an outcome, and a solution.

story impressions A prewriting strategy that introduces a list of words to be used in a story along with the order in which they should be used.

structural analysis An instructional unit dealing with meaningful word parts such as variants (word endings), compounds, and derivatives (affixes).

structured comprehension A reading strategy that moves from the sentence level to the paragraph level, assisting students by (a) providing students with the proper context, (b) reading the sentence and decoding any miscues, (c) clarifying student questions about the sentence, and (d) asking students a series of predetermined questions to further clarify the information.

structured overview A learning strategy designed to introduce new vocabulary as well as the overall organization of a selection that uses a graphic representation of terms essential to the selection through the use of the following steps: (a) listing the essential vocabulary; (b) arranging the words to show relationships between concepts: (c) adding vocabulary familiar to the students that assists in developing the relationships; (d) evaluating the diagram; (e) introducing the lesson by displaying the diagram and explaining the reason for the arrangement; and (f) continuing to relate information as the selection is read.

structured practice An opportunity for students to practice what has been demonstrated by the teacher while the teacher is still involved.

studying Student-directed instruction that expands and reinforces the knowledge gained in the classroom through various comprehension strategies.

study skills Reading tools that permit readers to expand on and build their knowledge through literacy.

stuttering A speech disorder whose basis is neurological.

style shifting The ability to adapt and adjust oral and written language to meet the needs and styles of various listeners and readers.

subordinate relationship The relationship of specific or supporting details in a passage to the overall text.

summarizing Condensing text by paraphrasing to include only the most important ideas.

superordinate relationship The relationship of the general or main idea of a passage to the overall text.

symbol system Any arbitrary conventional written or printed mark intended to communicate, such as letters, numerals, ideographs, and so forth.

syndrome A set of overt signs or observable behaviors occurring together.

syntactic cue system The system of language concerned with the word order of sentences, the placement of punctuation, and the use of capital letters to help a reader determine the grammatical sense of a selection, and in turn use that information to assist word recognition and comprehension.

syntactic system See *syntactic cue system*

syntax The component of language concerned with the order of words and their placement in phrases and sentences.

synthesizing Summarizing text by combining relationships between the ideas of several different selections through students' interpretation of the material.

teachable units Parcels of information small enough to be learned through direct instruction; a specific learning segment.

teacher-guided writing lessons Writing lessons based on students' specific needs that concentrate on discrete aspects of written language that are new to the learners, such as spelling, punctuation, and so forth, as well as more global aspects of language, such as prewriting, paraphrasing, and editing.

teaching hypothesis The instructional plan determined by the teacher to be most beneficial to a particular student's instructional needs following the collection and analysis of educational data.

telegraphic stage In oral language development, the stage in which a concept or an idea is expressed by two words.

temporary spelling (see *invented* or *constructed spelling*) The developmentally appropriate form of spelling a word that represents a stage of spelling.

test-taking strategies Planful behaviors related to preparing for and taking a test.

text-based collaborative learning Students work together with a partner or small group to clarify their reading of expository text.

text organization The establishment of relationships between words, sentences, paragraphs, and larger units, which is the key to reading comprehension.

text-related tests Tests that measure the content, skills, and subskills learned by a reader from recently completed text material.

textually explicit In QARs, the state of answers to questions that are stated literally and directly in the text material.

textually implicit In QARs, the state of answers to questions that are in the text but that require the student to synthesize material spanning several sentences or paragraphs.

thematic units of instruction Particular topics of instruction on which much of the instruction in a particular classroom is based, usually incorporating multiple disciplines and often arising naturally within the context of the school day.

think-links An instructional strategy to help teachers guide their students into thinking about what they have read by having the students write down key words about a selection, then connect the key words first with specific examples and then with descriptive words, thereby reconstructing the important elements of the material.

thought units Short phrases, selected from text, that contain only one idea.

tiered activities A way of differentiating instruction by differentiating the process learners use to achieve a common lesson objective.

topic A word or phrase that represents the major subject of a text selection or picture.

transactional model A model of the reading process that takes into account the dynamic nature of language and both the cognitive and aesthetic aspects of reading by maintaining the concept that meaning exists in reading only through the interaction between the author's words and the reader's background knowledge.

transactive Relating to the construction of meaning by the active interchange of ideas between reader and text or between speaker and listener.

transfer of training The ability to generalize the specific process involved in the recognition of certain unknown words to other unknown words encountered in the future.

understanding questions A type of question to help students monitor their comprehension at the word, sentence, and paragraph levels by homing in on possible barriers to meaning such as new words, unfamiliar facts, and the relationship between the text material and existing knowledge.

validity In standardized testing, the extent to which a test measures what it claims to measure and does what it claims to do.

vernacular dialects The language varieties commonly used in informal circumstances; prevalent among lower socioeconomic groups.

viewing A receptive language art related to visual literacy and the unique visual symbols found with the use of videotapes, certain CD-ROM software, and other visual media.

visual A representation of important characters or settings in a piece of literature, such as a teddy bear, a sailboat, or a frog.

visual acuity The degree of one's ability to see with clarity and sharpness.

visual art Any form of art that provides meaning when viewed, such as dioramas, murals, or paintings.

visual arts media Crayons, tempera paint, chalk, colored pencils, watercolors, and the like.

visual language Communication through visual representations; meaning through images.

visual perception The skills of visual awareness, such as the ability to discriminate visually, the concept of constancy in spatial orientation, and the ability to remember visual sequences.

visual synthesizing The process in reading that follows auditory blending and allows readers to analyze words mentally without having to sound them out.

visually impaired Unable to see with appropriate keenness and acumen even with corrective lenses, thus requiring large-print accommodations for reading.

visually representing A language art related to the production of visual representations for the comprehension of text, such as graphs, charts, maps, clusters, drawings, and murals.

voices of composing The points of view taken by an author in writing, including the expressive, the poetic or imaginative, and the expository.

WebQuest An inquiry-based technique that invites students to use the Internet to obtain information related to a particular topic or problem.

word learning strategies Using context and word parts to determine the meanings of words.

word map A graphic organizer for showing a concept in relation to its relevant attributes and to examples and nonexamples of the concept.

word wall A large surface for posting words being learned, studied, or used often in reading or writing.

working portfolio A portfolio that contains various works in progress, including a student's current project, works that may never be completed, work generated during various writing activities, ideas for future projects, copies of postwriting questionnaires, and anything else not selected for the showcase portfolio.

Writer's Workshop A block of instructional time devoted to student prewriting, drafting, revising, and editing of compositions for publication/sharing.

writing process Refers to all aspects of producing a written composition including prewriting, composing, revising, editing, and publishing/sharing.[1]

---

[1]The author is forever grateful to Susan Glynn Mulé for the initial preparation of this glossary. Thank you, Susan!

References

Aardema, V. (1981). *Bringing the rain to Kapiti Plain*. New York: Dial.

Adams, M. J. (1990). *Beginning to read: Thinking and learning about print*. Cambridge, MA: MIT Press.

Adger, C. T., Wolfram, W., & Christian, D. (2007). *Dialects in schools and communities*, 2nd edition. Mahwah, NJ: Erlbaum.

Alexander, F. (1993). National standards: A new conventional wisdom. *Educational Leadership, 50,* 9–10.

Alexander, J. E., & Cobb, J. (1992). Assessing attitudes in middle and secondary schools and community colleges. *Journal of Reading, 36,* 146–149.

Allington, R. (1994). The schools we have, the schools we need. *The Reading Teacher, 48,* 14–29.

Allington, R., & Walmsley, S. (Eds.). (1995). *No quick fix: Rethinking literacy programs in America's elementary schools*. Columbia University, NY: Teachers College Press, and Newark, DE: International Reading Association.

Almasi, J. (1996). A new view of discussion. In L. Gambrell & J. Almasi (Eds.), *Lively discussions! Fostering engaged reading* (pp. 2–24). Newark, DE: International Reading Association.

Alvermann, D. E. (Ed.). (2002). *Adolescents and literacies in a digital world*. New York: Peter Lang Publishing.

Alvermann, D. E., Moon, J. E., & Hagood, M. C. (1999). *Popular culture in the classroom: Teaching and researching critical media literacy*. Mahwah, NJ: Lawrence Erlbaum Associates.

Anderson, R. C., & Freebody, P. (1981). Vocabulary knowledge. In J. Guthrie (Ed.), *Comprehension and teaching: Research reviews* (pp. 77–117). Newark, DE: International Reading Association.

Anderson, T. H. (1980). Study strategies and adjunct aids. In R. J. Spiro, B. C. Bruce, & W. F. Brewer (Eds.), *Theoretical issues in reading comprehension*. Hillsdale, NJ: Erlbaum.

Anderson, V., & Roit, M. (1996). Linking reading comprehension instruction to language development for language-minority students. *Elementary School Journal, 96,* 295–310.

Andersson, B. V., & Gipe, J. P. (1983). Creativity as a mediating variable in inferential reading comprehension. *Reading Psychology, 4,* 313–325.

Andre, M. E. D. A., & Anderson, T. H. (1978/1979). The development and evaluation of a self-questioning study technique. *Reading Research Quarterly, 14,* 605–623.

Anonymous. (1997, December 1). Forty-seven states take steps toward improved music and arts education. The American Music Teacher, Dec. 1997/Jan. 1998. A publication of Music Teachers National Association.

Applegate, M. D., Quinn, K. B., & Applegate, A. J. (2002). Levels of thinking required by comprehension questions in informal reading inventories. *The Reading Teacher, 56*(2), 174–180.

Applegate, M. D., Quinn, K. B., & Applegate, A. J. (2008). *The critical reading inventory: Assessing students' reading and thinking*. Upper Saddle River, NJ: Prentice Hall.

Armstrong, T. (1993). *7 kinds of smart*. New York: Plume/Penguin.

Armstrong, T. (2000). *Multiple intelligences in the classroom* (2nd ed.). Alexandria, VA: Association for Supervision and Curriculum Development.

Arnold, R. D., & Sherry, N. (1975). A comparison of reading levels of disabled readers with assigned textbooks. *Reading Improvement, 12,* 207–211.

Asher, J. (1982). *Learning another language through actions: The complete teachers' guidebook*. Los Gatos, CA: Sky Oaks.

Au, K. (1993). *Literacy instruction in multicultural settings*. Fort Worth, TX: Harcourt Brace Jovanovich.

Au, K. H. (1979). Using the experience-text-relationship method with minority children. *The Reading Teacher, 32,* 677–679.

Au, K. H. (2006). *Multicultural issues and literacy achievement*. Mahwah, NJ: Erlbaum.

Au, K. H., & Kawakami, A. J. (1985). Research currents: Talk story and learning to read. *Language Arts, 62,* 406–411.

August, D., & Shanahan, T. (2008). Developing reading and writing in second language learners: Lessons from the report of the National Reading Panel on language-minority children and youth. Center for Applied Linguistics.

Aulls, M. W. (1978). *Developmental and remedial reading in the middle grades* (Abridged ed.). Boston: Allyn & Bacon.

Auman, M. (2002). *Step up to writing*. Colorado: Sopris West Educational Services.

Author unknown. (2003). ELD/SDAIE worksheet from professional development training session for the Department of Teacher Education. Sacramento, CA: California State University, Sacramento.

Azevedo, R., & Cromley, J. G. (2004). Does training on self-regulated learning facilitate students' learning with hypermedia? *Journal of Educational Psychology, 96,* 523–535.

Babbs, P. J. (1984). Monitoring cards help improve comprehension. *The Reading Teacher, 38,* 200–204.

Bader, L. A. (2005). *Reading and language inventory*. Upper Saddle River, NJ: Prentice Hall.

Baildon, R., & Baildon, M. (2008). Guiding independence: Developing a research tool to support student decision making in selecting online information sources. *The Reading Teacher, 61,* 636–647.

Baker, L. (1979). *Comprehension monitoring: Identifying and coping with text confusions* (Tech. Rep. No. 145). Champaign: University of Illinois, Center for the Study of Reading.

Baker, L., & Brown, A. L. (1984). Metacognitive skills and reading. In P. D. Pearson (Ed.), *Handbook of reading research*. New York: Longman.

Bangert-Drowns, R. L., Kulik, J. A., & Kulik, C. (1983). Effects of coaching programs on achievement test performance. *Review of Educational Research, 53,* 571–585.

Barnitz, J. G. (1985). *Reading development of nonnative speakers of English: Research and instruction* (Language in Education: Theory and Practice series, Monograph No. 63). ERIC Clearinghouse on Languages and Linguistics. Washington, DC: Center for Applied Linguistics, and Orlando,

FL: Harcourt Brace Jovanovich. (ERIC Document Reproduction Service No. ED256182)

Barnitz, J. G. (1986). Toward understanding the effects of cross-cultural schemata and discourse structure on second language reading comprehension. *Journal of Reading Behavior, 18,* 95–116.

Barnitz, J. G. (1994). Discourse diversity: Principles for authentic talk and literacy instruction. *Journal of Reading, 37,* 586–591.

Barnitz, J. G. (1997). Linguistic perspectives in literacy education: Emerging awareness of linguistic diversity for literacy instruction. *The Reading Teacher, 51,* 264–266.

Barnitz, J. G. (1998). Linguistic perspectives in literacy education: Revising grammar instruction for authentic composing and comprehending. *The Reading Teacher, 51,* 608–611.

Barnitz, J. G. (2003, April). *Literacy, language and urban neighborhood baseball: An autobiographical educational journey in the alley.* Paper presented at the annual meeting of the American Educational Research Association, Chicago, IL.

Barnitz, J. G. (2004, August 27). Literacy and baseball. [Radio talk show] Ron Swoboda (Sportscaster) for "Sports Talk," BIZ radio AM 990, WHSO, New Orleans.

Barnitz, J. G. (2006). No evacuee left behind: Brainstorming on literacy education after Hurricane Katrina. *Journal of Reading Education, 31*(Spring/Summer), 5–10.

Barnitz, J. G., & Barnitz, C. G. (1996). Celebrating with language and literature at birthday parties and other childhood events. *The Reading Teacher, 50,* 110–117.

Barnitz, J. G., Gipe, J. P., & Richards, J. C. (1999). Linguistic perspectives in literacy education: Exploring linguistic benefits of literature for children's language performance in teacher education contexts. *The Reading Teacher, 52,* 528–531.

Barone, D. (1995). "Be very careful not to let the facts get mixed up with the truth": Children prenatally exposed to crack/cocaine. *Urban Education, 30*(1), 40–55.

Barone, D. (1996). Children prenatally exposed to crack or cocaine: Looking behind the label. *The Reading Teacher, 49,* 278–289.

Barrett, H. C. (2007). Researching electronic portfolios and learner engagement: The REFLECT initiative. *Journal of Adolescent and Adult Literacy, 50,* 436–449.

Barrie, B. (1994). *Adam Zigzag.* New York: Delacourt.

Barron, R. F. (1969). The use of vocabulary as an advance organizer. In H. Herber & P. Sanders (Eds.), *Research in reading in the content areas: First year report.* Syracuse, NY: Syracuse University.

Bartlett, F. C. (1932). *Remembering: A study in experimental and social psychology.* New York: Cambridge University Press.

Bartolome, P. I. (1969). Teachers' objectives and questions in primary reading. *The Reading Teacher, 23,* 27–33.

Base, G. (1986). *Animalia.* New York: Abrams.

Baskin, B., & Harris, K. (1995). Heard any good books lately? The case for audiobooks in the secondary classroom. *Journal of Reading, 38,* 372–376.

Batey, C. (1996). *Parents are lifesavers: A handbook for parent involvement in schools.* Thousand Oaks, CA: Corwin.

Baugh, J. (1983). *Black street speech.* Austin: University of Texas.

Baugh, J. (1999). *Out of the mouths of slaves.* Austin: University of Texas.

Bean, T. W., & Pardi, R. (1979). A field test of a guided reading strategy. *Journal of Reading, 23,* 144–147.

Beattie, B. (2005). Putting the crack baby myth to bed: Researchers fail to link cocaine use and neonatal outcomes. *National Review of Medicine, 2*(13), 4–13.

Beck, I. L. (1981). Reading problems and instructional practices. In G. E. Mackinnon & T. G. Waller (Eds.), *Reading research:*

Advances in theory and practice (Vol. 2, pp. 53–95). New York: Academic Press.

Beck, I. L., & McKeown, M. G. (1981). Developing questions that promote comprehension of the story map. *Language Arts, 58,* 913–917.

Beck, I. L., McKeown, M. G., & Kucan, L. (2002). *Bringing words to life: Robust vocabulary instruction.* New York: Guilford.

Beck, I. L., McKeown, M. G., & McCaslin, E. S. (1983). Vocabulary development: All contexts are not created equal. *The Elementary School Journal, 83*(3), 177–181.

Bedford, A. W., & Kieff, J. E. (in press). Surviving the storm: *Creating opportunities for learning in response to Hurricane Katrina.* Olney, MD: Association for Childhood Education International.

Bedsworth, B. (1991). The neurological impress method with middle school poor readers. *Journal of Reading, 34,* 564–565.

Benedict, S., & Carlisle, L. (1992). *Beyond words: Picture books for older readers and writers.* Portsmouth, NH: Heinemann.

Berliner, D. C. (1981). Academic learning time and reading achievement. In J. T. Guthrie (Ed.), *Comprehension and teaching: Research reviews.* Newark, DE: International Reading Association.

Bernhardt, E. B. (1991). *Reading development in a second language: Theoretical, empirical, and classroom perspectives.* Norwood, NJ: Ablex.

Betancourt, J. (1993). *My name is Brain/Brian.* New York: Scholastic.

Betts, E. (1946). *Foundations of reading instruction.* New York: American Book.

Bidwell, S. M. (1990). Using drama to increase motivation, comprehension, and fluency. *Journal of Reading, 34,* 38–41.

Biemiller, A. (1999). *Estimating vocabulary growth for ESL children with and without listening comprehension instruction.* Paper presented at the annual conference of the American Educational Research Association, Montreal, Quebec, Canada.

Binch, C. (1994). *Gregory Cool.* New York: Dial Books for Young Readers.

Blachowicz, C. L. Z., & Fisher, P. (2004). Keep the "fun" in fundamental. In J. F. Baumann and E. J. Kame'enui (Eds.), *Vocabulary instruction: Research to practice* (pp. 218–237). New York: The Guilford Press.

Blachowicz, C. L. Z., & Zabroske, B. (1990). Context instruction: A metacognitive approach for at-risk readers. *Journal of Reading, 33,* 504–508.

Blair-Larsen, S., & Williams, K. E. (Eds.). (1999). *The balanced reading program: Helping all students achieve success.* Newark, DE: International Reading Association.

Blecher, S., & Jaffee, K. (1998). *Weaving in the arts: Widening the learning circle.* Portsmouth, NH: Heinemann.

Block, C. C. (1999). Comprehension: Crafting understanding. In L. Gambrell, L. Morrow, S. Neuman, & M. Pressley (Eds.), *Best practices in literacy instruction* (pp. 98–118). New York: Guilford.

Block, C. C., & Cavanaugh, C. (1998). Teaching thinking: How can we and why should we? In R. Bernhardt, C. Hedley, G. Cattaro, & V. Svolopoulous (Eds.), *Curriculum leadership: Rethinking schools for the 21st century* (pp. 301–320). Alexandria, VA: Association for Supervision and Curriculum Development.

Bloem, P. L., & Padak, N. D. (1996). Picture books, young adult books, and adult literacy learners. *Journal of Adolescent and Adult Literacy, 40,* 48–53.

Bloome, D. (1991). Anthropology and research on teaching the English language arts. In J. Flood, J. M. Jensen, D. Lapp, & J. R. Squire (Eds.), *Handbook of research on teaching the English language arts* (pp. 46–56). New York: Macmillan.

Bloome, D., & Egan-Robertson, A. (1993). The social construction of intertextuality in classroom reading and writing lessons. *Reading Research Quarterly, 25,* 305–333.

Boling, E., Castek, J., Zawilinski, L., Barton, K., & Nierlich, T. (2008). Collaborative literacy: Blogs and Internet projects. *The Reading Teacher, 61,* 504–506.

Boning, T., & Boning, R. (1957). I'd rather read than . . . *The Reading Teacher* (April), 196–200.

Borkowski, J. G., Wehing, R. S., & Turner, L. A. (1986). Attributional retraining and the teaching of strategies. *Exceptional Children, 53,* 130–137.

Bormuth, J. R. (1967). Comparable cloze and multiple-choice comprehension test score. *Journal of Reading, 10,* 291–299.

Bormuth, J. R. (1968a). The cloze readability procedure. *Elementary English, 45,* 429–436.

Bormuth, J. R. (1968b). Cloze test readability: Criterion reference scores. *Journal of Educational Measurement, 5,* 189–196.

Bormuth, J. R. (1975). The cloze procedure: Literacy in the classroom. In W. D. Page (Ed.), *Help for the reading teacher: New directions in research* (pp. 60–90). Urbana, IL: ERIC Clearinghouse on Reading and Communication Skills.

Bracken, B. (1998). *Bracken basic concept scale-revised: Examiner's manual.* San Antonio, TX: The Psychological Corporation, Harcourt Brace and Company.

Bradley, B. A., & Jones, J. (2007). Sharing alphabet books in early childhood classrooms. *The Reading Teacher, 60,* 452–463.

Brassell, D. (2004, Winter). A comprehensive emergent literacy program for inner-city Latino preschoolers: Perspectives and practices. *NABE Journal of Research and Practice, 2*(1), 109–128.

Braunger, J., & Lewis, J. (2006). *Building a knowledge base in reading,* 2nd ed. Newark, DE, and Urbana, IL: IRA and NCTE.

Brett, J. (1987). *Goldilocks and the three bears.* Boston: Houghton Mifflin.

Britton, J., Burgess, T., Martin, N., McLeod, A., & Rosen, H. (1975). *The development of writing abilities* (pp. 11–18). Schools Council Research Studies. London: Macmillan.

Brock, C. H., & Raphael, T. E. (2005). *Windows to language, literacy and culture: Insights from an English-language learner.* Newark, DE: International Reading Association.

Broda, H. W. (2007). *Schoolyard-enhanced learning: Using the outdoors as an instructional tool, K–8.* Portland, ME: Stenhouse.

Brown, A. L. (1980). Metacognitive development and reading. In R. J. Spiro, B. C. Bruce, & W. F. Brewer (Eds.), *Theoretical issues in reading comprehension* (pp. 453–481). Hillsdale, NJ: Erlbaum.

Brown, A. L., & DeLoache, J. (1978). Skills, plans, and self-regulation. In R. Siegler (Ed.), *Children's thinking: What develops?* Hillsdale, NJ: Erlbaum.

Brown, C. S. (1985, April). *Assessing perceptions of language and learning: Alternative diagnostic approaches.* Paper presented at the International Reading Association Convention, New Orleans, LA.

Brown, J. I., Fishco, V. V., & Hanna, G. S. (1993). *Nelson-Denny Reading Test, Forms G & H.* Itasca, IL: Riverside.

Brown, L. K., & Brown, M. (1986). *Dinosaurs' divorce: A guide for changing families.* College Park, MD: Atlantic Monthly Press.

Brozo, W. G. (1990). Learning how at-risk readers learn best: A case for interactive assessment. *Journal of Reading, 33,* 522–527.

Bruchac, J. (1993). *Fox song.* New York: Putnam.

Bruner, J. (1966). *Toward a theory of instruction.* Cambridge, MA: Harvard University Press.

Bryan, J. (1998). K–W–W–L: Questioning the known. *The Reading Teacher, 51,* 618–620.

Buikema, J. L., & Graves, M. F. (1993). Teaching students to use context to infer word meanings. *Journal of Reading, 36,* 450–457.

Burmeister, L. E. (1978). *Reading strategies for middle and secondary school teachers.* Reading, MA: Addison-Wesley.

Burnett, F. H. (1962). *The secret garden.* New York: J. P. Lippincourt.

Burns, P. C. (1980). *Assessment and correction of language arts difficulties.* Columbus, OH: Merrill.

Byars, B. (1975). *The lace snail.* New York: Viking.

Calkins, L. (1994). *The art of teaching writing.* Portsmouth, NH: Heinemann.

Campbell, L., Campbell, B., & Dickinson, D. (1999). *Teaching and learning through multiple intelligences.* Needham Heights, MA: Allyn & Bacon.

Cannon, J. (1997). *Verdi.* New York: Harcourt Children's Books.

Cantrell, S. (1998/1999). Effective teaching and literacy learning: A look inside primary classrooms. *The Reading Teacher, 52,* 370–378.

Cardarelli, A. F. (1988). The influence of reinspection on students' IRI results. *The Reading Teacher, 41,* 664–667.

Carle, E. (1987). *The very hungry caterpillar.* New York: Scholastic.

Carlisle, J. F., & Stone, C. A. (2005). *Exploring the role of morphemes in word reading.* Reading Research

Carlo, M. S., August, D., McGlaughlin, B., Snow, C. E., Dressler, C., Lippman, D. N., Lively, T. J., & White, C. E. (2004). Closing the gap: Addressing vocabulary needs of English-language learners in bilingual and mainstreamed classes. *Reading Research Quarterly, 39,* 188–215.

Carr, E., & Ogle, D. (1987). K–W–L plus: A strategy for comprehension and summarization. *Journal of Reading, 30*(7), 626–631.

Carr, E., & Wixson, K. K. (1986). Guidelines for evaluating vocabulary instruction. *Journal of Reading, 29,* 588–595.

Carrell, P. L., Devine, J., & Eskey, D. E. (Eds.). (1988). *Interactive approaches to second language reading.* Cambridge, England: Cambridge University Press.

Carver, R. P. (1992). Commentary: Effect of prediction activities, prior knowledge, and text type upon amount comprehended: Using reading theory to critique schema theory research. *Reading Research Quarterly, 27,* 164–174.

Cary, S. (2007). *Working with English language learners: Answers to teachers' top ten questions.* 2nd edition. Portsmouth, NH: Heinemann.

Caskey, H. J. (1970). Guidelines for teaching comprehension. *The Reading Teacher, 23,* 649–654, 669.

Cassady, J. K. (1998). Wordless books: No-risk tools for inclusive middle-grade classrooms. *Journal of Adolescent & Adult Literacy, 41,* 428–432.

Caverly, D., Mandeville, T., & Nicholson, S. (1995). PLAN: A study-reading strategy for informational text. *Journal of Adolescent & Adult Literacy, 39,* 190–199.

Cazden, C. B., John, V. P., & Hymes, D. (Eds.). (1972). *Functions of language in the classroom.* New York: Teachers College Press.

Cecil, N., & Lauritzen, P. (1994). *Literacy and the arts for the integrated classroom: Alternative ways of knowing.* White Plains, NY: Longman.

Cecil, N. L. (1995). *The art of inquiry: Questioning strategies for K–6 classrooms.* Winnipeg, Canada: Peguis.

Chant, S. A., & Pelow, R. A. (1979, May). *Activities for functional reading and language: Preschool through middle school*. Paper presented at the annual meeting of the International Reading Association, Atlanta, GA.

Chase, A. C., & Duffelmeyer, F. A. (1990). VOCAB-LIT: Integrating vocabulary study and literature study. *Journal of Reading, 34,* 188–193.

Chasnoff, I. (1991). Drugs, alcohol, pregnancy, and the neonate. *JAMA, 266*(11), 1567–1568.

Cherry, L. (1990). *The great kapok tree: A tale of the Amazon rain forest.* New York: Harcourt Brace and Co.

Cheyney, A. B. (1992). *Teaching reading through the newspaper* (3rd ed.). Newark, DE: International Reading Association.

Chomsky, N. (1972). *Language and mind.* New York: Harcourt Brace Jovanovich.

Clarke, L. W., & Holwadel, J. (2007). "Help! What is wrong with these literature circles and how can we fix them?" *The Reading Teacher, 61,* 20–29.

Clay, M. M. (1985). *The early detection of reading difficulties.* Auckland, New Zealand: Heinemann.

Clay, M. M. (1993). *An observation survey of early literacy achievement.* Portsmouth, NH: Heinemann.

Clay, M. M. (2000a). *Concepts about print.* Portsmouth, NH: Heinemann.

Clay, M. M. (2000b). *Running records for classroom teachers.* Portsmouth, NH: Heinemann.

Cleland, C. J. (1981). Highlighting issues in children's literature through semantic webbing. *The Reading Teacher, 34,* 642–646.

Clements, A. (1997). *Double trouble in Walla Walla.* Brookfield, CT: Millbrook.

Clemmons, J., Laase, L., Cooper, D., Areglado, N., & Dill, M. (1993). *Portfolios in the classroom: A teacher's sourcebook.* New York: Scholastic.

Clymer, T. L. (1963). The utility of phonic generalizations in the primary grades. *The Reading Teacher, 16,* 252–258. (Reprinted 1996, *The Reading Teacher, 50,* 182–187.)

Cochran-Smith, M. (1991). Learning to teach against the grain. *Harvard Educational Review, 61,* 279–310.

Cohn, M. L. (1969). Structured comprehension. *The Reading Teacher, 22,* 440–444, 489.

Coiro, J. (2003). Reading comprehension on the Internet: Expanding our understanding of reading comprehension to encompass new literacies. *The Reading Teacher, 56,* 458–464.

Coiro, J. (2005). Making sense of online text. *Educational Leadership, 63*(2), 30–35.

Coiro, J., Knobel, M., Lankshear, C., & Leu, D. (2007). *Handbook of research on new literacies.* New York: Erlbaum.

Coiro, J., & Schmar-Dobler, B. (2005). *Reading comprehension on the Internet: Exploring the comprehension strategies used by sixth-grade skilled readers as they search for and locate information on the Internet.* Unpublished manuscript. Available online at http://ctell1.uconn.edu/coiro/research.html.

Collier, V. P. (1987). Age and rate of acquisition of second language for academic purposes. *TESOL Quarterly, 21,* 617–641.

Collier, V. P. (1989). How long? A synthesis of research on academic achievement in a second language. *TESOL Quarterly, 23,* 509–631.

Collins, A., & Smith, E. E. (1980). *Teaching the process of reading comprehension* (Tech. Rep. No. 182). Champaign: University of Illinois, Center for the Study of Reading.

Collins COBUILD learner's dictionary. (2003). London: Harper Collins.

Compton-Lilly, C. (2007). What can video games teach us about teaching reading? *The Reading Teacher, 60,* 718–727.

Conner, U. (1996). *Contrastive rhetoric: Cross-cultural aspects of second-language writing.* New York: Cambridge University Press.

Cooper, J. D., Warncke, E. W., Ramstad, P., & Shipman, D. A. (1979). *The what and how of reading instruction.* Upper Saddle River, NJ: Prentice Hall/Merrill.

Cooper, L. J. (1952). *The effect of adjustment of basal reading materials on achievement.* Unpublished doctoral dissertation, Boston University.

Cooter, R. B., & Chilcoat, G. W. (1990). Content-focused melodrama: Dramatic renderings of historical text. *Journal of Reading, 34,* 274–277.

Cooter, R. B. Jr., Flynt, E. S., & Cooter, R. B. (2007). *Comprehensive reading inventory: Measuring reading development in regular and special education classrooms.* Upper Saddle River, NJ: Pearson Education.

Corcoran, C. A., & Davis, A. D. (2005). A study of the effects of readers' theater on second and third grade special education students' fluency growth. *Reading Improvement, 42*(2), 105–112.

Coulmas, F. (1989). *The writing systems of the world.* Oxford, England: Basil Blackwell.

Cowan, J. R., & Sarmad, Z. (1976). Reading performance of bilingual children according to the type of school and home environment. *Language Learning, 26,* 353–376.

Cudd, E. T., & Roberts, L. L. (1987). Using story frames to develop reading comprehension in a first grade classroom. *The Reading Teacher, 41,* 74–79.

Cudd, E. T., & Roberts, L. L. (1989). Using writing to enhance content area learning in the primary grades. *The Reading Teacher, 42*(6), 392–404.

Cummins, J. (1981). The role of primary language development in promoting educational success for language minority students. In *Schooling and language minority students: A theoretical framework.* Los Angeles: Office of Bilingual Education.

Cummins, J. (1994). The acquisition of English as a second language. In K. Spangenberg-Urbschat & R. Pritchard (Eds.), *Kids come in all languages: Reading instruction for ESL students* (pp. 36–62). Newark, DE: International Reading Association.

Cunningham, J. (1982). Generating interactions between schemata and text. In J. Niles & L. Harris (Eds.), *New inquiries in reading research and instruction* (pp. 42–47). Washington, DC: National Reading Conference.

Cunningham, P. (1999). What should we do about phonics? In L. Gambrell, L. Morrow, S. Neuman, & M. Pressley (Eds.), *Best practices in literacy instruction* (pp. 68–89). New York: Guilford.

Cunningham, P. M. (2005). *Phonics they use: Words for reading and writing* (4th ed.). Boston: Allyn & Bacon.

Curtis, L. M. (2007). *The role of music in early literacy learning: A kindergarten study.* Unpublished doctoral dissertation, Kansas State University. (UMI# 3274536)

Curtis, M. E., & McCart, L. (1992). Fun ways to promote poor readers' word recognition. *Journal of Reading, 35,* 398–399.

Dale, E. (1965). Vocabulary measurement: Techniques and major findings. *Elementary English, 42,* 82–88.

Dale, E., O'Rourke, J., & Bamman, H. A. (1971). *Techniques of teaching vocabulary.* Palo Alto, CA: Field Educational Publications.

Dale, E., O'Rourke, J., & Barbe, W. (1986). *Vocabulary building: A process approach.* Columbus, OH: Zaner-Bloser.

D'Alessandro, M. (1990). Accommodating emotionally handicapped children through a literature-based reading program. *The Reading Teacher, 44,* 288–293.

Daniels, H. (2002). *Literature circles: Voice and choice in book clubs & reading groups.* Portland, ME: Stenhouse Publishers.

Danielson, K. E. (1992). Picture books to use with older students. *Journal of Reading, 35,* 652–654.

Dantonio, M., & Beisenherz, P. C. (2001). *Learning to question, questioning to learn: Developing effective teacher questioning practices.* Boston: Allyn & Bacon.

Davey, B. (1983). Think-aloud–modeling the cognitive processes of reading comprehension. *Journal of Reading, 27,* 44–47.

Davidson, J. L. (1982). The group mapping activity for instruction in reading and thinking. *Journal of Reading, 26,* 52–56.

Davis, A. L. (1972). English problems of Spanish speakers. In D. L. Shores (Ed.), *Contemporary English: Change and variation* (pp. 123–133). New York: Lippincott.

Davis, C. (1978). The effectiveness of informal assessment questions constructed by secondary teachers. In P. D. Pearson & J. Hansen (Eds.), *Reading: Disciplined inquiry in process and practice* (pp. 13–15). 27th Yearbook of the National Reading Conference, Clemson, SC.

Davis, F. B. (1944). Fundamental factors of comprehension in reading. *Psychometrika, 9,* 185–197.

Day, J. D. (1980). *Training summarization skills: A comparison of teaching methods.* Unpublished doctoral dissertation, University of Illinois, Urbana.

Dean, D. (2008). *Bringing grammar to life.* Newark, DE: International Reading Association.

DeFina, A. A. (1992). *Portfolio assessment: Getting started.* New York: Scholastic.

Degen, B. (1983). *Jamberry.* New York: Harper & Row.

Delgado-Gaitan, C. (2002). Words in and out of print: The power of literacy in community. In D. L. Schallert, C. M. Fairbanks, J. Worthy, B. Maloch, & J. V. Hoffman (eds.), *51st Yearbook of the National Reading Conference* (pp. 16–22). Oak Creek, WI: National Reading Conference, Inc.

DeSylvia, D. A., & Klug, C. D. (1992). Drugs and children: Taking care of the victims. *Journal of the American Optometric Association, 63*(1), 59–62.

Devine, T. G. (1981). *Teaching study skills: A guide for teachers.* Boston: Allyn & Bacon.

Dewey, J. (1916). *Democracy and education.* New York: Macmillan.

Dietrich, S. (2008). *Effects of an explicit, systematic vocabulary intervention on first grade English language learners.* Unpublished doctoral dissertation, Walden University.

Diller, D. (1999). Opening the dialogue: Using culture as a tool in teaching young African American children. *The Reading Teacher, 52,* 820–827.

Dimino, J., Gersten, R., Carnine, D., & Blake, G. (1990). Story grammar: An approach for promoting at-risk secondary students' comprehension of literature. *Elementary School Journal, 91,* 19–32.

Dionisio, M. (1989). Write? Isn't this reading class? *The Reading Teacher, 36,* 746–749.

Dolch, E. (1953). *Dolch basic sight vocabulary.* Champaign, IL: Garrard.

Doty, D. E., Popplewell, S. R., & Byers, G. O. (2001). Interactive CD-ROM storybooks and young readers' reading comprehension. *Journal of Research on Computing in Education, 33,* 374–384.

Draper, S. M. (2002). *Double Dutch.* NY: Atheneum.

Drewe, S. B. (1998). *Creative dance inspirations: Facilitating expression.* Calgary, Alberta, Canada: Detselig Enterprises.

Dreyer, S. (1987). *The bookfinder: Guide to children's literature about the needs and problems of youth aged 2–15.* Circle Pines, MN: American Guidance Services.

Drummond, M. J. (1994). *Learning to see: Assessment through observation.* York, ME: Stenhouse Publishers.

Duffelmeyer, F. A., & Baum, D. D. (1992). The extended anticipation guide revisited. *Journal of Reading, 35,* 654–656.

Duffelmeyer, F. A., & Black, J. (1996). The names test: A domain-specific validation study. *The Reading Teacher, 50,* 148–150.

Duffelmeyer, F. A., & Duffelmeyer, B. B. (1989). Are IRI passages suitable for assessing main idea comprehension? *The Reading Teacher, 42,* 358–363.

Duffelmeyer, F. A., Kruse, A., Merkley, D., & Fyfe, S. (1994). Further validation and enhancement of the Names Test. *The Reading Teacher, 48,* 118–128.

Duffelmeyer, F. A., Robinson, S. S., & Squier, S. E. (1989). Vocabulary questions on informal reading inventories. *The Reading Teacher, 43,* 142–148.

Duffy, G. G., Roehler, L. R., & Herrmann, B. A. (1988). Modeling mental processes helps poor readers become strategic readers. *The Reading Teacher, 41,* 762–767.

Dunkeld, C. (1978). Students' notetaking and teachers' expectations. *Journal of Reading, 21,* 542–546.

Dunn, L. M., Dunn, L. L., & Dunn, D. M. (2006). *Peabody picture vocabulary test, fourth edition: Examiner's manual and norms booklet.* Circle Pines, MN: American Guidance Services.

Durkin, D. (1978). *Teaching them to read* (3rd ed.). Boston: Allyn & Bacon.

Durkin, D. (1978/1979). What classroom observations reveal about reading comprehension instruction. *Reading Research Quarterly, 14,* 481–533.

Durkin, D. (1981). Reading comprehension instruction in five basal reading series. *Reading Research Quarterly, 14,* 515–544.

Durrell, D. D. (1963). *Phonograms in primary grade words.* Boston: Boston University Press.

Dyer, H. S. (1968). Research issues on equality of educational opportunity: School factors. *Harvard Educational Review, 38,* 38–56.

Dyson, A. (2003). *The brothers and sisters learn to write: Popular literacies in childhood and school cultures.* New York: Teachers College Press.

Eanet, M. G., & Manzo, A. V. (1976). REAP—a strategy for improving reading/writing study skills. *Journal of Reading, 19,* 647–652.

Echevarria, J., Vogt, M., & Short, D. J. (2003). *Making content comprehensible for English learners: The SIOP model* (2nd ed.). Boston: Allyn & Bacon.

Edminston, B., Enciso, P., & King, M. (1987). Empowering readers and writers through drama: Narrative theater. *Language Arts, 64,* 219–229.

Eisner, E. (1981). The role of the arts in cognition and curriculum. *Phi Delta Kappan, 63,* 48–52.

Ekwall, E. E., & Shanker, J. L. (1988). *Diagnosis and remediation of the disabled reader* (3rd ed.). Boston: Allyn & Bacon.

Ekwall, E. E., & Shanker, J. L. (2000). *Ekwall/Shanker reading inventory.* Boston: Allyn & Bacon.

Elbow, P. (2000). *Everyone can write: Essays toward a hopeful theory of writing and teaching.* New York: Oxford University.

Elley, W. (1991). Acquiring literacy in a second language: The effect of book-based programs. *Language Learning, 41*(3), 375–411.

Ellis, E., & Farmer, T. (2000). *The clarifying routine: Elaborating vocabulary instruction.* Kansas City, MO: Edge Enterprises.

Emberly, B. (Adapted by). (1967). *Drummer Hoff.* New York: Prentice Hall.

Emig, J. (1983). *The web of meaning: Essays on writing, teaching, learning, and thinking.* Portsmouth, NH: Heinemann.

Englert, C. S., & Thomas, C. C. (1987). Sensitivity to text structure in reading and writing: A comparison between learning disabled and non-learning disabled students. *Learning Disabilities Quarterly, 10,* 93–105.

Enright, D. S., & McCloskey, M. L. (1988). *Integrating English: Developing English language and literacy in the multilingual classroom.* Reading, MA: Addison-Wesley.

Ericson, L., & Juliebo, M. F. (1998). *The phonological awareness handbook for kindergarten and primary teachers.* Newark, DE: International Reading Association.

Estes, T. H., Estes, J. J., Richards, H. C., & Roettger, D. (1981). *Estes attitude scales: Measures of attitude toward school subjects.* Austin, TX: Pro-Ed.

Fang, Z. (2008). Going beyond the Fab Five: Helping students cope with the unique linguistic challenges of expository reading in intermediate grades. *Journal of Adolescent & Adult Literacy, 51,* 476–487.

Farr, R. (1992). Putting it all together: Solving the reading assessment puzzle. *The Reading Teacher, 46,* 26–37.

Farr, R., & Carey, R. F. (1986). *Reading: What can be measured.* Newark, DE: International Reading Association.

Farstrup, A. E., & Samuels, S. J. (Eds.). (2008). *What research has to say about vocabulary instruction.* Newark, DE: International Reading Association.

Farver, J. M., Nakamoto, J., & Lonigan, C. J. (2007). Assessing preschoolers' emergent literacy skills in English and Spanish with the Get Ready to Read! screening tool. *Annals of Dyslexia, 57*(2), 161–178.

Fay, L. (1965). Reading study skills: Math and science. In J. A. Figurel (Ed.), *Reading and inquiry.* Newark, DE: International Reading Association.

Fennessey, S. (1995). Living history through drama and literature. *The Reading Teacher, 49,* 16–19.

Ferdman, B. M., Weber, R. M., & Ramirez, A. G. (Eds.). (1994). *Literacy across languages and cultures.* Albany: SUNY.

Fernald, G. M. (1943). *Remedial techniques in basic school subjects.* New York: McGraw-Hill.

Fisher, D., Frey, N., & Lapp, D. (2008). Shared readings: Modeling comprehension, vocabulary, text structures, and text features for older readers. *The Reading Teacher, 61,* 548–556.

Fitzgerald, J. (1999). What is this thing called "balance"? *The Reading Teacher, 53*(2), 100–107.

Fitzgerald, J., & Spiegel, D. L. (1983). Enhancing children's reading comprehension through instruction in narrative structure. *Journal of Reading Behavior, 15,* 1–17.

Flavell, J. H. (1976). Metacognitive aspects of problem solving. In L. B. Resnick (Ed.), *The nature of intelligence.* Hillsdale, NJ: Erlbaum.

Flood, J., Heath, S. G., & Lapp, D. (Eds.). (2007). Handbook of research on teaching literacy through the communicative and visual arts, Vol. II. New York: Erlbaum.

Flood, J., & Wood, K. (1998). Viewing: The neglected communication process or "When what you see isn't what you get." *The Reading Teacher, 52,* 300–304.

Flores, B. M. (1984). *Language interference or influence: Toward a theory for Hispanic bilingualism.* Doctoral dissertation, University of Arizona, Tucson.

Flores, B., Cousin, P. T., & Diaz, E. (1998). Transforming deficit myths about learning, language, and culture. In M. F. Opitz (Ed.), *Literacy instruction for culturally and linguistically diverse students: A collection of articles and commentaries* (pp. 27–38). Newark, DE: International Reading Association.

Flynt, E. S., & Cooter, R. B. (2004). *Flynt-Cooter reading inventory for the classroom.* Columbus, OH: Prentice Hall/Merrill.

Fountas, I. C., & Pinnell, G. S. (2001). *Guiding readers and writers, grades 3-6: Teaching comprehension, genre, and content literacy.* Portsmouth, NH: Heinemann.

Fouse, B., & Morrison, J. (1997). Using children's books as an intervention for attention-deficit disorder. *The Reading Teacher,* 50, 442–445.

Fowler, G. L. (1982). Developing comprehension skills in primary students through the use of story frames. *The Reading Teacher, 37,* 176–179.

Fox, B. J. (2000). *Word identification strategies: Phonics from a new perspective* (2nd ed.). Upper Saddle River, NJ: Merrill/Prentice Hall.

Frase, L. T., & Schwartz, B. J. (1975). Effect of question production on prose recall. *Journal of Educational Psychology, 67,* 628–635.

Frayer, D. A., Frederick, W. C., & Klausmeier, H. J. (1969). *A schema for testing the level of concept mastery* (Tech. Rep. No. 16). Madison: University of Wisconsin, R & D Center for Cognitive Learning.

Frazee, B. (1993). Core knowledge: How to get started. *Educational Leadership, 50,* 28–29.

Freedman, G., & Reynolds, E. G. (1980). Enriching basal reader lessons with semantic webbing. *The Reading Teacher, 33,* 677–684.

Freeman, Y. S., & Freeman, D. E. (2006). *Teaching reading and writing in Spanish and English in bilingual and dual language classrooms,* 2nd ed. Portsmouth, NH: Heinemann.

Freeman, Y. S., Freeman, D. E., & Mercuri, S. (2006). *Dual language essentials for teachers and administrators.* Portsmouth, NH: Heinemann.

Freire, P. (1992). *Pedagogy of the oppressed.* New York: Continuum.

Fry, E. B. (1980). Test review: Metropolitan Achievement Tests. *The Reading Teacher, 34,* 196–201.

Fry, E. B., & Kress, J. (2006). *The reading teacher's book of lists.* San Francisco: Jossey-Bass.

Fukunaga, N. (2006). "Those anime students": Foreign language literacy development through Japanese popular culture. *Journal of Adolescent & Adult Literacy,* 50, 206–222.

Furness, E. L. (1971). Proportion, purpose, and process in listening. In S. Duker (Ed.), *Teaching listening in the elementary school* (pp. 53–57). Metuchen, NJ: Scarecrow.

Gag, W. (1928). *Millions of cats.* New York: Coward, McCann & Geoghegan.

Gag, W. (1938). *Snow White and the seven dwarfs* (original story by Jacob Grimm freely translated and illustrated). Eau Claire, WI: E. M. Hale and Company.

Gallant, R. (1964). *An investigation of the use of cloze tests as a measure of readability of materials for the primary grades.* Unpublished doctoral dissertation, Indiana University, Bloomington.

Gambrell, L. B., & Bales, R. (1986). Mental imagery and the comprehension monitoring performance of fourth- and fifth-grade poor readers. *Reading Research Quarterly, 11,* 454–464.

Gambrell, L. B., & Jawitz, P. B. (1993). Mental imagery, text illustrations, and children's story comprehension and recall. *Reading Research Quarterly, 28,* 264–276.

Gambrell, L. B., Koskinen, P. S., & Kapinus, B. A. (1991). Retelling and the reading comprehension of proficient and less-proficient readers. *Journal of Educational Research, 84,* 356–362.

Gambrell, L. B., & Mazzoni, S. (1999). Principles of best practice: Finding the common ground. In L. Gambrell, L. Morrow, S. Neuman, & M. Pressley (Eds.), *Best practices in literacy instruction* (pp. 11–21). New York: Guilford.

Gambrell, L. B., Pfeiffer, W., & Wilson, R. (1985). The effects of retelling upon reading comprehension and recall of text information. *Journal of Educational Research, 7,* 216–220.

Gambrell, L. B., Wilson, R. M., & Gantt, W. N. (1981). Classroom observations of task-attending behaviors of good and poor readers. *Journal of Educational Research, 24,* 400–404.

Garcia, G. C. (Ed.). (2003). *English learners: Reaching the highest level of English literacy.* Newark, DE: International Reading Association.

Garcia, G., & Pearson, P. D. (1991). *Literacy assessment in a diverse society.* (Tech. Rep. No. 525). Champaign: University of Illinois, Center for the Study of Reading. (Also in E. H. Hiebert [Ed.], *Literacy for a diverse society* [pp. 253–278]. New York: Teachers College.)

Gardner, H. (1983). *Frames of mind: The theory of multiple intelligences.* New York: Basic Books.

Gardner, H. (1995). Reflections on multiple intelligences. *Phi Delta Kappan, 77,* 200–209.

Gardner, H. (1999). *Intelligence reframed: Multiple intelligences for the 21st century.* New York: Basic Books.

Garner, R. (1980). Monitoring of understanding: An investigation of good and poor readers' awareness of induced miscomprehension of text. *Journal of Reading Behavior, 12,* 55–64.

Garner, R. (1987). *Metacognition and reading comprehension.* Norwood, NJ: Ablex.

Gee, J. P. (2003). Reading as situated language: A sociocognitive perspective. In P. A. Mason & J. Shay Schumm (Eds.), *Promising practices for urban reading instruction* (pp. 362–380). Newark, DE: International Reading Association. (Reprinted from *Journal of Adolescent and Adult Literacy* (2001), *44,* 714–725.)

Gee, J. P. (2008). *Social linguistics and literacies: Ideology in discourse,* 3rd ed. New York: Routledge.

Geissal, M. A., & Knafle, J. D. (1977). A linguistic view of auditory discrimination tests and exercises. *The Reading Teacher, 31,* 624–644.

Gentry, J. R. (1982). An analysis of developmental spellings in Gnys at wrk. *The Reading Teacher, 36,* 192–200.

Gentry, J. R. (1987). *Spel . . . is a four-letter word.* New York: Scholastic.

Gentry, J. R. (1996). *My kid can't spell! Understanding and assisting your child's literacy development.* Portsmouth, NH: Heinemann.

Gersten, R. (1996). The double demands of teaching English language learners. *Educational Leadership, 53*(5), 18–22.

Gibbons, G. (1993). *Whales.* New York: Holiday House.

Gillespie, C. (1990/1991). Questions about student-generated questions. *Journal of Reading, 34,* 250–257.

Gipe, J. P. (1977). *An investigation of the effectiveness of four techniques for teaching word meanings with third- and fifth-grade students.* Unpublished doctoral dissertation, Purdue University.

Gipe, J. P. (1978/1979). Investigating techniques for teaching word meanings. *Reading Research Quarterly, 14,* 624–644.

Gipe, J. P. (1980). Use of a relevant context helps kids learn new word meanings. *The Reading Teacher, 33,* 398–402.

Glasgow, J. (1996). It's my turn! Motivating young readers. *Learning & Leading with Technology, 24*(3), 20–23.

Glasgow, J. (1996/1997). It's my turn! Part 2: Motivating young readers using CD-ROM storybooks. *Learning & Leading with Technology, 24*(4), 18–22.

Glasser, W. (1969). *Schools without failure.* New York: Harper & Row.

Glasser, W. (1975). *Reality therapy.* New York: Harper & Row.

Glazer, S. M. (1992). *Reading comprehension: Self-monitoring strategies to develop independent readers.* New York: Scholastic.

Glazer, S. M. (1993). Children and self-assessment: A "risky" experience. *Teaching PreK–8, 23*(8), 106–108.

Glazer, S. M., & Brown, C. S. (1993). *Portfolios and beyond: Collaborative assessment in reading and writing.* Norwood, MA: Christopher-Gordon.

Goldenberg, C. (1992/1993). Instructional conversations: Promoting comprehension through discussion. *The Reading Teacher, 46,* 316–326.

Golinkoff, R. M. (1975/1976). A comparison of reading comprehension processes in good and poor comprehenders. *Reading Research Quarterly, 11,* 623–659.

Goodlad, J. (2004). *A place called school: Twentieth anniversary edition.* New York: McGraw-Hill. (Original work published 1984).

Goodman, K. S. (1968). The psycholinguistic nature of the reading process. In K. S. Goodman (Ed.), *The psycholinguistic nature of the reading process.* Detroit, MI: Wayne State.

Goodman, K. S. (1973). *Theoretically based studies of patterns of miscues in oral reading performance.* Washington, DC: U.S. Department of Health, Education and Welfare, Office of Education, Bureau of Research.

Goodman, K. S. (1982). Revaluing readers and reading. *Topics in Learning and Learning Disabilities, 1,* 87–93.

Goodman, K. S. (1994). Reading, writing, and written texts: A transactional sociopsycholinguistic view. In R. B. Ruddell, M. R. Ruddell, & H. Singer (Eds.), *Theoretical models and processes of reading* (4th ed., pp. 1093–1130). Newark, DE: International Reading Association.

Goodman, K. S. (1996). *On reading.* Portsmouth, NH: Heinemann.

Goodman, K. S. (2006). *The truth about DIBELS: What it is—what it does.* Portsmouth, NH: Heinemann.

Goodman, K. S., & Buck, S. (1973). Dialect barriers to reading comprehension revisited. *The Reading Teacher, 27,* 6–12. (Reprinted in *The Reading Teacher* (1997), *50,* 454–459.)

Goodman, Y. M. (1996). Revaluing readers while readers revalue themselves: Retrospective miscue analysis. *The Reading Teacher, 49,* 600–609.

Goodman, Y., & Burke, C. (1972). *Reading miscue inventory manual: Procedure for diagnosis and evaluation.* New York: Macmillan.

Goodman, Y., & Marek, A. (1996). *Retrospective miscue analysis: Revaluing readers and reading.* Katonah, NY: Owen.

Goodman, Y. M., Watson, D. J., & Burke, C. L. (1987). *Reading miscue inventory: Alternative procedures.* New York: Owen.

Goswami, U., & Mead, F. (1992). Onset and rime awareness and analogies in reading. *Reading Research Quarterly, 27,* 152–162.

Gough, P. B. (1984). Word recognition. In P. D. Pearson (Ed.), *Handbook of reading research* (pp. 225–253). New York: Longman.

Gould, M. (1982). *Golden daffodils.* Reading, MA: Addison-Wesley.

Grady, E. (1992). *The portfolio approach to assessment.* Bloomington, IN: Phi Delta Kappa Educational Foundation.

Graham, S., MacArthur, C. A., & Fitzgerald, J. (2007). *Best practices in writing instruction.* New York: Guilford Press.

Graves, D. (1983). *Writing: Teachers and children at work.* Portsmouth, NH: Heinemann.

Graves, D. (1988). *Writing and reading process: A closer look.* Portsmouth, NH: Heinemann.

Graves, D., & Kittle, P. (2005). *Inside writing: How to teach the details of the craft.* Portsmouth, NH: Heinemann.

Graves, M. F. (2006). *The vocabulary book: Learning & instruction.* New York: Teachers College.

Graves, D., & Murray, D. (1980). Revision in the writer's workshop and in the classroom. *Journal of Education, 162,* 38–56.

Greene, P. J. (1981). *The morpheme conceptualization barrier: Adult non-inflected language speakers' acquisition of English morpheme structures.* Unpublished doctoral dissertation, University of New Orleans.

Greene, M. (1988). *The dialectic of freedom.* New York: Teachers College Press.

Greenlaw, M. J. (1992). Using informational books to develop reference skills. In E. B. Freeman & D. G. Person (Eds.), *Using nonfiction trade books in the elementary classroom* (pp. 131–145). Urbana, IL: National Council of Teachers of English.

Griffith, P. L., & Olson, M. W. (1992). Phonemic awareness helps beginning readers break the code. *The Reading Teacher, 45,* 516–523.

Grognet, A. G., Pfannkuche, A., Quang, N. H., Robson, B., Convery, A., Holdzkom, D., et al. (1976). *A manual for Indochinese refugee education.* Arlington, VA: The National Indochinese Clearinghouse, Center for Applied Linguistics.

Gunning, T. (1995). Word building: A strategic approach to the teaching of phonics. *The Reading Teacher, 48,* 484–488.

Gunning, T. (2001). *Building words: A resource manual for teaching word analysis and spelling strategies.* Boston: Allyn & Bacon.

Guszak, F. J. (1967). Teachers' questions and levels of reading comprehension. In T. C. Barrett (Ed.), *The evaluation of children's reading achievement.* Newark, DE: International Reading Association.

Guthrie, J. T., Seifert, M., Burnham, N. A., & Caplan, R. I. (1974). The maze technique to assess, monitor reading comprehension. *The Reading Teacher, 28,* 161–168.

Guzzetti, B., & Gamboa, M. (2004). Zines for social justice: Adolescent girls writing on their own. *Reading Research Quarterly, 39,* 406–436.

Haberman, M. (1991). The pedagogy of poverty versus good teaching. *Phi Delta Kappan, 73,* 290–294.

Hadaway, N., & Mundy, J. (1999). Children's informational picture books visit a secondary ESL classroom. *Journal of Adolescent & Adult Literacy, 42,* 464–475.

Hadaway, N., Vardell, S., & Young, T. (2004). *What every teacher should know about English learners.* Boston: Pearson.

Haddon, M. (2004). *The curious incident of the dog in the night.* New York: Doubleday.

Haggard, M. (1986). The vocabulary self-collection strategy: Using student interest and world knowledge to enhance vocabulary growth. *Journal of Reading, 29,* 634–642.

Hair, L. M. (2009). *Addressing word poverty and comprehension through the Text Talk direct instruction method.* Unpublished doctoral dissertation: Walden University.

Hakuta, K., & Cancino, H. (2001). Trends in second language acquisition research. In S. Beck & L. Nabors Olah (Eds.), *Perspectives on language and literacy: Beyond the here and now* (pp. 225–246). Cambridge, MA: Harvard Educational Review.

Hall, W. S., & Freedle, R. (1975). *Culture and language.* New York: Halstead.

Haller, E. J., & Waterman, M. (1985). The criteria of reading group assignments. *The Reading Teacher, 38,* 772–781.

Halliday, M. A. K. (1978). Language as a social semiotic. Baltimore: University Park.

Hanf, M. B. (1971). Mapping: A technique for translating reading into thinking. *Journal of Reading, 14,* 225–230, 270.

Hansell, T. S. (1978). Stepping up to outlining. *Journal of Reading, 22,* 248–252.

Harmon, J. M. (1998). Vocabulary teaching and learning in a seventh-grade literature-based classroom. *Journal of Adolescent and Adult Literacy, 41,* 518–529.

Harris, A. J., & Sipay, E. R. (1990). *How to increase reading ability* (9th ed.). New York: Longman.

Harris, T. L., & Hodges, R. E. (Eds.). (1995). *The literacy dictionary: The vocabulary of reading and writing.* Newark, DE: International Reading Association.

Harste, J., Woodward, V., & Burke, C. (1984). *Language stories and literacy lessons.* Portsmouth, NH: Heinemann.

Hart, D. (1994). *Authentic assessment: A handbook for educators.* Reading, MA: Addison-Wesley.

Harvey, S., & Goudvis, A. (2000). *Strategies that work: Teaching comprehension to enhance understanding.* York, ME: Stenhouse.

Hayes, D. A. (1989). Helping students GRASP the knack of writing summaries. *Journal of Reading, 33,* 96–101.

Heath, S. (1983). *Ways with words: Language, life and work in communities and classrooms.* Cambridge, England: Cambridge University Press.

Heath, S. B. (1993). Inner city life through drama: Imagining the language classroom. *TESOL Quarterly, 27,* 177–192.

Heckelman, R. G. (1969). A neurological-impress method of remedial reading instruction. *Academic Therapy, 4,* 277–282.

Heckelman, R. G. (1986). N. I. M. revisited. *Academic Therapy, 21,* 411–420.

Heilman, A. W., & Holmes, E. A. (1978). *Smuggling language into the teaching of reading.* Columbus, OH: Prentice Hall/Merrill.

Heimlich, J. E., & Pittelman, S. D. (1986). *Semantic mapping: Classroom applications.* Newark, DE: International Reading Association.

Helfeldt, J. P., & Henk, W. A. (1990). Reciprocal question-answer relationships: An instructional technique for at-risk readers. *Journal of Reading, 33,* 509–515.

Henk, W. A., & Selders, M. L. (1984). A test of synonymic scoring of cloze passages. *The Reading Teacher, 38,* 282–287.

Hennings, D. G. (1991). Essential reading: Targeting, tracking, and thinking about main ideas. *Journal of Reading, 34,* 346–353.

Henry, L. A. (2006). SEARCHing for an answer: The critical role of new literacies while reading on the Internet. *The Reading Teacher, 59,* 614–627.

Herber, H. L. (1970). *Teaching reading in content areas.* Upper Saddle River, NJ: Prentice Hall.

Herrell, A. (1998). *Exemplary practices in teaching English language learners.* Fresno: California State University, Fresno.

Herrmann, B. A. (1988). Two approaches for helping poor readers become more strategic. *The Reading Teacher, 42,* 24–28.

Hiebert, E. H. (Ed.). (1991). *Literacy for a diverse society: Perspectives, practices and policies.* New York: Teachers College Press.

Hiebert, E. H., Lehr, F., & Osborn, J. (2004). A focus on vocabulary. Second in the Research-Based Practices in Early Reading Series published by the Regional Educational Laboratory at Pacific Resources for Education and Learning. Available at www.prel.org.

Hill, M. (1991). Writing summaries promotes thinking and learning across the curriculum—but why are they so difficult to write? *Journal of Reading, 34,* 536–539.

Hirtz, D. (2007, January 31). Neurological disorders afflict millions. Bethesda, MD: National Institutes of Neurological Disorders and Stroke. Retrieved January 8, 2009 from: www.apparelyzed.com/forums/index.php?showtopic=3536.

Hobbs, R. (2001, Spring). The great debates circa 2001: The promise and the potential of media literacy. *Community Media Review,* 25–27.

Hobbs, R. (2005). What's news? *Educational Leadership, 63*(2), 58–61.

Hodges, M. (1990). *St. George and the dragon.* Boston: Little, Brown.

Hoover, M. R., & Fabian, E. M. (2000). A successful program for struggling readers. *The Reading Teacher, 53,* 474–476.

Hopkins, L. B. (1987). *Click, rumble, roar: Poems about machines.* New York: Crowell.

Houston, G. (1992). *My great-aunt Arizona.* New York: HarperCollins.

Howard, E. R., Christian, D., & Genesee, F. (2004). *The development of bilingualism and biliteracy from Grade 3 to 5: A summary of findings from the CAL/CREDE study of two-way immersion education.* Center for Applied Linguistics.

Hoyt, L. (1999). *Revisit, reflect, retell: Strategies for improving reading comprehension.* Portsmouth, NH: Heinemann.

Hughes, T. O. (1975). *Sentence combining: A means of increasing reading comprehension.* Bloomington, IN: ERIC Clearinghouse on Reading. (ERIC Document Reproduction Service No. ED112421)

Hunt, J. (1989). *Illuminations.* New York: Bradbury.

Hutchins, P. (1976). *Don't forget the bacon!* New York: Morrow.

Inspiration Software. (1998–1999). *Inspiration.* Portland, OR: Author.

International Dyslexia Association. (2008). Formal definition of dyslexia. Retrieved January 7, 2009 from www.interdys.org/FAQWhatIs.htm.

International Reading Association. (1988). *New directions in reading instruction.* Newark, DE: Author.

International Reading Association & National Council of Teachers of English. (1996). *Standards for the English language arts.* Newark, DE: International Reading Association; and Urbana, IL: National Council of Teachers of English.

IRI/Skylight Publishing. (1995). *Integrating curricula with multiple intelligences: Teams, themes, and threads.* Palatine, IL: Author.

Irwin, P. A., & Mitchell, J. N. (1983). A procedure for assessing the richness of retellings. *Journal of Reading, 26,* 391–396.

Ivey, G., & Broaddus, K. (2001). Just plain reading: A survey of what makes students want to read in middle school classrooms. *Reading Research Quarterly, 36,* 350–377.

Jackson, L. A. (1981). Whose skills system? Mine or Penny's? *The Reading Teacher, 35,* 260–262.

Jacobowitz, T. (1990). AIM: A metacognitive strategy for constructing the main idea of text. *Journal of Reading, 33,* 620–624.

Jacobson, J. M. (1990). Group vs. individual completion of a cloze passage. *Journal of Reading, 33,* 244–251.

Jensen, E. (1998). *Teaching with the brain in mind.* Alexandria, VA: Association for Supervision and Curriculum Development.

Jensen, E. (2008). A fresh look at brain based education. *Phi Delta Kappan, 89*(6), 408–417.

Johns, J. (2005). *Basic reading inventory: Preprimer through grade twelve & early literacy assessments.* Dubuque, IA: Kendall/Hunt.

Johnson, D. D., & Pearson, P. D. (1984). *Teaching reading vocabulary.* New York: Holt, Rinehart and Winston.

Johnson, N. J., & Rose, L. M. (1997). *Portfolios: Clarifying, constructing, and enhancing.* Lancaster, PA: Technomic Publishing Company.

Johnson-Weber, M. (1989). Picture books for junior high. *Journal of Reading, 33,* 219–220.

Johnston, P. (1984). Prior knowledge and reading comprehension test bias. *Reading Research Quarterly, 19,* 219–239.

Johnston, P. (1992). Nontechnical assessment. *The Reading Teacher, 46,* 60–62.

Johnston, P., & Costello, P. (2005). Principles for literacy assessment. *Reading Research Quarterly, 40,* 256–267.

Johnston, P., & Winograd, P. (1985). Passive failure in reading. *Journal of Reading Behavior, 17,* 279–301.

Jorgenson, G. W. (1977). Relationship of classroom behavior to the accuracy of the match between material difficulty and student ability. *Journal of Educational Psychology, 69,* 24–32.

Jorm, A. (1977). Effect of word imagery on reading performance as a function of reader ability. *Journal of Educational Psychology, 69,* 46–54.

Joyce, B., Weil, M., & Calhoun, E. (2000). *Models of teaching* (6th ed.). Needham Heights, MA: Allyn & Bacon.

Juel, C. (1988). Learning to read and write: A longitudinal study of 54 children from first through fourth grades. *Journal of Educational psychology, 78,* 243–255.

Juel, C. (1991). Cross-age tutoring between student athletes and at-risk children. *The Reading Teacher, 45,* 178–186.

Justice, L., Bowles, R., & Skibbe, L. (2006). Measuring preschool attainment of print concept knowledge: A study of typical and at-risk 3- to 5-year old children. *Language, Speech, and Hearing Services in Schools, 3,* 1–12.

Kamil, M. L., Mosenthal, P. B., Pearson, P. D., & Barr, R. (Eds.). (2000). *Handbook of reading research, Vol. III.* Mahwah, NH: Erlbaum.

Kamm, K. (1979). Focusing reading comprehension instruction: Sentence meaning skills. In C. Pennock (Ed.), *Reading comprehension at four linguistic levels.* Newark, DE: International Reading Association.

Kant, I. (1963). *Critique of pure reason* (2nd ed.). (N. Kemp Smith, Trans.). London: Macmillan. (Original work published 1787).

Kaplan, R. B. (1966). Cultural thought patterns in intercultural education. *Language Learning, 16,* 1–20.

Kaplan, W. with Tanaka, S. (1998). *One more border: The true story of one family's escape from war-torn Europe.* Toronto, Ontario, Canada: Groundwood Books; and Berkeley, CA: Publishers Group West.

Karlsen, B., & Gardner, E. F. (1995, 2003). *Stanford diagnostic reading tests* (4th ed.). San Antonio, TX: Harcourt. (2003 edition available online at www.harcourt.com.)

Kavale, K. (1979). Selecting and evaluating reading tests. In R. Schreiner (Ed.), *Reading tests and teachers: A practical guide* (pp. 9–34). Newark, DE: International Reading Association.

Kavale, K., & Schreiner, R. (1979). The reading processes of above average readers: A comparison of the use of reasoning strategies in responding to standardized comprehension measures. *Reading Research Quarterly, 15,* 102–128.

Kennedy, E. C. (1977). *Classroom approaches to remedial reading* (2nd ed.). Itasca, IL: Peacock.

Kibby, M. (1995). The organization and teaching of things and the words that signify them. *Journal of Adolescent and Adult Literacy, 39,* 208–223.

Kiefer, B. Z. (1995). *The potential of picture books: From visual literacy to aesthetic understanding.* Englewood Cliffs, NJ: Merrill Prentice Hall.

Kletzien, S. B. (1991). Strategy use by good and poor comprehenders reading expository text of differing levels. *Reading Research Quarterly, 26,* 67–86.

Kletzien, S. B., & Bednar, M. R. (1990). Dynamic assessment for at-risk readers. *Journal of Reading, 33,* 528–533.

Klingner, J., & Vaughn, S. (1999). Promoting reading comprehension, content learning, and English acquisition through Collaborative Strategic Reading (CSR). *The Reading Teacher, 52,* 738–747.

Klingner, J., Vaughn, S., Arguelles, M.E., Hughes, M.T., & Leftwich, S. A. (2004). Collaborative strategic reading: "Real world" lessons from classroom teachers. *Remedial and Special Education, 25,* 291–302.

Koda, K., & Zehler, M. (Eds.). (2007). *Learning to read across languages: Cross-linguistic relationships in first- and second-language literacy development.* New York: Routledge.

Kolers, P. A. (1975). Pattern-analyzing disability in poor readers. *Developmental Psychology, 11,* 282–290.

Koskinen, P. A., & Blum, I. H. (1986). Paired repeated reading: A classroom strategy for developing fluent reading. *The Reading Teacher, 40,* 70–75.

Kozol, J. (1991). *Savage inequalities: Children in America's schools.* New York: Crown.

Krashen, S. D. (1993). *The power of reading.* Englewood, CO: Libraries Unlimited.

Krashen, S. D. (2003). *Explorations in language acquisition and use.* Portsmouth, NH: Heinemann.

Krashen, S. D. (2004). *The power of reading: Insights from the research.* Portsmouth, NH: Heinemann.

Krashen, S. D., & Terrell, T. (1983). *The natural approach: Language acquisition in the classroom.* Oxford, England: Pergamon.

Labbo, L. (2000). 12 things young children can do with a talking book in a classroom computer center. *The Reading Teacher, 53,* 542–546.

Labbo, L. D., & Teale, W. H. (1990). Crossage reading: A strategy for helping poor readers. *The Reading Teacher, 43,* 362–369.

LaBerge, D., & Samuels, S. J. (1974). Toward a theory of automatic information processing in reading. *Cognitive Psychology, 6,* 293–323.

Labov, W. (1975). *The study of nonstandard English.* Urbana, IL: National Council of Teachers of English.

Lackney, J. A. (2004). 12 design principles based on brain-based learning research. *Design share: The international forum for innovative schools.* Retrieved February 21, 2004, from www.designshare.com/Research/BrainBasedLearn98.htm.

Laframboise, K. (2000). Said webs: Remedy for tired words. *The Reading Teacher, 53,* 540–542.

Laminack, L., & Wood, K. (1996). *Spelling in use: Looking closely at spelling in whole language classrooms.* Urbana, IL: National Council of Teachers of English.

Langer, J. (1981). From theory to practice: A prereading plan. *Journal of Reading, 25,* 152–156.

Langer, J. A. (2001). Beating the odds: Teaching middle and high school students to read and write well. *American Educational Research Journal, 38,* 837–880.

Lankshear, C., & Knobel, M. (2003). New literacies: Changing knowledge and classroom learning. Buckingham, UK: Open University Press.

Lazear, D. (1994). *Multiple intelligence approaches to assessment: Solving the assessment conundrum.* Tucson, AZ: Zephyr.

Lenhart, A., Madden, M., & Hitlin, P. (2005). *Teens and technology: Youth are leading the transition to a fully wired and mobile nation.* Washington, DC: PEW Internet & American Life Project.

Leslie, L., & Caldwell, J. (2006). *Qualitative reading inventory.* New York: HarperCollins College.

Leslie, L., & Cooper, J. (1993). Assessing the predictive validity of prior-knowledge assessment. In D. J. Leu & C. K. Kinzer (Eds.), *Examining central issues in literacy research, theory and practice* (pp. 93–100). Chicago: National Reading Conference.

Leu, D. J., Kinzer, C. K., Coiro, J., & Cammack, D. (2004). Toward a theory of new literacies emerging from the Internet and other information and communication technologies. In R. B. Ruddell & N. Unrau (Eds.), *Theoretical models and processes of reading* (5th ed., pp. 1568–1611). Newark, DE: International Reading Association.

Lewin, C. (2000). Exploring the effects of talking book software in UK primary classrooms. *Journal of Research in Reading, 23* (2), 149–157.

Lewis, C., & Fabos, B. (2005). Instant messaging, literacies, and social identities. *Reading Research Quarterly, 40,* 470–501.

Lindamood, P. C., & Lindamood, P. (2004). *Lindamood Auditory Conceptualization Test (LAC-3).* Austin, TX: PRO-ED.

Lindfors, J. W. (1989). The classroom: A good environment for language learning. In P. Rigg & V. G. Allen (Eds.), *When they don't all speak English: Integrating the ESL student into the regular classroom* (pp. 39–54). Urbana, IL: National Council of Teachers of English.

Lipson, M., & Wixson, K. (1991). *Assessment and instruction of reading disability: An interactive approach.* New York: HarperCollins.

Lonigan, C., Farer, J. M., Eppe, S., Wagner, R. K., Torgesen, J., & Rashotte, C. (2002). *Preschool Comprehensive Test of Phonological and Print Processing (P-CTOPPP): Spanish version.* Tallahassee, FL: Authors.

Lowenfeld, V. (1970). *Creative and mental growth* (5th ed.). New York: Macmillan.

Lundsteen, S. (1979). *Listening: Its impact on reading and other language arts* (Rev. ed.). Urbana, IL: National Council of Teachers of English.

Mahiri, J. (1998). *Shooting for excellence: African American and youth culture.* New York: National Council of Teachers of English and Teachers College Press.

Mahiri, J. (2004). *What they don't learn in school: Literacy in the lives of urban youth.* New York: Peter Lang.

Mandler, J. (1984). *Stories, scripts and scenes: Aspects of schema theory.* Hillsdale, NJ: Erlbaum.

Mandler, J. M., & Johnson, N. S. (1977). Remembrance of things parsed: Story structure and recall. *Cognitive Psychology, 9,* 111–151.

Manis, F. R., Lindsey, K. A., & Bailey, C. E. (2004). Development of reading in grades K–2 in Spanish-speaking English language learners. *Learning Disabilities Research & Practice, 19,* 214–224.

Mantle-Bromley, C., & Foster, A. M. (2005). Educating for democracy: The vital role of the language arts teacher. *English Journal, 94*(5), 70–74.

Manzo, A. V. (1969). The ReQuest procedure. *Journal of Reading, 13,* 123–126.

Manzo, A. V. (1975). Guided reading procedure. *Journal of Reading, 18,* 287–291.

Manzo, A. V. (1985). Expansion modules for the ReQuest, CAT, GRP, and REAP reading/study procedures. *Journal of Reading, 28,* 498–502.

Markman, E. M. (1979). Realizing that you don't understand: Elementary school children's awareness of inconsistencies. *Child Development, 50,* 643–655.

Markman, E. M. (1981). Comprehension monitoring. In W. P. Dickson (Ed.), *Children's oral communication skills.* New York: Academic Press.

Martin, B. (1970). *The haunted house.* New York: Holt, Rinehart and Winston.

Martin, B. (1983). *Brown bear, brown bear, what do you see?* New York: Holt.

Martinez, M., Roser, N., & Strecker, S. (1998/1999). "I never thought I could be a star": A readers theatre ticket to fluency. *The Reading Teacher, 52,* 326–334.

Marzano, R. J. (2003). *What works in schools: Translating research into action.* Alexandria, VA: Association for Supervision and Curriculum Development.

Mason, J. M., & Stewart, J. P. (1990). Emergent literacy assessment for instructional use in kindergarten. In L. M. Morrow & J. K. Smith (Eds.), *Assessment for instruction in early literacy* (pp. 155–175). Englewood Cliffs, NJ: Prentice-Hall.

Massey, D. D. (2007). "The Discovery Channel said so" and other barriers to comprehension. *The Reading Teacher, 60,* 656–666.

Mathewson, G. C. (1994). Model of attitude influence upon reading and learning to read. In R. B. Ruddell, M. R. Ruddell, & H. Singer (Eds.), *Theoretical models and processes of reading* (4th ed., pp. 1131–1161). Newark, DE: International Reading Association.

McAuliffe, S. (1993). A study of the differences between instructional practice and test preparation. *Journal of Reading, 36,* 524–530.

McBroom, D. B. (2009). *Developing the expressive and productive academic language of limited English proficient learners.* Unpublished doctoral dissertation, Walden University, Minneapolis, MN.

McCormick, S., & Cooper, J. O. (1991). Can SQ3R facilitate secondary learning disabled students' literal comprehension of expository text? *Reading Psychology, 12,* 239–271.

McDermott, G. (1986). *Anansi the spider.* New York: Owlet Paperbacks. (First published, 1972, Holt Rinehart and Winston.)

McGee, L. M., & Schickedanz, J. A. (2007). Repeated interactive read-alouds in preschool and kindergarten. *The Reading Teacher, 60,* 742–751.

McGinley, W., & Denner, P. (1987). Story impressions: A pre-reading/writing activity. *Journal of Reading, 31,* 248–253.

McKenna, M. C. (1976). Synonymic versus verbatim scoring of the cloze procedure. *Journal of Reading, 20,* 141–143.

McKeown, M. (1985). The acquisition of word meaning from context by children of high and low ability. *Reading Research Quarterly, 20,* 482–496.

McLaughlin, M. (1989). *Dragonflies.* New York: Walker and Company.

McMahon, S., & Raphael, T. (Eds.). (1997). *The book club connection: Literacy learning and classroom talk.* New York: Teachers College Press; and Newark, DE: International Reading Association.

McNeil, J. D. (1974). False prerequisites in the teaching of reading. *Journal of Reading Behavior, 6,* 421–427.

McNinch, G. H. (1981). A method for teaching sight words to disabled readers. *The Reading Teacher, 35,* 269–272.

McTaggert, J. (2006). The graphic novel: Everything you ever wanted to know but were afraid to ask. Unpublished manuscript available from the author at www.theteachersdesk.com.

McWhorter, J. (2000). *Spreading the word: Language and dialect in America.* Portsmouth, NH: Heinemann.

Meier, T. (2008). *Black communications and learning to read: Building on children's linguistic and cultural strengths.* New York: Erlbaum.

Memory, D. M. (1990). Teaching technical vocabulary: Before, during, or after the reading assignment? *Journal of Reading Behavior, 22,* 39–53.

Mercer, C. (1997). *Students with learning disabilities* (5th ed.). Upper Saddle River, NJ: Prentice Hall.

Merwin, J. C. (1973). Educational measurement of what characteristic, of whom (or what), by whom, and why. *Journal of Educational Measurement, 10,* 1–6.

Miller, G. R., & Coleman, E. B. (1967). A set of 36 prose passages calibrated for complexity. *Journal of Verbal Learning and Verbal Behavior, 6,* 851–854.

Miller, T. (1998). The place of picture books in middle-level classrooms. *Journal of Adolescent & Adult Literacy, 41,* 376–381.

Mills, G. E. (2003). *Action research: A guide for the teacher researcher* (2nd ed.). Upper Saddle River, NJ: Merrill/Prentice Hall.

Mills, H., O'Keefe, T., & Stephens, D. (1992). *Looking closely: Exploring the role of phonics in one whole language classroom.* Urbana, IL: National Council of Teachers of English.

Mitchell, J. V. (Ed.). (1985). *The ninth mental measurements yearbook.* Lincoln, NE: University of Nebraska Press.

Mo, W., & Shen, W. (2000, Spring). A mean wink at authenticity: Chinese images in Disney's "Mulan." *New Advocate, 13*(2), 129–142.

Mochizuki, K. (1993). *Baseball saved us.* New York: Lee & Low.

Moe, A. J., & Manning, J. C. (1984). Developing intensive word practice exercises. In J. F. Baumann & D. D. Johnson (Eds.), *Reading instruction for the beginning teacher: A practical guide* (pp. 16–27). Minneapolis, MN: Burgess.

Montessori, M. (1967). *The absorbent mind.* New York: Dell.

Morningstar, J. (1999). Home response journals: Parents as informed contributers in the understanding of their child's literacy development. *The Reading Teacher, 5,* 690–697.

Morrice, C., & Simmons, M. (1991). Beyond reading buddies: A whole language crossage program. *The Reading Teacher, 44,* 572–577.

Morrow, L. M. (1985a). Reading and retelling stories: Strategies for emergent readers. *The Reading Teacher, 38,* 870–875.

Morrow, L. M. (1985b, April). *Story retelling: A diagnostic approach for evaluating story structure, language and comprehension.* Paper presented at the International Reading Association Convention, New Orleans, LA.

Morrow, L. M. (1988). Retelling as a diagnostic tool. In S. Glazer, L. Searfoss, & L. Gentile (Eds.), *Re-examining reading diagnosis: New trends and procedures in classrooms and clinics* (pp. 128–149). Newark, DE: International Reading Association.

Morrow, L. M. (Ed.). (1995). *Family literacy: Connections in schools and communities.* Newark, DE: International Reading Association.

Morrow, L. M., & Gambrell, L. B. (2000). Literature based reading instruction. In M. L. Kamil, P. B. Mosenthal, P. D. Pearson, & R. Barr (Eds.), *Handbook of reading research,* Vol. III (pp. 563–586). Mahwah, NJ: Erlbaum.

Morrow, L. M., & Smith, J. (1990). The effects of group size on interactive storybook reading. *Reading Research Quarterly, 25,* 213–231.

Morrow, L. M., & Temlock-Fields, J. (2004). Use of literature in home and at school. In B. H. Wasik (Ed.), *Handbook of family literacy* (pp. 83–99). Mahwah, NJ: Erlbaum.

Moustafa, M., & Maldonado-Colon, E. (1999). Whole-to-parts phonics instruction: Building on what children know to help them know more. *The Reading Teacher, 52,* 448–458.

Nagy, W. E., Anderson, R. C., & Herman, P. (1987). Learning word meanings from context during normal reading. *American Educational Research Journal, 24,* 237–270.

Nagy, W. E., Anderson, R. C., Schommer, M., Scott, J., & Stallman, A. (1989). Morphological families in the internal lexicon. *Reading Research Quarterly, 24,* 262–282.

Nagy, W. E., & Scott, J. A. (2000). Vocabulary processes. In M. L. Kamil, P. Mosenthal, P. D. Pearson, & R. Barr (Eds.), *Handbook of reading research* (Vol. 3, pp. 269–284). Mahwah, NJ: Erlbaum.

Nathan, R., Temple, C., Juntunen, K., & Temple, F. (1989). *Classroom strategies that work: An elementary teacher's guide to process writing.* Portsmouth, NH: Heinemann.

National Reading Panel. (2000). *National Reading Panel report.* Retrieved January 8, 2009 from www.nationalreadingpanel.org/.

National Standards for Arts Education (1994). *Standards for the arts.* Reston, VA: Music Educators National Conference.

National Stuttering Association. (2000). General *Information on stuttering.* Retrieved January 8, 2009 from www.nsastutter.org/.

Neal, J. C., & Moore, K. (1991/1992). The very hungry caterpillar meets Beowulf in secondary classrooms. *Journal of Reading, 35,* 290–296.

Nelson, K. (1986). *Event knowledge: Structure and function in development*. Hillsdale, NJ: Erlbaum.

Neville, D. D., & Searls, E. F. (1991). A meta-analytic review of the effect of sentence-combining on reading comprehension. *Reading Research and Instruction, 31*, 63–76.

New York City Board of Education. (1956, 1963). *Teaching English to Puerto Rican Pupils in Grades 1 and 2*. New York: Author.

Newkirk, T. (1982). Young writers as critical readers. *Language Arts, 59*, 451–457.

Newmann, F. M., & Wehlage, G. G. (1993). Five standards of authentic instruction. *Educational Leadership, 50*, 8–12.

Nicholson, T., Lillas, C., & Rzoska, M. A. (1988). Have we been misled by miscues? *The Reading Teacher, 42*, 6–10.

Nieto, S. (1999). *The light in their eyes: Creating multicultural learning communities*. New York: Teachers College Press.

Nikkel, S. (1996, December). *The effects of interactive computer software on literacy acquisition*. Paper presented at the annual meeting of the National Reading Conference, Charleston, SC.

Nilsson, N. L. (2008). A critical analysis of eight informal reading inventories. *The Reading Teacher, 61*, 526–536.

Nist, S. L., & Simpson, M. L. (1989). PLAE, a validated study strategy. *Journal of Reading, 33*, 182–186.

Nist, S. L., & Simpson, M. L. (1990). The effects of PLAE upon students' test performance and metacognitive awareness. In J. Zutell & S. McCormick (Eds.), *Literacy theory and research: Analyses from multiple paradigms* (pp. 321–327). Chicago: National Reading Conference.

Nist, S. L., Simpson, M. L., Olejnik, S., & Mealey, D. L. (1989). *The relation between self-selected text learning variables and test performance*. Unpublished manuscript.

Nolan, T. E. (1991). Self-questioning and prediction: Combining metacognitive strategies. *Journal of Reading, 35*, 132–138.

Norton, D. (1993). *The effective teaching of language arts* (4th ed.). New York: Merrill.

Norton-Meier, L. (2005). Trust the fungus: Lessons in media literacy learned from the movies. *Journal of Adolescent & Adult Literacy, 48*, 608–611.

O'Brien, D. G., & Bauer, E. B. (2005). New literacies and the institution of old learning. *Reading Research Quarterly, 40*, 120–131.

Ogle, D. M. (1986). K–W–L: A teaching model that develops active reading of expository text. *The Reading Teacher, 39*, 564–570.

Ohlhausen, M., & Jepsen, M. (1992). Lessons from Goldilocks: "Someone has been choosing my books but I can make my own choices now!" *The New Advocate, 5*, 31–46.

Olivares, R. A. (1993). *Using the newspaper to teach ESL learners*. Newark, DE: International Reading Association.

Olshavsky, J. E. (1976/1977). Reading as problem solving: An investigation of strategies. *Reading Research Quarterly, 12*, 654–674.

Opitz, M. (Ed.). (1998). *Literacy instruction for culturally and linguistically diverse students: A collection of articles and commentaries*. Newark, DE: International Reading Association.

Opitz, M. (2000). *Rhymes & reasons: Literature and language play for phonological awareness*. Portsmouth, NH: Heinemann.

Opitz, M., & Rasinski, T. (1998). *Good-bye round robin: 25 effective oral reading strategies*. Portsmouth, NH: Heinemann.

Otto, C. (2002). *Spiders*. New York: Scholastic.

Otto, W., & Smith, R. J. (1980). *Corrective and remedial teaching* (3rd ed.). Boston: Houghton Mifflin.

Paine, S. (1993). *The world of the sea otter*. San Francisco: Sierra Club Books.

Palincsar, A. (1987, January). Reciprocal teaching: Can student discussions boost comprehension? *Instructor*, 56–60.

Palincsar, A. S., & Brown, A. L. (1984). Reciprocal teaching of comprehension-fostering and comprehension-monitoring activities. *Cognition and Instruction, 1*(2), 117–175.

Palincsar, A. S., & Brown, A. L. (1986). Interactive teaching to promote independent learning from text. *The Reading Teacher, 39*, 771–777.

Pallotta, J. (1986). *The icky bug alphabet book*. New York: Trumpet Club.

Pappas, C., Kiefer, B., & Levstik, L. (1999). *An integrated language perspective in the elementary school: An action approach* (3rd ed.). New York: Longman.

Paris, S., & Myers, M. (1981). Comprehension monitoring, memory, and study strategies of good and poor readers. *Journal of Reading Behavior, 13*, 7–22.

Paterson, K. (1977). *Bridge to Terabithia*. New York: Crowell.

Payne, R. K. (1998). *A framework for understanding poverty*. Highlands, TX: RFT Publishing.

Pearson Digital Learning. (2006). Waterford Early Reading Program (WERP). Available online at www.pearsondigital.com.

Pearson, P. D. (1985). Changing the face of reading comprehension instruction. *The Reading Teacher, 38*, 724–738.

Pearson, P. D., Hiebert, E. H., & Kamil, M. L. (2007). Vocabulary assessment: What we know and what we need to learn. *Reading Research Quarterly, 42*(2), 282–296.

Pearson, P. D., & Johnson, D. D. (1978). *Teaching reading comprehension*. New York: Holt, Rinehart and Winston.

Peregoy, S. F., & Boyle, O. F. (2004). *Reading, writing and learning in ESL: A resource book for K–12 teachers* (4th ed.). Boston: Allyn & Bacon.

Peterson, R., & Eeds, M. (1990). *Grand conversations: Literature groups in action*. New York: Scholastic.

Phelps, S. (2005). *Ten years of research on adolescent literacy, 1994–2004: A review*. Naperville, IL: Learning Point Associates.

Phelps, S. F. (2006). Introduction to Part I: Situating adolescents' literacies. In D. E. Alverrmann, K. A. Hinchman, D. W. Moore, S. F. Phelps, & D. R. Waff (Eds.), *Reconceptualizing the literacies in adolescents' lives* (2nd ed., pp. 3–4). Mahwah, NJ: Erlbaum.

Piaget, J., & Inhelder, B. (1969). *The psychology of the child*. New York: Basic Books.

Piazza, C. (1999). *Multiple forms of literacy: Teaching literacy and the arts*. Upper Saddle River, NJ: Merrill/Prentice Hall.

Piercey, D. (1982). *Reading activities in content areas*. Boston: Allyn & Bacon.

Pikulski, J. J., & Tobin, A. W. (1982). The cloze procedure as an informal assessment technique. In J. J. Pikulski & T. Shanahan (Eds.), *Approaches to the informal evaluation of reading* (pp. 42–62). Newark, DE: International Reading Association.

Piper, T. (2003). *Language and learning: The home school years*. Columbus, OH: Prentice Hall.

Piper, T. P. E. (2006). *Language and learning: The home and school years*. Mahwah, NJ: Erlbaum.

Piro, J. M. (2002). The picture of reading: Deriving meaning in literacy through image. *The Reading Teacher, 56*, 126–134.

Pitcher, S. M., Albright, L. K., DeLaney, C. J., Walker, N. T., Seunarinesingh, K., Mogge, S., et al. (2007). Assessing adolescents' motivation to read. *Journal of Adolescent & Adult Literacy, 50*, 378–396.

Pittelman, S. D., Heimlich, J. E., Berglund, R. L., & French, M. P. (1991). *Semantic feature analysis: Classroom applications*. Newark, DE: International Reading Association.

Polette, K. (1989). Using ABC books for vocabulary development in the secondary school. *English Journal, 78*, 78–80.

Powell, W., & Dunkeld, C. (1971). Validity of the IRI reading levels. *Elementary English, 48,* 637–642.

Powell, W. R. (1970). Reappraising the criteria for interpreting informal inventories. In D. DeBoer (Ed.), *Reading diagnosis and evaluation.* Newark, DE: International Reading Association.

Puma, M., Karweit, N., Price, C., Ricciuti, A., Thompson, W., & Vaden-Kiernan, M. (1997). *Prospects: Student outcomes, final report.* Washington, DC: U.S. Department of Education, Office of Educational Research and Improvement.

Putnam, R. (2000). *Bowling alone: The collapse and revival of American community.* NY: Simon & Schuster.

Quigley, S., King, C., McAnally, P., & Rose, S. (Eds.). (1998). *Reading Milestones: An alternative reading program* (2nd ed.). Austin, TX: Pro-Ed.

Rabe, B. (1981). *The balancing girl.* New York: Dutton.

Raines, S. (2000). Educators influencing legislators: Commentary and the Kentucky case. *The Reading Teacher, 53,* 642–643.

RAND Reading Study Group. (2002). *Reading for understanding: Toward an R & D program in reading comprehension.* Santa Monica, CA: RAND. Retreived on January 8, 2009 from www.rand.org/multi/achievementforall.

Rankin, E. F., & Culhane, J. W. (1969). Comparable cloze and multiple-choice comprehension scores. *Journal of Reading, 13,* 193–198.

Raphael, T. E. (1982). Question-answering strategies for children. *The Reading Teacher, 36,* 186–190.

Raphael, T. E. (1986). Teaching question-answer relationships, revisited. *The Reading Teacher, 39,* 516–522.

Raphael, T. E., & Au, K. H. (2005). QAR: Enhancing comprehension and test taking across grades and content areas. *The Reading Teacher, 59,* 206–221.

Raphael, T. E., & Pearson, P. D. (1985). Increasing students' awareness of sources of information for answering questions. *American Educational Research Journal, 22,* 217–235.

Rasinski, T. (Ed.). (1995). *Parents and teachers: Helping children learn to read and write.* Fort Worth, TX: Harcourt Brace.

Rasinski, T. (2003). *The fluent reader: Oral reading strategies for building word recognition, fluency, and comprehension.* New York: Scholastic.

Reutzel, D. R. (1985). Story maps improve comprehension. *The Reading Teacher, 38,* 400–404.

Reutzel, D. R. (1986). Clozing in on comprehension: The cloze story map. *The Reading Teacher, 39,* 524–528.

Reynolds, R. E., Taylor, M. A., Steffensen, M. S., Shirey, L. L., & Anderson, R. C. (1981). *Cultural schemata and reading comprehension* (Tech. Rep. No. 201). Champaign: University of Illinois, Center for the Study of Reading.

Rhodes, L. K., & Dudley-Marling, C. (1988). *Readers and writers with a difference: A holistic approach to teaching learning disabled and remedial students.* Portsmouth, NH: Heinemann.

Rhodes, L. K., & Shanklin, N. (1993). *Windows into literacy: Assessing learners K–8.* Portsmouth, NH: Heinemann.

Richards, J., & McKenna, M. (2003). *Integrating multiple literacies in K–8 classrooms: Cases, commentaries, and practical applications.* Mahwah, NJ: Erlbaum.

Richards, J. C. (1985). *Theoretical orientation and first- and third-grade teachers' reading instruction.* Unpublished doctoral dissertation, University of New Orleans.

Richards, J. C., & Gipe, J. (1996). I wonder . . . ? A strategy to help children listen actively to stories. *The Whole Idea, 7*(1), 10–11.

Richards, J. C., & Gipe, J. P. (1992). Activating background knowledge: Strategies for beginning and poor readers. *The Reading Teacher, 45,* 474–476.

Richards, J. C., & Gipe, J. P. (1993). Recognizing information about story characters: A strategy for young and at-risk readers. *The Reading Teacher, 47,* 78–79.

Richards, J. C., Gipe, J. P., & Necaise, M. A. (1994). Find the features and connect them. *The Reading Teacher, 48,* 187–188.

Richards, M. (2000). Be a good detective: Solve the case of oral fluency. *The Reading Teacher, 53,* 534–539.

Richek, M. A. (1987). DRTA: 5 variations that facilitate independence in reading narratives. *Journal of Reading, 30,* 632–636.

Rickford, J. R. (1999). *African American Vernacular English: Features, evolution, educational implications.* Oxford: Blackwell.

Rickford, J. R., & Rickford, R. J. (2000). *Spoken soul: The story of Black English.* Wiley Publ.

Rigg, P. (1989). Language Experience Approach: Reading naturally. In P. Rigg & V. G. Allen (Eds.), *When they don't all speak English: Integrating the ESL student into the regular classroom* (pp. 65–76). Urbana, IL: National Council of Teachers of English.

Rigg, P., & Allen, V. G. (Eds.). (1989). *When they don't all speak English: Integrating the ESL student into the regular classroom.* Urbana, IL: National Council of Teachers of English.

Robelen, E. W. (1998). Reengaging young people. In *ASCD, Infobrief: Educating for Democratic Life* (pp. 1–8). Alexandria, VA: Association for Supervision and Curriculum Development.

Roberts, T. (1976). "Frustration level" reading in the infant school. *Educational Research, 19,* 41–44.

Robinson, F. P. (1970). *Effective study* (4th ed.). New York: Harper & Row.

Roe, B. D., & Burns, P. C. (2007). *Informal reading inventory: Preprimer to twelfth grade, seventh edition.* Boston: Houghton Mifflin.

Rogers, L. K. (1999). Spelling cheerleading. *The Reading Teacher, 53,* 110–111.

Rosenblatt, L. (1978). Aesthetic reading. In T. L. Harris & R. E. Hodges (Eds.), *The literacy dictionary: The vocabulary of reading and writing* (1995, p. 5). Newark, DE: International Reading Association.

Rosenblatt, L. (1983). *Literature as exploration.* New York: Modern Languages Association of America.

Rosenblatt, L. (1991). Efferent reading. In T. L. Harris & R. E. Hodges (Eds.), *The literacy dictionary: The vocabulary of reading and writing* (1995, p. 69). Newark, DE: International Reading Association.

Rosenblatt, L. M. (1994). The transactional theory of reading and writing. In R. B. Ruddell, M. R. Ruddell, & H. Singer (Eds.), *Theoretical models and processes of reading* (4th ed., pp. 1057–1092). Newark, DE: International Reading Association.

Roswell, F., & Chall, J. (1997). *Roswell-Chall auditory blending test.* Cambridge, MA: Educators Publishing Service.

Routman, R. (1991). *Invitations: Changing as teachers and learners K–12.* Portsmouth, NH: Heinemann.

Routman, R. (2000). *Conversations: Strategies for teaching, learning, and evaluating.* Portsmouth, NH: Heinemann.

Ruddell, R. B. (1964). A study of the cloze comprehension technique in relation to structurally controlled reading material. In J. A. Figurel (Ed.), *Improvement of reading through classroom practice* (pp. 298–303). Newark, DE: International Reading Association.

Ruddell, R.B., & Unrau, N. J. (1996). The role of responsive teaching in focusing reader intention and developing reader motivation. In J. T. Guthrie & A. Wigfield (Eds.), *Reading engagement: Motivating readers through integrated instruction* (pp. 102–125). Newark, DE: International Reading Association.

Rumelhart, D. E. (1975). Notes on a schema for stories. In D. G. Bobrow & A. M. Collins (Eds.), *Representation and under-*

standing: Studies in cognitive science. New York: Academic Press.

Rumelhart, D. E. (1980). Schemata: The building blocks of cognition. In R. J. Spiro, B. C. Bruce, & W. F. Brewer (Eds.), *Theoretical issues in reading comprehension* (pp. 33–58). Hillsdale, NJ: Erlbaum.

Rumelhart, D. E. (1994). Toward an interactive model of reading. In R. B. Ruddell, M. R. Ruddell, & H. Singer (Eds.), *Theoretical models and processes of reading* (pp. 864–894). Newark, DE: International Reading Association.

Rupley, W., Logan, J., & Nichols, W. (1998/1999). Vocabulary instruction in a balanced reading program. *The Reading Teacher, 52,* 336–346.

Russell, D. H., & Russell, E. (1979). *Listening aids through the grades* (2nd ed.). New York: Teachers College Press.

Rutland, A. D. (1987). Using wordless picture books in social studies. *History and Social Science Teacher, 22,* 193–196.

Rylant, C. (1982). *When I was young in the mountains*. New York: Dutton.

Sadow, M. W. (1982). The use of story grammar in the design of questions. *The Reading Teacher, 35,* 518–522.

Samuels, S. J. (1979). The method of repeated readings. *The Reading Teacher, 32,* 403–408. (Reprinted 1997, *The Reading Teacher, 50,* 376–381.)

Samuels, S. J. (1988). Decoding and automaticity: Helping poor readers become automatic at word recognition. *The Reading Teacher, 41,* 756–761.

Samuels, S. J. (1994). Toward a theory of automatic information processing in reading, revisited. In R. B. Ruddell, M. R. Ruddell, & H. Singer (Eds.), *Theoretical models and processes of reading* (4th ed., pp. 816–837). Newark, DE: International Reading Association.

San Souci, R. D. (1998). *Cendrillon: A Caribbean Cinderella*. New York: Simon & Schuster Books for Young Readers.

Saunders, W., O'Brien, G., Lennon, D., & McLean, J. (1998). Making the transition to English literacy successful: Effective strategies for studying literature with transition students. In R. Gersten & R. Jimenez (Eds.), *Promoting learning for culturally and linguistically diverse students: Classroom applications from contemporary research* (pp. 99–132). Belmont, CA: Wadsworth.

Sautter, R. (1994). An arts education school reform strategy. *Phi Delta Kappan, 75,* 432–437.

Sax, G. (1980). *Principles of educational and psychological measurement and evaluation* (2nd ed.). Belmont, CA: Wadsworth.

Schachter, S. W. (1978). Developing flexible reading habits. *Journal of Reading, 22,* 149–152.

Schell, L. M., & Hanna, G. S. (1981). Can informal reading inventories reveal strengths and weaknesses in comprehension subskills? *The Reading Teacher, 35,* 263–268.

Schirduan, V., & Case, K. (2000). Focusing on the positive: The self-concept of students with ADHD in schools using MI theory. *Multiple Intelligences: Theory and Practice, 1*(1), 3–5.

Schmelzer, R. V. (1975). *The effect of college student constructed questions on the comprehension of a passage of expository prose* Doctoral dissertation, University of Minnesota. *Dissertation Abstracts International, 36,* 2162A.

Schmidt, P. R. (1999). KWLQ: Inquiry and literacy learning in science. *The Reading Teacher, 52,* 789–792.

Schön, D. A. (1987). *Educating the reflective practitioner*. San Francisco: Jossey-Bass.

Schumm, J. S., & Mangrum, C. T. (1991). FLIP: A framework for content area reading. *Journal of Reading, 35,* 120–124.

Schwartz, E., & Sheff, A. (1975). Student involvement in questioning for comprehension. *The Reading Teacher, 29,* 150–154.

Schwartz, R. M. (1988). Learning to learn: Vocabulary in content area textbooks. *Journal of Reading, 32,* 108–117.

Scott, J. A., Lubliner, S., & Hiebert, E. H. (2006). Constructs underlying word selection and assessment tasks in the archival research on vocabulary instruction. In J. V. Hoffman, D. L. Schallert, C. M. Fairbanks, J. Worthy, & B. Maloch (Eds.), *55th yearbook of the National Reading Conference* (pp. 264–275). Oak Creek, WI: National Reading Conference.

Scott, J. A., & Nagy, W. E. (1997). Understanding the definitions of unfamiliar verbs. *Reading Research Quarterly, 32,* 184–200.

Scruggs, T. E., & Mastropieri, M.A. (1992). *Teaching test-taking skills*. Cambridge, MA: Brookline Books.

Seaborg, M., & Sturtevant, E. (1996, December). *E-mail keypals: Multiple dimensions of an e-mail penpal program*. Paper presented at the National Reading Conference, Charleston, SC.

Search Institute. (1997). *40 developmental assets*. Minneapolis, MN: Author.

Searfoss, L. (1993). Assessing classroom environments. In S. Glazer & C. Brown (Eds.), *Portfolios and beyond: Collaborative assessment in reading and writing* (pp. 11–26). Norwood, MA: Christopher-Gordon.

Seuss, Dr. (1960). *Green eggs and ham*. New York: Beginner Books.

Seuss, Dr. (1963). *Dr. Seuss's ABC: An amazing alphabet book!* New York: Random House.

Shafer, R. E., Staab, C., & Smith, K. (1983). *Language functions and school success*. Glenview, IL: Scott, Foresman.

Shamir, A., & Korat, O. (2007). How to select CD-ROM storybooks for young children: The teacher's role. *The Reading Teacher, 59*(6), 532–543.

Shamir, A., Korat, D., & Barbi, N. (2008). The effects of CD-ROM storybook reading on low SES kindergartners' emergent literacy as a function of learning context. *Computers & Education, 51*(1), 354–367.

Shannon, P. (1989). *Broken promises: Reading instruction in twentieth-century America*. Granby, MA: Bergin & Garvey.

Shannon, P. (1990). *The struggle to continue: Progressive reading instruction in the United States*. Portsmouth, NH: Heinemann.

Shaw, N. (1989). *Sheep on a ship*. Boston: Houghton Mifflin.

Shefelbine, J. (1998). *Fun with Zip and Zap*. New York: Scholastic.

Shnayer, S. W. (1969). Relationships between reading interest and comprehension. In J. A. Figurel (Ed.), *Reading and realism*. Newark, DE: International Reading Association.

Short, J. R., & Dickerson, B. (1980). *The newspaper: An alternative textbook*. Carthage, IL: Fearon Teacher Aids.

Shuy, R. W. (1981). A holistic view of language. *Research in the Teaching of English, 15,* 101–111.

Shuy, R. W. (1988). Sentence level language functions. In J. R. Staton, R. W. Shuy, J. K. Peyton, & L. Reed (Eds.), *Dialogue journal communication*. Norwood, NJ: Ablex.

Sidelnick, M., & Svoboda, M. (2000). The bridge between drawing and writing: Hannah's story. *The Reading Teacher, 54,* 174–184.

Silva, C., & Yarborough, B. (1990). Help for young writers with spelling difficulties. *Journal of Reading, 34,* 48–53.

Simpson, M. L. (1986). PORPE: A writing strategy for studying and learning in the content areas. *Journal of Reading, 29,* 407–414.

Simpson, M. L. (1987). Alternative formats for evaluating content area vocabulary understanding. *Journal of Reading, 31,* 20–27.

Simpson, M. L., & Nist, S. L. (1984). PLAE: A model for planning successful independent learning. *Journal of Reading, 29,* 218–223.

Simpson, M. L., & Nist, S. L. (1990). Textbook annotation: An effective and efficient study strategy for college students. *Journal of Reading, 34,* 122–129.

Simpson, M. L., Stahl, N. A., & Hayes, C. G. (1989). PORPE: A research validation. *Journal of Reading, 33,* 22–28.

Sinatra, R. C., Stahl-Gemake, J., & Berg, D. N. (1984). Improving reading comprehension of disabled readers through semantic mapping. *The Reading Teacher, 38,* 22–29.

Singer, H. (1978). Active comprehension: From answering to asking questions. *The Reading Teacher, 31,* 901–908.

Sippola, A. E. (1995). K–W–L–S. In T. Rasinski, et al. (Eds.), *Teaching comprehension and exploring multiple literacies: Strategies from* The Reading Teacher (pp. 37–38). Newark, DE: International Reading Association.

Skinner, B. F. (1957). *Verbal behavior.* Upper Saddle River, NJ: Merrill/Prentice Hall.

Smith, P., & Tompkins, G. (1988). Structured notetaking: A new strategy for content area readers. *Journal of Reading, 32,* 46–53.

Smith, R. J., & Johnson, D. D. (1980). *Teaching children to read.* Reading, MA: Addison-Wesley.

Smith, S. P., & Jackson, F. H. (1985). Assessing reading/learning skills with written retellings. *Journal of Reading, 28,* 622–630.

Smitherman, G. (1985). What go round come round: King in perspective. In C. K. Brooks (Ed.), *Tapping potential: English and language arts for the black learner.* Urbana, IL: National Council of Teachers of English.

Smitherman, G., & Villanueva, V. (Eds.). (2003). *Language diversity in the classroom: From intention to practice.* Carbondale: Southern Illinois University.

Snell, C. A. (2007). *The impact of daily writing on kindergarten students' phonemic awareness.* Unpublished doctoral dissertation, Walden University, Minneapolis, MN. (UMI # 3261224)

Snow, C. E., Burns, M. S., & Griffin, P. (Eds.). (1998). *Preventing reading difficulties in young children.* Washington, DC: National Academy Press.

Solley, B. (2000). *Writers' workshop: Reflections of elementary and middle school teachers.* Boston: Allyn & Bacon.

Soto, G. (1993). *Too many tamales.* New York: Putnam.

Spache, G. (1963). *Toward better reading.* Champaign, IL: Garrard.

Spache, G. (1976). *Diagnosing and correcting reading disabilities.* Boston: Allyn & Bacon.

Spangenberg-Urbschat, K., & Pritchard, R. (Eds.). (1994). *Kids come in all languages: Reading instruction for ESL students.* Newark, DE: International Reading Association.

Speaker, R., & Speaker, P. (1991). Sentence collecting: Authentic literacy events in the classroom. *Journal of Reading, 35,* 92–95.

Speaker, R. B. Jr., & Barnitz, J. G. (1999). Linguistic perspectives in literacy education: Electronic and linguistic connections in one diverse twenty-first century classroom. *The Reading Teacher, 52,* 874–877.

Spiegel, D. (1999). The perspective of the balanced approach. In S. Blair-Larsen & K. Williams (Eds.), *The balanced reading program: Helping all students achieve success* (pp. 8–23). Newark, DE: International Reading Association.

Squires, D., & Bliss, T. (2004). Teacher visions: Navigating beliefs about literacy learning. *The Reading Teacher, 57,* 756–763.

Stahl, N. A., King, J. R., & Henk, W. A. (1991). Enhancing students' notetaking through training and evaluation. *Journal of Reading, 34,* 614–622.

Stahl, S. A., & Fairbanks, M. M. (1986). The effects of vocabulary instruction: A model-based meta-analysis. *Review of Educational Research, 56,* 72–110.

Stanovich, K. E. (1980). Toward an interactive-compensatory model of individual differences in the development of reading fluency. *Reading Research Quarterly, 16,* 32–71.

Staton, J. (1987). The power of responding in journals. In T. Fulwiler (Ed.), *The journal book* (pp. 47–63). Portsmouth, NH: Heinemann.

Staton, J. (1988). Discussing problems. In J. Staton, R. W. Shuy, J. K. Peyton, & L. Reed (Eds.), *Dialogue journal communication: Classroom, linguistic, social and cognitive views* (pp. 202–244). Norwood, NJ: Ablex.

Staton, J., Shuy, R. W., Peyton, J. K., & Reed, L. (Eds.). (1988). *Dialogue journal communication: Classroom, linguistic, social and cognitive views.* Norwood, NJ: Ablex.

Stauffer, R. G. (1975). *Directing the reading-thinking process.* New York: Harper & Row.

Stauffer, R. G. (1981). Strategies for reading instruction. In M. Douglas (Ed.), *45th Yearbook of the Claremont Reading Conference.* Claremont, CA: Claremont Graduate School Curriculum Laboratory.

Steffensen, M. S. (1987). The effect of context and culture on children's L2 reading: A review. In J. Devine, P. L. Carrell, & D. E. Eskey (Eds.), *Research in reading in English as a second language* (pp. 41–54). Washington, DC: Teachers of English to Speakers of Other Languages.

Steptoe, J. (1987). *Mufaro's Beautiful Daughters: An African tale.* New York: Lothrop, Lee & Shepard.

Sternberg, R. J. (1991). Are we reading too much into reading comprehension tests? *Journal of Reading, 34,* 540–545.

Stevenson, J., & Baumann, J. (1979, May). *Vocabulary development: Semantic feature analysis and semantic mapping.* Microworkshop presented at the 24th annual meeting of the International Reading Association, Atlanta, GA.

Sticht, T. G., & Beck, L. J. (1976, August). *Experimental literacy assessment battery (LAB)* (Final Rep. No. AFHRL-TR-76-51). Lowry Air Force Base, CO: Air Force Human Resources Laboratory, Technical Training Division.

Sticht, T. G., & James, J. H. (1984). Listening and reading. In P. D. Pearson (Ed.), *Handbook of reading research* (pp. 293–317). New York: Longman.

Stieglitz, E. (2002). *The Stieglitz informal reading inventory: Assessing reading behaviors from emergent to advanced levels.* Boston: Allyn & Bacon.

Strickland, D. (2000). Classroom intervention strategies: Supporting the literacy development of young learners at risk. In D. Strickland & L. Morrow (Eds.), *Beginning reading and writing* (pp. 99–110). New York: Teachers College Press; and Newark, DE: International Reading Association.

Strode, S. L. (1993). An adaptation of REAP for the developmental reader. *Journal of Reading, 36,* 568–569.

Sulzby, E. (1985). Kindergartners as writers and readers. In M. Farr (Ed.), *Advances in writing research: Vol. 1. Children's early writing development* (pp. 127–199). Norwood, NJ: Ablex.

Sunstein, B., & Lovell, J. (2000). *The portfolio standard: How students can show us what they know and are able to do.* Portsmouth, NH: Heinemann.

Swearingen, R., & Allen, D. (2000). *Classroom assessment of reading processes.* Boston: Houghton Mifflin.

Taba, H. (1967). *Teacher's handbook for elementary social studies.* Reading, MA: Addison-Wesley.

Taylor, B. H., Harris, L. A., & Pearson, P. D. (1988). *Reading difficulties: Instruction and assessment.* New York: Random.

Taylor, W. L. (1953). Cloze procedure: A new tool for measuring readability. *Journalism Quarterly, 30,* 415–433.

Teale, W. H., & Sulzby, E. (1989). Emergent literacy: New perspectives. In D. S. Strickland & L. M. Morrow (Eds.), *Emerging literacy: Young children learn to read and write* (pp. 1–15). Newark, DE: International Reading Association.

Temple, C., Nathan, R., Burris, N., & Temple, F. (1988). *The beginning of writing* (2nd ed.). Boston: Allyn & Bacon.

Templeton, S. (1991). *Teaching the integrated language arts.* Boston: Houghton Mifflin.

Tharp, R., & Gallimore, R. (1988). *Rousing minds to life: Teaching, learning, and schooling in social context.* New York: Cambridge University Press.

Therrien, W. J. (2004). Fluency and comprehension gains as a result of repeated reading: A meta-analysis. *Remedial and Special Education, 25*(4), 252–261.

Thomas, A., Fazio, L., & Stiefelmeyer, B. (1999a). *Families at school: A guide for educators.* Newark, DE: International Reading Association.

Thomas, A., Fazio, L., & Stiefelmeyer, B. (1999b). *Families at school: A handbook for parents.* Newark, DE: International Reading Association.

Thonis, E. W. (1976). *Literacy for America's Spanish speaking children.* Newark, DE: International Reading Association.

Thorndyke, P. (1977). Cognitive structures in comprehension and memory of narrative discourse. *Cognitive Psychology, 9,* 77–110.

Tiedt, I. (2000). *Teaching with picture books in the middle school.* Newark, DE: International Reading Association.

Tierney, R. J., Carter, M. A., & Desai, L. E. (1991). *Portfolio assessment in the reading-writing classroom.* Norwood, MA: Christopher-Gordon.

Tierney, R. J., & Pearson, P. D. (1994). Learning to learn from text: A framework for improving classroom practice. In R. B. Ruddell, M. R. Ruddell, & H. Singer (Eds.), *Theoretical models and processes of reading* (4th ed., pp. 496–513). Newark, DE: International Reading Association.

Tierney, R. J., Readence, J. E., & Dishner, E. K. (1990). *Reading strategies and practices: A compendium* (3rd ed.). Boston: Allyn & Bacon.

Tinajero, J. V., & Schifini, A. (1997). *INTO English!* Carmel, CA: Hampton-Brown Books.

Tomlinson, C. (1999). *The differentiated classroom: Responding to the needs of all learners.* Alexandria, VA: Association for Supervision and Curriculum Development.

Tompkins, G., & Hoskisson, K. (1991). *The language arts curriculum: Content and teaching strategies.* New York: Merrill.

Topping, K. (1995). Cued spelling: A powerful technique for parent and peer tutoring. *The Reading Teacher, 48,* 374–383.

Torgesen, J. K., & Bryant, B. R. (2004). *Test of phonological awareness, 2nd edition: plus (TOPA-2+).* Austin, TX: Pro-Ed.

Torp, L. & Sage, S. (1998). *Problems as possibilities: Problem-based learning for K–12 education.* Alexandria, VA: Association for Supervision and Curriculum Development.

Tovani, C. (2000). *I read it, but I don't get it: Comprehension strategies for adolescent readers.* Portland, ME: Stenhouse.

Trabasso, T. R., Sabatini, J. P., Massaro, D. W., & Calfee, R.. (Eds.). (2005). *From orthography to pedagogy: Essays in honor of Robert L. Venezky.* New York: Routledge.

Trachtenburg, P. (1990). Using children's literature to enhance phonics instruction. *The Reading Teacher, 43,* 648–654.

Troike, R. C. (1972). English and the bilingual child. In D. L. Shores (Ed.), *Contemporary English: Change and variation.* Philadelphia: Lippincott.

Upton, A. (1973). *Design for thinking: A first book on semantics.* Palo Alto: Pacific Press.

Valmont, W. (1972). Creating questions for informal reading inventories. *The Reading Teacher, 25,* 509–512.

Valmont, W. J. (1983). Cloze and maze instructional techniques: Differences and definitions. *Reading Psychology, 4,* 163–167.

Van Allsburg, C. (1981). *Jumanji.* New York: Houghton Mifflin.

Venezky, R. L. (1999). *The American way of spelling: The structure and origins of American English orthography.* New York: Guilford.

Vera, D. (2007). *The use of popular culture environmental print to increase the emergent literacy skills of prekindergarten children in one high-poverty urban school district.* Unpublished doctoral dissertation, Texas A & M, College Station, TX. (UMI # 3270408).

Villaume, S., & Hopkins, L. (1995). A transactional and sociocultural view of response in a fourth-grade literature discussion group. *Reading Research and Instruction, 34,* 190–203.

Vogt, M., & Nagano, P. (2003, November). Turn it on with light bulb reading! Sound-switching strategies for struggling readers. *The Reading Teacher, 57*(3), 214–221.

Vygotsky, L. S. (1962). *Thought and language* (E. Hanfmann & G. Vaker, Trans.) Cambridge, MA: MIT Press.

Vygotsky, L. S. (1978). *Mind in society: The development of higher psychological processes.* Cambridge, MA: Harvard University Press.

Wagoner, S. A. (1983). Comprehension monitoring: What it is and what we know about it. *Reading Research Quarterly, 17,* 328–346.

Wajnryb, R. (1990). *Grammar dictation.* Oxford, England: Oxford University Press.

Walker, B. J. (2000). *Diagnostic teaching of reading: Techniques for instruction and assessment* (4th ed.). Upper Saddle River, NJ: Merrill/Prentice Hall.

Walker, B. J. (2003). *Diagnostic teaching of reading: Techniques for instruction and assessment* (5th ed.). Upper Saddle River, NJ: Merrill/Prentice Hall.

Waller, M. B. (1992/1993). Helping crack-affected children succeed. *Educational Leadership, 50,* 57–60.

Wardhaugh, R. (2002). *An introduction to sociolinguistics* (4th ed.). Oxford, England: Blackwell.

Wasik, B. A., & Bond, M. A. (2001). Beyond the pages of a book: Interactive book reading and language development in preschool classrooms. *Journal of Educational Psychology, 93,* 243–250.

Watts-Taffe, S., & Truscott, D. M. (2000). Using what we know about language and literacy development for ESL students in the mainstream classroom. *Language Arts, 77*(3), 258–265.

Weaver, C. (1998). *Teaching grammar in context.* Portsmouth, NH: Heinemann.

Weaver, C. (2002). *Reading process and practice* (3rd ed.). Portsmouth, NH: Heinemann.

Weinstein, S. (2007). A love for the thing: The pleasures of rap as a literate practice. *Journal of Adolescent & Adult Literacy, 50,* 270–281.

West, K. C. (2008). Weblogs and literary response: Socially situated identities and hybrid social languages in English class blogs. *Journal of Adolescent & Adult Literacy, 51,* 588–598.

Wheeler, R. S., & Swords, R. (2006). *Code-switching: Teaching standard English in urban classrooms.* Urbana, IL: National Council of Teachers of English.

Whitin, P. (1996). *Sketching stories, stretching minds: Responding visually to literature.* Portsmouth, NH: Heinemann.

Wiesendanger, K. D., & Bader, L. (1992). SCAIT: A study technique to develop students' higher comprehension skills when reading content area material. *Journal of Reading, 35,* 399–400.

Wiig, E. H., Secord, W., & Semel, E. (2006). *CELF-Preschool 4.* San Antonio, TX: Pearson Education.

Wilde, S. (1996). Foreword. In L. Laminack & K. Wood (Eds.), *Spelling in use: Looking closely in whole language classrooms* (pp. x–xi). Urbana, IL: National Council of Teachers of English.

Wilde, S. (1997). *What's a schwa sound anyway? A holistic guide to phonetics, phonics, and spelling.* Portsmouth, NH: Heinemann.

Wilhelm, J. D. (1997). *"You Gotta BE the Book": Teaching engaged and reflective reading with adolescents.* New York: Teachers College Press.

Wilson, C. N. (2007). *Developing narrative language through the use of dramatic play in preschoolers.* Unpublished doctoral dissertation, Texas Woman's University. (UMI # 3271431), Denton, TX.

Wilson, R. M. (1981). *Diagnostic and remedial reading for classroom and clinic* (4th ed.). Columbus, OH: Prentice Hall/Merrill.

Winograd, P., & Johnston, P. (1980). *Comprehension monitoring and the error detection paradigm* (Tech. Rep. No. 153). Champaign: University of Illinois, Center for the Study of Reading.

Wiseman, D. (1992). *Learning to read with literature.* Boston: Allyn & Bacon.

Wolfram, W. (1991). *Dialects and American English.* Upper Saddle River, NJ: Prentice Hall and Center for Applied Linguistics.

Wong Fillmore, L., & Snow, C. (2000, August 23). *What teachers need to know about language.* Washington, DC: Center for Applied Linguistics. (ERIC Document Reproduction Service No. ED444379)

Woods, M. L., & Moe, A. J. (2007). *Analytical reading inventory.* Columbus, OH: Prentice Hall/Merrill.

Worthy, M. J., & Bloodgood, J. (1992/1993). Enhancing reading instruction through Cinderella tales. *The Reading Teacher, 46,* 290–301.

Wylie, R. E., & Durrell, D. D. (1970). Teaching vowels through phonograms. *Elementary English, 47,* 787–791.

(Yoon) Kim, Y. H., & Goetz, E. (1994). Context effects on word recognition and reading comprehension of poor and good readers: A test of the interactive-compensatory hypothesis. *Reading Research Quarterly, 29,* 179–187.

Yopp, H. (1995). A test for assessing phonemic awareness in young children. *The Reading Teacher, 49,* 20–29.

Yopp, H. K., & Yopp, R. H. (1996). *Oo-pples and boo-noo noos: Songs and activities for phonemic awareness.* San Diego: Harcourt Brace.

Young, T., & Crow, M. (1992). Using dialogue journals to help students deal with their problems. *The Clearing House, 65* (May/June), 307–310.

Zimmerman, I. L., Steiner, V. G., & Pond, R. (2002). *Preschool Language Scale-4 (PLS-4); English and Spanish versions.* San Antonio, TX: Psychological Corporation.

Zipoli, R. R. Jr. (2007). *Enhancing vocabulary intervention for kindergarten students: Strategies integration of semantically-related and embedded word review.* Unpublished doctoral dissertation, University of Connecticut.

Zutell, J. (1996). The directed spelling thinking activity (DSTA): Providing an effective balance in word study instruction. *The Reading Teacher, 50,* 98–108.

INDEX